Ainsworth Rand Spofford

American Almanac and Treasury of Facts, Statistical, Financial and

Political

Ainsworth Rand Spofford

American Almanac and Treasury of Facts, Statistical, Financial and Political

ISBN/EAN: 9783337336691

Printed in Europe, USA, Canada, Australia, Japan

Cover: Foto ©Suzi / pixelio.de

More available books at **www.hansebooks.com**

AN

AMERICAN ALMANAC

AND

Treasury of Facts.

STATISTICAL, FINANCIAL, AND POLITICAL,

FOR THE YEAR

1878.

EDITED BY

AINSWORTH R. SPOFFORD,

LIBRARIAN OF CONGRESS.

———◆———

NEW YORK AND WASHINGTON:

THE AMERICAN NEWS COMPANY.

—

1878.

PREFACE.

THIS volume aims to supply a want long felt for a compact and comprehensive reference book, giving the statistics of all nations, and especially of the United States, at the latest date and at a moderate price.

Other annual publications of great value occupy special fields. The Statesman's Year-Book deals with the political statistics of governments, excluding miscellaneous information; the Almanach de Gotha is a cyclopædia of knowledge regarding the reigning dynasties of the globe; the British Almanac and Whitaker's Almanac are replete with facts respecting Great Britain, paying little attention to other countries. The *Tribune, World,* and *Herald* Almanacs have their full tables of elections in detail, touching but lightly upon other than political topics. McPherson's Hand-Books of Politics form an invaluable official record of political votes and movements. Major Poore's admirable Congressional Directory supplies the freshest official lists of Congress and the departments of the government. The *Statistician,* a comparatively recent candidate for public favor, issued at San Francisco, furnishes a wide range of carefully digested information.

To all these this volume is under obligation, and to official documents and other publications too numerous to name. The Department and Bureau documents of the United States are rich in statistics of the greatest value, but so widely scattered in voluminous records and reports having little permanent interest, and so imperfectly indexed, as to baffle even the inquirer who has them always within reach. To glean the most important and practically useful facts out of the multitudinous reports concerning the Public Lands, the Finances, the Post-office system, the Tariff and Internal Revenue, the Currency, the Patent Office and Pension Bureau, Commerce and Navigation, the Army and Navy, the Reports of the Commissioner of Education, and the statistics of the Census, has been one object of the editor. To select, arrange, and condense the multitude of statistics derived from foreign as well as American sources, presenting them in compact tabular form, so that results may be quickly seized without laborious search, has been the chief aim. The editor's profession has taught

him the supreme value of moments ; and if this book should prove a time-saving and useful manual to his countrymen, his highest ambition will be gratified. The work is the fruit of many evening hours, laborious, but welcomed as a relief from severer cares.

In a volume embracing nearly half a million of figures to be verified, errors are unavoidable, but it is hoped that they have been reduced to a minimum. Defects of arrangement will be observed, due mainly to the exigencies of fitting large matter into small space, and the continuity of related subjects is thus broken, though all will be readily found by the index.

The commanding importance of questions of economic science has led to the devotion of much space to financial topics, including coinage, currency, revenue, expenditure, public debts, taxation, etc., which it is thought will prove of more value and interest than nearly obsolete questions of party politics, or tedious lists of minor officials. The editor has no ambition to be ranked among statisticians, and distinctly disclaims responsibility in the tabular information presented for any thing beyond the accuracy of his compilations from other sources. In most cases the authorities are given, and the reader is left to his own judgment. For matters outside of the tables, the editor is wholly responsible. He here expresses his thanks to the officers of the National and State governments who have supplied him with information, and to the members of his family who have cheered and aided him in his labors.

105 C STREET, SOUTH-EAST,
WASHINGTON, December 25, 1877.

TABLE OF CONTENTS.

ECLIPSES, FESTIVALS, ETC., IN 1878.
MOVABLE FESTIVALS, ETC.

Septuagesima Sunday, February 17.
Sexagesima Sunday, February 24. Quinquagesima Sunday,
March 3. Ash Wednesday, March 6. Quadragesima Sunday, March
10. Mid-Lent, March 31. Palm Sunday, April 14. Good Friday,
April 19. Easter Sunday, April 21. Low Sunday, April 28. Roga-
tion Sunday, May 26. Ascension Day, May 30. Whit Sunday, June 9.
Trinity Sunday, June 16. Corpus Christi, June 20.
Advent Sunday, December 1.

CHRONOLOGICAL CYCLES.

Dominical Letter, F. Epact, 26. Lunar Cycle, or Golden Number, 17. Solar Cycle, 11. Roman Indiction, 6. Julian Period, 6591.
Dionysian Period, 207. Jewish Lunar Cycle, 14.

ECLIPSES IN 1878.

There will be four Eclipses this year, two of the Sun, two of the
Moon, and a transit of Mercury over the Sun's disc.
I. An annular Eclipse of the Sun, February 2, invisible in
America.
II. A partial Eclipse of the Moon, February 17, in the morning,
partly visible at Washington.

	BEGINS. H. M.	MIDDLE. H. M.	END. H. M.
Washington	4 35 morn.	6 3 morn.	7 35 morn.

III. A total Eclipse of the Sun, July 29, in the afternoon. Visible
at Washington, and generally in the United States as a partial eclipse.
The total will be visible at Galveston, the middle being at about 4 h.
28 m. P.M. The Eclipse will be nearly total at New Orleans, Austin,
Santa Fé, and Denver, Col.

	BEGINS. H. M.	MIDDLE. H. M.	END. H. M.
Washington	4 36 eve.	5 30 eve.	6 25 eve.

IV. A partial Eclipse of the Moon, August 12, in the evening.
Size, 7.15 digits. The Moon will rise more or less eclipsed east of
Kansas, west of which no Eclipse will be visible.

	BEGINS. H. M.	MIDDLE. H. M.	END. H. M.
Washington	5 34 eve.	7 0 eve.	8 26 eve.

V. A transit of Mercury, May 6, visible at Washington.

	BEGINS. H. M.	MIDDLE. H. M.	END. H. M.
Washington	10 4 morn.	1 53 eve.	5 40 eve.

MORNING STARS.	EVENING STARS.
VENUS from Feb. 20 to Dec. 5.	VENUS until Feb. 20, and after Dec. 5.
MARS after Sept. 18.	MARS from Jan. 1 until Sept. 18.
JUPITER from Jan. 5 to April 25.	JUPITER until Jan. 5, and after April 25.
SATURN from March 13 to June 23.	SATURN until Mar. 13, and after June 23.

1st Month.]   **JANUARY, 1878.**   **[31 Days.**

		Moon's Phases.		Washington.			
Day of Month.	Day of Week.		DAY.	H. M.	Sun Rises.	Sun Sets.	Moon Rises.
		New Moon......	3	8 55 morn.			
		First Quarter....	11	1 39 eve.			
		Full Moon......	18	7 3 eve.			
		Last Quarter....	25	10 42 morn.			
					H. M.	H. M.	H. M.
1	Tues.	1863 Lincoln's Emancipation Proclamation.			7 19	4 49	5 48
2	Wed.	1788 Georgia ratified the Constitution.			7 19	4 50	6 47
8	Thur.	1777 Battle of Princeton.			7 19	4 51	sets.
4	Fri.	1858 Death of Rachel.			7 19	4 52	6 1
5	Sat.	1781 Richmond, Va., burned by Arnold.			7 19	4 52	7 4
6	**Sun.**	1844 First telegraph between Baltimore and Washington.			7 19	4 53	8 6
7	Mon.	1718 General Putnam born.			7 19	4 54	9 4
8	Tues.	1815 Defeat of the British at New Orleans.			7 19	4 55	10 3
9	Wed.	1788 Connecticut ratified the Constitution.			7 19	4 56	10 59
10	Thur.	1840 Penny Postage established in England.			7 19	4 57	11 57
11	Fri.	1757 Alexander Hamilton born.			7 19	4 58	morn.
12	Sat.	1808 Salmon P. Chase born.			7 18	4 59	57
13	**Sun.**	1825 Slavery abolished in Mexico.			7 18	5 0	2 0
14	Mon.	374 St. Chrysostom born.			7 18	5 1	3 4
15	Tues.	1759 British Museum opened.			7 18	5 2	4 3
16	Wed.	1841 Banks resumed specie paym'ts.			7 17	5 3	5 16
17	Thur.	1600 Calderon de la Barca born.			7 17	5 5	6 12
18	Fri.	1782 Daniel Webster born.			7 16	5 6	rises.
19	Sat.	1848 Gold discovered in California.			7 16	5 7	6 12
20	**Sun.**	1779 David Garrick died.			7 15	5 8	7 28
21	Mon.	1793 Louis XVI. beheaded.			7 15	5 9	8 41
22	Tues.	1788 Byron born.			7 14	5 10	9 53
23	Wed.	1806 William Pitt died.			7 14	5 11	11 4
24	Thur.	1712 Frederick the Great born.			7 13	5 12	morn.
25	Fri.	1759 Robert Burns born.			7 12	5 13	15
26	Sat.	1837 Michigan admitted into the Union.			7 12	5 15	1 18
27	**Sun.**	1756 Mozart born			7 11	5 16	2 37
28	Mon.	1859 William H. Prescott died.			7 10	5 17	3 42
29	Tues.	1861 Kansas admitted to the Union.			7 9	5 18	4 41
30	Wed.	1049 King Charles I. beheaded.			7 8	5 19	5 32
81	Thur.	1849 Abolition of the Corn Laws.			7 8	5 20	6 25

2d Month.]   **FEBRUARY, 1878.**   **[28 Days.**

Moon's Phases.		WASHINGTON.
New Moon......	DAY. 2	H. M. 3 9 morn.
First Quarter....	10	8 9 morn.
Full Moon......	17	6 9 morn.
Last Quarter....	23	10 5 eve.

Day of Month.	Day of Week.			Sun Rises.	Sun Sets.	Moon Rises.
				H. M.	H. M.	H. M.
1	Fri.	1552	Sir Edward Coke born.	7 7	5 21	6 47
2	Sat.	1848	Treaty of Guadalupe Hidalgo signed.	7 6	5 23	sets.
3	**Sun.**	1811	Horace Greeley born.	7 5	5 24	6 57
4	Mon.	1555	John Rogers burned.	7 4	5 25	7 54
5	Tues.	1788	Sir Robert Peel born.	7 3	5 26	8 51
6	Wed.	1788	Massachusetts ratified the Constitution.	7 2	5 27	9 49
7	Thur.	1812	Charles Dickens born.	7 1	5 28	10·57
8	Fri.	1587	Mary Queen of Scots beheaded.	7 0	5 29	11 47
9	Sat.	1773	Wm. Henry Harrison born.	6 59	5 30	morn.
10	**Sun.**	1876	Reverdy Johnson died.	6 58	5 32	51
11	Mon.	1735	Daniel Boone born.	6 57	5 33	1 53
12	Tues.	1809	Abraham Lincoln born.	6 55	5 34	2 56
13	Wed.	1689	William III. and Mary proclaimed.	6 54	5 35	4 7
14	Thur.	1859	Oregon admitted to the Union.	6 53	5 36	4 51
15	Fri.	1710	Louis XV. born.	6 52	5 38	5 37
16	Sat.	1857	Dr. E. K. Kane died.	6 51	5 39	6 17
17	**Sun.**	1815	The War of 1812 ended.	6 49	5 40	rises.
18	Mon.	1564	Galileo born.	6 48	5 41	7 30
19	Tues.	1821	Florida ceded to U. S. by Spain.	6 47	5 42	8 56
20	Wed.	1716	David Garrick born.	6 46	5 44	9 59
21	Thur.	1801	John Henry Newman born.	6 44	5 45	11 13
22	Fri.	1732	George Washington born.	6 43	5 46	morn.
23	Sat.	1848	John Quincy Adams died.	6 42	5 47	26
24	**Sun.**	1863	Territory of Arizona organized.	6 40	5 48	1 35
25	Mon.	1791	First U. S. bank chartered.	6 38	5 49	2 37
26	Tues.	1848	French Republic proclaimed.	6 37	5 51	3 30
27	Wed.	1807	Henry W. Longfellow born.	6 36	5 52	4 14
28	Thur.	1820	Rachel born.	6 34	5 53	4 49

3d Month.]   MARCH, 1878.   [31 Days.

Moon's Phases.		WASHINGTON.

Day of Month.	Day of Week.		DAY.	H. M.		SUN RISES.	SUN SETS.	MOON RISES.
		New Moon......	3	10 9 eve.				
		First Quarter....	11	10 53 eve.				
		Full Moon.......	18	3 59 eve.				
		Last Quarter.....	25	11 42 morn.				

				H. M.	H. M.	H. M.
1	Fri.	1867 Nebraska admitted to the Union.		6 33	5 54	5 20
2	Sat.	1853 Territory of Washington organized.		6 32	5 55	5 44
3	Sun.	1845 Florida admitted to the Union.		6 30	5 56	6 6
4	Mon.	1791 Vermont admitted to the Union.		6 29	5 57	sets.
5	Tues.	1770 Boston Massacre.		6 27	5 57	7 42
6	Wed.	1836 Massacre of the Alamo, Tex. Ash Wednesday.		6 26	5 58	8 39
7	Thur.	1274 St. Thomas Aquinas died.		6 24	5 59	9 39
8	Fri.	1702 Accession of Queen Anne: William III. died.		6 23	6 0	10 40
9	Sat.	1451 Americus Vespucius born.		6 21	6 1	11 42
10	Sun.	First Sunday in Lent.		6 20	6 2	morn.
11	Mon.	1702 First London daily paper issued		6 18	6 3	45
12	Tues.	1684 Bishop Berkeley born.		6 17	6 4	1 44
13	Wed.	1841 Steamer President lost.		6 15	6 5	2 39
14	Thur.	1782 Thomas H. Benton born.		6 13	6 6	3 28
15	Fri.	1820 Maine admitted to the Union.		6 12	6 7	4 21
16	Sat.	1751 James Madison born.		6 10	6 8	4 45
17	Sun.	1776 British evacuated Boston.		6 9	6 9	5 16
18	Mon.	1766 Stamp Act repealed.		6 7	6 10	rises.
19	Tues.	1813 David Livingstone born.		6 6	6 11	7 33
20	Wed.	1727 Sir Isaac Newton died.		6 4	6 12	8 49
21	Thur.	1413 Henry V. of Eng. crowned.		6 3	6 13	10 5
22	Fri.	1765 Stamp Act passed.		6 1	6 14	11 18
23	Sat.	1749 La Place born.		5 59	6 15	morn.
24	Sun.	1603 Queen Elizabeth died.		5 58	6 16	26
25	Mon.	1609 Hudson River discovered.		5 56	6 17	1 23
26	Tues.	1827 Beethoven died.		5 54	6 18	2 13
27	Wed.	1512 Florida discovered by Ponce de Leon.		5 53	6 19	2 50
28	Thur.	1793 Henry R. Schoolcraft born.		5 51	6 19	3 22
29	Fri.	1772 Swedenborg died.		5 50	6 20	3 49
30	Sat.	1867 Alaska acquired by treaty with Russia.		5 48	6 21	4 11
31	Sun.	1850 John C. Calhoun died.		5 47	6 22	4 34

4th Month.]   **APRIL, 1878.**   **[30 Days.**

Day of Month.	Day of Week.	Moon's Phases.				Washington. SUN RISES.	SUN SETS.	MOON RISES.
			DAY.	H. M.				
		New Moon......	2	4 6 eve.				
		First Quarter....	10	9 47 morn.				
		Full Moon......	17	0 49 morn.				
		Last Quarter....	24	3 25 morn.				
						H. M.	H. M.	H. M.
1	Mon.	1789	First House Representatives organized at New York.			5 46	6 23	4 55
2	Tues.	1792	U. S. Mint estab. at Phila.			5 44	6 24	5 15
3	Wed.	1783	Washington Irving born.			5 42	6 25	sets.
4	Thur.	1841	President Harrison died.			5 41	6 26	8 32
5	Fri.	1794	Execution of Danton.			5 39	6 27	9 35
6	Sat.	1789	First Senate organized at New York.			5 37	6 28	10 38
7	**Sun.**	1780	William Ellery Channing born			5 36	6 29	11 38
8	Mon.	1848	Donizetti died.			5 34	6 30	morn.
9	Tues.	1626	Lord Bacon died.			5 33	6 31	33
10	Wed.	1816	U. S. Bank incorporated.			5 31	6 32	1 23
11	Thur.	1713	Peace of Utrecht.			5 30	6 33	2 8
12	Fri.	1777	Henry Clay born.			5 28	6 34	2 42
13	Sat.	1593	Thomas Wentworth Strafford born.			5 27	6 35	3 14
14	**Sun.**	1865	President Lincoln assassinated			5 25	6 36	3 43
15	Mon.	1814	John L. Motley born.			5 24	6 37	4 9
16	Tues.	1786	Sir John Franklin born.			5 23	6 38	4 39
17	Wed.	1790	Benjamin Franklin died.			5 21	6 39	rises.
18	Thur.	1847	Battle of Cerro Gordo.			5 20	6 40	8 54
19	Fri.	1775	Battles of Lexington and Concord. Good Friday.			5 18	6 41	10 6
20	Sat.	1808	Napoleon III. born.			5 17	6 42	11 11
21	**Sun.**	1836	Battle of San Jacinto. Easter Sunday.			5 16	6 42	morn.
22	Mon.	1509	Accession of Henry VIII.			5 14	6 43	5
23	Tues.	1616	Shakespeare died.			5 13	6 44	48
24	Wed.	1704	Boston *News Letter*, first paper in the U. S.			5 11	6 45	1 22
25	Thur.	1599	Oliver Cromwell born.			5 10	6 46	1 52
26	Fri.	1711	David Hume born.			5 9	6 47	2 15
27	Sat.	1737	Edward Gibbon died.			5 8	6 48	2 39
28	**Sun.**	1788	Maryland ratified the Constitution.			5 6	6 49	2 59
29	Mon.	1856	Peace proclaimed after Crimean War.			5 5	6 50	3 21
30	Tues.	1812	Louisiana admitted to the Union.			5 4	6 51	3 40

5th Month.]   MAY, 1878.   [31 Days.

Moon's Phases.		WASHINGTON.			

Day of Month.	Day of Week.		DAY.	H. M.	SUN RISES.	SUN SETS.	MOON RISES.
		New Moon......	2	7 42 morn.			
		First Quarter....	9	5 24 eve.			
		Full Moon... ..	16	9 23 morn.			
		Last Quarter....	23	8 34 eve.			
		New Moon. ...	31	8 40 eve.			

			H. M.	H. M	H. M.
1	Wed.	1775 Boston besieged by American army.	5 2	6 52	4 9
2	Thur.	1494 Jamaica discovered.	5 1	6 53	4 39
3	Fri.	1845 Thomas Hood died.	5 0	6 54	sets.
4	Sat.	1780 John J. Audubon born.	4 59	6 55	9 33
5	Sun.	1821 Napoleon Bonaparte died.	4 58	6 56	10 29
6	Mon.	1859 Alex. von Humboldt died.	4 57	6 57	11 21
7	Tues.	1869 Union Pacific Railroad completed.	4 55	6 58	morn.
8	Wed.	1871 Treaty of Washington with Great Britain.	4 54	6 59	5
9	Thur.	1502 Columbus sailed, 4th voyage.	4 53	7 0	43
10	Fri.	1876 Centennial Exhibition opened.	4 52	7 1	1 20
11	Sat.	1858 Minnesota admitted to the Union.	4 51	7 2	1 44
12	Sun.	1763 Andrew Jackson born.	4 50	7 2	2 12
13	Mon.	1607 First settlement at Jamestown, Va.	4 49	7 3	2 37
14	Tues.	1610 Henry IV. killed by Ravaillac.	4 49	7 4	3 7
15	Wed.	1847 Daniel O'Connell died.	4 48	7 5	3 40
16	Thur.	1801 Wm. Henry Seward born.	4 47	7 6	rises.
17	Fri.	1829 John Jay died.	4 46	7 7	8 52
18	Sat.	1804 Napoleon I. proclaimed emperor	4 45	7 8	9 42
19	Sun.	1780 Dark Day in New England.	4 44	7 9	10 41
20	Mon.	1506 Christopher Columbus died.	4 43	7 10	11 20
21	Tues.	1849 Maria Edgeworth died.	4 43	7 10	11 52
22	Wed.	1688 Alexander Pope born.	4 42	7 11	morn.
23	Thur.	1836 Edward Livingstone died.	4 41	7 12	18
24	Fri.	1864 Territory of Montana organized.	4 41	7 13	40
25	Sat.	1803 Ralph Waldo Emerson born.	4 40	7 14	1 3
26	Sun.	1781 Bank of North America established.	4 39	7 14	1 23
27	Mon.	1199 King John crowned.	4 39	7 15	1 47
28	Tues.	1807 Louis Agassiz born.	4 38	7 16	2 11
29	Wed.	1848 Wisconsin admt'd to the Union	4 38	7 17	2 42
30	Thur.	Decoration Day, soldiers' graves	4 37	7 17	3 12
31	Fri.	1791 First U. S. copyright law.	4 37	7 18	3 52

6th Month.] **JUNE, 1878.** **[30 Days.**

		Moon's Phases.		WASHINGTON.			SUN RISES.	SUN SETS.	MOON SETS.
				DAY.	H. M.				
Day of Month.	Day of Week.	First Quarter ...		7	10 47 eve.				
		Full Moon......		14	6 43 eve.				
		Last Quarter....		22	2 7 eve.				
		New Moon......		30	7 23 morn.				

			H. M.	H. M.	H. M.
1	Sat.	1792 Kentucky admitted; 1796, Tennessee admitted.	4 36	7 19	sets.
2	Sun.	1773 John Randolph born.	4 36	7 19	9 16
3	Mon.	1861 Stephen A. Douglas died.	4 36	7 20	10 4
4	Tues.	1859 Battle of Magenta.	4 35	7 21	10 44
5	Wed.	1723 Adam Smith born.	4 35	7 21	11 18
6	Thur.	1770 Patrick Henry died.	4 35	7 22	11 47
7	Fri.	1765 First American Congress, N.Y.	4 35	7 23	morn.
8	Sat.	1845 Andrew Jackson died.	4 34	7 23	14
9	Sun.	1870 Charles Dickens died.	4 34	7 24	40
10	Mon.	1580 Camoens died.	4 34	7 24	1 8
11	Tues.	1727 Accession of George II.	4 34	7 25	1 38
12	Wed.	1846 Oregon treaty signed.	4 34	7 25	2 14
13	Thur.	1786 Gen. Winfield Scott born.	4 34	7 26	2 55
14	Fri.	1777 U. S. flag, 13 stars and stripes, adopted.	4 34	7 26	rises.
15	Sat.	1836 Arkansas admitted to the Union.	4 34	7 26	8 31
16	Sun.	1846 Pius IX. elected Pope.	4 34	7 27	9 14
17	Mon.	1775 Battle of Bunker Hill.	4 34	7 27	9 50
18	Tues.	1815 Battle of Waterloo.	4 34	7 28	10 18
19	Wed.	1863 West Virginia admitted to the Union.	4 34	7 28	10 44
20	Thur.	1782 Great Seal of United States adopted.	4 34	7 28	11 5
21	Fri.	1788 New Hampshire ratified the Constitution.	4 34	7 28	11 25
22	Sat.	1815 Napoleon's final abdication.	4 35	7 28	11 48
23	Sun.	1859 Battle of Solferino.	4 35	7 29	morn.
24	Mon.	1497 New Foundland discovered by Cabot.	4 35	7 29	11
25	Tues.	1788 Virginia ratified Constitution.	4 35	7 29	38
26	Wed.	1830 George IV. died.	4 36	7 29	1 8
27	Thur.	1805 Francis W. Newman born.	4 36	7 29	1 46
28	Fri.	1836 James Madison died.	4 37	7 29	2 31
29	Sat.	1852 Henry Clay died.	4 37	7 29	3 24
30	Sun.	1834 Indian country set apart by Congress.	4 37	7 29	sets.

7th Month.]   JULY, 1878.   [31 Days.

Moon's Phases.			WASHINGTON.			
		DAY.	H. M.	SUN RISES.	SUN SETS.	MOON SETS.
First Quarter....		7	3 12 morn.			
Full Moon......		14	5 47 morn.			
Last Quarter....		22	7 8 morn.			
New Moon.......		29	4 32 eve.			

Day of Month.	Day of Week.			H. M.	H. M.	H. M.
1	Mon.	1690 Battle of the Boyne.		4 38	7 29	8 40
2	Tues.	1850 Sir Robert Peel died.		4 38	7 29	9 18
3	Wed.	1866 Battle of Sadowa.		4 39	7 29	9 49
4	Thur.	1776 Declaration of Independence signed.		4 39	7 28	10 17
5	Fri.	1755 Sarah Siddons born.		4 40	7 28	10 45
6	Sat.	1535 Sir Thomas More beheaded.		4 41	7 28	11 11
7	**Sun.**	1844 Native American riots in Philadelphia.		4 41	7 28	11 40
8	Mon.	1778 Massacre at Wyoming Valley.		4 42	7 27	morn.
9	Tues.	1755 Gen. Braddock's defeat—Monongahela.		4 42	7 27	11
10	Wed.	1810 Ney captured Ciudad Rodrigo.		4 43	7 27	51
11	Thur.	1767 John Quincy Adams born.		4 44	7 26	1 40
12	Fri.	1831 Belgium separated from Holland.		4 44	7 26	2 36
13	Sat.	1787 Ordinance of 1787 passed Congress.		4 45	7 26	3 38
14	**Sun.**	1873 Great Fire in Chicago.		4 46	7 25	rises.
15	Mon.	1828 Houdon the sculptor died.		4 46	7 24	8 19
16	Tues.	1790 District of Columbia establis'd		4 47	7 24	8 45
17	Wed.	1797 Paul Delaroche born.		4 48	7 23	9 8
18	Thur.	1778 British evacuation of Phila.		4 49	7 23	9 30
19	Fri.	1786 Fitch's first steamer on the Delaware.		4 50	7 22	9 51
20	Sat.	1806 John Sterling born.		4 51	7 21	10 13
21	**Sun.**	1796 Robert Burns died.		4 52	7 21	10 38
22	Mon.	1621 Earl of Shaftesbury born.		4 52	7 20	11 6
23	Tues.	1803 Emmett's insurrection in Ireland.		4 53	7 19	11 40
24	Wed.	1783 Simon Bolivar born.		4 54	7 18	morn.
25	Thur.	1868 Territory of Wyoming organized.		4 55	7 18	21
26	Fri.	1788 New York ratified the Constitution.		4 56	7 17	1 12
27	Sat.	1789 State Department established.		4 57	7 16	2 10
28	**Sun.**	1794 Robespierre guillotined		4 58	7 15	3 18
29	Mon.	1108 Philip I. of France died.		4 58	7 14	4 61
30	Tues.	1784 Diderot died.		4 59	7 13	sets.
31	Wed.	1875 Andrew Johnson died.		4 60	7 12	8 15

8th Month.]   **AUGUST, 1878.**   **[31 Days.**

Moon's Phases.	WASHINGTON.

Day of Month.	Day of Week.		DAY.	H. M.	SUN RISES.	SUN SETS.	MOON SETS.
		First Quarter....	5	8 11 morn.			
		Full Moon......	12	7 8 eve.			
		Last Quarter....	20	11 0 eve.			
		New Moon......	28	0 51 morn.			

				H. M.	H. M.	H. M.
1	Thur.	1876 Colorado admitted to the Union.		5 0	7 11	8 46
2	Fri.	1830 Charles X. abdicated.		5 1	7 10	9 14
3	Sat.	1492 Columbus sailed from Palos to America.		5 2	7 9	9 43
4	**Sun.**	1792 Percy Bysshe Shelley born.		5 3	7 8	10 16
5	Mon.	1858 First Atlantic cable landed.		5 4	7 7	10 53
6	Tues.	1775 Daniel O'Connell born.		5 5	7 6	11 39
7	Wed.	1789 War Department established.		5 6	7 5	morn.
8	Thur.	1779 Benjamin Silliman born.		5 6	7 4	30
9	Fri.	1842 First Treaty of Washington signed.		5 7	7 2	1 23
10	Sat.	1821 Missouri admitted to the Union.		5 8	7 1	2 34
11	**Sun.**	1763 J. V. Moreau born.		5 9	7 0	3 40
12	Mon.	1775 C. Malte-Brun born.		5 10	6 59	rises.
13	Tues.	1838 Banks in the U. S. resumed specie payment.		5 11	6 58	7 12
14	Wed.	1714 C. Joseph Vernet born.		5 12	6 56	7 34
15	Thur.	1769 Napoleon I. born.		5 13	6 54	7 55
16	Fri.	1777 Battle of Bennington.		5 14	6 53	8 16
17	Sat.	1786 Frederick the Great died.		5 15	6 52	8 40
18	**Sun.**	1812 Frigate Constitution captured.		5 16	6 51	9 7
19	Mon.	1780 P. J. de Beranger born.		5 17	6 50	9 38
20	Tues.	1745 Francis Asbury born.		5 17	6 48	10 15
21	Wed.	1567 Francis de Sales born.		5 18	6 47	10 58
22	Thur.	1485 Battle of Bosworth Field.		5 19	6 45	11 54
23	Fri.	1769 Cuvier born.		5 20	6 44	morn.
24	Sat.	1814 British army entered Washington.		5 21	6 43	56
25	**Sun.**	1814 Battle of Bladensburg.		5 22	6 41	2 6
26	Mon.	1346 Battle of Crecy.		5 23	6 40	3 19
27	Tues.	1776 Battle of Long Island.		5 24	6 38	4 46
28	Wed.	1749 J. W. von Goethe born.		5 25	6 37	sets.
29	Thur.	1632 John Locke born.		5 26	6 35	7 14
30	Fri.	1814 Alexandria taken by British.		5 26	6 34	7 43
31	Sat.	1688 John Bunyan died.		5 27	6 32	8 15

9th Month.]   SEPTEMBER, 1878.   [30 Days.

Day of Month.	Day of Week.	Moon's Phases.			WASHINGTON.		
			DAY.	H. M.	SUN RISES.	SUN SETS.	MOON SETS.
		First Quarter..	3	3 18 eve.			
		Full Moon	11	10 41 morn.			
		Last Quarter...	19	1 22 eve.			
		New Moon.....	26	9 2 morn.			

			H. M.	H. M.	H. M.
1	**Sun.**	1715 Louis XIV. died.	5 28	6 31	8 51
2	Mon.	1789 Treasury Department estab.	5 29	6 29	9 35
3	Tues.	1783 Definitive treaty of peace with England.	5 30	6 28	10 36
4	Wed.	1870 French Republic proclaimed.	5 31	6 26	11 24
5	Thur.	1513 Balboa discov. Pacific Ocean.	5 32	6 25	morn.
6	Fri.	1757 La Fayette born.	5 33	6 23	26
7	Sat.	1707 Buffon born.	5 34	6 22	1 32
8	**Sun.**	1781 Battle of Eutaw Springs, S. C.	5 35	6 21	2 36
9	Mon.	1850 California admitted to the Union. Utah Ter. organized.	5 35	6 20	3 39
10	Tues.	1813 Perry's victory on Lake Erie.	5 36	6 18	4 39
11	Wed.	1777 Battle of Brandywine.	5 37	6 17	rises.
12	Thur.	1847 Battle of Chepultepec.	5 38	6 15	6 32
13	Fri.	1759 French lose Canada. Battle of Quebec.	5 39	6 14	6 45
14	Sat.	1872 Geneva decision on Alabama Claims announced.	5 40	6 12	7 11
15	**Sun.**	1789 J. Fenimore Cooper born.	5 41	6 10	7 38
16	Mon.	1812 Burning of Moscow.	5 42	6 9	8 12
17	Tues.	1787 Constitution of the U. S. adopted by convention.	5 43	6 7	8 54
18	Wed.	1793 Washington laid corner-stone of the Capitol.	5 44	6 6	9 43
19	Thur.	1779 Lord Brougham born.	5 44	6 4	10 40
20	Fri.	1697 Peace of Ryswick.	5 45	6 2	11 45
21	Sat.	1832 Sir Walter Scott died.	5 46	6 1	morn.
22	**Sun.**	1789 Post-Office Department estab.	5 47	5 59	54
23	Mon.	1836 Madame Malibran died.	5 48	5 58	2 7
24	Tues.	1846 Battle of Monterey.	5 49	5 56	3 21
25	Wed.	1734 Louis René Rohan born.	5 50	5 54	4 35
26	Thur.	1846 Thomas Clarkson died.	5 51	5 53	5 51
27	Fri.	1854 U. S. Steamer Arctic lost.	5 52	5 51	sets.
28	Sat.	1746 Sir William Jones born.	5 53	5 50	6 47
29	**Sun.**	1066 William the Conqueror landed in England.	5 54	5 48	7 28
30	Mon.	1399 Henry IV. of England crowned	5 55	5 46	8 18

10th Month.]   OCTOBER, 1878.   [31 Days.

		Moon's Phases.		WASHINGTON.			
Day of Month.	Day of Week.	First Quarter.. Full Moon..... Last Quarter... New Moon....	DAY. 3 11 19 25	II. M. 1 53 morn. 3 46 morn. 2 2 morn. 5 50 eve.	SUN RISES.	SUN SETS.	MOON SETS.

					II. M.	H. M.	H. M.
1	Tues.	1833	U. S. Deposits removed from U. S. Bank.		5 55	5 43	9 16
2	Wed.	1833	First railroad in the U. S.		5 56	5 42	10 18
3	Thur.	1803	Samuel Adams died.		5 57	5 40	11 14
4	Fri.	1777	Battle of Germantown.		5 58	5 39	morn.
5	Sat.	1813	Death of Tecumseh. Battle of the Thames.		5 59	5 37	29
6	**Sun.**	1821	Jenny Lind born.		6 0	5 35	1 32
7	Mon.	1780	Battle of Kings Mountain, N.C.		6 1	5 34	2 34
8	Tues.	1754	Henry Fielding died.		6 2	5 32	3 30
9	Wed.	1874	International Postal Treaty at Berne.		6 3	5 31	4 29
10	Thur.	1871	Great Fire at Chicago.		6 4	5 29	5 26
11	Fri.	1809	Meriwether Lewis died.		6 5	5 28	rises.
12	Sat.	1492	Columbus discovered America at San Salvador.		6 6	5 26	5 42
13	**Sun.**	1822	Canova died.		6 7	5 25	6 15
14	Mon.	1644	Wm. Penn born in London.		6 8	5 23	6 56
15	Tues.	1797	Treaty of Campo Formio.		6 9	5 22	7 38
16	Wed.	1725	First paper in New York, *New York Gazette.*		6 10	5 21	8 32
17	Thur.	1777	Surrender of Burgoyne at Saratoga.		6 11	5 19	9 33
18	Fri.	1865	Lord Palmerston died.		6 12	5 18	10 39
19	Sat.	1781	Surrender of Cornwallis at Yorktown.		6 13	5 16	11 49
20	**Sun.**	1784	Lord Palmerston born.		6 14	5 15	morn.
21	Mon.	1805	Battle of Trafalgar.		6 15	5 14	59
22	Tues.	1685	Edict of Nantes revoked.		6 16	5 13	2 9
23	Wed.	1872	Theophile Gautier died.		6 18	5 11	3 23
24	Thur.	1852	Daniel Webster died.		6 19	5 10	4 37
25	Fri.	1415	Battle of Agincourt.		6 20	5 8	5 56
26	Sat.	1807	Treaty of Fontainebleau.		6 21	5 8	sets.
27	**Sun.**	1492	Columbus discovered Cuba.		6 22	5 6	6 5
28	Mon.	1874	Rhinehart, sculptor, died.		6 23	5 5	7 0
29	Tues.	1864	John Leech died.		6 24	5 4	8 4
30	Wed.	1735	John Adams born.		6 25	5 2	9 12
31	Thur.	1864	Nevada admitted to the Union.		6 26	5 1	10 19

IIth Month.]   NOVEMBER, 1878.   [30 Days.

Moon's Phases.		WASHINGTON.	

			DAY.	H. M.
		First Quarter....	1	4 43 eve.
		Full Moon......	9	9 26 eve.
		Last Quarter....	17	0 50 eve.
		New Moon......	24	4 3 morn.

Day of Month.	Day of Week.		SUN RISES.	SUN SETS.	MOON SETS.
			H. M.	H. M.	H. M.
1	Fri.	1700 Charles II. of Spain died.	6 27	5 0	11 24
2	Sat.	1783 Washington's farewell orders to American armies.	6 28	4 59	morn.
3	Sun.	1800 Battle of Hohenlinden.	6 29	4 58	25
4	Mon.	1791 St. Clair's defeat by Indians in Ohio.	6 31	4 57	1 27
5	Tues.	1811 Indians defeated by Harrison at Tippecanoe.	6 32	4 56	2 22
6	Wed.	1860 Lincoln elected President.	6 33	4 55	3 20
7	Thur.	1665 London *Gazette* first published.	6 34	4 54	4 17
8	Fri.	1835 New York and Erie Railroad begun.	6 35	4 53	5 15
9	Sat.	1872 Great fire in Boston.	6 36	4 52	6 14
10	Sun.	1876 Centennial Exhibition closed.	6 37	4 51	rises.
11	Mon.	1864 John R. McCulloch died.	6 38	4 50	5 37
12	Tues.	1857 Financial panic in England.	6 39	4 49	6 29
13	Wed.	1862 Johann L. Uhland died.	6 40	4 48	7 29
14	Thur.	1831 G. W. F. Hegel died.	6 41	4 47	8 32
15	Fri.	1708 Earl of Chatham born.	6 43	4 47	9 39
16	Sat.	1717 D'Alembert born.	6 44	4 46	10 47
17	Sun.	1800 First meeting of Congress in Washington.	6 45	4 45	11 55
18	Mon.	1647 Pierre Bayle born.	6 46	4 44	morn.
19	Tues.	1794 Jay's treaty with England signed.	6 47	4 44	1 6
20	Wed.	1272 Edward I. crowned.	6 48	4 43	2 15
21	Thur.	1789 North Carolina ratified the Constitution.	6 49	4 43	3 29
22	Fri.	1643 Cavelier de la Salle born.	6 50	4 42	4 45
23	Sat.	1873 Steamer Ville du Havre lost.	6 51	4 42	6 4
24	Sun.	1784 Zachary Taylor born.	6 52	4 41	sets.
25	Mon.	1783 Evacuation of New York by British.	6 53	4 40	5 44
26	Tues.	1806 Berlin decree by Napoleon.	6 55	4 40	6 50
27	Wed.	1635 Madame de Maintenon born.	6 56	4 40	8 0
28	Thur.	1776 Washington crossed the Delaware.	6 57	4 40	9 10
29	Fri.	1802 Ohio admitted to the Union.	6 58	4 39	10 13
30	Sat.	1700 Charles XII. wins battle of Narva.	6 59	4 39	11 14

12th Month.]   DECEMBER, 1878.   [31 Days.

		Moon's Phases.	WASHINGTON.			
Day of Month.	Day of Week.		DAY. H. M.	SUN RISES.	SUN SETS.	MOON SETS.
		First Quarter.... 1	11 29 morn.			
		Full Moon....... 9	2 42 eve.			
		Last Quarter.... 16	9 56 eve.			
		New Moon...... 23	4 16 eve.			
		First Quarter.... 31	8 49 morn.			
				H. M.	H. M.	H. M.
1	Sun.	1841 Greenough's " Washington " placed in the Capitol.		7 0	4 39	morn.
2	Mon.	1805 Battle of Austerlitz.		7 1	4 39	13
3	Tues.	1818 Illinois admitted to the Union.		7 2	4 38	1 11
4	Wed.	1783 Washington's farewell to the army.		7 2	4 38	2 7
5	Thur.	1782 Martin Van Buren born.		7 3	4 38	3 6
6	Fri.	1823 Max Müller born.		7 4	4 38	4 5
7	Sat.	1787 Delaware ratified the Constitution.		7 5	4 38	5 5
8	Sun.	1765 Eli Whitney born.		7 6	4 38	6 6
9	Mon.	1807 American ports closed to the British.		7 7	4 38	rises.
10	Tues.	1817 Mississippi admitted to the Union.		7 8	4 38	5 23
11	Wed.	1816 Indiana admitted to the Union.		7 9	4 38	6 25
12	Thur.	1787 Pennsylvania ratified the Constitution.		7 9	4 39	7 32
13	Fri.	1850 Territory of N. Mexico orga'd.		7 10	4 39	8 39
14	Sat.	1819 Alabama admitted to the Union		7 11	4 39	9 48
15	Sun.	1814 The Hartford Convention met.		7 12	4 39	10 55
16	Mon.	1773 Destruction of tea in Boston harbor.		7 12	4 40	morn.
17	Tues.	1770 Beethoven born.		7 13	4 40	3
18	Wed.	1865 Amendment abolishing slavery declared adopted.		7 14	4 40	1 14
19	Thur.	1154 Henry II. of England crowned.		7 14	4 41	2 26
20	Fri.	1767 Emmerich Vattel died.		7 15	4 41	3 42
21	Sat.	1639 Jean Racine born.		7 15	4 42	4 56
22	Sun.	1620 Pilgrims settled at Plymouth, Mass.		7 16	4 42	6 6
23	Mon.	1783 Washington resigned his commission.		7 16	4 43	7 12
24	Tues.	1814 Treaty of Peace signed at Ghent.		7 17	4 43	sets.
25	Wed.	1642 Sir Isaac Newton born. Christmas Day.		7 17	4 44	6 48
26	Thur.	1716 Thomas Gray born.		7 17	4 44	7 55
27	Fri.	1595 Sir Francis Drake died.		7 18	4 45	8 59
28	Sat.	1846 Iowa admitted to the Union.		7 18	4 46	10 0
29	Sun.	1845 Texas admitted to the Union.		7 18	4 47	11 0
30	Mon.	1870 Juan Prim died.		7 19	4 47	11 57
31	Tues.	1814 Jules Simon born.		7 19	4 48	morn.

HEADS OF THE PRINCIPAL NATIONS OF THE WORLD IN 1878.

Governments.	Rulers.	Title.	Year of Birth.	Date of Accession.
Argentine Republic....	Nicolás Avellaneda......	President.....	1838	Oct. 12, 1874
Austria-Hungary........	Franz Joseph I.........	Emperor.....	1830	Dec. 2, 1848
Belgium..............	Leopold II.............	King.......	1835	Dec. 10, 1865
Bolivia...............	Gen. Daza.............	President.....		May 4, 1876
Brazil...............	Pedro II., Alcántara....	Emperor....	1825	April 7, 1831
Chili.................	Anibal Pinto..........	President.....		Sept.18, 1876
China................	Kuanglu (Tsai-Tien)....	Emperor....	1871	Jan., 1875
Colombia.............	Aquileo Parra.........	President.....		April 1, 1876
Costa Rica...........	Vicente Herrera........	President.....		Provisional.
Denmark	Christian IX..........	King....	1818	Nov.15, 1863
Ecuador.............	José de Vintimille.....	President....		Sept. 8, 1876
France..............	M. E. P. M. de MacMahon	President....	1808	May 24, 1873
Germany.............	Wilhelm I............	Emperor....	1797	Jan. 18, 1871
Alsace-Lorraine......	Eduard von Möller.....	Oberpräsid't.	1814	Nov., 1871
Anhalt...............	Friedrich............	Duke......	1831	May 22, 1871
Baden...............	Friedrich I...........	Grand Duke..	1826	Apl. 24, 1852
Bavaria............	Ludwig II............	King.......	1845	Mar.10, 1864
Bremen..............		Burgomasters		
Brunswick...........	Wilhelm I............	Duke......	1806	Apl. 20, 1831
Hamburg............		Burgomasters		
Hesse...............	Ludwig III...........	Grand Duke..	1806	June 16,1848
Lippe...............	G. F. Waldemar.......	Prince......	1824	Dec. 8, 1875
Lubeck..............		Burgomasters		
Mecklenb'rg-Schwerin	Friedrich Franz II.....	Grand Duke..	1823	Mar. 7, 1842
Mecklenburg-Strelitz..	Friedrich Wilhelm I.....	Grand Duke..	1819	Sept. 6, 1860
Oldenburg...........	Peter I..............	Grand Duke..	1827	Feb.27, 1853
Prussia..............	Wilhelm I............	King........	1797	Jan. 2, 1861
Reuss-Greiz.........	Henrich XXII.........	Prince......	1846	Nov. 8, 1859
Reuss-Schleiz........	Heinrich XIV.........	Prince......	1832	July 10, 1867
Saxe-Altenburg......	Ernst...............	Duke......	1826	Aug. 3, 1853
Saxe-Coburg & Gotha.	Ernst II.............	Duke......	1818	Jan. 29, 1844
Saxe-Meiningen......	Georg II............	Duke......	1826	Sept.20,1866
Saxe-Weimar........	Karl Alexander........	Grand Duke..	1818	July 8, 1853
Saxony.............	Albert I.............	King.......	1828	Oct. 29, 1873
Schaumburg-Lippe....	Adolf...............	Prince......	1817	Nov.21, 1860
Schwarzburg-Rudolph	Georg...............	Prince......	1832	Nov.26, 1869
Schwarzburg-Sonders.	Günther II...........	Prince......	1801	Aug. 19,1835
Waldeck............	Georg Victor.........	Prince......	1831	May 14, 1845
Wortemberg.........	Karl I...............	King.......	1823	June 25,1864
Gt. Britain & Ireland....	Victoria I...........	Queen&E.ofI.	1819	June 20,1837
Greece..............	Georgios I...........	King.......	1845	June 6, 1863
Guatemala...........	J. Rufino Barrios......	President....		May 7, 1873
Haiti...............	Boisrond-Canal........	President....		July 19, 1876
Hawaiian Islands......	Kalakaua............	King.......	1836	Feb. 12, 1874
Honduras...........	Crecencio Gomez.......	President....		June 16,1876
Italy................	Humbert I............	King.......	1844	Jan. 9, 1878
Japan...............	Mutsu Ilito...........	Mikado....	1859	Feb.13, 1867
Mexico.............	Porfirio Diaz..........	President....	1830	Mar.12, 1877
Morocco............	Muley-Hassan.........	Sultan.....	1831	Sept.25,1873
Netherlands.........	Willem III...........	King.......	1817	Mar 17,1949
Nicaragua..........	Pedro Chamorro.......	President....		Nov.10, 1875
Paraguay...........	Joao Bautista Gill.....	President....		Nov.25,1874
Persia..............	Nassr-ed-Deen........	Shah.......	1800	Sept.10.1848
Peru...............	Mariano Ignacio Prado...	President....		Aug. 2, 1876
Portugal............	Luis I..............	King.......	1838	Nov. 11,1861
Russia..............	Alexander II..........	Emperor....	1818	Mar. 2, 1855
Santo Domingo........	Bonaventura Baez......	President....		Dec. 10, 1876
San Salvador.........	Rafael Zaldivar.......	President....		Apl. 30, 1876
Spain..............	Alfonso XII..........	King.......	1857	Dec.80, 1874
Sweden and Norway....	Oscar II............	King.......	1829	Sept.18,1872
Switzerland..........	J. Heer..............	President....		1877
Turkey..............	Abdul-Hamid-Khan.....	Sultan......	1842	Aug.31, 1876
Egypt..............	Ismail I.............	Khedive.....	1830	Jan. 18, 1863
Roumania..........	Karl I. Domnu........	Prince......	1839	May 10, 1866
Servia.............	Milan IV. Obrenovic...	Prince......	1853	July 2, 1860
United States........	Rutherford B. Hayes....	President....	1822	Mar. 5, 1877
Uruguay............	L. Latorre...........	President....		Mar.11, 1876
Venezuela	Antonio Guzman Blanco.	President.....		Apl. 15, 1873

A BRIEF HISTORY OF ALMANACS.

AMONG the most ancient as well as the most widely diffused productions of the press, the Almanac holds a conspicuous place. The
word is generally derived from the Arabic *al-manah*, the reckoning ;
and the book commonly embraces the calendar for one year, with a more
or less extended ephemeris of the movements of the planetary system, and a record of the eclipses, festivals, or special days, etc., to
which is sometimes added statistical matter or general information.
Frequently, however, almanacs have been made the vehicle for super-
stitions, weather predictions, superannuated jokes, vulgar allusions,
and prophetical impostures.   The credulity of the uneducated has been
imposed on in all ages by prognostics of the weather, every day of the
year being set down as a propitious or unpropitious season for certain transactions.   Even modern almanacs prepared for country circulation continue to perpetuate this absurd and misleading practice.
The utmost which science can effect in forecasting the weather barely extends to the twenty-four hours' "probabilities," now termed
"weather indications," published by the Signal Office of the United
States Army.   The science of meteorology affords no means for almanac predictions of the weather set down a year in advance, and all
such pretended forecasts are impositions upon popular credulity.

Ages before the invention of printing, something akin to the al-
, manac was in use among all civilized nations of antiquity—the Egyp-
tians, Greeks, Romans, etc.   The Chinese also used them from time
immemorial.   The earliest manuscript almanacs noticed date from
A.D. 1150, and several of the fourteenth century are found in English libraries.   In France, the noted astrologer Nostradamus began
the publication of the almanac which bore his name in 1550 ; and the
celebrated *Almanach de Liége*, by Laensberg, dates from 1635.   Its great
success led to numerous imitations, and the *Double* or *Triple Liége-
ois*, the patriarch of French almanacs, has maintained itself to this
day in the favor of the common people, although representing little but tradition, ignorance, and prejudice.   The French press now
annually swarms with almanacs in every variety of attractiveness of

title, price, and style of manufacture. There is the *Almanach comique, the Almanach pittoresque, dramatique, critique, lunatique, prophétique, chanton, satirique, démocratique, astrologique, anecdotique, astronomique*, etc. There is the *Almanach du laboreur, du cultivateur, du jardinier, des dames, des muses*, and so on. The *Almanach Royal*, founded in 1699, and known variously as the *Almanach Imperial, Royal* or *National* according to the changes of the government, is the principal official almanac now printed in France, though the *Almanach de France* has also a large circulation.

In Germany, the celebrated *Almanach de Gotha*, which first appeared in 1764, and has been continuously published and enlarged for 114 years, has become recognized as an authority upon the genealogy of the royal and noble families of Europe, while its official lists and statistical information (not always accurate) regarding the organization, finances, etc., of all the governments of the world render it a much-sought-for book of reference.

The earliest English almanacs are of the sixteenth century, and for two hundred years most almanacs were issued by pretended astrologers, one of the most famous of whom was William Lilly, who began to print his Ephemeris in 1644. Another famed English almanac was that of " Francis Moore, Physician," a quack doctor of Westminster, who began his career of imposture in 1698. Poor Robin's Almanack began in 1663, and is still published. John Partridge's Merlinus Liberatus was started in 1681. R. White's Celestial Atlas or Ephemeris began in 1750, and is still published. These almanacs abounded in direful portents of the baneful effects of comets or blazing stars, and were filled with absurdities about lucky and unlucky days, nativities, judgments of things to come, epidemic diseases, murrain in cattle, prodigious shipwrecks, monstrous floods, and other events referred to supernatural or planetary agencies which are directly due to natural causes. In short, it may be said of the almanacs of earlier days (and even of some still circulated) that they are simply repositories for all the errors of antiquity.

Not until the year 1827 was there a single almanac printed in Great Britain free from these anachronisms and absurdities. In that year Charles Knight, the industrious writer and printer, and publisher for the Society for the Diffusion of Useful Knowledge, conceived the idea of bringing out the British Almanac. The market was then filled with Poor Robin's, Francis Moore's, Lilly's, and Partridge's astronomical almanacs, which had been published from the time of James I., under the monopoly of the London Stationers' Company, till their exclusive privilege was broken up in 1775 by a famous suit, in which the Court decided against the legality of the patent for printing almanacs. The powerful Stationers' Company, however, by buying up competitors, contrived to continue possessed of an exclusive market for stamped almanacs, and with a reckless-

ness disgraceful to the age, were still perpetuating the follies and in-
decencies to which we have referred. Not only so, but the British
Government levied a tax of nearly thirty cents on every almanac issued in Great Britain, and the number sold, even with this heavy im-
position, exceeded 450,000 copies annually. Says Mr. Knight:

"In 1897, when the almanac stamp was fifteen pence, the people of England,
calling themselves enlightened, voluntarily taxed themselves to pay an annual sum
of fifteen thousand pounds to the Government for permission to read the trash
which first obtained currency and belief when every village had its witch and every
churchyard its ghost ; when agues were cured by charms and stolen spoons discovered by incantation. * * * *
"I immediately went to work to elaborate the scheme of a rational and useful
almanac. It was completed in a few days, and I took it to consult Mr. Brougham.
What an incalculable source of satisfaction to a projector, even of so apparently
humble a work as an almanac, to find a man of ardent and capacious mind, quick to
comprehend, frank to approve, not deeming a difficult undertaking impossible,
ready not only for counsel, but for action! 'It is now the middle of November,'
said the rapid genius of unprocrastinating labor ; 'can you have your almanac out
before the end of the year?' 'Yes, with a little help in the scientific matters.'
'Then tell Mr. Coates to call a meeting of the General Committee at my chambers
at half-past eight to-morrow morning. You shall have help enough. You may
have your choice of good men for your astronomy and meteorology, your tides and
your eclipses. Go to work, and never fear.'
"*The British Almanac* was published before the 1st of January. Late as it was
in the field, high as was its unavoidable price—half-a-crown, to cover the heavy
stamp duty and allow a profit to the retailers—ten thousand were sold in a week.
* * * * The two objects which have been always kept in view were set forth
in 1828: First, That the subjects selected shall be generally useful, either for present information or future reference. Secondly, That the knowledge conveyed shall
be given in the most condensed and explicit manner, so as to be valuable to every
class of readers."—[Passages of a Working Life, by Charles Knight.]

The marked success of the British Almanac has been permanent ;
and this is due to the fact that its high character has been maintained, and many articles of permanent value have enriched its columns during every year of the half-century since its foundation. The
stamp duty on almanacs (one of those odious taxes on the spread of
intelligence which so long survived) was repealed in 1834, and this,
with the example of the British Almanac, has tended steadily to improve the standard of these publications. Among the most useful
and comprehensive of the English almanacs are Whitaker's
Almanac, first issued in 1869 ; Thom's Irish Almanac and Official
Directory of Great Britain and Ireland, begun in 1844 ; Oliver &
Boyd's Edinburgh Almanac, established 1816 ; the Financial Reform Almanac, started in 1867 ; and the Statesman's Year-Book,
first published in 1864.

The annals of almanacs in America begin with the first introduction of printing in the New World north of Mexico. In 1639 appeared at Cambridge "an Almanac calculated for New England, by
Mr. William Pierce, Mariner." This was printed by Stephen
Daye, and no copy of it has been preserved. It was the first book
printed in the colonies, preceding by a twelvemonth the famous
Bay Psalm Book, or New England Version of the Psalms, published by the same printer at Cambridge in 1640. Cambridge continued to issue almanacs almost every year, and in 1676 the first

Boston Almanac was printed by John Foster, who published the same year the first book ever printed in Boston. The first Philadelphia almanac was put forth in 1686, edited by Daniel Leeds, and printed by William Bradford. New York followed with its first almanac in 1697 by J. Clapp. Samuel Clough issued his first almanac in Boston in 1700, which was continued until A.D. 1708, under the title of The New England Almanac, a copy of which for 1703, a dingy little book of twelve leaves, measuring three and a half inches by five and a half, is before us. The title is as follows: " The New England ALMANAC for the Year of our Lord MDCCIII. Being Third after Leap-year, and from the CREATION, 5652, Discovery of *America*, by *Columbus*, 211, Reign of our Gracious *Queen* ANNE, (which began *March* 8, 1702,) the 2, year. Wherein is contained Things necessary and common in such a COMPOSURE. Licensed by His Excellency the GOVERNOUR. *Boston*, Printed by *B. Green* and *J. Allen*, for the Booksellers, and are to be sold at their shops. 1703." The second page bears the traditional and repulsive wood-cut professing to show what parts the moon governs in man's body, corresponding to the twelve signs of the Zodiac. The weather predictions are curious. For April 26 is foretold "misling weather mixt with some dripling showers." The eclipses of the year 1703, "in the judgment both of Divines and Astrologers," are supposed to "portend great alterations, mutations, changes and troubles to come upon the world." The "Comet or Æthereal Blaze," seen in 1702, is said to have led to " blood-shed, droughts, clashing of armies, and terrible diseases among men."

Of Almanacs which have been published in long series in this country, the following list embraces some of the more notable: Nathaniel Ames's Astronomical Diary and Almanac, started at Boston in 1725, and continued more than half a century, about 60,000 copies of which were sold annually; Titan Leeds's American Almanac, Philadelphia, 1726; T. Godfrey's Pennsylvania Almanac, begun at Philadelphia in 1729; Poor Richard's Almanac, by Richard Saunders (Benjamin Franklin), continued by others as " Poor Richard improved," Philadelphia, 1733-1786; Father Abraham's Almanac, by Abraham Weatherwise, Philadelphia, 1759-1799; Nathanael Low's Astronomical Diary or Almanac, Boston, 1762-1827; Isaiah Thomas's Massachusetts, Connecticut, Rhode Island, New Hampshire, and Vermont Almanac, Worcester, Mass., and Boston, 1775-1822; R. B. Thomas's Farmer's Almanac, Boston, 1793-1877; the Massachusetts Register and Almanac, Boston, established by Mein and Fleming, 1767-1877; Webster's Calendar, or the Albany Almanac, 1784-1877, the oldest family almanac continuously published extant in the United States; Bickerstaff's Boston and New England Almanac, 1768-1814, continued as Bickerstaff's Rhode Island Almanac, Providence, 1815-1877; Poor Will's Almanac,

Philadelphia, 1770 to 1840, or later ; the Virginia Almanac, Williamsburg and Richmond, 1751 to 1829, and later ; the South Carolina and Georgia Almanac, Charleston, 1760 to 1800, and later ; North American Calendar, Wilmington, Del., 1796 to 1844, and later ; Dudley Leavitt's New England Almanac, Exeter and Concord, N. H., 1797 to 1877 ; Thomas Spofford's Farmer's Almanac, Boston, 1817 to 1845 ; John Gruber's Town and Country Almanac, Hagerstown, Md., 1822 to 1877 ; the Maine Farmer's Almanac, by D. Robinson, Hallowell, 1818 to 1877 ; Daboll's New England Almanac, New London, Conn., 1777–1877 ; and Allen's New England Almanac, Hartford, 1806 to 1833, or later. Many of these almanacs are preserved in private families, though but few are to be found in our public libraries. It was an early habit in New England to preserve the almanacs from year to year, carefully stitched together, and to annotate them frequently with family records or current events. The generally worthless character which has been attributed to the English almanacs of the last century must be modified as regards some of the American family almanacs. Benjamin Franklin, the illustrious printer and statesman, is justly declared by a French encyclopædist to have put forth the first popular almanac which spoke the language of reason. In truth, the homely maxims and pithy proverbial counsels of Poor Richard, although not all originated by Franklin, constitute to this day a breviary of life and conduct admirable in most respects for the use of the young.

In the later days of the American Revolution, the almanacs put forth by Nathanael Low, at Boston, price "4 coppers single," contained political articles vigorously defending the liberties of the people, and exerted a great influence at the New England fireside in inspiring young and old with the love of freedom.

Virginia was early in the field with Warne's Almanac, printed at Williamsburg, in 1731. The first almanac printed in Connecticut was issued at New London in 1765, by T. Green. The first Rhode Island Almanac was issued at Newport in 1728, by James Franklin, and the first Providence Almanac, by Benjamin West, in 1763. The first in Maryland of which we have any trace appeared at Annapolis in 1763.

Of Agricultural and Medical Almanacs, the latter an outgrowth of the present century, the name is legion. Comic almanacs appear to have been first published in the United States about 1834, and have had an enormous circulation. Of the religious or denominational almanacs, the Church Almanac of the Protestant Episcopal Church was begun in 1830 ; the Catholic Almanac and Directory (continued under various names to the present time) in 1833 ; the Methodist Almanac in 1834 ; the Universalist Register in 1836 ; the Baptist Almanac in 1842 (?) ; the Congregational Almanac in 1846 ; the American Unitarian Register and Year-Book in 1846 ; the Presbyterian Histori-

cal Almanac in 1858; and the Family Christian Almanac in 1821. Most, if not all of these are still continued annually.

The class of Political almanacs, or almanacs issued by public journals, began with the first Whig Almanac issued by Horace Greeley in 1838, continued since 1855 as the Tribune Almanac. The chief feature of this publication has been its full tables of election statistics. The World Almanac was first issued in 1868; and the New York Herald Almanac in 1872. The Evening Journal Almanac of Albany dates from 1860, and the Public Ledger Almanac, Philadelphia, from 1870. Many other journals east and west publish annual almanacs.

Of more extensive publications under the name of almanacs published in this country, The National Calendar, edited by Peter Force, was the prototype. This work was published at Washington from 1820 to 1836 (with a three years' interval from 1825 to 1827, when no calendar was issued), and was a useful official register of the Government, with abstracts of public documents and other valuable information. The American Almanac and Repository of Useful Knowledge, first published at Cambridge, Mass., in 1830 (two years after the first issue of the British Almanac), was continued annually under various editors and publishers till the year 1861, when the publication ceased. This carefully edited publication embodied much astronomical and meteorological information, that department frequently extending to one hundred pages. The official statistics of Congress and the general government, and of the various States, with a chronicle of events and obituary notices, made up the remainder of the work. The United States Almanac, or Complete Ephemeris, edited by John Downes, appeared at Philadelphia for the years 1843, 1844, and 1845. It was nearly one half made up of astronomical matter and tables, valuable chiefly to those versed in the higher mathematics. The National Almanac and Annual Record for the years 1863 and 1864 was published at Philadelphia by George W. Childs, and contained a vast amount of useful and thoroughly digested information. The American Year-Book and National Register, edited by David N. Camp, appeared from the Hartford press for the year 1869, in an octavo of 824 pages, and was the most extensive attempt to combine a work of general information and reference with the calendar which the country has seen. It has not been continued.

Many almanacs are printed in this country in foreign languages. The pioneer of the German Almanacs was issued by Sower of Germantown, Pa., in 1738, and continued by him and his successors to the present day. Franklin's Poor Richard's Almanac was translated into German by A. Armbruster, who was in partnership with Franklin from 1754 to 1758. German almanacs are now printed and circulated in large editions in nearly all the Middle and Western

States of the Union. In French, the Almanach Français des États Unis, established in 1848 in New York, is still published.

Of Nautical Almanacs, the class of Ephemerides which are indispensable to the navigator and astronomer, the first was published by the Bureau of Longitudes at Paris in 1679, and has been continued to this time, appearing since 1783 under the title of *Le Connaissance des Temps*. The British Nautical Almanac was commenced in 1767, and now forms a large volume published by the Admiralty. In Germany, the Astronomisches Jahrbuch, founded in 1776, still continues to be published by the Royal Academy of Sciences, at Berlin. The first number of the American Ephemeris and Nautical Almanac, published at Washington, was for the year 1855, by the late Admiral C. H. Davis, under the authority of the Navy Department. These publications are still continued annually, each being issued some three years in advance, with full calculations of eclipses, planetary motions, fixed stars, occultations, etc.

HOW INTEREST EATS.

ONE of the causes of bankruptcy is that so few persons properly estimate the difference between a high and low rate of interest, and therefore often borrow money at a ruinous rate that no legitimate business can stand. Very few have figured on the difference between six and eight per cent. One dollar loaned for one hundred years at six per cent, with the interest collected annually and added to the principal, will amount to $340. At eight per cent it amounts to $2203, or nearly seven times as much. At three per cent, the usual rate of interest in England, it amounts to $19.25; whereas at ten per cent, which has been a very common rate in the United States, it is $13,809, or about seven hundred times as much. At twelve per cent it amounts to $84,075, or more than four thousand times as much. At eighteen per cent it amounts to $15,145,007. At twenty-four per cent (which we sometimes hear talked of) it reaches the enormous sum of $2,551,799,404.

One hundred dollars borrowed at six per cent, with the interest compounded annually, will amount to $1842 in fifty years, while the same $100 borrowed at eight per cent will amount to $4690 in fifty years. One thousand dollars, at ten per cent, compounded, will run up to $117,390 in fifty years.

AGE OF NOTABLE PERSONS.

NAME.	BORN.	DIED.	NAME.	BORN.	DIED.
Abbott, Jacob......	1803	....	Aristides............	....	B.C. 468?
Abbott, John S. C..	1805	1877	Aristophanes.......	B.C. 444?	B.C. 380?
Abd-el-Kader.......	1807	1873	Aristotle............	B.C. 384	B.C. 322
Abelard, Pierre	1079	1142	Arminius, J.........	1560	1609
About, Edmond....	1828	....	Armstrong, John...	1755	1843
Adams, Charles F...	1807	....	Arnold, Benedict...	1740	1801
Adams, John.......	1735	1826	Arnold, Thomas...	1795	1842
Adams, J. Quincy..	1767	1848	Arrianus...........	90?	170?
Adams, Samuel....	1722	1803	Asbury, Francis....	1745	1816
Adams, William T..	1822	....	Astor, John'Jacob..	1763	1848
Addison, Joseph...	1672	1719	Athanasius, Saint..	296?	373
Æschines...........	B.C. 387	B.C. 314	Athenæus	....	200?
Æschylus	B.C. 525	B.C. 456	Attila...............	....	453
Æsop	?	B.C. 570?	Auber, Daniel F. E.	1782	1871
Agassiz, Louis.....	1807	1873	Audubon, John J..	1780	1851
Aguesseau, H. F. d'	1668	1751	Auerbach, Berthold	1812	....
Aguilar, Grace.....	1816	1847	Augustine, Saint....	354	430
Ainsworth, Wm. H.	1805	...	Augustus Cæsar....	B.C. 63	14
Airy, George B.....	1801	....	Aurelian, Emperor.	213	275
Akenside, Mark....	1721	1770	Austen, Jane.......	1775	1817
Albert, Prince......	1819	1861	Bach, J. Sebastian..	1685	1750
Albert Edward	1841	....	Bache, Alex. Dallas.	1806	1867
Albertus Magnus...	1193?	1280	Bacon, Francis.....	1561	1626
Alcibiades..........	B.C. 450?	B.C. 404	Bacon, Roger	1214	1292?
Alcott, A. Bronson.	1799	....	Badger, George E..	1795	1866
Alcott, Wm. A.....	1798	1859	Baillie, Joanna.....	1762	1851
Aldrich, T. Bailey..	1836	....	Bainbridge, Wm...	1774	1833
Alembert, Jean L. d'	1717	1783	Baker, Edward D...	1811	1861
Alexander the Great	B.C. 356	B.C. 323	Balboa, Vas. Nunez de	1475	1517
Alexander I. of Russia	1777	1825	Baldwin, Abraham.	1754	1807
Alexander II. "	1818	....	Balfe, Michael Wm.	1808	1870
Alfieri, Vittorio.....	1749	1803	Balzac, Honoré de..	1799	1850
Alfred the Great....	849	901?	Bancroft, George...	1800	....
Alison, Sir Archibald	1792	1867	Banks, Nathaniel P.	1816	....
Allen, Ethan.......	1737	1789	Banks, Sir Joseph..	1743	1820
Allston, Washington	1779	1843	Barbour, James....	1775	1842
Alva, Ferd., Duke of	1508	1582	Barbour, Philip P..	1783	1841
Ames, Fisher.......	1758	1808	Barlow, Francis C..	1834	....
Anacreon...........	B.C. 563?	B.C. 478?	Barlow, Joel.......	1755	1812
Anaxagoras........	B.C. 500?	B.C. 428	Barnes, Albert.....	1798	1870
Andersen, Hans C..	1805	1875	Barney, Joshua	1759	1818
Anderson, Robert..	1805	1871	Barré, Isaac.......	1726	1802
André, John, Major.	1751	1780	Barron, James.....	1768	1851
Andrew, John A...	1818	1867	Barrow, Isaac......	1630	1677
Anne (Queen of Eng'd)	1664	1714	Bartolozzi, F.......	1725?	1813?
Anthony, St., the Great	250	356	Bates, Edward	1793	1869
Antonelli, Giacomo.	1806	1877	Baxter, Richard....	1615	1691
Antoninus, Marcus Au.	121	180	Bayard, Chevalier de	1475?	1524
Antoninus Pius, Titus	86	161	Bayle, Pierre.......	1647	1706
Aquinas, St. Thomas	1224?	1274	Beaumont, Francis.	1586	1616
Arago, Dominique F.	1786	1853	Beauregard, P. G. T.	1818	....
Archimedes.......	B.C. 287?	B.C. 212	Beaumarchais, P. de	1732	1799
Ariosto, Lodovico..	1474	1533	Becket, St. Thos. A.	1119	1170

NAME.	BORN.	DIED.	NAME.	BORN.	DIED.
Bede, *the Venerable.*	672?	735	Brougham, H., Lord	1779	1868
Beecher, Henry W.	1813	....	Brown, Aaron V...	1795	1859
Beecher, Lyman....	1775	1863	Brown, Benj. Gratz.	1826	....
Beethoven, Ludwig.	1770	1827	Brown, H. K.......	1814	....
Belisarius..........	505?	565	Brown, John.......	1800	1859
Bell, John..........	1797	1869	Browne, Charles F.	1834	1867
Bellini, Vincenzio..	1802	1835	Browne, Sir Thomas	1605	1682
Benjamin, Judah P.	1812	....	Browning, Eliz. B..	1809	1861
Bennett, J. Gordon.	1795	1872	Browning, Orville H.	1810	....
Bentham, Jeremy..	1748	1832	Browning, Robert..	1812	....
Benton, Thomas H.	1782	1853	Brownlow, Wm. G.	1805	1877
Béranger, P. J. de.	1780	1857	Brownson, Orestes A.	1803	1876
Berkeley, George..	1684	1753	Bruce, Robert......	1274	1329
Berkley, Sir Wm...	1610?	1677	Brutus, Marcus Jun. B.C.	85	B.C. 42
Berrien, John M...	1781	1856	Bryant, Wm. Cullen	1794	....
Bibb, George M....	1772	1859	Buchanan, James...	1791	1868
Binney, Horace	1780	1875	Buckle, Henry Thos.	1822	1862
Birney, James G...	1792	1857	Buffon, Geo. L. L...	1707	1788
Bismarck, Prince von	1815	....	Bulwer Lytton, Lord	1805	1873
Black, Jeremiah S.	1810	....	Bunsen, C. K. J., Baron	1791	1860
Blackstone, Sir W..	1723	1780	Bunyan, John......	1628	1688
Blaine, James G...	1830	....	Burges, Tristam....	1770	1853
Blair, Francis P....	1791	1877	Burke, Edmund....	1728?	1797
Blair, Jr., Fran. P..	1821	1875	Burlingame, Anson.	1822	1870
Blair, Montgomery.	1813	....	Burns, Robert......	1759	1796
Boileau, Nicholas..	1636	1711	Burnside, Amb. E..	1824	....
Boccaccio, Giovanni	1313	1375	Burr, Aaron........	1756	1836
Bolingbroke, H. St. J.	1678	1751	Burton, Richard F.	1821	....
Bolivar, Simon.....	1783	1830	Burton, Robert.....	1576	1640
Bonaparte, Jerome.	1784	1860	Butler, Benj. F., of N.Y.	1795	1858
Bonaparte, Joseph.	1768	1844	Butler, Benj. F., of Mass.	1818	....
Bonaparte, Louis...	1778	1846	Butler, Joseph	1692	1752
Bonaparte, Lucien..	1775	1840	Butler, Samuel.....	1612	1680
Bonaparte, Napoleon	1769	1821	Byron, G. N. G., Lord	1788	1824
Bonheur, Rosalie...	1822	....	Cabot, Sebastian...	1477?	1557?
Boone, Daniel......	1735	1820	Cæsar, Caius Julius B.C.	100	B.C. 44
Booth, Junius B...	1796	1852	Calderon de la Barca	1600	1681
Booth, Edwin......	1833	....	Calhoun, John C...	1782	1850
Borgia, Lucrezia...	?	1523	Caligula, Caius Cæsar	12	41
Boswell, James.....	1740	1795	Calvin, John.......	1509	1564
Bossuet, Jacques B.	1627	1704	Cameron, Simon...	1790	....
Boucicault, Dion...	1822	....	Camoens, Luis de..	1524?	1579?
Boudinot, Elias.....	1740	1821	Campbell, Alex....	1788	1866
Boutwell, George S.	1818	....	Campbell, James A.	1811	....
Boyd, Linn........	1800	1859	Campbell, Thomas.	1777	1844
Brackenridge, H. M.	1786	1871	Canning, George...	1770	1827
Bradley, Joseph P.	1813	....	Canova, Antonio...	1757	1822
Bragg, Braxton.....	1817	1876	Carey, Henry C....	1798	....
Breckinridge, J. C..	1821	1875	Carlyle, Thomas...	1795	....
Bremer, Fredrika...	1801	1865	Carroll, Charles....	1737	1832
Bright, John.......	1811	....	Cass, Lewis........	1782	1866
Bristow, Benj. H...	1833	....	Catharine I.	1684?	1727
Broderick, David C.	1818	1859	Catharine II........	1729	1796
Bronte, Charlotte ..	1816	1855	Cato, the Censor... B.C.	234?	B.C. 149

NAME.	BORN.	DIED.	NAME.	BORN.	DIED.
Cato, *uticensis*	B.C. 95	B.C. 46	Colburn, Warren...	1793	1858
Catron, John	1778	1865	Cole, Thomas	1801	1848
Catullus, Valerius..	B.C. 87	B.C. 47?	Coleridge, Samuel T.	1772	1834
Cavour, Camillo....	1810	1861	Colfax, Schuyler....	1823	....
Caxton, William...	1412?	1491?	Collamer, Jacob....	1792	1865
Cellini, Benvenuto..	1500	1571?	Collins, William....	1720	1756
Cenci, Beatrice	?	1599	Collins, Wm. Wilkie	1825	....
Cervantes-Saavedra.	1547	1616	Columbus, Christopher	1436?	1506
Chalmers, Thomas.	1780	1847	Combe, George.....	1788	1858
Champlain, S. de...	1570	1635	Comte. Auguste....	1798	1857
Channing, Wm. E..	1780	1842	Condé, Prince de...	1621	1686
Chantrey, Sir F....	1781	1841	Condorcet, Marq. de	1743	1794
Charlemagne........	742	814	Confucius..........	B.C. 551?	B.C. 478?
Charles I...........	1600	1649	Congreve, William.	1670	1729
Charles II.........	1630	1685	Constantine *the Great*	272?	337
Charles XII........	1682	1718	Cook, James.......	1728	1779
Charles the Bold....	1433	1477	Cooley, Thomas M.	1824	...
Charlevoix,P.F.X.de	1682	1761	Cooper, Sir Astley..	1708	1841
Chase, Samuel......	1741	1811	Cooper, J. Fenimore	1789	1851
Chase, Salmon P....	1808	1873	Cooper, Peter.......	1791	....
Chastellux, Marq. de	1734	1788	Copernicus, Nicolaus	1473	1543
Chateaubriand, F.A.	1769?	1848	Copley, John S.....	1737	1815
Chatham, Earl of...	1708	1778	Corday, Charlotte..	1768	1793
Chatterton, Thomas	1752	1770	Corneille, Pierre....	1606	1684
Chaucer, Geoffrey..	1328	1400	Cornwallis, Charles.	1738	1805
Chesterfield, Earl of	1694	1773	Correggio (A. Allegri)	1494	1534
Chevalier, Michel...	1806	....	Cortez, Hernando...	1485	1547?
Choate, Rufus......	1799	1859	Corwin, Thomas....	1794	1865
Chopin, F..........	1810	1849	Cousin, Victor......	1792	1867
Christina, Queen...	1626	1669	Cowley, Abraham..	1618	1667
Chrysostom, St.John	347?	407	Cowper, William...	1731	1800
Church, Fred. E....	1826	....	Crabbe, George.....	1754	1832
Churchill, Charles..	1731	1764	Cranmer, Thomas..	1489	1556
Cibber, Colley......	1671	1757	Crawford, Thomas..	1814	1857
Cicero, Marcus Tull.	B.C. 106	B.C. 43	Crawford,William H.	1772	1834
Cincinnatus,Luc.Q..	B.C. 519?	B.C. 439?	Crebillon, P. J. de..	1674	1762
Clarendon, Earl of..	1608	1674	Crichton, James....	1560	1583
Clarke, Adam.......	1760	1832	Crittenden, John J.	1786	1863
Clarkson, Thomas..	1760	1846	Crœsus.	B.C. 590?	B.C. 546?
Claude Lorraine....	1600	1682	Croker, John Wilson	1780	1857
Clay, Cassius M....	1810	....	Cromwell, Oliver....	1599	1658
Clay, Henry........	1777	1852	Cruikshank, George	1792	....
Clayton, John M...	1796	1856	Curran, John Philpot	1750	1817
Clemens, Samuel L.	1835	....	Curtis, Benjamin R.	1809	1874
Cleopatra..	B.C. 69	B.C. 30	Curtis, Geo. Ticknor	1812	....
Clifford, Nathan....	1803	....	Curtis, George Wm.	1824	....
Clinton, De Witt. ..	1769	1828	Cushing, Caleb.....	1800	....
Clinton, George....	1739	1812	Cushman, Charlotte.	1816	1876
Clive, Robert, Lord	1725	1774	Custer, George A...	1839	1876
Cobb, Howell.......	1815	1868	Cuvier,G.C.L.D ,Bar.	1769	1832
Cobbett, William...	1762	1835	Cyrus *the Great*.....	....	B.C. 529?
Cobden, Richard...	1804	1865	Daguerre,Louis J.M.	1789	1851
Coke, Sir Edward...	1552	1633	Dahlgren, John A..	1809	1870
Colbert, Jean Baptiste	1619	1683	Dallas, Alexander J.	1759	1817

NAME.	BORN.	DIED.	NAME.	BORN.	DIED.
Dallas, George M...	1792	1864	Dunglison, Robley..	1798	1869
Dana, James D.....	1813	....	Durand, Asher B....	1796	....
Dana, Richard H...	1787	....	Dürer, Albrecht....	1471	1528
Dana, Richard H., Jr.	1815	....	Dwight, Timothy...	1752	1817
Dante...	1265	1321	Early, Jubal A.....	1818	....
Danton, Geo. Jacques	1759	1794	Eastlake, Sir Chas. L.	1793	1865
Darius............. B.C.	550?	B.C. 435?	Eaton, John Henry.	1790	1856
Darwin, Charles R.	1809	....	Edgeworth, Maria..	1767	1849
Davenport, Edw. L.	1816	1877	Edwards, Jonathan.	1703	1758
Davies, Charles.....	1798	1874	Eliot, Sir John.....	1590	1632
Davis, Charles H....	1807	1877	Elizabeth, Queen...	1533	1603
Davis, David........	1815	....	Elliott, Ebenezer...	1781	1849
Davis, Henry Winter	1817	1865	Elliott, Jesse D.....	1782	1845
Davis, Jefferson ...	1808	....	Ellsworth, Oliver...	1745	1807
Davy, Sir Humphry	1778	1829	Emerson, Ralph Waldo	1803	....
Dayton, Jonathan..	1760	1824	Emmet, Robert....	1780	1803
Dayton, William L.	1807	1864	Epaminondas ...... B.C.	418?	B.C. 362
Deane, Silas........	1737	1789	Epictetus	?	125?
Dearborn, Henry...	1751	1829	Epicurus.......... B.C.	342?	B.C. 270
Decatur, Stephen...	1779	1820	Erasmus, Desiderius	1465	1536
Defoe, Daniel......	1661?	1731	Ericsson, John.....	1803	....
De Kalb, J., Baron	1732?	1780	Erskine, Thos., Lord	1750	1823
Delaroche, Paul....	1797	1856	Euclid, Geom....... B.C.	300?	....
Democritus.... ..... B.C.	460?	B.C. 357?	Eugene, Prince....	1663	1736
Demosthenes....... B.C.	385?	B.C. 322?	Euler, Leonard....	1707	1783
DeQuincey, Thomas	1785	1859	Euripides.......... B.C.	480?	B.C. 406
Derby, Edward, Earl	1799	1869	Eusebius Pamphili..	263?	340?
Descartes, René....	1596	1650	Evarts, William M.	1818	....
Dickens, Charles....	1812	1870	Evelyn, John.......	1620	1706
Dickinson, Daniel S.	1800	1866	Everett. Edward...	1794	1865
Dickinson, John....	1732	1808	Ewing, Thomas....	1789	1871
Diderot, Denis......	1713	1784	Farragut, David G..	1801	1870
Diocletian..........	245	313	Faust, Johann... .	....	1470?
Diogenes....... ... B.C.	412?	B.C. 323?	Fénelon, F. de S....	1651	1715
Dionysius the Elder, B.C.	430?	B.C. 367?	Ferdinand V. of Spain	1452	1516
Disraeli, Benjamin.	1805	....	Fessenden, W. Pitt.	1806	1869
Disraeli, Isaac......	1766?	1848	Feuillet, Octave....	1812	....
Dix, John A........	1798	....	Fichte, J. Gottlieb..	1762	1814
Dixon, W. Hepworth	1821	....	Field, Cyrus W.....	1819	....
Doddridge, Philip..	1702	1751	Field, David Dudley	1805	....
Domitian, Titus F.A.	51?	96	Field, Stephen J....	1816	....
Donizetti, Gaetano..	1798	1848	Fielding, Henry....	1707	1754
Doré, Paul Gustave.	1833	....	Fillmore, Millard...	1800	1874
Douglas, Stephen A.	1813	1861	Fish, Hamilton.....	1808	....
Dow, Gerhard......	1613	1680?	Fitch, John........	1743	1798
Drake, Sir Francis..	1539?	1595	Fletcher, John.....	1576	1625
Draper, John Wm..	1811	...	Floyd, John B......	1805	....
Drayton, Michael...	1563	1631	Ford, John	1586	1639?
Dryden, John......	1631	1700	Forrest, Edwin.....	1806	1872
Duane, William J..	1780	1865	Forster, John......	1812	1876
Du Chaillu, Paul B..	1830	....	Forsyth, John......	1780	1841
Dudevant (Geo. Sand)	1804	1876	Fourier, Charles. .	1772	1837
Duguesclin, Bertrand	1314?	1380	Fox, Charles James	1749	1806
Dumas, Alexandre..	1803	1870	Fox, George...... .	1624	1691

NAME.	BORN.	DIED.	NAME.	BORN.	DIED.
Foxe, John........	1517	1587	Grey, Lady Jane...	1537	1554
Francis de Sales, St.	1567	1622	Grier, Robert C....	1794	1870
Franklin, Benjamin.	1706	1790	Grimm, Jacob L. C.	1785	1863
Franklin, Sir John.	1786	1847	Griswold, Rufus W.	1815	1857
Frederick I........ ...	1657	1713	Groto, George......	1794	1871
Frederick II., *the Great*	1712	1786	Grotius............	1583	1645
Fremont, John C...	1813	....	Grow, Galusha A...	1823	....
Freneau, Philip....	1752	1832	Grundy, Felix......	1777	1840
Froissart, Jean.....	1337	1410?	Guicciardini, Fran.	1482	1510
Froude, Jas. Anthony	1818	....	Guido (Guido Reni).	1574?	1642
Fuller, Thomas....	1608	1661	Guizot, F. P. G.....	1787	1874
Fulton, Robert.....	1765	1815	Gurney, Joseph J..	1788	1847
Galen, Claudius....	130	200	Gustavus Vasa.....	1496	1560
Galileo (Galilei)....	1564	1642	Gustavus Adolphus	1594	1632
Gallatin, Albert....	1761	1849	Gutenberg, Johann.	1400	1478?
Galt, John........	1779	1839	Guthrie, James.....	1792	1869
Gambetta, Leon....	1838	....	Haeckel, Ernst H...	1834	....
Garibaldi, Giuseppe	1807	....	Hafiz.............. ..	?	1389?
Garrick, David.....	1716	1779	Hahnemann, Sam...	1755	1843
Garrison, W. Lloyd.	1804	....	Hakluyt, Richard...	1553?	1616
Gaskell, Eliz. C.....	1811	1865	Hale, John P.	1806	1873
Gates, Horatio.....	1728	1806	Hale, Sir Matthew..	1609	1676
Gautier, Théophile.	1811	1872	Halévy, Jacques....	1799	1862
Genghis Khan......	1163	1227	Haliburton, T. C...	1797	1865
George I...........	1660	1727	Hall, Charles F....	1821	1871
George II........ ..	1683	1760	Hall, Joseph, Bp...	1574	1656
George III.........	1738	1820	Hall, Robert........	1764	1831
George IV.........	1762	1830	Hallam, Henry.....	1777	1859
Gerry, Elbridge....	1744	1814	Halleck, Fitz-Greene	1790	1867
Ghiberti, Lorenzo..	1378	1455	Halleck, Henry W..	1815	1872
Gibbon, Edward...	1737	1794	Hamilton, Alex.....	1757	1804
Gibson, John......	1790	1866	Hamilton, Sir Wm..	1788	1856
Giddings, Joshua R.	1795	1864	Hamlin, Hannibal..	1809	...
Giles, Wm. Branch.	1762	1830	Hampden, John....	1594	1643
Gillmore, Quincy A.	1825	....	Hancock, John.....	1737	1793
Giotto..............	1276	1336	Hancock, Winfield S.	1824	....
Girard, Stephen...,	1750	1831	Handel, Geo. Fred..	1685	1759
Gladstone, Wm. E..	1809	....	Hannibal........... B.C.	247	B.C. 183?
Godwin, William...	1756	1836	Haroun-al-Raschid..	765	809
Goethe, J. W. von..	1749	1832	Harrison, Benjamin	1740	1791
Goldsmith, Oliver..	1728	1774	Harrison, Wm. Henry	1773	1841
Goodrich, Sam. G..	1793	1860	Harte, F. Bret......	1839	....
Goodyear, Charles..	1900	1860	Harvey, William....	1578	1657
Gottschalk, L. M...	1829	1869	Hastings, Warren ..	1733	1818
Gough, John B.....	1817	....	Hawthorne, Nath...	1804	1864
Gounod, Felix C....	1818	....	Haydn, Franz Joseph	1732	1809
Gower, John.......	1327?	1408?	Hayes, Rutherford B.	1822	..
Grant, Ulysses S....	1822	...	Hayne, Robert Y...	1791	1839
Grattan, Henry....	1746	1820	Hazlitt, William....	1778	1830
Gray, Asa..........	1810	....	Headley, Joel T....	1811	....
Gray, Thomas......	1716	1771	Hegel, Georg W. F.	1770	1831
Greeley, Horace....	1811	1872	Heine, Heinrich....	1799	1856
Greene, Nathaniel..	1742	1786	Helmholtz, H. L. F.	1821	....
Greenough, Horatio	1805	1852	Heloise	1100	1164

NAME.	BORN.	DIED.	NAME.	BORN.	DIED.
Helps, Arthur	1817	1875	Hunt, Leigh........	1784	1859
Helvetius, Claude A.	1715	1771	Hunter, Robt. M. T.	1809	...
Hemans, Felicia D.	1794	1835	Huntington, Daniel.	1816	....
Hendricks, Thos. A.	1819	....	Huss, Johann......	1376?	1415
Henry I of England	1068	1135	Huxley, Thos. H...	1825	....
Henry II........ ..	1133	1189	Irving, Washington	1783	1859
Henry III..........	1207	1272	Isabella of Castile..	1451	1504
Henry IV...... ...	1366?	1413	Isocrates........... B.C.	436?	B.C. 328
Henry V...........	1388	1422	Jackson, Andrew...	1767	1845
Henry VI.	1421	1471	Jackson, Thomas J.	1824	1863
Henry VII........	1456	1509	James I............	1566	1625
Henry VIII.......	1491	1547	James II...........	1633	1701
Henry IV. of France	1553	1610	James, George P. R.	1801	1860
Henry, Joseph.....	1797	....	Jameson, Anna.... .	1797	1860
Henry, Patrick.....	1736	1799	Jay, John..........	1745	1829
Hentz, Caroline Lee	1800	1856	Jefferson, Thomas..	1743	1826
Heraclitus.......... B.C.	535?	....	Jeffrey, Francis ...	1773	1850
Herbert, Edward...	1581	1648	Jeffreys, George....	1640?	1689
Herbert, George....	1593	1633	Jerome, Saint......	345?	420?
Herodotus.......... B.C.	484?	B.C. 408?	Jerome of Prague..	1378?	1416
Herrick, Robert....	1591	1674	Jerrold, Douglas...	1803	1857
Herschel, Sir J. F. M.	1792	1871	Joan of Arc.......	1412?	1431
Herschel, Sir Wm..	1738	1822	Johnson, Andrew...	1808	1875
Hesiod.............. B.C.	840?	....	Johnson, Cave.....	1793	1866
Hildreth, Richard..	1807	1865	Johnson, Reverdy..	1796	1876
Hipparchus......... B.C.	150?	....	Johnson, Richard M.	1780	1850
Hippocrates........ B.C.	460	B.C. 357	Johnson, Samuel...	1709	1784
Hitchcock, Edward	1793	1864	Johnston, Albert S.	1803	1862
Hobbes, Thomas....	1588	1679	Johnston, Joseph E.	1807	....
Hogarth, William..	1697	1764	Joinville, Prince de	1818	....
Holbach, Baron von	1723	1789	Jones, John Paul...	1747?	1792
Holbein, Hans	1494 ?	1543?	Jones, Sir William..	1746	1794
Holland, Josiah G..	1819	....	Jonson, Ben........	1574	1637
Holmes, Oliver W..	1809	....	Joseph II...........	1741	1790
Holt, Joseph.......	1807	....	Josephine..........	1763?	1814
Homer.............. B.C.	850 ?	776?	Josephus, Flavius..	38?	100?
Hood, Thomas......	1798	1845	Juarez, Benito Pablo	1806	1872
Hooker, Joseph....	1814	....	Julian, Emperor....	331	363
Hooker, Richard...	1553 ?	1600	Justin Martyr.......	105?	160?
Hopkinson, Francis	1737	1791	Justinian...........	483	565
Horatius,Q. Flaccus, B.C.	65	B.C. 8	Juvenalis, Decimus J.	40?	120?
Hortense, Queen...	1783	1837	Kames (H. Home, Lord)	1696	1782
Hosmer, Harriet....	1831	....	Kane, Elisha K.....	1820	1857
Houdon, Jean A....	1741	1828	Kant, Immanuel....	1724	1804
Houston, Samuel...	1793	1863	Kaulbach, W. von..	1805	1874
Howard, John......	1726	1790	Kean, Charles......	1811	1868
Howe, Julia Ward..	1819	....	Kean, Edmund.....	1787?	1833
Howe, Samuel G...	1801	1876	Kearny, Philip.....	1815	1862
Hughes, Thomas...	1823	....	Keats, John........	1796	1821
Hugo, Victor Marie	1802	....	Kemble, Frances A.	1811	....
Hull, Isaac.........	1775	1843	Kemble, John P.....	1757	1823
Humboldt, Alex.von	1769	1859	Kempis, Thomas à.	1380	1471
Humboldt,K.W.von	1767	1835	Kendall, Amos.....	1789	1869
Hume, David.......	1711	1776	Kennedy, John P...	1795	1870

NAME.	BORN.	DIED.	NAME.	BORN.	DIED.
Kent, James........	1763	1847	Lesseps, Ferdinand de	1805	....
Kepler, Johann.....	1571	1630	Lessing, Gotthold E.	1729	1781
Key, Francis S.....	1779	1843	Lesueur, Eustache..	1617	1655
King, Preston......	1806	1865	Lever, Charles......	1806	1872
King, Rufus........	1755	1827	Lewes, Geo. Henry	1817	....
King, T. Starr......	1824	1864	Lewes, Marian Evans	1820	...
King, William R...	1786	1853	Lewis, Sir G. C.....	1806	1863
Kingsley, Charles..	1819	1875	Lewis, Meriwether.	1774	1809
Klopstock, Fried. G.	1724	1803	Lieber, Francis....	1800	1872
Knowles, J. Sheridan	1784	1862	Liebig, Justus von.	1803	1873
Knox, Henry.......	1750	1806	Lincoln, Abraham..	1809	1865
Knox, John........	1505	1572	Lind, Jenny........	1821	....
Kock, Chas. Paul de	1794	1871	Linnæus, Carl von..	1707	1778
Kosciuszko, Tadeusz	1746	1817	Liszt, Franz........	1811	...
Kossuth, Louis.....	1802	....	Livingston, Edward	1764	1836
La Bruyère, Jean de	1646?	1696	Livingston, Robert R.	1747	1813
La Fayette, Marquis de	1757	1834	Livingstone, David	1813	1873
La Fontaine, Jean..	1621	1695	Livius, Titus P..... B.C. 59	A.D.	17
Lamartine, Alph. de	1790	1869	Locke, John........	1632	1704
Lamb, Charles......	1775	1834	Lockhart, J. G.....	1794	1854
Lamennais, F. R. de,	1782	1854	Longfellow, H. W..	1807	....
La Motte Fouqué, F. de	1777	1843	Longstreet, James..	1820	....
Landor, Walter Savage	1775	1864	Lossing, Benson J..	1813	....
Landseer, Sir Edwin	1802?	1873	Louis IX. (St. Louis)	1215	1270
Lane, James H.....	1814	1866	Louis XIV. (le Grand)	1638	1715
Lane, Joseph.......	1801	....	Louis XV..........	1710	1774
La Place, P. S. de...	1749	1827	Louis XVI.........	1754	1793
La Rochefoncauld, F. de	1613	1680	Louis Philippe......	1773	1850
La Salle, R. Cavelier de	1643?	1687	Lovejoy, Owen.....	1811	1864
Las Casas, B........	1474	1566	Lover, Samuel.....	1797	1868
Latimer, Hugh.....	1490?	1555	Loyola, St. Ignatius de	1491	1553
Laud, William......	1573	1645	Lucanus, Marcus A.	39 ?	65
Laurens, Henry.....	1724	1792	Lucianus...........	120 ?	200?
Laurens, John......	1753?	1782	Lucretius,CarusTitus, B.C. 95	B.C. 52?	
Lavater, Johann C..	1741	1801	Luther, Martin.....	1483	1546
Law, John..........	1671?	1729	Lycurgus...........	.... B.C.	825?
Lawrence, Abbott..	1792	1855	Lyell, Sir Charles..	1797	1875
Lawrence, Sir Thomas	1769	1830	Lyon, Nathaniel....	1819	1861
Ledyard, John......	1751	1789	Macaulay, T. B., Lord	1800	1859
Lee, Ann...........	1736	1784	Macchiavelli, Niccolo	1469	1527
Lee, Arthur........	1740	1792	McCulloch, John R.	1789	1864
Lee, Charles....... .	1731	1782	McClellan, George B.	1826	....
Lee, Henry.........	1756	1818	McDowell, Irvin...	1818	....
Lee, Richard Henry	1732	1794	McDuffie, George..	1788	1851
Lee, Robert E......	1807	1870	McHenry, James...	1753 ?	1816
Leech, John........	1817	1864	Mackintosh, Sir James	1765	1832
Legaré, Hugh S.....	1797	1843	McLean, John......	1785	1861
Legendre, Adrien M.	1752?	1833	Maclise, Daniel.....	1811?	1870
Leibnitz, Gottfried W.	1646	1716	MacMahon, M. E. P. M.	1808	....
Leicester, Earl of...	1532?	1588	McPherson, James B.	1829	1864
Leo X	1475	1521	Macready, Wm. C..	1793	1873
Leonidas..........	?	480?	Madison, James....	1751?	1836
Le Sage, Alain René	1668	1747	Magellan, Fernando	1470 ?	1521
Leslie, Chas. Robert	1794	1859	Maintenon, Mme. de	1635	1719

NAME.	BORN.	DIED.	NAME.	BORN.	DIED.
Maistre, Joseph de.	1754	1821	Meagher, Thos. F..	1823	1867
Maistre, Xavier de..	1763	1852	Medici, Catharine de	1519	589
Malebranche, Nicolas	1638	1715	Medici, Lorenzo de	1448	1492
Malibran, Maria F..	1806	1836	Mehemet Ali.......	1769	1849
Malte-Brun, Conrad	1775	1826	Meissonier,Jean L.E.	1813	....
Malthus, Thos. R...	1760	1831	Melanchthon, Philip	1497	1560
Mandeville, Sir John	1300 ?	1372	Melville, Herman..	1819	....
Mangum, Willie P..	1792	1861	Mendelssohn, Moses	1729	1786
Mann, Horace.. ..	1796	1859	Mendelssohn-Bartholdy	1809	1847
Mansard, François.	1598	1666	Mengs, Anton Rafael	1728	1779
Mansfield, Lord....	1705	1793	Meredith,William M.	1799	1873
Manzoni, Alessandro	1785	1873	Merle d'Aubigné,J.H.	1794	1872
Marat, Jean Paul...	1744	1793	Metastasio, Pietro B.	1698	1782
Marcy, Wm. L.....	1786	1857	Metternich,C.Prince von	1773	1859
Margaret of Valois	1492	1549	Meyerbeer, Giacomo	1794	1864
Margaret of France	1552 ?	1615	Michael-Angelo....	1474	1564
Maria Louisa.......	1791	1847	Michelet, Jules....	1798	1874
Maria Theresa of			Mifflin, Thomas....	1744	1800
Austria...	1638	1683	Mill, John Stuart..	1806	1873
Maria Theresa of			Miller, Hugh.......	1802	1856
Hungary..........	1717	1780	Miller, Samuel F...	1816	....
Marie Antoinette...	1755	1793	Milman, Henry Hart	1791	1868
Marie de Medicis...	1573	1642	Milne-Edwards, H.	1800	....
Marino Falieri......	1278	1355	Miltiades..........	....	B.C. 490?
Marion, Francis....	1732	1795	Milton, John......	1608	1674
Marius, Caius....... B.C. 157		B.C. 86	Mirabeau,H.G.R.de	1749	1791
Marlborough, Duke of	1650	1722	Mitchell, Donald G.	1822	....
Marlowe, C..	1564	1593	Mitchel, Ormsby M.	1810	1862
Marmont, Auguste.	1774	1852	Mithridates........ B.C. 131?		B.C. 63
Marryat, Frederick	1792	1848	Mohammed or Mahomet	570?	632
Marshall, John.....	1755	1835	Molière, Jean B. P. de	1622	1673
Marston, John.....	?	1635?	Moltke, H. C. B. von	1800	....
Martialis, Marcus V.	43	104 ?	Monk, George.....	1608	1670
Martineau, Harriet..	1802	1876	Monroe, James....	1758	1831
Marvell, Andrew...	1620	1678	Montagu, Lady M.W.	1690	1762
Mary I..............	1516	1558	Montaigne, Michel de	1533	1592
Mary II............	1662	1694	Montalembert,Comte de	1810	1870
Mary Stuart........	1542	1587	Montesquieu, Charles	1689	1755
Mason, George.....	1726	1792	Montgomery, James	1771	1854
Mason, James M...	1798	1871	Montgomery, Richard	1736	1775
Mason, Lowell.....	1792	1872	Montrose, Marquis of	1612	1650
Massillon, Jean Bapt.	1663	1742	Moore, Thomas....	1779	1852
Massinger, Philip..	1584	1640	More, Hannah.....	1745	1833
Mather, Cotton....	1663	1728	More, Henry......	1614	1687
Mather, Increase...	1639	1723	More, Sir Thomas..	1480	1535
Mathew, Theobald.	1790	1856	Morean, J. Victor..	1763	1813
Mathews, Charles..	1776	1835	Morgan, Daniel....	1736	1802
Maury, Matthew F.	1806	1873	Morgan, S. O., Lady	1783	1859
Maximilian I.......	1459	1519	Morris, George P..	1802	1864
Maximilian II.....	1527	1576	Morris, Gouverneur	1752	1816
Maximilian (Mexico)	1832	1867	Morris, Robert.....	1734	1806
Mazarin, J., *Cardinal*	1602	1661	Morse, Jedediah...	1761	1826
Mazzini, Giuseppe	1805	1872	Morse, Samuel F.B.	1791	1872
Meade, George G..	1815	1872	Morton, Oliver P..	1823	1877

NAME.	BORN.	DIED.	NAME.	BORN.	DIED.
Motley, John L....	1814	1877	Patti, Carlotta.....	1840	....
Mowatt, Anna Cora	1818	1870	Paulding, James K.	1779	1860
Mozart, J. C. W. A.	1756	1791	Peabody, George..	1795	1869
Müller, F. Max....	1823	....	Peale, Rembrandt..	1778	1860
Murat, Joachim....	1771	1815	Pedro II., of Brazil	1825	....
Muratori, L. A.....	1672	1750	Peel, Sir Robert...	1788	1850
Murchison, Sir R..	1792	1871	Peirce, Benjamin..	1809	....
Murillo, Bartolomeo E.	1618	1682	Pellico, Silvio.....	1789	1854
Murray, Lindley...	1745	1826	Pendleton, Edmund	1721	1803
Musset, Alfred de..	1810	1857	Pendleton, Geo. II..	1825	....
Napoleon I........	1769	1821	Penn, William.....	1644	1718
Napoleon II.......	1811	1832	Pepys, Samuel.....	1632	1703
Napoleon III	1808	1873	Percival, James G.	1795	1857
Nast, Thomas......	1840	....	Pericles............	? B.C. 420	
Neal, John.........	1793	1866	Perry, Matthew C..	1795	1858
Neander, Johann A.W.	1789	1850	Perry, Oliver H....	1785	1819
Necker, Jacques...	1732	1804	Pestalozzi, J. H....	1746	1827
Nelson, Horatio...	1758	1805	Peter the Hermit...	1050?	1115
Nelson, Samuel....	1792	1873	Peter I., the Great..	1672	1725
Nepos, Cornelius..	? B.C. 40?		Petrarch, Francesco	1304	1374
Nero...............	37	68	Phidias............	B.C. 490? B.C. 432	
Newman, Francis Wm.	1805	....	Philip I............	1478	1506
Newman, John II..	1801	....	Philip II...........	1527	1598
Newton, Sir Isaac..	1642	1727	Phillips, Wendell..	1811	....
Ney, Michel.......	1769	1815	Pickering, Timothy	1745	1829
Nicholas I.........	1796	1855	Pierce, Franklin...	1804	1869
Niebuhr, B. G.....	1776	1831	Pierpont, John....	1785	1866
Nott, Eliphalet.....	1773	1866	Pierrepont, Edwards	1817	....
O'Connell, Daniel..	1775	1847	Pike, Zebulon M ..	1779	1813
Offenbach, Jacques	1819	....	Pillow, Gideon J..	1806	....
Origen.............	185 ?	254	Pinckney, Charles..	1758	1824
Orr, James L......	1822	1873	Pinckney, Charles C.	1746	1825
Ossoli, Margaret Fuller	1810	1850	Pinckney, Thomas.	1750	1828
Otis, James........	1725	1783	Pindarus	B.C. 518	442?
Overbeck, Friedrich	1789	1869	Pinkney, William..	1764	1822
Ovidius Naso, P....	B.C. 43 A.D. 18		Pitt, William......	1759	1806
Owen, Robert......	1771	1858	Pius IX............	1792	...
Owen, Robert Dale	1801	1877	Pizarro, Francisco..	1471	1541
Oxenstiern, Axel..	1583	1654	Plato..............	B.C. 429? B.C. 347	
Paganini, Niccolo..	1784	1840	Plautus, Marcus A.	B.C. 254? B.C. 184	
Page, William.....	1811	....	Pliny, the Elder....	23	79
Paine, Thomas.....	1737	1809	Pliny, the Younger,	61	116?
Paley, William.....	1743	1805	Plutarch...........	46?	125?
Palfrey, John G....	1796	....	Poe, Edgar Allan..	1809	1849
Palissy, Bernard...	1508?	1590	Poinsett, Joel R...	1779	1851
Palmerston, Lord..	1784	1865	Polk, James K.....	1795	1849
Paracelsus.........	1493	1541	Polo, Marco........	1254	1324?
Park, Mungo......	1771	1805	Polybius	B.C. 204? B.C. 122?	
Parker, Theodore..	1810	1860	Pompadour, J.A.P.de	1722	1764
Parton, James....	1822	....	Pompeius.........	B.C. 106 B.C. 48	
Parton, Sara Payson	1811	1872	Pope, Alexander...	1688	1744
Pascal, Blaise......	1623	1662	Porson, Richard...	1759	1808
Patrick, Saint	?	493?	Porter, David......	1780	1848
Patti, Adelina.....	1843	..	Porter, David D...	1814	....

NAME.	BORN.	DIED.	NAME.	BORN.	DIED.
Potter, Paul.......	1625	1654	Richard I.... ...	1157	1199
Poussin, Nicolas...	1594	1665	Richard II....	1366	1400
Powers, Hiram....	1805	1873	Richard III........	1452	1485
Pozzo-di-Borgo,C.A.	1768	1842	Richardson, Samuel	1689	1761
Praxiteles..........	....	B.C. 365?	Richelieu, Cardinal..	1585	1642
Prentice, George D.	1802	1870	Richter, Jean Paul F.	1763	1825
Prescott,William II.	1796	1859	Rienzi, Nicola G...	?	1354
Preston, William C.	1794	1860	Rinehart,Wm. II....	1825	1874
Priestley, Joseph..	1799	1851	Ristori, Adelaide...	1821	....
Prior, Matthew.... .	1664	1721	Rives, William C...	1793	1868
Probus, Marcus A..	230	282	Robert Bruce.......	1276?	1329
Proctor, Bryan W..	1789	1864	Roberts, David.....	1796	1864
Propertius, Sextus A.	? B.C. 51?		Robertson, William	1721	1793
Proudhon, Pierre J.	1809	1865	Robespierre, M. M. I.	1758	1794
Ptolemy I., Soter... B.C. 367		B.C. 283	Rochambeau, J. B. de	1725	1817
Ptolemy II., Philadel.	309	B.C. 247	Rochofoucauld, F. de la	1613	1680
Ptolemy, Claudius..	136?	161?	Rogers, Samuel....	1763	1855
Pufendorf, S. Baron von	1632	1694	Roland, Madame ..	1754	1793
Pugin, A. W. N....	1811	1852	Romilly, Sir Samuel	1757	1818
Pulaski, Casimir....	1747	1779	Rosa, Euph. Parepa	1836	1874
Putnam, Israel.....	1718	1790	Rosa, Salvator.....	1615	1673
Pythagoras.........	570? B.C. 500?		Rosecrans, William S.	1819	....
Quarles, Francis...	1592	1644	Rossini, Gioacchino	1792	1868
Quincy, Josiah, Jr.	1744	1775	Rousseau, Jean J...	1712	1778
Quincy, Josiah.....	1772	1864	Rubens, Peter Paul	1577	1640
Quintilianus, Marcus F.	42?	118?	Rupert, Prince.....	1619	1682
Quitman, John A...	1799	1858	Rush, Benjamin....	1746	1818
Rabelais, François.	1495?	1553?	Rush, Richard.	1780	1859
Rachel, Eliza. Felix	1820	1858	Ruskin, John..	1819	....
Racine, Jean......	1639	1699	Russell, John, Earl	1792	....
Raleigh, Sir Walter.	1552	1618	Russell, Wm., Lord	1639	1683
Ramsay, Allan.....	1686	1758	Rutledge, Edward..	1749	1800
Ramsay, David.....	1749	1815	Rutledge, John.....	1739	1800
Randolph, Edmund	1753	1813	Ruyter, Michael A. de	1707	1676
Randolph, John....	1773	1833	Saadi, or Sadi......	1176?	1291
Randolph, Peyton..	1723	1775	Sachs, Hans..	1494	1578
Ranke, Leopold....	1795	....	St. Clair, Arthur...	1735	1818
Raphael	1483	1520	Sainte-Beuve, C. A.	1804	1869
Rawlins, John A. .	1831	1869	Saint-Pierre, J.B.H. de	1737	1814
Raymond, Henry J.	1820	1869	Saint-Simon, Duc de	1675	1755
Raynal, Abbé......	1711	1796	Sallustius, Caius C.. B.C. 86		B.C. 34
Read, George.......	1733	1798	Santa Aña, Antonio L.	1798	1876
Read, T. Buchanan	1822	1872	Sargent, Epes......	1812	....
Reade, Charles.....	1814	...	Sarpi, Paolo (Father		
Recamier, Jean F.J.A.	1779	1849	Paul).............	1552	1623
Red Jacket.........	1752	1830	Savonarola, Girolamo	1452	1498
Reed Joseph.......	1741	1785	Saxe, H. Maurice de	1696	1750
Reid, Mayne.......	1818	....	Saxe, John G.......	1816	...
Reid, Thomas......	1710	1796	Scheffer, Ary.......	1795	1858
Rembrandt, Paul...	1607	1669	Schenck, Robert C.	1809	....
Renan, J. Ernest...	1823	....	Schiller, Johann C. F.	1759	1805
Retz, Cardinal de...	1614	1679	Schlegel, Aug. W. von	1767	1845
Reynolds, Sir Joshua	1723	1792	Schlegel, F. C.W. von	1772	1829
Ricardo, David.....	1772	1823	Schleiermacher, F. E.	1768	1834

NAME.	BORN.	DIED.	NAME.	BORN.	DIED.
Schoolcraft, Henry R.	1793	1864	South, Robert......	1633	1716
Schopenhauer, Arthur	1788	1860	Southey, Robert....	1774	1843
Schubert, Franz....	1797	1828	Souvestre, Emile...	1806	1854
Schurz, Carl.	1829	....	Sparks, Jared......	1789	1866
Schuyler, Philip....	1733	1804	Spencer, John C....	1788	1855
Scott, Sir Walter...	1771	1832	Spenser, Edmund..	1553?	1599
Scott, Winfield.....	1786	1866	Spinoza, Benedict de	1632	1677
Scribe, Augustine E.	1791	1861	Spurzheim, Johann K.	1776	1832
Sedgwick, Cath. M.	1789	1867	Staël-Holstein, A. L..	1766	1813
Sedgwick, John....	1813	1864	Stanhope, P. H., Earl	1805	1875
Sedgwick, Theodore	1746	1813	Stanton, Edwin M..	1814	1869
Selden, John.......	1584	1654	Steele, Sir Richard.	1671	1729
Seneca, Lucius A...	....	C5	Stephens, Alex. H..	1812	....
Sergeant, John.....	1779	1852	Sterne, Laurence...	1713	1768
Servetus, Michael..	1509	1553	Steuben, Fred. W. A.	1730	1794
Sévigné, Marie de R.	1626	1696	Stevens, Thaddeus.	1793	1868
Seward, Wm. Henry,	1801	1872	Stevenson, Andrew.	1784	1857
Seymour, Horatio..	1810	....	Stewart, Charles...	1778	1869
Shaftesbury, 1st Earl of	1621	1683	Stewart, Dugald....	1753	1828
Shaftesbury, 2d Earl of	1671	1712	Stockton, Richard..	1730	1781
Shakespeare, William	1564	1616	Stockton, Robert F.	1796	1866
Sharp, Granville....	1725	1813	Stoddert, Benjamin	1751	1813
Shell, Richard L ...	1791	1851	Story, Joseph......	1779	1845
Shelby, Isaac.......	1750	1826	Stowe, Harriet B...	1812	....
Shelley, Percy Bysshe	1792	1822	Strabo............. B.C.	60? A.D.	22?
Shenstone, Wm....	1714	1763	Strafford, Earl of..	1593	1641
Sheridan, Philip H..	1831	....	Stuart, Alex. H. H..	1807	....
Sheridan, Richard B.	1751	1816	Stuart, Gilbert.....	1755	1828
Sherman, John.....	1823	....	Stuart, James E. B..	1832	1864
Sherman, Roger....	1721	1793	Sue, Eugène........	1804	1857
Sherman, William T.	1820	....	Suetonius, Caius....	70?	?
Shields, James... .	1810	....	Sulla, L. Cornelius, B.C.	138 B.C.	78
Siddons, Sarah.....	1755	1831	Sullivan, James....	1744	1808
Sidney, Algernon...	1617?	1683	Sullivan, John.....	1741	1795
Sidney, Sir Philip..	1554	1586	Sully, Max., Duc de	1560	1641
Sigourney, Lydia H.	1791	1865	Sully, Thomas......	1783	1872
Silliman, Benjamin.	1779	1864	Sumner, Charles...	1811	1874
Simms, Wm. Gilmore	1806	1870	Swedenborg, Eman.	1688	1772
Simon, Jules.......	1814	?	Swift, Jonathan....	1667	1745
Sismondi, J.C.L.S. de	1773	1842	Tacitus, Caius Corn.	61?	120?
Slidell, John.......	1793	1871	Taglioni, Marie.....	1804	....
Smith, Adam.......	1723	1790	Talfourd, T. N.....	1795	1854
Smith, Gerrit......	1797	1874	Talleyrand-Perigord	1754	1838
Smith, Capt. John..	1579	1631	Talma, François Jos.	1763	1826
Smith, Joseph......	1805	1844	Tamerlane.........	1336	1405
Smith, Sydney.....	1771	1845	Taney, Roger B....	1777	1864
Smithson, Jas. L. M..	1765	1829	Tasso, Torquato...	1544	1595
Smollett, Tobias G..	1721	1771	Taylor, Bayard....	1825	
Socrates........... B.C.	469? B.C.	399	Taylor, Isaac.......	1796?	1865
Solon.............. B.C.	638? B.C.	558?	Taylor, Jeremy....	1613	1667
Somerville, Mary...	1780	1872	Taylor, Zachary....	1784	1850
Sophocles.......... B.C.	495? B.C.	405?	Tegner, Esaias.....	1782	1846
Soto, Hernandez de.	1496?	1542	Temple, Sir William	1628	1699
Soult, Nicolas Jean.	1769?	1851	Tennyson, Alfred..	1809?	....

NAME.	BORN.	DIED.	NAME.	BORN.	DIED.
Terentius..........	B.C. 194	B.C. 159	Veronese, Paul....	1532?	1588
Tertullian,Quint.S.F.	160?	240?	Vespasian, Titus Flav.	9	79
Thackeray, W. M..	1811	1863	Vespucci, Amerigo.	1451	1512
Themistocles......	B.C. 519?	B.C. 449	Victor Emmanuel II.	1820	....
Theophrastus......	B.C. 372?	B.C. 287?	Victoria, Alexandrina	1819	....
Thierry, J. N. A...	1795	1856	Villemain, Abel F..	1790	1867
Thiers, Louis Adolphe	1797	1877	Vinci, Leonardo da.	1452	1519
Thomas, George H.	1816	1870	Virgilius Maro, P. B.C.	70	B.C. 22
Thomson, James...	1700	1748	Volney, C. F. C. de	1757	1820
Thorwaldsen, Bertel	1770	1844	Voltaire, F. M. A. de	1694	1778
Thucydides........	B.C. 471?	B.C. 401?	Wade, Benjamin F.	1800	....
Tiberius, Claudius..	B.C. 42	A.D. 37	Wagner, Richard...	1813	....
Tieck, Ludwig.....	1773	1853	Waite, Morrison R.	1816	....
Tilden, Samuel J...	1814	....	Walker, Robert J..	1801	1869
Tillotson, John.....	1630	1694	Wallenstein, A. W. E.	1583	1634
Tintoretto.........	1512	1594	Walpole, Horace...	1717	1797
Titian..............	1477	1576	Walpole, Sir Robert	1676	1745
Titus Flavius......	40	81	Walton, Izaak.....	1593	1683
Tocqueville, A. C. H. de	1805	1859	Warburton, William	1698	1779
Tompkins,Daniel D.	1774	1825	Warren, Joseph....	1741	1775
Tooke, J. Horne...	1736	1812	Washburne, Elihu B.	1816	....
Toombs, Robert...	1810	....	Washington, George	1732	1799
Toussaint L'Ouverture	1743	1803	Watt, James.......	1736	1819
Trajan, Marcus U..	52	117	Watts, Isaac.......	1679	1748
Trollope, Anthony..	1815	....	Wayland, Francis..	1796	1865
Trumbull, John....	1756	1843	Wayne, Anthony...	1745	1796
Trumbull, Jonathan	1740	1809	Wayne, James M...	1790	1867
Truxton, Thomas..	1755	1822	Weber, Karl M. von	1786	1826
Tucker, St. George.	1752	1827	Webster, Daniel....	1782	1852
Tuckerman, H. T..	1813	1871	Webster, Noah.....	1758	1843
Tupper, Martin F..	1810	....	Welles, Gideon.....	1802	....
Turenne, Henri....	1611	1675	Wellington, Duke of	1769	1852
Turgot, A. R. J.....	1727	1781	Wesley, Charles....	1708	1788
Turner, J. M. W...	1775	1851	Wesley, John......	1703	1791
Twiggs, David E...	1790	1862	West, Benjamin....	1738	1820
Tyler, John........	1790	1862	Whately, Richard..	1787	1863
Tyndale, William..	1485?	1536	Wheaton, Henry...	1785	1848
Uhland, Johann L.	1787	1862	Wheeler,William A.	1819	....
Ulloa, Antonio.....	1716	1795	Whewell, William..	1794	1866
Upshur, Abel P....	1790	1844	Whitefield, George.	1714	1770
Ure, Andrew........	1778	1857	Whitney, Eli.......	1765	1825
Usher, James.....	1580	1656	Whittier, John G...	1807	....
Vallandigham, C. L.	1822	1871	Wickliffe, Charles A.	1788	1869
Van Buren, Martin.	1782	1862	Wieland, C. M......	1733	1813
Vanderbilt, C......	1794	1877	Wilberforce, Wm...	1759	1833
Van Dyck,Anthony,	1599	1641	Wilkes, Charles....	1801	1877
Vane, Sir Henry...	1612	1662	Wilkes, John.......	1727	1797
Vasari, George.....	1512	1574	Wilkie, Sir David..	1785	1841
Vattel, Emmerich de	1714	1767	Wilkinson, James..	1757	1825
Vauban, Sebastian.	1633	1707	William the Conqueror	1027	1087
Vega, Lope de.....	1562	1635	William of Orange.	1650	1702
Velasquez, D. R. de S.	1599	1660	William IV.........	1765	1837
Verdi, Giuseppe....	1814	....	William, the Silent..	1533	1584
Vernet, Horace.....	1789	1863	Williams, Roger....	1606	1683

NAME.	BORN.	DIED.	NAME.	BORN.	DIED.
Wilmot, David.....	1814	1868	Worcester, Joseph E.	1784	1835
Wilson, Alexander..	1766	1813	Wordsworth, Wm..	1770	1850
Wilson, Henry.....	1812	1875	Wraxall, Sir N. W..	1751	1831
Wilson, James.... .	1742	1799	Wren, Sir Christopher	1632	1723
Wilson, John.... ..	1785	1854	Wright, Silas.......	1795	1847
Winckelmann, J. J.	1717	1768	Wycherly, William.	1640?	1715
Winthrop, John....	1588	1649	Wycliffe, John.....	1324?	1384
Winthrop, Robert C.	1809	....	Wythe, George.....	1726	1806
Wirt, William......	1772	1834	Xavier, St. Francis.	1506	1552
Wise, Henry A.....	1806	1876	Xenophon.......... B.C.	444?	B.C. 359?
Wiseman, Cardinal.	1802	1865	Xerxes.............	?	B.C. 465
Wolcott, Oliver.....	1760	1833	Young, Brigham...	1801	1877
Wolfe, James.......	1726	1759	Young, Edward....	1684	1765
Wollstonecraft, Mary	1759	1797	Zeno.............. B.C.	362?	B.C. 264?
Wolsey, Thomas...	1471	1530	Zenobia...........	?	275?
Woodbury, Levi....	1789	1851	Zschokke, J. H. D..	1770	1848
Woodworth, Samuel	1785	1842	Zwingli, Ulric......	1484	1531
Wool, John E......	1784	1869			

THE CAPITAL OF THE UNITED STATES.*

WASHINGTON CITY, the capital of the United States of America, and the seat of the Federal Government since 1800, is situated on the eastern bank of the Potomac River, 106 miles above its mouth, and 105 miles in a straight line west of the Atlantic Ocean, in 38° 53' 39" N. lat., and 77° 2' 48" long. W. of Greenwich. The population of the city in 1875 was 125,000 (estimated).

Washington is almost alone among the capitals of great nations of modern times in the fact of its creation for the sole purpose of a seat of government, apart from any questions of commercial greatness or population. While London, Paris, Berlin, St. Petersburg, Vienna, and Madrid are respectively the commercial capitals and the most populous cities of the nations they represent, Washington never was, and probably will never be, the leading city of the United States, or the great metropolis of a commercial and a manufacturing population. In trade and manufactures it is overshadowed, no doubt permanently, by the neighboring great commercial capitals of Baltimore and Philadelphia, from which it is distant only 39 and 137 miles respectively, while New York is but 227 miles distant by railway. There are those who maintain that superior advantages result to Washington as a pleasant, salubrious, and perennially attractive residence, from the absence of all manufacturing establishments, so fruitful in smoke and other drawbacks to health and comfort.

The history of the selection of Washington as the seat of government shows that there was a protracted conflict in the Congress of the Republic over the claims of rival localities, and that the confluence of the Potomac and Anacostia was finally selected as a compromise. After the cession to the United States by Maryland in 1788, and Virginia in 1789, of a Federal district ten miles square, the site of the city and the location of the public squares and buildings were selected by President Washington in person on the Maryland side of the Potomac, in accordance with the act of Congress of March 30, 1791. At the time of this location, the city was almost

* From Johnson's New Universal Cyclopædia, 1877.

precisely in the geographical centre between the northern and the southern limits of the Union. On April 15th, 1791, the corner-stone of the Federal territory was laid by three commissioners appointed by the President, together with the officials of Alexandria, Va. ; and in the following year the lines of boundary directed by the President's proclamation were permanently marked by square milestones. The place was called "the Federal City" by Washington, and in the records of the time, until September 9, 1791, when the commissioners directed that the Federal district should be called "the Territory of Columbia," and the Federal city "the City of Washington." Major L'Enfant, a French engineer, prepared the topographical plan of Washington City, under the direction of President Washington and Thomas Jefferson, Secretary of State. L'Enfant took as a basis for his design the topography of Versailles, the seat of the government of France, and introduced the scheme of broad transverse avenues intersecting the main streets of the city, with constantly recurring squares, circles, and triangular reservations, which form at this day the main features of the plan of the city. Having determined upon the location of the capitol as the initial point, a true meridian line was drawn through it, crossed by another due east and west line, by the accurate measurement of which the acute angles were determined, and the avenues and streets laid down by strict measurement. The ideas of the founders of the city proposed a seat of government of ample territorial proportions, and provided for the future wants of a swarming population, as well as for the embellishment of the fine natural features of the city by the aid of art. The grand scope of the superficial design, contrasted with the poverty of the results achieved in the shape of public improvements for many years, led to the proverbial designation of Washington as the "city of magnificent distances." Thus, the public streets throughout were projected on the scale of 160 feet down to 70, no street in the city being less than the latter width. The aggregate length of the streets and avenues is 264 miles, and they are wider than those of any other city in the world. There are 21 avenues in all, which bear the names of various States in the Union. Pennsylvania Avenue, the principal street of Washington, is a magnificent thoroughfare, 160 feet wide (just double the width of Broadway, New York), running from the Capitol to the Treasury Department, where it is deflected to the north, and continued past the President's house westward to Georgetown, at the width of 130 feet. On the other side of the Capitol it runs 160 feet wide to the Anacostia River. This avenue was originally laid out in three roadways, with a double row of Lombardy poplars, planted at the instance of Mr. Jefferson, between the central or main street and that on each side. These trees were cut down in 1832, and the avenue thrown into one broad thoroughfare, now (1877) paved with smooth concrete, consti-

tuting the most splendid and attractive *corso* or driveway in the
country. Massachusetts Avenue is over four and a half miles long,
running in an unbroken course 160 feet in width, from the northwest
boundary of Washington at Twenty-second Street to the Anacostia,
beyond Lincoln Park. The other avenues are named—Maine, New
Hampshire, Vermont, Connecticut, Rhode Island, New York, New Jersey, Maryland, Delaware, Virginia, North Carolina, South Carolina,
Georgia, Louisiana, Missouri, Tennessee, Kentucky, Ohio, and Indiana. To these must be added the newly laid out Executive Avenue,
which starts from Pennsylvania Avenue at the President's House, '
and follows a serpentine course through the Washington Monument
grounds, in full view of the Potomac, till it reaches the grounds of
the Department of Agriculture, whence it passes through the Smithsonian reservation and the Mall to the Botanic Garden at the foot of
the Capitol. Executive Avenue affords a fine drive about two
miles in length, and will soon be adorned with shade-trees through
its whole extent, as it now is in the grounds of the Smithsonian Institution. The Mall, through which the drive runs, was originally covered with majestic oaks, which were cut down about 1820, under an
unwise agreement of the commissioners of Washington with the
proprietors, that they should be entitled to all the wood on the lands
reserved by the United States. East Capitol Street, running at a
uniform breadth of 160 feet from the east front of the Capitol to
Lincoln Park, was originally designed to be the chief street of the
city, and has recently become one of the most attractive, many fine
residences having been located upon it. K Street, 148 feet wide,
extending from Rock Creek, the Georgetown boundary, to the Anacostia, is one of the most splendid thoroughfares of the city. Sixteenth Street, 160 feet wide, runs from Lafayette Square, opposite
the President's house, due north to the boundary, where it climbs
the heights towards Columbian College, presenting a fine view of
the city and environs. Boundary Street, running along the northern
limit of the city, is also a fine driveway or boulevard.

Every grand transverse avenue was laid out 160 feet wide. The
crossings of the streets and avenues created opportunity for frequent
parks or reservations as centres of attraction, interspersed with business blocks and dwelling-houses. Besides these fractional reservations, there were set apart more extensive parks or squares, including the following: The Capitol grounds, 52 acres; President's
grounds, 20 acres; Lafayette Square, 7 acres; the Park, or Mall
(not yet fully opened), about 100 acres; Judiciary Square, 19 acres;
the Arsenal grounds, 44½ acres; the Navy Yard, 27 acres; Farra-
gut Square, 1¼ acres; McPherson Square, 1¼ acres; Franklin
Square, 4 acres; Rawlins Square, 1¼ acres; Lincoln Park, Capitol
Hill, 6¼ acres; Stanton Place, Capitol Hill, 3¼ acres. Besides these
are numerous smaller squares and several circular plots of ground,

the most conspicuous of which are Washington Circle, midway between Washington and Georgetown; Fourteenth Street Circle, at the
corner of Massachusetts and Vermont Avenues; Scott Circle, at the
junction of Massachusetts Avenue and Sixteenth Street; Nineteenth
Street Circle, at the intersection of Connecticut, Massachusetts, and
New Hampshire Avenues with P Street; and Thirteenth Street
Circle, at the junction of Rhode Island and Vermont avenues.
Numerous triangular reservations at the intersections of streets and
avenues have been enclosed and beautified with trees and shrubs.

Notwithstanding the magnitude and farsightedness of the original
plans for the laying out of the Federal capital, more than half a
century was suffered to elapse before any portion of the city could
be said to have assumed the beauty and attraction due alike to its
natural advantages and to the liberality of the schemes for its
adornment. The narrowest views of economy prevailed in Congress, and all attempts to expend even the smallest sums of public
money upon making the Federal capital attractive, or even of con-
tributing to its salubrity as a residence by draining its numerous
marshes, or rendering its muddy streets and avenues accessible by
suitable pavements, were steadily defeated. The descriptions which
have come down to us of the appearance of Washington in early
days concur in representing it as a gigantic failure. Mrs. John
Adams, the first occupant of the White House, A.D. 1800, has de-
scribed, in letters familiar to the public, the rude and uncomfortable
condition of the city, when Congress first came to occupy the new
capital. For ten years before the public offices were removed from
Philadelphia, the area of the future capital embraced scarcely 500
inhabitants. Oliver Wolcott wrote in 1800, "The Capitol is situated
on an eminence near the centre of the immense country here called
the city. There is one good tavern about forty rods from the Capitol,
and several other houses are built and erecting." John Cotton
Smith, Congressman, wrote, "The Pennsylvania Avenue was then
nearly the whole distance a deep morass, covered with elder bushes."
The place was simply a backwoods town in the wilderness, and Senators and Representatives in Congress were for years in the habit of
finding such comfort as they could in lodgings in Georgetown, three
miles distant, though within the District of Columbia. Yet the
nascent capital of the republic was not without its experiences of the
soaring ambition of the early owners of land in the vicinity of the capital, that was to arise in such magnitude out of the primitive swamps
and forests which had so long occupied the site of Washington.
When the bluff overlooking the Potomac was selected as the site for
the Capitol, the owners of lots on the plateau facing eastward, where
the edifice was to front, immediately put up the prices of their lots to 75
cents or $1 a square foot. The result was that settlers in Washington,
avoiding Capitol Hill, purchased land and erected their houses in the

swampy district lying between the Capitol and the Potomac, where lots could be obtained at the low price of from 10 to 25 cents a square foot. Thus it came to pass that the broad plateau of Capitol Hill, the highest, most commanding, and most salubrious portion of Washington, remained unsettled for more than half a century, save by a small straggling population. The shops and residences of the citizens grew steadily in the northwestern direction, following the valley on either side of Pennsylvania Avenue, and extending slowly towards the northern limits of the city, as well as westward towards Georgetown. In 1839, George Combe, the British traveller, wrote of Washington, "The town looks like a large straggling village reared in a drained swamp." It was not until the year 1851 that any thing was done towards laying out or adorning the numerous public parks and reservations contemplated by L'Enfant sixty years before. In that year A. J. Downing, the landscape gardener, was employed by President Fillmore, pursuant to a small appropriation by Congress; and his plans for roadways planted with a picturesque selection of trees, were partially carried out in the park occupied by the Smithsonian Institution. The death of the artist in 1852, and the neglect of Congress, suspended these needed improvements for twenty years longer. All visitors to Washington before 1871 cannot fail to remember the crude and unkempt condition of the Capitol grounds, and the neglected aspect of the approaches to all the noble public buildings which adorn the capital. The streets and avenues were in a chronic state of neglect, the drifting of dust alternating with the deepest mud, and the thoroughfares of the city being at times almost impassable. At length, in 1871, under the combined influence of a more liberal spirit in Congress, and the energetic determination of some of the private citizens, a new order of things was inaugurated. Congress having abolished the municipal governments of Washington and Georgetown, and created for the District of Columbia a Territorial government, with a governor, legislature, and board of public works, the latter body became invested with exclusive power over the streets, sewers, and avenues of Washington and Georgetown, with authority to improve the same on a comprehensive plan. Endowed with these great powers, and the ability to raise money by tax and loan, the new government went vigorously into the business of improving the Federal city. An extensive system of sewerage and of street pavements was drawn up, through which the greater portion of the city was reclaimed from neglect and filth, the great ditch known as the Washington Canal was filled up, and about 160 miles of streets and avenues were paved with stone, wood, or concrete. Many streets were completely re-graded, the public squares were all fenced and planted with shade-trees, while in the streets and avenues about 29,000 umbrageous trees have been set out. These comprise elm,

maple, linden, tulip, ash, Carolina poplar, and other native forest trees. The magnitude and extent of these improvements, carried on with a vigor and rapidity almost without precedent in American municipal history, of course entailed a corresponding amount of extravagance. While the seat of government reaps solid and permanent benefit from some of these improvements, others, hastily executed, have already fallen into decay: Whatever may be the verdict of history upon the much controverted acts of the Territorial government during whose short reign of three years the city of Washington was so transformed, it cannot be doubted that a new era for the Federal capital dates from these improvements. Coincident with them, the erection of an unprecedented number of public buildings and private residences has contributed to render the city at once more attractive and more habitable to residents old and new. The net result of the operations of the board of public works is the substantial completion of these vast improvements and the creation of a public debt of more than $20,000,-000, which still hangs over the city, unadjusted by the legislation of Congress, while the interest thereon is paid partly by taxation of the property of the district and partly out of the public treasury.

The government of Washington was strictly municipal in character, with a mayor and city council, until 1871, when Congress created a Territorial government for the District of Columbia, repealing the charters of the cities of Washington and Georgetown, and merging them into the same government. This government was abolished by act of June 20, 1874, and a provisional government of three commissioners, appointed by the President and Senate, was constituted until Congress should devise a more permanent form. The affairs of the District, including those of Washington, still continue to be managed by these commissioners under the direct legislation of Congress for the levying and disbursement of taxes and for all public improvements. The financial operations of the government are administered directly by the Treasury Department. The assessed valuation of real estate in Washington in 1876 was a little less than eighty millions of dollars. The rate of tax levied that year was 1½ per cent, with the same amount on personal property. The government property in buildings and reservations has never been subjected to tax. Congress exercises, under the Constitution, the power of exclusive legislation.

Since the retrocession of Alexandria and the territory on the west bank of the Potomac to Virginia in 1846, the city of Washington, together with the District of Columbia, embraces only 64 square miles. The city extends 4½ miles in one direction by about 2½ in the other, and its circumference is 14 miles, having a water front on the Potomac of 4 miles, and on the Anacostia of 3½ miles. The city proper covers 6111 acres, being about 9½ square miles; and out of this territory the government reservations comprise 541 acres, while the avenues and streets embrace 2554 acres (or 3095 acres in all),

leaving only 3016 acres to the squares on which private residences
are built. There is thus a much larger proportion of land reserved
from buildings in Washington than in any large city on the globe
—a circumstance which conduces in the highest degree to the public health, securing as it does large open spaces and abundant venti-
lation in every quarter of the city. The returns of the Board of
Health exhibit a death-rate of slightly more than 2 per cent. per
annum—considerably below the average mortality of cities in all
countries. The continuous heat of summer, though often intense, is
mitigated by breezes which blow up the valley of the Potomac,
while in winter snow seldom falls, and for many days together the
thermometer rarely indicates a temperature below the freezing
point. By the original plan, the city is divided into four sections,
starting from the Capitol as a centre, with North and South Capitol
Street as the dividing line on one side, and East and West Capitol
Street (the latter not opened) on the other. The streets and avenues
are numbered by what is known as the Philadelphia plan—100 num
bers to each square ; and the streets running east and west are
called by the letters of the alphabet from A to W inclusive, while
those running north and south bear numerical names from First to
Twenty-eighth Street inclusive. This poverty of street nomencla-
ture will probably be superseded by more expressive designations.

The site of the city of Washington is admirably adapted by nature
for the building up of an attractive and imposing city. Situated in
part on the tongue of land lying at the confluence of two broad riv-
ers, from which the ground rises in natural and not abrupt ridges
into the expanded plateau of Capitol Hill, about 100 feet above the
Potomac, the surface of the city presents a gentle undulation which
gives variety and constant transition of prospect, without producing
any obstructions to travel. The city proper is surrounded on the
east, north, and west by an amphitheatre of well-wooded hills, embracing in most cases the ancient forest growth of tall timber,
which was partly cut off or burned on the Maryland side (as on the
Virginia) during the ravages of the civil war. Viewed from the
vantage-ground of the Capitol dome, or even the western portico,
the environs of Washington present a landscape of rare beauty and
picturesqueness. The near view includes the mass of the city,
thickly covered with dwellings, stores, and shops, intersected by the
two great arteries of Pennsylvania Avenue, running to the Treasury, and Maryland Avenue, running westward to the Potomac. At
frequent intervals, through the perspective of roofs, rise the tall
steeples of churches and the massive white marble edifices of the
various government buildings. Turning westward, the bright
broad current of the Potomac—nearly one mile wide opposite the
Capitol—sweeps southward ; while there comes in on the left, join-
ing its broad stream at Greenleaf's Point (on which the government

arsenal is situated), the deep current of the Anacostia, or Eastern Branch of the Potomac. To the south, on the heights beyond the Eastern Branch, is seen the long mass of the Government Insane Asylum building. On the Virginia shore rises a long picturesque range of hills. amid which may be discerned Arlington Heights, with its pillared edifice erected by George Washington Parke Custis, now occupied by the government, and its National Cemetery or city of the dead, where 15,000 Union soldiers are interred, while the spire of Fairfax Seminary, six miles distant, rises above the horizon in the direction of Alexandria. The latter little city, with its houses, churches, and shipping lying along the harbor, is clearly visible, and the river is at almost all seasons dotted with the sails of river craft, and with steamers plying up and down. To the northwest, over the roofs of the Executive Mansion and the new State Department, rise the lofty and picturesque heights of Georgetown, attaining at the adjoining village of Tenallytown, just outside the borders of the District of Columbia, a height of some 400 feet above the level of the sea. To the north are seen the buildings of Howard University crowning Seventh Street hill; and beyond, the tower of the Soldiers' Home, a free refuge for the disabled soldiers of the army, comprising a beautiful park of 500 acres in extent. It was this delightful and comprehensive view which drew from Baron von Humboldt the remark, as he stood on the western crest of Capitol Hill and surveyed the scene, " I have not seen a more charming panorama in all my travels."

The Capitol is the most conspicuous object in the scenery of Washington, its lofty white dome being visible from all directions for miles around the city. It is situated very nearly in the geographical centre of the city, the great plateau of Capitol Hill extending from the east front about one mile and gently sloping towards the Anacostia, while from the west front the ground falls off by a partly abrupt and partly gradual decline to the level of the Potomac. This building, constructed in the purely classic style, with a centre and two projecting wings of great extent, is ornamented on the eastern front with 68 Corinthian columns. The entire length of the building is 751 feet 4 inches, with a breadth of from 121 to 324 feet in the different portions. The whole edifice covers nearly 3½ acres. The height of the centre and wings from the ground to the roof is 70 feet. From the main or central building springs a lofty iron dome, 135½ feet in diameter at its base, and containing 8,009,200 pounds, or 3575 tons of cast and wrought iron. The apex of the dome is surmounted by a tholus or lantern 15 feet in diameter and 50 feet high, and this is crowned by a bronze statue of Freedom, designed by Crawford, facing the east, the height of which is 19½ feet. The total height from the eastern front of the Capitol to the crest of the statue of Freedom is 285½ feet. The advantageous position, great

architectural mass, and harmonious and imposing effect of the Capitol, seen from most points of view, are such as to have secured for it the almost unanimous praise of the best judges of all countries as the most impressive modern edifice in the world. The material of the central building is Virginia freestone; that of the wings is white marble, from Massachusetts quarries; while the fluted marble columns are from the Cockeysville (Md.) quarries, near Baltimore. The solidity and durability of the structure are in harmony with its character and cost. The total expenditure upon the Capitol for erection, extension, and repairs has been a little more than thirteen millions of dollars. Owing to the fact that the main building was constructed many years before the wings, there is some want of harmony between the older and newer portions, but this is more perceptible in the interior than the exterior. The chief want in the latter direction is a greater projection of the eastern and western fronts of the central building, so as to afford a more ample support to the enormous superincumbent weight and mass of the dome. The Capitol has had several superintending architects. The central building was designed chiefly by R. H. Latrobe, and the wings and dome by Thomas U. Walter. The present central structure dates from 1818 (completed 1827), and the extension or wings from 1851. The first Capitol building, erected on the same site, was commenced in 1793, the corner-stone having been laid by George Washington, September 18th of that year—seven years before the removal of Congress to Washington. Two wings were first constructed, the north wing being occupied by Congress in 1800, and the south wing, connected by a wooden passage, in 1811. Before the completion of this first Capitol building, the whole was fired and destroyed by the British army at the invasion of Washington in August, 1814; after which Congress found temporary apartments in other buildings until the completion of the central portion of the present Capitol in 1827, which was surmounted by a wooden dome, afterwards replaced (between 1855 and 1863) by the present one of iron. The corner-stone of the Capitol extension was laid July 4th, 1851, the new Hall of Representatives in the south wing was occupied in 1857, and the Senate Chamber in 1859. The work was continuously prosecuted during the civil war, the great dome rising foot by foot, while hostile armies were struggling for the possession of the capital, until the great statue of Freedom crowned the summit on December 12th, 1863.

The rotunda forms the central attraction of the Capitol, and consists of a circular hall 96 feet in diameter, by 180 feet in height to the canopy above, on the concave interior of which is painted a mammoth fresco by Brumidi, representing allegorical and historical subjects. The eight panels which surround the rotunda, nearly on a level with the spectator, are adorned by historical paintings, most of

which have become familiar to all, through their repeated multiplication by the art of the engraver.   These comprise Col. Trumbull's
four paintings, *The Declaration of Independence*, *The Surrender of
Burgoyne*, *The Surrender of Cornwallis*, and *The Resignation of General Washington ; The Landing of Columbus,* by Vanderlyn ; *The Em-
barkation of the Pilgrims,* by Weir ; *The Baptism of Pocahontas*, by
Chapman ; and *De Soto's Discovery of the Mississippi*, by Powell.
The portico of the eastern front of the Capitol presents two sculptured groups on either side—one by Persico, representing the discovery of America by Columbus ; the other by Greenough, being
an allegorical representation of the first settlement of America.
Neither group can be esteemed happy in conception or pleasing in
treatment.   In niches on the right and left of the main entrance
door are two colossal statues by Persico, representing Peace and
War.   But the best embodiment of the sculptor's art in the external
decorations of the Capitol is the group, by Thomas Crawford, on
the tympanum of the eastern front of the Senate wing.   This represents the progress of civilization in the United States.   The great
bronze doors by Randolph Rogers, which adorn the eastern front
entrance of the Capitol, represent in sculptured *alto-relievo* events in
the discovery of America and life of Columbus, while the similar
doors in bronze which constitute the main entrance to the Senate
wing, designed by Thomas Crawford, represent Revolutionary bat-
tles and prominent civic events in the history of the country.

The Senate Chamber, occupying the centre of the north wing, is
113 by 81 feet in dimensions, with seats for 76 Senators, the galleries
furnishing accommodations for over 1000 spectators.   The Senate
Chamber is without artistic decoration, except in the glass panels of
the ceiling, which have symbolic designs.   The most elaborate decorations in the Capitol are beneath the Senate Chamber, in the
corridors and connecting passages, where the vaulted ceilings
and walls are completely covered with designs in fresco and
distemper, representing natural scenery, birds, animals, flowers,
and heads of historical characters in great variety of graceful
combination.   Several of the Senate committee-rooms are richly
and elaborately frescoed—notably the naval committee-room, with
its frescos of sea-gods and goddesses and other nautical subjects, exquisitely painted in the style of some of the panels
unearthed at Pompeii ; and the military committee-room, which has
five paintings of Revolutionary battle scenes done in pure fresco by
Brumidi.   The grand staircase of white marble, ascending from
the basement story to the Senate floor on the west, presents one of
the finest gems of interior architecture in the world.   The long
apartment in the rear of the Senate Chamber, known as the Marble
Room, is constructed wholly of marble, the ceiling resting upon
four Corinthian columns of Italian marble, while the walls are

wholly of variegated Tennessee marble, highly polished. Adjoining the Marble Room is the President's Room, which presents a crowded assemblage of decorations too numerous and ornate for so small an apartment. On the opposite side is the room of the Vice-President, presenting a marked contrast to the former, being furnished in severely simple though pleasing taste. The Senate post-office, just beyond, has a ceiling elaborately frescoed with emblematic designs.

The south wing of the Capitol is occupied by the House of Representatives and its offices and committee-rooms. The Hall of the House is the largest legislative chamber in the world, measuring 139 feet in length by 93 feet in width, and 36 feet in height. The galleries are capable of accommodating about 1500 persons, while the floor affords ample space for 300 members, each of whom is provided with a writing-desk. On the right of the Speaker's chair is Vanderlyn's full-length portrait of Washington, and on the left a fine portrait of La Fayette by Ary Scheffer, presented by that artist to Congress.

The Library of Congress occupies the whole western projection of the central building. It consists of three communicating halls, lined throughout with iron shelves and alcoves, finished in ornate but chaste and beautiful style. The floor is of black and white marble, and no wood has been used in any part of the construction of the library, which is thus impregnably fireproof. The Library embraces over 315,000 volumes, and a new building is proposed, to contain its overflowing stores, together with the copyright bureau, which is attached by law to the office of the Librarian of Congress. Copies of every work secured by copyright, including books, periodicals, musical compositions, prints, chromos, photographs, engravings, etc., must be deposited in this office, and hundreds of thousands of these publications are already gathered here, the number constantly increasing. The law department of the library is located in the basement of the Capitol, occupying the room formerly used by the Supreme Court of the United States. It has 35,000 volumes. The vestibule, or entrance to this library, is marked by six columns of what may be styled an American order of architecture, being carved in imitation of Indian-corn stalks, while the capitals of the columns represent the silken corn in full ear. In like manner, the columns in the upper vestibule are crowned by capitals representing the flower and leaf of the tobacco plant, instead of the traditional acanthus.

The Supreme Court room and offices occupy the old Senate Chamber in the central building and rooms adjacent. The Court of Claims, which has jurisdiction of cases involving claims on the government of the United States, is located immediately beneath. The old hall of the House of Representatives, through which one passes from the rotunda to reach the present hall of the House, is built in

the form of a semicircle, surrounded by columns of variegated marble from the Potomac River. This hall was devoted by act of 1864 to the purposes of a national memorial hall, each State in the Union being invited to contribute statues of two of its most distinguished citizens in marble or bronze. As yet, only Rhode Island, Connecticut, Massachusetts, Vermont, New York, and New Jersey have sent contributions to this hall of fame. In this hall, too, is the exquisite piece of sculpture by Franzoni, representing the Muse of History on the winged car of Time, with a clock for recording the hours.

The Capitol contains, besides these, the historical paintings in the rotunda, and the frescos, a considerable number of works of art of various merit. At the head of the grand staircase west of the House is Leutze's large painting, representing an emigrant train crossing the Rocky Mountains. Powell's picture of *Perry's Victory on Lake Erie* is at the head of the eastern staircase in the Senate wing. Two paintings of American scenery on the Colorado and Yellowstone, by Thomas Moran, are in the corridor to the east of the Senate gallery. Statues of Franklin and Jefferson by Powers, and of Hancock, Hamilton and Baker, by Horatio Stone, are among the decorations of the Capitol.

The Treasury Department, situated at the corner of Fifteenth Street and Pennsylvania Avenue, is an imposing edifice, in the pure Ionic style of architecture, with a stone balustrade running around the entire roof of the building. It has four fronts, the eastern of which, facing the city, represents the older part of the building, constructed 1836–41, and is of Virginia freestone. The other three fronts (built 1855–64) are of solid granite from the State of Maine. The monolithic columns in the south front are among the largest in the world, being 31½ feet high and 4½ feet in diameter. The building measures 468 feet by 264, exclusive of porticos and stairways, contains 195 rooms, exclusive of attic and sub-basement, and cost $3,000,000. It was designed by Robert Mills and T. U. Walter. The great building of the State Department, which when finished will accommodate the War and Navy Departments as well, is the latest erection among the public buildings of Washington, and is a massive piece of architecture in the Italian Renaissance style, from designs by A. B. Mullett, surmounted by a mansard roof. The material of the basement is Maine granite, and the entire superstructure is of granite from the quarries near Richmond, Va. The building was commenced in 1871, and the southern portion finished and occupied by the State Department in 1875. The dimensions of the entire edifice will be 567 feet by 471, and it will have four façades, looking to the east, west, north, and south respectively. The two buildings now occupied by the War Department and the Navy Department are situated on Seventeenth Street, near the corner of Pennsylvania Avenue, and are plain edifices of

brick, which will shortly give place to the magnificent new structure erected in part for their use, the total cost of which will approach $7,000,000.

The Department of the Interior, best known as the Patent Office building, is located near the centre of the city, occupying the entire square between F and G streets, and running from Seventh to Ninth. This splendid building is of severely simple, though massive proportions, the architecture being pure Doric, the edifice measuring 453 by 331 feet, with a elevation of 75 feet. The older part of the structure, erected 1837–42, and fronting on F Street, is of freestone. The three remaining fronts, constructed 1850–64, are of Maryland marble; and the interior, fronting on a court in the centre, is of New England granite. The Parthenon at Athens furnished the models of the columns, capitals, and tympanum of this building. In it are located, besides the Patent Office, which occupies by far the larger portion of its 191 rooms, the Indian Office, and the Office of the Public Lands, together with the offices of the Secretary of the Interior and clerks. The patent business of the United States is of enormous extent, and the models exhibited in this building number upwards of 160,000, while the annual registry of new patents now averages about 15,000. The cost of the Patent Office building was $2,700,000.

The building of the Post Office Department is located immediately opposite the Patent Office, occupying the square embraced between Seventh and Eighth streets on one side, and E and F streets on the other. It is constructed of Maryland marble. It is 300 feet long by 204 wide, with a central quadrangle of 195 by 95 feet. The order of architecture is pure Corinthian. The building, erected about 1855, cost $1,700,000.

The Department of Agriculture occupies a large brick building with brownstone trimmings in the Renaissance style, 170 by 61 feet, situated on a public reservation adjoining the Smithsonian Institution. It was erected in 1868, at a cost of $140,000. Its appendages consist of greenhouses and graperies, and experimental grounds, covering about ten acres, with terraces beautifully laid out in front, and planted with beds of assorted flowers grouped in excellent taste. The business of the Agricultural Department is the distribution of seeds, plants, agricultural reports, and information, chiefly through members of Congress.

The Naval Observatory of the United States is situated on the banks of the Potomac, midway between Washington and Georgetown. The grounds occupy 19 acres. The main building of the observatory, erected in 1844, is surmounted by a dome, from the flagstaff of which a signal ball, dropped daily at the hour of twelve, indicates the hour of mean noon by electric wires to the telegraph company running to all parts of the United States. Another domed edifice in the immediate vicinity of the observatory contains the

great equatorial telescope, mounted in 1873 with an object-glass of twenty-six inches, made at a cost of $47,000. This is the largest refractor in the world.

The Army Medical Museum, formerly Ford's Theatre, is on Tenth Street, between E and F, and contains the hospital records of the United States army in over 10,000 MS. volumes, and a vast assemblage of curious and instructive specimens representing the effects upon the human body of wounds, morbid conditions, surgical operations, etc. The microscopic section of this museum has been carried to a high point of perfection, and exhibits wonderful results; while the models assembled of hospitals, barracks, ambulances, surgical instruments, etc., constitute the finest museum of the kind in existence. The library of the surgeon-general's office, here deposited, embraces about 40,000 volumes, and is by far the most complete medical collection in the United States.

The government printing-office and book-bindery occupy a plain brick building 300 by 175 feet, at the corner of North Capitol and H streets. This is said to be the largest printing establishment in the world, and its equipment is very complete, as many as 1,000,000 volumes having been turned out in a single year.

The Washington Navy Yard, established 1804, occupies 27 acres on the Anacostia River, at the foot of Eighth Street, about one mile southeast of the Capitol. It embraces two ship-houses, several boat-houses, and shops for the manufacture of ordnance, together with buildings for officers' quarters. This yard, though practically disused for the construction of naval vessels, is an important dépôt for the manufacture of naval supplies. Above it are the extensive though not attractive buildings known as the Marine Barracks, the headquarters of the marine corps of the United States Navy.

The President's House, known also as the Executive Mansion, and popularly called the White House, stands on Pennsylvania Avenue, occupying a reservation of about 20 acres of ground midway between the Treasury and the Departments of State, War, and Navy. It is a plain edifice of freestone, painted white, 170 feet long by 86 feet wide, with a colonnade of eight simple Doric columns in front, and a semicircular portico in the rear. The grounds are adorned with fountains, flowers, and shrubbery, and form a pleasing retreat in the midst of buildings and streets devoted to commercial and public business. The building is adorned by excellent portraits of the ex-Presidents of the United States. The largest apartment, known as the East Room, is 80 by 40 feet in dimensions, and 22 feet high. The adjoining Blue Room, a beautiful apartment finished in blue and gold, is devoted to receptions, diplomatic and social. The Green Room and Red Room (so called from their furnishings) are each 30 by 20 feet. The rooms of the second floor are occupied by the executive office and the President's secretaries, together with apart-

ments for the Presidential family. The first President's house, commenced in 1792, was occupied by President John Adams in 1800, and was burned by the British army in 1814. The present edifice was constructed 1818–29 and there have been appropriated for its erection and maintenance up to the present time about $1,800,000.

Besides the public buildings erected by the government, various public offices occupy rented buildings in different parts of the city. The Department of Justice is accommodated in the upper stories of the Freedmen's Bank building, opposite the Treasury. The Pension Office and its valuable records occupy the upper portions of a fire-proof building on the corner of Pennsylvania Avenue and Twelfth Street. The Bureau of Education is in the same building. The Bureau of Statistics is on Fifteenth Street, and the Coast Survey rents the fine buildings, with fireproof store-rooms attached, erected especially for its use on New Jersey Avenue, near the Capitol. The large operations of the signal service of the army are conducted in two buildings on G Street, west of the War Department, and the army paymaster's office, commissary bureau, Nautical Almanac office, etc., are bestowed in hired apartments elsewhere.

The fine arts are not well represented in Washington, though numerous ambitious attempts have been made to decorate the city with statuary. The earliest executed of these, including the bronze equestrian statues of Gen. Jackson in La Fayette Square, and of Washington in the circle on Pennsylvania Avenue, both by Clark Mills, belong to the grotesque and exaggerated style, which is gradually giving place to better models. H. K. Brown's fine equestrian statue of Gen. Winfield Scott in bronze, erected in 1874, occupies the circle at the intersection of Massachusetts and Rhode Island Avenues on Sixteenth Street. Rawlins Square is distinguished by a full-length statue in bronze of Gen. Rawlins, Secretary of War in 1869, executed by Bailly in 1873. The Soldiers' Home is ornamented by a very superior work of art in bronze, being a colossal full-length statue of Gen. Scott by Launt Thompson. Ball's fine bronze statue emblematic of Emancipation, erected in Lincoln Park in 1876, represents Abraham Lincoln freeing a slave in chains. Greenough's marble statue of Washington, classical in style and colossal in size, is situated immediately before the eastern front of the Capitol.

The only public institution devoted exclusively to the fine arts is the Corcoran Gallery of Art, on the corner of Pennsylvania Avenue and Seventeenth Street, erected in 1859 from designs by Renwick, and opened with a collection of paintings, statuary, bronzes, and casts from the antique in 1873. This gallery, founded by the liberality of W. W. Corcoran, of Washington, is managed by a board of trustees, and is open to the public free during three days of the week, with an admission fee of twenty-five cents on Mondays, Wednesdays, and Fridays.

The Washington National Monument, so long a truncated column of 174 feet in height, was commenced in 1848 by an association incorporated by Congress. After an expenditure of $230,000, raised by voluntary subscription, the monument came to a stand-still for twenty years. By act of Congress passed in 1876, appropriating the sum of $200,000, this monument is to be finished, and will form a lofty and imposing plain obelisk, 70 feet square at the base, and 470 feet high. It is constructed of great blocks of crystal Maryland marble, lined with blue gneiss stone, and while simple and majestic in form, without attempt at ornament, will constitute a mausoleum that will last for ages, erected by the people of the whole country to its greatest citizen, on a scale worthy of the nation.

The cemeteries of Washington are not numerous. The Congressional Cemetery, located on the banks of the Anacostia, one mile east from the Capitol, embraces 30 acres. It has about 200 square cenotaphs of freestone, erected to the memory of members of Congress who have died in Washington, and contains also the graves of many distinguished officials and citizens. Oak Hill Cemetery, on Georgetown Heights, is the most attractive and beautiful place of sepulture about Washington, occupying the undulating hills above Rock Creek, and thickly planted with noble forest trees and shrubbery. Glenwood Cemetery, at the extremity of Lincoln Avenue, north of the city, and Rock Creek Cemetery, near the Soldiers' Home, with Mount Olivet, are the principal other cemeteries. The Soldiers' Home, a national institution for the invalid soldiers of the regular army, was established in 1851 by a purchase of 200 acres three miles north of the Capitol, with a sum of money levied by Gen. Scott on the city of Mexico. It has been more than doubled in extent of grounds, and is kept up by a fund derived from retaining 12¼ cents a month from the pay of each private in the army. The buildings are handsome and costly, and the grounds, laid out in meadows, groves, and lakes, afford seven miles of beautiful drives, serving as a free public park for the city of Washington. At the Soldiers' Home, President Lincoln and some of his predecessors were wont to find relaxation during the heated term of summer.

Of minor public buildings erected by the government, may be mentioned the Naval Hospital, a handsome edifice at the corner of Ninth and Pennsylvania Avenue East ; the Columbia Institution for the Deaf and Dumb, founded 1857, with its picturesque semi-Gothic buildings, occupying 100 acres at Kendall Green, and accommodating 100 pupils; the Government Hospital for the Insane (opened 1855), a commodious structure on the crest of hills on the east bank of the Anacostia, opposite Washington, with 419 acres and 600 patients, belonging to the army and navy and the District of Columbia ; and the Reform School of the District of Columbia (150 acres), established in 1871, on the Bladensburg turnpike, three miles from the Capitol.

Charitable institutions abound in Washington, and many of them have received continuous or occasional aid from the Treasury by act of Congress. The principal ones are Providence Hospital, a large edifice on Capitol Hill, accommodating 200 patients; the Louise Home, a fine building on Massachusetts Avenue, erected and endowed by W. W. Corcoran in 1871 for indigent gentlewomen; the Columbia Hospital for Women; the National Soldiers' and Sailors' Orphans' Home; the Washington Orphan Asylum; St. Joseph's and St. Vincent's Orphan Asylums; St. John's Hospital for Children; the Freedman's Hospital, and the Home for the Aged, under the care of the Little Sisters of the Poor.

The markets of Washington are profusely supplied with all the products of the soil and of the waters, the best qualities of meats, and the finest game, at low rates. The two principal markets are the Central, erected in 1870, an ornate structure of brick on Pennsylvania Avenue, between Seventh and Ninth streets, and the Northern Liberty Market, running from K to L streets, on Fifth, erected in 1874.

The water supply of Washington is brought by a capacious aqueduct from the Great Falls of the Potomac, sixteen miles above the city. It affords a daily supply of 80,000,000 gallons to the reservoir, the consumption, however, only reaching 23,000,000 gallons *per diem*. The aqueduct cost $3,500,000. The public parks and squares are well supplied with fountains, none of which, however, are of remarkable size or artistic beauty.

Washington is connected with the Virginia shore by three bridges across the Potomac. The Long Bridge, which has a track for the Washington and Alexandria Railroad, and a carriage-way for vehicles and pedestrians, is laid on piers. The Aqueduct Bridge at Georgetown is the only toll bridge in the District. The Chain Bridge at Little Falls, four miles above, has given place to an iron truss bridge erected in 1874. Across the Eastern Branch, or Anacostia, runs the Navy Yard Bridge, an iron structure erected in 1875; and Benning's Bridge, of wood, lies about a mile above the Navy Yard.

One of the most conspicuous and imposing edifices at the national capital is the Smithsonian Institution, located on the Mall. It is constructed of dark red sandstone, in the rounded Norman or Romanesque style of architecture, from designs by Renwick, and forms by far the most picturesque public edifice in Washington. This elegant building is the repository of the National Museum, and of all objects of art, natural history, geology, etc., belonging to the government, and is the centre of international and scientific exchanges of great magnitude and value, while its numerous publications are recognized as important contributions to science throughout the world. Its fine scientific library was removed to the Capitol in 1866, and forms an adjunct to the Library of Congress.

There are several colleges or universities, the chief of which are Columbian University, with its law and medical department, and preparatory school of over 100 pupils; Gonzaga College (Roman Catholic); Howard University for colored youth; and the law school of the National University.

Five daily newspapers and twelve weekly periodicals, with several monthlies, are issued; but as yet the capital possesses no journal of first-rate power and importance to the country, the local papers being overshadowed by the keen competition of the metropolitan press.

As the political capital of the United States, Washington enjoys a distinction to which no other metropolis, however extensive its population, commerce, shipping, or manufactures, can lay claim. The vast and varied interests connected with the legislation for a people of 45,000,000, now embracing 38 States and 9 Territories, draw to Washington an annually increasing number of citizens from motives of interest or curiosity; while its mild and salubrious climate in the winter season renders it an attractive resort for persons of wealth and leisure from all quarters. The society of Washington is marked by a degree of freedom and liberality of intercourse such as prevails in scarcely any other city in the Union. While the vast majority of the population is distinctively American, the presence of travellers and sojourners from all parts of the world, and the residence of the diplomatic corps, representing foreign nations, render the society cosmopolitan in the best sense of the term. The opening of the fashionable season is nearly coincident with the opening of Congress on the first Monday in December. From that time until the Lenten holidays, there is a constant succession of receptions, balls, dinners, etc., invitations to which are freely distributed; while the partly official, partly social receptions, termed levees, given by the President, the members of the cabinet, and the Speaker of the House of Representatives, are open to all comers. The President receives the calls of the public daily from 12 to 3 P.M., except on Sundays and cabinet days, Tuesdays and Fridays. New Year's Reception at the White House is attended by foreign ministers in their official costumes, by the officers of the army and navy in full uniform, and by officers of the government, Senators and Representatives, and the public generally.

The chief places of amusement are Ford's Opera House, corner of Louisiana Avenue and Ninth Street, and the National Theatre. There are several public halls, where concerts and lectures are of frequent occurrence during the season. The principal hotels are the Arlington, Riggs House, Ebbitt House, Willard's, the National, and the Metropolitan. Washington has 120 church edifices, few of which are remarkable for architectural beauty, divided between fifteen different religious denominations. Nearly all parts of the

city and of Georgetown are accessible by street cars, there being ten street railway companies and branches in active operation.

Washington is to a great extent a city of boarding-houses, and thousands of its citizens depend upon the rental of apartments, etc., for a portion of their incomes. The number of officers and clerks in government employ is nearly 5000, and, as most of these have families, there is an extensive local market for goods and commodities of all kinds, which is met by a large and excellent variety of stores and merchandise.

During the civil war of 1861-65, Washington was the centre of military operations of prodigious magnitude. On the return of peace and the assured restoration of the Union, confidence in the future revived, and Washington, which had been so long retarded by the incubus of war, began to extend its growth by the erection of multitudes of new buildings, and other evidences of prosperity. From this period may be said to date that new Washington, which, with its magnificent public improvements and multitude of private edifices of taste and elegance, has taken the place of the mean little village which but a few years ago appeared so unworthy the capital of a great nation. There were erected in 1875 nearly 1400 new buildings, at a cost of about $3,500,000, and in 1876, 1160 houses.

The environs of Washington abound in natural beauties, which need only the hand of wealth and taste to render them more attractive than those of any other American city. Favorite drives out of town take the visitor to Soldiers' Home, whence an enchanting view of city, river, and hilly landscape is unrolled ; to Rock Creek Valley, notable for its picturesque wildness and wealth of flowers and forest trees ; to the heights above Georgetown, by the splendid driveway of K Street and Connecticut Avenue, climbing hills which command the widest and most impressive prospect in the District of Columbia ; and to Arlington Heights, on the Virginia shore, with its city of the dead containing 15,000 Union soldiers' graves, and its lovely views down and across the Potomac to where the Capitol lifts its airy dome into the eastern sky.

The question whether it is good policy to build up a great city expressly for a seat of government is not now an open one. Washington has been built, and was laid out by the fathers of the republic on a scale of greatness commensurate with the permanent wants of a capital for a populous and powerful nation, destined to hold a front rank in civilization. The question of the removal of the seat of government westward, or nearer to the present or prospective centre of the country, is no longer agitated. The present capital, with its storied memories, founded by the first President, whose name it bears, is felt to be a worthy centre of the political union of a great people, symbolized by the inscription engraved on the dome of the Capitol, " *E pluribus unum.*"

THE ELECTORAL SYSTEM OF CHOOSING THE PRESIDENT.

HISTORY OF ITS ORIGIN.

It appears from Mr. Madison's invaluable Report of the Debates on the Adoption of the Federal Constitution, that in the first scheme of government submitted to the Convention, by Edmund Randolph, of Virginia, the Electoral system of choosing the President had no place. On the contrary, by the seventh article of Mr. Randolph's plan, it was " resolved that a National Executive be instituted, to be chosen by the National Legislature, for the term of —— years." On the same day, May 29th, 1787, Mr. Charles Pinckney, of South Carolina, submitted " the draft of a Federal Government " which he had prepared. In Mr. Pinckney's plan, while the members of the Senate of the United States were to be chosen by the House of Delegates (*i.e.*, of Representatives), the Representatives were to be chosen by the people under State regulations ; but the mode of electing the President was not defined. When these schemes for a government came up for consideration, the greatest difference of opinion was revealed as to the mode of electing the Chief Executive. Mr. James Wilson, of Pennsylvania, declared himself first and last in favor of an election of President by the people. Experience in the States, said he, had shown that the election of a First Magistrate by the people at large was both convenient and successful. The objects of choice in such cases must be persons whose merits had general notoriety.

Roger Sherman, of Connecticut, was for the appointment of President by the Legislature (*i.e.*, Congress), and was for making him absolutely dependent on that body, as it was the will of that which was to be executed.

The next day Mr. Wilson repeated his arguments in favor of an election by the people, and submitted the first germ of the Electoral system subsequently adopted, in the following amendment :

" That the States shall be divided into —— districts, and that per-

sons qualified to vote in each district for members of the first branch of the National Legislature elect —— members for their respective districts to be Electors of the Executive Magistracy ; that the said Electors of the Executive Magistracy meet at ——, and they, or any —— of them, so met, shall proceed to elect by ballot, but not out of their own body —— person, in whom the Executive authority of the National Government shall be vested."

Mr. Elbridge Gerry, of Massachusetts, liked the principle of Mr. Wilson's motion, but feared it would be unpopular.   He seemed to prefer the taking of the suffrages of the States instead of the Electors.   He was not clear that the people ought to act directly even in the choice of Electors, being too little informed of personal characters in large districts, and liable to deceptions.   At the same time, he was opposed to the election by the National Legislature.

Mr. Williamson, of North Carolina, could see no advantage in the introduction of Electors chosen by the people, who would stand in the same relation to the latter as the State Legislatures stood, while the expedient would involve great trouble and expense.

The vote being taken on Mr. Wilson's suggestion of Electors, it was defeated by two States affirmative to eight negative.   The question recurred on electing the Executive by the National Legislature for the term of seven years, which was agreed to—yeas, eight States ; nays, two States.

This action was reconsidered on the 9th of June, 1787, when Mr. Gerry, of Massachusetts, moved that the National Executive should be elected by the Executives of the States.   " If the appointment was made by Congress," said he, " it would lessen that independence of the Executive which ought to prevail · would give birth to intrigue and corruption, and to partiality in the Executive to the friends who promoted him."   He supposed the State Executives would most likely select the fittest man.

Mr. Randolph, of Virginia, strongly opposed Mr. Gerry's mode of appointing a President.   The confidence of the people would not be secured by it.

The vote was then taken, and Mr. Gerry's motion defeated by a large majority.

On the 15th of June, the New Jersey members proposed a third scheme for a constitution, in which the Presidential office was made elective by the United States in Congress.

On the 18th of June, Alexander Hamilton, of New York, who had been hitherto silent on the business before the Convention, made a vigorous speech against some popular features of the plans proposed, and advocating, among other things, the election of one branch of the Legislature and the Executive for life.   He submitted a sketch of his own plan for a constitution of government, the fourth article of which provided that " the supreme executive authority of the

United States should be vested in a Governor, to be elected to serve during good behavior, the election to be made by Electors chosen by the people in election districts."

These various plans were referred to a committee, which, after many consultations, reported back the clause relating to the choice of President, with the provision that he should be chosen by the National Legislature. A long debate ensued. Gouverneur Morris, of Pennsylvania, was pointedly against his being so chosen. The President would be the mere creature of the Legislature if appointed by that body. He ought to be elected by the people at large—by the freeholders of the country. If the people should elect, they would never fail to prefer some man distinguished for character or services, and some man of continental reputation ; if the Legislature elect, it will be the work of intrigue, cabal, and faction ; it will be like the election of a Pope by a conclave of Cardinals. He moved to strike out " National Legislature," and insert " citizens of the United States."

Roger Sherman thought the sense of the United States would be better expressed by the Legislature than by the people at large. The latter would never be as sufficiently informed of characters, and besides, will never give a majority of votes to any one man.

Mr. Wilson renewed his advocacy of an election by the people.

Mr. Pinckney opposed a popular election, which, he said, was liable to the most obvious and striking objections. The people would be led by a few active and distinguished men. Congress, being most immediately interested in the laws made by themselves, would be most attentive to the choice of a good man to carry them properly into execution.

Mr. Gouverneur Morris declared that if there was any combination it must be among the people's representatives in the Legislature. The people of the States could not combine, nor would they be led by distinguished men. An Executive chosen by the Legislature would not be independent of them. Appointments made by numerous bodies were always worse than those made by the people at large.

Mr. George Mason, of Virginia, conceived it would be as unnatural to refer the choice of a proper person for a Chief Magistrate to the people as it would to refer a trial of colors to a blind man. The extent of the country rendered it impossible that the people could have the requisite capacity to judge of the respective pretensions of the candidates.

The question being taken on an election by the people instead of the Legislature, it was decided in the negative—ayes, 1 (Pennsylvania); nays, 9, being all the other States voting.

Luther Martin, of Maryland, now moved that the Executive be chosen by Electors appointed by the several Legislatures. This was defeated—ayes, 2 (Delaware and Maryland); nays, 8. The question

recurring on the words " to be chosen by the National Legislature," it passed unanimously.

This was reconsidered the next day, when Oliver Ellsworth, of Connecticut, moved to strike out the appointment by Congress, and to insert, " to be chosen by Electors appointed by the Legislatures of the States." This was carried—ayes, 6 ; nays, 3 ; and Massachusetts divided.   On the second clause of the amendment, " shall the Electors be chosen by the State Legislatures," eight States voted in the affirmative and two in the negative.

This action was again reconsidered on the 24th of July, when Mr. Houston, of Georgia, renewed the plan of appointment by Congress, instead of Electors appointed by the State Legislatures. He doubted whether capable men would undertake the service of Electors.

Mr. Gerry opposed the motion. He thought there was no ground to apprehend this danger.   The election of the Executive Magistrate would be considered as of vast importance, and would create great earnestness.   The best men, the Governors of States, would not hold it derogatory from their character to be the Electors. He moved that the Legislatures of the States should vote by ballot for the Executive in the same proportions as it had been proposed they should choose Electors.   This was laid on the table, and the question recurring on Mr. Houston's motion, that the Executive be appointed by the National Legislature, it was carried by a vote of seven States in the affirmative to four in the negative. A controversy then sprang up over the term of the Executive. Mr. Wilson said the perplexities into which the Convention was now thrown proceed from the election by the Legislature, which he was sorry had been reinstated.

Mr. Gouverneur Morris said, of all possible modes of appointment, that by the Legislature is the worst.   If the Legislature is to appoint and to impeach, the Executive will be the mere creature of it.

Mr. Wilson moved that the Executive be chosen by Electors, to be taken by lot from the National Legislature.

Mr. Gerry said this was committing too much to chance.

Mr. King said we ought to be governed by reason, and not by chance.   As nobody seemed to be satisfied, he wished the matter to be postponed.

Mr. Wilson said he did not move this as the best mode, but as a compromise.   His opinion remained unshaken, that we ought to resort to the people for the election.

The question was then postponed.

The next day Mr. Gerry repeated his remark, that an election at all by the National Legislature was radically and incurably wrong, and moved that the Executive be " appointed by the Governors and Presidents of the States, with the advice of their Councils."

Mr. Madison made a sagacious speech, prefaced by the statement that there were objections against every mode that had been, or

perhaps can be, proposed. A National Executive will be subservient to the State Legislatures, if the latter had the power of election. An appointment by the State Executive was liable to the insuperable objection, that there would be intrigue with the Legislature by the candidates and their partisans.

" The option before us then lay between an appointment by Electors chosen by the people, and an immediate appointment by the people. He thought the former mode free from many of the objections which had been urged against it, and greatly preferable to an appointment by the National Legislature. As the Electors would be chosen for the occasion, would meet at once, and proceed immediately to an appointment, there would be very little opportunity for cabal or corruption.

" As a further precaution, it might be required that they should meet at some place distant from the seat of government. The second difficulty arose from the disproportion of qualified voters in the Northern and Southern States, and the disadvantages which this mode would throw on the latter. The answer to this objection was, in the first place, that this disproportion would be continually decreasing under the influence of the republican laws introduced in the Southern States, and the more rapid increase of their population; in the second place, that local considerations must give way to the general interest. As an individual from the Southern States, he was willing to make the sacrifice."

Mr. Gerry said :

" A popular election in this case is radically vicious. The ignorance of the people would put it in the power of some one set of men dispersed through the Union, and acting in concert, to delude them into any appointment. He observed that such a society of men existed in the order of the Cincinnati. They are respectable, united, and influential. They will, in fact, elect the Chief Magistrate in every instance, if the election be referred to the people."

Mr. John Dickinson, of Pennsylvania, said he had long leaned towards an election by the people, which he regarded as the best and purest source.

The question being taken, the Convention again indorsed the plan of election by Congress for the term of seven years, by a vote of six States to three. The whole proceedings were then referred to a committee of detail, and the Convention adjourned to the 6th of August (ten days), to give them time to prepare and report the Constitution. On that day, the Committee reported the clause concerning the President in this form: " He shall be elected by ballot by the Legislature, during the term of seven years." After protracted discussions (not, however, involving the election of President), the whole scheme was again referred, on the 31st of August, to a committee of eleven.

On the 4th of September, Mr. Brearly, of New Jersey, from this committee, reported in substance the present Electoral system for

choosing the President, in lieu of the plan so often adopted by the Convention for electing the Executive by Congress:

"Each State shall appoint, in such manner as its Legislature may direct, a number of Electors equal to the whole number of Senators and members of the House of Representatives to which the State may be entitled in the Legislature."

To this was added a proviso, that if an equal number of votes should be given to two persons by the Electors, the Senate should immediately choose, by ballot, one of them for President ; and if no person should have a majority, then from the five highest on the list the Senate should choose the President.

An explanation of this change being called for, Gouverneur Morris, from the committee, said that nobody had appeared to be satisfied with an appointment of the President by the Legislature. Many were even anxious for an immediate choice by the people. It was indispensably necessary to make the Executive independent of the Legislature. As the Electors would vote at the same time throughout the United States, and at so great a distance from each other, the great evil of cabal was avoided. It would be impossible also to corrupt them.

Mr. Mason, of Virginia, declared that the plan was liable to the strong objection that nineteen times out of twenty the President would be chosen by the Senate—an improper body for the purpose.

Mr. Pinckney, of South Carolina, said that the Electors would be strangers to the several candidates, and of course unable to decide on their comparative merits. It would also throw the whole appointment, in fact, into the Senate.

Mr. Wilson thought the plan, on the whole, a valuable improvement on the former. It gets rid of one great evil—that of cabal and corruption ; and continental characters would multiply as the States more and more coalesce, so as to enable the Electors in every part of the Union to know and judge of them. He thought, however, it would be better to refer the eventual appointment to the Legislature rather than to the Senate.

Mr. Randolph concurred in the latter proposition.

Mr. Rutledge, of South Carolina, was greatly opposed to the plan reported by the committee. It would throw the whole power into the Senate.

Mr. Wilson moved to strike out "Senate," and insert the word "Legislature."

Mr. Madison considered it a primary object to render an eventual resort to any part of the Legislature improbable.

Mr. Wilson's motion was then defeated—ayes, 3 States ; nays, 7 States.

Mr. Hamilton disliked the whole scheme of government, though

he liked the new modification on the whole better than that in the first report.

The question was taken on the report for appointing a President by Electors, and carried by a vote of nine States against two.

An amendment was moved that the Electors meet at the seat of the general government, but only one State voted for this provision.

Mr. Spaight, of North Carolina, said if the election by Electors was to be crammed down, he would prefer their meeting all together and deciding finally, without any reference to the Senate, and again moved that the Electors meet at the seat of government.

This was again voted down.

An amendment was then adopted adding the words, " but the election shall be on the same day throughout the United States."

Roger Sherman suggested that it would be better that the House of Representatives should elect, in case of a tie, or the want of a majority in the Electoral vote. He moved to strike out the words " the Senate shall immediately choose," and insert " the House of Representatives shall immediately choose by ballot one of them for President, the members from each State having one vote."

Mr. Mason liked this mode best, as lessening the aristocratical influence of the Senate.

The question being taken, ten States voted yea, and one State (Delaware) voted nay.

Thus the Electoral system was at length incorporated into the Constitution on the 6th of September, 1787—the Convention having been in continuous session over four months. Ten days later the Convention adjourned.

It will be noted (and the fact is most remarkable) that the members of the Convention voted three several times (and once by a unanimous vote of all the States) to make the President elective by the two Houses of Congress; that they voted once to make him elective by a body of Electors chosen by the State Legislatures only · and that they voted finally to make him elective by a body of Electors chosen as the State Legislatures might ordain. The proposition to choose the President by direct vote of the people, though offered and voted on, found so little favor, that only a single State supported it in the Convention, in which twelve States were represented.

A CERTAIN Irish author, in describing a change in religious creed on the part of an eminent person, observed that " he abandoned the errors of the Church of Rome, and embraced those of the Church of England."

IN Voltaire's collected works there are 33,000,000 alphabetical characters. In the Bible, only 3,566,480.

THE HISTORY OF THE INCOME-TAX.

In considering the question of the expediency of a tax upon incomes as a part of our revenue system, it is well to know precisely what has been done as to an income-tax by former legislation. The country having once derived from an income-tax what would now be equivalent to the heavy proportion of one fifth the annual revenue of the Government, and that within a period not far removed, it will be seen at once how important an item this would form in any reorganization of our system of taxation, which should look to imposing a share of the burdens of government upon property rather than upon the consumption of commodities.

The first income-tax was passed by Congress July 1, 1862, and took effect in the year 1863. It taxed all incomes over $600 and under $10,000 at the rate of three per cent, and on all over $10,000 it levied a tax of five per cent. Owing to the late time of its taking effect, it brought into the Treasury but a small sum prior to the year 1864, when there was collected under the head of income-tax a little over $15,000,000. By the act of March 3, 1865, the income-tax law was amended so as to increase the three per cent tax to five per cent, and the five per cent tax on incomes over $10,000 was changed to a ten per cent tax upon the excess over $5000 income, the exemption of $600 remaining the same. The most of the tax for the year 1865, however, was collected under a former law, and brought into the Treasury not less a sum than $21,000,000 for the fiscal year 1834–65. The following year, 1865–66, the war having ceased, and the country being in a high state of development in all its resources, the income-tax rose to a point the highest ever reached in the history of the tax. The returns for the fiscal year ending June 30, 1866, showed a total revenue from the income tax of $60,547,882.43. This was but little diminished in the following year, 1866–67, when the net revenue from the income-tax footed up $57,040,640.67.

The income-tax act was further amended, March 2, 1867, so as to increase the exemption, then standing at $600, up to $1000. At the same time all discrimination as to the taxing of large incomes a higher rate was abolished, and the tax fixed at five per cent on all

incomes in excess of $1000. The act also contained the limitation or proviso that the taxes on incomes should be levied and collected until, and including, the year 1870, and no longer. Under this modified tax there was collected, in the year 1868, the large sum of $32,027,-610.78; in 1869, $25,025,068.86; and in the fiscal year ending June 30, 1870, $27,115,046.11.

The agitation against the income-tax, which led finally to its repeal, was perhaps far more owing to the excess of the rate charged than to any real objection to the tax itself. Special Commissioner David A. Wells, in his report on the revenue system for the year 1869, set forth the fact that an income-tax of five per cent was greater than had ever been imposed by any other nation, except in time of war, or in extraordinary national exigencies. He recommended the reduction of the tax from five per cent to three per cent on all incomes over $1000, accompanying the suggestion with an expression of opinion that an assessment of three per cent would probably yield to the Treasury a sum almost, if not quite equal to that collected at five per cent. The reason assigned for this was, that while the reduction of the rate would afford a great and welcome relief to the classes then paying it, it would at the same time bring within reach of the income-tax law great numbers who had hitherto avoided giving in their receipts at all, or had made imperfect or fraudulent returns, in order to escape the excessive tax. "A tax of five per cent," said Commissioner Wells, "is evidently too high for revenue purposes." He also recommended that the exemption from the income-tax on account of rent, in addition to the $1000 exemption, should be fixed at the maximum of $200. The existing law, as construed in collection, permitted any one to deduct the full amount paid for rent from his annual income. Evidently, no claim could properly be made for the exemption of rent to any large extent which would not be equally valid in support of the exemption of any other class of expenditure. Certainly high rents are as much a luxury as any form of expenditure, and are as little to be considered in exemption from income taxation.

The same report of Commissioner Wells (being the last during his term of office) set forth the doctrine, that through an income-tax a larger proportion is contributed to the revenue by the classes best able to afford it than by any other method of taxation whatever. These classes owe most to the protection of the government, and it is certainly a wide departure from the true doctrine and methods of taxation that they should be exempted from the burdens of its support, with the single exception of the tax on consumption, through the tariff, which they bear in common with the poorest in the community.

In meeting the proposition then seriously advocated in many quarters, that the income-tax should be wholly removed, Mr. Wells called

the attention of the country to the fact that the tax was paid during 1868 by only 250,000 persons out of the entire population of almost 40,000,000, and yet that the returns of these persons represented an aggregate income of not less than $800,000,000. Even allowing for the families of these 250,000 contributors, it is evident that only about a million of the population were interested in having the tax repealed, while the remaining 39,000,000 out of 40,000,000 of people in the United States, were interested in having it maintained.

Both the Secretary of the Treasury and the Commissioner of Internal Revenue supported the recommendation of Special Commissioner Wells in 1869–70 that the income-tax should be retained, although willing to have it reduced to a uniform rate of three per cent on incomes exceeding $1000, with a proper minimum exemption on account of the rent of a family. The question came up in Congress two or three times before the impending expiration of the income-tax by limitation of law. After something of a contest, the tax was renewed for one year only, by act of July 14, 1870, the rate at the same time being reduced to 2½ per cent. The exemption was increased to $2000, so that nobody paid the tax for the year 1870–71, except those in such easy circumstances as to be in receipt of more than $2000 per annum. Pending the discussion in the Senate in 1871, on the bill to repeal in effect all income-tax, the tax was opposed by Mr. Scott, of Pennsylvania, Governor Buckingham, of Connecticut, and others, while it was strongly defended by Senator Sherman, and Mr. Morrill, of Vermont. The repeal finally passed the Senate, January 26, 1871, by the close vote of 26 yeas to 25 nays.

In the House of Representatives, the question was raised of jurisdiction between the two Houses, the Senate having presumed to pass a bill connected with the income-tax, while the Constitutional provision declares that all bills for raising revenue must originate in the House of Representatives. This controversy was finally compromised, however. The House, on the 9th of February, 1871, came to a vote on the question of taking up the Senate Bill to repeal the income-tax, when the yeas were 104 and the nays 105, thus showing about as close a division of opinion on the measure as in the Senate, which passed the repeal by one vote only. Thus the matter ran on to the very last day of the session, March 3, 1871, when the House, without taking the yeas and nays, concurred in the report of a committee of conference, which indorsed the Senate Bill, and thus gave effect to the income-tax repeal. The last taxes levied under the law were paid in the year 1871.

A SCOTCH laborer being asked the meaning of metaphysics, defined it as follows: "When the chiel wha listens dinna ken what the chiel wha speaks means, and when the chiel wha speaks dinna ken what he means himsel', that's metapheesics!'

FREE HOMESTEADS ON THE PUBLIC LANDS.

THE fact is not so widely known as it should be, that any one willing to work can secure, a farm on the public domain of the United States, free of cost.

By our present laws, any citizen or applicant for citizenship, over twenty-one years of age, may enter one quarter section (that is, 160 acres) of any unappropriated public lands, which are subject to pre-emption at $1.25 per acre. Or he may enter by pre-emption 80 acres of such unappropriated lands, valued and classed at $2.50 per acre by the Government.

This privilege extends to women who may be the heads of families, and each person availing himself or herself of its benefits must make affidavit before the Register of the Land Office of the district in which the entry is to be made, that he or she is the head of a family, or else twenty-one years of age. The affidavit must also set forth that the land entered is for the exclusive use and benefit of the applicant, and for the purpose of actual settlement and cultivation, and not either directly or indirectly for the use or benefit of any other person.

The applicant under the Homestead Law must pay the sum of ten dollars, on filing his affidavit with the Register, and is thereupon permitted to enter the 160 acres, or 80 acres, on payment of five dollars, as the case may be. But no certificate is given or patent issued for the land until the expiration of five years from the date of the entry above provided for. If, at the expiration of five years, or at any time within two years thereafter, the person making such entry or his direct heirs shall prove by two credible witnesses that he, she, or they have resided upon and cultivated the land for five years immediately following the date of its original entry, and shall make affidavit that no part of the land has been alienated, then the settler is entitled to the issue of a patent for the land, without further delay. This patent is a valid title from the United States, and those who have earned it by actual residence and cultivation of the land during the full term of five years have nothing to pay, except the original ten dollars for 160 acres, or five

dollars for an 80-acre homestead. Any one who chooses to complete his title before the expiration of the five years, with a view to sell or remove, can do so only by payment to the United States of the valuation price of the land, at $1.25 or $2.50 per acre, as the case may be. But he has at all times the prior right to do this, and so become full owner of the land he has settled, as against any other person.

There is a proviso in the law, that no lands acquired under the provisions of the Homestead Act shall be liable for any debts of the settler, contracted prior to the issuing of the patent for his homestead.

There is another proviso, intended to guard the interests of the Government, and compel all pre-emptors of public lands to act in good faith, which declares that if, at any time after the filing of the required affidavit, and before the expiration of the five years' probationary residence, the pre-emptor shall change his residence, or abandon the land for more than six months at any time, then the land shall revert to the United States Government. No individual is permitted to acquire more than 160 acres under the provisions of the Homestead Act ; but there is no limit to the quantity of land which may be purchased by individuals. All existing pre-emption rights are maintained unimpaired by the provisions of the act.

The five years' residence required of all other settlers under the Homestead Law, is waived in favor of all soldiers or sailors who served ninety days or longer in the United States army or navy during the war of 1861–65, and were honorably discharged. Every such soldier (or his widow, or children, in case of his decease) is entitled to free entry of 160 acres of the public lands on condition of actual residence and cultivation of the same for one year only.

Any settler on the public lands who has set out and cultivated for two years as much as 5 acres of trees on an 80-acre homestead, or 10 acres on a homestead of 160 acres, is entitled to receive a free patent for his land at the end of three years, instead of five. And any person who has planted and cultivated for ten years 40 acres of timber on any quarter section of the public lands is entitled to a patent for each 160 acres so improved, on payment of $10, provided that only one quarter in any section shall be thus granted. This is the only exception to the limitation of free homesteads to 160 acres to any one person, unless in the case of a settler under the army provision, who is not debarred, through having occupied a homestead under the law previously, from acquiring a second 160 acres through his service in the army.

Such is a succinct outline of the terms under which the unoccupied public lands of the United States are open to settlement. For information as to what portions of the public domain yet remain unappropriated, direct application should be made by letter to the Commissioner of the General Land Office, Washington.

[Condensed from the Revised Statutes of the U.S., pp. 422–426, 434.]

CENTENNIAL INTERNATIONAL EXHIBITION OF 1876.

[Compiled, with additions, from the Philadelphia Ledger Almanac and Johnson's New Universal Cyclopædia.]

THE International Exhibition of Arts, Manufactures and Products of the Soil and Mine, provided for in Acts of Congress approved March 3, 1871, and June 1, 1872, providing for the appointment of the Centennial Commission and the Centennial Board of Finance, was officially opened in Fairmount Park, Philadelphia, by the President of the United States, May 10, and officially closed by him, November 10, 1876. It was open for pay admissions one hundred and fifty-nine days, the pay gates being closed on Sundays.

In the following tables and text we present information showing the number of nations represented at the Exhibition, the amount of space occupied by the exhibitors of each nation, the number and character of the buildings erected within the enclosure, and a table of the number of admissions to the Exhibition for the whole season.

Nations Represented at the Exhibition, and the Space Occupied by them in the Principal Buildings.

AREA OF CENTENNIAL EXHIBITION GROUNDS, 236 ACRES; AREA OF BUILDINGS ABOUT 75 ACRES.

NATIONS.	Main Building, 1880 by 464 ft.; 20 acres. Cost, $1,600,000.	Carriage Annex, 346 by 231 ft.	Machinery Hall, 960 by 1402 ft., and Annex, 208 by 210 ft. Cost, $792,000.	Horticultural Hall, 350 by 160 ft. Cost, $251,937.	Horticultural Grounds, 40 acres.	Memorial Hall, 365 by 210 ft. Cost, $1,500,000. Art Annex, 854 by 136 ft. (Sculp. Fl. sp.)	Photograph Hall, 98 by 143 ft. (Plct's W. sp.)	Agricultural Hall, 465 by 680 ft.	Estimate of space occupied and special other Exhibition buildings.	Total space occupied, exclusive of wall space for pictures.
Argentine Republic	2,861							684	3,468	6,329
Austro-Hung'y	24,727	154	1,243		800	115	4,646	2,392	1,600	31,086
Belgium	15,598		9,875			320	5,514		200	25,493
Brazil	6,899		5,056			74	1,496	4,668	1,200	17,897
Canada	24,118	1,015	4,300			28	2,319	10,387	9,700	49,543
Chili	3,424								3,000	6,424
China	6,628								1,594	8,222
Denmark	2,562		685			17	538	806	40	4,010
Egypt	5,026								80	5,106
France	45,460		1,129	100	19,590	465	18,115	15,713	7,910	89,995
Germany	29,625	237	10,098	120		493	8,031	4,878	780	46,231
Great Britain and Ireland	64,155	4,130	33,208	1,050	8,000	339	12,163	12,924	1,100	114,296
India and British Colonies	24,193	63		750			126		400	25,406
Hawaii Islands	1,575			50						1,625
Italy	8,943	140	283			7,423	4,740	4,290	150	21,224
Japan	17,531					128	1,665		900	20,396
Luxemburg, Grand Duchy	247									247
Liberia								1,536		1,536
Mexico	6,567					77	3,296		60	6,691
Netherlands	15,948				6,700		4,356	4,276	101	27,024
Norway	6,959					26	1,439	3,090	200	10,275
Orange Free St.	1,058									1,058
Peru	1,462									1,462
Portugal	5,988							6,182		12,170
Russia	11,141	672	5,967¾			75	2,162	6,895	850	25,524¾
San Domingo					75					75
Spain and Colonies	11,253		1,224	1,840	8,500	93	2,960	6,061	9,200	38,173
Siam									1,000	1,000
Sweden	17,799		3,186			76	3,637	2,603	2,700	26,861
Switzerland	6,693		283							6,981
Tunis	2,015								60	2,065
Turkey	3,347									3,347
Venezuela								1,270		1,220
Total Foreign Countries	363,102	6,411	76,042¾	5,985	43,500	9,621	76,790	96,372	42,094	689,127¾
United States	136,684	80,617	308,210	18,577	239,173	2,360	46,829	157,315	370,000	1,232,930

Other principal exhibition buildings not heretofore mentioned were the following:

WOMEN'S PAVILION.—This building was 208 by 208 feet. The following nations occupied in the aggregate one fourth the floor space: Great Britain and Ireland, Canada and colonies, Brazil, France, Belgium, Netherlands, Denmark, Sweden, Norway, Italy, Germany, Spain and colonies, Tunis, Japan, Egypt, and Mexico. There was a separate Art Gallery in the Women's Pavilion, the wall space of which was also largely occupied by exhibits from the women of the above nations.

SHOE AND LEATHER BUILDING.—This was 314 by 160 feet. Great Britain occupied 615 square feet, Germany 580 square feet, and Russia 850 square feet.

POMOLOGICAL BUILDING, 182 by 192 feet, used for successive exhibitions of fruits and vegetables according to season, and finally of poultry.

BREWERS' HALL, for the exhibition of brewing apparatus and materials, 272 by 96 feet. This was constructed wholly at the expense of American brewers.

FARM WAGON ANNEX to Agricultural Hall, 144 by 196 feet.

SAW MILL ANNEX to Machinery Hall, 276 by 80 feet.

MACHINE SHOPS AND BOILER HOUSES, annexes to Machinery Hall.

CAR HOUSE, for the exhibition of railroad freight cars, 140 by 44 feet.

BUTTER AND CHEESE FACTORY, annex to Agricultural Hall, 100 by 116 feet. Occupied jointly by exhibitors of dairy products from the United States and Canada.

THE STOCK YARDS.—As an auxiliary to the agricultural exhibits, an area of 20 acres at Belmont and Girard avenues was enclosed, in which successive exhibits were made of horses and dogs, sheep, goats and swine, and horned cattle. The exhibits were almost wholly from the United States and Canada.

PRIVATE EXHIBITION BUILDINGS.—There were thirty or more exhibition buildings erected on the grounds by individual exhibitors from the United States, some of them scarcely inferior in interest to the principal buildings mentioned above.

THE AUXILIARY BUILDINGS.—At the time of the opening of the Exhibition there were 190 buildings within the inclosure, and before the close there were upward of 200. Of these, 101 were buildings used for exhibition purposes or for State or national headquarters. The remainder were ornamental structures and pavilions, restaurants, bazaars, boiler-houses, guard and fire-engine houses, offices, etc., used solely for the transaction of business, official or private. The dimensions of the five principal exhibition buildings are given in the preceding table.

The following nations had buildings on the grounds:

Austro-Hungary, Hungarian pavilion ; Brazil, Commissioners' pavilion ; Canada, log and timber house for exhibition of woods and lumber ; Chili, frame structure for exhibition of models of amalgamating machinery ; France, government pavilion for exhibition of illustrations and models of public works, charts, etc., 100 by 50 feet, also three individual exhibition buildings ; Germany, Commissioners' pavilion ; Great Britain and Ireland, three government buildings for use of Commissioners from the United Kingdom, and a boiler-house ; Japan, Japanese dwelling for workmen, 102 by 48 feet, and Japanese bazaar ; Morocco, Moorish villa, 17 by 23 feet, for display and sale of national products ; Portugal, Commissioners' pavilion ; Spain and colonies, Government exhibition building, 80 by 100 feet, and building for Spanish soldiers, also Cuban acclimation garden ; Sweden, Swedish school-house, 40 by 50 feet, and meteorograph ; Tunis, café and bazaar ; Turkey, Turkish café, 51 by 65 feet, sponge-fishers' building, and numerous small bazaars under various designations ; United States of America, Government building, 504 by 306 feet, area 102,840 square feet; ordnance laboratory, 53 by 23 feet ; U. S. Army post hospital, 40 by 14 feet; transit of Venus buildings, including transit house, photographic house and equatorial house ; also lighthouse and steam ayren for fog signal and fog bell, and U. S. signal stations. Twenty-six States were represented by 26 buildings erected either for exhibition of State pro-

ducts or for State headquarters, Kansas and Colorado uniting in one large building, and Pennsylvania having two buildings. Philadelphia also erected a pavilion for the accommodation of city officials. The States having separate buildings were as follows: Arkansas, California, Colorado, Connecticut, Delaware, Illinois, Indiana, Iowa, Kansas, Maryland, Massachusetts, Michigan, Mississippi, Missouri, New Hampshire, New Jersey, New York, Nevada, Ohio, Pennsylvania, Rhode Island, Tennessee, Vermont, Virginia, West Virginia, and Wisconsin.

The money for constructing the buildings and getting the grand Exhibition into working order was derived mainly from the following sources:

The State of Pennsylvania contributed	$1,000,000
The City of Philadelphia	1,500,000
The Government of the United States	1,500,000
Subscriptions to capital stock	2,500,000
Total	$6,500,000

Besides the advance of $1,500,000, the United States Congress appropriated $505,000 for the erection of the U. S. Government Building, and for organizing and defraying the expenses of the highly creditable display by the various departments and bureaus of the Government and by the Smithsonian Institution. The amounts invested by Pennsylvania and Philadelphia were permanent. That invested by the United States was a loan, to be repaid out of the profits of the Exhibition, if any. At the winding up of the entire business of the Exhibition, there was found to be a surplus on hand, after paying all expenses of administration. The Centennial Board of Finance took the ground that this belonged to the stockholders, who were entitled to share it pro rata. As no actual profits had been derived from the Exhibition, they viewed the subscriptions of the stockholders as a lien upon the surplus funds. The United States authorities, on the other hand, maintained that it was the clear intent of Congress in the act of February 16, 1876, advancing the $1,500,000, that the United States should be fully repaid before any dividends were made. To decide the question, an amicable suit was brought in the United States Court, and decided in the spring of 1877 in favor of the Government. The $1,500,000 was accordingly returned to the United States, the stockholders receiving about 25 per cent on their investments. The financial result of the Exhibition was more favorable than that of any other International Exhibition, except one.

The awards of the Exhibition for meritorious products were decided by a board of 225 judges, chosen from the most distinguished specialists in the several branches of art and science in this country and abroad. The results of the Exhibition, by the almost unanimous judgment of the public, at home and abroad, were in the highest degree successful. It brought together a far wider concourse of American people than was ever gathered on any other occasion. The great resources of the country were exhibited in a manner approximating, though not reaching, completeness. The administrative functions and the military and naval constructions of the Government were shown in a connected manner. The vast mechanical industries of the continent, assembled and illustrated in Machinery Hall, were in the highest degree impressive and instructive. The superiority of some of the foreign exhibits in decorative art and the finer class of manufactures, especially in ornamental articles, did much to stimulate emulation among our own artists and artisans. The educational effects of the Exhibition are beyond computation. Hardly one of the ten millions of visitors but must have learned something of real importance from this inexhaustible mine, to be stored up in memory. The whole Exhibition period, in short, was an epoch of national and international education. The good-will and friendly relations established between so many worthy representatives of most of the countries on the globe and our own people cannot fail to have permanent results in fostering the arts of peace and national brotherhood.

International Exhibitions or World's Fairs.

Where held.	Year.	Opened	Closed.	Acres under Cover.	Number of Visitors.	Cost.	Receipts.
London	1851	May 1..	Oct. 11..	23	6,170,000	$1,454,000	$2,121,612
New York....	1853	July 14.	Nov. 10..	5¼	600,000	500,000	
Paris........	1855	May 15.	Nov. 15..	30	4,533,464	4,000,000	640,595
London	1862	May 1..	Oct. 25..	24	6,211,103	2,300,000	2,042,632
Paris.........	1867	April 1.	Oct. 31..	40½	9,300,000	4,596,763	2,103,675
Vienna........	1873	May 1..	Oct. 31..	56	7,254,867	9,850,000	1,032,380
Philadelphia..	1876	May 10.	Nov. 10.	75	9,910,966	8,500,000	4,308,660

GREATEST DAYS COMPARED.

Cities.	Greatest Days.	Visitors.	Cities.	Greatest Days.	Visitors.
Phila...	Thursd., Sept. 28, 1876..	274.919	Paris....	Sunday, Sept. 9, 1855..	123,017
Paris...	Sunday, Oct. 27, 1867..	173,920	London..	Tuesday, Oct. 7, 1851..	109,915
Vienna.	Sunday, Nov. 2, 1873..	103,674	London..	Thurs. Oct. 30, 1862..	67,891

Centennial International Exhibition at Philadelphia, 1876.

Opened from May 10 to Nov. 10, 159 days. Total number of visitors, 9,910,966; total receipts from admissions, $3,813,749.75.

DAYS OF LARGE ATTENDANCE.

Days.	Visitors.	Days.	Visitors.	Days.	Visitors.
Opening Day.......	76,712	Sept. 30............	103.385	Nov. 2.............	115,208
Sept. 9............	99,934	Oct. 18.............	124,777	Nov. 8.............	90,583
Sept. 20........	101,498	Oct. 25	106.986	Nov. 9, Philadelphia	
Sept. 28. Pennsylva-		Oct. 27	95,563	Day..............	176,753
nia Day.........	274,919	Nov. 1.............	107,715		

DAILY AVERAGES FOR EACH MONTH.

Month.	Cash Admissions.		Free.	Total.
	50 cents.	25 cents.		
May, 19 days...............	19,946	......	6,527	26,473
June, 26 days...............	26,756	.....	9,835	30,622
July, 26 days...............	24,472	9	10,351	34,863
Aug., 27 days...............	27,924	5,730	9,875	53,530
Sept., 26 days..............	60,816	21,144	11,873	93,834
Oct., 26 days...............	85,796	992	12,668	102,458
Nov., 9 days	99,532	2,567	13,215	115,315
Daily average...............	45,601	4,739	11,991	62,333

MONTHLY SUMMARY OF ATTENDANCE AND RECEIPTS.

Months.	Days open.	Number of Admissions.					Receipts.
		50 cents.	25 cts.	Paid.	Free.	Total.	
May........	19	373,980	....	378,980	305,960	184,940	$189,490 35
June.......	26	695,666	.....	695,666	307,159	1,002,825	347,833 40
July.......	26	636,278	240	636,518	269,929	906,447	318,199 25
August....	27	733,953	154,731	908,684	266,630	1,175,314	415,659 25
September.	26	1,581,233	549,758	2,130,991	308,698	2,439,689	928,056 00
October....	26	2,308,716	25,814	2,334,530	329,381	2,663,911	1,160,811 50
November..	9	895,794	23,111	918,956	118,985	1,037,840	453,700 00
Total	159	....	....	8,004,274	1,906,692	9,910,966	$3,813,749 75

Total free admissions. .... 1,906,692 | Average total daily admissions......62,333
Average daily cash admissions   50,340 | Average daily cash receipts.... $23,985 85

RECEIPTS FROM ROYALTIES, CONCESSIONS, ETC.

The total receipts of the Exhibition were :

From admission fees............................$3,813.749 75
From concessions................................ 289,900 00
For percentages and royalties.................. 205,010 75

$4,309,660 50

The following are given as the receipts from a part of the concession contracts :

Catalogue Co.	$100,000	Guide Book Co.	$5,000
Restaurants.	36,000	Whitman's Confectionery	5,000
Cafés in Main Building	20,000	Safe-deposit Vaults	5,000
Soda-water Fountains	20,000	California Wine Booth	5,000
Cigar Stands	18,000	Cafés in Agricultural Hall	4,500
Narrow-gauge Railway, about.	16,000	Cut Flowers	3,000
Rolling Chair Co	13,000	Glass Works	3,000
Globe Hotel	10,300	Dairymen's Association	3,000
Public Comfort Restaurant	8,500	Photograph Co	3,000
Pop-corn	8,000	Tobacco Exhibit	3,000
Cafés in Machinery Hall	7,900	Vienna Bakery	3,000
Centennial Bank	5,000	American Fusee Co	1,000

HOW MANY BOOKS ARE THERE IN THE WORLD?

THE following estimate of the total number of printed books which exist in all languages, is quoted in Gabriel Peignot's " Manuel de Bibliophile," vol. i., published 1823 :

Number of works from invention of printing (say 1450) to
1536... 42,000
Number of works, 2d century from invention of printing
1536–1636.. 575,000
Number of works, 3d century from invention of printing,
1636–1736.. 1,125,000
Number of works, 4th century from invention of printing,
1736–1822 (incomp.)............................... 1,839,960

3,861,960

The first century was obtained by diligent computation from Maittaire, Panzer, and the other catalogues of publications of the fifteenth century. Passing then to the last century, and availing himself of all the literary and bibliographical journals, catalogues of booksellers and of libraries, etc., he arrives at the figures quoted, viz., 1,839,960. Using these as a basis for computation of the two intermediate centuries, of which no more approximate estimate could be made, from defect of data to proceed upon, he calculates the product of each quarter century in progressive ratio, and obtains the results above recorded. Estimating each work at an average of three volumes, the total product of the printed literature of the globe is about ten millions of volumes. Our literary cipherer next estimates that three fourths of the whole may have been destroyed by use, or accident, leaving in all the public and private libraries of the globe only 2,250,000 *different* volumes.

Peignot considers the estimate exaggerated, the facts vague, and their verification impossible,

From the *Financial Review*, 1877.

COMPOUND INTEREST TABLE.

Showing the Accumulation of Principal and Interest on one Dollar, at various rates per Annum, from 3 to 10 per cent., the Interest being compounded semi-annually.

No. of Years.	3 per cent.	4 per cent.	4½ per cent.	5 per cent.	6 per cent.	7 per cent.	7½ per cent.	8 per cent.	10 per cent.
1....	$1.0302	$1.0404	$1.0455	$1.0506	$1.0609	$1.0712	$1.0743	$1.0816	$1.1025
2...	1.0613	1.0824	1.0930	1.1028	1.1255	1.1475	1.1530	1.1692	1.2155
3....	1.0934	1.1261	1.1438	1.1596	1.1940	1.2292	1.2387	1.2646	1.3400
4....	1.1261	1.1715	1.1918	1.2184	1.2667	1.3168	1.3308	1.3678	1.4773
5 ...	1.1605	1.2188	1.2431	1.2800	1.3439	1.4105	1.4298	1.4794	1.6257
6 ...	$1.1956	$1.2681	$1.3004	$1.3448	$1.4257	$1.5110	$1.5360	$1.6002	$1.7957
7 ...	1.2317	1.3193	1.3643	1.4129	1.5125	1.6186	1.6502	1.7307	1.9747
8....	1.2689	1.3726	1.4264	1.4845	1.6047	1.7339	1.7729	1.8720	2.1827
9....	1.3073	1.4231	1.4913	1.5596	1.7024	1.8574	1.9047	2.0247	2.4064
10 ...	1.3463	1.4858	1.5592	1.6385	1.8061	1.9897	2.0462	2.1899	2.6530
11....	$1.3875	$1.5458	$1.6301	$1.7234	$1.9161	$2.1315	$2.1982	$2.3687	$2.9250
12....	1.4295	1.6082	1.7041	1.8086	2.0326	2.2833	2.3617	2.5619	3.2248
13....	1.4727	1.6732	1.7820	1.9001	2.1564	2.4459	2.5372	2.7710	3 5558
14 ...	1.5172	1.7408	1.8631	1 9963	2.2878	2.6201	2.7258	2.9971	3.9198
15....	1.5630	1.8111	1.9479	2.0933	2.4271	2.8068	2.9284	3.2417	4.3216
16....	$1.6103	$1.8843	$2.0365	$2.2027	$2.5749	$3.0067	$3.1461	$3.5062	$4.7645
17....	1 6589	1.9604	2.1272	2.3142	2.7317	3.2208	3.3800	3.7923	5.2529
18 ...	1.7091	2.0396	2.2210	2.4313	2.8981	3.4502	3.6312	4.1018	5.7883
19....	1.7607	2.12.0	2.3252	2.5541	3.0746	3.6900	3.9011	4.4365	6.3816
20....	1.8140	2.2073	2.4310	2.6837	3.2618	3.9592	4.1911	4.7985	7.0362
21....	$1.8690	$2.2970	$2.5415	$2.8196	$3.4605	$4.2412	$4.5026	$5.1900	$7.7574
22....	1.9233	2.3898	2.6572	2.9324	3.6712	4.5433	4.8373	5.6136	8.5525
23 ...	1.9835	2.4853	2.7781	3.1123	3.8948	4.8669	5.1909	6.0716	9.4293
24 ...	2.0131	2.5868	2.9045	3.2699	4.1320	5.2136	5.5832	6.5670	10.3957
25....	2.1032	2.6913	3.0367	3.4351	4.3836	5.5849	5.9982	7.1030	11.4612
26....	$2.1698	$2.8006	$3.1749	$3.6094	$4.6506	$5.9827	$6.4441	$7.6826	$12.6359
27....	2.2314	2.9131	3.3193	3.7921	4.9638	6.4088	6.9231	8 3094	13.9811
28....	2.3019	3 0318	3.4703	3.9341	5.2343	6.8653	7.4377	8.9975	15.3501
29....	2.3715	3.1513	3.6282	4.1858	5.5531	7.3543	7.9906	9.7208	16.9334
30....	2.4432	3.2818	3.7933	4.3977	5.8913	7.8781	8.5846	10.5143	18.6691
31....	$2.5170	$3.4141	$3.9660	$4.6203	$6.2500	$8.4391	$9.2227	$11.3742	$20.5837
32....	2.5931	3.5523	4.1465	4.8542	6.6307	9.0402	9.9087	12.3024	22.6924
33 ...	2.6715	3.6958	4.3351	5.0999	7.0345	9.6841	10.6453	13.3062	25.0184
34...	2.7322	3.8451	4.5324	5.3591	7.4629	10.3738	11.4366	14.3920	27.5828
35....	2.8331	4.0005	4.7387	5.6294	7.9174	11.1126	12.2867	15.5664	30.4081
36....	$2.9211	$4.1621	$4.9543	$5.9141	$8.3996	$11.9041	$13.2000	$16.8367	$33.5249
37....	3.0044	4.3302	5.1798	6.2138	8.9111	12.7620	14.1811	18.2105	36.9612
38....	3.1004	4.5052	5.4146	6.5284	9.4538	13.6709	15.2353	19.6965	40.7497
39....	3.1941	4.6872	5.6610	6.8589	10.0295	14.6446	16.3677	21.3088	44.9266
40....	3.2907	4.8766	5.9238	7.2061	10.6403	15.6877	17.5814	23.0422	49.5316
41....	$3.3901	$5.0736	$6.1986	$7.5709	$11.2833	$16.8050	$18.8915	$24.9221	$54.6086
42....	3.4926	5.2785	6.4807	7.9542	11.9758	18.0020	20.2956	26.9561	60.2059
43...	3.5982	5.4925	6.7756	8.3569	12.7051	19.2842	21.8043	29.1857	66.3771
44...	3.7070	5.7147	7.0840	8.7800	13.8832	20.6577	23.2'50	31.5348	73.1807
45....	3.8191	5.9456	7.4062	9.2445	14.7287	22.1290	25.1663	34.1080	80.6817
46....	$3.9315	$6.1858	$7.7430	$9.6915	$15.6257	$23.7052	$27.0363	$36.8813	$88.9516
47....	4.0452	6.4357	8.0954	10.1822	16.5773	25.3936	29.0466	39.8908	98.0692
48....	4.1655	6.6957	8.4638	10.6957	17.5968	27.2022	31.2057	43.1459	107.1213
49....	4.2914	6.9662	8.8490	11.2383	18.6597	29.1397	33.5253	46.6666	118.1012
50....	4.4211	7.2477	9.2516	11.8072	19.7941	31.2141	36.0154	50.4746	130.2066

[From Hill's Manual of Social and Business Forms, Chicago, 1875.]

STATUTES OF LIMITATIONS.

State Laws with Reference to Limitation of Actions, showing the Limit of Time on which Action may be brought.

STATES AND TERRITORIES.	Assault, slander, replevin, etc. Years.	Open accounts. Years.	Notes. Years.	Judgments. Years.	Sealed and witnessed instruments. Years.
Alabama.................	1	3	6	20	10
Arkansas...............	1	3	5	10	10
California.............	3	2	4	5	5
Colorado..............	1	2	2	3	3
Connecticut...........	1	6	6	6	17
Dakota.................	2	6	6	20	20
Delaware..............	1	3	6	20	20
District of Columbia .	1	3	3	12	12
Florida	2	5	5	20	20
Georgia...............	1	4	6	7	20
Idaho.................	3	2	4	5	5
Illinois.	1	5	10	20	10
Indiana...............	2	6	20	20	20
Iowa..................	2	5	10	20	10
Kansas	1	3	5	5	15
Kentucky..............	1	5	5	15	15
Louisiana.............	1	3	5	10	20
Maine.................	2	6	20	20	20
Maryland.............	3	3	3	12	12
Massachusetts........	2	6	20	20	20
Michigan	2	6	6	10	10
Minnesota............	2	6	6	10	20
Mississippi	1	3	6	7	7
Missouri..............	1	4	5	5	10
Montana.............	2	2	4	5	4
Nebraska.............	2	6	20	20	10
Nevada...............	2, 6	6	20	20	20
New Hampshire	1	—	—	10	10
New Jersey...........	2	6	6	20	20
New Mexico..........	1	3	10	10	10
New York.............	1	6	15	15	15
North Carolina.......	1	3	10	10	10
Ohio.................	1	6	15	15	15
Ontario (U. Canada)...	1	5	5	30	30
Oregon	2	1	6	10	20
Pennsylvania.........	1	6	6	20	20
Quebec (L. Canada)...	1, 2	5	5	30	30
Rhode Island.........	1	6	6	20	20
South Carolina	2	6	6	20	20
Tennessee.............	1	6	6	20	—
Texas.................	1	2	4	10	10
Utah..................	1	2	4	5	7
Vermont..............	2	6	14	8	8
Virginia	5	5	5	10	20
Washington Territory	2	3	6	9	20
West Virginia	5	5	6	10	10
Wisconsin............	2	6	6	20	20
Wyoming.............	1	6	15	10	21

Tom Brown says of the ancient and singular custom of making fools of people on the 1st of April: "I never could inform myself what gave the first rise to so odd a frolic; but methinks they might let it alone: for since three parts in four of the people are fools every day in the year, what occasion is there to set a day apart for it?"

GOVERNMENT MANAGEMENT OF RAILWAYS.

[Abridged from the *Journal des Économistes*, August, 1877.]

THE attentive observer of politics and of the railway system of the different countries of Europe has remarked of late years a strong tendency to the absorption by the State of lines so long worked by charter companies. Bavaria, near the close of 1875, purchased the railways of the Eastern Bavarian Company ; Saxony has assumed the lines of the railway company from Leipzig to Dresden. The Italian Legislative chambers have recently voted the purchase by the State of a portion of the roads belonging to the railway system of the peninsula.

Does this absorption, this purchase of railways by the State, answer to an economical want ? Do the results of working by the State, hitherto obtained, justify us in predicting a better management of the lines heretofore worked by the companies, when they shall be worked by the Government ? What is the solution to be arrived at from the point of view of the general interest, in different countries ? Is it that the working of railways by the State is to be preferred to that by private companies, or will the contrary solution rather have to be admitted ?

When two railways situated in the same country, the one belonging to the Government, the other to a private company, are in almost identical conditions as to working—that is to say, if the receipts per mile of each road, and the variations of the longitudinal sections, are approximately the same—we arrive at the following economical deductions :

1. The working coefficient, or the ratio of expenses to receipts in running the roads, is greater on the government railway than on the private one.

2. In order to obtain the same receipts, the Government is subjected to a greater expense than the private company.

3. The rate of interest paid on account of construction capital exceeds on the private railway that realized by the Government railway.

4. The expenses of working per passenger and per ton of freight under the system of the State are greater than those of the private railway.

These results, founded upon the figures of the working of many years given us by statistics, are a characteristic mark of the inferiority of the working of railways by the State, compared to the working by private companies.

The economic inferiority of railway management by the State when compared with that by private companies results from several causes. The working of a railroad is above all things an industry—the industry of transportation, and as such it ought to be managed commercially. A private company should manage, and it does generally manage its railway, in the same manner as the manufacturer or merchant manages his factory or his trade. In the hands of the State, on the contrary, the railway falls into the jurisdiction of one of the ministers, and it is managed administratively. The State has to do with administration, and not with commerce.

In England and in Austria, where the railways are managed on the most commercial plan by the companies which own them, or which have obtained the charters, the commercial agents of these companies traverse the country to secure freights, just as the clerks of any merchant would travel to open up markets for the goods of

their patron. Private companies interest themselves in finding out means of producing new sources of traffic, of attracting new freights to their lines. If all the railways belonged to the Government, and were worked by it, these methods, employed by the railway companies to make the most out of the lines which they have in their hands, would soon fall into disuse, for they are conformed neither to the habits nor to the character of the State and of its functionaries. This is a first cause of the economic inferiority of State railways in comparison with private ones —a cause which is exhibited in a diminution of the receipts.

The expenses of working a railway are no less important than the receipts. A rational and economical management requires that the expenses should constantly follow the same variations, the same law as the traffic. For the merchant and manufacturer this rule is elementary, and railways ought equally to observe it. If the traffic falls off, the expenses should fall off likewise, otherwise the working coefficient will be increased. The expense of the working force represents a very important figure in the management of a railway. If the traffic falls off, the railway companies reduce a part of their *personnel*. In railway management the smallest economy must not be neglected, for the amount of that saving multiplied by the number of miles of trains or of way, or by that of tons of freight, yields at the end of the year important sums, and establishes the fact that in railways there is nothing so little, no economy so trifling, as not to merit the attention of those responsible for the direction. In this respect the economic inferiority of working railways by the State compared to that of private companies is well established. Governments in general are not accustomed to dismiss a part of the official staff of a railway which it works when the traffic upon these railways diminishes. This *personnel* is composed in effect almost entirely of old soldiers, towards whom the State has, so to speak, contracted a moral obligation of keeping them till their age renders them unfit for working service, when it gives them a retiring pension.

One point of economy in which the superiority of privately managed railroads over those of the State is incontestable, and in which the economic results obtained by private industry greatly outrun those reached by the State, consists in the utilization of the working force. Let us cite an example in the railway running from Vienna to Berlin. On the Austrian portion of this railway, the *personnel* of the train is composed, besides the engineer and the fireman, of one conductor in charge of the train, and two conductors charged with the care of the tickets. Now, on the same line of railway when it enters Saxony, where it is managed by the Government, the same train comprehends, besides the engineer and fireman, four conductors and three brakemen. The Saxon train has always three officers more than the Austrian train. In the latter the brakes are cared for by the three conductors of the train, who, during the trip, are seated upon the platforms, and during the stops superintend the handling of baggage, etc. The Saxon train has all these extra brakemen, and while the train is *en route* the conductors are seated in a reserved compartment of a car, and chatting among themselves like ordinary travellers. Estimating the expense of one brakeman at only 1500 francs per year, each regular train of travellers on the Government railway of Saxony will cost at least 4500 francs per year more than on the system of the Austrian company. One sees at once the importance reached by the figures of these additional expenses of running when the number of regular passenger trains per day is so considerable. Thus the railway companies make much better and more economic use of the officers on their trains than the railways of the State, and that, too, without any prejudice to the security of the train, and the good execution of the service. With rare exceptions it may be asserted, that the *personnel* employed by the Government for any given work is more numerous than that occupied upon a similar labor with a private company.

The comparison of the methods pursued by State railways and by private ones to accomplish the best use of the material consumed in running trains leads to conclusions of the same character as the preceding. Railway companies are in the habit of giving to their employés, who by their attention or zeal succeed in ac-

complishing economies in consumption, a premium representing a part of the saving. They by whose care the rails, the locomotive, or the cars are saved for running use, or the expenses in any direction are reduced, are suitably rewarded. The employés thus encouraged are induced to study economy in the interest of the company, and this stimulus operates to induce each person employed to study how to augment the receipts or diminish the expenses. This is an idea which has not hitherto penetrated into the administrative spheres of the government of railways, and yet there is none more important commercially than this. It has been introduced into every department of business.

One of the principles taught by political economy is that in the domain of labor, in that of industry and of commerce, the sphere of activity of the State begins nearly where the *rôle* of the individual ends, or where the activity of private industry ceases. Wherever, in the vast field of industrial action, individual efforts can be successfully applied, the Government should leave free room to that agency, and not enter into competition with it.

If the State, in almost all countries, has constructed highways, canals, etc., it is because that at the time when these public works were executed, it alone was capable of undertaking them, and of managing them after their construction was finished. The association of capital, which, in more recent times, has created companies of great powers and credit, superior to that of many governments, was then almost unknown. The intervention of the State is unnecessary in the construction or management of railways, except in case of lines recognized to be of general utility, but with a small traffic, and consequently where the expenses of construction are such that private industry would not find from the profits of working them a sufficient reward for its labor and its capital. The *rôle* of the Government should be limited to exercise a control over its railways. From the point of view of political economy, the construction, the purchase, and the working of railways by the State was an economic blunder; it was, moreover, a hindrance to the freedom of industry. The Government administers, instead of operating in the interest of commerce and of industry; the agents of the State have not, in the conduct of affairs purely industrial and commercial, those qualities which private industry and individual interest alone can confer.

It is claimed, however, that the management of railways by the Government would lead to a simplification of the rates, a reform of regulations, and a reduction of freights and fares. Now this simplification and reform of regulations may be obtained without recourse to the radical solution of the purchase and working of railways by the State. A reform of this kind was brought about long ago in Austria by an agreement between the numerous railways of that country, whom their own interests led to this progressive measure. As to a lower tariff, if we look at practical examples, the rates charged by the two Bavarian roads are no lower since the Government management took effect than under the former tariff. Moreover, even were the rates charged by the Government railways lowered, it would by no means constitute an economic superiority in their favor. The Government, in order to construct or to purchase railways, is obliged to appeal to the private treasury of the citizens; it contracts a loan, the interest of which can only be discharged by the levying of a tax. If, then, the State derives no net profit from the working of its railways, if it transports at the price it receives, the tax to be paid by the citizens will be augmented, in this case, by the entire sum necessary to discharge that interest. No such solution as that is admissible. Let it not be said that if the State effects, on the one hand, a lower price for transportation by railway, it may well, on the other hand, increase the tax upon the people, and that a compensation will be arrived at in that manner. This might be true if the increase of tax sustained by each citizen were proportionate to the use he made of the railway. Such a distribution of the taxes is impossible in practice, and it would happen that he who could make little or no use of the railway would pay the tax for him who constantly uses it, which would be a gross injustice. The State is obliged, in fairness, to impose such a tariff upon railway traffic as will enable it, by the aid of the profits real-

ized, to pay for the capital invested in the railways which it works. What, then, becomes of the theory of those who hoped that the Government, if it were to buy up all the railways, would carry for the public at the mere cost of working the road ? From the moment that the railways should become the property of the Government and be managed   it, they would become subject to political influence. The minister of the railways would find himself absolute master in questions which touch industry and commerce most intimately; he would dispose of one of the most considerable elements of national wealth—transportation ; he would be chief of an army of functionaries scattered over the whole country, and in continual contact with the whole nation ; the railways would pass very probably into the *rôle* of *propaganda*, or the means of yielding a pressure of political influence in the hands of the minister or of a majority of the legislative body. Who would occupy him self with the development of traffic, with the increase of receipts, with the curtailment of expenses, with the proper and economic use of the railway *personnel?* From that day, the railways would have lost their essential character, they would have ceased to be an industry, they would become only a bureau, and would constitute only one section of the more or less complicated machinery of the Government.

AMERICAN TRADE WITH CHINA.

[From the Bankers' Magazine, N. Y.]

" The commerce of our Pacific steamers is made up of a larger variety of commodities than is by many persons supposed. From January to July the steamers bring principally teas and silks, and great expedition is used in the transport of these goods. Tea deteriorates with age, and the sooner a new crop can be put on the market, the better will be the tea, and the greater will be the proportionate profits of the shipper and consignee. When the steamer arrives at San Francisco, the railroad cars are drawn up at her side and the chests of tea or bales of silk are transported at once without the necessity of a second handling. The work goes on with great rapidity ; in a few hours the transfer is complete, and the train is on its way to the eastward. It has the right of way over every thing but a passenger-train ; nothing is allowed to stop or delay it. It contains from twenty-five to thirty cars; it climbs the Sierras, and winds through the snow-sheds ; crosses the alkali plains of Nevada and Utah, and steadily ascends the long slope of the Rocky Mountains, till it halts at the water-shed between the Atlantic and the Pacific, more than 8000 feet above the level of the sea. Then down the mountains and through the broad valley of the Missouri, across the fertile prairies of the Mississippi, striking the lakes, and crossing the Alleghanies, the train comes at length to the seaboard. Twelve days suffice for the journey, and in one instance, a tea-train carried its cargo in nine days and a few hours from San Francisco to New York.

" With the present system of commerce, a man may do four times as much business as formerly. A decade or two ago, it took the best part of a year to send a cargo of tea or silk from China or Japan and get the returns therefor ; from six to twelve months' capital was locked up, and there was no way of releasing it. Now the steamers and the railway are able to deliver cargo in New York in twenty-eight days from Yokohama, and in thirty-three days from Hong Kong. If we multiply those figures by four for Hong Kong, and by five or six for Yokohama, we shall not be far from the best time of the old sailing-ships.

" Nearly every steamer takes $1,000,000 or so in silver coin, chiefly in trade dollars. Mexican dollars have long been a well-known commodity, and are in constant demand ; the trade dollar was created to supply this want, and is rapidly doing so."

AMERICAN LIBRARIES CONTAINING 10,000 VOLUMES AND UPWARDS.

[From the Special Report on Public Libraries in the United States; Bureau of Education, 1876.]

LOCATION.	NAME OF LIBRARY.	FOUNDED.	VOLUMES.
Alabama:			
Montgomery	State Library	1828	14,000
California:			
Oakland	University of California	1869	13,600
Sacramento	State	1850	37,000
San Francisco	Law	—	12,500
San Francisco	Mechanics' Institute	1855	24,108
San Francisco	Mercantile	1853	41,563
San Francisco	Odd Fellows	1854	26,883
San Francisco	Pacific	1859	12,000
San Francisco	St. Ignatius College	1855	11,000
Santa Clara	Santa Clara College	1851	10,000
Vallejo	Vallejo	1856	12,000
Connecticut:			
Hartford	Historical Society	1825	16,000
Hartford	State	1854	12,000
Hartford	Trinity College	1824	15,000
Hartford	Watkinson Reference	1858	26,788
Hartford	Young Men's Institute	1838	24,000
Middletown	Berkeley Divinity School	1855	16,000
Middletown	Wesleyan University	1833	26,000
New Haven	Yale College	1700	114,200
New Haven	Young Men's Institute	1826	10,000
Waterbury	Silas Bronson	1870	20,000
Delaware:			
Dover	State	1832	11,000
Wilmington	Institute	1857	11,000
District of Columbia:			
Georgetown	Georgetown College	1791	32,268
Washington	Attorney-General's Office	1853	12,000
Washington	City (Y. M. C. A.)	1811	15,000
Washington	Library of Congress	1802	300,000
Washington	Department of State	1789	20,000
Washington	Department of War	1832	13,000
Washington	Gonzaga College	1858	10,000
Washington	House of Representatives	1780	125,000
Washington	Howard University	1869	10,700
Washington	Patent Office	1839	23,000
Washington	Surgeon-General's Office	1865	40,000
Washington	United States Senate	1852	25,000
Florida:			
Tallahassee	State	1845	10,000
Georgia:			
Athens	University of Georgia	1831	27,600
Atlanta	State	1835	20,000
Macon	Mercer University	1840	12,000
Illinois:			
Chicago	Baptist Union Theological Seminary	1869	15,000
Chicago	Public	1872	48,100
Chicago	University	1855	18,000
Evanston	Northwestern University	1856	33,000
Springfield	State	....	42,000
Urbana	Industrial University	1868	10,600
Indiana:			
Crawfordsville	Wabash College	1833	10,482
Greencastle	Indiana Asbury University	1837	10,400
Indianapolis	Public	1872	17,000
Indianapolis	State	1825	10,841
Notre Dame	University	1843	10,000

LOCATION.	NAME OF LIBRARY	FOUNDED.	VOLUMES.
Iowa:			
Des Moines	State	1838	14,000
Kansas:			
Topeka	State	1857	10,500
Kentucky:			
Danville	Theological Seminary	1853	10,000
Frankfort	State	1621	30,000
Lexington	Kentucky University	1865	12,934
Lexington	Library Association	1800	17,000
Louisville	Public	1871	50,000
Louisiana:			
Baton Rouge	State University	1860	15,000
New Orleans	Librairie de la Famille	1872	25,000
New Orleans	Louisiana State	1813	21,832
New Orleans	Public School and Lyceum	1844	16,000
Maine:			
Augusta	State	1832	95,000
Bangor	Mechanics' Association	1828	13,737
Bangor	Theological Seminary	1820	15,000
Brunswick	Bowdoin College	1802	35,860
Portland	Institute and Public	1867	15,644
Waterville	Colby University	1813	14,100
Maryland:			
Annapolis	Naval Academy	1845	17,678
Anapolis	Louisiana State	1826	40,000
Baltimore	Archiepiscopal	—	10,000
Baltimore	Loyola College	1853	21,500
Baltimore	Maryland Historical Society	1844	15,000
Baltimore	Maryland Institute	1847	16,433
Baltimore	Mercantile	1839	31,032
Baltimore	Odd Fellows'	1840	19,835
Baltimore	Peabody Institute	1857	57,458
Baltimore	St. Mary's Theological Seminary	1791	15,000
Hagerstown	College of St. James	1842	11,000
Woodstock	Woodstock College	1869	18,000
Massachusetts:			
Amherst	Amherst College	1821	38,533
Andover	Theological Seminary	1807	34,000
Boston	American Academy Arts and Sciences	1780	16,000
Boston	Athenæum	1807	108,000
Boston	Congregational	1853	22,895
Boston	General Theological	1860	12,000
Boston	Handel and Haydn Society	1815	11,699
Boston	Library Society	1794	25,000
Boston	Loring's Private Circulating	1859	10,000
Boston	Massachusetts Historical Society	1791	23,000
Boston	Mercantile	1820	21,500
Boston	N. E. Historic-Genealogical Society	1845	12,337
Boston	Public	1852	299,869
Boston	Social Law	1804	13,000
Boston	Society of Natural History	1831	10,000
Boston	State	1826	37,000
Brookline	Public	1857	16,609
Cambridge	Harvard University	1638	190,000
Concord	Public	1851	10,601
Fall River	Public	1860	12,754
Fitchburg	Public	1859	11,000
Haverhill	Public	1874	20,000
Lawrence	Public	1872	13,328
Lowell	City	1844	17,589
Lowell	Middlesex Mechanics' Association	1825	12,782
Lynn	Public	1862	19,808
Medford	Tufts College	1854	16,000
New Bedford	Public	1853	31,000
Newburyport	Public	1854	16,218
Newton	Public	1870	10,088
Newton	Theological Institution	1826	13,000
Northampton	Public	1860	10,474
Peabody	Peabody Institute	1853	16,505
Pittsfield	Berkshire Athenæum	1871	14,000
Salem	Athenæum	1810	20,000
Salem	Essex Institute	1848	30,655
Springfield	City Library Association	1857	36,790
Taunton	Public	1866	12,726

LOCATION.	NAME OF LIBRARY	FOUNDED.	VOLUMES.
Massachusetts (*Continued*):			
Wellesley	Wellesley College	1875	10,000
Williamstown	Williams College	1793	27,500
Worcester	American Antiquarian Society	1812	60,497
Worcester	College of the Holy Cross	1843	12,000
Worcester	Public	1859	31,609
Michigan:			
Ann Arbor	University of Michigan	1841	28,400
Detroit	Public	1865	22,882
Detroit	Young Men's Society	1833	12,790
Lansing	State	1828	39,886
Minnesota:			
Minneapolis	University of Minnesota	1869	10,000
St. Paul	State	1849	10,000
Mississippi:			
Jackson	State	1838	16,000
Missouri:			
Columbia	University of Missouri	1840	13,400
Jefferson City	State	1833	13,000
St. Louis	College of the Christian Brothers	1860	22,000
St. Louis	Public School	1865	33,097
St. Louis	St. Louis Mercantile	1810	42,013
St. Louis	University of St. Louis	1829	25,000
Nebraska:			
Lincoln	State	1856	13,133
New Hampshire:			
Concord	State	1818	13,500
Hanover	Dartmouth College	1770	52,550
Manchester	City	1854	17,527
Portsmouth	Athenæum	1817	11,607
New Jersey:			
Madison	Drew Theological Seminary	1867	10,875
Newark	Library Association	1847	22,000
New Brunswick	Rutgers College	1770	10,614
New Brunswick	Theological Seminary Reformed Church	1784	26,000
Princeton	College of New Jersey	1750	41,500
Princeton	Theological Seminary Presby'n Church	1821	26,779
Red Bank	Shrewsbury Model School	1873	10,740
Trenton	State	1796	20,000
New York:			
Albany	State	1818	95,000
Albany	Young Men's Association	1833	13,000
Auburn	Theological Seminary	1821	10,000
Brooklyn	Brooklyn Heights Female Seminary	1835	10,000
Brooklyn	Eastern District School	1866	10,000
Brooklyn	Hawkins' (Private Circulating)	1848	17,000
Brooklyn	Long Island Historical Society	1863	26,000
Brooklyn	Mercantile	1857	50,257
Brooklyn	St. Francis College		13,970
Brooklyn	Youth's Free	1834	10,000
Buffalo	Grosvenor	1859	18,000
Buffalo	Young Men's Association	1835	27,597
Clinton	Hamilton College	1812	22,000
Fordham	St. John's College	1840	15,000
Geneva	Hobart College	1824	13,000
Hamilton	Madison University	1820	13,000
Ithaca	Cornell	1866	10,000
Ithaca	Cornell University	1868	39,000
New York	American Geographical Society	1852	10,000
New York	American Institute	1833	10,600
New York	Apprentices'	1820	53,000
New York	Astor	1849	152,446
New York	College of St. Francis Xavier	1847	21,000
New York	College of the City of New York	1850	20,600
New York	Columbia College	1757	34,750
New York	Cooper Union	1858	17,500
New York	Eclectic (Private Circulating)	1869	30,300
New York	Gen. Theol. Seminary Prot. Episc. Church	1820	15,400
New York	Law Institute	1828	20,000
New York	Manhattan College	1863	13,000
New York	Mercantile	1820	160,613
New York	New York Historical Society	1804	60,000
New York	New York Hospital	1796	10,600
New York	New York Society	1754	65,000

LOCATION.	NAME OF LIBRARY.	FOUNDED.	VOLUMES.

New York (*Continued*) :

New York	Union Theological Seminary	1836	34,000
New York	Young Men's Christian Association	1852	10,552
Rochester	Athenæum and Mechanics' Association	1829	21,000
Rochester	Theological Seminary	1851	10,000
Rochester	University	1850	12,000
Schenectady	Union College	1795	25,800
Syracuse	Central	1856	13,300
Syracuse	University	1871	10,000
Troy	Young Men's Association	1834	21,424
West Point	Military Academy	1812	25,000

North Carolina :

Chapel Hill	University of North Carolina	1795	22,100
Raleigh	State	1831	40,000
Trinity	Trinity College	1849	10,000

Ohio :

Cincinnati	Lane Theological Seminary	1829	12,000
Cincinnati	Mount St. Mary's Seminary	1849	15,100
Cincinnati	Public	1867	71,405
Cincinnati	St. Xavier College	1840	17,000
Cincinnati	Young Men's Mercantile	1835	36,193
Cleveland	Public	1868	24,000
Columbus	State	1817	40,000
Dayton	Public School	1854	13,000
Delaware	Ohio Wesleyan University	1845–'56	13,900
Gambier	Kenyon College	1865	13,705
Granville	Denison University	1831	13.000
Hudson	Western Reserve College	1827	10,000
Marietta	Marietta College	1835	20,700
Oberlin	Oberlin College	1834	14,000

Pennsylvania :

Allegheny City	Western Theological Seminary	1827	15,000
Carlisle	Dickinson College	1783	27,508
Easton	Lafayette College	1832	21,100
Gettysburg	Pennsylvania College	1832	19,550
Gettysburg	Theological Seminary (Lutheran)	1823	11,000
Harleysville	Cassel's (Circulating)	1835	10,175
Harrisburg	State	1816	30,500
Haverford	Haverford College	1833	11,450
Lancaster	Franklin and Marshall College	1836–'53	11,500
Lancaster	Theological Seminary (Reformed)	1825	10,000
Latrobe	St. Vincent's College	1846	13.000
Meadville	Allegheny College	1820	10 500
Meadville	Theological School	1845	12,308
Philadelphia	Academy of Natural Sciences	1812	30,000
Philadelphia	American Philosophical Society	1743	20,000
Philadelphia	Apprentices' Library Company	1820	21,000
Philadelphia	Athenæum	1814	20,000
Philadelphia	College of Physicians	1789	18,753
Philadelphia	Franklin Institute	1824	16,000
Philadelphia	German Society	1817	16,000
Philadelphia	Historical Society of Pennsylvania	1824	16,000
Philadelphia	Library Company and Loganian	1731	104,000
Philadelphia	Mercantile	1821	125,668
Philadelphia	Pennsylvania Hospital	1763	12 500
Philadelphia	Southwark	1831	10,015
Philadelphia	University of Pennsylvania	1755	25,573
Philadelphia	Wagner Free Institute	1855	15,000
Pittsburgh	Mercantile	1847	13,012

Rhode Island :

Newport	People's	1870	14 799
Newport	Redwood Library and Athenæum	1730	20,634
Providence	Athenæum	1836	34,492
Providence	Brown University	1768	45,000

South Carolina :

Charleston	Library Society	1748	15,000
Columbia	Theological Seminary	1829	18 884
Columbia	University of South Carolina	1805	28 250
Due West	Erskine College	1839	12,500

Tennessee :

Columbia	Athenæum	1852	12,000
Nashville	State	1854	20,000
Nashville	University of Nashville	1785	10,000

LOCATION.	NAME OF LIBRARY.	FOUNDED.	VOLUMES.
Texas:			
Galveston	Free	1871	10,000
Tyler	Bowdon Literary Society	1871	11,257
Vermont:			
Burlington	University of Vermont	1800	16,021
Middlebury	Middlebury College	1800	15,500
Montpelier	State	1825	14,600
Virginia:			
Alexandria	Theol. Seminary Prot. Episcopal Church	1823	10,000
Ashland	Randolph Macon College	1834	10,000
Charlottesville	University of Virginia	1825	40,000
Emory	Emory and Henry College	1837	13,580
Hampden Sidney	Union Theological Seminary	1825	10,000
Lexington	Washington and Lee University	1796	16,000
Richmond	State	1822	35,000
Salem	Roanoke College	1853	17,000
Wisconsin:			
Madison	State	1836	23,000
Madison	State Historical Society	1849	33,347
Milwaukee	Young Men's Association	1847	15,000

LIBRARIES OF THE WORLD CONTAINING 100,000 VOLUMES OR UPWARDS AT LATEST DATES.*

	City.	Country.	Name of Library.	Volumes.	When Founded.
1.	Albany, N. Y.	United States	N. Y. State Library	100,000	1818
2.	Athens	Greece	University	125,000	1837
3.	Augsburg	Bavaria	City	100,000	1537
4.	Bamberg	"	Royal	120,000	} ....
			And pamphlets	150,000	
5.	Bâle	Switzerland	Public	100,000	....
6.	Berlin	Prussia	Royal	700,000	1650
7.	Berlin	"	University	115,000	....
8.	Bologna	Italy	University	200,000	1690
9.	Bonn	Prussia	University	180,000	1818
10.	Bordeaux	France	City	123,000	1738
11.	Boston	United States	Public Library	235,000	} 1852
			Branches	65,000	
12.	Boston	" "	Athenæum	108,000	1807
13.	Breslau	Prussia	University	340,000	1811
14.	Brussels	Belgium	Royal	250,000	1400
15.	Buda-Pest	Hungary	Public	200,000	1804
16.	Buda-Pest	"	University	105,000	....
17.	Cambridge	England	University	250,000	1475
18.	Cambridge, Mass.	United States	Harvard College	190,000	1638
19.	Carlsruhe	Baden	Grand Ducal	110,000	....
20.	Cassel	Prussia	National	120,000	1580
21.	Christiania	Sweden	University	200,000	1811
22.	Copenhagen	Denmark	Royal	500,000	1550
23.	Copenhagen	"	University	200,000	1731
24.	Cracow	Poland	University	140,000	1364
25.	Darmstadt	Germany	Grand Ducal	380,000	1700
26.	Dresden	Saxony	Royal Public	500,000	} 1555
			And pamphlets	400,000	
27.	Dublin	Ireland	Trinity College	150,000	1601
28.	Edinburgh	Scotland	Faculty of Advocates	300,000	1680
29.	Edinburgh	"	University	130,000	1580
30.	Erlangen	Bavaria	University	110,000	1743
31.	Florence	Italy	National	200,000	1864
32.	Frankfort	Germany	City	150,000	....
33.	Freiburg	Switzerland	University	250,000	1454
34.	Giessen	Germany	University	150,000	1607
35.	Glasgow	Scotland	University	105,000	1473
36.	Gotha	Germany	Ducal	240,000	1640

* Corrected from Johnson's New Universal Cyclopædia, 1873.

	City.	Country.	Name of Library.	Volumes.	When Founded.
37..	Göttingen......	Germany.......	University............	400,000	1734
38..	Hague.........	Netherlands....	Royal..........	100,000	1795
39..	Halle.........	Prussia...	University............	100,000	1696
40..	Hamburg.....	Germany......	City....	300,000	1529
41..	Hanover........	"	Royal Public...	170,000	1690
42..	Heidelberg....	"	University............	300,000	1703
43..	Helsingfors....	Russia..........	University........	140,000	1630
44..	Jena..........	Germany......	University............	180,000	1548
45..	Kiel..........	Denmark.....	University............	150,000	1665
46..	Königsberg....	Prussia........	Royal and University...	220,000	1544
47..	Leipzig.......	Saxony........	City....	100,000	1677
48..	Leipzig........	"	University............	350,000	1543
49..	Lisbon........	Portugal......	National....	100,000	1796
50..	Liverpool....	England.......	Public.................	100,000	1850
51..	London.	France....	British Museum..	1,150,000	1753
52..	Lyons..........	France....	City....	120,000	....
53..	Madrid........	Spain....	National....	220,000	1712
54..	Manchester.....	England......	Public....	120,000	1852
55..	Marburg.......	Germany......	University............	120,000	1527
56..	Mentz........	"	City....	110,000	....
57..	Mexico........	Mexico....	National....	100,000	....
58..	Milan........	Italy....	Ambrosian....	100,000	1609
59..	Milan........	"	Brera....	185,000	1763
60..	Modena........	"	Este....	100,000	....
61..	Moscow........	Russia....	University....	160,000	1755
62..	Munich........	Bavaria...... {	Royal.... .... / And pamphlets.........	400,000 / 400,000	} 1660
63..	Munich........	"	University...........	280,000	1573
64..	Münster.. ...	Prussia........	Royal Paul....	100,000	....
65..	Naples........	Italy....	National....	200,000	1780
66..	New Haven ...	United States..	Yale College........ ...	105,000	1700
67..	New York.....	"	Astor	150,000	1849
68..	New York.....	" "	Mercantile............ .	160,000	1820
69..	Oxford........	England	Bodleian.............	330,000	1598
70..	Padua........	Italy....	University....	100,000	1629
71..	Paris..........	France....	National................	2,000,000	1350
72..	Paris..........	"	Arsenal................	225,000	1781
73..	Paris..........	"	St. Genevieve..........	200,000	1624
74..	Paris..........	"	Sorbonne...............	140,000	....
75..	Paris..........	"	Mazarin...............	160,000	1660
76..	Paris..........	"	Institute...............	100,000	1759
77..	Philadelphia....	United States..	Library Co. of Phila....	104,000	1731
78..	Philadelphia....	" "	Mercantile.............	126,000	1821
79..	Parma....... ..	Italy....	Public.	140,000	....
80..	Prague........	Austria..	University....	152,000	1350
81..	Rome....	Italy....	Vatican................	105,000	1378
82..	Rome..........	"	Casanata..............	160,000	1700
83..	Rome........ ..	"	Angelica..............	100,000	1605
84..	Rouen........	France....	City..................	120,000	1809
85..	Rostock	Germany......	University...........	140,000	1419
86..	St. Petersburg.	Russia.......	Imperial..............	1,100,000	1714
87..	St. Petersburg.	"	Academy of Sciences....	190,000	1726
88..	Stockholm.....	Sweden....	Royal....	125,000	1540
89..	Strasburg.....	Germany....	City..................	300,000	1531
90..	Stuttgart.......	"	Royal Public..........	180,000	1765
91..	Treves........	Prussia....	City..................	100,000	1773
92..	Tübingen.....	Germany.....	University............	220,000	1477
93..	Turin	Italy....	University............	150,000	1426
94..	Upsal........	Sweden....	University............	150,000	1621
95..	Venice........	Italy....	St. Mark's............	120,000	1468
96..	Vienna........	Austria........	Imperial Public........	400,000	1440
97..	Vienna........	"	University............	210,000	1777
98..	Washington....	United States...	Library of Congress....	300,000	1802
99..	Weimar........	Germany......	Grand Ducal...........	170,000	....
100..	Wolfenbüttel...	"	Brunswick Ducal.......	270,000	1604
101..	Würzburg.....	Bavaria.... ...	University............	200,000	1403
102..	Zurich........ ...	Switzerland....	City..................	100,000	1832

THE CURIOSITIES OF STATISTICS.

THE American people, like their European ancestry, may be said to have a passion for facts. They instinctively demand the basis upon which every statement rests, and all things must show their reason for being. The statistics of every art, trade, and manufacture are sought for with interest and swallowed with avidity. Sometimes we are reproached for our overweening taste for romance, and our vast consumption of books of fiction ; but the demand for books of fact, the steady and enormous sale, of encyclopædias, dictionaries, and popular scientific books, is something far in advance of what is common in other nations, and evinces the popular taste for the solid and the practical. No people in the world hunt so eagerly after precedents as the Americans, and it is only candid to add, that no people, when found, so systematically disregard them.

Next to a Bible and a dictionary of language, there is no book perhaps more common than a biographical dictionary. Our interest in our fellow-men is perennial ; and we seek to know not only their characteristics, and the distinguishing events of their lives, but also the time of their birth into the world and their exit from it. This is a species of statistics upon which one naturally expects certainty, since no person eminent enough to be recorded at all is likely to have had the epoch of his death, at least, unremarked. Yet the seeker after exact information in the biographical dictionaries will find, if he extends his quest among various authorities, that he is afloat on a sea of uncertainties. Not only can he not find out the date of decease of navigators like Sir John Franklin and La Perouse, who sailed into the unexplored regions of the globe, and were never heard of more, save by the finding of a few traces where they perished, but the men who died at home, in the midst of friends and families, are frequently recorded as deceased at dates so discrepant that no ingenuity can reconcile them. In Haydn's Dictionary of Dates, Sir Henry Havelock is said to have died November 25th, 1857, while Maunder's Treasury of Biography gives November 21st, the London Almanac November 27th, and the Life of Havelock, by his brother-in-law, November 24th. Here are four distinct dates of death given, by

authorities equally accredited, to a famous general, who died within twenty years. Of the death of the notorious Robespierre, guillotined in 1794, we find in Chalmers' Biographical Dictionary that he died July 10th, in Rees' Cyclopædia, July 28th, and in Alison's History of Europe, July 29th. Doubtless it is some comfort to reflect, in view of his many crimes, that the bloody tyrant of the Jacobins is really dead, irrespective of the date, about which biographers may dispute. Of the English mechanician Joseph Bramah, inventor of the Bramah lock, we learn from the English Cyclopædia that he died in 1814, and from Rose's Biographical Dictionary that he died in 1815.

Now, although a large share of the errors and discrepancies that abound in biographical dictionaries and other books of reference may be accounted for by misprints, others by reckoning old style instead of new, or *vice versâ*, and many more by the carelessness of editors and transcribers, it is plain that all the variations cannot thus be accounted for. Nothing is more common in printing-offices than to find a figure 6 inverted serving as a 9, a 5 for a 3, or a 3 for an 8, while 8, 9, and 0 are frequently interchanged. In such cases, a lynx-eyed proof-reader may not always be present to prevent the falsification of history; and it is a fact not sufficiently recognized, that to the untiring vigilance, intelligence, and hard conscientious labors of proof-readers, the world owes a deeper debt of gratitude than it does to many a famous maker of books. It is easy enough, Heaven knows, to make books, but to make them correct, *Hic labor, hoc opus est.*

A high authority in encyclopædical lore tells us that the best accredited authorities are at odds with regard to the birth or death of individuals in the enormous ratio of from twenty to twenty-five per cent of the whole number in the biographical dictionaries. The Portuguese poet Camoens is said by some authorities to have been born in 1517, and by others in 1525. Chateaubriand is declared by the English Cyclopædia to have been born September 4th, 1768; September 14th, 1768, by the *Nouvelle Biographie générale* of Dr. Hoefer; and September 4th, 1769, by the Conversations-Lexicon. Of course it is clear that all these authorities cannot be right, but which of the three is so, is matter of extreme doubt, leaving the student of facts perplexed and uncertain at the very point where certainty is not only most important, but most confidently expected.

Of another kind are the errors that sometimes creep into works of reference of high credit, by accepting too confidently statements publicly made. In one edition of the Dictionary of Congress a certain honorable member from Pennsylvania, in uncommonly robust health, was astonished to find himself recorded as having died of the National Hotel disease, contracted at Washington in 1856. In this case the editor of the work was the victim of too much confidence in the newspapers. In the Congressional Directory, where brief biographies of Congressmen are given, one distinguished member was printed as hav-

ing been elected to Congress at a time which, taken in connection with his birth-date in the same paragraph, made him precisely one year old when he took his seat in Congress.

The statistics of the population of the globe, especially in remote ages, are among the things that must be set down as far more curious than valuable. It was long believed that the ancient world was vastly more populous than the modern, and that, too, on no better authority than that of such historians as Appian and Diodorus Siculus, who made out the population of Gaul to have been 200,000,000 at about the beginning of the Christian era, though in modern days it ' is scarcely more than one sixth as much. Polybius tells us that the Romans could muster 700,000 men able to bear arms; and Julius Cæsar, according to Appian, in one of his freebooting excursions into what is now France, encountered 4,000,000 Gauls, killed 1,000,000, and made 1,000,000 prisoners. Is there any modern general, in any wars however bloody, carried on in countries however populous, who could boast conquests anywhere approaching these figures, even when divided by ten? Diodorus tells us in one place that the population of Egypt was 3,000,000—a moderate number enough ; but then, in another place, he would have us believe that the number of cities in Egypt was 18,000, which, if there were but 3,000,000 people, is an evident contradiction, as it would give only 167 inhabitants to each city. The truth is, probably, he knew as much about the matter as we do of the population or the number of cities in the moon. Not a solitary writer of antiquity cites any census to prove his statements as to population, and of course no census existed. Diodorus tells us of the army of Ninus, the mythical founder of Babylon, that it consisted of 1,700,000 foot and 200,000 horse, and deprecates the scepticism of his contemporaries by saying that they must not form a notion of the ancient populousness of the earth by the degenerate and sparsely peopled times in which they lived. Thus a writer cotemporary with Cæsar and Augustus, in that very age now represented as the most populous, complains of the desolation which then prevailed, exalts the good old times when armies contained 2,000,000 men, and quotes ancient fables in support of his opinions. "To count," said Dr. Johnson, "is a modern practice : the ancient method was to guess: and when numbers are guessed they are always magnified." Yet writers of great reputation have repeated, almost down to our own days, the wildest exaggerations of antiquity. Even Montesquieu, writing near the middle of the last century, affirmed that by the best computations which the subject would admit of, there were not in his day, on the face of the earth, the fiftieth part of mankind which existed in the time of Julius Cæsar. The historian Hume remarks on this, that any such comparison must be imperfect, since we know not exactly the numbers of any country in Europe, or even of any city, at present : how then, he adds, can we pretend to calculate those of an-

cient cities and States?" Hume wrote just about 1752, when as yet
no enumeration of the people had been taken even in England, the
first census of the United Kingdom having been no farther back than
1801.   In fact, the United States, just after becoming an independent
republic, was the first nation to set the example of a census distinctly
required in its fundamental law.   Our first decennial census was
taken in 1790.

As a fair example of the curiosities of statistics, take the army of
Xerxes when it crossed the Hellespont to invade Greece.   Herodotus
gives it as 1,700,000 foot, 100,000 horse, and 517,000 naval forces;
total, 2,317,000; and adds that the number was swollen by the atten-
dants to 5,200,000 men; and all this to invade a country, which in no
age known to history contained over 1,500,000 inhabitants ! Another
favorite myth of historians is the story of that famous Alexandrian
Library of 700,000 volumes, burned by the Caliph Omar, A.D. 640,
with a rhetorical dilemma in his mouth. Unfortunately for this highly
dramatic tale, no two writers are agreed as to the circumstances, except as to the single fact, that there was a library at Alexandria, and
that it ceased to exist in the seventh century.   To ask a modern inquirer to believe that 700,000 books were gathered in one body 800
years before the invention of printing, while the largest library in
the world, four centuries after the multiplication of books by printing
began, contained less than 200,000 volumes, is altogether too great a
stretch of credulity.   Even in reporting the size of modern libraries,
exaggeration holds sway.   The library of George IV., inherited by
that graceless ignoramus from a book-collecting father, and presented to the British nation with ostentatious liberality only after he
had failed to sell it to Russia, was said in the publications of the time
to contain about 120,000 volumes.   But an actual enumeration when
the books were lodged in the King's library at the British Museum,
where they have ever since remained, showed that there were only
65,250 volumes, being but little more than half the reported number.
Many libraries public and private are equally over-estimated.   It is
so much easier to guess than to count, and the stern test of arithmetic
is too seldom applied, notwithstanding the fact that 100,000 volumes
can easily be counted in a day by two or three persons, and so on in
the same proportion.   Here, as in the statistics of population, the same
proverb holds good, that the unknown is always the magnificent, and
on the surface of the globe we inhabit, the unexplored country is
always the most marvellous since the world began.

Can any one tell us what is the true population of China?   Variously set down in the books for the past 200 years at from 200,000,000
to 500,000,000, have we any right to strike an average, and call it, as
does the Almanach de Gotha, 433,500,000?   That teeming Oriental population excludes all calculation and baffles all conjecture.   Though the
fecundity of the human race there reaches its maximum, perhaps,

and approaches the marvellous, though generation after generation goes spawning on, apparently unchecked by wars, and undecimated by disease, no man can tell its numbers. Here are some statistics of the population of Chinese cities : In the Almanach de Gotha of 1877, there are set down four cities in China containing 1,000,000 or more of inhabitants, each ; nine more having upwards of 500,000 each ; ten cities of 250,000, or upwards ; and twenty-five cities with more than 100,000 people each. If these statistics are true, Europe and America must hide their diminished heads. It is very probable, perhaps, that these swarming populations of Asia actually count as many human creatures as they claim, but it is only fair to the rest of mankind to remark, that there is no proof of the fact. Trustworthy or harmonious estimates do not exist, and census there is none. Mr. George A. Seward, the American Minister to China, wrote in 1877 : " In a country where we must make a long inquiry to learn whether the population may more reasonably be set down at 200,000,000 or 400,000,000 of souls, it may be expected that data of a more refined sort will be lacking."

In illustration of the general indifference, if not incapacity, of the Oriental mind for statistical science, take the following remarkable letter published by Mr. Layard, the Oriental traveller, and written by a Turkish Cadi in reply to some inquiries concerning the commerce and population of his own city :

" MY ILLUSTRIOUS FRIEND, AND JOY OF MY LIVER !

" The thing you ask of me is both difficult and useless. Although I have passed all my days in this place, I have neither counted the houses, nor have I inquired into the number of the inhabitants ; and as to what one person loads on his mules, and another stows away in the bottom of his ship, that is no business of mine. But, above all, as to the previous history of this city, God only knows the amount of dirt and confusion that the infidels may have eaten before the coming of the sword of Islam. It were unprofitable for us to inquire into it. O my soul! O my lamb! seek not after the things which concern thee not. Thou camest unto us and we welcomed thee : go in peace.

" Of a truth thou hast spoken many words ; and there is no harm done, for the speaker is one and the listener is another. After the fashion of thy people, thou hast wandered from one place to another, until thou art happy and content in none. We (praise be to God) were born here, and never desire to quit it. Is it possible, then, that the idea of a general intercourse between mankind should make any impression on our understandings? God forbid !

" Listen, O my son ! There is no wisdom equal unto the belief in God! He created the world : and shall we liken ourselves unto him in seeking to penetrate into the mysteries of his creation? Shall we say—behold this star spinneth around that star, and this other star with a tail goeth and cometh in so many years? Let it go! He, from whose hand it came, will guide and direct it.

" But thou wilt say unto me, stand aside, O man, for I am more learned than thou art, and have seen more things. If thou thinkest that thou art in this respect better than I am, thou art welcome. I praise God that I seek not that which I require not. Thou art learned in the things I care not for ; and as for that which thou hast seen, I defile it. Will much knowledge create thee a double belly, or wilt thou seek paradise with thine eyes?

"O my friend! If thou wilt be happy, say, There is no God but God! Do no
evil, and thus wilt thou fear neither man nor death; for surely thine hour will
come!
" The meek in spirit (El Fakir),

                                            " IMAUM ALI ZADÈ."

That there may be such a thing as a science of statistics, it would
probably require some hardihood to deny. That principles are, or
may be, discovered, by the aid of which known facts or figures may
be so summarized as to yield only true and trustworthy results, may
be presumed to follow as a natural fruit of the healthy workings of
the human intellect. But that we have attained to a point where we
can trust, without examination, what are commonly treated and published as statistics, is carrying credulity rather farther than is creditable to our good sense. The truth is, and it is every now and then
demonstrated in a very startling manner, there is nothing that can
lie at once so extensively and so dangerously as figures. Men talk of
the essential falsehood of most of what goes under the name of history, but are some of our statistics a whit better?

The newspapers once gave wide currency to a tabulated statement
of the annual consumption of ale and beer in the United States, which
some wiseacre had manipulated for the public instruction, from the
tables of production of that staple beverage as rendered to the Internal Revenue Bureau for taxation. This cheerful piece of statistics
sets out with the cool assumption : " It is estimated that the amount
of beer consumed in each State is equal to the amount produced."
It then goes on, after reducing gallons to glasses, as follows :

" A table showing the number of glasses of fermented liquors consumed in each
State during the current year has been prepared. From this it appears that in New
York and New Jersey the average amount is two hundred and forty-eight glasses
for every man, woman, and child ; in California it is one hundred and sixty-five
glasses ; in Pennsylvania, New Hampshire, and Nevada, ninety-nine glasses ; in
Maryland and Massachusetts, eighty-three glasses; in Missouri, seventy-one glasses;
in Michigan and Nebraska, fifty-five glasses ; in Iowa and the District of Columbia,
fifty glasses ; in Washington Territory and Idaho, forty-five glasses ; in Connecticut, Colorado, and Wyoming Territory, forty-one glasses ; in Indiana and Utah,
thirty-eight glasses; in Oregon, thirty-five glasses; in Louisiana, thirty-three
glasses ; in Rhode Island, twenty-nine glasses ; in Kansas, twenty-seven glasses ;
in Kentucky, twenty-six glasses ; in West Virginia, sixteen glasses ; in Delaware,
fifteen glasses ; in Arizona, fourteen glasses ; in Dakota, seven glasses ; in Texas,
four glasses ; in Tennessee, Virginia, and Maine, three glasses ; in Georgia and
Vermont, two glasses ; in South Carolina, Alabama, Arkansas, Mississippi, and
North Carolina, one glass each."

Here we are invited to believe that " each man, woman, and child "
in Massachusetts drinks more than twice as much of the mild stimu-
lants known as ale and beer as in Indiana ; that Californians con-
sume three times as much as Michiganders, six times as much as
Kentuckians, and fifty-five times as much as Tennesseeans and Vir-

ginians. The people of New Hampshire, it appears, drink a great deal more beer than those of Missouri. Who ever saw any lager beer in New Hampshire? And, we were about to ask, who ever saw any thing else in Germanized Missouri? New Jersey, it seems, has a statistical capacity of two hundred and forty-eight glasses for each of her " men, women, and children ;" while Texas could swallow but four glasses per head per annum, Georgia only two, and Mississippi and Arkansas only one. The three great States of Ohio, Illinois, and Wisconsin, with their beer-consuming capitals of Cincinnati, Chicago, and Milwaukee, are left out of the computation entirely ; another instance of statistical accuracy, wonderful to behold. No allowance is made for exportation, which, as everybody knows, absorbs more than half the product of certain States. New York and New Jersey are great exporting centres for the neighboring States, and to a great degree for the rest of the Union, while California supplies all the Pacific States and Territories : thus accounting, in the case of all three, for the great apparent preponderance of consumption in those States.

Yet this foolish item, a bundle of inaccuracies, a compound of blunders, where each suppression of fact is supplemented by a suggestion of falsehood, was gravely disseminated over the country as an important contribution to statistical knowledge !

It reminds us, in its illogical absurdity, of a certain nautical problem once gravely propounded for the puzzling of small wits : " Given the captain's name and the year of our Lord, to determine the longitude of the ship."

Seriously, if one were to undertake to bring all statistical science into contempt, he could not well improve upon the statements just considered. Whoever expects to draw any enlightenment as to the real consumption of fermented liquors in this country from the shallow sciolism of these tables, or to point a temperance moral or adorn a tale of drunkenness by such facts and figures, must be far gone in lunacy. By and by, perhaps, we shall see it gravely set down that the intellectual and moral deterioration of the States is in the direct ratio of their bibulous capacity, and that the latter is precisely equivalent to the amount of taxed liquor manufactured in each. We shall be pointed with holy horror to the two hundred and forty-eight glasses of liquid demoralization which each man, woman, and child in New York is proved by the Internal Revenue Bureau to have consumed, as a sufficient cause for all the homicides, burglaries, and divorces in that unhappy State, and we shall be invited to admire the touching contrast presented by Maine and Virginia, whose abstemiousness contents itself with three glasses apiece per annum ; while in the hotter climes of the Carolinas and Alabama the exemplary citizens illustrate all the virtues upon one glass of beer each per annum, mint juleps not counted !

In the returns of the last census of the United States are

contained very suggestive tables of "statistics of the wealth, taxation, and public indebtedness" of all the States in the Union. These formidable arrays of figures are very properly prefaced by the careful Superintendent of the Census, General Francis A. Walker, with a *caveat* as to the degree of confidence to be placed, especially in the estimates of the aggregate value of real and personal property throughout the country. These values are arrived at, under the provision of the Census Law, in two ways. First, by recording the assessed valuation of real estate and personal property in each, for purposes of local taxation ; and secondly, by setting down the actual value of each description of property, as estimated by the Deputy Marshals empowered to take the census in each locality. It is the aggregate footings of the returns obtained by each of these processes which are made public in the volume of "social statistics" of the census of 1870.

As the sole value of all statistics whatever is dependent upon their accuracy, the careful student of these tables will be compelled to receive them with a large allowance of scepticism. Considering that no property, of any description, anywhere in the United States, is taxed at its real market value, and that in most States real estate is valued on the tax schedules at rates ludicrously remote from its real value, while the great bulk of personal property is scarcely invoiced at all, it is evident that we can put no faith in the first table of the census—that, namely, which gives the wealth of the States as assessed on the local tax duplicates. Not even the approximate value of property can thus be arrived at, since, in some States, large classes, both of real and of personal property, are exempted from taxation by law, while in other States the same kind of property is taxed. Moreover, in some States, taxed property is assessed at not more than a third of its selling price, while, in others, it is assessed at fifty, seventy-five, or even ninety per cent of its market value. This various usage of States is still further complicated by the diversity of system which prevails in county valuation and assessment within the same State. It is manifest, therefore, that the sole value of any estimate of our public wealth, founded on the figures of these assessments, is to furnish an approximate basis of a valuation of property for taxation merely.

As to the second table of estimates in our census, called the "true value," it being based upon the varying and imperfect judgment of men but little skilled in the work of valuing property, appointed for a temporary enumeration merely, and without any experience which could justly entitle them to be regarded as experts, we apprehend that it is chiefly guess-work, and very poor guess-work at that. Certainly the Superintendent of the Census puts the case none too strongly when he says of the results : "At the best, these figures represent but the opinion of one man, or of a body of men, in each State, acting under advice in the collection of material, and in the calculation of

•

the several elements of the public wealth." And he elsewhere cautiously expresses himself thus: "The result reached must, at best, be characterized rather as an *impression* than an *opinion.*"

Let any one try his own hand at an estimate of the wealth of even a dozen of the men best known to him who may have property invested in varied ways, and see how he will come out. Possibly he may come approximately near the facts in some cases, but in others he will do well if he guesses within fifty per cent of the actual worth of the worldly possessions of his neighbors. How much more complicated with liability to error must be the chance estimates of men put to value the property of a whole ward or township, and to return the result in a very few days.

These reflections being premised, we come to the tables of wealth themselves ; and the first notable fact about them is the extraordinary discrepancy between the comparative valuations by the census-takers in 1860 and 1870, as between the assessed values of property, and the estimated, or "true value." Thus, the aggregate assessed value of real and personal property in the United States and Territories was, in 1870, $14,178,986,732, while the estimated real value, as returned by the deputy marshals, aggregated $30,068,518,507. This, it will be perceived, is much more than double the assessed values for purposes of taxation. Now let us see what proportion the assessed values have to the census estimates of value in 1860. We find that the aggregate amount of real and personal property assessed that year was $12,084,560,005, and the "true value," as estimated by the census enumerators, was only $16,159,616,068. This gives a ratio of assessed value to real value of about *three fourths*, whereas in 1870 the census marshals make out a ratio of assessed value to "true value" of less than *one half.* This surprising result is not alluded to in the statement of the Superintendent of the Census ; yet it is sufficient, unexplained, to throw a valid suspicion over the whole tables, considered as a basis of comparison between the years 1860 and 1870.

How much are the people of the United States worth ? is a question incapable of accurate solution. The present attempted tabulation of public wealth (in the sense of the aggregate of private wealth) makes nowhere any estimate of the property of the general government, leaving the public lands, as well as all other national property, wholly out of the account. If the United States, without counting the government wealth, are worth, as the census-takers would have us believe, an aggregate of *thirty thousand millions* of dollars, then our national debt, formidable as it appears, is less than 7 per cent of the gross value of the property owned by our population. Can this be true ? There are no figures known to us which can either prove or disprove it conclusively. But it seems sufficiently improbable at first sight.

If we turn from the United States to Great Britain, we are con-

fronted by the fact, that while the British census makes no attempt
at estimating the property of the people, the independent estimates
of statistical writers vary hopelessly and irreconcilably. Mr. J. R. Mc-
Culloch lays it down as a dictum, that "sixty years is the shortest
time in which the capital of an old and densely peopled country can
be expected to be doubled." Yet Joseph Lowe assumes the wealth
of the United Kingdom to have doubled in eighteen years, from 1823
to 1841; while George R. Porter, in his widely accredited book on the
"Progress of the Nation," and Leone Levi, a publicist of high reputation, make out (by combining their estimates) that the private
wealth of England increased fifty per cent in seventeen years, at
which rate it would double in about twenty-nine years, instead of
sixty, as laid down by McCulloch. Mr. Levi calculates the aggregate
private wealth of Great Britain in 1858 at $29,178,000,000, being a
fraction less than the guesses of the census enumerators at the National wealth of the United States twelve years later, in 1870.
Can one guess be said to be any nearer the fact than the other? May
we not be pardoned for treating all estimates as utterly fallacious that
are not based upon known facts and figures? Why do we hear so
much of the "approximate correctness" of so many statistical tables,
when in point of fact the primary data are incapable of proof, and
the averages and conclusions built upon them are all assumed?
"Statisticians," says one of the fraternity, "are generally held to be
eminently practical people: on the contrary, they are more given to
theorizing than any other class of writers, and are generally less
expert in it."

Are we then to conclude that there are no certainties in human
affairs, no statistics capable of verification, no facts that are not to
be suspected of being fictions? Are we to take the attitude of the
blasé old worldling, and say with him, "there's nothing new nor
true, and it's no matter"? Shall we echo, on a larger theatre of
affairs, the complaint of that unhappy little girl we read of, who, on
discovering beyond doubt or controversy that all things are not what
they seem, seriously announced to her mamma, "The world is hol-
low, and my doll is stuffed with sawdust, and if you please, I would
like to be a nun"? Let us hope that there are some things left that
are real. In spite of the compound errors, blunders, and assump-
tions of too many of the statisticians, it is not to be doubted that we
stand on our feet, that the earth is our inheritance, that we live and
love, and that problems insoluble by any arithmetic that we possess
can afford to wait for their solution. There is a middle ground between the hard Pyrrhonism, which pushes the domain of doubt to
such extremes as to lead one to question even his own existence, and
that easy credulity that accepts as unquestioned whatever is written
down. The true attitude is that of inquiry, of scepticism, not that
invincible scepticism which refuses to yield to evidence however

sound, but that which answers to the primary meaning of the word—
to weigh, to consider. Remembering that it is ever better to have
no opinion at all of a matter than to have a false one, let us hold
fast by the intellect, and prove all things before accepting them.
Dogmatism, and assertion, and assumption may endure for a day, but
the truth only is eternal, and will abide

> " Till the earth grows old,
> And the stars grow cold,
> And the leaves of the judgment book unfold."

THE GERMAN IMPERIAL BANK (REICHSBANK).

[From Crump's English Manual of Banking, London, 1877.]

THE German Imperial Bank is under the supervision of the Government. The
capital is 120,000,000 Reichsmarks (about $30,000,000), consisting of 40,000 shares of
3000 Rm. each. The bank buys and sells gold, discounts bills not having more than
three months to run, and not less than three (exceptionally two) signatures; makes
advances for not longer than three months on specie, on German Government securities up to three fourths of their value, on non-German Government securities up
to one half of their value, on bills of exchange up to 90 per cent, or on merchandise
up to two thirds of its value. It buys and sells stocks and shares on commission,
makes payments and collections, receives money on deposit and valuables for safe
custody. Part of its funds may be invested in German Government securities or
German railway debentures.

The bank issues notes, of which one third must be covered by gold or German
paper money, and two thirds in bills on Germany of not longer currency than three
months. The bank is obliged to cash its notes at Berlin in legal money (gold or
Reichskassenscheine), and to issue its notes against gold bars at the price of 1392
Rm. per 1 lb.

The profits are divided as follows :

(1) The shareholders receive 4½ per cent.

(2) One fifth of the remainder goes to the reserve fund till the latter reaches 25
per cent of the capital.

(3) Half of what then remains is divided among the shareholders ; half goes to
the Imperial treasury till the shareholders get 8 per cent. After that the shareholders get one fourth, and the treasury three fourths.

Should the profit be less than 4½ per cent, it is brought up to this figure out of the
reserve fund.

In 1875 there existed in Germany besides the Bank of Prussia, thirty-two other
banks issuing notes under widely different charters. The law of 1875 forbade the
circulation of these notes outside the state which had granted the charter, unless
these banks submitted to certain rules, the most important of which were (1) always
to keep one third of the notes covered by gold, and two thirds by three-months'
bills, and (2) to pay the notes at Berlin or Frankfort. Eighteen banks (exclusive of
the Reichsbank) submitted to these rules, and consequently their notes are allowed
to circulate throughout the whole of the Empire. The other banks either gave up
their circulations in favor of the Reichsbank, or continue a local issue.

The notes of the German banks are not legal tender, and the lowest denomination is 100 Reichsmarks ($25).

The German Imperial Bank is located at Berlin, and has 154 branches, scattered
widely over Germany.

STRIKES, PAST AND PRESENT.

THE word "strike," as expressing the refusal of workmen to labor on terms offered by employers, is modern, though the act which it denotes is by no means so, as strikes occurred in England more than five centuries ago. Not long after the great plague of 1349, English laborers refused to work for the small wages then current; fruitful crops went to waste for want of harvesters; buildings in course of construction were left unfinished, and even workmen employed on the king's palace deserted their business. Labor could not be had in town or country, except at prices considered ruinous by employers. These strikes of the fourteenth century were succeeded by several repressive statutes rigorously suppressing all combinations of workmen, imposing fines and imprisonment as well as the pillory on all mechanics, servants, or laborers who refused to serve for the former wages. The "statute of labor" of Edward III. provided that every man and woman not possessed of landed property, or other means of livelihood, should work for any employer requiring their labor, at the old rate of wages.

But the general prevalence of strikes or combinations to raise the wages of labor may be said to belong distinctively to the present century. Though most prominent for the last forty years in Great Britain, they belong to no country. Hardly a nation in Europe has been free from striking combinations and trades-unions, and the year 1877 has witnessed the great power and disastrous effects of even suddenly organized strikes upon the great and varied interests of trade and transportation. Those easy-going theorists who fancied that the United States is the one country so favored with vast natural resources, abundant means of living, and good wages for all workers, as that we were insured for all time against the evil effects of strikes, have found reason to amend their opinions.

In Great Britain, where strikes and trades-unions have assumed a magnitude unknown in any other country, the most extensive movements of the workmen in combining against employers occurred between 1850 and 1860. In an account of the lock-out of Operative Engineers in 1851-52, by Thomas Hughes, it is stated that this move-

ment was the first of a new class of strikes. It was originated by the society of engineers, machinists, millwrights, etc., engaged in the iron trades, which had, in 1851, 121 branches in different towns of the United Kingdom, and 11,829 members, with an income of over $110,-000 annually. The society was pledged to attempt the abolition of over-time and piece-work in the iron trades, which were deemed injurious to the business interests of workmen. They demanded the abandonment of self-acting machines, and the employment of mechanics in their stead. Their organization against employers was perfect. On the other hand, the employers' association came into the field, held meetings, and resolved that the efforts of the society were an infringement on the right of every British subject to dispose of his labor or capital according to his individual views of his own interest, and would compel the industrious and careful to share his profits with the slothful and inexpert. By the end of 1851 the amalgamated society of workmen having pledged themselves to leave their workshops if their demands were not complied with, the members of the masters' association pledged themselves to close their establishments in that event. This resolute bearing took the workmen by surprise. The strife became bitter; a lock-out took place January 10, 1852, as well against non-society men and laborers as against the amalgamated society; 3500 members of the latter and 1500 skilled workmen not members of the society, with 10,000 laborers, were at once thrown completely out of employment. An appeal was issued to the trade and the public in behalf of the society, and a subscription of $4000 from private persons was the result. During the strife the society paid to non-society members and laborers, from their own funds, nearly twice as much as they received from outside subscription. Unsuccessful efforts were made to get the dispute referred to arbitration. The masters opened their workshops after a month, but little business was done, though no interference took place on the part of the men turned out with those who chose to go to work. Finally, on the 30th of March, the discontent of the men so long out of employment prevailed over the dogged resolution of the executive council of the society, and overtures were made to the employers' association, but the latter refused all compromise. By the end of April, almost all the men had gone back to work, under the old arrangements, the bread of their families depending upon it. The cost of the lock-out to the society of workmen was about £42,000, or over $200,000, to which should be added the amount of wages lost to the men during their three months' idleness.

This strike may serve as an example of the history of the results of the majority of such combinations, although in some cases workmen have partially succeeded. In the memorable strike of the building trades in London in 1859–60, were included bricklayers, masons, plasterers, carpenters, joiners, painters, plumbers, and glaziers. In these

important trades 38,000 workmen were employed, under 450 masters.
The strike was to secure a reduction in the hours of labor from ten to
nine hours. The builders replied that to grant the demand would be
equivalent to taxing the public more than ten per cent. On the 6th
of August, 1859, 225 of the largest master-builders, employing 24,000
artisans, closed their shops, and the associated laborers raised subscriptions and got along from month to month. Late in September
the association of masters opened their shops to such operatives as
would agree to a declaration recognizing the freedom of labor and
acknowledging the independence of both employers and workmen.
The recusants refused this declaration, and the shops were gradually
filled with laborers from the country. At last the strikers gave in, in
February, 1860, and the old hours of labor were maintained. The
net result of the strike was the expenditure of £23,000 for the support
of the needy, while the amount of wages sacrificed by them was about
ten times that amount, and the losses entailed upon the masters by
the stoppage of their trade, the loss of profits and interest on capital,
were still greater, and the inconvenience to the public from the stoppage of many works of much importance was incalculable.

The strike of the flint-glass makers in 1858 involved, by March,
1859, 1100 workmen. Its cause was the disregard by some employers of the regulations of the workmen's union restricting the number
of apprentices, and fixing a minimum of wages. The strike led to a
general lock-out of operatives through Great Britain, and the avowed
object on the part of the masters' association of extinguishing the
glass-makers' union. The dispute, after a duration of months, ended
in a compromise offered by the operatives and accepted by the masters, the men withdrawing or qualifying the rules which were obnox-
ious.

The great strike of the cotton factory operatives at Preston, in 1853,
was for a ten per cent increase of wages. It lasted six months, and
being made at an unpropitious time, when gloomy prospects of trade
prevailed, aggravated by the Russian war, it failed, the whole body
of spinners and weavers again applying for work and being received
back at the old rates. This cotton strike is styled, in a report of the
British Social Science Association, a contest unprecedented in history,
and which, if the lessons of experience be not without effect, will
never again be repeated.

In the West Yorkshire coal strike and lock-out of 1858, 3200 men
were engaged. The strike was against a reduction of wages caused
by a fall in the price of coal. It lasted something over two months,
with the public feeling enlisted rather in favor of the men. At length,
coal becoming scarce, a compromise was effected, the laborers returning to work at a reduction of 7½ per cent on their former wages, which
were still, however, 22 per cent higher than five years before ; while
the masters withdrew the conditions they had insisted upon as pre-

liminary to receiving back the men. The cost of this strike has been reckoned at £100,000 in all, of which £54,000 fell on the men, namely, £46,000 in wages, and £8000 in subscriptions.

The printers' strikes in Great Britain, although numerous, have invariably been local, affecting only one office in the same locality. London, Liverpool, and many other cities have been the localities of strikes, which in each case were aided by the National Typographical Association, founded in 1845, and having about 4300 members. One of the objects of the association has been to enable some of the printing trades to emigrate. In all, sixty-six disputes, or trade differences, between employing printers and compositors, occurred from 1850 to 1860, and in each of these cases the funds of the association were employed to aid. In thirty-seven of these cases the offices were closed to members of the Union, and non-society men took their places. The London Society of Compositors was established to protect the wages of labor, which in that city varied from 33 shillings to 36 shillings per week, working ten hours and a half per day.

As the net result of English experience on this question, it is found that strikes have materially diminished during the last fifteen years. Parliamentary law has been invoked, trades-unions have been legalized, arbitration has worked well in many cases, and in place of any restraints on the combinations of workmen, old restrictions have been repealed. The practical results of strikes have been conflicting : some have been successful in raising wages or reducing the hours of labor ; a much larger number have failed. It has been shown that the state of trade, of prices, and of profits left no margin for compliance with the demands of workmen, while employers were sometimes positive gainers by the suspension of business. It is urged against strikes that profits in any business cannot rise above a certain average, and, as a consequence, advances in wages will come spontaneously from competition ; while, if such advances are brought about by a strike, the value of the labor unemployed while it lasts is lost, both to the workmen and to the public. Strikes have sometimes caused the transfer of manufactures and industry to other localities ; and it is claimed that the emigration of capital from England to America proves that its profits have long been at a minimum in Great Britain, and can bear no further reduction. The great misery and want, even leading to crime, which strikes have occasioned to working people, and the load of debt under which the strikers sometimes labor through life, are also pointed to in deprecation of them.

On the other hand, it is claimed that the occasional failure of strikes is no proof of their impolicy; that the profits of trades are very great, and the fortunes of capitalists are frequently built up in a few years ; that competition may benefit the public through a fall in prices, but does not benefit the laborer ; that the suffering caused to the workmen by strikes is justified by the law of present sacrifice for future

gain ; and that many strikes have been crowned with immediate or ultimate success, and have compelled employers to yield terms which they at first refused.

Amid these conflicting views, one notable fact seems incontestably shown by the history of strikes; namely, that strikes for a rise of wages frequently succeed, but strikes to prevent a fall commonly fail. The obvious reason is, that the demand for higher wages comes in prosperous times, when profits are good and can bear a reduction; whereas the lowering of wages by employers very rarely comes except in times of depression, when there is more labor upon the market than demand for its products. There is no doubt that one beneficial result of the agitation growing out of strikes has been to bring prominently to public view the equities which govern between labor and capital ; to encourage industrial partnerships and co-operation for the benefit of laborers ; to liberalize the rules and policy of trades-unions ; to abate the tyranny of employers on the one hand, and of workmen's societies on the other ; and to lead to a wider disposition for conciliation and arbitration in all differences between employers and employed.

In the United States, the history of strikes up to the present year is rather a succession of isolated movements to better their material condition on the part of certain trades, than any general or concerted schemes for raising the wages of labor. The trades and occupations which have witnessed the most of these workingmen's movements are the coal-miners, the iron-workers, the cotton and woollen spinners, the railroad employés, and the printers, although there have been numerous instances of strikes among day-laborers and skilled workmen in almost all employments, including the building trades, railroad construction, shipping and freighting industries, and even farm labor. In this country, where all voluntary organizations are free, no laws have ever been passed to prevent the action of organized societies of workmen for the protection of their own interests. Here is a partial list of some of these societies in the United States, a few of which control considerable funds and wield a large amount of power in their respective industries :

	Established.	Branches.	Membership.
International Typographical Union, .	1852	175	10,950
Machinists and Blacksmiths, . .	1859	164	8,000
Iron Moulders' Association, . .	1859	152	7,500
Brotherhood of Locomotive Engineers,	1863	192	14,000
Journeymen Tailors' National Trade Union, ...	1865	40	2,800
Coopers' International Union,	1870	68	5,000
Cigar Makers' Union, . . .	1871	103	5,000
Miners' National Union, . . .	1873	347	33,315
United Sons of Vulcan, . . .	1874	..	4,000

Some of these Unions are scattered over many States, while others are chiefly local in the large cities. All of them assert the right to secure higher wages, or to protect themselves against lowering wages, by stopping work. Nearly all of them go further, and assert the right to reach the ends of a strike by constraining others than members of the Unions to quit work, or at least to refrain from taking the place of strikers. In numerous cases the Unions have held out for weeks, subsisting upon reduced receipts, and aided partially by funds subscribed, and by the private charities of friends or relatives. As a rule, the operations of unions in striking for higher wages, when accompanied with constraint of other laborers, have failed to command the sympathy of the community, and have been of short duration. When an organization of laborers passes from refusing themselves to labor (which is their right), to violently compelling other men to cease labor, they at once pass from the ranks of law-abiding citizens into those of rioters and resisters of the law. There is no principle in human society more universally recognized or resting upon a stronger foundation, than that no man has the right to interfere with the rights of his neighbors, nor can any body of men assume that right. No man nor association can take from others the right to work and to enjoy the fruits of their labor. The moment violence is used, and willing laborers are compelled to become idlers and drones, that moment a strike passes the limit of public sympathy, and makes those engaged in it rioters and outlaws.

It was this principle, joined with the almost universal indignation at the violence committed and the destruction of property, added to the interruption in the traffic across the country, which made the great railroad strikes of 1877 so short-lived. Millions of private and corporate property were destroyed, many lives lost, and hundreds of thousands of laborers, depending on their work for daily bread, thrown out of employment, through an endeavor on the part of the employés of a railroad to secure better wages on a falling market. Widespread and disastrous as were the immediate results of this strike, enormous as was the public loss and inconvenience, frightful as were the passions aroused, and astounding as were their effects as exhibited in the conflagration of buildings, the wreck of railway trains, the stoppage of multitudes of industries other than those immediately concerned, and the pillage, havoc, violence, and murder that broke out almost simultaneously among the mobs in so many cities, the whole history of the struggle occupied barely two weeks. And it may be added, the whole mischief might have been prevented if the timely decision and pluck in putting down the rioters manifested in some cities had been made the rule in all.

The great railroad riots of 1877, unprecedented in their circumstances as well as in their extent by any thing in the history of the country, began at Martinsburg, on the Baltimore and Ohio Railroad,

on the night of the 16th of July. A ten per cent reduction in the wages of the railroad men employed by the Baltimore and Ohio Railroad Company had recently gone into effect, and this was the immediate cause of the strike. It was claimed by the firemen and engineers that they could not live and maintain families on the niggardly wages to which they were reduced. On the other hand, it was asserted by officers of the company that they could not continue to pay the old wages and earn interest on the capital of the road. The firemen began the movement by leaving work at Martinsburg, West Virginia, on the 16th of July, and when other men offered to take their places drove them from the engines. The Vice-President telegraphed Governor Matthews, of West Virginia, that trains were in the hands of rioters and the town authorities powerless to suppress them, and asking for military aid. The Governor telegraphed to Colonel Faulkner to aid the authorities with the two militia companies of Martinsburg. Colonel Faulkner, with the Berkeley County Light Infantry Guard, took charge of one of the detained freight trains, and strove to protect it while sent westward. The strikers seized the locomotive, and a collision speedily occurred between them and the militia, in which several shots were fired and two or three wounded. The volunteer fireman and engineer who had taken charge of the train ran away in the mêlée, and Colonel Faulkner, declaring that he had done his duty, and if the train men deserted their posts he could do nothing more, marched his company to the armory and disbanded them, leaving the rioters in possession of the field. It was charged and not denied, that the local militia were in sympathy with the strikers. Next day, the strikers having gained headway, marched about, fully 1000 strong, bidding defiance alike to the military and the authorities. All the freight trains which came into Martinsburg from the East and the West were blockaded there, until seventy-five to one hundred engines, with trains attached to them, were congregated, and none allowed to depart. The rioters stood with drawn revolvers, compelling engineers and firemen to run every train on to the sidings. Passenger trains were not interfered with, as the strike was entirely confined to the transportation men. Governor Matthews, finding that he could not rely on the West Virginia troops, telegraphed to the President of the United States for aid. After requiring more specific information, the Secretary of War was directed to send United States troops to Martinsburg, and eight companies of artillery, acting as infantry, left Washington the same night, 250 strong, fully supplied with ammunition, under command of General French.

The strikers, who had found great sympathy among the citizens and even local troops, so that they were emboldened to defy the authorities, and even stoned the Governor in his hotel, now had to face the stern fact that they must resist the United States if they per-

sisted in their movement, the President's proclamation, dated July 18th, 1877, setting forth that the laws of the United States required all insurrection in any State to be promptly suppressed, and warning all persons engaged in domestic violence and obstruction of the laws to disperse within twenty-four hours. On the 19th, two trains were started out, all violent demonstrations on the part of the mob being stopped for a time. The arrested trains stretched two miles away on each side of Martinsburg, and the locomotives stood with their fires banked, ready to start. Transportation would have been resumed and continued but for the breaking out of similar strikes in other places. The first successes of the mob at Martinsburg unquestionably emboldened the discontented employés of every railroad in the country to see what they could do by striking to better their condition.

The very day that the troops were dispatched from Washington, a strike broke out at Keyser, Maryland, on the same railway, while trains that had left Martinsburg were stopped by rioters at Cumberland. Governor Carroll at once issued a proclamation, calling on the rioters to disperse, and sent the Fifth Maryland Regiment to Cumberland to protect the trains. Before it could leave Baltimore, however, a ferocious mob, easily aroused in that city, made a rush at the regiment, hurling stones and brickbats. The streets were thronged with angry men, whose cries and shouts spread terror abroad, while the soldiers with fixed bayonets marched steadily forward to the station, scattering the crowd and entering the train. The Sixth Regiment was also called out, though before they could get together the rioters increased to a vast surging mob, several thousand strong, taking possession of various parts of the city. A collision occurred on Front Street, where the soldiers were attacked by a shower of stones, mingled with pistol shots. They returned the fire, but by a fatal mistake fired over the heads of the mob. This only exasperated the rioters, who opened fire on the troops, compelling the latter to level their pieces and fire point blank into the dense and yelling mass. Men falling on the sidewalks or reeling back with bullets in their breasts scared the crowd, which soon scattered, to gather elsewhere. The torch was applied in various places to railroad cars and offices, and many conflicts took place in the streets between the policemen, who behaved most bravely, and the ungovernable mob. Governor Carroll, of Maryland, now called on the President for aid, and General Barry, commanding the United States garrison at Fort McHenry, Baltimore, was ordered to report to the Governor of Maryland with guns and all his men, though the disturbances were happily quelled before the troops of the United States were called out. In Baltimore, between 30 and 40 of the mob were wounded, while 9 were killed outright, all of them rioters, several of the militia being seriously injured.

The strike now spread into Pennsylvania, and the men employed

on the Pennsylvania Railroad struck at Pittsburgh the very day after the riot in Baltimore. The alleged cause of this strike was a new order of the company requiring double trains to be taken out with only one crew of men, which, it was claimed, would enable the company to discharge laborers, and thereby reduce its force. Besides this, there was an old grievance of a former reduction of wages. The strikers ran out the trains at Pittsburgh, took possession of the main tracks, and stopped all trains going East or West. The Brotherhood of Engineers held a meeting and resolved to stand by the strikers. A committee was appointed to demand from the Pennsylvania Railroad Company that the double-train system be abandoned, and the two per cent reduction in wages be restored. This demand was promptly refused, and the officers began to prepare to defend their property and open up the road. The Pittsburgh militia, three regiments strong, were called out, but only manifested, as at Martinsburg, that no reliance whatever could be placed upon them. Troops were then called for from Philadelphia, and were received at Pittsburgh by a violent and howling mob, armed with stones, sticks, and every thing they could lay hands on. Enraged at the rapid fire that followed from the Philadelphia militia, which mowed down about 20 of the mob, the rioters fled, but quickly reassembled in immense throngs, which brought together working men, tramps, and miners from every quarter, filling the city with uproar, and uttering threats of vengeance. Gun factories and stores dealing in arms were seized, and 3000 rioters marched down Fifth Avenue, with drums beating and flags flying, and shouting curses on the troops and General Pearson, who commanded them. The latter withdrew to the round-house —a sign of weakness which was taken advantage of, for they were quickly besieged in their place of safety, and shouts of "Burn them! burn the wretches!" were raised by the rioters. A long blockade had accumulated from the stoppage of cars for an extent of more than two miles, many of which were loaded with coal and coke, and these were now set on fire by petroleum, making a tremendous conflagration. The round-house began to burn amid the darkness of the night; the mob, seized with a sudden panic lest the Gatling gun the soldiers had drawn in with them should be turned upon them, suddenly turned and fled. The soldiers, who if they had remained longer would have been roasted alive, formed in line and marched out, the mob regathering and opening fire upon them. The troops, however, succeeded in scattering, not being able to make headway against the mob.

Sunday morning dawned on a city full of madness on the one hand, and fear and trembling on the other. Pittsburgh was in a state of anarchy, possessed by rioters composed of the worst elements in the community. Men with sledges broke open cars loaded with all sorts of valuables, and indiscriminate pillage was made of private and public prop-

erty. Two round-houses were burned, containing 125 first-class locomotives, together with the extensive railway machine-shops, depot, and offices of the United States Transfer Company. The freight depot of the Pittsburgh, Cincinnati and St. Louis Railroad, the depot of Adams Express Company, the Pan-Handle Railway Depot, and finally the great Union Depot on Liberty Street, a large four story-building, 2000 feet long—all these were totally consumed, besides a large amount of property too tedious to enumerate. The direct losses of the Pennsylvania Railway Company alone were estimated at two and a half millions of dollars—a debt still remaining unadjusted, but which must ultimately be paid out of the taxes of Alleghany County, in which Pittsburgh is situated. The firemen were not allowed to move a finger toward putting out the fire. The mayor and citizens seemed absolutely cowed and powerless, great crowds of the latter standing and looking on while these wild scenes of riot and destruction went forward.

Meanwhile Governor Hartranft telegraphed to Washington for aid, and another proclamation was issued, and United States troops dispatched from the various garrisons along the coast. With returning confidence inspired by this movement, Pittsburgh once more resumed an orderly aspect. The mobs melted away in the presence of the public determination that no more destruction should take place.

At Harrisburg a formidable riot was organized by the strikers, and a vast crowd assembled, threatening the property of the railroad company. About 2000 troops assembled at the State arsenal at the capital. The citizens organized a vigilance committee to guard the principal buildings, and kept so completely the upper hand, that the riot was quelled without any bloodshed. The people of the city of Reading did not fare so well. The strikers took possession of the Lebanon Valley Railroad tracks, set on fire the bridge, one of the finest in the State, and seized the Philadelphia and Reading Railroad Depot, with all its trains. The Easton Grays and two militia companies from Allentown were quickly summoned, and were received at a deep cut near Penn and Seventh Streets with howls and showers of coal. The soldiers received orders to fire, which they did at first over the heads of the mob, but finally point blank, aiming a volley into the very midst of the crowd, which turned and rushed, with wild shouts and cries of blood and vengeance, from the cut. Next day more soldiers arrived, when a company from Allentown openly deserted the defence of the city and refused to act against the mob. It was plain that the State militia could not be relied on. About 600 United States troops of the First Artillery arrived that evening, and their measured tread and determined aspect preserved order thenceforward. The journals state that 10 men were killed and 40 wounded at Reading, besides 20 soldiers.

The strike seemed to spread like an insurrection from road to road

and from city to city. If order was restored in one place, the trains were so obstructed at other points that no through freight could be run. Mail trains were not stopped by the rioters, but some of the companies refused to run any trains unless safe passage to all was guaranteed by the Government. By the middle of the week (July 23d) strikes had occurred on all the following roads :

Baltimore and Ohio, Pennsylvania Central, Erie, Lake Shore and Michigan Southern, Pittsburgh, Fort Wayne and Chicago, Pittsburgh, Cincinnati and St. Louis, Vandalia, Ohio and Mississippi, Cleveland, Columbus, Cincinnati and Indianapolis, Philadelphia and Reading. Philadelphia and Erie, Erie and Pittsburgh, Chicago, Alton and St. Louis, Canada Southern, and some minor roads.

The journals at this date announced :

" No through freight is arriving at New York, Philadelphia, Boston, or Baltimore.

" On the Baltimore and Ohio Railroad, where the strike began, the blockade continues at Cumberland, Keyser, and Grafton.

" On the Pennsylvania Central the blockade is complete.

" On the Lake Shore no trains are running. No trains leave Cleveland or Toledo.

" On the Erie road the blockade at Hornellsville is perfect, way trains only running on the branches.

" On the Central and Hudson, trains are running to Buffalo, but a strike is expected.

" On the Ohio and Mississippi the road is blockaded at Vincennes.

" The Central Pacific, Union Pacific, Louisville and Lexington, Cincinnati and Muskingum, St. Louis, Iron Mountain and Southern, St. Louis, Kansas City and Northern have acceded to the demands of the strikers."

Meanwhile the War Department at Washington acted with the utmost promptitude and vigor, summoning troops and marines from their stations all along the coast, and sending them into the interior wherever the rioters held sway. Major-General Hancock was sent to Philadelphia to direct military movements, and although great mobs, amounting to thousands, gathered in that city, and a train of cars was burned, the firm front presented by Mayor Stokley and the citizens, with the arrival of the United States troops, made it apparent by the 24th of July that no serious disturbances would take place in Philadelphia. At Scranton, on the Lehigh and Susquehanna division of the New Jersey Central, the strikers were recruited by a vast mob of coal-miners, making common cause. The company, which was engaged both in mining coal and transportation, refusing to grant the demand of 25 per cent advance in wages, the mines were flooded by the hands, though the railway strike was over in two or three days.

In New York, the Central and Hudson River Railroad was interrupted at various points by the strikers, who held meetings demanding a restoration of the 10 per cent reduction that had been made on

the 1st of July. The following table shows the rate of this reduction :

	Old Rate.	New Rate.
Engineers, per day, . . .	$3 50	$3 15
Firemen, per day, .	1 75	1 58
Brakemen, per day, . . .	1 75	1 58
Switchmen, per month, .	40 00	36 00
Yard hands, . .	$40 to $55.	$36 to $49 50.
Shop hands, per month, .	$45 to $125.	$38 50 to $112 50.

President Vanderbilt refused to restore wages in the face of menaces, but held out good promises for the future, if order were preserved, which promises were amply redeemed afterward. Trains were stopped at Syracuse, Buffalo, and West Albany, but the strikers were dispersed without bloodshed or serious destruction of property.

On the Erie road, a great meeting of firemen, brakemen, and trackmen was held at Hornellsville on the 20th of July, and a strike resolved upon, making known their demand for larger wages, which the company declined to comply with. Gangs of strikers took possession of the trains and tore up railway tracks, but militia arriving from Rochester, and Governor Robinson, of New York, issuing a proclamation offering a reward of $500 for the arrest and conviction of any one interfering with railway trains, the mob were speedily cowed. The firemen and brakemen agreed to go to work again at the 10 per cent reduction, while on the company's part it was stipulated that no men were to be discharged except those who had destroyed the company's property.

In Ohio the Lake Shore road was visited with a strike at Cleveland ; and on July 21st to the 25th, mobs gathered at Newark, Toledo, and Cincinnati, and elsewhere, mainly composed of roughs and tramps, striving to close up factories and rolling-mills. Governor Young ordered out the militia and issued a proclamation, and this, with public meetings of the citizens, soon put down all violence, limiting the evil accomplished to the stoppage of freight between the West and the East.

Chicago was the centre of one of the most furious mob movements, mainly engineered by the most radical of Communists, and was only saved from pillage and conflagration by the prompt organization and vigorous handling of its police force. Yelling crowds patrolled the streets, seizing upon arms and ordering all the workmen in machine-shops, factories, and elevators to quit labor. The mob was harangued by Communist orators with such words as these, " We know what we are fighting for and what we are doing : let us kill those d—d aristocrats." It was at one time feared that Chicago would be a scene of blood, and the Governor of Illinois telegraphed, like the Governors of Maryland, Pennsylvania, and West Virginia, for the aid of Federal

troops, which, however, was not ultimately required. At St. Louis, the Working Men's Party, as it was called, almost put out of sight the railroad strikers by their high-handed movements, by closing mills and factories, and compelling laborers and mechanics to stop work. Numerous strikes occurred throughout Missouri, but these, as well as the St. Louis movement, were soon put down.

The whole country by the second week of the strikes was aroused to such indignation at the arrogant despotism of the strikers, and the violence, destruction, and bloodshed they had been guilty of, that there is no doubt the rioters would ultimately have fared more hardly at the hands of the people than of the soldiery, had they not been promptly put down by the show of military power. The blockade of supplies put the strikers in the attitude of saying to the producers of the West and the consumers of the East, "You shall suffer, and if need be starve, until we get our wages advanced. No more food shall be taken to market until we grant permission." The press of the whole country, almost without exception, enforced the true view of the case, and the prompt and vigorous action of the general Government in placing the whole power of the military at the points where it was most needed, proved that our republican government, contrary to what is sometimes asserted, is not weak nor halting in the presence of popular violence and insurrection.

No language, says a modern critic, supplies so many illustrations of the art of carrying things too far, as the German. That language has seven deadly sins, viz.:

1. Too many volumes in the language.
2. Too many sentences in a volume.
3. Too many words in a sentence.
4. Too many syllables in a word.
5. Too many letters in a syllable.
6. Too many strokes in a letter.
7. Too much black in a stroke.

"As good almost kill a Man as kill a good Booke ; who kills a Man kills a reasonable creature, God's Image ; but he who destroys a good Booke kills reason itself. A good Booke is the precious life blood of a master spirit embalmed and treasured on purpose to a life beyond life."—*Milton's Areopagitica.*

TOM BROWN used to remark of bad wine (such as was ordinarily served at taverns in his day, as it still is in our own), that it was "a better argument for sobriety than all the volumes of morality could afford."

[From the (official) Statistical Abstract of the United Kingdom, 1877.]

QUANTITIES OF WHEAT AND FLOUR IMPORTED INTO THE UNITED KINGDOM, 1861–1876.

Wheat.—Total of Grain and Flour in equivalent Weight of Grain (1 cwt. of wheat flour = 1¼ cwt. of wheat in grain).

FROM WHAT COUNTRIES.	1861.	1862.	1863.	1864.	1865.	1866.	1867.	1868.	1869.	1870.	1871.	1872.	1873.	1874.	1875.	1876.
	Cwts.	Cwts.	Cwts.	Cwts.	Cwts.	Cwts.	Cwts.	Cwts.	Cwts.	Cwts.	Cwts.	Cwts.	Cwts.	Cwts.	Cwts.	Cwts.
Austrian Territories	465,683	831,185	107,379	43,765	612,725	1,390,935	706,619	1,530,515	1,345,786	463,683	836,243	456,966	311,240	255,208	420,192	661,683
British N. America	3,387,949	5,118,609	3,198,187	1,831,397	639,456	69,601	835,008	794,505	3,396,511	3,402,690	3,732,776	2,155,170	4,315,709	4,598,315	4,069,565	2,770,975
Chili	314,246	347,341	282,311	193,231	169,862	341,099	2,097,978	1,477,526	550,349	643,347	689,951	1,677,904	1,837,587	2,307,016	902,660	1,012,642
Denmark	674,325	419,144	394,991	776,176	637,763	643,007	664,963	811,173	779,884	640,548	295,432	611,283	475,354	455,384	831,850	802,090
Egypt	1,474,490	3,304,079	2,382,636	867,462	10,063	13,831	1,471,756	3,237,380	1,029,299	106,701	908,847	2,801,042	1,271,794	297,925	2,112,138	2,249,252
France	1,359,898	1,961,835	1,957,403	2,654,424	6,036,902	8,025,530	2,140,882	946,863	2,153,350	1,069,120	182,262	4,553,731	3,259,619	1,124,712	3,573,777	1,663,800
Germany	6,658,402	7,930,849	5,724,696	6,842,721	7,294,371	6,801,465	7,873,216	7,546,698	7,046,883	4,487,773	4,268,283	5,183,601	3,019,406	4,012,066	6,613,544	3,487,672
Holland	60,872	12,794	11,709	13,786	51,616	93,096	13,534	60,132	205,760	26,306	12,398	61,912	99,378	9,823	62,472	83,127
Russia	4,040,488	5,755,799	4,594,984	5,129,410	8,093,989	9,181,472	14,166,794	10,855,836	9,187,296	10,326,844	15,648,943	17,038,977	9,693,997	5,793,976	10,157,847	8,911,783
Spain	1,297,257	316,822	11,393	1,890	133,755	865,679	472,640	2,982	44,161	8,936	16,990	643,087	1,734,640	418,450	157,217	270,473
Sweden	66,352	19,290	26,810	60,479	26,906	30,000	13,244	24,509	62,905	37,322	20,538	41,582	44,069	54,077	100,052	63,450
Turkey & dependencies	1,002,768	1,759,566	415,534	482,994	571,135	629,433	2,447,218	3,066,607	2,886,020	493,646	1,421,746	829,942	430,882	623,177	1,312,494	1,561,257
United St's	15,610,472	21,785,057	11,969,179	10,077,431	1,498,679	956,229	6,091,783	7,258,389	15,930,257	15,057,236	16,625,531	9,681,349	21,775,110	27,206,082	26,372,151	22,223,403
Oth. Count's	693,574	499,361	132,908	131,443	172,579	474,301	1,253,603	890,529	418,617	211,907	722,947	1,463,296	3,442,483	2,561,529	2,870,722	6,002,006
Total....	37,646,705	50,042,394	30,687,692	28,887,203	25,843,552	29,371,679	39,136,780	36,606,045	44,447,772	36,906,110	44,562,227	47,612,896	51,681,197	49,322,693	59,546,681	51,904,433

QUANTITIES OF MAIZE OR INDIAN CORN IMPORTED INTO THE UNITED KINGDOM, 1861–1876.

COUNTRIES.	1861.	1862.	1863.	1864.	1865.	1866.	1867.	1868.	1869.	1870.	1871.	1872.	1873.	1874.	1875.	1876.
	Cwts.	Cwts.	Cwts.	Cwts.	Cwts.	Cwts.	Cwts.	Cwts.	Cwts.	Cwts.	Cwts.	Cwts.	Cwts.	Cwts.	Cwts.	Cwts.
Austrian Territories	193,490	1,425,892	205,576	79,533	26,017	45,863	639,563	1,079,564	2,927,056	1,225,914	156,049	155,656	134,328	96,767	1,198,707	63,749
British N.A.	506,249	255,693	394,440	9,641	802,173	832,678	338,032	339,683	83,847	12,400	1,346,009	3,617,896	10,762,353	1,380,228	673,176	1,878,413
Egypt	256,049	18,135	431,494	9,239		3,903	219,998	657,726	10,896	11,214	75,905	372,001	38,950	12,749	63,490	132,571
France	74,050	935,070	42,989	107,129	71,985	464,161	1,000,824	178,401	166,312	971,682	90,623	10,992	5,703	90,429	263,531	829,606
Russia	628,969		957,236	1,401,343	1,131,756	461,930	247,460	664,381	604,618	2,511,725	2,096,483	423,851	1,354,395	508,561	504,115	
Turkey & dependencies	3,734,751	2,241,968	5,880,430	4,311,796	3,997,849	5,372,873	1,030,968	4,097,191	11,008,607	11,821,290	5,548,271	2,588,023	4,063,564	1,629,705	4,449,555	9,590,950
United St's	7,385,717	6,511,718	4,648,386	294,963	1,766,305	6,653,811	4,799,285	4,009,770	1,354,844	92,063	7,312,546	16,980,683	712,963	13,454,617	12,038,606	27,065,440
Oth. Count's	609,192	331,890	344,734	12,991	49,399	161,744	887,509	634,862	1,351,963	779,506	196,372	443,653		650,518	1,082,700	701,001
Total....	13,214,366	11,094,819	12,736,594	6,295,938	7,096,083	14,392,863	8,540,429	11,472,286	17,064,119	16,756,783	16,825,025	24,682,670	13,823,431	17,693,025	20,488,450	39,968,869

[Condensed, with additions, from the Financial Review, 1877.]

TABLE FOR INVESTORS.

THE following table shows the rate per cent of annual income to be realized from stocks or bonds bearing any given rate of yearly dividends or interest, from 1 to 20 per cent, when purchased at various prices from 10 to 300 per cent. This table applies equally well to both stocks and bonds, and has nothing to do with the length of time which a bond has to run to maturity.

For example : To ascertain what rate of annual interest will be realized on a bond or stock which bears 7 per cent per annum and can be purchased at 92 (i.e., at 92 per cent of its par value, whatever the par may be), find 92 in the column of "purchase price" and follow that line across to the column headed "7 per cent," which will show the correct figures—in the present instance, 7,6 per cent.

Purchase Price.	3 per cent.	3.65 per cent.	4 per cent.	4½ p'r cent.	5 per cent.	6 per cent.	7 per cent.	7 3/10 per cent.	8 per cent	9 per cent.	10 per cent.	12 per cent.	15 per cent.
10	30	36.50	40	45	50	60	70	73	80	90	100	120	150
15	20	24.33	26.66	30	33.33	40	46.66	48.66	53.33	60	66.66	80	100
20	15	18.25	20	22.50	25	30	35	36.50	40	45	50	60	75
22	13.63	16.59	18.18	20.45	22.72	27.27	31.81	33.18	36.36	40.90	45.45	54.54	68.18
24	12.50	15.20	16.66	18.75	20.83	25	29.16	30.41	33.33	37.50	41.66	50	62.50
26	11.53	14.03	15.38	17.30	19.23	23.07	26.92	28.07	30.76	34.61	38.46	46.15	57.69
28	10.71	13.03	14.28	16.07	17.85	21.42	25	26.07	28.57	32.14	35.71	42.85	53.57
30	10	12.16	13.33	15	16.66	20	23.33	24.33	26.66	30	33.33	40	50
32	9.37	11.40	12.50	14.06	15.62	18.75	21.87	22.81	25	28.12	31.25	37.50	46.87
34	8.82	10.73	11.76	13.23	14.70	17.64	20.58	21.47	23.52	26.47	29.41	35.29	44.11
36	8.33	10.13	11.11	12.50	13.88	16.66	19.44	20.27	22.22	25	27.77	33.33	41.66
38	7.89	9.60	10.52	11.84	13.15	15.78	18.42	19.21	21.05	23.68	26.31	31.57	39.47
40	7.50	9.12	10	11.25	12.50	15	17.50	18.25	20	22.50	25	30	37.50
42	7.14	8.69	9.52	10.71	11.90	14.28	16.66	17.38	19.04	21.42	23.80	28.57	35.71
44	6.81	8.29	9.09	10.22	11.36	13.63	15.90	16.59	18.18	20.45	22.72	27.27	34.09
46	6.52	7.93	8.69	9.78	10.86	13.04	15.21	15.86	17.39	19.56	21.73	26.08	32.60
48	6.25	7.60	8.33	9.37	10.41	12.50	14.58	15.20	16.66	18.75	20.83	25	31.25
50	6	7.30	8	9	10	12	14	14.60	16	18	20	24	30
51	5.88	7.15	7.84	8.82	9.80	11.76	13.72	14.31	15.68	17.64	19.60	23.52	29.41
52	5.76	7.01	7.69	8.65	9.61	11.53	13.46	14.03	15.38	17.30	19.23	23.07	28.84
53	5.66	6.88	7.54	8.49	9.43	11.32	13.20	13.77	15.09	16.98	18.86	22.64	28.30
54	5.55	6.75	7.40	8.33	9.25	11.11	12.96	13.51	14.81	16.66	18.51	22.22	27.77
55	5.45	6.63	7.27	8.18	9.09	10.90	12.72	13.27	14.54	16.36	18.18	21.81	27.27
56	5.35	6.51	7.14	8.03	8.92	10.70	12.50	13.03	14.28	16.07	17.85	21.42	26.78
57	5.26	6.40	7.01	7.89	8.77	10.52	12.27	12.80	14.03	15.78	17.54	21.05	26.31
58	5.17	6.29	6.89	7.75	8.62	10.34	12.06	12.58	13.79	15.51	17.24	20.68	25.86
59	5.08	6.18	6.77	7.62	8.47	10.16	11.86	12.37	13.55	15.25	16.94	20.33	25.42
60	5	6.08	6.66	7.50	8.33	10	11.66	12.16	13.33	15	16.66	20	25
61	4.91	5.97	6.55	7.37	8.19	9.83	11.47	11.95	13.11	14.75	16.39	19.67	24.59
62	4.83	5.88	6.45	7.25	8.06	9.67	11.29	11.77	12.90	14.51	16.12	19.35	24.19
63	4.76	5.79	6.34	7.14	7.93	9.52	11.11	11.58	12.69	14.28	15.87	19.04	23.80
64	4.68	5.70	6.25	7.03	7.81	9.37	10.93	11.40	12.50	14.06	15.62	18.75	23.43
65	4.61	5.61	6.15	6.92	7.69	9.23	10.76	11.23	12.30	13.84	15.38	18.46	23.07
66	4.54	5.53	6.06	6.81	7.57	9.09	10.60	11.06	12.12	13.63	15.15	18.18	22.72
67	4.47	5.44	5.97	6.71	7.46	8.95	10.44	10.89	11.94	13.43	14.92	17.91	22.38
68	4.41	5.36	5.88	6.61	7.35	8.82	10.29	10.73	11.76	13.23	14.70	17.64	22.05
69	4.34	5.28	5.79	6.52	7.24	8.69	10.14	10.57	11.59	13.04	14.49	17.39	21.73
70	4.28	5.21	5.71	6.42	7.14	8.57	10	10.42	11.43	12.85	14.28	17.14	21.42
71	4.22	5.14	5.63	6.33	7.04	8.45	9.85	10.28	11.26	12.67	14.08	16.90	21.12
72	4.16	5.06	5.55	6.25	6.94	8.33	9.72	10.13	11.11	12.50	13.89	16.66	20.83
73	4.10	5	5.47	6.16	6.84	8.21	9.58	10	10.95	12.32	13.69	16.43	20.54
74	4.05	4.93	5.40	6.08	6.75	8.10	9.45	9.86	10.81	12.16	13.51	16.21	20.27
75	4	4.86	5.33	6	6.66	8	9.33	9.73	10.66	12	13.33	16	20
76	3.94	4.80	5.26	5.92	6.57	7.89	9.21	9.60	10.52	11.84	13.15	15.78	19.73
77	3.89	4.74	5.19	5.84	6.49	7.79	9.09	9.48	10.38	11.68	12.98	15.58	19.48
78	3.84	4.67	5.12	5.76	6.41	7.69	8.97	9.35	10.25	11.53	12.82	15.38	19.23
79	3.79	4.62	5.06	5.69	6.32	7.59	8.86	9.24	10.12	11.39	12.65	15.18	18.98
80	3.75	4.56	5	5.62	6.25	7.50	8.75	9.12	10	11.25	12.50	15	18.75
81	3.70	4.50	4.93	5.55	6.17	7.40	8.64	9.01	9.87	11.11	12.34	14.81	18.51
82	3.65	4.45	4.87	5.48	6.09	7.31	8.53	8.90	9.75	10.97	12.19	14.63	18.29
83	3.61	4.39	4.81	5.42	6.02	7.22	8.43	8.79	9.63	10.84	12.04	14.45	18.04
84	3.57	4.34	4.76	5.35	5.95	7.14	8.33	8.69	9.52	10.71	11.90	14.28	17.85
85	3.52	4.29	4.70	5.29	5.88	7.05	8.23	8.58	9.41	10.58	11.76	14.11	17.64

TABLE FOR INVESTORS—(Continued).

Purchase Price	3 per cent.	3.65 per cent.	4 per cent.	4½p'r cent.	5 per cent.	6 per cent.	7 per cent.	7⅕% per cent.	8 per cent.	9 per cent.	10 per cent.	12 per cent.	15 per cent.
86...	3.48	4.24	4.65	5.23	5.81	6.97	8.13	8.48	9.30	10.46	11.62	13.95	17.41
87...	3.44	4.19	4.59	5.17	5.74	6.89	8.04	8.39	9.19	10.34	11.49	13.79	17.24
88...	3.40	4.14	4.54	5.11	5.68	6.81	7.94	8.29	9.09	10.22	11.36	13.63	17.01
89...	3.37	4.10	4.49	5.05	5.61	6.74	7.86	8.20	8.98	10.11	11.23	13.48	16.85
90...	3.33	4.05	4.44	5	5.55	6.66	7.77	8.11	8.88	10	11.11	13.33	16.66
91...	3.29	4.01	4.39	4.94	5.49	6.59	7.69	8.02	8.79	9.89	10.98	1.318	16.43
92...	3.26	3.96	4.34	4.80	5.43	6.52	7.60	7.93	8.69	9.78	10.86	1.304	16.30
93...	3.22	3.92	4.30	4 83	5.37	6.45	7.52	7.84	8.60	9.67	10.75	1 290	16.12
94...	3.19	3.88	4.25	4.78	5.31	6.38	7.44	7.76	8.51	9.57	10.65	1.276	15.95
95...	3.15	3.64	4.21	4.73	5.26	6.31	7.36	7.68	8.42	9.47	10.55	1.263	15.78
96...	3.10	3.80	4.16	4.68	5.20	6.25	7.29	7.60	8.33	9.37	10.41	12.50	15.72
97...	3.09	3.76	4.12	4.63	5.15	6 18	7.21	7.52	8.24	9.27	10.30	12.37	15.46
98...	3.06	3.72	4.08	4.59	5.10	6.12	7.14	7.45	8.16	9.18	10.20	12 24	15.30
99...	3.03	3.68	4 04	4.54	5.05	6.06	7.07	7.37	8.08	9.00	10.10	12.12	15.15
100...	3	3 65	4	4.50	5	6	7	7.30	8.	9	10	12	15
101...	2.97	3.61	3.96	4.45	4.95	5.94	6.93	7.22	7.92	8.91	9.90	11.88	14.85
102...	2.94	3.57	3.92	4.41	4.90	5.88	6.86	7.15	7.84	8.82	9.80	11.76	14.70
103...	2.91	3.54	3.88	4.36	4.85	5.82	6.79	7.08	7.76	8 73	9.70	11.65	14.56
104...	2.88	3.50	3.84	4.32	4 80	5.76	6.72	7.01	7.69	8.65	9.01	11.53	14.42
105...	2.85	3.47	3.80	4.28	4.76	5.71	6.66	6.95	7.61	8.57	9.52	11.42	14.28
106...	2.83	3.44	3.77	4.24	4.71	5.66	6.60	6.88	7.54	8.49	9.43	11.32	14.15
107...	2.80	3.41	3.73	4.20	4.67	5.60	6.54	6.82	7.47	8.41	9.34	11.21	14.01
108...	2.77	3.37	3.70	4.16	4.62	5.55	6.48	6.75	7.40	8.33	9.25	11.11	13.88
109...	2.75	3.34	3.66	4.12	4.58	5.50	6.42	6.69	7.33	8.25	9.17	11	13.76
110...	2.72	3.31	3.63	4.09	4.54	5.45	6.36	6.63	7.27	8.18	9.09	10.90	13 63
111...	2.70	3.28	3.60	4.05	4.50	5.40	6.30	6 57	7.20	8.10	9	10.81	13 51
112...	2.67	3.25	3.57	4.01	4·46	5.35	6.25	6.51	7.14	8.03	8.92	10.71	13.39
113...	2.65	3.23	3.54	3.98	4.42	5.30	6.19	6.46	7.07	7.96	8.84	10.61	13.27
114...	2.63	3.20	3.50	3.94	4.38	5.26	6.14	6.40	7.01	7.89	8 77	10.52	13.15
115...	2.60	3.17	3.47	3.91	4.35	5.21	6.08	6.34	6.95	7.82	8.69	10.43	13.04
116...	2.58	3.14	3 44	3.87	4.31	5.17	6.03	6.29	6.89	7.75	8 61	10.34	12.93
117...	2.56	3.11	3.41	3.84	4.27	5.12	5.98	6.23	6.83	7.69	8.54	10.25	12.83
118··	2.54	3.09	3.38	3.81	4.23	5.08	5.93	6.18	6.77	7.62	8.47	10.16	12.71
119...	2.52	3.06	3.36	3.78	4.20	5.04	5.88	6.13	6.72	7 56	8.40	10.08	12.60
120...	2.50	3·04	3.33	3.75	4.16	5	5.83	6 08	6.66	7.50	8 33	10	12.50
121...	2.47	3.01	3.30	3.71	4.13	4 95	5.78	6.03	6.61	7.43	8.26	9.91	12.39
122...	2.45	2.99	3.27	3.68	4.09	4.91	5.73	5.96	6.55	7.37	8.19	9.83	12.29
123...	2.43	2 96	3.25	3.65	4.06	4.87	5.69	5.93	6 50	7.31	8.13	9.76	12.19
124...	2.41	2 94	3 22	3.62	4.03	4 83	5.65	5.88	6.45	7.25	8 06	9.67	12.09
125...	2.40	2.90	3.20	3.60	4	4.80	5.60	5.80	6.40	7.20	8	9.60	12
130...	2.30	2.80	3.08	3.46	3.84	4.61	5.38	5.61	6.15	6.92	7.69	9.23	11.53
135...	2.22	2.66	2.96	3.33	3.70	4.44	5.18	5.33	5.92	6.66	7.40	8 88	11.11
140...	2.14	2 60	2.85	3.21	3.57	4.28	5	5.21	5.71	6 42	7.14	8.57	10.71
145...	2.06	2.51	2.75	3.10	3.44	4.13	4.82	5.03	5.51	6.20	6.89	8.27	10.34
150...	2	2.43	2.66	3	3.33	4	4 66	4.86	5 33	6	6.66	8	10
155...	1.93	2.35	2.58	2.90	3.22	3 87	4.51	4.70	5.16	5.80	6.45	7.74	9.67
160...	1.87	2.28	2.50	2.81	3.12	3.75	4.37	4.56	5	5.62	6.25	7.50	9.37
165...	1.81	2.21	2.42	2.72	3.03	3.63	4.24	4.42	4.84	5.45	6.06	7.27	9.09
170...	1.76	2.14	2.35	2.64	2.94	3.52	4.11	4.29	4.70	5.29	5.88	7.05	8.82
175...	1.71	2.08	2.28	2.57	2.85	3.42	4.	4.17	4.57	5.14	5·71	6 85	8.57
180...	1.66	2.02	2.22	2.50	2.77	3.33	3.88	4.05	4.44	5	5.55	6.66	8.33
185...	1.62	1.97	2.16	2.43	2.70	3.24	3.78	3.94	4.32	4.86	5.40	6.48	8.10
190...	1.57	1 92	2.10	2.36	2 63	3.15	3.68	3.84	4.21	4.73	5.26	6.31	7.89
195...	1.53	1.89	2.05	2.30	2.56	3.07	3.58	3.79	4.10	4.61	5.13	6.15	7.69
200...	1.50	1.82	2	2.25	2.50	3.	3.50	3.65	4	4.50	5	6	7.50
210...	1.42	1.73	1.90	2.14	2.38	2.85	3.33	3 47	3.80	4.28	4.76	5 71	7.14
220...	1.36	1.65	1.81	2.04	2.27	2 72	3.18	3.31	3.63	4.09	4.54	5.45	6.81
225...	1.33	1.62	1.77	2	2.22	2.66	3.11	3.24	3.55	4	4.44	5.33	6.66
230...	1.30	1.58	1 73	1.97	2.17	2.60	3.04	3.17	3.47	3 91	4.34	5.21	6.52
240...	1.25	1.52	1.66	1.87	2·08	2.50	2.91	3.04	3.33	3.73	4.16	5	6.25
250...	1.20	1.46	1.60	1.80	2	2.40	2.80	2.92	3.20	3.60	4	4.80	6
275...	1.09	1.32	1.45	1.63	1.81	2.18	2.54	2.65	2.90	3.27	3.63	4.36	5.45
300...	1	1 20	1.33	1.50	1.66	2	2.33	2.40	2.66	3	3.33	4	5

VALUE OF CURRENCY, GOLD BEING AT A GIVEN RATE

(Values Expressed in Cents.)

Gold Rate	Value of Currency	Gold Rate	Value of Currency	Gold Rate	Value of Currency	Gold Rate	Value of Currency	Gold Rate	Value of Currency
100	100.000000	108	92.592592	116	86.206896	124	80.645161	132	75.757576
100⅛	99.875156	108⅛	92.485549	116⅛	86.114107	124⅛	80.563948	132⅛	75.685903
100¼	99.750623	108¼	92.378753	116¼	86.021505	124¼	80.482897	132¼	75.614367
100⅜	99.626400	108⅜	92.272203	116⅜	85.929108	124⅜	80.402010	132⅜	75.542965
100½	99.502487	108½	92.165899	116½	85.836910	124½	80.321285	132½	75.471691
100⅝	99.378882	108⅝	92.059839	116⅝	85.744909	124⅝	80.240722	132⅝	75.400565
100¾	99.255583	108¾	91.954023	116¾	85.653105	124¾	80.160320	132¾	75.329567
100⅞	99.132590	108⅞	91.848450	116⅞	85.561497	124⅞	80.080080	132⅞	75.258702
101	99.009901	109	91.743119	117	85.470085	125	80.000000	133	75.187970
101⅛	98.887515	109⅛	91.638030	117⅛	85.378869	125⅛	79.920080	133⅛	75.117371
101¼	98.765432	109¼	91.533181	117¼	85.287846	125¼	79.840319	133¼	75.046904
101⅜	98.643650	109⅜	91.428571	117⅜	85.197018	125⅜	79.760718	133⅜	74.976570
101½	98.522167	109½	91.324201	117½	85.106383	125½	79.681275	133½	74.906367
101⅝	98.400984	109⅝	91.220068	117⅝	85.015940	125⅝	79.601990	133⅝	74.836295
101¾	98.280098	109¾	91.116173	117¾	84.925690	125¾	79.522863	133¾	74.766355
101⅞	98.159509	109⅞	91.012514	117⅞	84.835631	125⅞	79.443893	133⅞	74.696545
102	98.039216	110	90.909091	118	84.745763	126	79.365079	134	74.626865
102⅛	97.919216	110⅛	90.805902	118⅛	84.656085	126⅛	79.286422	134⅛	74.557316
102¼	97.799511	110¼	90.702948	118¼	84.566596	126¼	79.207921	134¼	74.487896
102⅜	97.680098	110⅜	90.600226	118⅜	84.477297	126⅜	79.129575	134⅜	74.418605
102½	97.560975	110½	90.497737	118½	84.388186	126½	79.051383	134½	74.349442
102⅝	97.442144	110⅝	90.395480	118⅝	84.299262	126⅝	78.973346	134⅝	74.280408
102¾	97.323601	110¾	90.293454	118¾	84.210526	126¾	78.895463	134¾	74.211503
102⅞	97.205346	110⅞	90.191657	118⅞	84.121977	126⅞	78.817734	134⅞	74.142725
103	97.087379	111	90.090090	119	84.033613	127	78.740157	135	74.074074
103⅛	96.969697	111⅛	89.988751	119⅛	83.945435	127⅛	78.662733	135⅛	74.005550
103¼	96.852300	111¼	89.887640	119¼	83.857442	127¼	78.585462	135¼	73.937153
103⅜	96.735187	111⅜	89.786756	119⅜	83.769633	127⅜	78.508342	135⅜	73.868883
103½	96.618357	111½	89.686099	119½	83.682008	127½	78.431372	135½	73.800738
103⅝	96.501809	111⅝	89.585666	119⅝	83.594566	127⅝	78.354554	135⅝	73.732719
103¾	96.385542	111¾	89.485458	119¾	83.507307	127¾	78.277886	135¾	73.664825
103⅞	96.269555	111⅞	89.385475	119⅞	83.420229	127⅞	78.201368	135⅞	73.597056
104	96.153846	112	89.285714	120	83.333333	128	78.125000	136	73.529412
104⅛	96.038415	112⅛	89.186176	120⅛	83.246618	128⅛	78.048780	136⅛	73.461892
104¼	95.923261	112¼	89.086860	120¼	83.160083	128¼	77.972709	136¼	73.394495
104⅜	95.808383	112⅜	88.997764	120⅜	83.073729	128⅜	77.896787	136⅜	73.327223
104½	95.693780	112½	88.888889	120½	82.987552	128½	77.821012	136½	73.260073
104⅝	95.579450	112⅝	88.790233	120⅝	82.901554	128⅝	77.745344	136⅝	73.193047
104¾	95.465394	112¾	88.691794	120¾	82.815735	128¾	77.669003	136¾	73.126143
104⅞	95.351609	112⅞	88.593577	120⅞	82.730093	128⅞	77.594568	136⅞	73.059361
105	95.238090	113	88.495575	121	82.644628	129	77.519380	137	72.992701
105⅛	95.124851	113⅛	88.397790	121⅛	82.559339	129⅛	77.444337	137⅛	72.926162
105¼	95.011876	113¼	88.300221	121¼	82.474227	129¼	77.369439	137¼	72.859745
105⅜	94.899170	113⅜	88.202867	121⅜	82.389289	129⅜	77.294686	137⅜	72.793448
105½	94.786730	113½	88.105727	121½	82.304527	129½	77.220077	137½	72.727273
105⅝	94.674556	113⅝	88.008801	121⅝	82.219938	129⅝	77.145612	137⅝	72.661218
105¾	94.562648	113¾	87.912088	121¾	82.135523	129¾	77.071291	137¾	72.595281
105⅞	94.451003	113⅞	87.815587	121⅞	82.051282	129⅞	76.997112	137⅞	72.529460
106	94.339623	114	87.719298	122	81.967213	130	76.923077	138	72.463768
106⅛	94.228504	114⅛	87.623220	122⅛	81.883316	130⅛	76.849183	138⅛	72.398190
106¼	94.117647	114¼	87.527352	122¼	81.799591	130¼	76.775432	138¼	72.332730
106⅜	94.007050	114⅜	87.431694	122⅜	81.716037	130⅜	76.701822	138⅜	72.267389
106½	93.896713	114½	87.336244	122½	81.632653	130½	76.628352	138½	72.202166
106⅝	93.786635	114⅝	87.241000	122⅝	81.549439	130⅝	76.555024	138⅝	72.137060
106¾	93.676815	114¾	87.145969	122¾	81.466395	130¾	76.481835	138¾	72.072072
106⅞	93.567251	114⅞	87.051142	122⅞	81.383520	130⅞	76.408787	138⅞	72.007201
107	93.457944	115	86.956519	123	81.300813	131	76.335878	139	71.942446
107⅛	93.348891	115⅛	86.862106	123⅛	81.218274	131⅛	76.263107	139⅛	71.877808
107¼	93.240093	115¼	86.767896	123¼	81.135902	131¼	76.190476	139¼	71.813285
107⅜	93.131548	115⅜	86.673889	123⅜	81.053696	131⅜	76.117965	139⅜	71.748879
107½	93.023255	115½	86.580086	123½	80.971660	131½	76.045627	139½	71.684588
107⅝	92.915215	115⅝	86.486486	123⅝	80.889788	131⅝	75.973649	139⅝	71.620412
107¾	92.807424	115¾	86.393088	123¾	80.808081	131¾	75.901328	139¾	71.556351
107⅞	92.699881	115⅞	86.299889	123⅞	80.726539	131⅞	75.829384	139⅞	71.492404

EQUIVALENT IN CURRENCY OF ONE DOLLAR IN GOLD.

(Currency Rates Expressed in Cents.)

Rate	$1 in Gold will buy.	Rate	$1 in Gold will buy.	Rate	$1 in Gold will buy.	Rate	$1 in Gold will buy.	Rate	$1 in Gold will buy.
60	$1.6666667	68	$1.4705882	76	$1.3157895	84	$1.1904762	92	$1.0869565
60⅛	1.6632017	68⅛	1.4678899	76⅛	1.3136289	84⅛	1.1887073	92⅛	1.0854817
60¼	1.6597510	68¼	1.4652015	76¼	1.3114754	84¼	1.1869436	92¼	1.0840108
60⅜	1.6563147	68⅜	1.4625228	76⅜	1.3093229	84⅜	1.1851851	92⅜	1.0825440
60½	1.6528925	68½	1.4598540	76½	1.3071895	84½	1.1834319	92½	1.0810811
60⅝	1.6494845	68⅝	1.4571949	76⅝	1.3050571	84⅝	1.1816839	92⅝	1.0796221
60¾	1.6460905	68¾	1.4545454	76¾	1.3029316	84¾	1.1799410	92¾	1.0781671
60⅞	1.6427105	68⅞	1.4519056	76⅞	1.3008130	84⅞	1.1782032	92⅞	1.0767160
61	1.6393443	69	1.4492754	77	1.2987013	85	1.1764706	93	1.0752688
61⅛	1.6359918	69⅛	1.4466546	77⅛	1.2965961	85⅛	1.1747430	93⅛	1.0738255
61¼	1.6326531	69¼	1.4440438	77¼	1.2944984	85¼	1.1730205	93¼	1.0723861
61⅜	1.6293279	69⅜	1.4414414	77⅜	1.2924071	85⅜	1.1713031	93⅜	1.0709505
61½	1.6260163	69½	1.4388489	77½	1.2903226	85½	1.1695900	93½	1.0695187
61⅝	1.6227180	69⅝	1.4362657	77⅝	1.2882448	85⅝	1.1678839	93⅝	1.0680908
61¾	1.6194332	69¾	1.4336918	77¾	1.2861736	85¾	1.1661802	93¾	1.0666667
61⅞	1.6161616	69⅞	1.4311270	77⅞	1.2841091	85⅞	1.1644832	93⅞	1.0652463
62	1.6129032	70	1.4285714	78	1.2820513	86	1.1627907	94	1.0638298
62⅛	1.6096579	70⅛	1.4260249	78⅛	1.2800000	86⅛	1.1611030	94⅛	1.0624161
62¼	1.6064257	70¼	1.4234875	78¼	1.2779553	86¼	1.1594203	94¼	1.0610079
62⅜	1.6032061	70⅜	1.4209591	78⅜	1.2759111	86⅜	1.1577424	94⅜	1.0596026
62½	1.6000000	70½	1.4184397	78½	1.2738853	86½	1.1560694	94½	1.0582011
62⅝	1.5968064	70⅝	1.4159292	78⅝	1.2718601	86⅝	1.1544011	94⅝	1.0568032
62¾	1.5936255	70¾	1.4134275	78¾	1.2698413	86¾	1.1527377	94¾	1.0554090
62⅞	1.5904571	70⅞	1.4109347	78⅞	1.2678288	86⅞	1.1510791	94⅞	1.0540184
63	1.5873016	71	1.4084507	79	1.2658228	87	1.1494253	95	1.0526316
63⅛	1.5841584	71⅛	1.4059754	79⅛	1.2638231	87⅛	1.1477762	95⅛	1.0512484
63¼	1.5810277	71¼	1.4035088	79¼	1.2618299	87¼	1.1461318	95¼	1.0498688
63⅜	1.5779093	71⅜	1.4010508	79⅜	1.2598425	87⅜	1.1444921	95⅜	1.0484928
63½	1.5748031	71½	1.3990014	79½	1.2578616	87½	1.1428571	95½	1.0471204
63⅝	1.5717092	71⅝	1.3961606	79⅝	1.2558870	87⅝	1.1412268	95⅝	1.0457517
63¾	1.5686274	71¾	1.3937282	79¾	1.2539185	87¾	1.1396011	95¾	1.0443864
63⅞	1.5655580	71⅞	1.3913043	79⅞	1.2519562	87⅞	1.1379801	95⅞	1.0430248
64	1.5625000	72	1.3888889	80	1.2500000	88	1.1363636	96	1.0416667
64⅛	1.5594542	72⅛	1.3864818	80⅛	1.2480499	88⅛	1.1347518	96⅛	1.0403121
64¼	1.5564202	72¼	1.3840830	80¼	1.2461059	88¼	1.1331445	96¼	1.0389610
64⅜	1.5533981	72⅜	1.3816926	80⅜	1.2441679	88⅜	1.1315417	96⅜	1.0376135
64½	1.5503876	72½	1.3793103	80½	1.2422360	88½	1.1299435	96½	1.0362694
64⅝	1.5473888	72⅝	1.3769363	80⅝	1.2403101	88⅝	1.1283498	96⅝	1.0349288
64¾	1.5444015	72¾	1.3745704	80¾	1.2383901	88¾	1.1267606	96¾	1.0335917
64⅞	1.5414258	72⅞	1.3722127	80⅞	1.2364760	88⅞	1.1251758	96⅞	1.0322581
65	1.5384615	73	1.3698630	81	1.2345679	89	1.1235955	97	1.0309278
65⅛	1.5355086	73⅛	1.3675214	81⅛	1.2326656	89⅛	1.1220196	97⅛	1.0296010
65¼	1.5325670	73¼	1.3651877	81¼	1.2307692	89¼	1.1204481	97¼	1.0282776
65⅜	1.5296371	73⅜	1.3628620	81⅜	1.2288786	89⅜	1.1188811	97⅜	1.0269576
65½	1.5267176	73½	1.3605442	81½	1.2269939	89½	1.1173184	97½	1.0255997
65⅝	1.5238095	73⅝	1.3582343	81⅝	1.2251149	89⅝	1.1157601	97⅝	1.0243297
65¾	1.5209125	73¾	1.3559322	81¾	1.2232416	89¾	1.1142061	97¾	1.0230179
65⅞	1.5180266	73⅞	1.3536379	81⅞	1.2213740	89⅞	1.1126565	97⅞	1.0217114
66	1.5151515	74	1.3513513	82	1.2195122	90	1.1111111	98	1.0204082
66⅛	1.5122873	74⅛	1.3490725	82⅛	1.2176560	90⅛	1.1097919	98⅛	1.0191083
66¼	1.5094340	74¼	1.3468013	82¼	1.2158055	90¼	1.1080332	98¼	1.0178117
66⅜	1.5065913	74⅜	1.3445378	82⅜	1.2139605	90⅜	1.1065007	98⅜	1.0165184
66½	1.5037594	74½	1.3422819	82½	1.2121212	90½	1.1049724	98½	1.0152284
66⅝	1.5009381	74⅝	1.3400335	82⅝	1.2102875	90⅝	1.1034483	98⅝	1.0139417
66¾	1.4981288	74¾	1.3377926	82¾	1.2084592	90¾	1.1019284	98¾	1.0126582
66⅞	1.4953271	74⅞	1.3355593	82⅞	1.2066365	90⅞	1.1004126	98⅞	1.0113780
67	1.4925373	75	1.3333333	83	1.2048193	91	1.0989011	99	1.0101010
67⅛	1.4897579	75⅛	1.3311148	83⅛	1.2030075	91⅛	1.0973937	99⅛	1.0088272
67¼	1.4869888	75¼	1.3289037	83¼	1.2012012	91¼	1.0958904	99¼	1.0075567
67⅜	1.4842300	75⅜	1.3266998	83⅜	1.1994003	91⅜	1.0943912	99⅜	1.0062893
67½	1.4814815	75½	1.3245033	83½	1.1976048	91½	1.0928962	99½	1.0050251
67⅝	1.4787431	75⅝	1.3223140	83⅝	1.1958146	91⅝	1.0914052	99⅝	1.0037641
67¾	1.4760148	75¾	1.3201320	83¾	1.1940298	91¾	1.0899182	99¾	1.0025063
67⅞	1.4732965	75⅞	1.3179572	83⅞	1.1922504	91⅞	1.0884354	99⅞	1.0012516

PRICES OF BRITISH THREE PER CENT CONSOLS FOR EIGHTY-EIGHT YEARS, 1789-1876.

[From the London Economist's Commercial History and Review, 1877.]

Years.	Highest Price.	Lowest Price.	Years.	Highest Price.	Lowest Price.	Years.	Highest Price.	Lowest Price.	Years.	Highest Price.	Lowest Price.
1789..	81.2	71.6	1811	66.7	61.7	1833	91.7	86.5	1855	93.2	85.6
1790..	80.9	70.5	1812	63.0	55.1	1834	93.2	89.0	1856	96.1	90.5
1791..	89.7	75.7	1813	67.5	54.5	1835	93.1	89.1	1857	97.9	86.5
1792..	97.1	72.5	1814	67.5	54.5	1836	93.0	86.6	1858	98.9	94.6
1793..	81.0	70.5	1815	72.5	61.5	1837	94.1	90.2	1859	97.4	88.2
1794..	72.4	62.7	1816	65.7	53.9	1838	95.5	91.9	1860	95.5	91.1
1795..	70.5	61.0	1817	84.2	62.0	1839	94.1	89.2	1861	94.4	89.1
1796..	70.6	53.2	1818	82.0	73.0	1840	93.5	85.7	1862	94.7	91.5
1797..	56.5	47.5	1819	79.0	64.9	1841	90.6	87.1	1863	94.0	89.7
1798..	58.0	47.2	1820	70.2	65.6	1842	97.2	90.1	1864	92.0	87.1
1799..	69.0	52.6	1821	78.7	68.7	1843	99.9	92.1	1865	91.5	86.1
1800..	67.2	60.0	1822	83.0	75.4	1844	101.4	97.9	1866	91.5	84.0
1801..	70.0	54.2	1823	85.7	72.0	1845	100.6	91.9	1867	96.4	89.9
1802..	79.0	66.0	1824	97.2	91.1	1846	97.2	87.9	1868	96.1	92.0
1803..	73.0	50.2	1825	93.5	73.9	1847	90.0	78.7	1869	94.2	91.5
1804..	59.9	53.7	1826	84.6	76.5	1848	94.5	80.0	1870	94.5	88.5
1805..	62.0	57.0	1827	89.6	81.7	1849	97.9	90.6	1871	94.0	91.4
1806..	64.6	58.5	1828	89.6	83.5	1850	98.5	95.0	1872	93.7	91.2
1807..	61.4	57.6	1829	95.7	86.5	1851	99.1	95.6	1873	94.0	91.7
1808..	69.1	62.6	1830	93.9	74.6	1852	101.6	98.7	1874	93.6	91.2
1809..	70.4	63.4	1831	84.9	78.1	1853	101.0	85.1	1875	95.6	92.4
1810..	71.0	63.2	1832	89.0	82.5	1854	95.9	86.9	1876	97.0	93.5

MERCHANT SHIPPING OF THE WORLD IN 1876.

[From the London Economist's Commercial History and Review, 1877.]

Countries.	Sailing Vessels.	Tonnage.	Steam Vessels.	Tonnage.	Total Tonnage.
British	20,265	5,807,365	3,290	3,362,992	9,170,357
United States	7,288	2,390,521	605	789,728	3,180,249
Norwegian	4,749	1,410,903	122	55,674	1,466,777
Italian	4,601	1,292,076	114	97,582	1,389,658
German	3,456	875,995	226	226,888	1,102,853
French	3,858	725,048	814	834,334	1,069,382
Spanish	2,915	557,320	230	176,250	733,570
Greek	2,121	426,905	11	7,133	434,038
Dutch	1,432	399,993	126	134,600	534,593
Swedish	2,121	399,128	219	88,660	487,788
Russian	1,785	391,052	151	105,962	497,914
Austrian	983	338,684	78	81,269	419,953
Danish	1,348	188,953	67	60,697	249,650
Portuguese	456	107,010	26	22,277	129,294
South American	273	95,459	81	59,213	154,792
Central American	153	57,044	6	8,132	61,076
Turkish and Egyptian	305	48,289	30	28,264	76,553
Belgian	54	23,341	35	40,700	64,044
Asiatic	42	16,019	11	10,877	26,996
Liberian	3	454	....	....	454

I.—SUMMARY OF POPULAR AND ELECTORAL VOTES FOR PRESIDENT AND VICE-PRESIDENT OF THE UNITED STATES, 1789-1876.

Year of Election.	No. of States.	Total Elec. V.	POLITICAL PARTY.	*PRESIDENTS. CANDIDATES.	States.	VOTE. Popular.	Electoral	*VICE-PRESIDENTS. CANDIDATES.	Elect. Vote.
1789	†10	73	....	George Washington	..	....	69	....	...
			....	John Adams........	..	....		....	34
			....	John Jay..........	..	....		... .	9
			....	R. H. Harrison.....	..	....		....	6
			....	John Rutledge......	.	....		....	6
			....	John Hancock......	..	....		....	4
			....	George Clinton.....	..	....		....	3
			....	Samuel Huntingdon	..	....		....	2
			....	John Milton........	..	....		....	2
			....	James Armstrong..	..	....		....	1
			... .	Benjamin Lincoln..	..	....		....	1
			....	Edward Telfair. ..	..	....		....	1
				Vacancies........			4	....	4
1792	15	135	Federalist..	George Washington	..	....	132	....	...
			Federalist..	John Adams....	..	....		....	77
			Republican	George Clinton.....	..	....		....	50
			....	Thomas Jefferson..	..	....		... .	4
			....	Aaron Burr........	..	....		....	1
				Vacancies........	..	....	3	....	3
1796	16	138	Federalist..	John Adams.......	..	....	71	....	...
			Republican	Thomas Jefferson..	.	....		....	68
			Federalist..	Thomas Pinckney..	..	....		....	59
			Republican	Aaron Burr.....	..	....		... .	30
			....	Samuel Adams....	..	....		.. ..	15
			....	Oliver Ellsworth ..	..	....		....	11
			....	George Clinton.....	..	....		....	7
			....	John Jay..........	..	....		....	5
			....	James Iredell......	..	....		....	3
			....	George Washington	..	....		... .	2
			... .	John Henry.... ...	..	....		....	2
			, ...	S. Johnson	..	....		....	2
			....	Charles C. Pinckney	..	....		....	1
1800	16	138	Republican	Thomas Jefferson..	..	....	‡73	....	‡73
			Republican	Aaron Burr.......	..	....		....	‡73
			Federalist..	John Adams.......	..	....		....	65
			Federalist..	Charles C. Pinckney	..	....		....	64
			....	John Jay..........	..	....		....	1

* Previous to the election of 1804 each elector voted for two candidates for President ; the one receiving the highest number of votes, if a majority, was declared elected President ; and the next highest Vice-President.

† Three States out of thirteen did not vote, viz. : New York, which had not passed an electoral law ; and North Carolina and Rhode Island, which had not adopted the Constitution.

‡ There having been a tie vote, the choice devolved upon the House of Representatives. A choice was made on the 36th ballot, which was as follows : Jefferson—Georgia, Kentucky, Maryland, New Jersey, New York, North Carolina, Pennsylvania, Tennessee, Vermont, and Virginia—10 States ; Burr—Connecticut, Massachusetts, New Hampshire, and Rhode Island —4 States ; Blank—Delaware and South Carolina—2 States.

120   AN AMERICAN ALMANAC FOR 1878.

SUMMARY OF POPULAR AND ELECTORAL VOTES—*(Continued).*

Year of Election	No. of States	Total Elec. V.	POLITICAL PARTY	PRESIDENTS. Candidates	States	Popular.	Electoral	VICE-PRESIDENTS. Candidates	Elect. Vote.
1804	17	176	Republican	Thomas Jefferson..	15		162	George Clinton..	162
			Federalist..	Charles C. Pinckney	2		14	Rufus King.....	14
1808	17	176	Republican	James Madison. ..	12		122	George Clinton..	113
			Federalist..	Charles C. Pinckney	5		47	Rufus King.....	47
				George Clinton....			6	John Langdon..	9
				....			...	James Madison.	3
								James Monroe..	3
				Vacancy.........			1		1
1812	18	218	Republican.	James Madison....	11		128	Elbridge Gerry..	131
			Federalist..	De Witt Clinton...	7		89	Jared Ingersoll..	86
				Vacancy			1		1
1816	19	221	Republican.	James Monroe.....	16		183	D. D. Tompkins.	183
			Federalist..	Rufus King........	3		34	John E. Howard	22
							...	James Ross.....	5
							...	John Marshall..	4
							...	Robt. G. Harper.	3
				Vacancies			4		4
1820	24	235	Republican	James Monroe.....	24		231	D. D. Tompkins.	218
			Opposition.	John Q. Adams...			1	Rich. Stockton..'	8
								Daniel Rodney..	4
								Robt. G. Harper	1
								Richard Rush...	1
				Vacancies.......			3		8
1824	24	261	Republican.	Andrew Jackson...	10	155,872	*99	John C. Calhoun	182
			Coalition...	John Q. Adams....	8	105,321	84	Nathan Sanford.'	30
			Republican.	Wm. H. Crawford..	3	44,282	41	Nathaniel Macon	24
			Republican.	Henry Clay........	3	46,587	37	Andrew Jackson	13
								M. Van Buren...	9
								Henry Clay.....	2
				Vacancy					1
1828	24	261	Democratic	Andrew Jackson...	15	647,231	178	John C. Calhoun	171
			Nat. Repub.	John Q. Adams ...	9	509,097	83	Richard Rush...	83
							...	William Smith..	7
1832	24	288	Democratic	Andrew Jackson...	15	687,502	219	M. Van Buren...	189
			Nat. Repub.	Henry Clay.......	7	530,189	49	John Sergeant...	49
				John Floyd..... }	1	33,108	11	Henry Lee......	11
			Anti-Mason	William Wirt.... }	1		7	Amos Ellmaker.	7
							..	William Wilkins	30
				Vacancies.......			2		2
1836	26	294	Democratic.	Martin Van Buren.	15	761,549	170	R. M. Johnson†.	147
			Whig	Wm. H. Harrison }	7				Francis Granger.	77
			Whig.......	Hugh L. White... }	2	736,656	26	John Tyler......	47
			Whig... ...	Daniel Webster.. }	1		14	William Smith..	23
			Whig......	W. P. Mangum... }	1		11		...

* No choice having been made by the Electoral College, the choice devolved upon the House of Representatives. A choice was made on the first ballot, which was as follows: Adams—Connecticut, Illinois, Kentucky, Louisiana, Maine, Maryland, Massachusetts, Missouri, New Hampshire, New York, Ohio, Rhode Island, and Vermont—13 States; Jackson— Alabama, Indiana, Mississippi, New Jersey, Pennsylvania, South Carolina, and Tennessee— 7 States; Crawford—Delaware, Georgia, North Carolina, and Virginia—4 States.

† No candidate having received a majority of the votes of the Electoral College, the Senate elected R. M. Johnson Vice-President, who received 33 votes; Francis Granger received 16.

SUMMARY OF POPULAR AND ELECTORAL VOTES—(*Continued*).

Year of Election.	No. of States.	Total Elec. V.	POLITICAL PARTY.	CANDIDATES.	States.	VOTE. Popular.	Electoral	CANDIDATES.	Elect. Vote.
								VICE-PRESIDENTS.	
1840	26	294	Whig	Wm. H. Harrison..	19	1,275,017	234	John Tyler......	234
			Democratic	Martin Van Buren.	7	1,128,702	60	R. M. Johnson..	48
			Liberty	James G. Birney...	..	7,059	...	....	...
			....	....	..	....	...	L. W. Tazewell.	11
			....	....	..	....	...	James K. Polk..	1
1844	26	275	Democratic	James K. Polk.....	15	1,337,243	170	Geo. M. Dallas..	170
			Whig	Henry Clay..........	11	1,299,068	105	T. Frelinghuysen	105
			Liberty	James G. Birney...	..	62,300	...	....	...
1848	30	290	Whig	Zachary Taylor.....	15	1,360,101	163	Millard Fillmore	163
			Democratic	Lewis Cass.........	15	1,220,544	127	Wm. O. Butler..	127
			Free Soil...	Martin Van Buren..	..	291,263	...	Chas. F. Adams.	...
1852	31	296	Democratic	Franklin Pierce....	27	1,601,474	254	Wm. R. King...	254
			Whig	Winfield Scott.....	4	1,386,578	42	Wm. A. Graham	42
			Free Dem..	John P. Hale.......	..	156,149	...	Geo. W. Julian..	...
1856	31	296	Democratic	James Buchanan...	19	1,838,169	174	J. C. Breckinr'ge	174
			Republican.	John C. Fremont..	11	1,341,264	114	Wm. L. Dayton.	114
			American..	Millard Fillmore...	1	871,534	8	A. J. Donelson..	8
1860	33	303	Republican.	Abraham Lincoln..	17	1,866,352	180	Hannibal Hamlin	180
			Democratic.	J. C. Breckinridge..	11	845,763	72	Joseph Lane....	72
			Cons. Union	John Bell........	3	589,581	39	Edward Everett.	39
			Ind. Dem...	S. A. Douglas......	2	1,375,157	12	H. V. Johnson..	12
1864	*36	314	Republican.	Abraham Linclon..	22	2,216,067	212	Andrew Johnson	212
			Democratic	Geo. B. McClellan..	3	1,808,725	21	G. H. Pendleton.	21
				Vacancies.........	11	....	81	....	81
1868	†37	317	Republican.	Ulysses S. Grant...	26	3,015,071	214	Schuyler Colfax.	214
			Democratic.	Horatio Seymour ..	8	2,709,613	80	F. P. Blair, Jr...	80
				Vacancies.........	3	....	23	....	23
1872	37	366	Republican.	Ulysses S. Grant...	31	3,597,070	286	Henry Wilson...	286
			Dem. & Lib.	Horace Greeley.....	6	2,834,079	...	B. Gratz Brown.	47
			Democratic.	Charles O'Conor...	..	29,408	...	Geo. W. Julian..	5
			Temp'rance	James Black.......	..	5,608	...	A. H. Colquitt...	5
			....	Thos. A. Hendricks	..	....	42	John M. Palmer.	3
			....	B. Gratz Brown.....	..	....	18	T. E. Bramlette.	3
			....	Charles J. Jenkins..	..	....	2	W. S. Groesbeck	1
			....	David Davis.......	..	....	1	Willis B. Machen	1
			....	‡ Not Counted...	..	....	17	N. P. Banks.....	1
								....	14
1876	38	369	Republican.	Rutherford B.Hayes	21	4,033,950	185	Wm. A. Wheeler	185
			Democratic.	Samuel J. Tilden...	17	4,284,885	184	T. A. Hendricks	184
			Greenback..	Peter Cooper......	..	81,740	...	....	...
			Prohibition	Green Clay Smith..	..	9,522	...	....	...
			....	Scattering.	..	2,636	...		

* Eleven States did not vote, viz.: Alabama, Arkansas, Florida, Georgia, Louisiana, Mississippi, North Carolina, South Carolina, Tennessee, Texas, and Virginia.

† Three States did not vote, viz.: Mississippi, Texas, and Virginia.

‡ Three electoral votes of Georgia cast for Horace Greeley, and the votes of Arkansas, 6, and Louisiana, 8, cast for U. S. Grant, were rejected. If all had been included in the count, the electoral vote would have been 300 for U. S. Grant, and 66 for opposing candidates.

II.—ELECTORAL VOTE, BY STATES, FOR PRESIDENT AND VICE-PRESIDENT, 1789-1876.

ELECTORAL VOTE OF 1789.*

No returns of the popular vote for President are preserved with any fulness previous to 1824. During the earlier elections the States, or a majority of them, chose the Presidential Electors by their Legislatures, and not by popular vote. Even as late as 1824, six States thus voted, while one State (South Carolina) continued to choose Presidential Electors by her Legislature until 1868.

STATES.†	Geo. Washington, of Va.	John Adams, of Mass.	John Jay, of N.Y.	R. H. Harrison, of Md.	John Rutledge, of S. C.	John Hancock, of Mass.	Geo. Clinton, of N.Y.	Sam'l Hunting-ton, of Ct.	John Milton, of Ga.	Jas. Armstrong, of Ga.	Benj. Lincoln, of Mass.	Edward Telfair, of Ga.	Vacancies.	Total.
1 Connecticut....	7	5	...	...	...	...	...	2	...	...	...	...	...	7
2 Delaware......	3	...	3	...	...	...	...	...	...	...	...	...	...	3
3 Georgia........	5	...	...	...	...	...	...	...	2	1	1	1	...	5
4 Maryland......	6	...	...	6	...	...	...	...	...	...	...	...	2	8
5 Massachusetts.	10	10	...	...	...	...	...	...	...	...	...	...	...	10
6 N. Hampshire.	5	5	...	...	...	...	...	...	...	...	...	...	...	5
7 New Jersey....	6	1	5	...	...	...	...	...	...	...	...	...	...	6
8 Pennsylvania .	10	8	...	...	...	...	2	...	...	...	...	...	...	10
9 South Carolina	7	...	...	...	...	6	1	...	...	...	...	...	...	7
10 Virginia......	10	5	1	...	...	...	1	3	...	...	...	...	2	12
Total.......	69	34	9	6	6	4	3	2	2	1	1	1	4	73

* From 1789 to the election of 1804 the Electors voted for President and Vice-President on the same ballot, the one receiving the highest number of votes being President.

† New York, North Carolina, and Rhode Island did not vote, the New York Legislature having failed to agree on the mode of choosing electors, and North Carolina and Rhode Island not having ratified the Constitution in time to take part in the election.

ELECTORAL VOTE OF 1792.

STATES.	Geo. Washington, of Va.	J. Adams, of Mass.	Geo. Clinton, of N.Y.	T. Jefferson, of Va.	A. Burr, of N.Y.	Vacancies.	Total.
1 Connecticut......	9	9	...	...	...	...	9
2 Delaware........	3	3	...	...	...	...	3
3 Georgia..........	4	...	4	...	...	...	4
4 Kentucky........	4	...	...	4	...	...	4
5 Maryland........	8	8	...	...	...	2	10
6 Massachusetts..	16	16	...	...	...	...	16
7 New Hampshire.	6	6	...	...	...	...	6
8 New Jersey......	7	7	...	...	...	...	7
9 New York.......	12	...	12	...	...	...	12
10 North Carolina..	12	...	12	...	...	...	12
11 Pennsylvania....	15	14	1	...	...	...	15
12 Rhode Island....	4	4	...	...	...	...	4
13 South Carolina...	8	7	...	...	1	...	8
14 Vermont...	3	3	...	...	...	1	4
15 Virginia.........	21	...	21	...	...	...	21
Total	132	77	50	4	1	3	135

ELECTORAL VOTE OF 1796.

STATES.	John Adams, of Mass.	Thos. Jefferson, of Va.	Thos. Pinckney, of S.C.	Aaron Burr, of N.Y.	Samuel Adams, of Mass.	Oliver Ellsworth, of Conn.	Geo. Clinton, of N.Y.	John Jay, N.Y.	Jas. Iredell, N.C.	Geo. Washington, of Va.	John Henry, of Md.	S. Johnson, N.C.	C. C. Pinckney.	Total.
1 Connecticut...	9	....	4	....	....	....	5	....	....	....	....	....	....	9
2 Delaware	3	....	3	....	....	....	....	....	....	....	....	....	....	3
3 Georgia	....	4	....	....	....	....	4	....	....	....	....	....	....	4
4 Kentucky......	....	4	....	4	....	....	....	....	....	....	....	....	....	4
5 Maryland.. ...	7	4	4	3	....	....	....	....	....	2	....	....	....	10
6 Massachusetts.	16	....	13	....	....	1	....	....	....	....	2	....	....	16
7 N. Hampshire.	6	....	....	....	....	6	....	....	....	....	....	....	....	6
8 New Jersey....	7	....	7	....	....	....	....	....	....	....	....	....	....	7
9 New York.....	12	....	12	....	....	....	....	....	....	....	....	....	....	12
10 North Carolina	1	11	1	6	....	....	....	....	3	1	....	....	1	12
11 Pennsylvania..	1	14	2	13	....	....	....	....	....	....	....	....	....	15
12 Rhode Island..	4	....	....	....	....	4	....	....	....	....	....	....	....	4
13 South Carolina	....	8	8	....	....	....	....	....	....	....	....	....	....	8
14 Tennessee.....	....	3	....	3	....	....	....	....	....	....	....	....	....	3
15 Vermont......	4	....	4	....	....	....	....	....	....	....	....	....	....	4
16 Virginia.......	1	20	1	1	15	....	3	....	....	1	....	....	....	21
Total........	71	68	59	30	15	11	7	5	3	2	2	2	1	138

ELECTORAL VOTE OF 1800.

STATES.	Thos. Jefferson, of Va.	A. Burr, of N.Y.	John Adams, of Mass.	C. C. Pinckney, of S.C.	John Jay, of N.Y.	Total.	STATES.	Thos. Jefferson, of Va.	A. Burr, of N.Y.	John Adams, of Mass.	C. C. Pinckney, of S.C.	John Jay, of N.Y.	Total.
1 Connectic't	....	....	9	9	....	9	10 N. Carolina	8	8	4	4	..	12
2 Delaware...	....	....	3	3	....	3	11 Pennsylv'ia	8	8	7	7	..	15
3 Georgia....	4	4	....	....	....	4	12 Rhode Isl'd	....	..	4	3	1	4
4 Kentucky..	4	4	....	....	....	4	13 S. Carolina.	8	8	....	....	..	8
5 Maryland...	5	5	5	5	....	10	14 Tennessee..	3	3	....	....	..	3
6 Massach'tts	....	....	16	16	....	16	15 Vermont...	....	..	4	4	..	4
7 N. H'pshire	....	..	6	6	....	6	16 Virginia....	21	21	....	....	..	21
8 New Jersey	....	..	7	7	....	7	Total....	73	73	65	64	1	138
9 New York.	12	12	....	....	....	12							

The vote for Thomas Jefferson and Aaron Burr being equal, there was no choice for President by the Electoral votes. On the 11th February, 1801, the House of Representatives proceeded to the election of a President. On the first ballot eight States voted for Jefferson, six for Burr, and the votes of two were divided. Balloting continued without a choice until February 17th, 1801, when on the 36th ballot ten States voted for Jefferson, four for Burr, and two in blank. Thomas Jefferson was thus elected President, and Aaron Burr, Vice-President.

ELECTORAL VOTE OF 1804.*

STATES.	Thos. Jefferson, of Va.	C. C. Pinckney, of S. C.	Geo. Clinton, of N. Y.	Rufus King, of N. Y.	Total.
	PRESIDENT.		*VICE-PRES'T.*		
1 Connecticut....		9		9	9
2 Delaware......		3		3	3
3 Georgia........	6		6		6
4 Kentucky.....	8		8		8
5 Maryland......	9	2	9	2	11
6 Massachusetts.	19		19		19
7 N. Hampshire.	7		7		7
8 New Jersey....	8		8		8
9 New York.....	19		19		19
10 North Carolina	14		14		14
11 Ohio...........	3		3		3
12 Pennsylvania..	20		20		20
13 Rhode Island..	4		4		4
14 South Carolina	10		10		10
15 Tennessee.....	5		5		5
16 Vermont.......	6		6		6
17 Virginia.......	24		24		24
Total.........	162	14	162	14	176

* By Article XII. of the Amendments to the Constitution, which was declared in force September 25th, 1804, the Electors are required to ballot separately for President and Vice-President. The election of 1804 was the first under this amendment.

ELECTORAL VOTE OF 1808.

STATES.	James Madison, of Va.	C. C. Pinckney, of S. C.	Geo. Clinton, of N. Y.	Vacancies.	Geo. Clinton, of N. Y.	Rufus King, of N. Y.	John Langdon, of N. H.	James Madison, of Va.	James Monroe, of Va.	Vacancies.	Total.
	PRESIDENT.				*VICE-PRESIDENT.*						
1 Connecticut....		9				9					9
2 Delaware.......		3				3					3
3 Georgia........	6				6						6
4 Kentucky......	7			1	7					1	8
5 Maryland......	9	2			9	2					11
6 Massachusetts.		19				19					19
7 New Hampshire		7				7					7
8 New Jersey....	8				8						8
9 New York.....	13		6		13			3	3		19
10 North Carolina	11	3			11	3					14
11 Ohio...........	3						3				3
12 Pennsylvania..	20				20						20
13 Rhode Island..		4				4					4
14 South Carolina	10				10						10
15 Tennessee.....	5				5						5
16 Vermont.......	6						6				6
17 Virginia.......	24				24						24
Total.........	122	47	6	1	113	47	9	3	3	1	176

ELECTORAL VOTE OF 1812.

STATES	PRESIDENT — James Madison, of Va.	PRESIDENT — Geo. Clinton, of N.Y.	PRESIDENT — Vacancies	VICE-PRES'T — Elbridge Gerry, of Mass.	VICE-PRES'T — Jared Ingersoll, of Pa.	VICE-PRES'T — Vacancies	Total
1 Connecticut	..	9	..	..	9	..	9
2 Delaware	..	4	..	..	4	..	4
3 Georgia	8	..	..	8	..	..	8
4 Kentucky	12	..	..	12	..	..	12
5 Louisiana	3	..	..	3	..	..	3
6 Maryland	6	5	..	6	5	..	11
7 Massachusetts	..	22	..	2	20	..	22
8 New Hampshire	..	8	..	1	7	..	8
9 New Jersey	..	8	..	..	8	..	8
10 New York	..	29	..	..	29	..	29
11 North Carolina	15	..	..	15	..	..	15
12 Ohio	..	7	1	..	7	1	8
13 Pennsylvania	25	..	..	25	..	..	25
14 Rhode Island	..	4	..	..	4	..	4
15 South Carolina	11	..	..	11	..	..	11
16 Tennessee	8	..	..	8	..	..	8
17 Vermont	8	..	..	8	..	..	8
18 Virginia	25	..	..	25	..	..	25
Total	128	89	1	131	86	1	218

ELECTORAL VOTE OF 1816.

STATES	PRESIDENT — James Monroe, of Va.	PRESIDENT — Rufus King, of N.Y.	PRESIDENT — Vacancies	VICE-PRESIDENT — D. D. Tompkins, of N.Y.	VICE-PRESIDENT — John E. Howard, of Md.	VICE-PRESIDENT — James Ross, of Penn.	VICE-PRESIDENT — John Marshall, of Va.	VICE-PRESIDENT — R. G. Harper, of Md.	VICE-PRESIDENT — Vacancies	Total
1 Connecticut	...	9	...	...		5	4	...		9
2 Delaware	...	3	1	...				3	1	4
3 Georgia	8			8						8
4 Indiana	3			3						3
5 Kentucky	12			12						12
6 Louisiana	3			3						3
7 Maryland	8		3	8					3	11
8 Massachusetts	..	22	..		22					22
9 New Hampshire	8			8						8
10 New Jersey	8			8						8
11 New York	29			29						29
12 North Carolina	15			15						15
13 Ohio	8			8						8
14 Pennsylvania	25			25						25
15 Rhode Island	4			4						4
16 South Carolina	11			11						11
17 Tennessee	8			8						8
18 Vermont	8			8						8
19 Virginia	25			25						25
Total	183	34	4	183	22	5	4	3	4	221

ELECTORAL VOTE OF 1820.

STATES.	James Monroe, of Va.	John Q Adams, of Mass.	Vacancies	D.D.Tompkins, of N.Y.	R. Stockton, of N.Y.	Daniel Rodney, of Del.	K. G. Harper, of Md.	Richard Rush, of Pa.	Vacancies	Total.
	PRESIDENT.			VICE-PRESIDENT.						
1 Alabama	3			3						3
2 Connecticut	9			9						9
3 Delaware	4					4				4
4 Georgia	8			8						8
5 Illinois	3			3						3
6 Indiana	3			3						3
7 Kentucky	12			12						12
8 Louisiana	3			3						3
9 Maine	9			9						9
10 Maryland	11			10			1			11
11 Massachusetts	15			7	8					15
12 Mississippi	2		1	2					1	3
13 Missouri	3			3						3
14 New Hampshire	7	1		7				1		8
15 New Jersey	8			8						8
16 New York	29			29						29
17 North Carolina	15			15						15
18 Ohio	8			8						8
19 Pennsylvania	24		1	24					1	25
20 Rhode Island	4			4						4
21 South Carolina	11			11						11
22 Tennessee	7		1	7						8
23 Vermont	8			8						8
24 Virginia	25			25						25
Total	231	1	3	218	8	4	1	1	3	235

BRIEF HISTORY OF NATIONAL POLITICAL CONVEN-TIONS.

[From Greeley & Cleveland's Political Text-Book, 1860, and other sources.]

NATIONAL CONVENTIONS for the nomination of candidates for President and Vice-President are of comparatively recent origin. In the earlier political history of the United States, under the Federal Constitution, candidates for President and Vice-President were nominated by congressional and legislative caucuses. Washington was elected as first President under the Constitution, and re-elected for a second term by a unanimous, or nearly unanimous, concurrence of the American people; but an opposition party gradually grew up in Congress, which became formidable during its second term, and which ultimately crystallized into what was then called the Republican Party. John Adams, of Massachusetts, was prominent among the leading Federalists, while Thomas Jefferson, of Virginia, was pre-eminently the author and oracle of the Republican Party, and, by common consent, they were the opposing candidates for the Presidency, on Washington's retirement in 1796-7.

The first Congressional Caucus to nominate candidates for President and Vice-President is said to have been held in Philadelphia, in the year 1900, and to have nominated Mr. Jefferson for the first office, and Aaron Burr for the second. These candidates were elected after a desperate struggle, beating John Adams, and Charles C. Pinckney, of South Carolina. In 1804, Mr. Jefferson was re-elected President, with George Clinton, of New York, for Vice, encountering but slight opposition; Messrs. Charles C. Pinckney and Rufus King, the opposing candidates, receiving only 14 out of 176 electoral votes. We have been unable to find any record as to the manner of their nomination.

In January, 1808, when Mr. Jefferson's second term was about to close, a Re-

POPULAR VOTE OF 1824.

STATES.	Andrew Jackson, Republican.		John Quincy Adams, Coalition.		William H. Crawford, Republican.		Henry Clay, Republican.		Total Vote.
	Vote.	Maj.	Vote.	Maj.	Vote.	Maj.	Vote.	Maj.	
1 Alabama.......	9,443	5,280	2,416	.....	1,680	.....	67	......	13,606
2 Connecticut.....			7,587	5,609	1,978	.....			9,565
3 Delaware*									
4 Georgia*									
5 Illinois..........	1,901	1359	·1,54?	......	219	....	1,047	......	4,709
6 Indiana..........	7,343	‡2,028	3,09?	.....			5,315	.....	15,758
7 Kentucky.......	6,453	.....					16,782	10,329	23,235
8 Louisiana*......									
9 Maine..........	2,330	.....	6,870	4,540					9,200
10 Maryland	14,523	.....	14,632	§109	3,640	....	695	.....	33,496
11 Massachusetts..			30,687	24,071	6,616	....			37,303
12 Mississippi.....	3,234	1,421	1,694	.....	119	....			5,047
13 Missouri.......	987	.....	311	....			1,401	103	2,699
14 New Hampshire	643	......	4,107	3,464					4,750
15 New Jersey.....	10,985	679	9,110	.....	1,196	....			21,291
16 New York*									
17 North Carolina..	20,415	4,794			15,621	....			36,036
18 Ohio...........	18,457	.....	12,280	.....			19,255	§798	49,992
19 Pennsylvania...	36,100	24,845	5,440	.....	4,206	....	1,609	.....	47,355
20 Rhode Island...			2,145	1,945	200	....			2,345
21 South Carolina*									
22 Tennessee......	20,197	19,669	216	.....	312	....			20,725
23 Vermont*									
24 Virginia.......	2,861	......	3,189	.....	8,489	2,023	416	.....	14,955
Total.........	155,872	56,683	105,321	39,629	44,282	2,023	46,587	10,432	352,062
Jackson's Plurality.....	†50,551								

* The Electors of Delaware, Georgia, Louisiana, New York, South Carolina, and Vermont were chosen by the State Legislatures.
† Plurality over Adams.   ‡ Plurality over Clay.'   § Plurality over Jackson.

publican Congressional Caucus was held at Washington, to decide as to the relative claims of Madison and Monroe for the succession, the Legislature of Virginia, which had been said to exert a potent influence over such questions, being, on this occasion, unable to agree as to which of her favored sons should have the preference. Ninety-four out of the 136 Republican members of Congress attended this caucus, and declared their preference of Mr. Madison, who received 83 votes, the remaining 11 being divided between Mr. Monroe and George Clinton. The opposition supported Mr. Pinckney, but Mr. Madison was elected by a large majority.

Toward the close of Mr. Madison's earlier term he was nominated for re-election by a Congressional Caucus, held at Washington in May, 1812. In September of the same year, a convention of the opposition, representing eleven States, was held in the city of New York, which nominated De Witt Clinton, of New York, for President. He was also put in nomination by the Republican Legislature of New York. The ensuing canvass resulted in the re-election of Mr. Madison, who received 128 electoral votes to 89 for De Witt Clinton.

In 1816, the Republican Congressional Caucus nominated James Monroe, who received in the caucus 65 votes, to 54 for Wm. H. Crawford, of Georgia. The opposition, or Federalists, named Rufus King, of New York, who received only 34 electoral votes out of 217. There was no opposition to the re-election of Mr. Monroe in 1820, a single (Republican) vote being cast against him, and for John Quincy Adams.

In 1824, the Republican Party could not be induced to abide by the decision of a Congressional Caucus. A large majority of the Republican members formally refused to participate in such a gathering, or be governed by its decision ; still, a caucus was called, and attended by the friends of Mr. Crawford alone. Of the 261 Members of Congress at this time, 216 were Democrats or Republicans ; yet only 66

[Continued on page 131.]

ELECTORAL VOTE OF 1824.

STATES.	A. Jackson, of Tenn.	J. Q. Adams, of Mass.	W. H. Crawford, of Ga.	Henry Clay, of Ky.	Vacancies.	J. C. Calhoun, of S. C.	N. Sanford, of N. Y.	N. Macon, of N. C.	A. Jackson, of Tenn.	M. Van Buren, of N. Y.	Henry Clay, of Ky.	Vacancies.	Total.
	PRESIDENT.					VICE-PRESIDENT.							
1 Alabama	5					5							5
2 Connecticut		8							8				8
3 Delaware		1	2			1					2		3
4 Georgia			9							9			9
5 Illinois	2	1				3							3
6 Indiana	5					5							5
7 Kentucky				14		7	7						14
8 Louisiana	3	2				5							5
9 Maine		9				9							9
10 Maryland	7	3	1			10			1				11
11 Massachusetts		15				15							15
12 Mississippi	3					3							3
13 Missouri				3					3				3
14 New Hampshire		8				7			1				8
15 New Jersey	8					8							8
16 New York	1	26	5	4		29	7						36
17 North Carolina	15					15							15
18 Ohio				16			16						16
19 Pennsylvania	28					28							28
20 Rhode Island		4				3						1	4
21 South Carolina	11					11							11
22 Tennessee	11					11							11
23 Vermont		7				7							7
24 Virginia			24					24					24
Total	99	84	41	37		182	30	24	13	9	2	1	261

No candidate having received a majority of the votes for President, the House of Representatives elected JOHN QUINCY ADAMS. See p. 120.

POPULAR VOTE OF 1828.

STATES.	Andrew Jackson, Democratic. Vote.	Majority.	John Quincy Adams, National Republican. Voto.	Majority.	Total Vote.
1 Alabama	17,138	15,200	1,938	....	19,076
2 Connecticut	4,448	....	13,829	9,381	18,277
3 Delaware	4,349	......	4,769	420	9,118
4 Georgia	18,709	18,709	....		18,709
5 Illinois	6,763	5,182	1,581	......	8,344
6 Indiana	22,237	5,185	17,052	......	39,289
7 Kentucky	39,064	7,912	31,172		70,236
8 Louisiana	4,605	508	4,097		8,702
9 Maine	13,927	....	20,773	6,846	34,700
10 Maryland	24,578	....	25,750	1,181	50,367
11 Massachusetts	6,019	....	29,836	23,817	35,855
12 Mississippi	6,763	5,182	1,581		8,344
13 Missouri	8,232	4,810	3,422	....	11,654
14 New Hampshire	20,692	....	24,076	3,384	44,708
15 New Jersey	21,950	....	23,738	1,609	45,708
16 New York	140,763	5,350	135,413	....	276,176
17 North Carolina	37,857	23,939	13,918		51,775
18 Ohio	67,597	4,201	63,396		130,998
19 Pennsylvania	101,652	50,804	50,848	....	152,500
20 Rhode Island	821	....	2,754	1,933	3,575
21 South Carolina	Electors	chosen by	Legislature.		
22 Tennessee	44,090	41,850	2,940		46,380
23 Vermont	8,215	....	24,794	16,579	32,989
24 Virginia	26,752	14,651	12,101	....	38,853
Total	647,231	203,483	509,097	65,349	1,150,328
Jackson's Majority		138,134			

ELECTORAL VOTE OF 1828.

STATES.	A. Jackson, of Tenn.	J. Q. Adams, of Mass.	J. C. Calhoun, of S.C.	R. Rush, of Pa.	Wm. Smith, of S.C.	Total.	STATES.	A. Jackson, of Tenn.	J. Q. Adams, of Mass.	J. C. Calhoun, of S.C.	R. Rush, of Pa.	Wm. Smith, of S.C.	Total.
1 Alabama	5	....	5	..	...	5	14 N. Hampshire	....	8	...	8	..	8
2 Connecticut	....	8	..	8	...	8	15 New Jersey	....	8	...	8	..	8
3 Delaware	....	3	..	3	...	3	16 New York	20	16	20	16	..	36
4 Georgia	9	....	2	..	7	9	17 North Carolina	15	....	15	..	.	15
5 Illinois	3	....	3	..	...	3	18 Ohio	16	....	16	..	.	16
6 Indiana	5	....	5	..	...	5	19 Pennsylvania	28	....	28	..	.	28
7 Kentucky	14	....	14	..	...	14	20 Rhode Island	....	4	...	4	.	4
8 Louisiana	5	....	5	..	...	5	21 South Carolina	11	....	11	..	.	11
9 Maine	1	8	1	8	...	9	22 Tennessee	11	..	11	..	.	11
10 Maryland	5	6	5	6	...	11	23 Vermont	....	7	...	7	.	7
11 Massachusetts	....	15	..	15	...	15	24 Virginia	24	....	24	..	.	24
12 Mississippi	3	....	3	..	...	3							
13 Missouri	3	....	3	..	...	3	Total	178	83	171	83	7	261

POPULAR VOTE OF 1832.

STATES.	Andrew Jackson Democratic. Vote.	Majority.	Henry Clay, National Republican. Vote.	Majority.	Total Vote.
1 Alabama	*	....	....	....	....
2 Connecticut	11,269	....	17,755	6,486	29,024
3 Delaware	4,110	....	4,276	166	8,386
4 Georgia	20,750	20,750	....	....	20,750
5 Illinois	14,147	8,718	5,429	....	19,576
6 Indiana	31,552	16,080	15,472	....	47,024
7 Kentucky	36,247	....	43,396	7,149	79,643
8 Louisiana	4,049	1,521	2,528	....	6,577
9 Maine	33,291	6,087	27,204	....	60,495
10 Maryland	19,156	....	19,160	4	38,316
11 Massachusetts	14,545	....	33,003	18,458	47,549
12 Mississippi	5,919	5,919	....	....	5,919
13 Missouri	†5,192	5,192	....	....	5,192
14 New Hampshire	25,486	6,476	19,010	....	44,496
15 New Jersey	23,856	463	23,393	....	47,249
16 New York	168,497	13,601	154,896	....	323,393
17 North Carolina	24,862	20,299	4,563	....	29,425
18 Ohio	81,246	4,707	76,539	....	157,785
19 Pennsylvania	90,983	34,267	56,716	....	147,699
20 Rhode Island	2,126	....	2,810	684	4,936
21 South Carolina	Electors	chosen by	Legislature.		
22 Tennessee	28,740	27,304	1,436	....	30,176
23 Vermont	7,870	....	11,152	3,282	19,022
24 Virginia	33,609	22,158	11,451	....	45,060
Total	687,502	193,542	530,189	36,229	‡1,217,691
Jackson's Majority		157,313			

* Unanimous for Jackson.　　† Majority.
‡ This total does not include 33,108 votes cast for John Floyd and William Wirt.

ELECTORAL VOTE OF 1832.

STATES.	PRESIDENT.					VICE-PRESIDENT.						Total.
	A. Jackson, of Tenn.	H. Clay, of Ky.	John Floyd, of Va.	Wm. Wirt, of Md.	Vacancies.	M. Van Buren, of N. Y.	John Sergeant, of Pa.	Wm. Wilkins, of Pa.	Henry Lee, of Mass.	Amos Ellmaker, of Pa.	Vacancies.	
1 Alabama	7					7						7
2 Connecticut		8					8					8
3 Delaware		3					3					3
4 Georgia	11					11						11
5 Illinois	5					5						5
6 Indiana	9					9						9
7 Kentucky		15					15					15
8 Louisiana	5					5						5
9 Maine	10					10						10
10 Maryland	3	5			2	3	5				2	10
11 Massachusetts		14					14					14
12 Mississippi	4					4						4
13 Missouri	4					4						4
14 New Hampshire	7					7						7
15 New Jersey	8					8						8
16 New York	42					42						42
17 North Carolina	15					15						15
18 Ohio	21					21						21
19 Pennsylvania	30							30				30
20 Rhode Island		4					4					4
21 South Carolina			11						11			11
22 Tennessee	15					15						15
23 Vermont				7						7		7
24 Virginia	23					23						23
Total	219	49	11	7	2	180	49	30	11	7	2	288

POPULAR VOTE OF 1836.

STATES.	Martin Van Buren, Democratic.		Wm.H.Harrison, etc.* Whig, etc.		Total Vote.
	Vote.	Majority.	Vote.	Majority.	
1 Alabama	19,063	3,431	15,637		34,705
2 Arkansas	2,400	1,162	1,238		3,638
3 Connecticut	19,231	768	18,466		37,700
4 Delaware	4,155		4,738	583	8,893
5 Georgia	22,126		24,930	2,804	47,066
6 Illinois	18,097	3,114	14,983		33,080
7 Indiana	32,480		41,281	8,801	73,751
8 Kentucky	33,435		36,935	3,520	70,360
9 Louisiana	3,653	270	3,383		7,086
10 Maine	22,900	7,061	15,249		37,539
11 Maryland	22,167		25,852	3,685	48,019
12 Massachusetts	33,501		41,093	7,592	74,594
13 Michigan	7,360	3,360	4,000		11,860
14 Mississippi	9,979	291	9,688		19,667
15 Missouri	10,995	2,658	8,337		19,332
16 New Hampshire	18,722	12,494	6,228		24,950
17 New Jersey	25,347		26,862	545	58,209
18 New York	166,815	28,273	138,543		305,358
19 North Carolina	26,910	3,284	23,626		50,586
20 Ohio	96,948		105,405	8,457	202,383
21 Pennsylvania	91,475	4,364	87,111		178,586
22 Rhode Island	2,964	254	2,710		5,674
23 South Carolina	Electors	chosen	by the	Legisla-	ture.
24 Tennessee	26,120		35,962	9,842	62,092
25 Vermont	14,037		20,091	6,954	35,028
26 Virginia	30,261	6,693	23,368		53,629
Total	761,549	77,076	736,656	58,783	1,496,905
Van Buren's Majority		24,893			

* This column includes the vote given for Harrison, White, Webster, and Mangum.

ELECTORAL VOTE OF 1836.

STATES.	PRESIDENT. M. Van Buren, of N.Y.	W. H. Harrison, of Ohio.	Hugh L. White, of Tenn.	Daniel Webster, of Mass.	W. P. Mangum, of N.C.	* VICE-PRESIDENT. R. M. Johnson, of Ky.	Fr. Granger, of N.Y.	John Tyler, of Va.	William Smith, of Ala.	Total.
1 Alabama...................	7					7				7
2 Arkansas	3					3				3
3 Connecticut	8					8				8
4 Delaware		3					3			3
5 Georgia....................			11					11		11
6 Illinois....................	5					5				5
7 Indiana...................		9					9			9
8 Kentucky.................		15					15			15
9 Louisiana................	5					5				5
10 Maine	10					10				10
11 Maryland		10					10			10
12 Massachusetts				14				14		14
13 Michigan................	3					3				3
14 Mississippi.............	4					4				4
15 Missouri.................	4					4				4
16 New Hampshire........	7					7				7
17 New Jersey.............		8					8			8
18 New York...............	42					42				42
19 North Carolina.........	15					15				15
20 Ohio		21					21			21
21 Pennsylvania...........	30					30				30
22 Rhode Island	4					4				4
23 South Carolina					11			11		11
24 Tennessee...............			15					15		15
25 Vermont.................		7					7			7
26 Virginia	23								23	23
Total	170	73	26	14	11	147	77	47	23	294

* No candidate for Vice-President having received a majority of the votes cast, the Senate elected R. M. Johnson Vice-President.

[HISTORY OF CONVENTIONS—Continued from page 127.]
responded to their names at roll-call, 64 of whom voted for Mr. Crawford, as the Republican nominee for President. This nomination was very extensively repudiated throughout the country, and three competing Republican candidates were brought into the field through legislative and other machinery, viz., Andrew Jackson, Henry Clay, and John Quincy Adams. The result of this famous "scrub-race" for the Presidency was, that no one was elected by the people, Gen. Jackson receiving 99 electoral votes, Mr. Adams 84, Mr. Crawford 41, and Mr. Clay 37. The election then devolved on the House of Representatives, when Mr. Adams was chosen, receiving the votes of 13 States, against 7 for Gen. Jackson and 4 for Mr. Crawford. This was the end of "King Caucus."

Gen. Jackson was immediately thereafter put in nomination for the ensuing term by the Legislature of Tennessee, having only Mr. Adams for an opponent in 1828, when he was elected by a decided majority, receiving 178 electoral votes, to 83 for Mr. Adams.

The first political National Convention in this country of which we have any record was held at Philadelphia in September, 1830, styled the United States Anti-Masonic Convention. It was composed of 96 delegates. Francis Granger, of New York, presided, but no business was transacted.

In compliance with its call, a National Anti-Masonic Convention was held at Baltimore in September, 1831, which nominated William Wirt, of Maryland, for President, and Amos Ellmaker, of Pennsylvania, for Vice-President.

[Continued on page 137.]

132 AN AMERICAN ALMANAC FOR 1878.

POPULAR VOTE OF 1840.

STATES.	W. H. Harrison, Whig. Vote.	Maj.	M. Van Buren, Democratic. Vote.	Maj.	Jas.G.Birney, LibertyParty. Vote.	Maj.	Total Vote.
1 Alabama	28,471	....	33,991	5,520	......	.....	62,462
2 Arkansas	5,160	....	6,049	889	......	.....	11,209
3 Connecticut	31,601	6,131	25,296	....	174	.....	57.071
4 Delaware	5,967	1,083	4,884	....	......	.....	10,851
5 Georgia	40,261	8,328	31,933	....	......	.....	72,194
6 Illinois	45,537	....	47,476	1,790	149	.....	93,162
7 Indiana	65,302	13,607	51,695	....	......	.....	116,997
8 Kentucky	58,480	25,873	32,616	....	......	.....	91,105
9 Louisiana	11,297	3,680	7,617	....	......	.....	18.914
10 Maine	46,612	217	46,201	....	194	.....	93,007
11 Maryland	33,528	4,776	28,752	....	......	.....	62.2?0
12 Massachusetts	72,874	19,305	51,948	....	1,621	.....	126,443
13 Michigan	22,933	1,514	21.098	....	321	.....	44,352
14 Mississippi	19,518	2,523	16.995	....	......	.....	36,513
15 Missouri	22,972	....	29,760	6,788	......	.....	52,732
16 New Hampshire	26,158	....	32,670	6,386	126	.....	58,954
17 New Jersey	33,351	2,248	31,034	....	69	.....	64,454
18 New York	225,817	10.500	212,519	....	2,798	.....	441,134
19 North Carolina	46,376	12,158	34.218	....	......	.....	80,594
20 Ohio	148,157	22,479	124,782	....	903	.....	273,842
21 Pennsylvania	144,021	2	143,676	....	343	.....	288,040
22 Rhode Island	5,278	1,935	3,301	....	42	.....	8,621
23 South Carolina	Electors	chosen	by the	Legisla-	ture.		....
24 Tennessee	60,391	12,102	48,289	....	......	.....	108,680
25 Vermont	32,445	14,117	18,009	....	319	.....	50,773
26 Virginia	42,501	....	43,893	1,392	......	.....	66,394
Total	1,275,017	162,571	1,128,702	22,765	7,059	.....	2,410,778
Harrison's Majority		139,256					

ELECTORAL VOTE OF 1840.

STATES.	PRESIDENT. W. H. Harrison, of Ohio.	M. Van Buren, of N. Y.	VICE-PRESIDENT. John Tyler, of Virginia.	R. M. Johnson, of Ky.	L. W. Tazewell, of Va.	J. K. Polk, of Tennessee.	Total.
1 Alabama	...	7	...	7	......	...	7
2 Arkansas	...	3	...	3	......	...	3
3 Connecticut	8	...	8	...	......	...	8
4 Delaware	3	...	3	...	......	...	3
5 Georgia	11	...	11	...	......	...	11
6 Illinois	...	5	...	5	......	...	5
7 Indiana	9	...	9	...	......	...	9
8 Kentucky	15	...	15	...	......	...	15
9 Louisiana	5	...	5	...	......	...	5
10 Maine	10	...	10	...	......	...	10
11 Maryland	10	...	10	...	......	...	10
12 Massachu's	14	...	14	...	......	...	14
13 Michigan	3	...	3	...	......	...	3
14 Mississippi	4	...	4	...	......	...	4
15 Missouri	...	4	...	4	......	...	4
16 N.Hamps're	...	7	...	7	......	...	7
17 New Jersey	8	...	8	...	......	...	8
18 New York	42	...	42	...	......	...	42
19 N. Carolina	15	...	15	...	......	...	15
20 Ohio	21	...	21	...	......	...	21
21 Pennsylv'ia	30	...	30	...	......	...	30
22 Rhode Isl'd	4	...	4	...	......	...	4
23 S. Carolina	...	11	...	...	11	...	11
24 Tennessee	15	...	15	...	......	...	15
25 Vermont	7	...	7	...	......	...	7
26 Virginia	...	23	...	22	...	1	23
Total	234	60	234	48	11	1	234

POPULAR VOTE OF 1844.

STATES.	James K. Polk, Democratic.		Henry Clay, Whig.		J. G. Birney, Liberty Party.		Total Vote.
	Vote.	Maj.	Vote.	Maj.	Vote.	Maj.	
1 Alabama	37,740	11,656	26,084				63,824
2 Arkansas	9,546	4,042	5,504				15,050
3 Connecticut	29,841		32,832	1,048	1,943		64,616
4 Delaware	5,996		6,278	282			12,274
5 Georgia	44,177	2,071	42,106				86,283
6 Illinois	57,920	8,822	45,528		3,570		107,018
7 Indiana	70,181	208	67,867		2,106		140,154
8 Kentucky	51,988		61,255	9,267			113,243
9 Louisiana	13,782	699	13,083				26,865
10 Maine	45,719	6,505	34,378		4,836		84,933
11 Maryland	32,676		35,984	3,308			68,660
12 Massachusetts	52,846		67,418	3,712	10,860		131,124
13 Michigan	27,759	*3,422	24,337		3,632		55,728
14 Mississippi	25,126	5,920	19,206				44,332
15 Missouri	41,369	10,118	31,251				72,620
16 New Hampshire	27,160	5,133	17,866		4,161		49,187
17 New Jersey	37,495		38,318	692	131		75,944
18 New York	237,588	*5,106	232,482		15,812		485,882
19 North Carolina	39,287		43,232	3,945			82,519
20 Ohio	149,117		155,057	†5,940	8,050		312,224
21 Pennsylvania	167,535	3,194	161,203		3,138		331,876
22 Rhode Island	4,807		7,322	2,348	107		12,296
23 South Carolina							
24 Tennessee	59,917		60,030	113			119,947
25 Vermont	18,041		26,770	4,775	8,954		48,765
26 Virginia	49,570	5,893	43,677				93,247
Total	1,337,243	64,261	1,299,068	29,490	62,300		2,698,611
Polk's Plurality		*38,175					

* Plurality over Clay.   † Plurality over Polk.

ELECTORAL VOTE OF 1844.

STATES.	PRESIDENT. James K. Polk, of Tenn.	Henry Clay, of Ky.	VICE-PRES'T. G. M. Dallas, of Pa.	T. Frelinghuysen, of N. J.	Total.	STATES.	PRESIDENT. James K. Polk, of Tenn.	Henry Clay, of Ky.	VICE-PRES'T. G. M. Dallas, of Pa.	T. Frelinghuysen, of N. J.	Total.
1 Alabama	9	....	9	....	9	15 Missouri	7	....	7	....	7
2 Arkansas	3	....	3	....	3	16 N. Hampshire	6	....	6	....	6
3 Connecticut	....	6	....	6	6	17 New Jersey	....	7	....	7	7
4 Delaware	....	3	....	3	3	18 New York	36	....	36	....	36
5 Georgia	10	....	10	....	10	19 North Carolina	....	11	....	11	11
6 Illinois	9	....	9	....	9	20 Ohio	....	23	....	23	23
7 Indiana	12	....	12	....	12	21 Pennsylvania	26	....	26	....	26
8 Kentucky	....	12	..	12	12	22 Rhode Island	....	4	....	4	4
9 Louisiana	6	...	6	....	6	23 South Carolina	9	....	9	....	9
10 Maine	9	....	9	....	9	24 Tennessee	....	13	....	13	13
11 Maryland	....	8	....	8	8	25 Vermont	....	6	....	6	6
12 Massachusetts	....	12	....	12	12	26 Virginia	17	...	17	....	17
13 Michigan	5	....	5	....	5						
14 Mississippi	6	....	6	....	6		170	105	170	105	275

POPULAR VOTE OF 1848.

STATES.	Zachary Taylor, Whig. Vote.	Maj.	Lewis Cass, Democratic. Vote.	Maj.	Van Buren, Free Soil. Vote.	Maj.	Total Vote.
1 Alabama.	30,482	.. ..	31,363	881	......	.....	61,845
2 Arkansas.......	7,588	......	9,300	1,712	......		16,888
3 Connecticut.....	30,314	*3,268	27,046	......	5,005	.....	62,355
4 Delaware.......	6,421	443	5,898	......	80	.....	12,399
5 Florida.........	3,116	1,269	1,847	......			4,963
6 Georgia........ ..	47,544	2,742	44,802	......			92,346
7 Illinois.........	53,047	......	56,300	13,253	15,774	.....	126,121
8 Indiana........	69,907	......	74,745	†4,838	8,100	.....	152,752
9 Iowa........ ...	11,064	......	12,093	†1,009	1,126	.....	24,308
10 Kentucky..... .	67,141	17,421	49,720	......	......	.....	116,861
11 Louisiana.....	18,217	2,847	15,370	.... ..	......	.....	33,587
12 Maine..........	35,125	......	39,880	†4,755	12,096	.....	87,101
13 Maryland......	37,702	3,049	34,526	......	125	.....	72,355
14 Massachusetts..	61,072	‡23,014	35,281	......	38,058	.....	134,411
15 Michigan.......	23,940	......	30,687	†6,747	10,389	.....	65,016
16 Mississippi.....	25,922	......	26,537	615	......	.....	52,459
17 Missouri.......	32,671	......	40,077	7,406	......	... ..	72,748
18 New Hampshire	14,781	......	27,763	5,422	7,560	.....	50,104
19 New Jersey....	40,015	2,285	36,901	......	829	.....	77,745
20 New York.....	218,603	‡98,093	114,318	......	120,510	.....	453,431
21 North Carolina.	43,550	8,681	34,869	......	......	.....	78,419
22 Ohio..........	138,360	......	154,775	†16,415	35,354	.....	328,489
23 Pennsylvania...	185,513	3,074	171,176	......	11,263	.....	367,952
24 Rhode Island...	6,779	2,403	3,646	......	730	.....	11,155
25 South Carolina..	Electors	chosen	by the	Legislat	ure.	......	......
26 Tennessee......	64,705	6,286	58,419	......	......	.....	126,124
27 Texas........	4,500	......	10,668	6,150	......	.....	15,177
28 Vermont..... ..	23,122	‡9,285	10,948	......	13,837	.....	47,907
29 Virginia.... ...	45,124	......	46,586	1,453	9	.....	91,719
30 Wisconsin......	13,747	......	15,001	†1,254	10,418	.....	39,166
Total.........	1,360,101	50,500	1,220,544	23,648	291,263	.....	2,871,908
Taylor's Plurality........		*139,557					

* Plurality over Cass.   † Plurality over Taylor.   ‡ Plurality over Van Buren.

ELECTORAL VOTE OF 1848.

STATES.	PRESI-DENT. Zachary Taylor, of La.	Lewis Cass, of Mich.	VICE-PRES'T. Millard Fillmore of N.Y.	W. O. Butler, of Ky.	Total.	STATES.	PRESI-DENT. Zachary Taylor, of La.	Lewis Cass, of Mich.	VICE-PRES'T. Millard Fillmore of N.Y.	W. O. Butler, of Ky.	Total.
1 Alabama.......	....	9	....	9	9	17 Missouri........	....	7	....	7	7
2 Arkansas....	...	3	....	3	3	18 N. Hampshire..	....	6	....	6	6
3 Connecticut. ..	6	...	6	...	6	19 New Jersey ..	7	....	7	...	7
4 Delaware	3	...	3	....	3	20 New York.	36	....	36	...	36
5 Florida........	3	...	3	...	3	21 North Carolina.	11	....	11	..	11
6 Georgia	10	...	10	...	10	22 Ohio........	...	23	...	23	23
7 Illinois........	....	9	....	9	9	23 Pennsylvania ..	26	....	26	...	26
8 Indiana........	....	12	....	12	12	24 Rhode Island ..	4	....	4	...	4
9 Iowa...........	....	4	....	4	4	25 South Carolina.	...	9	...	9	9
10 Kentucky	12	...	12	...	12	26 Tennessee......	13	....	13	...	13
11 Louisiana......	6	...	6	...	6	27 Texas..........	...	4	...	4	4
12 Maine	...	9	...	9	9	28 Vermont... ...	6	...	6	...	6
13 Maryland.. ...	8	...	8	...	8	29 Virginia........	...	17	..	17	17
14 Massachusetts.	12	...	12	...	12	30 Wisconsin	...	4	...	4	4
15 Michigan.	....	5	....	5	5						
16 Mississippi....	....	6	....	6	6	Total........	163	127	163	127	290

POPULAR VOTE OF 1852.

STATES.	Franklin Pierce, Democratic.		Winfield Scott, Whig.		John P. Hale, Free Democratic.		Total Vote.
	Vote.	Maj.	Vote.	Maj.	Vote.	Maj.	
1 Alabama	26,881	11,843	15,038				41,919
2 Arkansas	12,173	4,769	7,404				19,577
3 California	40,626	5,119	35,407		100		76,133
4 Connecticut	33,249	*2,892	30,357		3,160		66,766
5 Delaware	6,318	*25	6,293		62		12,673
6 Florida	4,318	1,443	2,875				7,193
7 Georgia	34,705	18,045	16,660				51,365
8 Illinois	80,597	5,697	64,934		9,966		155,497
9 Indiana	95,340	7,510	80,901		6,929		183,170
10 Iowa	17,763	303	15,856		1,604		35,223
11 Kentucky	53,806		57,068	2,997	265		111,139
12 Louisiana	18,647	1,392	17,255				35,902
13 Maine	41,609	1,036	32,543		8,030		82,182
14 Maryland	40,020	4,900	35,066		54		75,140
15 Massachusetts	44,560		52,683	18,114	28,023		125,275
16 Michigan	41,842	746	33,859		7,237		82,938
17 Mississippi	26,876	9,328	17,548				44,424
18 Missouri	38,353	8,369	29,984				68,337
19 New Hampshire	29,997	7,155	16,147		6,695		52,839
20 New Jersey	44,305	5,399	38,556		350		83,211
21 New York	262,083	1,872	234,882		25,329		522,294
22 North Carolina	39,744	627	39,058		59		78,861
23 Ohio	169,220	*16,694	152,526		31,682		353,428
24 Pennsylvania	198,568	10,809	179,174		8,525		386,267
25 Rhode Island	8,735	465	7,626		644		17,005
26 South Carolina	Electors	chosen	by the	Legislat	ure. .		
27 Tennessee	57,018		58,898	1,880			115,916
28 Texas	13,552	8,557	4,995				18,547
29 Vermont	13,044		22,173	508	8,621		43,838
30 Virginia	73,858	15,286	58,572				132,430
31 Wisconsin	33,658	2,604	22,240		8,814		64,712
Total	1,601,474	133,334	1,386,578	5,385	156,149		3,144,201
Pierce's Majority		58,747					

* Plurality over Scott.   † Plurality over Pierce.

ELECTORAL VOTE OF 1852.

STATES.	PRESIDENT. Franklin Pierce of N. H.	PRESIDENT. Winfield Scott of N. J.	VICE-PRESIDENT. W. R. King, of Ala.	VICE-PRESIDENT. W. A. Graham, of N. C.	Total.	STATES.	PRESIDENT. Franklin Pierce of N. H.	PRESIDENT. Winfield Scott of N. J.	VICE-PRESIDENT. W. R. King, of Ala.	VICE-PRESIDENT. W. A. Graham, of N. C.	Total.
1 Alabama	9		9		9	17 Mississippi	7		7		7
2 Arkansas	4		4		4	18 Missouri	9		9		9
3 California	4		4		4	19 N. Hampshire	5		5		5
4 Connecticut	6		6		6	20 New Jersey	7		7		7
5 Delaware	3		3		3	21 New York	35		35		35
6 Florida	3		3		3	22 North Carolina	10		10		10
7 Georgia	10		10		10	23 Ohio	23		23		23
8 Illinois	11		11		11	24 Pennsylvania	27		27		27
9 Indiana	13		13		13	25 Rhode Island	4		4		4
10 Iowa	4		4		4	26 South Carolina	8		8		8
11 Kentucky		12		12	12	27 Tennessee		12		12	12
12 Louisiana	6		6		6	28 Texas	4		4		4
13 Maine	8		8		8	29 Vermont		5		5	5
14 Maryland	8		8		8	30 Virginia	15		15		15
15 Massachusetts		13		13	13	31 Wisconsin	5		5		5
16 Michigan	6		6		6	Total	254	42	254	42	296

POPULAR VOTE OF 1856.

STATES.	James Buchanan, Democratic. Vote.	Maj.	John C. Fremont, Republican. Vote.	Maj.	M. Fillmore, American. Vote.	Maj.	Total Vote.
1 Alabama.....	46,739	18,187	....		28,552	.....	75,291
2 Arkansas	21,910	11,123	....	......	10,787	.....	32,697
3 California.....	53,365	*17,200	20,691	......	36,165	.....	110,221
4 Connecticut...	34,995		42,715	5,105	2,615	.....	80,325
5 Delaware	8,004	1,521	308	......	6,175		14,487
6 Florida.....	6,353	1,525			4,833	.....	11,191
7 Georgia.......	56,578	14,350	....		42,228	.....	98,900
8 Illinois........	105,348	19,159	96,189	......	37,444	.....	238,981
9 Indiana.......	118,670	1,900	94,375	......	22,386	.....	235,431
10 Iowa.........	36,170	....	43,954	‡7,784	9,180	.....	89,304
11 Kentucky.....	74,642	6,912	314	......	67,416	.....	142,372
12 Louisiana....	22,164	1,453	......	......	20,709	.....	42,873
13 Maine........	39,060	....	67,379	24,974	8,325	.....	109,784
14 Maryland.....	39,115	....	281	......	47,460	8,064	86,856
15 Massachusetts	39,240	....	108,190	49.324	19,626	.....	167,056
16 Michigan	52,136	....	71,762	17,9•6	1,660	.....	125,558
17 Mississippi ...	35,446	11,251			24,195	.....	59,641
18 Missouri......	58,164	9,640	....		48,524	.....	106,688
19 N. Hampshire	32,789		38,345	5,134	422	.....	71,556
20 New Jersey...	46,943	*18,605	28,338	......	24,115	.....	99,396
21 New York ..	195,878		276,007	‡80,129	124,604	.....	596,489
22 N. Carolina...	48,246	11,360	......		36,886	.....	85,132
23 Ohio...	170,874	.....	187,497	‡16,623	28,126	.....	396,497
24 Pennsylvania.	230,710	1,025	147,510	......	82,175	.....	460,395
25 Rhode Island.	6,680	.....	11,467	3,112	1,675	.....	19,822
26 S. Carolina...	Electors	chosen	by the	Legis-	lature.	....	....
27 Tennessee	73,638	7,460	....		66,178	.....	139,816
28 Texas........	31,169	15,530	....		15,639	.....	46,808
29 Vermont......	10,569	....	39,561	23,447	545	.....	50,675
30 Virginia......	89,706	29,105	291	.	60,310	.....	150,307
31 Wisconsin	52,843	....	66,090	12,668	579	.....	119,512
Total.......	1,838,169	142,353	1,341,264	146,730	874,534	8,064	4,053,967
Buchanan's Plurality....	†496,905						

* Plurality over Fillmore.   † Plurality over Fremont.   ‡ Plurality over Buchanan.

ELECTORAL VOTE OF 1856.

STATES.	PRES. Buchanan.	Fremont.	Fillmore.	V.-PRES. Breckinridge.	Dayton.	Donelson.	Total.	STATES.	PRES. Buchanan.	Fremont.	Fillmore.	V.-PRES. Breckinridge.	Dayton.	Donelson.	Total.
1 Alabama.....	9	..	..	9	..	..	9	17 Mississippi ..	7	..	..	7	..	..	7
2 Arkansas ...	4	...	..	4	...	..	4	18 Missouri.....	9	...	..	9	...	..	9
3 California ...	4	...	..	4	...	..	4	19 N. Hampshire		5	..		5	..	5
4 Connecticut..	...	6	..	...	6	..	6	20 New Jersey..	7	...	..	7	...	..	7
5 Delaware	3	..	..	3	...	..	3	21 New York...	...	35	..	...	35	..	35
6 Florida......	3	..	..	3	...	..	3	22 N. Carolina..	10	...	..	10	...	..	10
7 Georgia......	10	...	..	10	...	..	10	23 Ohio........	...	23	..	...	23	..	23
8 Illinois	11	...	..	11	...	..	11	24 Pennsylvania	27	...	..	27	...	..	27
9 Indiana......	13	...	..	13	...	..	13	25 Rhode Island	...	4	..	...	4	..	4
10 Iowa.........	...	4	..	...	4	..	4	26 S. Carolina..	8	...	..	8	...	..	8
11 Kentucky.....	12	...	..	12	...	..	12	27 Tennessee....	12	...	..	12	...	..	12
12 Louisiana....	6	...	..	6	...	..	6	28 Texas........	4	...	..	4	...	..	4
13 Maine........	...	8	..	...	8	..	8	29 Vermont... ..	...	5	..	...	5	..	5
14 Maryland.....	...	...	8	...	...	8	8	30 Virginia......	15	...	..	15	...	..	15
15 Massachus'ts.	...	13	..	...	13	..	13	31 Wisconsin	...	5	..	...	5	..	5
16 Michigan	...	6	..	...	6	..	6	Total ...	174	114	8	174	114	8	296

POPULAR VOTE OF 1860.

States.	A. Lincoln, Republican.		S. A. Douglas, Ind. Dem.		J.C. Breckinridge, Democratic.		John Bell, Const. Union.		Total Vote.
	Vote.	Maj.	Vote.	Maj	Vote.	Maj.	Vote.	Maj.	
1 Alabama.	....	....	13,651	....	48,831	7,355	27,825	......	90,307
2 Arkansas.			5,227	....	28,732	3,411	20,094	......	54,053
3 California	39,173	*657	38,516	....	34,334		6,817	......	118,840
4 Conn'icut	43,692	10,238	15,522	....	14,641	.....	3,291	......	77,146
5 Delaware.	3,815	....	1,023	....	7,347	†3,488	3,864	......	16,049
6 Florida...			367	....	8,543	2,739	5,437	......	14,347
7 Georgia..			11,590	....	51,889	†9,003	42,886	......	106,365
8 Illinois...	172,161	5,629	160,215	....	2,404	......	3,913	......	338,608
9 Indiana..	139,033	5,923	115,509	....	12,295	......	5,306	......	272,143
10 Iowa.....	70,409	12,487	55,111	....	1,048	......	1,763	......	128,331
11 Kentucky	1,364	....	25,651	....	53,143	......	66,058	‡12,915	146,216
12 Louisiana			7,625	....	22,681	†2,477	20,204		50,510
13 Maine....	62,811	27,704	26,693	....	6,368	......	2,046	......	97,918
14 Maryland	2,294	....	5,066	....	42,482	†722	41,760	......	92,502
15 Mass....	106,533	43,801	34,372	....	5,939	....	22,331	......	169,175
16 Michigan,	88,480	22,213	65,057	....	805	......	405	......	154,747
17 Minn'sota	22,069	9,339	11,920	....	748	......	62	......	34,799
18 Mississ'pi			3,283	....	40,797	12,474	25,040	......	69,120
19 Missouri..	17,028	....	58,801	†429	31,317	.....	58,372	......	165,518
20 N. Hamp.	37,519	9,085	25,881	....	2,112	.....	441	......	65,953
21 N. Jersey.	58,324	....	62,801	4,477	....				121,125
22 New York	362,646	50,136	312,510	....					675,156
23 N. Carol'a			2,701	....	48,330	648	44,990	......	96,030
24 Ohio.....	231,610	20,779	187,232	....	11,405	.....	12,194	......	442,441
25 Oregon...	5,270	*1,319	3,951	....	3,006	.....	183	......	12,410
26 Penn.....	268,030	59,618	16,765	....	178,871	.....	12,776	......	476,442
27 R. Island.	12,244	4,537	7,707	....					19,951
28 S. Carol'a	Electors	chosen	by the	Le-	gisla-	ture.	......	......	....
29 Tennesse'e			11,350	....	64,709	.....	60,274	‡4,565	145,333
30 Texas.....					47,548	32,110	15,438	......	62,986
31 Vermont.	33,808	24,772	6,849	....	218	......	1,969	......	42,844
32 Virginia..	1,929	....	16,290	....	74,323	......	74,681	‡358	167,223
33 Wiscon'n	86,110	20,040	65,021	....	888	......	161	......	152,180
Total...	1,866,352	326,391	1,375,157	4,477	845,763	58,737	589,581	......	4,676,853
Lincoln's Plurality *401,195									

* Plurality over Douglas.   † Plurality over Bell.   ‡ Plurality over Breckinridge.

[HISTORY OF CONVENTIONS—Continued from page 131.]

The candidates accepted the nomination, and received the electoral vote of Vermont only.

There was no open opposition in the Democratic Party to the nomination of Gen. Jackson for a second term in 1832, but the party was not so well satisfied with Mr. Calhoun, the Vice-President, so a convention was called to meet at Baltimore, in May, 1832, to nominate a candidate for the second office.

Mr. Van Buren received more than two thirds of all the votes cast, and was declared nominated.

The National Republicans met in convention at Baltimore, December 12th, 1831. Seventeen States and the District of Columbia were represented by 157 delegates, who cast a unanimous vote for Henry Clay, of Kentucky, for President.

In May, 1835, a Democratic National Convention, representing twenty-one States, assembled at Baltimore. A rule was adopted, that two thirds of the whole number of votes should be necessary to make a nomination, or to decide any question connected therewith. On the first ballot for President, Mr. Van Buren was nominated unanimously, receiving 265 votes.

In 1835, Gen. William H. Harrison, of Ohio, was nominated for President, with

ELECTORAL VOTE OF 1860.

STATES.	PRESIDENT.				VICE-PRESIDENT.				Total.
	A. Lincoln, of Ill.	J.C.Breckinridge, of Ky.	John Bell, of Tenn.	S. A. Douglas, of Ill.	H. Hamlin, of Maine.	Joseph Lane, of Oregon.	Edward Everett, of Mass.	H. V. Johnson, of Ga.	
1 Alabama.......... ...		9				9			9
2 Arkansas....		4				4			4
3 California...........	4				4				4
4 Connecticut.........	6				6				6
5 Delaware...........		3				3			3
6 Florida		3				3			3
7 Georgia.............		10				10			10
8 Illinois.............	11				11				11
9 Indiana.............	13				13				13
10 Iowa...............	4				4				4
11 Kentucky..........			12				12		12
12 Louisiana..........		6				6			6
13 Maine.............	8				8				8
14 Maryland..........		8				8			8
15 Massachusetts	13				13				13
16 Michigan...........	6				6				6
17 Minnesota..........	4				4				4
18 Mississippi.........		7				7			7
19 Missouri...........				9				9	9
20 New Hampshire.....	5				5				5
21 New Jersey........	4			3	4			3	7
22 New York..........	35				35				35
23 North Carolina......		10				10			10
24 Ohio...............	23				23				23
25 Oregon..		3				3			3
26 Pennsylvania.......	27				27				27
27 Rhode Island.......	4				4				4
28 South Carolina.....		8				8			8
29 Tennessee..........			12				12		12
30 Texas..............		4				4			4
31 Vermont...........	5				5				5
32 Virginia...........			15				15		15
33 Wisconsin	5				5				5
Total	180	72	39	12	180	72	39	12	303

Francis Granger for Vice-President, by a Whig State Convention at Harrisburg. Pa. Gen. Harrison also received nominations in Maryland, New York, Ohio, and other States.

A Whig National Convention, representing twenty-one States, met at Harrisburg, Pa., December 4th, 1839. James Barbour, of Virginia, presided, and the result of the first ballot was the nomination of Gen. William H. Harrison, of Ohio, who received 148 votes, to 90 for Henry Clay, and 16 for Gen. Winfield Scott. John Tyler, of Virginia, was unanimously nominated as the Whig candidate for Vice-President.

A Convention of Abolitionists was held at Warsaw, N. Y., on the 13th of November, 1839, and nominated for President James G. Birney, of New York, and for Vice-President, Francis J. Lemoyne, of Pennsylvania. These gentlemen declined the nomination. Nevertheless, they received a total of 7609 votes, in various Free States.

A Democratic National Convention met at Baltimore, May 5th, 1840, to nominate candidates for President and Vice-President. The Convention then unanimously nominated Mr. Van Buren for re-election as President.

A Whig National Convention assembled in Baltimore on the 1st of May, 1844, in

POPULAR VOTE OF 1864.

STATES.	Abraham Lincoln, Republican.		Geo. B. McClellan, Democratic		Total Vote.
	Vote.	Majority.	Vote.	Majority.	
1 Alabama*					
2 Arkansas*					
3 California	62,134	18,293	43,841		105,975
4 Connecticut	44,691	2,406	42,285		86,976
5 Delaware	8,155		8,767	612	16,922
6 Florida*					
7 Georgia*					
8 Illinois	189,496	30,766	158,730		348,226
9 Indiana	150,422	20,189	130,233		280,655
10 Iowa	89,075	39,479	49,596		138,671
11 Kansas	16,441	12,750	3,691		20,132
12 Kentucky	27,786		64,301	36,515	92,087
13 Louisiana*					
14 Maine	61,803	17,592	44,211		106,014
15 Maryland	40,153	7,414	32,739		72,892
16 Massachusetts	126,742	77,997	48,745		175,487
17 Michigan	91,521	16,917	74,604		166,125
18 Minnesota	25,060	7,685	17,375		42,435
19 Mississippi*					
20 Missouri	72,750	41,072	31,678		104,428
21 Nevada	9,826	3,232	6,594		16,420
22 New Hampshire	36,400	3,529	32,871		69,271
23 New Jersey	60,723		68,024	7,301	128,747
24 New York	368,735	6,749	361,986		730,721
25 North Carolina*					
26 Ohio	265,154	59,586	205,568		470,722
27 Oregon	9,888	1,431	8,457		18,345
28 Pennsylvania	296,391	20,075	276,316		572,707
29 Rhode Island	13,692	5,222	8,470		22,162
30 South Carolina*					
31 Tennessee*					
32 Texas*					
33 Vermont	42,419	29,098	13,321		55,740
34 Virginia*					
35 West Virginia	23,152	12,714	10,438		33,590
36 Wisconsin	83,458	17,574	65,884		149,342
Total	2,216,067	451,770	1,808,725	44,428	4,024,792
Lincoln's Majority.		407,342			

The eleven States marked thus (*) did not vote.

which every State in the Union was represented, and Mr. Clay was nominated for President by acclamation.

A Democratic National Convention assembled at Baltimore on the 27th May, 1844, adopted the two-thirds rule, and, after a stormy session of three days, James K. Polk, of Tennessee, was nominated for President, and Silas Wright, of New York, for Vice-President. Mr. Wright declined the nomination, and George M. Dallas, of Pennsylvania, was selected.

The Liberty Party National Convention met at Buffalo on the 30th of August, 1843. James G. Birney, of Michigan, was unanimously nominated for President, with Thomas Morris, of Ohio, for Vice-President

A Whig National Convention met at Philadelphia on the 7th of June, 1848. After a rather stormy session of three days, Gen. Zachary Taylor, of Louisiana, was nominated for President, and Millard Fillmore, of New York, for Vice-President.

The Democratic National Convention for 1848 assembled in Baltimore on the 22d of May. The two-thirds rule was adopted, and Gen. Lewis Cass was nominated for President on the fourth ballot.

ELECTORAL VOTE OF 1864.

STATES.	A. Lincoln, of Ill.	G. B. McClellan, of N. J.	Vacancies	A. Johnson, of Tenn.	G. H. Pendleton, of O.	Vacancies	Total
1 Alabama			8			8	8
2 Arkansas			5			5	5
3 California	5			5			5
4 Connecticut	6			6			6
5 Delaware		3			3		3
6 Florida			3			3	3
7 Georgia			9			9	9
8 Illinois	16			16			16
9 Indiana	13			13			13
10 Iowa	8			8			8
11 Kansas	3			3			3
12 Kentucky		11			11		11
13 Louisiana			7			7	7
14 Maine	7			7			7
15 Maryland	7			7			7
16 Massachusetts	12			12			12
17 Michigan	8			8			8
18 Minnesota	4			4			4
19 Mississippi			7			7	7
20 Missouri	11			11			11
21 Nevada	2		1	2		1	3
22 New Hampshire	5			5			5
23 New Jersey		7			7		7
24 New York	33			33			33
25 North Carolina			9			9	9
26 Ohio	21			21			21
27 Oregon	3			3			3
28 Pennsylvania	26			26			26
29 Rhode Island	4			4			4
30 South Carolina			6			6	6
31 Tennessee			10			10	10
32 Texas			6			6	6
33 Vermont	5			5			5
34 Virginia			10			10	10
35 West Virginia	5			5			5
36 Wisconsin	8			8			8
Total	212	21	81	212	21	81	314

On the 9th of August, 1845, a Free Democratic or Free Soil Convention was held at Buffalo, which was attended by delegates from seventeen States. Charles Francis Adams, of Massachusetts, presided, and the Convention nominated Messrs. Van Buren and Adams as candidates for President and Vice-President.

The Whig National Convention of 1852 assembled at Baltimore on the 16th of June, and after an exciting session of six days, nominated Gen. Winfield Scott as President, on the fifty-third ballot.

The Democratic Convention of 1852 assembled at Baltimore on the 1st of June, and the two-thirds rule was adopted. Gen. Franklin Pierce, of New Hampshire, was nominated for President, on the forty-ninth ballot.

The Free Soil Democracy held a National Convention at Pittsburg, on the 11th August, 1852, Henry Wilson, of Mass., presiding. All the Free States were represented, with Delaware, Virginia, Kentucky, and Maryland. John P. Hale, of N. H., was nominated for President, with Geo. W. Julian, of Indiana, for Vice-President.

The Republican National Convention of 1856 met at Philadelphia on the 17th of June. Col. John C. Fremont was unanimously nominated, having received 359 votes on the first ballot against 196 for John McLean.

On February 22d, 1856, the American National Nominating Convention organized at Philadelphia, with 227 delegates in attendance. Millard Fillmore was declared to be the nominee, with Andrew Jackson Donelson, of Tenn., for Vice-President. The Democratic National Convention of 1856 met at Cincinnati on the 2d of June, and nominated James Buchanan on the seventeenth ballot. John C. Breckinridge, of Ky., was unanimously nominated for Vice-President.

A Republican National Convention assembled at Chicago on May 16th, 1860, delegates being in attendance from all the Free States, as also from Delaware, Maryland, Virginia, Kentucky, and Missouri. Abraham Lincoln was nominated for the Presidency on the third ballot, receiving 354 out of 466 votes; his principal competitors being William H. Seward, Salmon P. Chase, and Edward Bates.

POPULAR VOTE OF 1868.

STATES.	Ulysses S. Grant, Republican. Vote.	Majority.	Horatio Seymour, Democratic. Vote.	Majority.	Total Vote.
1 Alabama.........	76 366	4,278	72,088	....	148,454
2 Arkansas	22,112	3,034	19,078	....	41,190
3 California.......	54,583	506	54,077	....	108,660
4 Connecticut......	50,995	3,043	47,952	....	98,947
5 Delaware	7,623	....	10,980	3,357	18,603
6 Florida	Electors	chosen by	the Legis-	lature.	....
7 Georgia..........	57,134	....	102,722	45,588	159,856
8 Illinois..........	250,303	51,160	199,143	....	449,446
9 Indiana	176,548	9,568	166,980	....	343,528
10 Iowa.............	120,399	46,359	74,040	....	194,439
11 Kansas	31,048	17,058	13,990	....	45,038
12 Kentucky	39,566	....	115,890	76,324	155,456
13 Louisiana........	33,263	....	80,225	46,962	113,488
14 Maine...	70,493	28,033	42,460	....	112,953
15 Maryland	30,438	....	62,357	31,919	92,795
16 Massachusetts ...	136,477	77,069	59,408	....	195,885
17 Michigan........	128,550	31,481	97,069	....	225,619
18 Minnesota........	43,545	15,470	28,075	....	71,620
19 Mississippi*....	....	....	....	....	.... ..
20 Missouri	80,860	21,232	65,628	....	152,488
21 Nebraska	9,729	4,290	5,439	....	15,168
22 Nevada..........	6,480	1,262	5,218	....	11,698
23 New Hampshire..	38,191	6,967	31,224	....	69,415
24 New Jersey......	80,131	....	83,001	2,870	163,132
25 New York.......	419,883	....	429,883	10,000	849,766
26 North Carolina...	96,769	12,168	84,601	....	181,370
27 Ohio.............	280,223	41,617	238,606	....	518,829
28 Oregon...	10,961	....	11,125	164	22,086
29 Pennsylvania ...	342,280	28,898	313,382	....	655,662
30 Rhode Island	12,993	6,445	6,548	....	19,541
31 South Carolina...	62,301	17,064	45,237	....	107,538
32 Tennessee	56,628	30,499	26,129	....	82,757
33 Texas*..........	....	....	....	....	....
34 Vermont........	44,167	32,122	12,045	....	56,212
35 Virginia*	....	....	....	....	....
36 West Virginia....	29,175	8,869	20,306	....	49,481
37 Wisconsin	108,857	24,150	84,707	....	193,564
Total	3,015,071	522,642	2,709,613	217,184	5,724,684
Grant's Majority.............		305,458			

A Democratic National Convention assembled at Charleston, S. C., on the 23d of April, 1860, with full delegations present from every State. Dissensions arising, chiefly out of the question of slavery in the Territories, too great to be reconciled, the delegations from seven Southern States withdrew,and the convention adjourned, after fifty-seven ineffectual ballots for a candidate, to meet at Baltimore, June 18th. Here Stephen A. Douglas was nominated for President, and B. Fitzpatrick for Vice-President. The latter declined, and H. V. Johnson was substituted by the National Committee. The Convention of Seceders nominated John C. Breckinridge and Joseph Lane.

A "Constitutional Union" Convention from twenty States met at Baltimore, May 9th, 1860, and nominated John Bell and Edward Everett for the Presidency and Vice-Presidency.

1864.

The REPUBLICAN National Convention met at Baltimore, June 7th. The renomination, for President, of Abraham Lincoln, of Illinois, was made unanimous, he having received the votes of all the States except Missouri, cast for Gen. Grant.

ELECTORAL VOTE OF 1868.

STATES.	U. S. Grant, of Ill.	H. Seymour, of N. Y.	Vacancies.	S. Colfax, of Ind.	F. P. Blair, of Mo.	Vacancies.	Total.
1 Alabama......	8	...	...	8	...	...	8
2 Arkansas......	5	...	...	5	...	...	5
3 California.....	5	...	...	5	...	...	5
4 Connecticut....	6	...	...	6	...	...	6
5 Delaware......	...	3	...	...	3	...	3
6 Florida	3	...	...	3	...	...	3
7 Georgia.......	...	9	...	...	9	...	9
8 Illinois........	16	...	...	16	...	...	16
9 Indiana	13	...	...	13	...	...	13
10 Iowa	8	...	...	8	...	...	8
11 Kansas........	3	...	...	3	...	...	3
12 Kentucky.....	...	11	...	...	11	...	11
13 Louisiana......	...	7	...	...	7	...	7
14 Maine........	7	...	...	7	...	...	7
15 Maryland......	...	7	...	...	7	...	7
16 Massachusetts.	12	...	...	12	...	...	12
17 Michigan.....	8	...	...	8	...	...	8
18 Minnesota....	4	...	...	4	...	...	4
19 Mississippi.....	...	...	7	...	...	7	7

STATES.	U. S. Grant, of Ill.	H. Seymour, of N. Y.	Vacancies.	S. Colfax, of Ind.	F. P. Blair, of Mo.	Vacancies.	Total.
20 Missouri........	11	...	...	11	...	...	...
21 Nebraska......	3	...	...	3	...	...	3
22 Nevada.........	3	...	...	3	...	...	3
23 New Hampshire.	5	...	...	5	...	...	5
24 New Jersey.....	...	7	...	...	7	...	7
25 New York......	...	33	...	...	33	...	33
26 North Carolina.	9	...	...	9	...	...	9
27 Ohio............	21	...	...	21	...	...	21
28 Oregon.........	...	3	...	...	3	...	3
29 Pennsylvania...	26	...	...	26	...	...	26
30 Rhode Island...	4	...	...	4	...	...	4
31 South Carolina..	6	...	...	6	...	...	6
32 Tennessee......	10	...	...	10	...	...	10
33 Texas..........	...	...	6	...	...	6	6
34 Vermont	5	...	...	5	...	...	5
35 Virginia........	...	...	10	...	...	10	10
36 West Virginia...	5	...	...	5	...	...	5
37 Wisconsin.......	8	...	...	8	...	...	8
Total	214	80	23	214	80	23	317

For Vice-President, Andrew Johnson, of Tennessee, was nominated on the second ballot, his principal competitors being D. S. Dickinson and H. Hamlin.

The DEMOCRATIC National Convention met at Chicago, Ill., August 29th. Nominations—President, George B. McClellan, of New Jersey ; Vice-President, George H. Pendleton, of Ohio.

1868.

The REPUBLICAN National Convention met at Chicago, Ill., May 20th. Nominations—President, Ulysses S. Grant, of Illinois ; Vice-President, Schuyler Colfax, of Indiana.

The DEMOCRATIC National Convention met at New York, July 4th. Nominations —President, Horatio Seymour, of New York ; Vice-President, Francis P. Blair, Jr., of Missouri.

1872.

The LIBERAL REPUBLICAN Convention met at Cincinnati, Ohio, May 1st. Nominations—President, Horace Greeley, of New York, on the sixth ballot, by 482 votes, against 187 for David Davis, of Illinois ; Vice-President, B. Gratz Brown, of Missouri, on the second ballot.

The REPUBLICAN National Convention met at Philadelphia, Pa., June 5th. Nominations—President, Ulysses S. Grant, on the first ballot, unanimously ; Vice-President, Henry Wilson, of Massachusetts, receiving 364½ votes against 321½ for Schuyler Colfax.

The DEMOCRATIC National Convention met at Baltimore, Md., July 9th. Nominations—President, Horace Greeley, on the first ballot, receiving 686 votes to 33 scattering ; Vice-President, B. Gratz Brown, who received 713 votes.

The DEMOCRATIC (" Straight Out ") Convention met at Louisville, Ky., September 3d. Nominations—President, Charles O'Conor, of New York ; Vice-President, John Q. Adams, of Massachusetts. The nominations were declined.

POPULAR VOTE OF 1872.

STATES.	U. S. Grant, Republican. Vote.	Maj.	II. Greeley, Dem. & Lib. Rep. Vote.	Maj.	O'Conor, Dem. Vote.	Black, Temperance. Vote.	Total Vote.
1 Alabama....	90,272	10,828	79,444				169,716
2 Arkansas....	41,373	3,446	37,927				79,300
3 California...	54,020	12,234	40,718		1,068		95,806
4 Connecticut.	50,638	4,348	45,880		204	206	96,928
5 Delaware....	11,115	422	10,206		487		21,808
6 Florida.....	17,763	2,336	15,427				33,190
7 Georgia.....	62,550		76,356	9,806	4,000		142,906
8 Illinois......	241,944	53,948	184,938		3,058		429,940
9 Indiana.....	186,147	21,098	168,632		1,417		351,196
10 Iowa........	131,566	58,149	71,196		2,221		204,983
11 Kansas......	67,048	33,482	32,970		596		100,614
12 Kentucky...	88,766		99,995	8,855	2,374		191,135
13 Louisiana...	71,663	14,634	57,029				128,692
14 Maine	61,422	32,335	29,087				90,509
15 Maryland ...	66,760		67,687	908	19		134,466
16 Massachu'ts.	133,472	74,212	59,260				192,732
17 Michigan....	138,455	55,968	78,355		2,861	1,271	220,942
18 Minnesota...	55,117	20,694	34,423				89,540
19 Mississippi..	82,175	34,887	47,288				129,463
20 Missouri	119,196		151,434	29,809	2,429		273,059
21 Nebraska....	18,329	10,517	7,612				26,141
22 Nevada.....	8,413	2,177	6,236				14,649
23 N.Hampsh'e	37,168	5,444	31,424		100	200	68,892
24 New Jersey.	91,656	14,570	76,456		630		168,742
25 New York ..	440,736	51,800	387,281		1,454	201	829,672
26 N. Carolina.	94,769	24,675	70,094				164,863
27 Ohio	281,852	34,268	244,321		1,163	2,100	529,436
28 Oregon......	11,819	3,517	7,730		572		20,121
29 Pennsylv'ia.	349,589	135,918	212,041			1,630	563,260
30 Rhode Isl'd..	13,665	8,336	5,329				18,994
31 S. Carolina..	72,290	49,400	22,703		187		95,180
32 Tennessee..	85,655		94,391	8,736			180,046
33 Texas.......	47,406		66,500	16,595	2,499		116,405
34 Vermont....	41,481	29,961	10,927		593		53,001
35 Virginia....	93,468	1,772	91,654		42		185,164
36 W. Virginia.	32,315	2,264	29,451		600		62,366
37 Wisconsin ..	104,997	17,086	86,477		834		192,308
Total......	3,597,070	825,326	2,834,079	74,709	29,408	5,608	6,466,165
Grant's Majority......	727,975						

1876.

The REPUBLICAN National Convention met at Cincinnati, Ohio, June 14th. Nominations—President, Rutherford B. Hayes, of Ohio, on the seventh ballot, receiving 384 votes, to 351 for J. G. Blaine, and 21 for B. H. Bristow; Vice-President, William A. Wheeler, of New York.

The DEMOCRATIC National Convention met at St. Louis, Mo., June 27th. Nominations—President, Samuel J. Tilden, of New York, on the second ballot, receiving 535 votes, against 85 for Hendricks, 54 for Wm. Allen, 58 for W. S. Hancock, and 6 scattering; Vice-President, Thomas A. Hendricks, of Indiana.

A "National GREENBACK Convention," composed of men opposed to specie resumption and in favor of national paper money to take the place of bank issues, met at Indianapolis, May 17th, with nineteen States represented. Peter Cooper, of New York, and Samuel F. Cary, of Ohio, were nominated for President and Vice-President.

A "PROHIBITION Reform Party" Convention met at Cleveland, May 17th, and nominated Green Clay Smith, of Kentucky, and R. T. Stewart, of Ohio.

ELECTORAL VOTE OF 1872.

No.	States	Ulysses S. Grant, of Ill.	T. A. Hendricks, of Ind.	B. Gratz Brown, of Mo.	C. J. Jenkins, of Ga.	D. Davis, of Illinois.	Not Counted.	H. Wilson, of Mass.	B. G. Brown, of Mo.	G. W. Julian, of Ind.	A. H. Coiquitt, of Ga.	J. M. Palmer, of Illinois.	T. E. Bramlette, of Ky.	W. S. Groesbeck, of Ohio.	W. B. Machen, of Ky.	N. P. Banks, of Mass.	Not Counted.	Total.
		PRESIDENT.						**VICE-PRESIDENT.**										
1	Alabama	10						10										10
2	Arkansas						6										6	6
3	California	6						6										6
4	Connecticut	6						6										6
5	Delaware	3						3										3
6	Florida	4						4										4
7	Georgia			6	2		3		5		5					1		11
8	Illinois	21						21										21
9	Indiana	15						15										15
10	Iowa	11						11										11
11	Kansas	5						5										5
12	Kentucky		8	4					8				3		1			12
13	Louisiana						8										8	8
14	Maine	7						7										7
15	Maryland		8						8									8
16	Massachusetts	13						13										13
17	Michigan	11						11										11
18	Minnesota	5						5										5
19	Mississippi	8						8										8
20	Missouri		6	8		1			6	5		3		1				15
21	Nebraska	3						3										3
22	Nevada	3						3										3
23	New Hampshire	5						5										5
24	New Jersey	9						9										9
25	New York	35						35										35
26	North Carolina	10						10										10
27	Ohio	22						22										22
28	Oregon	3						3										3
29	Pennsylvania	29						29										29
30	Rhode Island	4						4										4
31	South Carolina	7						7										7
32	Tennessee		12						12									12
33	Texas		8						8									8
34	Vermont	5						5										5
35	Virginia	11						11										11
36	West Virginia	5						5										5
37	Wisconsin	10						10										10
	Total	286	42	18	2	1	17	286	47	5	5	3	3	1	1	1	14	366

POPULAR VOTE OF 1876.

STATES.	S. J. Tilden, Democratic. Vote.	Maj.	R. B. Hayes, Republican. Vote.	Maj.	Peter Cooper, Greenback.	G. C. Smith, Temperance.	*Scattering.	Total Vote.
1 Alabama......	102,002	33,772	68,230	......	.....	....	....	170,232
2 Arkansas.....	58,071	19,113	38,669	......	289	......	.....	97,029
3 California.....	76,405	......	79,269	2,738	47	.....	19	155,800
4 Colorado.....	Electors chosen		by Legis- lature.		...			....
5 Connecticut...	61,934	1,712	59,034	.. ....	774	378	36	122,156
6 Delaware	13,381	2,629	10,752	......				24,133
7 Florida†	22,923	......	23,849	926				46,772
8 Georgia.......	130,088	79,642	50,446	......				180,534
9 Illinois........	258,601	......	278,232	1,971	17,283	141	286	554,493
10 Indiana.......	213,526	§5,515	208,011	......	9,533	. ....	.....	431,070
11 Iowa	112,099	......	171,327	59,191	9.001	36	.....	292,463
12 Kansas...... .	37,902	......	78,322	32,511	7,770	110	23	194,133
13 Kentucky.....	159,690	59,772	97,156	......	1,944	818	.....	259,608
14 Louisiana‡....	70,508	......	75,135	4,627	......	......	.....	145,643
15 Maine	49,823	......	66,300	15,814	663	......	.....	116,786
16 Maryland	91,780	19,750	71,981	......	33	10	.....	163,804
17 Massachusetts.	108,777	......	150,063	40,423	779	84	.....	259,703
18 Michigan	141,095	......	166,534	15,542	9,000	766	71	317,526
19 Minnesota....	48,799	......	72,962	21,780	2,311	72	.....	124,144
20 Mississippi....	112,173	59,568	52,605	......				164,778
21 Missouri.......	203,077	54,389	145,029	......	3,498	64	97	351,765
22 Nebraska.....	17,554	. ....	31,916	10,326	2,320	1,509	117	53,506
23 Nevada.......	9,308	......	10,383	1,075	......			19,691
24 N. Hampshire.	38,500	......	41,539	2,954	76	.....	.....	80,124
25 New Jersey...	115,962	11,690	103,517	......	712	43	.....	220,234
26 New York. ...	521,949	26,508	489,207	......	1,987	2,359	1,828	1,017,380
27 North Carolina	125,427	17,010	108,417	... ..				233,844
28 Ohio	323,182	......	330,698	2,747	3,057	1,636	76	658,649
29 Oregon........	14,149	......	15,206	547	510	......	. ...	29,863
30 Pennsylvania..	366,158	......	384,122	9,375	7,187	1,319	83	758,869
31 Rhode Island .	10,712	......	15,787	4,947	68	60	. ...	26,627
32 South Carolina	90,900	......	91,870	964	......			182,776
33 Tennessee.....	133,166	43,600	89,566	......				222,732
34 Texas.........	104,755	59,955	44,800	......	......			149,555
35 Vermont......	20,254	......	44.092	23,838				64,346
36 Virginia......	139,670	44,112	95,558	......	......			235,228
37 West Virginia.	56,455	12,384	42,696	......	1,373	......	.....	100,526
38 Wisconsin	123,927	......	130,668	5,205	1,509	27	.....	256,131
Total	4,284,757	545,672	4,033,950	248,501	81,740	9,522	2,636	8,412,605
Tilden's Majority......	156,909		....	. ....				....

* Scattering, Includes the votes of the anti-Masonic and American Alliance tickets.

† Returning Board's count, Nov. 28, 1876. A majority of 94 to 1197 was claimed for Tilden by the Democrats, and the opinion of the Supreme Court of Florida gave Tilden 94 majority.

‡ Returning Board's count. The figures on the face of the returns, when opened by the Board, are claimed to have been : Tilden, 82,326 ; Hayes, 77,023. Tilden's majority, 5303.

§ Plurality over Hayes.

ELECTORAL VOTE OF 1876.

STATES.	PRESIDENT. R. B. Hayes, of Ohio.	PRESIDENT. S. J. Tilden, of N. Y.	VICE-PRESIDENT. W. A. Wheeler, of N. Y.	VICE-PRESIDENT. T.A.Hendricks, of Ind.	Total.	STATES.	PRESIDENT. R. B. Hayes, of Ohio.	PRESIDENT. S. J. Tilden, of N. Y.	VICE-PRESIDENT. W. A. Wheeler, of N. Y.	VICE-PRESIDENT. T.A.Hendricks, of Ind.	Total.
1 Alabama		10		10	10	21 Missouri......		15		15	15
2 Arkansas		6		6	6	22 Nebraska.....	3		3		3
3 California.....	6		6		6	23 Nevada......	3		3		3
4 Colorado......	3		3		3	24 N. Hampshire.	5		5		5
5 Connecticut...		6		6	6	25 New Jersey...		9		9	9
6 Delaware		3		3	3	26 New York.....		35		35	35
7 Florida*......	4		4		4	27 N. Carolina...		10		10	10
8 Georgia.......		11		11	11	28 Ohio.........	22		22		22
9 Illinois.......	21		21		21	29 Oregon*......	3		3		3
10 Indiana		15		15	15	30 Pennsylvania.	29		29		29
11 Iowa.........	11		11		11	31 Rhode Island.	4		4		4
12 Kansas.......	5		5		5	32 S. Carolina*..	7		7		7
13 Kentucky.....		12		12	12	33 Tennessee....		12		12	12
14 Louisiana*....	8		8		8	34 Texas........		8		8	8
15 Maine........	7		7		7	35 Vermont......	5		5		5
16 Maryland.....		8		8	8	36 Virginia......		11		11	11
17 Massachusetts.	13		13		13	37 West Virginia.		5		5	5
18 Michigan	11		11		11	38 Wisconsin....	10		10		10
19 Minnesota	5		5		5						
20 Mississippi ...		8		8	8	Total	185	184	185	184	369

* From Florida two sets of certificates were received ; from Louisiana, three ; from Oregon, two ; and from South Carolina, two. They were referred to an Electoral Commission, formed under the provisions of the Compromise Bill, approved January 29th, 1877 ; the Commission decided in favor of counting the Electoral Vote, as returned in the table.

POPULATION OF STATES ACCORDING TO STATE CENSUSES SINCE 1870.

STATES.	United States Census, 1870.	State Censuses.		Increase.	Per Cent Increase.
1 Iowa............. ..	1,194,020	1875	1,350,544	156,524	13
2 Kansas............	364,399	"	528,437	164,038	45
3 Louisiana.........	726,915	"	857,039	130,124	18
4 Massachusetts.....	1,457,351	"	1,651,912	194,561	13
5 Michigan	1,184,059	1874	1,334,031	149,972	13
6 Minnesota	439,706	1875	597,407	157,701	36
7 Missouri..........	1,721,295	1876	2,085,537	364,942	21
8 Nebraska..........	122,993	"	257,747	134,754	169
9 Nevada	42,491	1875	52,540	10,049	24
10 New Jersey........	906,096	"	1,019,413	113,317	13
11 New York	4,382,759	"	4,705,208	322,449	7
12 Oregon...........	90,923	"	104,920	13,997	15
13 Rhode Island......	217,353	"	258,239	40,886	19
14 South Carolina.....	705,606	"	923,447	217,841	31
15 Wisconsin	1,054,670	"	1,236,509	181,929	17
Total	14,610,636	......	16,963,020	2,352,384	16 average of 15 States.

TOTAL POPULAR VOTE AT PRESIDENTIAL ELECTIONS.

NOTE.—See page 122 for reason why no returns of the popular vote prior to 1824 are given.

Elec. tion. Date.	Candidates Elected.	Opposing Candidates.	States Voting.	Total Vote.	Increase. Vote.	Increase. Per Cent.
1824..	John Q. Adams.....	Jackson,Crawford, Clay	24	352,062	....	....
1828..	Andrew Jackson....	John Q. Adams........	24	1,156,328	*804,266	*228.4
1832 .	" "	Clay, Floyd, Wirt......	24	1,250,799	94,471	8.2
1836..	Martin Van Buren..	Wm. H. Harrison, etc..	26	1,498,205	247,406	19.8
1840..	Wm. H. Harrison...	Van Buren, Birney.....	26	2,410,778	912,573	60.9
1844..	James K. Polk......	Clay and Birney........	26	2,698,611	287,833	11.9
1848..	Zachary Taylor.....	Cass and Van Buren....	30	2,871,906	173,297	6.4
1852..	Franklin Pierce.....	Scott and Hale........	31	3,144,201	272,293	9.5
1856..	James Buchanan....	Fremont, Fillmore......	31	4,053,967	909,766	28.9
1860..	Abraham Lincoln...	Breckinridge, Bell, Douglas	33	4,676,853	622,886	15.4
1864..	" " ...	Geo. B. McClellan......	25	4,034,792	....	....
1868..	Ulysses S. Grant....	Horatio Seymour.......	34	5,724,684	....	....
1872..	" "	Horace Greeley, etc...	37	6,466,165	†1,789,312	†38.3
1876..	Rutherford B. Hayes	Samuel J. Tilden, etc...	38	8,412,733	1,946,568	30.1

* The Electors of six States for 1824 were chosen by the Legislatures; in 1828 they were all chosen by the people, except in South Carolina. This will explain the great increase of the popular vote at the election of 1828.

† Increase from 1860 to 1872.

Percentage of the Total Vote Cast received by Candidates for President at each Election from 1804 to 1876.

[From The Statistician, San Francisco, 1877.]

CANDIDATES.	Pop.	Elec.	CANDIDATES.	Pop.	Elec.	CANDIDATES.	Pop.	Elec.
1804.			Henry Clay	42.39	17.13	1856.		
Thos. Jefferson	92.05		John Floyd.. }	2.65		Jas. Buchanan..	45.34	58.79
C. C. Pinckney.	7.95		Wm. Wirt.... }		2.45	J. C. Fremont.	33.09	39.51
1808.			1836.			Mill'd Fillmore.	21.57	2.70
James Madison......	69.71		M. Van Buren..	50.83	57.82	1860.		
C. C. Pinckney.....	26.86		W.H.Harris'n }		24.83	Abra'm Lincoln	39.91	59.41
George Clinton......	3.43		H. L. White.. }	49.17	8.85	J.C. Breckinri'e	18.08	23.76
1812.			Dan. Webster }		4.76	John Bell......	12.61	12.87
James Madison.	58.99		W.P.Mangum }		3.74	S. A. Douglas..	29.40	3.96
De Witt Clinton	41.01		1840.			1864.		
1816.			W. H. Harrison	52.89	79.59	Abra'm Lincoln	55.06	90.99
James Monroe..	84.33		M. Van Buren..	46.82	20.41	G. B. McClellan	44.94	9.01
Rufus King ...	15.67		Jas. G. Birney..	.29		1868.		
1820.			1844.			Ulysses S.Grant	52.67	72.79
James Monroe..	99.57		James K. Polk.	49.55	61.82	Horat. Seymour	47.33	27.21
John Q. Adams.	.43		Henry Clay	48.14	38.18	1872.		
1824.			Jas. G. Birney.	2.31		Ulysses S.Grant	55.63	81.97
John Q. Adams.	29.92	32.18	1848.			HoraceGreeley*	43.83	18.03
And. Jackson...	44.27	37.93	Zachary Taylor.	47.36	56.21	Chas. O'Conor..	.45	.....
W. H. Crawford	12 58	15.71	Lewis Cass.....	42.50	43.79	J. R. Black.....	.09	.....
Henry Clay	13.23	14.18	M. Van Buren..	10.14		1876.		
1828.			1852.			R. B. Hayes....	47.95	51.14
And. Jackson..	55.97	68.20	Franklin Pierce	50.93	85.81	S. J. Tilden....	50.94	49.86
John Q. Adams	44.03	31.80	Winfield Scott .	44.10	14.19	Peter Cooper...	.97	.....
1832.			John P. Hale...	4.97		G. C. Smith....	.11	.....
And. Jackson..	54.96	76.57				Scattering......	.03	.....

* For those who received electoral votes in place of Horace Greeley, deceased, see ELECTORAL VOTE of 1872, p. 144.

III.—PRESIDENTIAL ELECTIONS, BY STATES.

[Arrangement and percentages from The Statistician, San Francisco, 1877.]

ALABAMA.

NOTE.—The figures in left-hand column show the number of the election, from the first Presidential election in 1789 to the twenty-third in 1876. Names indented denote unsuccessful candidates. The table marked "Increase" shows the addition to the popular vote cast in each State since the next preceding Presidential election. In cases where the popular vote was decreased, the sign † is prefixed to the figures showing the falling off.

ELECTION.		CANDIDATES FOR PRESIDENT.	VOTE FOR CANDIDATES.				TOTAL VOTE.			
No.	Year.		Popular	Per cent Popular.	Majority.	Electoral	Popular.	Increase Popular	Per cent Increase	Electoral
9	1820	James Monroe.....				3				3
10	1824	John Q. Adams....	2,416	17.8			13,606			5
		Andrew Jackson..	9,443	69.4	5,280	5				
		Wm. H. Crawford	1,690	12.8						
		Henry Clay.. ...	67	.5						
11	1828	Andrew Jackson...	17,138	89.8	15,200	5	19,076	5,470	40.2	5
		John Q. Adams..	1,938	10.2						
12	1832	Andrew Jackson...	*			7				7
13	1836	Martin Van Buren .	19,068	54.9	3,431	7	34,705	15,629	81.9	7
		Hugh L. White...	15,637	45.1						
14	1840	Wm. H. Harrison...	28,471	45.6			62,462	27,737	80.0	7
		Martin Van Buren	33,991	54.4	5,520	7				
15	1844	James K. Polk.....	37,740	59.1	11,656	9	63,824	1,362	2.2	9
		Henry Clay.....	26,084	40.9						
16	1848	Zachary Taylor	30,482	49.3			61,845	†1,979	†3.1	9
		Lewis Cass....	31,363	50.7	881	9				
17	1852	Franklin Pierce....	26,881	64.1	11,843	9	41,919	†19,926	†32.2	9
		Winfield Scott....	15,038	35.9						
18	1856	James Buchanan...	46,739	62.1	18,187	9	75,291	33,372	79.6	9
		Millard Fillmore.	28,552	37.9						
19	1860	J.C. Breckinridge..	48,831	54.1	7,355	9	90,307	15,016	20.0	9
		John Bell	27,825	30.8						
		S. A. Douglas....	13,651	15.1						
20	1864									
21	1868	Ulysses S. Grant...	76,366	51.4	4,278	8	148,454	58,147	64.4	8
		Horatio Seymour.	72,088	48.6						
22	1872	Ulysses S. Grant....	90,272	53.2	10,828	10	169,716	21,262	14.3	10
		Horace Greeley ..	79,444	46.8						
23	1876	Rutherford B. Hayes	68,230	40.1			170,232	516	.3	10
		Samuel J. Tilden.	102,002	59.9	33,772	10				

ARKANSAS.

13	1836	Martin Van Buren..	2,400	66.0	1,162	3	3,638			3
		Wm. H. Harrison..	1,238	34.0						
14	1840	Wm. H. Harrison...	5,160	46.0			11,209	7,571	208.1	3
		Martin Van Buren	6,049	54.0	889	3				
15	1844	James K. Polk.....	9,546	63.4	4,042	3	15,050	3,841	34.3	3
		Henry Clay .	5,504	36.6						
16	1848	Zachary Taylor....	7,588	44.9			16,888	1,838	12.2	3
		Lewis Cass......	9,300	55.1	1,712	3				
17	1852	Franklin Pierce....	12,173	62.2	4,780	4	19,577	2,089	15.9	4
		Winfield Scott....	7,404	37.8						
18	1856	James Buchanan...	21,910	67.0	11,123	4	32,697	13,190	67.0	4
		Millard Fillmore..	10,787	33.0						
19	1860	J. C. Breckinridge	28,732	53.1	3,411	4	54,053	21,356	65.3	4
		John Bell	20,094	37.2						
		S. A. Douglas.....	5,227	9.7						
20	1864									
21	1868	Ulysses S. Grant....	22,112	53.7	3,084	5	41,190	†12,863	†3.8	5
		Horatio Seymour.	19,078	46.8						
22	1872	Ulysses S. Grant....	41,373	52.2	3,446	6	79,300	33,110	92.5	6
		Horace Greeley ..	37,927	47.8						
23	1876	Rutherford B. Hayes	38,660	39.9			97,020	17,729	22.3	6
		Samuel J. Tilden.	58,071	59.8	19,113	6				
		Peter Cooper.....	249	.3						

* Unanimous.   † Decrease.

CALIFORNIA.

ELEC-TION. No.	Year	CANDIDATES FOR PRESIDENT.	VOTE FOR CANDIDATES. Popular	Per cent Popular.	Majority.	Electoral	TOTAL VOTE. Popular.	Increase Popular.	Per cent Increase.	Electoral
17	1852	Franklin Pierce....	40,626	53.4	5,119	4	70,133	†20,896	†21.5	4
		Winfield Scott..	35,407	46.5						
		John P. Hale.....	100	.1						
18	1856	James Buchauan...	53,365	48.4	*17,200	4	110,221	34,088	44.8	4
		John C. Fremont.	20,691	18.8						
		Millard Fillmore..	36,165	32.8						
19	1860	Abraham Lincoln..	39,173	33.0	*657	4	118,840	8,619	7.8	4
		J. C. Breckinridge	34,334	28.9						
		John Bell.......	6,817	5.7						
		S. A. Douglas ...	38,516	32.4						
20	1864	Abraham Lincoln..	62,134	58.6	18,293	5	105,075	†12,865	†10.8	5
		Geo. B. McClellan	43,841	41.4						
21	1868	Ulysses S. Grant...	54,583	50.2	506	5	108,660	2,685	2.5	5
		Horatio Seymour.	54,077	40.8						
22	1872	Ulysses S. Grant.	54,020	56.4	12,284	6	95,806	†12,854	†11.8	6
		Horace Greeley..	40,718	42.5						
		Charles O'Conor..	1,068	1.1						
23	1876	Rutherford B. Hayes	79,269	50.9	2,738	6	155,800	59,994	62.6	6
		Samuel J. Tilden.	76,465	49.1						
		Peter Cooper.....	47							
		Scattering.....	19							

COLORADO.

No.	Year	CANDIDATE	VOTE	Electoral			TOTAL	Electoral
23	1876	Rutherford B. Hayes	Legislature chose Electors.	3				3

CONNECTICUT.

No.	Year	CANDIDATES FOR PRESIDENT.	Popular	Per cent Popular.	Majority.	Electoral	Popular.	Increase Popular.	Per cent Increase.	Electoral
1	1789	George Washington				7				7
2	1792	George Washington				9				9
3	1796	John Adams........				9				9
4	1800	John Adams.....				9				9
5	1804	C. C. Pinckney..				9				9
6	1808	C. C. Pinckney..				9				9
7	1812	De Witt Clinton..				9				9
8	1816	Rufus King... ...				9				9
9	1820	James Monroe......				9				9
10	1824	John Q. Adams....	7,587	79.3	5,609	8	9,565			8
		Wm. H.Crawford.	1,978	20.7						
11	1828	Andrew Jackson...	4,448	24.3			18,277	8,712	91.1	8
		John Q. Adams..	13,829	75.7	9,381	8				
12	1832	Andrew Jackson...	11,269	38.8			29,024	10,747	58.9	8
		Henry Clay......	17,755	61.2	6,486	8				
13	1836	Martin Van Buren.	19,234	51.0	768	8	37,700	8,676	29.9	8
		Wm. H. Harrison	18,466	49.0						
14	1840	Wm. H. Harrison..	31,601	55.4	6,131	8	57,071	19,371	51.4	8
		Martin Van Buren	25,296	44.3						
		James G. Birney.	174	.3						
15	1844	James K. Polk.....	29,841	46.2			64,616	7,545	13.2	6
		Henry Clay......	32,832	50.8	1,048	6				
		James G. Birney.	1,943	3.0						
16	1848	Zachary Taylor....	80,314	48.6	*3,268	6	62,365	†2,251	†3.5	6
		Lewis Cass... ...	27,046	43.4						
		Martin Van Buren	5,005	8.0						
17	1852	Franklin Pierce....	33,249	49.8	*2,892	6	66,766	4,401	7.1	6
		Winfield Scott...	30,357	45.5						
		John P. Hale.....	3,160	4.7						
18	1856	James Buchanan..	34,995	43.6			80,325	13,559	20.3	6
		John C. Fremont.	42,715	53.2	5,105	6				
		Millard Fillmore.	2,615	3.2						

* Plurality.   † Decrease.

CONNECTICUT—Continued.

No.	Year	Candidates for President	Popular	Per cent Popular	Majority	Electoral	Popular	Increase Popular	Per cent Increase	Electoral
				Vote for Candidates				Total Vote		
19	1860	Abraham Lincoln..	43,692	56.6	10,238	6	77,146	†3,179	†3.9	6
		J. C. Breckinridge	14,641	19.0						
		John Bell........	3,291	4.3						
		S. A. Douglas....	15,522	20.1						
20	1864	Abraham Lincoln..	44,691	51.4	2,406	6	86,976	9,830	12.7	6
		Geo. B. McClellan	42,285	48.6						
21	1868	Ulysses S. Grant...	50,995	51.5	3,043	6	98,947	11,971	13.8	6
		Horatio Seymour...	47,952	48.5						
22	1872	Ulysses S. Grant...	50,638	52.3	4,348	6	96,928	†2,019	†2.1	6
		Horace Greeley..	45,880	47.3						
		Charles O'Conor.	204	.2						
		James Black....	206	.2						
23	1876	Rutherford B. Hayes	59,034	48.3			122,156	25,228	26.1	6
		Samuel J. Tilden.	61,934	50.7	1,712	6				
		Peter Cooper.	774	.7						
		G. C. Smith.....	378	.3						
		Scattering......	86							

DELAWARE.

No.	Year	Candidates for President	Popular	Per cent Popular	Majority	Electoral	Popular	Increase Popular	Per cent Increase	Electoral
				Vote for Candidates				Total Vote		
1	1789	George Washington				3				3
2	1792	George Washington				3				3
3	1796	John Adams......				3				3
4	1800	John Adams.....				3				3
5	1804	C. C. Pinckney..				3				3
6	1808	C. C. Pinckney...				3				3
7	1812	De Witt Clinton.				4				4
8	1816	Rufus King.....				3				3
9	1820	James Monroe....				4				4
10	1824	John Q. Adams...				1				
		Wm. H. Crawford				2				3
11	1828	Andrew Jackson...	4,349	47.7			9,118			3
		John Q. Adams...	4,769	52.3	420	3				
12	1832	Andrew Jackson...	4,110	49.0			8,386	†732	†8.0	3
		Henry Clay......	4,276	51.0	166	3				
13	1836	Martin Van Buren..	4,155	46.7			8,893	507	6.0	3
		Wm. H. Harrison.	4,738	53.3	583	3				
14	1840	Wm. H. Harrison...	5,967	55.0	1,083	3	10,851	1,958	24.0	3
		Martin Van Buren	4,881	45.0						
15	1844	James K. Polk.....	5,996	48.9			12,274	1,423	13.1	3
		Henry Clay.....	6,278	51.1	282	3				
16	1848	Zachary Taylor....	6,421	51.8	443	3	12,399	125	1.0	3
		Lewis Cass. ...	5,893	47.6						
		Martin Van Buren	80							
17	1852	Franklin Pierce ...	6,318	49.8	*25	3	12,673	274	2.2	3
		Winfield Scott...	6,293	49.7						
		John P. Hale....	62	.5						
18	1856	James Buchanan...	8,001	55.3	1,511	3	11,487	1,814	14.3	3
		John C. Fremont.	308	2.1						
		Millard Fillmore.	6,175	42.6						
19	1860	Abraham Lincoln..	3,815	23.7			16,019	1,562	10.8	3
		J. C. Breckinridge	7,317	45.8	*3,463	3				
		John Bell.......	3,864	24.1						
		S. A. Douglas.....	1,023	6.4						
20	1864	Abraham Lincoln	8,155	48.2			16,962	873	5.5	3
		Geo. B. McClellan	8,767	51.8	612	3				
21	1868	Ulysses S. Grant..	7,623	41.0			18,603	1,681	9.9	3
		Horatio Seymour.	10,980	59.0	3,357	3				
22	1872	Ulysses S. Grant...	11,115	51.0	422	3	21,838	3,205	17.2	3
		Horace Greeley..	10,206	46.8						
		Charles O'Conor.	487	2.2						
23	1876	Rutherford B. Hayes	10,752	44.6			24,133	2,325	10.6	3
		Samuel J. Tilden.	13,381	55.4	2,629	3				

* Plurality.　　　　† Decrease.

FLORIDA.

No.	Year	Candidates for President.	Popular	Per cent Popular.	Majority.	Electoral.	Popular.	Increase Popular.	Per cent Increase.	Electoral.
			VOTE FOR CANDIDATES.				TOTAL VOTE.			
16	1848	Zachary Taylor ...	3,116	62.8	1,269	3	4,963			3
		Lewis Cass......	1,847	37.2						
17	1852	Franklin Pierce....	4,318	60.0	1,443	3	7,193	2,230	44.9	3
		Winfield Scott...	2,875	40.0						
18	1856	James Buchanan..	6,358	56.8	1,525	3	11,191	3,998	55.6	3
		Millard Fillmore.	4,833	43.2						
19	1860	J. C. Breckinridge	8,543	59.5	2,739	3	14,347	3,156	28.2	3
		John Bell........	5,437	37.9						
		S. A. Douglas....	367	2.6						
20	1864									
21	1868	Ulysses S. Grant..				3				3
22	1872	Ulysses S. Grant...	17,763	53.5	2,336	4	33,190	18,843	131.3	4
		Horace Greeley ..	15,427	46.5						
23	1876	Rutherford B.Hayes	23,849	51.0	926	4	46,772	13,582	40.9	4
		Samuel J. Tilden	22,923	49.0						

GEORGIA.

No.	Year	Candidates for President.	Popular	Per cent Popular.	Majority.	Electoral.	Popular.	Increase Popular.	Per cent Increase.	Electoral.
			VOTE FOR CANDIDATES.				TOTAL VOTE.			
1	1789	George Washington				5				5
2	1792	George Washington				4				4
3	1796	Thomas Jefferson				4				4
4	1800	Thomas Jefferson..				4				4
5	1804	Thomas Jefferson..				6				6
6	1808	James Madison				6				6
7	1812	James Madison				8				8
8	1816	James Monroe				8				8
9	1820	James Monroe....				8				8
10	1824	Wm. H. Crawford				9				9
11	1828	Andrew Jackson...	18,709			9				9
12	1832	Andrew Jackson...	20,750			11				11
13	1836	Martin Van Buren..	22,126	47.0			47,056			11
		Hugh L. White...	24,930	53.0	2,804	11				
14	1840	Wm. H. Harrison..	40,261	55.8	8,328	11	72,194	25,138	53.4	11
		Martin Van Buren	31,933	44.2						
15	1844	James K. Polk.....	44,177	51.2	2,071	10	86,283	11,080	19.5	10
		Henry Clay......	42,106	48.8						
16	1848	Zachary Taylor.....	47,544	51.5	2,742	10	92,346	6,063	7.0	10
		Lewis Cass......	44,802	48.5						
17	1852	Franklin Pierce....	34,705	67.6	18,045	10	51,365	†40,981	†44.3	10
		Winfield Scott...	16,660	32.4						
18	1856	James Buchanan...	56,578	57.3	14,350	10	98,806	47,441	92.4	10
		Millard Fillmore.	42,228	42.7						
19	1860	J. C. Breckinridge	51,889	48.8	*9,003	10	106,365	7,559	7.6	10
		John Bell .....,.	42,896	40.3						
		S. A. Douglas....	11,590	10.9						
20	1864									
21	1868	Ulysses S. Grant...	57,134	35.7			159,856	53,491	50.3	9
		Horatio Seymour.	102,722	64.3	45,588	9				
22	1872	Ulysses S. Grant...	62,550	43.8			142,906	†16,950	†10.6	11
		Horace Greeley ..	76,356	53.4	9,806	3				
		Charles O'Conor..	4,000	2.8						
		B. Gratz Brown..				6				
		Charles J. Jenkins				2				
23	1876	Rutherford B.Hayes	50,446	27.9			180,534	87,628	26.3	11
		Samuel J. Tilden.	130,088	72.1	79,642	11				

* Plurality.   † Decrease.

ILLINOIS.

No.	Year	CANDIDATES FOR PRESIDENT.	Popular	Per cent Popular	Majority.	Electoral	Popular.	Increase Popular.	Per cent Increase.	Electoral
			VOTE FOR CANDIDATES.				TOTAL VOTE.			
9	1820	James Monroe.....	......	......	......	3	......	......	......	3
10	1824	John Q. Adams....	1,542	32.7	......	1	4,709	......	......	3
		Andrew Jackson.	1,901	40.4	*359	2				...
		Wm. H. Crawford	219	4.7	......	..				
		Henry Clay......	1,047	22.2	......	..				
11	1828	Andrew Jackson...	6,763	81.1	5,182	3	8,344	3,635	77.2	3
		John Q. Adams..	1,581	18.9	......	..				
12	1832	Andrew Jackson...	14,147	72.3	8,718	5	19,576	11,232	134.6	5
		Henry Clay......	5,429	27.7	......	..				
13	1836	Martin Van Buren..	18,097	54.7	3,114	5	33,080	13,504	69.0	5
		Wm. H. Harrison	14,983	45.3	......	..				
14	1840	Wm. H. Harrison ..	45,537	48.9	......	..	93,162	60,082	181.6	5
		Martin Van Buren	47,476	51.0	1,790	5				...
		James G. Birney.	149	.1	......	..				
15	1844	James K. Polk.....	57,920	54.1	8,822	9	107,018	13,856	14.8	9
		Henry Clay......	45,528	42.6	......	..				
		James G. Birney..	3,570	3.3	......	..				
16	1848	Zachary Taylor...	53,047	42.4	......	..	125,121	18,103	17.0	9
		Lewis Cass......	56,300	45.0	*3,253	9				
		Martin Van Buren	15,774	12.6	......	..				
17	1852	Franklin Pierce....	80,597	51.8	5,697	11	155,497	30,376	24.3	11
		Winfield Scott....	64,934	41.8	......	..				
		John P. Hale.....	9,906	6.4	......	..				
18	1856	James Buchanan...	105,348	44.1	*9,159	11	238,981	83,484	53.7	11
		John C. Fremont.	96,189	40.2	......	..				
		Millard Fillmore.	37,444	15.7	......	..				
19	1860	Abraham Lincoln...	172,161	50.8	5,629	11	338,693	99,712	41.7	11
		J. C. Breckinridge	2,404	.7	......	..				
		John Bell........	3,913	1.2	......	..				
		S. A. Douglas....	160,215	47.3	......	..				
20	1864	Abraham Lincoln..	189,496	54.4	30,766	16	348,226	9,533	2.8	16
		Geo. B. McClellan	158,730	45.6	......	..				
21	1868	Ulysses S. Grant...	250,303	55.7	51,160	16	449,446	101,220	29.1	16
		Horatio Seymour	199,143	44.3	......	..				
22	1872	Ulysses S. Grant...	241,914	56.3	53,948	21	420,040	†19,506	†4.4	21
		Horace Greeley...	184,938	43.0	......	..				
		Charles O'Conor..	3,058	.7	......	..				
23	1876	Rutherford B. Hayes	278,232	50.2	1,071	21	554,493	134,553	23.0	21
		Samuel J. Tilden.	258,601	46.6	......	..				
		Peter Cooper.....	17,283	3.1	......	..				
		G. C. Smith......	141		......	..				
		Scattering......	286		......	..				

INDIANA.

No.	Year	CANDIDATES FOR PRESIDENT.	Popular	Per cent Popular	Majority.	Electoral	Popular.	Increase Popular.	Per cent Increase.	Electoral
8	1816	James Monroe.....	......	......	......	3	......	......	......	3
9	1820	James Monroe.....	......	......	......	3	......	......	......	3
10	1824	John Q. Adams....	3,095	19.7	......	..	15,733	......	......	5
		Andrew Jackson.	7,343	46.6	*2,028	5				
		Henry Clay	5,315	33.7	......	..				
11	1828	Andrew Jackson...	22,237	56.6	5,185	5	39,289	23,556	149.5	5
		John Q. Adams..	17,052	43.4	......	..				
12	1832	Andrew Jackson...	31,552	67.1	16,080	9	47,024	7,735	19.7	9
		Henry Clay	15,472	32.9	......	..				
13	1836	Martin Van Buren..	32,480	44.0	......	..	73,761	26,737	56.8	9
		Wm. H. Harrison	41,281	56.0	8,801	9				
14	1840	Wm. H. Harrison..	65,302	55.8	13,607	9	116,997	43,236	58.6	9
		Martin Van Buren	51,695	44.2	......	..				
15	1844	James K. Polk.....	70,181	50.1	208	12	140,154	23,157	19.8	12
		Henry Clay	67,867	48.4	......	..				
		James G. Birney..	2,106	1.5	......	..				
16	1848	Zachary Taylor	69,907	45.8	......	..	152,732	12,558	9.0	12
		Lewis Cass......	74,745	48.9	*4,838	12				
		Martin Van Buren	8,100	5.3	......	..				

* Plurality.   † Decrease.

INDIANA—Continued.

No.	Year	Candidates for President	Popular	Per cent Popular	Majority	Electoral	Popular	Increase Popular	Per cent Increase	Electoral
17	1852	Franklin Pierce....	95,340	52 0	7,510	13	183,170	30,418	19.9	13
		Winfield Scott...	80,901	44.2						
		John P. Hale....	6,929	3.8						
18	1856	James Buchanan...	118,670	50.4	1,909	13	235,431	52,261	28.5	13
		John C. Fremont	94,375	40.1						
		Millard Fillmore.	22,386	9.5						
19	1860	Abraham Lincoln..	139,033	51 1	5,923	13	272,143	36,712	15.6	13
		J. C. Breckinridge	12,295	4.6						
		John Bell........	5,306	1.9						
		S. A. Douglas....	115,509	42.4						
20	1864	Abraham Lincoln..	150,422	53.6	20,169	13	280,655	8,512	3.2	13
		Geo. B. McClellan	130,233	46.4						
21	1868	Ulysses S. Grant...	176,548	51.4	9,568	13	343,528	62,873	22.4	13
		Horatio Seymour.	166,980	48.6						
22	1872	Ulysses S. Grant...	186,147	53.0	21,096	15	351,196	7,668	2.2	15
		Horace Greeley..	163,632	46.6						
		Charles O'Conor.	1,417	.4						
23	1876	Rutherford B.Hayes	208,011	48.3			431,070	79,674	22.7	15
		Samuel J. Tilden,	213,526	49.5	*5,515	15				
		Peter Cooper.....	9,533	2.2						

IOWA.

No.	Year	Candidates for President	Popular	Per cent Popular	Majority	Electoral	Popular	Increase Popular	Per cent Increase	Electoral
16	1848	Zachary Taylor	11,084	45.6			24,303			4
		Lewis Cass.......	12,093	49.8	*1,009	4				
		Martin Van Buren	1,126	4.6						
17	1852	Franklin Pierce....	17,763	50.4	808	4	35,223	10,920	44.9	4
		Winfield Scott...	15,856	45.0						
		John P. Hale.....	1,604	4.6						
18	1856	James Buchanan...	36,170	40.5			89,304	54,081	153.3	4
		John C. Fremont..	43,954	49.2	*7,784	4				
		Millard Fillmore.	9,180	10.3						
19	1860	Abraham Lincoln..	70,409	54.8	12,487	4	128,331	39,027	43.7	4
		J. C. Breckinridge	1,048	.9						
		John Bell.... ...	1,763	1.4						
		S. A. Douglas...	55,111	42.9						
20	1864	Abraham Lincoln ..	89,075	64.2	39,479	8	138,671	10,340	8.0	8
		Geo. B. McClellan	49,506	35.8						
21	1868	Ulysses S. Grant...	120,399	61.9	46,359	8	194,439	55,768	40.0	8
		Horatio Seymour	74,040	38.1						
22	1872	Ulysses S. Grant...	131,566	64.2	58,149	11	204,983	10,544	5.4	11
		Horace Greeley..	71,196	34.7						
		Charles O'Conor.	2,221	1.1						
23	1876	Rutherford B.Hayes	171,327	58.6	59,191	11	292,463	87,480	42.7	11
		Samuel J. Tilden	112,099	38.3						
		Peter Cooper	9,001	3.1						
		G. C. Smith......	36							

KANSAS.

No.	Year	Candidates for President	Popular	Per cent Popular	Majority	Electoral	Popular	Increase Popular	Per cent Increase	Electoral
20	1864	Abraham Lincoln..	16,441	81.7	12,750	3	20,132			3
		Geo. B. McClellan	3,691	18.3						
21	1868	Ulysses S. Grant...	31,048	69.0	17,058	3	45,038	24,906	123.7	3
		Horatio Seymour	13,990	31.0						
22	1872	Ulysses S. Grant...	67,048	66.6	33,482	5	100,614	55,576	123.4	5
		Horace Greeley..	32,970	32.8						
		Charles O'Conor.	596	.6						
23	1876	Rutherford B.Hayes	78,322	63.1	32,511	5	124,123	23,519	23.4	5
		Samuel J. Tilden	37,902	30.5						
		Peter Cooper....	7,776	6.3						
		G. C. Smith......	110	.1						
		Scattering	23							

* Plurality.

KENTUCKY.

No.	Year	Candidates for President.	Popular	Per cent Popular.	Majority.	Electoral.	Popular.	Increase Popular.	Per cent Increase.	Electoral.
2	1792	George Washington	......	.....	....	4	......	......	....	4
3	1796	Thomas Jefferson				4				4
4	1800	Thomas Jefferson..				4				4
5	1804	Thomas Jefferson..				8				8
6	1808	James Madison...				‡7				8
7	1812	James Madison....				12				12
8	1816	James Monroe....				12				12
9	1820	James Monroe.....				12				12
10	1824	Andrew Jackson.	6,453	27.8			23,235			14
		Henry Clay	16,782	72.2	10,329	14				
11	1828	Andrew Jackson...	39,064	55.6	7,912	14	70,256	47,021	202.3	14
		John Q. Adams	31,172	44.4						
12	1832	Andrew Jackson...	36,247	45.5			79,643	9,387	13.4	15
		Henry Clay	43,396	54.5	7,149	15				
13	1836	Martin Van Buren..	33,435	47.5			70,390	†9,253	†11.6	15
		Wm. H. Harrison	36,955	52.5	3,520	15				
14	1840	Wm. H. Harrison..	58,489	64.2	25,873	15	91,105	20,715	29.4	15
		Martin Van Buren	32,616	35.8						
15	1844	James K. Polk.....	51,988	45.9			113,243	22,138	24.3	12
		Henry Clay	61,255	54.1	9.267	12				
16	1848	Zachary Taylor....	67,141	57.5	17,421	12	116,861	3,618	3.2	12
		Lewis Cass......	49,720	42.5						
17	1852	Franklin Pierce...	53,806	48.4			111,139	†5,722	†4.9	12
		Winfield Scott...	57,068	51.4	2,997	12				
		John P. Hale....	265	.2						
18	1856	James Buchanan...	74,642	52.4	6,912	12	112,372	31,233	28.1	12
		John C. Fremont	314	.2						
		Millard Fillmore.	67,416	47.4						
19	1860	Abraham Lincoln..	1,364	.9			146,216	3,844	2.7	12
		J. C. Breckinridge	53,143	36.4						
		John Bell....	66,058	45.2	*12,915	12				
		S. A. Douglas....	25,651	17.5						
20	1864	Abraham Lincoln..	27,786	30.2			92,097	†54,129	†37.0	11
		Geo. B. McClellan	64,301	69.8	36,515	11				
21	1868	Ulysses S. Grant ...	39,566	25.5			135,456	63,369	68.8	11
		Horatio Seymour.	115,890	74.5	76,324	11				
22	1872	Ulysses S. Grant...	88,766	46.4			191,185	85,679	22.9	12
		Horace Greeley..	99,995	52.3	8,855					
		Charles O'Conor.	2,374	1.3						
		Thos.A.Hendricks				8				
		B. Gratz Brown..				4				
23	1876	Rutherford B.Hayes	97,156	37.4			259,608	68,473	35.8	12
		Samuel J. Tilden	159,690	61.5	59,772	12				
		Peter Cooper.....	1,944	.8						
		G. C. Smith.....	818	.3						

LOUISIANA.

No.	Year	Candidates for President.	Popular	Per cent Popular.	Majority.	Electoral.	Popular.	Increase Popular.	Per cent Increase.	Electoral.
7	1812	James Madison				3				3
8	1816	James Monroe				3				3
9	1820	James Monroe.....				3				3
10	1824	John Q. Adams ...				2				5
		Andrew Jackson.				3				
11	1828	Andrew Jackson...	4,605	52.9	508	5	8,702			5
		John Q. Adams..	4,097	47.1						
12	1832	Andrew Jackson. ..	4,049	61.6	1,521	5	6,577	†2,125	†24.4	5
		Henry Clay....	2,528	38.4						
13	1836	Martin Van Buren..	3,653	51.9	270	5	7,036	459	7.0	5
		Wm. H. Harrison	3,383	48.1						
14	1840	Wm. H. Harrison..	11,297	59.7	3,680	5	18,914	11,878	168.8	5
		Martin Van Buren	7,617	40.3						

* Plurality. † Decrease. ‡ One Electoral vote not cast.

LOUISIANA—Continued.

No.	Year	Candidates for President	Popular	Per cent Popular	Majority	Electoral	Popular	Increase Popular	Per cent Increase	Electoral
			Votes for Candidates.				**Total Vote.**			
15	1844	James K. Polk.....	13,782	51.3	699	6	26,865	7,951	42.0	6
		Henry Clay	13,083	48.7						
16	1848	Zachary Taylor	18,217	54.2	2,847	6	33,587	6,722	25.0	6
		Lewis Cass......	15,370	45.8						
17	1852	Franklin Pierce....	18,647	51.9	1,392	6	35,902	2,315	7.0	6
		Winfield Scott....	17,255	48.1						
18	1856	James Buchanan...	22,164	51.7	1,455	6	42,873	6,971	19.4	6
		Millard Fillmore.	20,709	48.3						
19	1860	J. C. Breckinridge	22,681	44.9	*2,477	6	50,510	7,637	17.8	6
		John Bell.......	20,204	40.0						
		S. A. Douglas....	7,625	15.1						
20	1864	....								
21	1868	Ulysses S. Grant....	33,263	29.3			113,488	62,978	124.6	7
		Horatio Seymour.	80,225	70.7	46,962	7				
22	1872	Ulysses S. Grant....	71,663	55.7	14,634	8	128,692	15,204	13.4	8
		Horace Greeley ..	57,029	44.3						
23	1876	Rutherford B.Hayes	75,135	51.5	4,499	8	145,771	17,079	13.3	8
		Samuel J. Tilden.	70,636	48.5						

MAINE.

No.	Year	Candidates for President	Popular	Per cent Popular	Majority	Electoral	Popular	Increase Popular	Per cent Increase	Electoral
9	1820	James Monroe.....				9				9
10	1824	John Q. Adams	6,870	74.7	4,540	9	9,200			9
		Andrew Jackson..	2,330	25.3						
11	1828	Andrew Jackson...	13,927	40.1		1	34,700	25,500	277.1	9
		John Q. Adams...	20,773	59.9	6,846	8				
12	1832	Andrew Jackson....	33,291	55.0	6,087	10	60,495	25,795	73.8	10
		Henry Clay	27,204	45.0						
13	1836	Martin Van Buren.	22,300	59.4	7,061	10	37,539	†22,956	†37.9	10
		Wm. H. Harrison.	15,239	40.6						
14	1840	Wm. H. Harrison...	46,612	50.2	217	10	93,007	55,468	147.7	10
		Martin Van Buren	46,201	49.6						
		James G. Birney..	194	.2						
15	1844	James K. Polk....	45,719	53.8	6,505	9	84,933	†8,074	†8.7	9
		Henry Clay	34,378	40.5						
		James G. Birney.	4,836	5.7						
16	1848	Zachary Taylor....	35,125	40.3			87,101	2,168	2.5	9
		Lewis Cass.......	39,880	45.8	*4,755	9				
		Martin Van Buren	12,096	13.9						
17	1852	Franklin Pierce....	41,609	50.6	1,096	8	82,182	†4,919	†5.6	8
		Winfield Scott....	32,543	39.6						
		John P. Hale.....	8,030	9.8						
18	1856	James Buchanan...	39,080	35.6			109,784	27,602	33.6	8
		John C. Fremont.	67,379	61.4	24,974	8				
		Millard Fillmore.	3,325	3.0						
19	1860	Abraham Lincoln...	62,811	64.1	27,704	8	97,918	†11,866	†10.8	8
		J. C. Breckinridge	6,368	6.5						
		John Bell.......	2,046	2.1						
		S. A. Douglas....	26,693	27.3						
20	1864	Abraham Lincoln...	61,803	58.3	17,592	7	106,014	8,096	8.2	7
		Geo. B. McClellan	44,211	41.7						
21	1868	Ulysses S. Grant...	70,498	62.4	28,033	7	112,953	6,939	6.5	7
		Horatio Seymour.	42,460	37.6						
22	1872	Ulysses S. Grant...	61,422	67.9	32,335	7	90,509	†22,444	†19.9	7
		Horace Greeley ..	29,087	32.1						
23	1876	Rutherford B.Hayes	66,300	56.8	15,814	7	116,786	26,277	29.0	7
		Samuel J. Tilden.	49,823	42.6						
		Peter Cooper.....	663	.6						

* Plurality.   † Decrease.

MARYLAND.

No.	Year	CANDIDATES FOR PRESIDENT.	Popular	Per cent Popular.	Majority.	Electoral	Popular	Increase Popular.	Per cent Increase	Electoral
1	1789	George Washington				‡6				8
2	1792	George Washington				8				10
3	1796	John Adams				7				10
4	1800	Thomas Jefferson				5				10
		Aaron Burr				5				
5	1804	Thomas Jefferson				9				11
		C. C. Pinckney				2				
6	1808	James Madison				9				11
		C. C. Pinckney				2				
7	1812	James Madison				6				11
		De Witt Clinton				5				
8	1816	James Monroe				8				11
9	1820	James Monroe				11				11
10	1824	John Q. Adams	14,632	43.7	*109	3	33,496			11
		Andrew Jackson	14,523	43.3		7				
		Wm.H.Crawford.	3,646	10.9		1				
		Henry Clay	695	2.1						
11	1828	Andrew Jackson	24,578	48.8		5	50,337	16,841	50.3	11
		John Q. Adams	25,759	51.2	1,181	6				
12	1832	Andrew Jackson	19,156	50.0		3	38,316	†12,021	†258	10
		Henry Clay	19,160	50.0	4	5				
13	1836	Martin Van Buren	22,167	46.2			48,019	9,703	25.4	10
		Wm. H. Harrison.	25,852	53.8	3,685	10				
14	1840	Wm. H. Harrison.	33,528	53.8	4,776	10	62,280	14,261	29.7	10
		Martin Van Buren	28,752	46.2						
15	1844	James K. Polk	32,676	47.5			68,060	6,380	10.2	8
		Henry Clay	35,9'4	52.5	3,306	8				
16	1848	Zachary Taylor	37,702	52.1	3,049	8	72,355	3,695	5.4	8
		Lewis Cass	34,528	47.7						
		Martin Van Buren	125	.2						
17	1852	Franklin Pierce	40,020	53.2	4,900	8	75,140	2,785	3.8	8
		Winfield Scott	35,066	46.7						
		John P. Hale	54	.1						
18	1856	James Buchanan	39,115	45.0			86,856	11,716	15.6	8
		John C. Fremont	281	.3						
		Millard Fillmore	47,460	54.7	8,064	8				
19	1860	Abraham Lincoln	2,294	2.4			92,502	5,646	6.5	8
		J.C.Breckinridge	42,482	46.0	*732	8				
		John Bell	41,760	45'2						
		S. A. Douglas	5,966	6.4						
20	1864	Abraham Lincoln	40,153	55.1	7,414	7	72,892	†19,610	†21.2	7
		Geo. B. McClellan	32,739	44.9						
21	1868	Ulysses S. Grant	30,438	32.8			92,795	19,903	27.3	7
		Horatio Seymour.	62,357	67.2	31,919	7				
22	1872	Ulysses S. Grant.	66,760	49.7			134,466	41,671	44.9	8
		Horace Greeley	67,687	50.3	908					
		Charles O'Conor.	19							
		T.A. Hendricks				8				
23	1876	Rutherford B.Hayes	71,981	44.0			163,804	29,338	21.8	8
		Samuel J. Tilden.	91,780	56.0	19,756	8				
		Peter Cooper	33							
		G. C. Smith	10							

MASSACHUSETTS.

No.	Year	CANDIDATES FOR PRESIDENT.	Popular	Per cent Popular.	Majority.	Electoral	Popular	Increase Popular.	Per cent Increase	Electoral
1	1789	George Washington				10				10
2	1792	George Washington				16				16
3	1796	John Adams				16				16
4	1800	John Adams				16				16
5	1804	Thomas Jefferson				19				19
6	1808	C. C. Pinckney				19				19
7	1812	De Witt Clinton				22				22

* Plurality.   † Decrease.   ‡ Two votes not cast.

MASSACHUSETTS—Continued.

No.	Year.	Candidates for President.	Popular	Per cent Popular.	Majority.	Electoral.	Popular.	Increase Popular.	Per cent Increase.	Electoral.
8	1816	Rufus King......				22				22
9	1820	James Monroe....				15				15
10	1824	John Q. Adams....	30,687	82.3	24,071	15	37,303			15
		Wm. H. Crawford	6,616	17.7						
11	1828	Andrew Jackson...	6,019	16.8			35,855	†11,448	†3.9	15
		John Q. Adams..	29,836	83.2	23,817	15				
12	1832	Andrew Jackson...	14,545	30.6			47,548	11,693	32.6	14
		Henry Clay......	33,003	69.4	18,458	14				
13	1836	Martin Van Buren.	33,501	44.9			74,594	27,046	56.9	14
		Daniel Webster..	41,003	55.1	7,592	14				
14	1840	Wm. H. Harrison..	72,874	57.6	19,305	14	126,443	51,849	69.5	14
		Martin Van Buren	51,948	41.1						
		James G. Birney.	1,621	1.3						
15	1844	James K. Polk.....	52,846	40.3			131,124	4,681	3.7	12
		Henry Clay......	67,418	51.4	3,712	12				
		James G. Birney.	10,860	8.3						
16	1848	Zachary Taylor....	61,072	45.4	*23,014	12	134,411	3,287	2.5	12
		Lewis Cass.......	35,281	26.3						
		Martin Van Buren	38,058	29.3						
17	1852	Franklin Pierce....	44,569	35.6			125,275	†9,136	†6.8	13
		Winfield Scott....	52,683	42.0	*8,114	13				
		John P. Hale.....	28,023	22.4						
18	1856	James Buchanan...	39,240	23.5			167,056	41,781	33.4	13
		John C. Fremont.	108,190	64.8	49,334	13				
		Millard Fillmore.	19,626	11.7						
19	1860	Abraham Lincoln..	106,533	63.0	43,891	13	169,175	2,119	1.3	13
		J. C. Breckinridge	5,939	3.5						
		John Bell.......	22,331	13.2						
		S. A. Douglas....	34,372	20.3						
20	1864	Abraham Lincoln..	126,742	72.2	77,997	12	175,487	6,312	3.7	12
		Geo. B. McClellan	48,745	27.8						
21	1868	Ulysses S. Grant..	136,477	69.7	77,069	12	195,885	20,398	11.6	12
		Horatio Seymour.	59,409	30.3						
22	1872	Ulysses S. Grant...	133,472	69.3	74,212	13	192,732	†3,153	†1.6	13
		Horace Greeley..	59,260	30.7						
23	1876	Rutherford B. Hayes	150,063	57.8	40,423	13	259,703	66,971	34.8	13
		Samuel J. Tilden.	108,777	41.9						
		Peter Cooper.....	779	.3						
		G. C. Smith......	84							

MICHIGAN.

No.	Year.	Candidates for President.	Popular	Per cent Popular.	Majority.	Electoral.	Popular.	Increase Popular.	Per cent Increase.	Electoral.
13	1836	Martin Van Buren.	7,360	64.8	3,360	3	11,360			3
		Wm. H. Harrison.	4,000	85.2						
14	1840	Wm. H. Harrison..	22,933	51.7	1,514	3	44,352	32,992	290.4	3
		Martin Van Buren	21,096	47.6						
		James G. Birney.	321	.7						
15	1844	James K. Polk....	27,759	49.8	*3,422	5	55,728	11,376	25.6	5
		Henry Clay......	24,337	43.7						
		James G. Birney.	3,632	6.5						
16	1848	Zachary Taylor....	23,940	36.8			65,016	9,288	16.7	5
		Lewis Cass.......	30,687	47.2	*6,747	5				
		Martin Van Buren	10,389	16.0						
17	1852	Franklin Pierce....	41,842	50.5	746	6	82,938	17,922	27.6	6
		Winfield Scott ...	33,859	40.8						
		John P. Hale.....	7,237	8.7						
18	1856	James Buchanan...	52,136	41.5			125,558	42,620	51.4	6
		John C. Fremont.	71,762	57.2	17,966	6				
		Millard Fillmore.	1,660	1.3						
19	1860	Abraham Lincoln..	88,480	57.2	22,213	6	154,747	29,189	23.2	6
		J. C. Breckinridge	805	.5						
		John Bell........	405	.3						
		S. A. Douglas....	65,057	42.0						

* Plurality.   † Decrease.

MICHIGAN—Continued.

No.	Year	CANDIDATES FOR PRESIDENT.	Popular	Per cent Popular.	Majority.	Electoral.	Popular.	Increase Popular.	Per cent Increase.	Electoral.
20	1864	Abraham Lincoln..	91,521	55.1	16,917	8	166,125	11,378	7.4	8
		Geo. B. McClellan	74,604	44.9						
21	1868	Ulysses S. Grant...	128,550	57.0	31,481	8	225,619	59,494	35.9	8
		Horatio Seymour.	97,069	43.0						
22	1872	Ulysses S. Grant...	138,455	62.7	55,968	11	220,942	†4,677	†2.1	11
		Horace Greeley...	78,355	35.4						
		Charles O'Conor..	2,861	1.3						
		James Black......	1,271	.6						
23	1876	Rutherford B.Hayes	166,534	52.5	15,542	11	317,526	96,584	43.7	11
		Samuel J. Tilden.	141,095	44.4						
		Peter Cooper....	9,060	2.9						
		G. C. Smith......	766	.2						
		Scattering.....	71							

MINNESOTA.

No.	Year	CANDIDATES FOR PRESIDENT.	Popular	Per cent Popular.	Majority.	Electoral.	Popular.	Increase Popular.	Per cent Increase.	Electoral.
19	1860	Abraham Lincoln..	22,069	63.4	9,339	4	34,799			4
		J. C. Breckinridge	748	2.2						
		John Bell........	62	.2						
		S. A. Douglas ...	11,920	34.2						
20	1864	Abraham Lincoln..	25,060	59.0	7,685	4	42,435	7,636	21.9	4
		Geo. B. McClellan	17,375	41.0						
21	1868	Ulysses S. Grant...	43,545	60.8	15,470	4	71,620	29,185	68.8	4
		Horatio Seymour.	28,075	39.2						
22	1872	Ulysses S. Grant...	55,117	61.6	20,694	5	89,540	17,920	25.0	5
		Horace Greeley...	34,423	38.4						
23	1876	Rutherford B.Hayes	72,962	58.8	21,780	5	124,144	34,604	38.5	5
		Samuel J. Tilden.	48,799	39.3						
		Peter Cooper.....	2,311	1.9						
		G. C. Smith... ..	72							

MISSISSIPPI.

No.	Year	CANDIDATES FOR PRESIDENT.	Popular	Per cent Popular.	Majority.	Electoral.	Popular.	Increase Popular.	Per cent Increase.	Electoral.
9	1820	James Monroe.....				*2				3
10	1824	John Q. Adams....	1,694	33.6			5,017			3
		Andrew Jackson.	3,234	64.1	1,421	3				
		Wm. H. Crawford	119	2 3						
11	1828	Andrew Jackson....	6 763	81.1	5,182	3	8,344	3,207	65.8	3
		John Q. Adams....	1,581	18.9						
12	1832	Andrew Jackson....			5,919	4				
13	1836	Martin Van Buren..	9,979	50.7	291	4	19,667	11,323	135.7	4
		Hugh L. White...	9,688	49.3						
14	1840	Wm. H. Harrison...	19,518	53.5	2,523	4	36,513	16,846	85.6	4
		Martin Van Buren	16,995	46.5						
15	1844	James K. Polk.....	25,126	56.7	5,920	6	41,332	7,819	21.4	6
		Henry Clay......	19,206	43.3						
16	1848	Zachary Taylor....	25,922	49.5			52,459	8,127	18.3	6
		Lewis Cass......	26,537	50.5	615	6				
17	1852	Franklin Pierce....	26,876	60.5	9,328	7	44,424	†8,035	†15.3	7
		Winfield Scott...	17,548	39.5						
18	1856	James Buchanan....	35,446	59.4	11,251	7	59,041	15,217	34.2	7
		Millard Fillmore.	24,195	40.6						
19	1860	J. C. Breckinridge	40,797	59.0	12,474	7	69,120	9,479	15.9	7
		John Bell........	25,040	36.2						
		S. A. Douglas....	3,283	4.8						
20	1864	....								
21	1868	....								
22	1872	Ulysses S. Grant...	82,175	63.5	34,887	8	129,468	60,343	87.3	8
		Horace Greeley..	47,288	36.5						
23	1876	Rutherford B.Hayes	52,605	31.9			164,778	35,315	27.2	8
		Samuel J. Tilden.	112,173	68.1	59,568	8				

* One Electoral vote not cast.   † Decrease.

MISSOURI.

No.	Year	Candidates for President.	Vote for Candidates — Popular	Per cent Popular	Majority.	Electoral	Total Vote — Popular.	Increase Popular.	Per cent Increase.	Electoral.
9	1820	James Monroe....				3				3
10	1824	John Q. Adams....	811	11.5		...	2,699			3
		Andrew Jackson.	987	30.6		...				...
		Henry Clay.....	1,401	51.9	103	3				...
11	1828	Andrew Jackson...	8,232	70.7	4,810	3	11,654	8,955	331.8	3
		John Q. Adams..	3,422	29.3		...				...
12	1832	Andrew Jackson...			5,192	4				4
13	1836	Martin Van Buren..	10,995	56.9	2,658	4	19,332	7,678	65.9	4
		Wm. H. Harrison.	7,401	38.3		...				...
		Hugh L. White...	936	4.8		...				...
14	1840	Wm. H. Harrison..	22,972	43.6		...	52,732	33,400	172.2	4
		Martin Van Buren	29,760	56.4	6,788	4				...
15	1844	James K. Polk.....	41,369	57.0	10,118	7	72,620	19,888	37.7	7
		Henry Clay.....	31,251	43.0		...				...
16	1848	Zachary Taylor....	32,671	45.0		...	72,748	128	.2	7
		Lewis Cass......	40,077	55.0	7,406	7				...
17	1852	Franklin Pierce...	38,353	56.2	8,369	9	68,337	†4,411	†6.1	9
		Winfield Scott...	29,984	43.8		...				...
18	1856	James Buchanan...	58,164	4.5	9,640	9	106,688	38,351	56.1	9
		Millard Fillmore.	48,524	45.5		...				...
19	1860	Abraham Lincoln..	17,028	10.3		...	165,518	58,830	55.1	9
		J. C. Breckinridge	31,317	18.9		...				...
		John Bell.......	58,372	35.8		...				...
		S. A. Douglas....	58,801	35.5	*429	9				...
20	1864	Abraham Lincoln..	72,750	69.7	41,072	11	104,428	†61,090	†36.9	11
		Geo. B. McClellan	31,678	30.3		...				...
21	1868	Ulysses S. Grant...	86,860	57.0	21,232	11	152,488	48,060	46.1	11
		Horatio Seymour.	65,628	43.0		...				...
22	1872	Ulysses S. Grant...	119,196	43.6		...	273,059	120,571	79.1	15
		Horace Greeley..	151,434	55.5	29,800					...
		Charles O'Conor.	2,429	.9		...				...
		Th's.A.Hendricks				6				...
		B. Gratz Brown..				8				...
		David Davis.....				1				...
23	1876	Rutherford B. Hayes	145,029	41.2		...	351,765	78,706	28.8	15
		Samuel J. Tilden.	203,077	57.8	54,889	15				...
		Peter Cooper.....	3,498	1 0		...				...
		G. C. Smith......	64			...				...
		Scattering.....	97			...				...

NEBRASKA.

No.	Year	Candidates for President.	Popular	Per cent Popular	Majority.	Electoral	Popular.	Increase Popular.	Per cent Increase.	Electoral.
21	1868	Ulysses S. Grant...	9,729	64.1	4,290	3	15,168			3
		Horatio Seymour.	5,439	35.9		...				...
22	1872	Ulysses S. Grant...	18,329	70.1	10,517	3	26,141	10,973	72.3	3
		Horace Greeley..	7,812	29.9		...				...
23	1876	Rutherford B.Hayes	31,916	59.7	10,326	3	53,506	27,365	104.7	3
		Samuel J. Tilden.	17,554	32 8		...				...
		Peter Cooper.....	2,320	4.3		...				...
		G. C. Smith......	1,599	3.0		...				...
		Scattering.....	117	.2		...				...

NEVADA.

No.	Year	Candidates for President.	Popular	Per cent Popular	Majority.	Electoral	Popular.	Increase Popular.	Per cent Increase.	Electoral.
20	1864	Abraham Lincoln..	9,826	59.8	3,232	†2	16,420			3
		Geo. B. McClellan	6,594	40.2		...				...
21	1868	Ulysses S. Grant...	6,480	55.4	1,262	3	11,698	†4,722	†28.8	3
		Horatio Seymour.	5,218	44.6		...				...
22	1872	Ulysses S. Grant...	8,413	57.4	2,177	3	14,649	2,951	25.2	3
		Horace Greeley..	6,236	42.6		...				...
23	1876	Rutherford B.Hayes	10,383	52.7	1,075	3	19,691	5,042	34.5	3
		Samuel J. Tilden.	9,308	47 3		...				...

* Plurality.　　　† Decrease.　　　‡ One vote not cast.

NEW HAMPSHIRE.

No.	Year	Candidates for President	Popular	Per cent Popular	Majority	Electoral	Popular	Increase Popular	Per cent Increase	Electoral
1	1789	George Washington				5				5
2	1792	George Washington				6				6
3	1796	John Adams				6				6
4	1800	John Adams				6				6
5	1804	Thomas Jefferson				7				7
6	1808	C. C. Pinckney				7				7
7	1812	De Witt Clinton				8				8
8	1816	James Monroe				8				8
9	1820	James Monroe				7				8
		John Q. Adams				1				
10	1824	John Q. Adams	4,107	86.5	3,464	8	4,750			8
		Andrew Jackson	643	13.5						
11	1828	Andrew Jackson	20,692	46.2			44,768			8
		John Q. Adams	24,076	53.8	3,384	8				
12	1832	Andrew Jackson	25,486	57.3	6,476	7	44,496	†272	1.6	7
		Henry Clay	19,010	42.7						
13	1836	Martin Van Buren	18,722	56.8	*12,494	7	32,950	†11,546	†26.0	7
		Wm. H. Harrison	6,228	18.9						
		Daniel Webster	8,000	24.3	‡					
14	1840	Wm. H. Harrison	26,158	44.4			58,954	26,004	78.8	7
		Martin Van Buren	32,670	55.4	6,386	7				
		James G. Birney	126	.2						
15	1844	James K. Polk	27,160	55.2	5,133	6	49,187	†9,767	†16.6	6
		Henry Clay	17,866	36.3						
		James G. Birney	4,161	8.5						
16	1848	Zachary Taylor	14,781	29.5			50,104	917	1.9	6
		Lewis Cass	27,763	53.4	5,422	6				
		Martin Van Buren	7,560	15.1						
17	1852	Franklin Pierce	29,997	56.8	7,155	5	52,839	2,735	5.4	5
		Winfield Scott	16,147	30.6						
		John P. Hale	6,695	12.6						
18	1856	James Buchanan	32,789	45.8			71,556	18,717	35.4	5
		John C. Fremont	38,345	53.6	5,134	5				
		Millard Fillmore	422	.6						
19	1860	Abraham Lincoln	37,519	56.9	9,086	5	65,953	†5,603	†7.8	5
		J. C. Breckinridge	2,112	3.2						
		John Bell	441	.7						
		S. A. Douglas	25,581	39.2						
20	1864	Abraham Lincoln	36,400	52.5	3,529	5	69,271	3,318	5.1	5
		Geo. B. McClellan	32,871	47.5						
21	1868	Ulysses S. Grant	38,191	55.0	6,967	5	69,415	144	.2	5
		Horatio Seymour	31,224	45.0						
22	1872	Ulysses S. Grant	37,168	54.0	5,444	5	68,802	†363	†.8	5
		Horace Greeley	31,424	45.6						
		Charles O'Conor	100	.1						
		James Black	200	.3						
23	1876	Rutherford B. Hayes	41,539	51.8	2,954	5	80,124	11,234	16.3	5
		Samuel J. Tilden	38,509	48.1						
		Peter Cooper	76	.1						

NEW JERSEY.

No.	Year	Candidates for President	Popular	Per cent Popular	Majority	Electoral	Popular	Increase Popular	Per cent Increase	Electoral
1	1789	George Washington				6				6
2	1792	George Washington				7				7
3	1796	John Adams				7				7
4	1800	John Adams				7				7
5	1804	Thomas Jefferson				8				8
6	1808	James Madison				8				8
7	1812	De Witt Clinton				8				8
8	1816	James Monroe				8				8
9	1820	James Monroe				8				8

    * Plurality.   † Decrease.   ‡ About 8,000.

NEW JERSEY—Continued.

No.	Year	Candidates for President	Popular	Per cent Popular	Majority	Electoral	Popular	Increase Popular	Per cent Increase	Electoral
10	1824	John Q. Adams....	9,110	42.8	...	...	21,291	...	...	8
		Andrew Jackson..	10,985	51.6	679	8				
		Wm. H. Crawford	1,196	5.6	...					
11	1828	Andrew Jackson...	21,950	48.0	...		45,708	24,417	114.7	8
		John Q. Adams..	23,758	52.0	1,809	8				
12	1832	Andrew Jackson...	23,856	50.5	463	8	47,249	1,541	3.3	8
		Henry Clay......	23,393	49.5						
13	1836	Martin Van Buren..	26,347	49.5	...	...	53,239	5,990	12.7	8
		Wm. H. Harrison.	26,892	50.5	545	8				
14	1840	Wm. H. Harrison..	33,351	51.7	2,248	8	64,454	11,215	21.1	8
		Martin Van Buren	31,034	48.2	...					
		James G. Birney.	69	.1						
15	1844	James K. Polk....	37,495	49.4	...	...	75,944	11,490	17.8	7
		Henry Clay......	38,318	50.4	692	7				
		James G. Birney.	131	.2						
16	1848	Zachary Taylor....	40,015	51.5	2,285	7	77,745	1,801	2.4	7
		Lewis Cass......	36,901	47.4						
		Martin Van Buren	829	1.1						
17	1852	Franklin Pierce....	44,305	53.3	5,399	7	83,211	5,466	7.0	7
		Winfield Scott...	38,556	46.3						
		John P. Hale.....	350	.4						
18	1856	James Buchanan...	46,943	47.2	*18,605	7	99,396	16,185	19.5	7
		John C. Fremont.	28,338	28.5						
		Millard Fillmore.	24,115	24.3						
19	1860	Abraham Lincoln..	58,324	48.2		4	121,125	21,729	21.9	7
		S. A. Douglas....	62,801	51.8	4,477	3				
20	1864	Abraham Lincoln..	60,723	47.2			128,747	7,622	6.3	7
		Geo. B. McClellan	68,024	52.8	7,301	7				
21	1868	Ulysses S. Grant...	80,131	49.1	...		163,132	34,385	26.7	7
		Horatio Seymour.	83,001	50.9	2,870	7				
22	1872	Ulysses S. Grant..	91,656	54.3	14,570	9	168,742	5,610	3.4	9
		Horace Greeley ..	76,456	45.3						
		Charles O'Conor.	630	.4						
23	1876	Rutherford B. Hayes.	103,517	47.0	...		220,234	51,492	30.5	9
		Samuel J. Tilden.	115,962	52.7	11,090	9				
		Peter Cooper.....	712		3					
		G. C. Smith......	43							

NEW YORK.

No.	Year	Candidates for President	Popular	Per cent Popular	Majority	Electoral	Popular	Increase Popular	Per cent Increase	Electoral
2	1792	George Washington				12				12
3	1796	John Adams.......				12				12
4	1800	Thomas Jefferson..				12				12
5	1804	Thomas Jefferson..				19				19
6	1808	James Madison....				13				13
		George Clinton...				6				
7	1812	De Witt Clinton...				29				29
8	1816	James Monroe....				29				29
9	1820	James Monroe....				29				29
10	1824	John Q. Adams....				26				36
		Andrew Jackson.				1				
		Wm. H. Crawford				5				
		Henry Clay				4				
11	1828	Andrew Jackson...	140,763	51.0	5,350	20	276,176			36
		John Q. Adams..	135,413	49.0		16				
12	1832	Andrew Jackson...	168,497	52.1	13,601	42	323,393	47,217	17.1	42
		Henry Clay	154,896	47.9						
13	1836	Martin Van Buren..	166,815	54.6	28,272	42	305,358	†18,085	†5.6	42
		Wm. H. Harrison	138,543	45.4						

* Plurality.　　† Decrease.

NEW YORK—Continued.

No.	Year	Candidates for President.	Popular	Per cent Popular.	Majority.	Electoral.	Popular.	Increase Popular.	Per cent Increase.	Electoral.
14	1840	Wm. H Harrison..	225,817	51.2	10,500	42	441,134	135,776	44.5	42
		Martin Van Buren	212,519	48.2						
		James G. Birney.	2,798	.6						
15	1844	James K. Polk.....	237,588	48.9	*5,106	36	485,882	44,748	10.1	36
		Henry Clay.......	232,482	47.8						
		James G. Birney.	15,812	3.3						
16	1848	Zachary Taylor....	218,603	48.2	*98,093	36	453,431	†32,451	†6.7	36
		Lewis Cass.......	114,318	25.2						
		Martin Van Buren	120,510	26.6						
17	1852	Franklin Pierce....	262,083	50.2	1,872	35	522,294	68,863	15.2	35
		Winfield Scott...	234,832	45.0						
		John P. Hale....	25,329	4.8						
18	1856	James Buchanan...	195,878	32.8	*80,129	35	596,489	74,195	14.2	35
		John C. Fremont.	276,007	46.3						
		Millard Fillmore.	124,604	20.9						
19	1860	Abraham Lincoln..	362,646	53.7	50,136	35	675,156	78,667	13.2	35
		S. A. Douglas....	312,510	46.3						
20	1864	Abraham Lincoln..	368,735	50.5	6,749	33	730,721	55,565	8.5	33
		Geo. B.McClellan	361,986	49.5						
21	1868	Ulysses S. Grant....	419,883	49.4	10,000	33	849,766	119,045	16.3	33
		Horatio Seymour.	429,883	50.6						
22	1872	Ulysses S. Grant....	440,736	53.1	51,800	35	820,672	†20,094	†2.4	35
		Horace Greeley..	387,281	46.7						
		Charles O'Conor.	1,454	.2						
		James Black.....	201							
23	1876	Rutherford B.Hayes	489,207	48.1			1,017,330	187,658	22.6	35
		Samuel J. Tilden.	521,949	51.3	26,568	35				
		Peter Cooper.....	1,987	.2						
		G. C. Smith......	2,359	.2						
		Scattering......	1,828	.2						

NORTH CAROLINA.

No.	Year	Candidates	Popular	Per cent Popular.	Majority.	Electoral.	Popular.	Increase Popular.	Per cent Increase.	Electoral.
2	1792	George Washington				12				12
3	1796	John Adams......				1				12
		Thomas Jefferson				11				
4	1800	Thomas Jefferson..				8				12
		John Adams....				4				
5	1804	Thomas Jefferson..				14				14
6	1808	James Madison..				11				14
		C. C. Pinckney...				3				
7	1812	James Madison....				15				15
8	1816	James Monroe....				15				15
9	1820	James Monroe.....				15				15
10	1824	Andrew Jackson..	20,415	56.7	4,794	15	36,036			15
		Wm. H. Crawford	15,621	43.3						
11	1828	Andrew Jackson...	37,857	73.1	23,939	15	51,775	15,739	43.7	15
		John Q. Adams...	13,918	26.9						
12	1832	Andrew Jackson...	24,862	84.5	20,299	15	29,425	†22,350	†43.1	15
		Henry Clay......	4,563	15.5						
13	1836	Martin Van Buren..	26,910	53.3	3,294	15	50,536	21,111	71.7	15
		Wm. H. Harrison	23,626	46.7						
14	1840	Wm. H. Harrison...	46,376	57.5	12,158	15	80,594	30,058	50.5	15
		Martin Van Buren	34,218	42.5						
15	1844	James K. Polk.....	39,287	47.6			82,519	1,925	2.4	11
		Henry Clay......	43,232	52.4	3,945	11				
16	1848	Zachary Taylor....	43,530	55.5	8,681	11	78,419	†4,100	†5.0	11
		Lewis Cass......	34,869	44.5						
17	1852	Franklin Pierce....	39,744	50.4	627	10	78,861	442	.6	10
		Winfield Scott...	39,058	49.5						
		John P. Hale....	59	.1						

* Plurality. † Decrease.

NORTH CAROLINA—Continued.

No.	Year	Candidates for President.	Popular	Per cent Popular.	Majority.	Electoral.	Popular.	Increase Popular.	Per cent Increase.	Electoral.
18	1856	James Buchanan...	48,246	56.7	11,360	10	85,132	6,271	8.0	10
		Millard Fillmore..	36,886	43.3						
19	1860	J. C. Breckinridge	48,339	50.3	649	10	96,030	10,898	12.8	10
		John Bell.......	44,990	46.9						
		S. A. Douglas....	2,701	2.8						
20	1864	....								
21	1868	Ulysses S. Grant...	16,769	53.4	12,168	9	181,370	85,340	88 9	9
		Horatio Seymour.	84,601	46.6						
22	1872	Ulysses S. Grant...	94,769	57.5	24,675	10	164,863	†16,507	†9.1	10
		Horace Greeley..	70,094	42.5						
23	1876	Rutherford B.Hayes	108,417	46.4			233,844	68,981	41.8	10
		Samuel J. Tilden.	125,427	53.6	17,010	10				

OHIO.

No.	Year	Candidates for President.	Popular	Per cent Popular.	Majority.	Electoral.	Popular.	Increase Popular.	Per cent Increase.	Electoral.
5	1804	Thomas Jefferson..				3				3
6	1808	James Madison....				3				3
7	1812	James Madison....				‡7				8
8	1816	James Monroe....				8				8
9	1820	James Monroe....				8				8
10	1824	John Q. Adams....	12,280	24.6			49,902			16
		Andrew Jackson.	18,457	36.9						
		Henry Clay.....	19,255	38.5	*798	16				
11	1828	Andrew Jackson...	67,597	51.6	4,201	16	130,993	81,001	162.0	16
		John Q. Adams..	63,396	48.4						
12	1832	Andrew Jackson...	81,246	51.5	4,707	21	157,795	26,792	20.4	21
		Henry Clay.....	76,539	48.5						
13	1836	Martin Van Buren.	96,948	47.9			202,353	44,568	28.3	21
		Wm. H. Harrison.	105,405	52.1	8,457	21				
14	1840	Wm. H. Harrison.	148,157	54.1	22,472	21	273,842	71,489	35.3	21
		Martin Van Buren	124,782	45.6						
		James G. Birney.	903	.3						
15	1844	James K. Polk....	149,117	47.7			312,224	33,382	14.0	23
		Henry Clay.....	155,057	49.7	*5,940	23				
		James G. Birney.	8,050	2 6						
16	1848	Zachary Taylor....	138,360	42.1			323,480	16,265	5.2	23
		Lewis Cass.....	154,775	47.1	*16,415	23				
		Martin Van Buren	35,854	10.8						
17	1852	Franklin Pierce....	169,220	47.9	*16,694	23	853,428	24,939	7.6	23
		Winfield Scott...	152,526	43.1						
		John P. Hale....	31,682	9.0						
18	1856	James Buchanan...	170,874	44.2			386,497	33,069	9.4	23
		John C. Fremont.	187,497	48.5	*16,622	23				
		Millard Fillmore.	28,126	7.3						
19	1860	Abraham Lincoln..	231,610	52.3	20,789	23	442,441	55,944	14.5	23
		J.C.Breckinridge	11,405	2.6						
		John Bell.	12,194	2.8						
		S. A. Douglas....	187,232	42.3						
20	1864	Abraham Lincoln..	265,154	56.3	59,586	21	470,722	28,281	6.4	21
		Geo. B. McClellan	205,568	43.7						
21	1868	Ulysses S. Grant..	2-0,223	54.0	41,617	21	518,829	48,107	10.2	21
		Horatio Seymour.	238,606	46.0						
22	1872	Ulysses S. Grant...	281,852	53.2	34,368	22	529,436	10,607	2.0	22
		Horace Greeley..	244,821	46.2						
		Charles O'Conor..	1,163	.2						
		James Black.....	2,100	.4						
23	1876	Rutherford B.Hayes	330,698	50.2	2,747	22	658,649	129,213	24.3	22
		Samuel J. Tilden.	323,182	49.1						
		Peter Cooper....	3,057	.5						
		G. C. Smith......	1,636	.2						
		Scattering......	76							

* Plurality.   † Decrease.   ‡ One vote not cast.

OREGON.

No.	Year	CANDIDATES FOR PRESIDENT.	Popular	Per cent Popular.	Majority.	Electoral	Popular.	Increase Popular.	Per cent Increase.	Electoral
							TOTAL VOTE.			
19	1860	Abraham Lincoln..	5,270	42 5	*1,319	3	12,410			3
		J. C. Breckinridge	3,006	24.2						
		John Bell.......	183	1.5						
		S. A. Douglas....	3,951	31.8						
20	1864	Abraham Lincoln..	9,888	53.9	1,431	3	18,345	5,935	47.8	3
		Geo. B. McClellan	8,457	46.1						
21	1868	Ulysses S. Grant...	10,961	49.6			22,086	3,741	20.4	3
		Horatio Seymour.	11,125	50.4	164	3				
22	1872	Ulysses S. Grant...	11,819	58.8	3,517	3	20,121	†1,965	†9.0	3
		Horace Greeley..	7,730	38.4						
		Charles O'Conor..	572	2.8						
23	1876	Rutherford B. Hayes	15,206	50.9	547	3	29,865	9,744	48.4	3
		Samuel J. Tilden.	14,149	47.4						
		Peter Cooper.....	510	1.7						

PENNSYLVANIA.

No.	Year	CANDIDATES FOR PRESIDENT.	Popular	Per cent Popular.	Majority.	Electoral	Popular.	Increase Popular.	Per cent Increase.	Electoral
1	1789	George Washington				10				10
2	1792	George Washington				15				15
3	1796	John Adams				1				15
		Thomas Jefferson				14				
4	1800	Thomas Jefferson..				8				15
		John Adams				7				
5	1804	Thomas Jefferson..				20				20
6	1808	James Madison.....				20				20
7	1812	James Madison....				25				25
8	1816	James Monroe				25				25
9	1820	James Monroe				‡24				25
10	1824	John Q. Adams....	5,440	11.5			47,355			28
		Andrew Jackson,	36,100	76.2	24,845	28				
		Wm. H. Crawford	4,206	8.9						
		Henry Clay......	1,609	3.4						
11	1828	Andrew Jackson...	101,652	66.7	50,804	28	152,500	105,145	222.0	28
		John Q. Adams..	50,848	33.3						
12	1832	Andrew Jackson...	90,983	61.6	34,267	30	147,699	†4,801	13 1	30
		Henry Clay......	56,716	38.4						
13	1836	Martin Van Buren.	91,475	51.2	4,364	30	178,586	30,887	20.9	30
		Wm. H. Harrison	87,111	48.8						
14	1840	Wm. H. Harrison..	144,021	50.0	2	30	288,040	109,451	61.3	30
		Martin Van Buren	143,676	49.9						
		James G. Birney..	343	.1						
15	1844	James K. Polk.....	167,535	50.5	3,194	26	331,876	43,836	15.2	26
		Henry Clay......	161,203	48.6						
		James G. Birney..	3,138	.9						
16	1848	Zachary Taylor...	185,513	50.4	3,074	26	367,932	36,076	10.8	26
		Lewis Cass.	171,176	46.6						
		Martin Van Buren	11,263	3.1						
17	1852	Franklin Pierce...	198,568	51.4	10,869	27	386,367	18,315	5.0	27
		Winfield Scott...	179,174	46.4						
		John P. Hale...	8,525	2.2						
18	1856	James Buchanan...	230,710	50.1	1,025	27	460,395	71,128	19.2	27
		John C. Fremont..	147,510	32.0						
		Millard Fillmore.	82,175	17.9						
19	1860	Abraham Lincoln..	268,080	56.3	50,618	27	476,442	16,017	3.3	27
		J. C. Breckinridge	178,871	37.5						
		John Bell...	12,776	2.7						
		S. A. Douglas....	16,765	3.5						
20	1864	Abraham Lincoln..	296,391	51.8	20,075	26	572,707	96,265	20.2	26
		Geo. B. McClellan	276,316	48 2						
21	1868	Ulysses S. Grant...	342,240	52.2	28,898	26	655,662	82,955	14.6	26
		Horatio Seymour.	313,382	47.8						

* Plurality.   † Decrease.   ‡ One vote not cast.

PENNSYLVANIA—Continued.

No.	Year	Candidates for President	Popular	Per cent Popular	Majority	Electoral	Popular	Increase Popular	Per cent Increase	Electoral
22	1872	Ulysses S. Grant...	349,589	62.1	135,918	29	563,260	†92,402	†14.1	20
		Horace Greeley..	212,041	37.6						
		James Black.....	1,630	.3						
23	1876	Rutherford B. Hayes	384,122	50.6	9,375	29	758,869	195,609	34.7	29
		Samuel J. Tilden.	366,158	48.3						
		Peter Cooper.....	7,187	.9						
		G. C. Smith......	1,319	.2						
		Scattering.....	83							

RHODE ISLAND.

No.	Year	Candidates for President	Popular	Per cent Popular	Majority	Electoral	Popular	Increase Popular	Per cent Increase	Electoral
2	1792	George Washington				4				4
3	1796	John Adams......				4				4
4	1800	John Adams.....				4				4
5	1804	Thomas Jefferson..				4				4
6	1908	C. C. Pinckney...				4				4
7	1812	De Witt Clinton..				4				4
8	1816	James Monroe.....				4				4
9	1820	James Monroe.....				4				4
10	1824	John Q. Adams....	2,145	91.5	1,945	4	2,345			4
		Wm. H. Crawford	200	8.5						
11	1828	Andrew Jackson....	821	23.0			3,575	1,230	52.5	4
		John Q. Adams..	2,754	77.0	1,933	4				
12	1832	Andrew Jackson....	2,126	43.1			4,936	1,361	38.1	4
		Henry Clay......	2,810	56.9	684	4				
13	1836	Martin Van Buren..	2,964	52.2	254	4	5,674	738	14.9	4
		Wm. H. Harrison.	2,710	47.8						
14	1840	Wm. H. Harrison...	5,278	61.2	1,935	4	8,621	2,947	51.9	4
		Martin Van Buren	3,301	38.3						
		James G. Birney.	42	.5						
15	1844	James K. Polk......	4,867	39.6			12,296	3,675	42.6	4
		Henry Clay......	7,322	59.5	2,348	4				
		James G. Birney.	107	.9						
16	1848	Zachary Taylor.....	6,779	60.8	2,403	4	11,155	†1,141	19.3	4
		Lewis Cass......	3,646	32.7						
		Martin Van Buren	730	6.5						
17	1852	Franklin Pierce....	8,735	51.4	465	4	17,005	5,850	52.4	4
		Winfield Scott....	7,626	44.8						
		John P Hale.....	644	3.8						
18	1856	James Buchanan...	6,680	33.7			19,822	2,817	16.5	4
		John C. Fremont.	11,467	57.8	3,112	4				
		Millard Fillmore..	1,675	8.5						
19	1860	Abraham Lincoln..	12,244	61.4	4,537	4	19,951	129	.7	4
		S. A. Douglas....	7,707	38.6						
20	1864	Abraham Lincoln..	13,692	61.8	5,222	4	22,162	2,211	11.1	4
		Geo. B. McClellan	8,470	38.2						
21	1868	Ulysses S. Grant...	12,993	66.5	6,445	4	19,541	†2,621	†11.8	4
		Horatio Seymour.	6,548	33.5						
22	1872	Ulysses S. Grant...	13,665	71.9	8,336	4	18,994	†547	†2.8	4
		Horace Greeley...	5,329	28.1						
23	1876	Rutherford B. Hayes	15,787	59.3	4,947	4	26,627	7,633	40.3	4
		Samuel J. Tilden.	10,712	40.2						
		Peter Cooper.....	68	.3						
		G. C. Smith.....	60	.2						

*SOUTH CAROLINA.

No.	Year	Candidates for President	Popular	Per cent Popular	Majority	Electoral	Popular	Increase Popular	Per cent Increase	Electoral
1	1789	George Washington				7				7
2	1792	George Washington				8				8
3	1796	Thomas Jefferson				8				8
4	1800	Thomas Jefferson..				8				8
5	1804	Thomas Jefferson..				10				10
6	1808	James Madison....				10				10

* No popular vote for Presidential Electors in South Carolina until the amendment of its Constitution in 1868.   † Decrease.

SOUTH CAROLINA—Continued.

No.	Year	Candidates for President.	Popular	Per cent Popular.	Majority.	Electoral.	Popular.	Increase Popular.	Per cent Increase.	Electoral.
7	1812	James Madison....				11				11
8	1816	James Monroe....				11				11
9	1820	James Monroe				11				11
10	1824	Andrew Jackson..				11				11
11	1828	Andrew Jackson...				11				11
12	1832	John Floyd......				11				11
13	1836	Willie P. Mangum				11				11
14	1840	Martin Van Buren				11				11
15	1844	James K. Polk.....				9				9
16	1848	Lewis Cass.......				9				9
17	1852	Franklin Pierce...				8				8
18	1856	James Buchanan...				8				8
19	1860	J. C. Breckinridge				8				8
20	1864									
21	1868	Ulysses S. Grant...	62,301	57.9	17,064	6	107,538			6
		Horatio Seymour	45,237	42.1						
22	1872	Ulysses S. Grant...	72,290	75.9	49,400	7	95,180	†12,358	†11.5	7
		Horace Greeley..	22,703	23.9						
		Charles O'Conor.	187	.2						
23	1876	Rutherford B.Hayes	91,870	50.3	964	7	182,776	87,506	92.0	7
		Samuel J. Tilden	90,906	49.7						

TENNESSEE.

No.	Year	Candidates for President.	Popular	Per cent Popular.	Majority.	Electoral.	Popular.	Increase Popular.	Per cent Increase.	Electoral.
3	1796	Thomas Jefferson				3				3
4	1800	Thomas Jefferson..				3				3
5	1804	Thomas Jefferson..				5				5
6	1808	James Madison....				5				5
7	1812	James Madison....				8				8
8	1816	James Monroe				8				8
9	1820	James Monroe.....				8				8
10	1824	John Q. Adams....	261	1.0			20,725			11
		Andrew Jackson.	20,197	97.5	19,669	11				
		Wm. H. Crawford	312	1.5						
11	1828	Andrew Jackson...	44,090	95.2	41,850	11	46,330	25,605	123.5	11
		John Q. Adams...	2,240	4.8						
12	1832	Andrew Jackson...	28,740	95.2	27,304	15	30,176	†16,154	†34.9	15
		Henry Clay......	1,436	4.8						
13	1836	Martin Van Buren..	26,120	42.1			62,082	31,906	105.7	15
		Hugh L. White...	35,962	57.9	9,842	15				
14	1840	Wm. H. Harrison...	60,391	55.6	12,102	15	108,680	46,598	75.1	15
		Martin Van Buren	48,289	44.4						
15	1844	James K. Polk.....	59,917	49.9			119,947	11,267	10.4	13
		Henry Clay.....	60,030	50.1	113	13				
16	1848	Zachary Taylor ...	64,705	52.6	6,286	13	123,194	3,177	2.7	13
		Lewis Cass	58,419	47.4						
17	1852	Franklin Pierce....	57,018	49.9			115,916	†7,208	†3.8	12
		Winfield Scott ...	58,898	50.1	1,880	12				
18	1856	James Buchanan...	73,638	52.7	7,460	12	139,816	23,900	20.6	12
		Millard Fillmore..	66,178	47.3						
19	1860	J. C. Breckinridge	64,709	44.5			145,333	5,517	3.9	12
		John Bell	69,274	47.7	*4,565	12				
		S. A. Douglas...	11,350	7.8						
20	1864									
21	1868	Ulysses S. Grant ...	56,636	68.4	30,499	10	82,737	†62,576	†43.1	10
		Horatio Seymour.	26,129	31.6						
22	1872	Ulysses S. Grant...	85,655	47.6			180,046	97,309	117.6	12
		Horace Greeley..	94,391	52.4	8,736					
		Thos.A.Hendricks				12				
23	1876	Rutherford B.Hayes	89,566	40.2			262,782	42,686	23.7	12
		Samuel J. Tilden.	133,166	59.8	43,600	12				

* Plurality.   † Decrease.   ‡ One vote not cast.

TEXAS.

No.	Year	CANDIDATES FOR PRESIDENT	Popular	Per cent Popular	Majority	Electoral	Popular	Increase Popular	Per cent Increase	Electoral
16	1848	Zachary Taylor....	4,509	29.7			15,177			4
		Lewis Cass......	10,668	70.3	6,159	4				
17	1852	Franklin Pierce....	13,552	73.1	8,557	4	18,547	3,370	22.2	4
		Winfield Scott....	4,995	26.9						
18	1856	James Buchanan...	31,169	66.6	15,530	4	46,808	28,261	152.3	4
		Millard Fillmore..	15,639	33.4						
19	1860	J.C. Breckenridge	47,548	75.5	32,110	4	62,986	16,178	34.5	4
		John Bell........	15,438	24.5						
20	1864	....								
21	1868	....								
22	1872	Ulysses S. Grant...	47,406	40.7			116,405	53,419	84.8	8
		Horace Greeley..	66,500	57.1	16,595					
		Charles O'Conor..	2,499	2.2						
		T. A. Hendricks.				8				
23	1876	Rutherford B. Hayes	44,800	30.0			149,555	33,150	28.5	8
		Samuel J. Tilden.	104,755	70.0	59,955	8				

VERMONT.

No.	Year	CANDIDATES FOR PRESIDENT	Popular	Per cent Popular	Majority	Electoral	Popular	Increase Popular	Per cent Increase	Electoral
2	1792	George Washington				‡3				4
3	1796	John Adams......				4				4
4	1800	John Adams.....				4				4
5	1804	Thomas Jefferson.				6				6
6	1808	James Madison...				6				6
7	1812	James Madison....				8				8
8	1816	James Monroe ...				8				8
9	1820	James Monroe				8				8
10	1824	John Q. Adams. ..				7				7
11	1828	Andrew Jackson...	8,205	24.9			32,989			7
		John Q. Adams..	24,784	75.1	16,579	7				
12	1832	Andrew Jackson...	7,670				19,022			7
		Henry Clay......	11,152							
		William Wirt ...				7				
13	1836	Martin Van Buren.	14,037	40.1			35,028			7
		Wm. H. Harrison.	20,991	59.9	6,954	7				
14	1840	Wm. H. Harrison ..	32,445	63.9	14,117	7	50,773	15,745	44.9	7
		Martin Van Buren	18,009	35.5						
		James G. Birney.	319	.6						
15	1844	James K. Polk.....	18,041	37.0			48,765	†2,008	†3.9	6
		Henry Clay......	26,770	54.9	4,775	6				
		James G. Birney.	3,954	8.1						
16	1848	Zachary Taylor	23,122	48.3	*9,285	6	47,907	†858	†1.8	6
		Lewis Cass......	10,948	22.8						
		Martin Van Buren	13,837	28.9						
17	1852	Franklin Pierce...	13,044	29.7			43,838	†4,069	†8.5	5
		Winfield Scott...	22,173	50.6	508	5				
		John P. Hale.....	8,621	19.7						
18	1856	James Buchanan...	10,569	20.8			50,675	6,837	15.6	5
		John C. Fremont.	39,561	78.1	28,447	5				
		Millard Fillmore.	545	1.1						
19	1860	Abraham Lincoln..	33,808	78.9	24,772	5	42,844	†7,831	†15.4	5
		J.C. Breckenridge	218	.5						
		John Bell...... ..	1,969	4.6						
		S. A. Douglas....	6,849	16.0						
20	1864	Abraham Lincoln..	42,419	76.1	29,098	5	55,740	12,896	30.1	5
		Geo. B. McClellan	13,321	23.9						
21	1868	Ulysses S. Grant...	44,167	78.0	32,122	5	56,212	472	.8	5
		Horatio Seymour.	12,045	21.4						
22	1872	Ulysses S. Grant...	41,481	79.3	29,961	5	53,001	†3,211	†6.0	5
		Horace Greeley..	10,927	20.6						
		Charles O'Conor..	593	1.1						
23	1876	Rutherford B. Hayes	44,092	68.5	23,838	5	64,346	11,345	21.4	5
		Samuel J. Tilden.	20,254	31.5						

* Plurality.　　† Decrease.　　‡ One vote not cast.

VIRGINIA.

No.	Year	CANDIDATES FOR PRESIDENT.	Popular	Per cent Popular	Majority	Electoral	Popular	Increase Popular	Per cent Increase	Electoral
1	1789	George Washington	......	......	......	†10	......	......	......	12
2	1792	George Washington	......	......	......	21	......	......	......	21
3	1796	John Adams	......	......	......	1	......	......	......	21
		Thomas Jefferson	......	......	......	20	......	......	......	...
4	1800	Thomas Jefferson..	......	......	......	21	......	......	......	21
5	1804	Thomas Jefferson...	......	......	......	24	......	......	......	24
6	1808	James Madison ...	......	......	......	24	......	......	......	24
7	1812	James Madison ...	......	......	......	25	......	......	......	25
8	1816	James Monroe.....	......	......	......	25	......	......	......	25
9	1820	James Monroe.....	......	......	......	25	......	......	......	25
10	1824	John Q. Adams....	3,189	21.3	......	...	14,955	......	......	24
		Andrew Jackson.	2,861	19.1	......	...	......	......	......	...
		Wm. H. Crawford	8,489	56.8	2,023	24	......	......	......	...
		Henry Clay	416	2.8	......	...	......	......	......	...
11	1828	Andrew Jackson...	26,752	68.9	14,651	24	38,853	23,898	159.8	24
		John Q. Adams..	12,101	31.1	......	...	......	......	......	...
12	1832	Andrew Jackson...	33,609	74.6	22,158	23	45,060	6,207	15.9	23
		Henry Clay	11,451	25.4	......	...	......	......	......	...
13	1836	Martin Van Buren..	30,261	56.4	6,893	23	53,629	8,509	19.0	23
		Wm. H. Harrison	23,368	43.6	......	...	......	......	......	...
14	1840	Wm. H. Harrison..	42,501	49.2	......	...	86,394	32,765	61.1	23
		Martin Van Buren	43,893	50.8	1,392	23	......	......	......	...
15	1844	James K. Polk.....	49,570	53.2	5,893	17	93,247	6,853	7.9	17
		Henry Clay......	43,677	46.8	......	...	......	......	......	...
16	1848	Zachary Taylor....	45,124	49.2	......	...	91,719	†1,528	†1.7	17
		Lewis Cass.......	46,586	50.8	1,453	17	......	......	......	...
		Martin V n Buren	9	......	......	...	......	......	......	...
17	1852	Franklin Pierce...	73,858	55.8	15,286	15	132,430	40,711	44.4	15
		Winfield Scott ...	58,572	44.2	......	...	......	......	......	...
18	1856	James Buchanan...	89,706	59.7	29,105	15	150,307	17,877	13.5	15
		John C. Fremont.	291	.2	......	...	......	......	......	...
		Millard Fillmore.	60,310	40.1	......	...	......	......	......	...
19	1860	Abraham Lincoln ..	1,929	1.2	......	...	167,223	16,916	11.8	15
		J. C. Breckinridge	74,323	44.4	......	...	......	......	......	...
		John Bell........	74,681	44.7	*358	15	......	......	......	...
		S. A. Douglas....	16,290	9.7	......	...	......	......	......	...
20	1864	......	......	......	......	...	......	......	......	...
21	1868	......	......	......	......	...	......	......	......	...
22	1872	Ulysses S. Grant...	93,468	50.5	1,772	11	185,164	17,911	10.7	11
		Horace Greeley ..	91,654	49.5	......	...	......	......	......	...
		Charles O'Conor.	42	......	......	...	......	......	......	...
23	1876	Rutherford B. Hayes	95,558	40.6	......	...	235,228	50,064	27.0	11
		Samuel J. Tilden.	139,670	59.4	44,112	11	......	......	......	...

WEST VIRGINIA.

No.	Year	CANDIDATES FOR PRESIDENT.	Popular	Per cent Popular	Majority	Electoral	Popular	Increase Popular	Per cent Increase	Electoral
20	1864	Abraham Lincoln..	23,152	68.9	12,714	5	33,590	......	......	5
		Geo. B. McClellan	10,438	31.1	......	...	......	......	......	...
21	1868	Ulysses S. Grant...	29,175	59.0	8,869	5	49,481	15,891	47.3	5
		Horatio Seymour.	20,306	41.0	......	...	......	......	......	...
22	1872	Ulysses S. Grant...	32,315	51.8	2,864	5	62,366	12,885	26.0	5
		Horace Greeley ..	29,451	47.2	......	...	......	......	......	...
		Charles O'Conor.	600	1.0	......	...	......	......	......	...
23	1876	Rutherford B. Hayes	42,698	42.5	......	...	100,526	38,160	61.2	5
		Samuel J. Tilden.	56,455	56.1	12,384	5	......	......	......	...
		Peter Cooper.....	1,373	1.4	......	...	......	......	......	...

* Plurality. † Decrease. ‡ Two votes not cast.

WISCONSIN.

Election		Candidates for President.	Vote for Candidates.				Total Vote.			
No.	Year.		Popular	Per cent Popular.	Majority.	Electoral.	Popular.	Increase Popular.	Per cent Increase.	Electoral.
16	1848	Zachary Taylor.....	13,747	35.1			39,166			4
		Lewis Cass........	15,001	28.3	*1,254	4				
		Martin Van Buren	10,418	26.6						
17	1852	Franklin Pierce....	33,658	52.0	2,604	5	64,712	25,546	65.2	5
		Winfield Scott....	22,240	34.4						
		John P. Hale.....	8,814	13.6						
18	1856	James Buchanan..	52,843	44.2			119,512	54,800	84.7	5
		John C. Fremont.	66,090	55.3	12,668	5				
		Millard Fillmore..	579	.5						
19	1860	Abraham Lincoln..	86,110	56.6	20,040	5	132,180	32,668	27.3	5
		J.C. Breckinridge	888	.6						
		John Bell........	161	.1						
		S. A. Douglas....	65,021	42.7						
20	1864	Abraham Lincoln..	83,458	55.9	17,574	8	149,342	†2,838	†1.8	8
		Geo. B. McClellan	65,884	44.1						
21	1868	Ulysses S. Grant...	108,857	56.2	24,150	8	193,564	44,222	29.6	8
		Horatio Seymour..	84,707	43.8						
22	1872	Ulysses S. Grant..	104,997	54.0	17,686	10	192,308	†1,256	†.7	10
		Horace Greeley..	86,477	45.0						
		Charles O'Conor..	834	.4						
23	1876	Rutherford B. Hayes	130,668	51.0	5,205	10	256,131	63,823	33.2	10
		Samuel J. Tilden.	123,927	48.4						
		Peter Cooper.....	1,509	.6						
		G. C. Smith......	27							

NUMBER OF SUCCESSFUL AND UNSUCCESSFUL CANDIDATES CHOSEN BY EACH STATE.

States.	Successful.	Unsuccessful.	No. Elections.	States.	Successful.	Unsuccessful.	No. Elections.	States.	Successful.	Unsuccessful.	No. Elections.	States.	Successful.	Unsuccessful.	No. Elections.
1 Alabama	9	5	14	11 Iowa.....	6	2	8	21 Missouri.	9	6	15	31 Rhode Is.	15	7	22
2 Arkansas	6	4	10	12 Kansas..	4		4	22 Neb......	3	..	3	32 S. C......	15	7	22
3 Califor'a.	7	..	7	13 Ky	11	11	22	23 Nevada..	4	..	4	33 Tenn....	12	8	20
4 Colorado	1	..	1	14 La......	13	3	16	24 N. H....	16	7	23	34 Texas....	2	4	6
5 Conn....	13	10	23	15 Maine...	12	3	15	25 N. J....	14	9	23	35 Vermont	15	7	22
6 Delawa'e	9	14	23	16 Md......	13	10	23	26 N. Y.....	18	4	22	36 Virginia.	15	6	21
7 Florida.	6	1	7	17 Mass....	13	10	23	27 N. C.....	16	5	21	37 W. Va...	3	1	4
8 Georgia.	15	7	22	18 Mich	9	2	11	28 Ohio....	14	5	19	38 Wiscona.	6	2	8
9 Illinois..	12	3	15	19 Minn....	5	.	5	29 Oregon..	4	1	5				
10 Indiana..	12	4	16	20 Miss.....	9	4	13	30 Penn....	21	2	23				

* Plurality.   † Decrease.

NUMBER OF ELECTORAL VOTES TO WHICH EACH STATE HAS BEEN ENTITLED AT EACH ELECTION, 1789-1876.

STATES.	1 1789	2 1792	3 1796	4 1800	5 1804	6 1808	7 1812	8 1816	9 1820	10 1824	11 1828	12 1832	13 1836	14 1840	15 1844	16 1848	17 1852	18 1856	19 1860	20 1864	21 1868	22 1872	23 1876
Ala..									3	5	5	7	7	7	9	9	9	0	0	8	8	10	10
Ark..													3	3	3	3	4	4	4	5	5	6	6
Cal..																	4	4	4	5	5	6	6
Col ..																							3
Conn.	7	9	9	9	9	9	9	9	9	8	8	8	8	8	6	6	6	6	6	6	6	6	6
Del..	3	3	3	3	3	3	4	4	4	3	3	3	3	3	3	3	3	3	3	3	3	3	3
Fla..																3	3	3	3	3	3	4	4
Ga...	5	4	4	4	6	6	8	8	8	9	9	11	11	11	10	10	10	9	9		11	11	11
Ill..									3	3	3	5	5	5	9	9	11	11	11	16	16	21	21
Ind..								3	3	5	5	9	9	9	12	12	13	13	13	13	13	15	15
Iowa.																4	4	4	4	8	8	11	11
Kan.																				3	3	5	5
Ky...		4	4	4	6	8	12	12	12	14	14	15	15	15	12	12	12	12	12	11	11	12	12
La...										3	3	3	5	5	5	5	6	6	6	7	7	8	8
Me...									9	9	9	10	10	10	9	9	8	8	8	7	7	7	7
Md...	8	10	10	10	11	11	11	11	11	11	10	10	10	8	8	8	8	8	7	7	8	8	8
Mass.	10	16	16	16	19	19	22	22	15	15	15	14	14	14	12	12	13	12	13	12	12	13	13
Mich.													3	3	5	5	6	6	6	8	8	11	11
Minn.																			4	4	4	5	5
Miss..									3	3	3	4	4	4	6	6	7	7	7	7	7	8	8
Mo..									3	3	3	4	4	4	7	7	9	9	9	11	11	15	15
Neb..																					3	3	3
Nev..																				3	3	3	3
N. H.	5	6	6	6	7	7	8	8	8	8	8	7	7	7	6	6	5	5	5	5	5	5	5
N. J..	6	7	7	7	8	8	8	8	8	8	8	8	8	7	7	7	7	7	7	7	7	9	9
N. Y..	8	12	12	12	19	19	29	29	29	36	36	42	42	42	36	36	35	35	35	33	33	35	35
N. C..	7	12	12	12	14	14	15	15	15	15	15	15	11	11	10	10	10	10	10	9	9	10	10
Ohio..					3	3	8	8	8	16	16	21	21	21	23	23	23	23	23	21	21	22	22
Or....																			3	3	3	3	3
Penn.	10	15	15	15	20	20	25	25	25	28	28	30	30	30	26	26	27	27	27	26	26	29	29
R. I..	3	4	4	4	4	4	4	4	4	4	4	4	4	4	4	4	4	4	4	4	4	4	4
S. C..	7	8	8	8	10	10	11	11	11	11	11	11	11	9	9	8	8	8	8	6	6	7	7
Tenn.			3	3	5	5	8	8	8	11	11	15	15	15	13	13	12	12	12	10	10	12	12
Tex..																4	4	4	4	6	6	8	8
Vt...				4	4	6	6	8	8	8	7	7	7	7	6	6	5	5	5	5	5	5	5
Va...	12	21	21	21	24	24	25	25	25	24	24	23	23	23	17	17	15	15	15	10	10	11	11
W.Va																				5	5	5	5
Wis...																4	5	5	5	8	8	10	10
Total.	91	135	138	138	176	176	218	221	235	261	261	288	294	294	275	290	296	296	303	314	317	366	369
No. of States	13	15	16	16	17	17	18	19	24	24	24	24	26	26	30	31	31	33	36	27	37	38	

RATIO OF REPRESENTATION IN THE HOUSE OF REPRESENTATIVES.

From 1789 to 1792, according to Constitution 30,000
"   1792 to 1803, based on 1st census, 1790 33,000
"   1803 to 1813,   "   2d   "   1800 33,000
"   1813 to 1823,   "   3d   "   1810 35,000
"   1823 to 1832,   "   4th   "   1820 40,000
"   1832 to 1843,   "   5th   "   1830 47,700
"   1843 to 1852,   "   6th   "   1840 70,680
"   1852 to 1863,   "   7th   "   1850 93,423
"   1863 to 1872,   "   8th   "   1860 127,381
"   1872 to ....,   "   9th   "   1870 131,425

CUSTOMS REVENUE OF THE UNITED STATES.

A Comparative Statement showing the Customs Revenue, Amount of Dutiable and Free Goods Imported, and the Average Rate of Duty in each Year from 1821 to 1877, inclusive.

[From the Official Reports on Commerce and Navigation.]

Year.	Receipts from Customs.	Imports.			Per cent on Dutiable	Per cent on Aggregate.
		Free.	Dutiable.	Total Amount Imported.		
1821.....	$18,475,704	$10,082,313	$32,503,411	$42,585,724	35.6	29.5
1822.....	24,066,066	7,298,708	75,942,833	83,241,541	31.7	28.9
1823.....	22,402,024	9,048,288	68,530,979	77,579,267	32.7	23.8
1824.....	25,486,817	12,563,773	67,985,234	80,549,007	37.5	31.6
1825.....	31,653,871	10,947,510	85,392,565	96,340,075	37.1	32.8
1826.....	26,083,862	12,567,769	72,406,708	84,974,477	34.6	20.7
1827.....	27,948,957	11,855,104	67,628,964	79,484,068	41.3	25.1
1828.....	20,951,252	12,379,176	76,130,648	88,509,824	39.3	33.8
1829.....	27,688,701	11,805,501	62,687,026	74,492,527	44.3	37.1
1830.....	28,389,505	12,746,245	58,130,675	70,876,920	48.8	40
1831.....	36,596,118	13,456,625	89,734,499	103,191,124	40.8	35.4
1832.....	29,341,176	14,249,453	86,779,813	101,029,266	33.8	29
1833.....	24,177,578	32,477,950	75,670,361	108,118,311	31.9	22.4
1834.....	18,960,706	68,393,180	58,128,152	126,521,332	32.6	15
1835.....	25,890,727	77,940,493	71,955,249	149,895,742	36.0	17.2
1836.....	30,818,328	92,056,481	97,923,554	189,990,035	31.6	16.2
1837.....	18,134,131	69,250,031	71,739,186	140,989,217	25.3	12.4
1838.....	19,702,825	60,860,005	52,857,399	113,717,404	37.8	17.3
1839.....	25,554,534	76,401,792	85,690,340	162,092,132	29.9	13.8
1840.....	15,104,791	57,196,204	49,945,315	107,141,519	30.4	14.1
1841.....	19,919,493	66,019,731	61,926,446	127,946,177	33.2	13.6
1842.....	16,662,747	30,627,486	69,534,601	100,162,087	23.1	16.6
1843.....	10,208,000	35,574,584	29,179,215	64,753,799	35.7	15.7
1844.....	29,236,357	24,766,881	83,668,154	108,435,035	35.1	26.9
1845.....	30,952,416	22,147,840	95,106,724	117,254,564	30.5	26.4
1846.....	26,712,668	24,767,739	96,924,058	121,691,797	26½	21.9
1847.....	23,747,865	41,772,636	101,773,002	146,545,638	22½	16.2
1848.....	31,757,071	22,716,603	132,282,325	154,999,928	24	20.4
1849.....	28,346,739	22,377,665	125,479,774	147,857,439	23	19.2
1850.....	39,668,686	22,710,382	145,427,936	178,138,318	25.2	22.3
1851.....	49,017,568	25,106,587	191,118,345	216,224,932	26	22.6
1852.....	47,339,326	29,602,934	183,252,508	212,945,442	26	22.2
1853.....	58,931,865	31,383,534	236,595,113	267,978,647	25	22
1854.....	64,224,190	33,285,821	271,276,560	304,562,381	23.5	21.1
1855.....	53,025,794	40,090,336	221,378,184	261,468,520	23	20.3
1856.....	64,022,863	56,955,706	257,684,236	314,439,942	23	20.3
1857.....	63,875,905	66,729,306	294,160,835	360,890,141	21.5	17.7
1858.....	41,789,621	80,319,275	202,293,875	282,613,150	20	14.8
1859.....	49,565,824	79,721,116	259,047,014	338,768,130	19	14.6
1860.....	53,187,511	90,841,749	279,872,327	362,166,254	19	14.7
1861.....	39,582,126	117,469,962	218,180,191	335,650,153	18.14	11.79
1862.....	49,056,398	69,136,705	136,635,024	205,771,729	35.90	23.84
1863.....	69,059,642	44,836,029	208,093,891	252,919,920	33.19	27.30
1864.....	102,316,153	54,241,944	275,320,951	329,562,895	37.16	31.04
1865.....	84,928,260	54,329,585	194,226,064	248,555,652	43.75	34.17
1866.....	179,046,630	69,728,618	375,783,540	445,512,158	47.65	40.19
1867.....	176,417,811	45,203,970	372,627,601	417,831,571	47.34	42.22
1868.....	164,464,599	29,379,149	342,245,659	371,624,808	48.05	44.25
1869.....	180,048,427	41,454,568	395,859,687	437,314,255	45.48	41.17
1870.....	192,878,265	46,508,795	415,845,856	462,354,651	46.37	41.71
1871.....	206,270,408	57,857,761	483,635,947	541,493,708	42.64	38.11
1872.....	216,370,287	61,010,902	579,327,864	640,338,766	37.34	33.77
1873.....	188,080,523	166,296,821	497,320,326	663,617,147	37.82	28.34
1874.....	163,103,834	180,117,061	415,748,693	595,865,754	39.20	27.54
1875.....	157,167,722	167,255,005	379,795,113	547,050,118	41.38	28.73
1876.....	148,071,985	156,298,594	320,379,277	476,677,871	46.21	31.06
1877.....	128,223,204	181,528,251	298,999,233	480,517,489	42.88	26.68

NOTE.—The percentages of duty are only approximately, not absolutely, correct, the rates being computed for the earlier years upon the gross value of merchandise, etc., imported, instead of upon the value of goods entering into consumption in the respective years.

45TH CONGRESS.—March 4, 1877, to March 4, 1879.

ALPHABETICAL LIST OF SENATORS.

Vice-President (President of the Senate), WILLIAM A. WHEELER, Malone, N. Y.

Allison, William B., Dubuque, Iowa.
Anthony, Henry B., Providence, R. I.
Armstrong, D H., St. Louis, Mo.
Bailey, James E., Clarksville, Tenn.
Barnum, William II., Lime Rock, Conn.
Bayard, Thomas F., Wilmington, Del.
Beck, James B., Lexington, Ky.
Blaine, James G., Augusta, Maine.
Booth, Newton, Sacramento, Cal.
Bruce, Blanche K., Floreyville, Miss.
Burnside, Ambrose E., Providence, R. I.
Butler. Manning C., Edgefield C. H., S.C.
Cameron, Angus, La Crosse, Wis.
Cameron, J. D., Harrisburg, Pa.
Chaffee, Jerome B., Denver, Col.
Christiancy, Isaac P., Lansing, Mich.
Cockrell, Francis M., Warrensburg, Mo.
Coke, Richard, Waco, Texas.
Conkling, Roscoe, Utica, N. Y.
Conover, Simon B., Tallahassee, Fla.
Davis, David, Bloomington, Ill.
Davis, Henry G., Piedmont, West Va.
Dawes, Henry L., Pittsfield, Mass.
Dennis, George R., Kingston, Md.
Dorsey, Stephen W., Helena, Ark.
Eaton, William W., Hartford, Conn.
Edmunds, George F., Burlington, Vt.
Eustis, James B., New Orleans, La.
Ferry, T. W., Grand Haven, Mich.
Garland, A. II., Little Rock, Ark.
Gordon, John B., Atlanta, Ga.
Grover, L. F., Salem, Oregon.
Hamlin, Hannibal, Bangor, Maine.
Harris, Isham G., Memphis, Tenn.
Hereford, Frank, Union, West Va.
Hill, Benjamin II., Atlanta, Ga.
Hoar, George F., Worcester, Mass.
Howe, Timothy O., Green Bay, Wis.

Ingalls, John J., Atchison, Kan.
Johnston, John W., Abingdon, Va.
Jones, Charles W , Pensacola, Fla.
Jones, John P., Gold Hill, Nev.
Kellogg, Wm. P., New Orleans, La
Kernan, Francis, Utica, N. Y.
Kirkwood, S. J., Iowa City, Iowa.
Lamar, L. Q. C., Oxford, Miss.
Matthews, Stanley, Glendale, Ohio.
Maxey, Samuel B., Paris, Texas.
McCreery, Thos. C., Owensborough, Ky.
McDonald, Joseph E., Indianapolis, Ind.
McMillan, Samuel J. R., St. Paul, Minn.
McPherson, J. R., Jersey City, N. J.
Merrimon, A. S., Raleigh, N. C.
Mitchell, John H., Portland, Oregon.
Morgan, John T., Selma, Ala.
Morrill, Justin S., Strafford, Vt.
Oglesby, Richard J., Decatur, Ill.
Paddock, Algernon S., Beatrice, Neb.
Patterson, John J., Charleston, S. C.
Plumb, J. B., Emporia, Kansas.
Randolph, Theo. F., Morristown, N. J.
Ransom, Matt W., Weldon, N. C.
Rollins, E. II., Concord, N. II.
Sargent, Aaron A., San Francisco, Cal.
Saulsbury, Eli, Dover, Del.
Saunders, A., Omaha, Neb.
Sharon, William, Virginia City, Nev.
Spencer, George E., Decatur, Ala.
Teller, Henry M., Central City, Col.
Thurman, Allen G., Columbus, O.
Wadleigh, Bainbridge, Milford, N. II.
Wallace, William A., Clearfield, Pa.
Whyte, William Pinkney, Baltimore, Md.
Windom, William, Winona, Minn.
Withers, Robert E., Wytheville, Va.

PRINCIPAL OFFICERS OF THE SENATE.

President of the Senate.—WILLIAM A. WHEELER, Vice-President of the U. S.
Chaplain.—Rev. Byron Sunderland, D.D.
Secretary of the Senate.—George C. Gorham.
Chief Clerk.—W. J. McDonald.
Sergeant-at-Arms.—John R. French.
Postmaster.—W. E. Creary.
Superintendent of Folding-Room.—L. D. Merchant.
Superintendent of Document-Room.—Amzi Smith.

Official Reporters of Debates.

D. F. Murphy.

Assistants.—Theo. F. Shuey. E. V. Murphy. Henry J. Gensler. R. S. Boswell

45TH CONGRESS.—March 4, 1877, to March 4, 1879.

SENATE.—List of Members by States, with their Terms of Office.

ALABAMA.		
Term Expires.		Residence.
1879	George E. Spencer, R	....Decatur.
1883	John T. Morgan, D	.........Selma.

INDIANA.		
Term Expires.		Residence.
1879	Dan. W. Voorhees, D	..Terre Haute.
1881	Jos. E. McDonald, D	..Indianapolis.

ARKANSAS.		
1879	Stephen W. Dorsey, R	....Helena.
1883	Aug. H. Garland, D	...Little Rock.

IOWA.		
1879	William B. Allison, R	...Dubuque.
1883	Samuel J. Kirkwood, R	..Iowa City.

CALIFORNIA.		
1879	Aaron A. Sargent, R	..Nevada City.
1881	Newton Booth, R	.....Sacramento.

KANSAS.		
1879	John J. Ingalls, R	.......Atchison.
1883	Preston B. Plumb, R	.....Emporia.

COLORADO.		
1879	Jerome B. Chaffee, R	......Denver.
1883	Henry M. Teller, R	...Central City.

KENTUCKY.		
1879	Thos. C. McCreery,D	..Owensboro'.
1883	James B. Beck, D	......Lexington.

CONNECTICUT.		
1879	William H. Barnum, D.	Lime Rock.
1881	William W. Eaton, D	....Hartford.

LOUISIANA.		
1879	James B. Eustis, D	.New Orleans.
1883	Wm. P. Kellogg, R.	.New Orleans.

DELAWARE.		
1881	Thos. F. Bayard, D	...Wilmington.
1883	Eli Saulsbury, D	.... Kenton.

MAINE.		
1881	Hannibal Hamlin, R	.......Bangor.
1883	James G. Blaine, R	......Augusta.

FLORIDA.		
1879	Simon B. Conover, R.	.Tallahassee.
1881	Charles W. Jones. D	....Pensacola.

MARYLAND.		
1879	George R. Dennis, D	....Kingston.
1881	Wm. Pinkney Whyte,D	..Baltimore.

GEORGIA.		
1879	John B. Gordon, D	........Atlanta.
1883	Benj. H. Hill, D	...........Atlanta.

MASSACHUSETTS		
1881	Henry L. Dawes, R	.....Pittsfield.
1883	George F. Hoar, R	.....Worcester.

ILLINOIS.		
1879	Richard J. Oglesby, R	...Decatur.
1883	David Davis, Ind	....Bloomington.

MICHIGAN.		
1881	Isaac P. Christiancy, R	...Lansing.
1883	Thos. W. Ferry, R	..Grand Haven.

SENATE.—LIST OF MEMBERS BY STATES—(*Continued*).

MINNESOTA.		
Term Expires.		Residence.
1881	Sam. J. R. McMillan, R..St. Paul.	
1883	William Windom, R......	Winona.

MISSISSIPPI.		
1881	Blanche K. Bruce, R...Floreyville.	
1883	Lucius Q. C. Lamar, D....Oxford.	

MISSOURI.		
1879	David H. Armstrong, D..St. Louis.	
1881	Francis M. Cockrell, D..Warrens'g.	

NEBRASKA.		
1881	Algernon S. Paddock, R..Beatrice.	
1883	Alvin Saunders, R.........Omaha.	

NEVADA.		
1879	John P. Jones, R........Gold Hill.	
1881	William Sharon, R.. Virginia City.	

NEW HAMPSHIRE.		
1879	Bainbridge Wadleigh, R..Milford.	
1883	Edward H. Rollins, R....Concord.	

NEW JERSEY.		
1881	Theo. F.Randolph, D..Morristown.	
1883	John R.McPherson,D..Jersey City.	

NEW YORK.		
1879	Roscoe Conkling, R........ Utica.	
1881	Francis Kernan, D...... ...Utica.	

NORTH CAROLINA.		
1879	Aug. S. Merrimon, D......Raleigh.	
1883	Matt.W. Ransom, D......Weldon.	

OHIO.		
1879	Stanley Matthews, R ....Glendale.	
1881	Allen G. Thurman, D...Columbus.	

OREGON.		
Term Expires.		Residence.
1879	John H. Mitchell, R......Portland.	
1883	Lafayette Grover, D........Salem.	

PENNSYLVANIA.		
1879	Jas.Donald Cameron,R..Harrisb'g.	
1881	William A. Wallace, D..Clearfield.	

RHODE ISLAND.		
1881	Ambrose E. Burnside, R..Provid'c.	
1883	Henry B. Anthony, R..Providence.	

SOUTH CAROLINA.		
1879	John J. Patterson, R..Charleston.	
1883	ManningC.Butler,D.,EdgefieldC.H.	

TENNESSEE.		
1881	James E. Bailey, D....Clarksville.	
1883	Isham G. Harris, D.....Memphis.	

TEXAS.		
1881	Samuel B. Maxey, D....... Paris.	
1883	Richard Coke, D...........Waco.	

VERMONT.		
1879	Justin S. Morrill, R.... Strafford.	
1881	George F.Edmunds, R..Burlington.	

VIRGINIA.		
1881	Robert E. Withers, D..Wytheville.	
1883	John W. Johnston, D...Abingdon.	

WEST VIRGINIA.		
1881	Frank Hereford, D.........Union.	
1883	Henry G. Davis, D......Piedmont.	

WISCONSIN.		
1879	Timothy O. Howe. R...Green Bay.	
1881	Angus Cameron, R......La Crosse.	

```
Republicans............................  ........ .. .............. 39
Democrats................................ ............................36
Independent...... ............. .......  .......................... 1
                                                                  —
    Total.................................... ...................  .......76
```

COMMITTEES OF THE SENATE—45TH CONGRESS, 1877-79.

Committee on Privileges and Elections.

B. Wadleigh, of N. H.
J. H. Mitchell, of Oregon.
Angus Cameron, of Wis.
S. J. R. McMillan, of Minn.
George F. Hoar, of Mass.
J. J. Ingalls, of Kan.
Eli Saulsbury, of Del.
A S. Merrimon, of N. C.
Benjamin H. Hill, of Ga.

Foreign Relations.

Hannibal Hamlin, of Me.
Timothy O. Howe, of Wis.
Roscoe Conkling, of N. Y.
Stanley Matthews, of Ohio.
S. J. Kirkwood, of Iowa.
T. C. McCreery, of Ky.
W. W. Eaton, of Conn.
John W. Johnston, of Va.
W. A. Wallace, of Pa.

Finance.

Justin S. Morrill, of Vt.
Henry L. Dawes, of Mass.
Thomas W. Ferry, of Mich.
John P. Jones, of Nev.
W. B. Allison, of Iowa.
Thomas F. Bayard, of Del.
Francis Kernan, of N. Y.
W. A. Wallace, of Pa.
D. W. Voorhees, of Ind.

Appropriations.

William Windom, of Minn.
Aaron A. Sargent, of Cal.
W. B. Allison, of Iowa.
Stephen W. Dorsey, of Ark.
James G. Blaine, of Me.
Henry G. Davis, of W. Va.
Robert E. Withers, of Va.
W. W. Eaton, of Conn.
James B. Beck, of Ky.

Commerce.

Roscoe Conkling, of N. Y.
George E. Spencer, of Ala.
S. J. R. McMillan, of Minn.
John J. Patterson, of S. C.
John P. Jones, of Nev.
John B. Gordon, of Geo.
George R. Dennis, of Md.
Matt W. Ransom, of N. C.
T. F. Randolph, of N. J.

Manufactures.

Edward H. Rollins, of N. H.
A. E. Burnside, of R. I.
J. D. Cameron, of Pa.
John W. Johnston, of Va.
J. R. McPherson, of N. J.

Agriculture.

A. S. Paddock, of Neb.
William Sharon, of Nev.
George F. Hoar, of Mass.
Henry G. Davis, of W. Va.
John B. Gordon, of Ga.

Military Affairs.

George E. Spencer, of Ala.
A. E. Burnside, of R. I.
B. Wadleigh, of N. H.
P. B. Plumb, of Kan.
J. D. Cameron, of Pa.
T. F. Randolph, of N. J.
Francis M. Cockrell, of Mo.
Samuel B. Maxey, of Texas.
M. C. Butler, of S. C.

Naval Affairs.

Aaron A. Sargent, of Cal.
Henry B. Anthony, of R. I.
Simon B. Conover, of Fla.
James G. Blaine, of Me.
William P. Whyte, of Md.
J. R. McPherson, of N. J.
C. W. Jones, of Fla.

Judiciary.

George F. Edmunds, of Vt.
Roscoe Conkling, of N. Y.
Timothy O. Howe, of Wis.
I. P. Christiancy, of Mich.
David Davis, of Ill.
Allen G. Thurman, of O.
J. E. McDonald, of Ind.

Post-Offices and Post-Roads.

T. W. Ferry, of Mich.
Hannibal Hamlin, of Me.
A. S. Paddock, of Neb.
Simon B. Conover, of Fla.
S. J. Kirkwood, of Iowa.
A. E. Burnside, of R. I.
Eli Saulsbury, of Del.
Samuel B. Maxey, of Tex.
James E. Bailey, of Tenn.

Public Lands.

Richard J. Oglesby, of Ill.
A. S. Paddock, of Neb.
Newton Booth, of Cal.
Jerome B. Chaffee, of Col.
P. B. Plumb, of Kan.
J. E. McDonald, of Ind.
Charles W. Jones, of Fla.
L. F. Grover, of Oregon.
A. H. Garland, of Ark.

Private Land-Claims.

Allen G. Thurman, of O.
Thomas F. Bayard, of Del.
George F. Edmunds, of Vt.
I. P. Christiancy, of Mich.
L. F. Grover, of Oregon.

Indian Affairs.

William B. Allison, of Ia.
Richard J. Oglesby, of Ill.
John J. Ingalls, of Kan.
A. Saunders, of Neb.
T. C. McCreery, of Ky.
Richard Coke, of Texas.
J. E. McDonald, of Ind.

Pensions.

John J. Ingalls, of Kan.
Blanche K. Bruce, of Miss.
S. J. Kirkwood, of Iowa.
W. P. Kellogg, of La.
Robert E. Withers, of Va.
James E. Bailey, of Tenn.
D. W. Voorhees, of Ind.

Revolutionary Claims.

J. W. Johnston, of Va.
Charles W. Jones, of Fla.
Benjamin H. Hill, of Ga.
Henry L. Dawes, of Mass.
S. J. R. McMillan, of Minn.

Claims.

S. J. R. McMillan, of Minn.
John H. Mitchell, of Or.
Angus Cameron, of Wis.
Henry M. Teller, of Col.
George F. Hoar, of Mass.
F. M. Cockrell, of Mo.
Frank Hereford, of W. Va.
I. G. Harris, of Tenn.
J. T. Morgan, of Ala.

COMMITTEES OF THE SENATE—(Continued).

District of Columbia.

S. W. Dorsey, of Ark.
G. E. Spencer, of Ala.
John J. Ingalls, of Kan.
E. H. Rollins, of N. H.
A. S. Merrimon, of N. C.
William H. Barnum, of Ct.
I. G. Harris, of Tenn.

Patents.

Newton Booth, of Cal.
B. Wadleigh, of N. H.
George F. Hoar, of Mass.
Francis Kernan, of N. Y.
J. T. Morgan, of Ala.

Territories.

John J. Patterson, of S. C.
Jerome B. Chaffee, of Col.
A. Saunders, of Neb.
W. P. Kellogg, of La.
A. H. Garland, of Ark.
L. F. Grover, of Oregon.
Frank Hereford, of W. Va.

Railroads.

John H. Mitchell, of Or.
Henry L. Dawes, of Mass.
S. W. Dorsey, of Ark.
H. M. Teller, of Col.
A. Saunders, of Neb.
Matt W. Ransom, of N. C.
W. H. Barnum, of Ct.
L. Q. C. Lamar, of Miss.
D. H. Armstrong, of Mo.
W. Windom, of Minn.
S. Matthews, of Ohio.

Mines and Mining.

William Sharon, of Nev.
Jerome B. Chaffee, of Col.
Newton Booth, of Cal.
P. B. Plumb, of Kan.
Frank Hereford, of W. Va.
Richard Coke, of Tex.
Benjamin H. Hill, of Ga.

Revision of the Laws of the United States.

I. P. Christiancy, of Mich.
S. Matthews, of Ohio.
David Davis, of Ill.
W. A. Wallace, of Pa.
Francis Kernan, of N. Y.

Education and Labor.

A. E. Burnside, of R. I.
John J. Patterson, of S. C.
Justin S. Morrill, of Vt.

Blanche K. Bruce, of Miss.
William Sharon, of Nev.
John B. Gordon, of Ga.
S. B. Maxey, of Texas.
James E. Bailey, of Tenn.
L. Q. C. Lamar, of Miss.

Civil Service and Retrenchment.

H. M. Teller, of Col.
Richard J. Oglesby, of Ill.
John J. Patterson, of S. C.
Newton Booth, of Cal.
T. C. McCreery, of Ky.
W. P. Whyte, of Md.
James B. Beck, of Ky.

Audit and Control the Contingent Expenses of the Senate.

J. P. Jones, of Nev.
E. H. Rollins, of N. H.
George R. Dennis, of Md.

Engrossed Bills.

T. F. Bayard, of Del.
Robert E. Withers, of Va.
H. B. Anthony, of R. I.

Rules.

James G. Blaine, of Me.
T. W. Ferry, of Mich.
A. S. Merrimon, of N. C.

Public Printing.

H. B. Anthony, of R. I.
A. A. Sargent, of Cal.
W. Pinkney Whyte, of Md.

Enrolled Bills.

Simon B. Conover, of Fla.
A. S. Paddock, of Neb.
D. H. Armstrong, of Mo.

Joint Committee on the Library.

Timothy O. Howe, of Wis.
George F. Edmunds, of Vt.
Matt W. Ransom, of N. C.

Public Buildings and Grounds.

H. L. Dawes, of Mass.
Justin S. Morrill, of Vt.
J. D. Cameron, of Pa.
Eli Saulsbury, of Del.
Charles W. Jones, of Fla.

SELECT COMMITTEES.

On the Levees of the Mississippi River.

Blanche K. Bruce, of Miss.
James G. Blaine, of Me.
W. P. Kellogg, of La.
Francis M. Cockrell, of Mo.
I. G. Harris, of Tenn.

On Transportation Routes to the Seaboard.

Angus Cameron, of Wis.
William Windom, of Minn.
Simon B. Conover, of Fla.
J. D. Cameron, of Pa.
Henry G. Davis, of W. Va.
L. Q. C. Lamar, of Miss.
James B. Beck, of Ky.
M. C. Butler, of S. C.

To Examine the Several Branches of the Civil Service.

J. B. Chaffee, of Col.
William Windom, of Minn.
H. Hamlin, of Me.
A. S. Merrimon, of N. C.
William W. Eaton, of Ct.

To take into Consideration the State of the Law respecting the Ascertaining and Declaration of the Result of the Elections of President and Vice-President of the United States.

Geo. F. Edmunds, of Vt.
R. Conkling, of N. Y.
T. O. Howe, of Wis.
S. J. R. McMillan, of Minn.
H. M. Teller, of Col.
David Davis, of Ill.
T. F. Bayard, of Del.
A. G. Thurman, of Ohio.
John T. Morgan, of Ala.

To Investigate the Finance Reports, Books, and Accounts of the Treasury Department.

H. G. Davis, of W. Va.
James B. Beck, of Ky.
W. B. Allison, of Iowa.
J. J. Ingalls, of Kan.
J. D. Cameron, of Pa.

45TH CONGRESS.—March 4, 1877, to March 4, 1879.

ALPHABETICAL LIST OF REPRESENTATIVES.

SAMUEL J. RANDALL, *Speaker*, Philadelphia, Pa.

Aiken, D. Wyatt, Cokesbury, S. C.
Aldrich, William, Chicago, Ill.
Atkins, John D. C., Paris, Tenn.
Bacon, William J., Utica, N. Y.
Bagley, George A., Watertown, N. Y.
Baker, John H., Goshen, Ind.
Baker, William H., Constantia, N. Y.
Ballou, Latimer W., Woonsocket, R. I.
Banks, Nathauiel P., Waltham, Mass.
Banning, Henry B., Cincinnati, O.
Bayne, Thomas M., Pittsburgh, Pa.
Beebe, George M., Moutlcello, N. Y.
Bell, Hiram P., Cumming, Ga.
Benedict, Charles B., Attica, N. Y.
Bicknell, George A., New Albany, Ind.
Bisbee, Horatio, Jr., Jacksonville, Fla.
Blackburn, Joseph C. S., Versailles, Ky.
Blair, Henry W., Plymouth, N. H.
Bland, Richard P., Lebanon, Mo.
Bliss, Archibald M., Brooklyn, N. Y.
Blount, James H., Macon, Ga.
Boone, Andrew R., Mayfield, Ky.
Bouck, Gabriel, Oshkosh, Wis.
Boyd, Thomas A., Lewiston, Ill.
Bragg, Edward S., Fond du Lac, Wis.
Breutano, Lorenzo, Chicago, Ill.
Brewer, Mark S., Pontiac, Mich.
Bridges, Samuel A., Allentown, Pa.
Briggs, James F., Manchester, N. H.
Bright, John M., Fayetteville, Tenn.
Brogden, Curtis H., Goldsboro', N. C.
Browne, Thomas M., Winchester, Ind.
Buckner, Aylett H., Mexico, Mo.
Bundy, Solomon, Oxford, N. Y.
Burchard, Horatio C., Freeport, Ill.
Burdick, Theodore W., Decorah, Iowa.
Butler, Benjamin F., Lowell, Mass.
Cabell, George C., Danville, Va.
Cain, Richard H., Charleston, S. C.
Caldwell, John W., Russellville, Ky.
Caldwell, William P., Gardner, Tenn.
Calkins, William H., La Porte, Ind.
Camp, John H., Lyons, N. Y.
Campbell, Jacob M., Johnstown, Pa.
Candler, Milton A., Atlanta, Ga.
Cannon, Joseph G., Tuscola, Ill.
Carlisle, John G., Covington, Ky.
Caswell, Lucien B., Fort Atkinson, Wis.
Chalmers, J. R., Friar's Point, Miss.
Chittenden, Simeon B., Brooklyn, N. Y.
Claflin, William, Newton, Mass.
Clark, Alvah A., Somerville, N. J.
Clark, John B., Jr., Fayette, Mo.
Clark, Rush, Iowa City, Iowa.
Clarke, John B., Brooksville, Ky.
Clymer, Hiester, Reading, Pa.

Cobb, Thomas R., Vincennes, Ind.
Cole, Nathan, St. Louis, Mo.
Collins, Francis D., Scranton, Pa.
Conger, Omar D., Port Huron, Mich.
Cook, Philip, Americus. Ga.
Covert, James W., Flushing, N. Y.
Cox, Jacob D., Toledo, O.
Cox, Samuel S., New York, N. Y.
Crapo, William W., New Bedford, Mass.
Cravens, Jordan E., Clarksville, Ark.
Crittenden, Thos. T., Warrensburg, Mo.
Culberson, David B., Jefferson, Tex.
Cummings, Henry J.B., Winterset, Iowa.
Cutler, Augustus W., Morristown, N. J.
Danford, Lorenzo, St. Clairsville, O.
Darrall, Chester B., Brashear, La.
Davidson, Robert H. M., Quincy, Fla.
Davis, Horace, San Francisco, Cal.
Davis, Joseph J., Louisburg, N. C.
Deering, Nathaniel C., Osage, Iowa.
Denison, Dudley C., Royalton, Vt.
Dibrell, George G., Sparta, Tenn.
Dickey, H. L., Greenfield, O.
Douglas, Beverly B., Aylett's, Va.
Dunnell, Mark H., Owatonna, Minn.
Durham, Milton J., Danville, Ky.
Dwight, Jeremiah W., Dryden, N. Y.
Eames, Benjamin T., Providence, R. I.
Eden, John R., Sullivan, Ill.
Eickhoff, Anthony, New York, N. Y.
Elam, Joseph B., Mansfield, La.
Ellis, E. John, New Orleans, La.
Ellsworth, Charles C., Greenville, Mich.
Errett, Russell, Pittsburgh, Pa.
Evans, I. Newton, Hatboro, Pa.
Evans, James L., Noblesville, Ind.
Evins, John H., Spartanburg, S. C.
Ewing, Thomas, Lancaster, O.
Felton, William H., Cartersville, Ga.
Field, Walbridge A., Boston, Mass.
Finley, Ebenezer B., Bucyrus, O.
Forney, William H., Jacksonville, Ala.
Fort, Greenbury L., Lacon, Ill.
Foster, Charles, Fostoria, O.
Franklin, Benjamin J., Kansas City, Mo.
Freeman, Chapman, Philadelphia, Pa.
Frye, William P., Lewiston, Me.
Fuller, Benoni S., Boonville, Ind.
Gardner, Mills, Washington C. H., O.
Garfield, James A., Mentor, O.
Garth, William W., Huntsville, Ala.
Gause, Lucien C., Jacksonport, Ark.
Gibson, Randall L., New Orleans, La.
Giddings, D. C., Brenham, Tex.
Glover, John M., La Grange, Mo.
Goode, John, Norfolk, Va.

Gunter, Thomas M., Fayetteville, Ark.
Hale, Eugene, Ellsworth, Maine.
Hamilton, Andrew H., Fort Wayne, Ind.
Hanna, John, Indianapolis, Ind.
Hardenbergh, Aug. A., Jersey City, N. J.
Harmer, Alfred C., Germantown, Pa.
Harris, Benj. W., E. Bridgewater, Mass.
Harris, Henry R., Greenville, Ga.
Harris, John T., Harrisonburg, Va.
Harrison, Carter H., Chicago, Ill.
Hart, E. Kirke, Albion, N. Y.
Hartridge, Julian, Savannah, Ga.
Hartzell, William, Chester, Ill.
Haskell, Dudley C., Lawrence, Kan.
Hatcher, Robert A., New Madrid, Mo.
Hayes, Philip C., Morris, Ill.
Hazelton, George C., Boscobel, Wis.
Hendee, George W., Morrisville, Vt.
Henderson, Thomas J., Princeton, Ill.
Henkle, Eli J., Brooklyn, Md.
Henry, Daniel M., Cambridge, Md.
Herbert, Hilary A., Montgomery, Ala.
Hewitt, Abram S., New York, N. Y.
Hewitt, Goldsmith W.,Birmingham,Ala.
Hiscock, Frank, Syracuse, N. Y.
Hooker, Charles E., Jackson, Miss.
House, John F., Clarksville, Tenn.
Hubbell, Jay A., Houghton, Mich.
Humphrey, H. L., Hudson, Wis.
Hungerford, John N., Corning, N. Y.
Hunter, Morton C., Bloomington, Ind.
Hunton, Eppa, Warrenton, Va.
Ittner, Anthony, St. Louis, Mo.
James, Amaziah B., Ogdensburg, N. Y.
Jones, Frank, Portsmouth, N. H.
Jones, James Taylor, Demopolis, Ala.
Jones, John S., Delaware, O.
Jorgensen, Joseph, Petersburg, Va.
Joyce, Charles H., Rutland, Vt.
Keifer, J. Warren. Springfield, O.
Keightley, Ed'n W., Constantine, Mich.
Kelley, William D., Philadelphia. Pa.
Kenna, John E., Kanawha C. H., W.Va.
Ketcham, John H., Dover Plains, N. Y.
Killinger, John W., Lebanon, Pa.
Kimmell, William, Baltimore, Md.
Knapp, Robert M., Jerseyville, Ill.
Knott, J. Proctor, Lebanon, Ky.
Landers, George M., New Britain, Ct.
Lapham, Elbridge G., Canandaigua,N.Y.
Lathrop, William, Rockford, Ill.
Leonard, John E., Monroe, La.
Ligon, Robert F., Tuskegee, Ala.
Lindsey, Stephen D., Norridgewock, Me.
Lockwood, Daniel N., Buffalo, N. Y.
Loring, George B., Salem. Mass.
Luttrell, John K., Santa Rosa, Cal.
Lynde, William Pitt, Milwaukee, Wis.
Mackey, L. A., Lock Haven, Pa.
Maish, Levi, York, Pa.
Manning, Van H., Holly Springs, Miss.
Marsh, Benjamin F., Warsaw, Ill.
Martin, Benjamin F., Pruntytown,W.Va.
Mayham, Stephen L., Schoharie, N. Y.
McCook, Anson G., New York. N. Y.
McGowan, J. H., Coldwater, Mich.
McKenzie, James A., Longview, Ky.
McKinley, William, jr., Canton, O.
McMahon, John A., Dayton, O.
Mills, Roger Q., Corsicana, Texas.
Mitchell, John I., Wellsboro, Pa.
Money, Hernando D., Winona, Miss.
Monroe, James, Oberlin, O.
Morgan, Charles H., Lamar, Mo.
Morrison, William R., Waterloo, Ill.

Morse, Leopold, Boston, Mass.
Muldrow, H. L., Starkville, Miss.
Muller, Nicholas, New York, N. Y.
Neal, Henry S., Ironton, O.
Norcross, Amasa, Fitchburg, Mass.
Oliver, Addison, Onawa, Iowa.
O'Neill, Charles, Philadelphia, Pa.
Overton, Edward, jr., Towanda, Pa.
Pacheco, Romualdo, S. Luis Obispo, Cal.
Page, Horace F., Placerville, Cal.
Patterson, George W., Westfield, N. Y.
Patterson, T. M., Denver, Col.
Peddie, Thomas B., Newark, N. J.
Phelps, James, Essex, Ct.
Phillips, William A., Salina, Kan.
Pollard, Henry M., Chillicothe, Mo.
Potter, Clarkson N., New Rochelle, N.Y.
Pound, Thad. C., Chippewa Falls, Wis.
Powers, Llewellyn, Houlton, Me.
Price, Hiram, Davenport, Iowa.
Pridemore, Auburn L., Jonesville, Va.
Pugh, John Howard, Burlington, N. J.
Quinn, Terence J., Albany, N. Y.
Rainey, Joseph H., Georgetown, S. C.
Randolph, James H., Newport, Tenn.
Rea, David, Savannah, Mo.
Reagan, John H., Palestine, Tex.
Reed, Thomas B., Portland, Me.
Reilly, James B., Pottsville, Pa.
Rice, Americus V., Ottawa, O.
Rice, William W., Worcester, Mass.
Riddle, Haywood Y., Lebanon, Tenn.
Robbins, William M., Statesville, N. C.
Roberts, Charles B., Westminster, Md.
Robertson, E. W., Baton Rouge, La.
Robinson, George D., Chicopee, Mass.
Robinson, Milton S., Anderson, Ind.
Ross, Miles, New Brunswick, N. J.
Ryan, Thomas, Topeka, Kan.
Sampson, Ezekiel S., Sigourney, Iowa.
Sapp, William F., Council Bluffs, Iowa.
Sayler, Milton, Cincinnati, O.
Scales, Alfred M., Greensboro', N. C.
Schleicher, Gustave, Cuero, Tex.
Sexton, Leonidas, Rushville, Ind.
Shallenberger, Wm. S., Rochester, Pa.
Shelley, Charles M., Selma, Ala.
Singleton, Otho R., Canton, Miss.
Sinnickson, Clement H., Salem, N. J.
Slemons, William F., Monticello, Ark.
Smalls, Robert, Beaufort, S. C.
Smith, A. Herr, Lancaster, Pa.
Smith, William E., Albany, Ga.
Southard, Milton I., Zanesville, O.
Sparks, William A. J., Carlyle, Ill.
Springer, William M., Springfield, Ill.
Starin, John H., Fultonville, N. Y.
Steele, Walter L., Rockingham, N. C.
Stenger, William S., Chambersburg. Pa.
Stephens, Alex. H., Crawfordville, Ga.
Stewart, J. H., Saint Paul, Minn.
Stone, John W., Grand Rapids, Mich.
Stone, Joseph C., Burlington, Iowa.
Strait, Horace B., Shakopee, Minn.
Swann, Thomas, Baltimore. Md.
Thompson, John M., Butler, Pa.
Thornburgh, Jacob M., Knoxville, Tenn.
Throckmorton, Jas. W., McKinney, Tex.
Tipton, Thomas F., Bloomington, Ill.
Townsend, Amos, Cleveland, O.
Townsend, Martin I., Troy, N. Y.
Townshend, R. W., Shawneetown, Ill.
Tucker, John R., Lexington, Va.
Turner, Thomas. Mount Sterling, Ky.
Turney, Jacob, Greensburg, Pa.

Vance, Robert B., Asheville, N. C.
Van Vorhes, Nelson H., Athens, O.
Veeder, William D., Brooklyn, N. Y.
Waddell, Alfred M., Wilmington, N. C.
Wait, John T., Norwich, Ct.
Walker, Gilbert C., Richmond, Va.
Walsh, William, Cumberland, Md.
Ward, William, Chester, Pa.
Warner, Levi, Norwalk, Ct.
Watson, Lewis F., Warren, Pa.
Welch, Frank, Norfolk, Neb.
White, Harry, Indiana, Pa.
White, Michael D., Crawfordsville, Ind.
Whitthorne, Wash'n C., Columbia, Tenn.
Williams, Jeremiah N., Clayton, Ala.
Williams, James, Kenton, Del.
Williams, Alpheus S., Detroit, Mich.
Williams, Andrew, Plattsburg, N. Y.
Williams, Richard, Portland, Or.
Williams, Charles G., Janesville, Wis.
Willis, Albert S., Louisville, Ky.

Willis, Benjamin A., New York, N. Y.
Willits, Edwin, Monroe, Mich.
Wilson, Benjamin, Wilsonburg, W. Va.
Wood, Fernando, New York, N. Y.
Wren, Thomas, Eureka, Nev.
Wright, Hendrick B., Wilkesbarre, Pa.
Yeates, Jesse J., Murfreesboro', N. C.
Young, Casey, Memphis, Tenn.

DELEGATES.

Cannon, George Q., Salt Lake City, Utah.
Corlett, William W., Cheyenne, Wy.
Fenn, Stephen S., Mount Idaho, Idaho.
Jacobs, Orange, Seattle, Wash.
Kidder, Jefferson P., Vermillion, Dak.
Maginnis, Martin, Helena, Montana.
Romero, Trinidad, New Mexico.
Stevens, Hiram S., Tucson, Arizona.

PRINCIPAL OFFICERS OF THE HOUSE.

Speaker.—SAMUEL J. RANDALL, of Pennsylvania.
Chaplain.—Rev. W. P. Harrison.
Clerk of the House.—George M. Adams.
Chief Clerk.—Green Adams.
Superintendent of Lower Document-Room.—Morgan Rawles.
Librarian.—W. M. Hardy.
Sergeant-at-Arms.—John G. Thompson.
Doorkeeper.—John W. Polk.
Superintendent of Folding-Room.—A. W. Fletcher.
Superintendent of Upper Document-Room.—Seaton Gales.
Postmaster.—James M. Steuart.
Stenographers.—Henry G. Hayes.
　　　　　　Andrew Devine.

Official Reporters of Debates.

John J. McElhone.　　　　William Blair Lord.
William Hincks.　　　　David Wolfe Brown.
　　　　　J. K. Edwards.

OFFICERS OF CONGRESS.

Public Printer.—John D. Defrees.
Librarian of Congress.—Ainsworth R. Spofford.

THE CONGRESS OF THE UNITED STATES.

45TH CONGRESS.—HOUSE OF REPRESENTATIVES.—March 4, 1877, to March 4, 1879.

SPEAKER ....SAMUEL J. RANDALL, D., of Pennsylvania.

[Democrats marked D. ; Republicans, R.; Members of the last House, *.]

(Names of contestants of seats placed directly under those of the sitting members, and indented.)

ALABAMA.

1 James T. Jones, D.
2 Hilary A. Herbert, D.
3 Jere. N. Williams,* D.
4 Charles M. Shelley, D.
   J. Haralson, R.
5 Robert F. Ligon, D.
6 GoldsmithW.Hewitt,*D.
7 William H. Forney,* D.
8 William W. Garth, D.

ARKANSAS.

1 Lucien C. Gause,* D.
2 William F. Slemons,* D.
3 Jordan E. Cravens, D.
4 Thomas M. Gunter,* D.

CALIFORNIA.

1 Horace Davis, R.
2 Horace F. Page,* R.
3 John K. Luttrell,* D.
4 Romualdo Pacheco, R.
   P. D. Wigginton, D.

COLORADO.

1 Thos. M. Patterson, D.

CONNECTICUT.

1 George M. Landers,* D.
2 James Phelps,* D.
3 John T. Wait,* R.
4 Levi Warner,* D.

DELAWARE.

1 James Williams,* D.

FLORIDA.

1 R. H. M. Davidson, D.
   Wm. J. Purman,* R.
2 Horatio Bisbee, Jr., R.
   J. J. Finley, D.

GEORGIA.

1 Julian Hartridge,* D.
2 William E. Smith,* D.
3 Philip Cook,* D.
4 Henry R. Harris,* D.
5 Milton A. Candler,* D.
6 James H. Blount,* D.
7 William H. Felton,* D.
8 Alex. H. Stephens,* D.
9 Hiram P. Bell, D.

ILLINOIS.

1 William Aldrich, R.
2 Carter H. Harrison,* D.
3 Lorenzo Brentano, R.
4 William Lathrop, R.
5 H. C. Burchard,* R.
6 Thos. J. Henderson,* R.
7 Philip C. Hayes, R.
8 Greenbury L. Fort,* R.
9 Thomas A. Boyd, R.
10 B. F. Marsh, R.
11 Robert M. Knapp, D.
12 Wm. M. Springer,* D.
13 Thomas F. Tipton, R.
14 Joseph G. Cannon,* R.
15 John R. Eden,* D.
16 Wm. A. J. Sparks,* D.
17 Wm. R. Morrison,* D.
18 William Hartzell,* D.
19 R. W. Townshend, D.

INDIANA.

1 Benoni S. Fuller,* D.
2 James R. Cobb, D.
3 George A. Bicknell, D.
4 Leonidas Sexton, R.
5 Thomas M. Browne, R.
6 Milton S. Robinson,* R.
7 John Hanna, R.
8 Morton C. Hunter,* R.
9 Michael D. White, R.
10 Wm. H. Calkins, R.
11 James L. Evans * R.
12 Andrew H Hamilton,* D.
13 John H. Baker,* R.

IOWA.

1 Joseph C. Stone, R.
2 Hiram Price, R.
3 Theo. W. Burdick, R.
4 Nathan C. Deering, R.
5 Rush Clark, R.
6 Ezek. S. Sampson,* R.
7 H. J. B. Cummings, R.
8 William F. Sapp, R.
9 Addison Oliver,* R.

KANSAS.

1 William A. Phillips,* R.
2 Dudley C. Haskell, R.
3 Thomas Ryan, R.

KENTUCKY.

1 Andrew R. Boone,* D.
2 James A. McKenzie, D.
3 John W. Caldwell, D.
4 J. Proctor Knott,* D.
5 Albert S. Willis, D.
6 John G. Carlisle, D.
7 Jos. C. S. Blackburn,* D.
8 Milton J. Durham,* D.
9 Thomas Turner, D.
10 John B. Clarke,* D.

LOUISIANA.

1 Randall L. Gibson,* D.
2 E. John Ellis,* D.
3 Chester B. Darrall,* R.
   J. H. Acklin, D.
4 Jos. R. B. Elam, D.
   George L. Smith, R.
5 John E. Leonard, R.
6 E. W. Robertson, D.
   Charles E. Nash, R.

MAINE.

1 Thomas B. Reed, R.
2 William P. Frye,* R.
3 Stephen D. Lindsey, R.
4 Llewellyn Powers, R.
5 Eugene Hale,* R.

HOUSE OF REPRESENTATIVES, BY STATES—(Continued).

MARYLAND.
1 Daniel M. Henry, D.
2 Charles B. Roberts,* D.
3 William Kimmell. D.
4 Thomas Swann,* D.
5 Eli J. Henkle,* D.
6 William Walsh,* D.

MASSACHUSETTS.
1 William W. Crapo,* R.
2 Benj. W. Harris,* R.
3 Walbridge A. Field, R.
  Benjamin Dean, D.
4 Leopold Morse, D.
5 Nathaniel P. Banks,* R.
6 George B. Loring, R.
7 Benjamin F. Butler, R.
8 William Claflin, R.
9 William W. Rice, R.
10 Amasa Norcross, R.
11 Geo. D. Robinson, R.

MICHIGAN.
1 Alpheus S. Williams,* D.
2 Edwin Willits, R.
3 Jonas H. McGowan, R.
4 Edwin W. Keightley, R.
5 John W. Stone, R.
6 Mark S. Brewer, R.
7 Omar D. Conger,* R.
8 Charles C. Ellsworth, R.
9 Jay A. Hubbell,* R.

MINNESOTA.
1 Mark H. Dunnell,* R.
2 Horace B. Strait,* R.
3 Jacob H. Stewart, R.

MISSISSIPPI.
1 Henry L. Muldrow, D.
2 Van H. Manning, D.
3 Hernando D. Money,* D.
4 Otho R. Singleton, D.
5 Charles E. Hooker,* D.
6 James R. Chalmers, D.
  J. R. Lynch, R.

MISSOURI.
1 Anthony Ittner, R.
2 Nathan Cole, R.
3 Lyne S. Metcalfe, R.
  R. G. Frost, D.
4 Robert A. Hatcher,* D.
5 Richard P. Bland,* D.
6 Charles H. Morgan,* D.
7 Thos. T. Crittenden, D.
8 Benj. J. Franklin,* D.
9 David Rea,* D.
10 Henry M. Pollard, R.
11 John B. Clark, Jr.,* D.
12 John M. Glover,* D.
13 Aylett H. Buckner,* D.

NEBRASKA.
1 Frank Welch, R.

NEVADA.
1 Thomas Wren, R.

NEW HAMPSHIRE.
1 Frank Jones,* D.
2 James F. Briggs, R.
3 Henry W. Blair,* R.

NEW JERSEY.
1 C. H. Sinnickson,* R.
2 John Howard Pugh, R.
3 Miles Ross,* D.
4 Alvah A. Clark. D.
5 Augustus W. Cutler,* D.
6 Thomas B. Peddie, R.
7 A. A. Hardenbergh,* D.

NEW YORK.
1 James W. Covert, D.
2 William D. Veeder, D.
3 Sim. B. Chittenden,* R.
4 Archibald M. Bliss,* D.
5 Nicholas Muller, D.
6 Samuel S. Cox,* D.
7 Anthony Eickhoff, D.
8 Anson G. McCook, R.
9 Fernando Wood,* D.
10 Abram S. Hewitt,* D.
11 Benjamin A. Willis,* D.
12 Clarkson N. Potter, D.
13 John H. Ketcham. R.
14 George M. Beebe,* D.
15 Stephen L. Mayham, D.
16 Terence J. Quinn, D.
17 Martin I. Townsend,* R.
18 Andrew Williams,* R.
19 Amaziah B. James, R.
20 John H. Starin, R.
21 Solomon Bundy, R.
22 George A. Bagley,* R.
23 William J. Bacon, R.
24 William H. Baker,* R.
25 Frank Hiscock, R.
26 John H. Camp, R.
27 Elbridge G. Lapham,* R.
28 Jeremiah W. Dwight, R.
29 John N. Hungerford, R.
30 E. Kirke Hart, D.
31 Charles B. Benedict, D.
32 Daniel N. Lockwood, D.
33 Geo. W. Patterson, R.

NORTH CAROLINA.
1 Jesse J. Yeates,* D.
2 Curtis H. Brogden, R.
3 Alfred M. Waddell,* D.
4 Joseph J. Davis,* D.
5 Alfred M. Scales,* D.
6 Walter L. Steele. D.
7 Wm. M. Robbins,* D.
8 Robert B. Vance,* D.

OHIO.
1 Milton Sayler,* D.
2 Henry B. Banning,* D.
3 Mills Gardner, R.
4 John A. McMahon,* D.
5 Americus V. Rice,* D.
6 Jacob D. Cox, R.
7 Henry L. Dickey, D.
8 J. Warren Keifer, R.
9 John S. Jones, R.
10 Charles Foster,* R.
11 Henry S. Neal, R.
12 Thomas Ewing, D.
13 Milton I. Southard,* D.
14 Ebenezer B. Finley, D.
15 N. H. Van Vorhes,* R.
16 Lorenzo Danford,* R.
17 Wm. McKinley, Jr., R.
18 James Monroe,* R.
19 James A. Garfield,* R.
20 Amos Townsend, R.

OREGON.
1 Richard Williams, R.
  S. W. McDowell, D.

PENNSYLVANIA.
1 Chapman Freeman,* R.
2 Charles O'Neill,* R.
3 Samuel J. Randall,* D.
4 William H. Kelley,* R.
5 Alfred C. Harmer, R.
6 William Ward, R.
7 Isaac N. Evans, R.
8 Hiester Clymer,* D.
9 A. Herr Smith,* R.
10 Samuel A. Bridges, D.
11 Francis D. Collins,* D.
12 Hendrick B. Wright,* D.
13 James B. Reilly,* D.
  J. L. Nutting, D.
14 John W. Killinger, R.
15 Edward Overton, R.
16 John I. Mitchell, R.
17 Jacob M. Campbell, R.
18 Wm. S. Stenger, D.
19 Levi Maish,* D.
20 Levi A. Mackey,* D.
21 Jacob Turney,* D.
22 Russell Errett, R.
23 Thomas M. Bayne, R.
24 Wm. S. Shallenberger, R.
25 Harry White, R.
26 John M. Thompson, R.
27 Lewis F. Watson, R.

RHODE ISLAND.
1 Benj. T. Eames,* R.
2 Latimer W. Ballou,* R.

SOUTH CAROLINA.
1 Joseph H. Rainey,* R.
  J. S. Richardson, D.
2 Richard H. Cain, R.
  M. P. O'Connor, D.
3 D. Wyatt Aiken, D.
4 John H. Evins, D.
5 Robert Smalls,* R.
  G. D. Tillman, D.

HOUSE OF REPRESENTATIVES, BY STATES—(*Continued*).

TENNESSEE.

1 James H. Randolph, R.
2 J. M. Thornburgh,* R.
3 George G. Dibrell,* D.
4 Haywood Y. Riddle,* D.
5 John M. Bright,* D.
6 John F. House,* D.
7 Wash C. Whitthorne,*D.
8 John D. C. Atkins,* D.
9 William P. Caldwell,* D.
10 Casey Young,* D.

TEXAS.

1 John H. Reagan,* D.
2 David B. Culberson,* D.
3 J.W. Throckmorton,*D.
4 Roger Q. Mills,* D.

5 De Witt C. Giddings, D.
6 Gustave Schleicher,* D.

VERMONT.

1 Charles H. Joyce,* R.
2 Dudley C. Denison,* R.
3 George W. Hendee,* R.

VIRGINIA.

1 Beverly B. Douglas,* D.
2 John Goode, Jr.,* D.
3 Gilbert C. Walker,* D.
4 Joseph Jorgensen, R.
  W. E. Hinton, D.
5 George C. Cabell,* D.
6 J. Randolph Tucker,* D.
7 John T. Harris,* D.

8 Eppa Hunton,* D.
9 A. L. Pridemore, D.

WEST VIRGINIA.

1 Benjamin Wilson,* D.
2 Benjamin F. Martin, D.
3 John E. Kenna, D.

WISCONSIN.

1 Charles G. Williams,* R.
2 Lucien B. Caswell,* R.
3 George C. Hazelton, R.
4 William P. Lynde,* D.
5 Edward S. Bragg, D.
6 Gabriel Bouck, D.
7 H. L. Humphrey, R.
8 Thaddeus C. Pound, R.

Delegates from Territories.

ARIZONA.

Hiram S. Stevens,* D.
William H. Hardy, R.

DAKOTA.

Jefferson P. Kidder,* R.

IDAHO.

Stephen S. Fenn,* D.

MONTANA.

Martin Maginnis,* D.

NEW MEXICO.

Trinidad Romero, R.

UTAH.

George Q. Cannon,* D.

WASHINGTON.

Orange Jacobs,* R.

WYOMING.

William W. Corlett, R.

Total Representatives 293

Democrats........ 253
Republicans 140
    Total... ....— 293

Democratic Majority... 13

COMMITTEES OF THE HOUSE OF REPRESENTATIVES—
45TH CONGRESS, 1877-79.

Elections.

John T. Harris, of Va.
William M. Springer, of Ill.
Milton A. Caudler, of Ga.
Jacob Turney, of Pa.
Thomas H. Cobb, of Ind.
Jer. N. Williams, of Ala.
E. John Ellis, of La.
John T. Wait, of Ct.
J. N. Thornburgh, of Tenn.
Jacob D. Cox, of O.
Frank Hiscock, of N. Y.

Ways and Means.

Fernando Wood, of N. Y.
J. Randolph Tucker, of Va.
Milton Sayler, of O.
W. M. Robbins, of N. C.
Henry R. Harris, of Ga.
Randall L. Gibson, of La.
James Phelps, of Ct.
William D. Kelley, of Pa.
James A. Garfield, of O.
Horatio C. Burchard, of Ill.
N. P. Banks, of Mass.

Appropriations.

J. D. C. Atkins, of Tenn.
James H. Blount, of Ga.
O. R. Singleton, of Miss.
Hiester Clymer, of Pa.
Abram S. Hewitt, of N. Y.
Wm. A. J. Sparks, of Ill.
Milton J. Durham, of Ky.
Eugene Hale, of Me.
Charles Foster, of O.
A. Herr Smith, of Pa.
John H. Baker, of Ind.

Banking and Currency.

A. H. Buckner, of Mo.
Thomas Ewing, of O.
A. A. Hardenburgh, of N.J.
Jesse J. Yeates, of N. C.
William Hartzell, of Ill.
Hiram P. Bell, of Ga.
E. Kirke Hart, of N. Y.
Benj. T. Eames, of R. I.
S. B. Chittenden, of N. Y.
Greenbury L. Fort, of Ill.
Wm. A. Phillips, of Kan.

Pacific Railroad.

J. W. Throckmorton, of Texas.
Wm. R. Morrison, of Ill.
John F. House, of Tenn.
John K. Luttrell, of Cal.
George M. Landers, of Ct.
J. R. Chalmers, of Miss.
J. B. Elam, of La.
Charles O'Neill, of Pa.
Henry W. Blair, of N. H.
Lucien B. Caswell, of Wis.
W. W. Rice, of Mass.
Nathan Cole, of Mo.
A. S. Hewitt, of N. Y.

Claims.

John M. Bright, of Tenn.
Levi Warner, of Ct.
Joseph J. Davis, of N. C.
James B. Reilly, of Pa.
H. L. Dickey, of O.
Daniel M. Henry, of Md.
D. N. Lockwood, of N. Y.
T. J. Henderson, of Ill.
C. C. Ellsworth, of Mich.
S. D. Lindsey, of Me.
H. J. B. Cummings, of Ia.

Commerce.

John H. Reagan, of Tex.
William H. Felton, of Ga.
C. B. Roberts, of Md.
A. M. Bliss, of N. Y.
Miles Ross, of N. J.
David Rea, of Mo.
John E. Kenna, of W. Va.
Morton C. Hunter, of Ind.
Mark H. Dunnell, of Minn.
Jay A. Hubbell, of Mich.
E. Overton, of Pa.

Public Lands.

Wm. R. Morrison, of Ill.
Benoni S. Fuller, of Ind.
Lucien C. Ganse, of Ark.
John B. Clark, Jr., of Mo.
H. B. Wright, of Pa.
G. W. Hewitt, of Ala.
William E. Smith, of Ga.
John H. Ketcham, of N. Y.
Romualdo Pacheco, of Cal.
William F. Sapp, of Ia.
Frank Welsh, of Neb.
Jeff. P. Kidder, of Dak.

Post-Offices and Post-Roads.

Alfred M. Waddell, of N.C.
Wm. F. Slemons, of Ark.
W. P. Caldwell, of Tenn.
Hernan. D. Money, of Miss.
D. C. Giddings, of Tex.
William W. Garth, of Ala.
Terence J. Quinn, of N. Y.
Joseph G. Cannon, of Ill.
Chapman Freeman, of Pa.
Andrew Williams, of N. Y.
Amos Townsend, of O.

District of Columbia.

Alph. S. Williams, of Mich.
Jos. C. S. Blackburn, of Ky.
Eppa Hunton, of Va.
Eli J. Henkle, of Md.
Hiester Clymer, of Pa.
Stephen L. Mayham, of N.Y.
Gabriel Bouck, of Wis.
George W. Hendee, of Vt.
William Claflin, of Vt.
Lorenzo Brentano, of Ill.
Horace Davis, of Cal.

Judiciary.

J. Proctor Knott, of Ky.
Wm. Pitt Lynde, of Wis.
John T. Harris, of Va.
Julian Hartridge, of Ga.
William S. Stenger, of Pa.
John A. McMahon, of O.
D. B. Culberson, of Tex.
William F. Frye, of Maine.
Benj. F. Butler, of Mass.
Omar D. Conger, of Mich.
Elb. G. Lapham, of N. Y.

War-Claims.

John R. Eden, of Ill.
George C. Cabell, of Va.
James B. Reilly, of Pa.
John W. Caldwell, of Ky.
Charles M. Shelley, of Ala.
William D. Veeder, of N.Y.
Addison Oliver, of Ia.
Milton S. Robinson, of Ind.
John M. Thompson, of Pa.
J. Warren Keifer, of O.
B. F. Martin, of West Va.

COMMITTEES OF THE HOUSE OF REPRESENTATIVES—(Continued).

Public Expenditures.
Robert A. Hatcher, of Mo.
William Hartzell, of Ill.
Chas. B. Benedict, of N. Y.
A. L. Pridemore, of Va.
Ebenezer B. Finley, of O.
Van H. Manning, of Miss.
R. H. M. Davidson, of Fla.
William H. Baker, of N. Y.
Ed. W. Keightley, of Mich.
Theodore W. Burdick, of Ia.
Thomas M. Bayne, of Pa.

Private Land-Claims.
Thomas M. Gunter, of Ark.
Wm. P. Caldwell, of Tenn.
James Williams, of Del.
Gabriel Bouck, of Wis.
R. W. Townshend, of Ill.
Thomas Turner, of Ky.
Dudley C. Denison, of Vt.
John H. Starin, of N. Y.
J. H. McGowan, of Mich.
Richard H. Cain, of S. C.
Geo. A. Bicknell, of Ind.

Manufactures.
Hendrick B. Wright, of Pa.
George C. Dibrell, of Tenn.
Levi Warner, of Ct.
Benjamin Wilson, of W.Va.
Carter H. Harrison, of Ill.
R. M. H. Davidson, of Fla.
Robert F. Ligon, of Ala.
Thos. B. Peddie, of N. J.
Anthony Ittner, of Mo.
Thomas F. Tipton, of Ill.
William J. Bacon, of N. Y.

Agriculture.
Aug. W. Cutler, of N. J.
John M. Glover, of Mo.
James W. Covert, of N. Y.
C. Wyatt Aiken, of S. C.
A. L. Pridemore, of Va.
Ebenezer B. Finley, of O.
Walter L. Steele, of N. C.
Nathaniel C. Deering, of Ia.
Philip C. Hayes, of Ill.
Lewis F. Watson, of Pa.
William H. Calkins, of Ind.

Indian Affairs.
Alfred M. Scales, of N. C.
Andrew R. Boone, of Ky.
Charles E. Hooker, of Miss.
Charles H. Morgan, of Mo.
J.W.Throckmorton,of Tex.
Thomas M. Gunter, of Ark.
George M. Beebe, of N. Y.
Horace F. Page, of Cal.
Nelson H. VanVorhes, of O.
M. I. Townsend, of N. Y.
J. H. Stewart, of Minn.
S. S. Fenn, of Idaho.

Military Affairs.
Henry B. Banning, of O.
Levi Maish, of Pa.
James Williams, of Del.

George G. Dibrell, of Tenn.
A. A. Clark, of N. J.
John H. Evins, of S. C.
Edward S. Bragg, of Wis.
Horace B. Strait, of Minn.
Harry White, of Pa.
Anson G. McCook, of N. Y.
Benjamin F. Marsh, of Ill.

Militia.
Miles Ross, of N. J.
Beverly B. Douglas, of Va.
Alfred M. Scales, of N. C.
Eli J. Henkle, of Md.
Frank Jones, of N. H.
David B. Culberson, of Tex.
Thomas Turner, of Ky.
William H. Calkins, of Ind.
Solomon Bundy, of N. Y.
I. Newton Evans, of Pa.
Robert Smalls, of S. C.

Naval Affairs.
W. C. Whitthorne, of Tenn.
John Goode, of Va.
Benjamin A. Willis, of N.Y.
Frank Jones, of N. H.
Leopold Morse, of Mass.
William Kimmell, of Md.
Benj. W. Harris, of Mass.
Lorenzo Danford, of O.
Alfred C. Harmer, of Pa.
John Hanna, of Ind.
T. T. Crittenden, of Mo.

Foreign Affairs.
Thomas Swann, of Md.
Samuel S. Cox, of N. Y.
And. H. Hamilton, of Ind.
William H. Forney, of Ala.
Gustave Schleicher, of Tex.
Samuel A. Bridges, of Pa.
Benj. Wilson, of W. Va.
James Monroe, of O.
Chas. G. Williams, of Wis.
William W. Crapo, of Mass.
John W. Killinger, of Pa.

Territories.
Benj. J. Franklin, of Mo.
Hay. Y. Riddle, of Tenn.
Jacob Turney, of Pa.
Jas. Taylor Jones, of Ala.
H. L. Muldrow, of Miss.
Leopold Morse, of Mass.
George A. Bagley, of N. Y.
William Aldrich, of Ill.
Thomas B. Reed, of Maine.
Henry S. Neal, of O.
M. Maginnis, of Montana.
J. E. Cravens, of Ark.

Revolutionary Pensions.
L. A. Mackey, of Pa.
Richard P. Bland, of Mo.
E. John Ellis, of La.
Chas. B. Benedict, of N. Y.
Walter L. Steele, of N. C.
B. F. Martin, of W. Va.
William Kimmell, of Md.

Geo. W. Patterson, of N. Y.
Mills Gardner, of O.
I. Newton Evans, of Pa.
Amasa Norcross, of Mass.

Invalid Pensions.
Americus V. Rice, of O.
Gold. W. Hewitt, of Ala.
Hay. Y. Riddle, of Tenn.
William Walsh, of Md.
Levi A. Mackey, of Pa.
James W. Covert, of N. Y.
C. H. Sinnickson, of N. J.
Joseph H. Rainey, of S. C.
Charles H. Joyce, of Vt.
Llewellyn Powers, of Maine.
L. S. Metcalfe, of Mo.

Railway and Canals.
Gustave Schleicher, of Tex.
George C. Cabell, of Va.
Thos. T. Crittenden, of Mo.
Charles M. Shelly, of Ala.
James A. McKenzie, of Ky.
Nicholas Muller, of N. Y.
A. A. Clark, of N. J.
James L. Evans, of Ind.
John I. Mitchell, of Pa.
John H. Camp, of N. Y.
George C. Hazleton, of Wis.

Mines and Mining.
George M. Beebe, of N. Y.
Joseph J. Davis, of N. C.
William H. Felton, of Ga.
Francis D. Collins, of Pa.
Andrew R. Boone, of Ky.
David Rea, of Mo.
Jas. Taylor Jones, of Ala.
Thomas Wren, of Nevada.
Jas. H. Randolph, of Tenn.
W. S. Shallenberger, of Pa.
John W. Stone, of Mich.
Hiram S. Stevens, of Arizo.

Education and Labor.
John Goode, Jr., of Va.
Benonl S. Fuller, of Ind.
Milton I. Southard, of O.
A. S. Willis, of Ky.
John M. Bright, of Tenn.
Hiram P. Bell, of Ga.
Van H. Manning, of Miss.
George B. Loring, of Mass.
Jacob M. Campbell, of Pa.
J. N. Hungerford, of N. Y.
Dudley C. Haskell, of Kan.

Revision of the Laws of the United States.
William Walsh, of Md.
Gilbert C. Walker, of Va.
Richard P. Bland, of Mo.
George A. Bicknell, of Ind.
Hilary A. Herbert, of Ala.
A. S. Willis, of Ky.
Wal. A. Field, of Mass.
Rush Clark, of Ia.
J. L. Leonard, of La.
Wm. McKinley, Jr., of O.
E. K. Har., of N. Y.

COMMITTEES OF THE HOUSE OF REPRESENTATIVES—(*Continued*).

Coinage, Weights, and Measures.

Alex. H. Stephens, of Ga.
Levi Maish, of Pa.
Robert B. Vance, of N. C.
John B. Clark, Jr , of Mo.
R. M. Knapp, of Ill.
H. L. Muldrow, of Miss.
John B. Clarke, of Ky.
Chester B. Darrall, of La.
Mark S. Brewer, of Mich.
Thomas Ryan, of Kan.
J. W. Dwight, of N. Y.

Patents.

Robert B. Vance, of N. C.
Beverly B. Douglas, of Va.
John B. Clarke, of Ky.
William E. Smith, of Ga.
D. Wyatt Aiken, of S. C.
R. W. Townshend, of Ill.
Aug. W. Cutler, of N. J.
William Ward, of Pa.
H. M. Pollard, of Mo.
James F. Briggs, of N. H.
Edwin Willits, of Mich.

Public Buildings and Grounds.

Philip Cook, of Ga.
Casey Young, of Tenn.
Benj. J. Franklin, of Mo.
Archibald M. Bliss, of N.Y.
Francis D. Collins, of Pa.
R. F. Ligon, of Ala.
James A. McKenzie, of Ky.
Joseph C. Stone, of Ia.
H. L. Humphrey, of Wis.
John S. Jones, of O.
William Lathrop, of Ill.

Accounts.

Charles B. Roberts, of Md.
John A. McMahon, of O.
J. R. Chalmers, of Miss.
Henry W. Blair, of N. H.
Thomas A. Boyd, of Ill.

Mileage.

Thomas R. Cobb, of Ind.
Anthony Eickhoff, of N. Y.
Samuel A. Bridges, of Pa.
Lorenzo Danford, of O.
Milton S. Robinson, of Ind.

Expenditures in the State Department.

William M. Springer, of Ill.
Gilbert C. Walker, of Va.
Stephen L. Mayham, of N.Y.
Mark H. Dunnell, of Minn.
Thomas M. Bayne, of Pa.

Expenditures in the Treasury Department.

John M. Glover, of Mo.
Henry R. Harris, of Ga.
William H. Forney, of Ala.

Lucien C. Gause, of Ark.
William D. Veeder, of N.Y.
H. L. Dickey, of O.
George A. Bagley, of N. Y.
Michael D. White, of Ind.
Joseph Jorgensen, of Va.

Expenditures in the War Department.

Jos. C. S. Blackburn, of Ky.
Milton A. Candler, of Ga.
Americus V. Rice, of O.
Chester B. Darrall, of La.
Benjamin T. Eames, of R. I.

Expenditures in the Navy Department.

Benjamin A. Willis, of N.Y.
W. C. Whitthorne, of Tenn.
John S. Carlisle, of Ky.
Horace F. Page, of Cal.
Jay A. Hubbell, of Mich.

Expenditures in the Post-Office Department.

Jer. N. Williams, of Ala.
Alph. S. Williams, of Mich.
John W. Caldwell, of Ky.
Lewis F. Watson, of Pa.
Curtis H. Brogden, of N. C.

Expenditures in the Interior Department.

William A. J. Sparks, of Ill.
Wm. M. Robbins, of N. C.
Dan. L. Lockwood, of N.Y.
Addison Oliver, of Ia.
Edwin Willits, of Mich.

Expenditures on Public Buildings.

William P. Lynde, of Wis.
Jesse J. Yeates, of N. C.
Terence J. Quinn, of N. Y.
Wm. F. Slemons, of Ark.
William S. Stenger, of Pa.
Amasa Norcross, of Mass.
Rich. Williams, of Oregon.

Expenditures in the Department of Justice.

Edward S. Bragg, of Wis.
Milton J. Durham, of Ky.
John R. Eden, of Ill.
A. A. Hardenbergh, of N.J.
Julian Hartridge, of Ga.
John H. Evins, of S. C.
Nicholas Muller, of N. Y.
Omar D. Conger, of Mich.
John T. Walt, of Ct.
Mills Gardner, of O.
Geo. D. Robinson, of Mass.

Reform in the Civil Service.

Carter H. Harrison, of Ill.
Philip Cook, of Ga.

William W. Garth, of Ala.
Jordan E. Cravens, of Ark.
Daniel W. Henry, of Md.
Charles H. Morgan, of Mo.
Hiram Price, of Ia.
Amaziah B. James, of N.Y.
J. Howard Pugh, of N. J.
Leonidas Sexton, of Ind.
C. N. Potter, of N. Y.

Mississippi Levees.

E. W. Robertson, of La.
Robert A. Hatcher, of Mo.
Hernan D. Money, of Miss.
H. Casey Young, of Tenn.
R. M. Knapp, of Ill.
George M. Landers, of Ct.
Benj. F. Martin, of W. Va.
Russell Errett, of Pa.
Thaddeus C. Pound, of Wis.
Geo. D. Robinson, of Mass.
Horatio Bisbee, Jr., of Fla.

On Rules.

The Speaker.
Alex. H. Stephens, of Ga.
Milton Sayler, of O.
Nath. P. Banks, of Mass.
James A. Garfield, of O.

On the Revision of the Laws Regulating the Counting of the Electoral Votes for President and Vice-President.

Milton I. Southard, of O.
Eppa Hunton, of Va.
Clarkson N. Potter, of N. Y.
John F. House, of Tenn.
George A. Bicknell, of Ind.
Hilary A. Herbert, of Ala.
John G. Carlisle, of Ky.
Benj. F. Butler, of Mass.
Thomas M. Browne, of Ind.
Curtis H. Brogden, of N. C.
Ezekiel S. Sampson, of Ia.

Printing.

Otho R. Singleton, of Miss.
Anthony Eickhoff, of N. Y.
Latimer W. Ballou, of R. I.

Enrolled Bills.

And. H. Hamilton, of Ind.
J. B. Elam, of La.
John E. Kenna, of W. Va.
Nelson H. Van Vorhes, of O.
Joseph H. Rainey, of S. C.

Library.

Samuel S. Cox, of N. Y.
Charles E. Hooker, of Miss.
Eugene Hale, of Maine.

CONSTITUTION OF THE UNITED STATES OF AMERICA.

We the People of the United States, in order to form a more perfect Union, establish justice, insure domestic tranquillity, provide for the common defence, promote the general welfare, and secure the blessings of liberty to ourselves and our posterity, do ordain and establish this Constitution for the United States of America.

ARTICLE I.

SECTION I.—All legislative powers herein granted shall be vested in a Congress of the United States, which shall consist of a Senate and House of Representatives.

SEC. II.—1. The House of Representatives shall be composed of members chosen every second year by the people of the several States, and the electors in each State shall have the qualifications requisite for electors of the most numerous branch of the State legislature.

2. No person shall be a representative who shall not have attained to the age of twenty-five years, and been seven years a citizen of the United States, and who shall not, when elected, be an inhabitant of that State in which he shall be chosen.

3. Representatives and direct taxes shall be apportioned among the several States which may be included within this Union, according to their respective numbers, which shall be determined by adding to the whole number of free persons, including those bound to service for a term of years, and excluding Indians not taxed, three fifths of all other persons. The actual enumeration shall be made within every three years after the first meeting of the Congress of the United States, and within every subsequent term of ten years, in such manner as they shall by law direct. The number of representatives shall not exceed one for every thirty thousand, but each State shall have at least one representative ; and until such enumeration shall be made, the State of New Hampshire shall be entitled to choose three, Massachusetts, eight, Rhode Island and Providence Plantations, one, Connecticut, five, New York, six, New Jersey, four, Pennsylvania, eight, Delaware, one, Maryland, six, Virginia, ten, North Carolina, five, South Carolina, five, and Georgia, three.

4. When vacancies happen in the representation from any State, the executive authority thereof shall issue writs of election to fill such vacancies.

5. The House of Representatives shall choose their speaker and other officers ; and shall have the sole power of impeachment.

SEC. III.—1. The Senate of the United States shall be composed of two senators from each State, chosen by the legislature thereof, for six years ; and each senator shall have one vote.

2. Immediately after they shall be assembled in consequence of the first election, they shall be divided as equally as may be into three classes. The seats of the senators of the first class shall be vacated at the expiration of the second year, of the second class at the expiration of the fourth year, and of the third class at the expiration of the sixth year, so that one third may be chosen every second year ; and if vacancies happen by resignation, or otherwise, during the recess of the legislature of any State, the executive thereof may make temporary appointments until the next meeting of the legislature, which shall then fill such vacancies.

3. No person shall be a senator who shall not have attained the age of thirty years, and been nine years a citizen of the United States, and who shall not, when elected, be an inhabitant of that State for which he shall be chosen.

4. The Vice-President of the United States shall be President of the Senate, but shall have no vote, unless they be equally divided.

5. The Senate shall choose their other officers, and also a president *pro tempore*, in the absence of the Vice-President, or when he shall exercise the office of President of the United States.

6. The Senate shall have the sole power to try all impeachments. When sitting for that purpose, they shall be on oath or affirmation. When the President of the United States is tried, the Chief Justice shall preside : and no person shall be convicted without the concurrence of two thirds of the members present.

7. Judgment in cases of impeachment shall not extend further than to removal from office, and disqualification to hold and enjoy any office of honor, trust or profit under the United States : but the party convicted shall nevertheless be liable and subject to indictment, trial, judgment and punishment, according to law.

SEC. IV.—1. The times, places and manner of holding elections for senators and representatives, shall be prescribed in the State by the legislature thereof ; but the Congress may at any time by law make or alter such regulations, except as to the places of choosing senators.

2. The Congress shall assemble at least once in every year, and such meeting shall be on the first Monday in December, unless they shall by law appoint a different day.

SEC. V.—1. Each house shall be judge of the elections, returns and qualifications of its own members, and a majority of each shall constitute a quorum to do business; but a smaller number may adjourn from day to day, and may be authorized to compel the attendance of absent members, in such manner, and under such penalties as each house may provide.

2. Each house may determine the rules of its proceedings, punish its members for disorderly behavior, and, with the concurrence of two thirds, expel a member.

3. Each house shall keep a journal of its proceedings, and from time to time publish the same, excepting such parts as may in their judgment require secrecy ; and the yeas and nays of the members of either house on any question shall, at the desire of one fifth of those present, be entered on the journal.

4. Neither house, during the session of Congress, shall, without the consent of the other, adjourn for more than three days, nor to any other place than that in which the two houses shall be sitting.

SEC. VI.—1. The senators and representatives shall receive a compensation for their services, to be ascertained by law, and paid out of the treasury of the United States. They shall in all cases, except treason, felony and breach of the peace, be privileged from arrest during their attendance at the session of their respective houses, and in going to and returning from the same ; and for any speech or debate in either house, they shall not be questioned in any other place.

2. No senator or representative shall, during the time for which he was elected, be appointed to any civil office under the authority of the United States, which shall have been created, or the emoluments whereof shall have been increased during such time : and no person holding any office under the United States, shall be a member of either house during his continuance in office.

SEC. VII.—1. All bills for raising revenue shall originate in the House of Representatives ; but the Senate may propose or concur with amendments as on other bills.

2. Every bill which shall have passed the House of Representatives and the Senate, shall, before it become a law, be presented to the President of the United

States ; if he approve he shall sign it ; but if not he shall return it, with his objections to that house in which it shall have originated, who shall enter the objections at large on their journal, and proceed to reconsider it. If after such reconsideration two thirds of that house shall agree to pass the bill, it shall be sent, together with the objections, to the other house, by which it shall likewise be reconsidered, and if approved by two thirds of that house, it shall become a law. But in all such cases the votes of both houses shall be determined by yeas and nays, and the names of the persons voting for and against the bill shall be entered on the journal of each house respectively. If any bill shall not be returned by the President within ten days (Sundays excepted) after it shall have been presented to him, the same shall be a law, in like manner as if he had signed it, unless the Congress by their adjournment prevent its return, in which case it shall not be a law.

3. Every order, resolution, or vote to which the concurrence of the Senate and House of Representatives may be necessary (except on a question of adjournment) shall be presented to the President of the United States ; and before the same shall take effect, shall be approved by him, or being disapproved by him, shall be repassed by two thirds of the Senate and House of Representatives, according to the rules and limitations prescribed in the case of a bill.

SEC. VIII.—The Congress shall have power—

1. To lay and collect taxes, duties, imposts and excises, to pay the debts and provide for the common defence and general welfare of the United States; but all duties, imposts and excises shall be uniform throughout the United States ;

2. To borrow money on the credit of the United States ;

3. To regulate commerce with foreign nations, and among the several States, and with the Indian tribes ;

4. To establish an uniform rule of naturalization, and uniform laws on the subject of bankruptcies throughout the United States ;

5. To coin money, regulate the value thereof, and of foreign coin, and fix the standard of weights and measures ;

6. To provide for the punishment of counterfeiting the securities and current coin of the United States;

7. To establish post-offices and post-roads ;

8. To promote the progress of science and useful arts, by securing for limited times to authors and inventors the exclusive right to their respective writings and discoveries ;

9. To constitute tribunals inferior to the Supreme Court ;

10. To define and punish piracies and felonies committed on the high seas, and offences against the law of nations;

11. To declare war, grant letters of marque and reprisal, and make rules concerning captures on land and water ;

12. To raise and support armies, but no appropriation of money to that use shall be for a longer term than two years ;

13. To provide and maintain a navy ;

14. To make rules for the government and regulation of the land and naval forces ;

15. To provide for calling forth the militia to execute the laws of the Union, suppress insurrections and repel invasions ;

16. To provide for organizing, arming, and disciplining, the militia, and for governing such part of them as may be employed in the service of the United States, reserving to the States respectively, the appointment of the officers, and the authority of training the militia according to the discipline prescribed by Congress ;

17. To exercise exclusive legislation in all cases whatsoever, over such district (not exceeding ten miles square) as may, by cession of particular States, and the acceptance of Congress, become the seat of the government of the United States, and to exercise like authority over all places purchased by the consent of the legislature of

the State in which the same shall be, for the erection of forts, magazines, arsenals, dock-yards, and other needful buildings ; and

13. To make all laws which shall be necessary and proper for carrying into execution the foregoing powers, and all other powers vested by this Constitution in the government of the United States, or in any department or officer thereof.

Sec. IX.—1. The migration or importation of such persons as any of the States now existing shall think proper to admit, shall not be prohibited by the Congress prior to the year one thousand eight hundred and eight, but a tax or duty may be imposed on such importation, not exceeding ten dollars for each person.

2. The privilege of the writ of *habeas corpus* shall not be suspended, unless when in cases of rebellion or invasion the public safety may require it.

3. No bill of attainder or *ex post facto* law shall be passed.

4. No capitation, or other direct, tax shall be laid, unless in proportion to the census or enumeration hereinbefore directed to be taken.

5. No tax or duty shall be laid on articles exported from any State.

6. No preference shall be given by any regulation of commerce or revenue to the ports of one State over those of another : nor shall vessels bound to, or from, one State, be obliged to enter, clear, or pay duties in another.

7. No money shall be drawn from the treasury, but in consequence of appropriations made by law ; and a regular statement and account of the receipts and expenditures of all public money shall be published from time to time.

8. No title of nobility shall be granted by the United States : and no person holding any office of profit or trust under them, shall, without the consent of the Congress, accept of any present, emolument, office, or title, of any kind whatever, from any king, prince, or foreign state.

Sec. X.—1. No State shall enter into any treaty, alliance, or confederation ; grant letters of marque and reprisal ; coin money ; emit bills of credit ; make any thing but gold and silver coin a tender in payment of debts ; pass any bill of attainder, *ex post facto* law, or law impairing the obligation of contracts, or grant any title of nobility.

2. No State shall, without the consent of the Congress, lay any imposts or duties on imports or exports, except what may be absolutely necessary for executing its inspection laws : and the net produce of all duties and imposts, laid by any State on imports or exports, shall be for the use of the treasury of the United States ; and all such laws shall be subject to the revision and control of the Congress.

3. No State shall, without the consent of Congress, lay any duty of tonnage, keep troops, or ships of war in time of peace, enter into any agreement or compact with another State, or with a foreign power, or engage in war, unless actually invaded, or in such imminent danger as will not admit of delay.

ARTICLE II.

Sec. I.—1. The executive power shall be vested in a President of the United States of America. He shall hold his office during the term of four years, and, together with the Vice-President, chosen for the same term, be elected, as follows :

2. Each State shall appoint, in such manner as the legislature thereof may direct, a number of electors, equal to the whole number of senators and representatives to which the State may be entitled in the Congress : but no senator or representative, or person holding an office of trust or profit under the United States, shall be appointed an elector.

3. The electors shall meet in their respective States, and vote by ballot for two persons, of whom one at least shall not be an inhabitant of the same State with themselves. And they shall make a list of all the persons voted for, and of the number of votes for each; which list they shall sign and certify, and transmit sealed to the seat of the government of the United States, directed to the President of the Senate. The President of the Senate shall, in the presence of the Senate and House of Representatives, open all the certificates, and the votes shall then be counted. The person having the greatest number of votes shall be the President, if such number be a majority of the whole number of electors appointed; and if there be more than one who have such majority, and have an equal number of votes, then the House of Representatives shall immediately choose by ballot one of them for President; and if no person shall have a majority, then from the five highest on the list the said House shall in like manner choose the President. But in choosing the President, the votes shall be taken by States, the representation from each State having one vote; a quorum for this purpose shall consist of a member or members from two thirds of the States, and a majority of all the States shall be necessary to a choice. In every case, after the choice of the President, the person having the greatest number of votes of the electors shall be the Vice-President. But if there should remain two or more who have equal votes, the Senate shall choose from them by ballot the Vice-President.

4. The Congress may determine the time of choosing the electors, and the day on which they shall give their votes; which day shall be the same throughout the United States.

5. No person except a natural-born citizen, or a citizen of the United States, at the time of the adoption of this Constitution, shall be eligible to the office of President; neither shall any person be eligible to that office who shall not have attained to the age of thirty-five years, and been fourteen years a resident within the United States.

6. In case of the removal of the President from office, or of his death, resignation or inability to discharge the powers and duties of the said office, the same shall devolve on the Vice-President, and the Congress may by law provide for the case of removal, death, resignation or inability, both of the President and Vice-President, declaring what officer shall then act as President, and such officer shall act accordingly, until the disability be removed, or a President shall be elected.

7. The President shall, at stated times, receive for his services, a compensation, which shall neither be increased nor diminished during the period for which he shall have been elected, and he shall not receive within that period any other emolument from the United States, or any of them.

8. Before he enter on the execution of his office, he shall take the following oath or affirmation:

"I do solemnly swear (or affirm) that I will faithfully execute the office of President of the United States, and will to the best of my ability, preserve, protect and defend the Constitution of the United States."

Sec. II.—1. The President shall be Commander-in-Chief of the Army and Navy of the United States, and of the militia of the several States, when called into the actual service of the United States; he may require the opinion, in writing, of the principal officer in each of the executive departments, upon any subject relating to the duties of their respective offices, and he shall have power to grant reprieves and pardons for offences against the United States, except in cases of impeachment.

2. He shall have power, by and with the advice and consent of the Senate, to make treaties, provided two thirds of the senators present concur; and he shall nominate, and by and with the advice and consent of the Senate, shall appoint ambassadors, other public ministers and consuls, judges of the Supreme Court, and all other officers of the United States, whose appointments are not herein otherwise provided for, and which shall be established by law: but the Congress may by law vest the appointment of such inferior officers, as they think proper, in the President alone, in the courts of law, or in the heads of departments.

3. The President shall have power to fill up all vacancies that may happen during the recess of the Senate, by granting commissions which shall expire at the end of their next session.

SEC. III.—He shall from time to time give to the Congress information of the state of the Union, and recommend to their consideration such measures as he shall judge necessary and expedient ; he may, on extraordinary occasions, convene both houses, or either of them, and, in case of disagreement between them, with respect to the time of adjournment, he may adjourn them to such time as he shall think proper ; he shall receive ambassadors and other public ministers ; he shall take care that the laws be faithfully executed, and shall commission all the officers of the United States.

SEC. IV.—The President, Vice-President and all civil officers of the United States, shall be removed from office on impeachment for, and conviction of, treason, bribery, or other high crimes and misdemeanors.

ARTICLE III.

SEC. I.—The judicial power of the United States, shall be vested in one Supreme Court, and in such inferior courts as the Congress may from time to time ordain and establish. The judges, both of the Supreme and inferior courts, shall hold their offices during good behavior, and shall, at stated times, receive for their services, a compensation, which shall not be diminished during their continuance in office.

SEC. II.—1. The judicial power shall extend to all cases, in law and equity, arising under this Constitution, the laws of the United States, and treaties made, or which shall be made, under their authority ; to all cases affecting ambassadors, other public ministers and consuls ; to all cases of admiralty and maritime jurisdiction ; to controversies to which the United States shall be a party ; to controversies between two or more States ; between a State and citizens of another State ; between citizens of different States ; between citizens of the same State, claiming lands under grants of different States ; and between a State, or the citizens thereof, and foreign States, citizens or subjects.

2. In all cases affecting ambassadors, other public ministers and consuls, and those in which a State shall be party, the Supreme Court shall have original jurisdiction. In all the other cases before mentioned, the Supreme Court shall have appellate jurisdiction, both as to law and fact, with such exceptions, and under such regulations as the Congress shall make.

3. The trial of all crimes, except in cases of impeachment, shall be by jury ; and such trial shall be held in the State where the said crimes shall have been committed ; but when not committed within any State, the trial shall be at such place or places as the Congress may by law have directed.

SEC. III.—1. Treason against the United States, shall consist only in levying war against them, or in adhering to their enemies, giving them aid and comfort. No person shall be convicted of treason unless on the testimony of two witnesses to the same overt act, or on confession in open court.

2. The Congress shall have power to declare the punishment of treason, but no attainder of treason shall work corruption of blood, or forfeiture except during the life of the person attainted.

ARTICLE IV.

SEC. I.—Full faith and credit shall be given in each State to the public acts, records, and judicial proceedings of every other State. And the Congress may by general laws prescribe the manner in which such acts, records and proceedings shall be proved, and the effect thereof.

SEC. II.—1. The citizens of each State shall be entitled to all privileges and immunities of citizens in the several States.

2. A person charged in any State with treason, felony, or other crime, who shall flee from justice, and be found in another State, shall on demand of the executive

authority of the State from which he fled, be delivered up to be removed to the State having jurisdiction of the crime.

3. No person held to service or labor in one State, under the laws thereof, escaping into another, shall, in consequence of any law or regulation therein, be discharged from such service or labor, but shall be delivered up on claim of the party to whom such service or labor may be due.

SEC. III.—1. New States may be admitted by the Congress into this Union ; but no new State shall be formed or erected within the jurisdiction of any other State ; nor any State be formed by the junction of two or more States, or parts of States, without the consent of the legislatures of the States concerned as well as of the Congress.

2. The Congress shall have power to dispose of and make all needful rules and regulations respecting the territory or other property belonging to the United States; and nothing in this Constitution shall be so construed as to prejudice any claims of the United States, or of any particular State.

SEC. IV.—The United States shall guarantee to every State in this Union a republican form of government, and shall protect each of them against invasion ; and, on application of the legislature, or of the executive (when the legislature cannot be convened), against domestic violence.

ARTICLE V.

The Congress, whenever two thirds of both houses shall deem it necessary, shall propose amendments to this Constitution, or, on the application of the legislatures of two thirds of the several States, shall call a convention for proposing amendments, which, in either case, shall be valid to all intents and purposes, as part of this Constitution, when ratified by the legislatures of three fourths of the several States, or by conventions in three fourths thereof, as the one or the other mode of ratification may be proposed by the Congress ; provided that no amendment which may be made prior to the year one thousand eight hundred and eight shall in any manner affect the first and fourth clauses in the ninth section of the first article ; and that no State, without its consent, shall be deprived of its equal suffrage in the Senate.

ARTICLE VI.

1. All debts contracted and engagements entered into, before the adoption of this Constitution, shall be as valid against the United States under this Constitution, as under the Confederation.

2. This Constitution, and the laws of the United States which shall be made in pursuance thereof; and all treaties made, or which shall be made, under the authority of the United States, shall be the supreme law of the land ; and the judges in every State shall be bound thereby, any thing in the constitution or laws of any State to the contrary notwithstanding.

3. The senators and representatives before mentioned, and the members of the several State legislatures, and all executive and judicial officers, both of the United States and of the several States, shall be bound by oath or affirmation, to support this Constitution ; but no religious test shall ever be required as a qualification to any office or public trust under the United States.

ARTICLE VII.

The ratification of the conventions of nine States, shall be sufficient for the establishment of this Constitution between the States so ratifying the same.

Done in convention by the unanimous consent of the States present the seventeenth day of September in the year of our Lord one thousand seven hundred and eighty-seven, and of the Independence of the United States of America the twelfth. In witness whereof, we have hereunto subscribed our names,

G°: WASHINGTON,

President, and Deputy from Virginia.

NEW HAMPSHIRE.	MASSACHUSETTS.	CONNECTICUT.
John Langdon,	Nathaniel Gorham,	Wm. Saml. Johnson,
Nicholas Gilman.	Rufus King.	Roger Sherman.

NEW YORK.	DELAWARE.	NORTH CAROLINA.
Alexander Hamilton.	Geo. Read,	Wm Blount,
NEW JERSEY.	Gunning Bedford, Jr.,	Rich'd Dobbs Spaight,
Wil. Livingston,	John Dickinson,	Hugh Williamson.
David Brearley,	Richard Bassett,	
Wm Patterson,	Jaco: Broom.	
Jona. Dayton.		SOUTH CAROLINA.

PENNSYLVANIA.	MARYLAND.	J. Rutledge,
B. Franklin,	James McHenry,	Charles C. Pinckney,
Thomas Mifflin,	Dan. Jenifer, of St.	Charles Pinckney,
Robt Morris,	Thomas,	Pierce Butler.
Geo Clymer,	Dan Carroll.	
Thos Fitzsimons,		
Jared Ingersoll,	VIRGINIA.	GEORGIA.
James Wilson,	John Blair,	William Few,
Gouv. Morris.	James Madison, Jr.	Abr. Baldwin.

Attest : William Jackson, Secretary.

The following-named Delegates from the States indicated were present but did not sign the Constitution :

MASSACHUSETTS.	NEW JERSEY.	VIRGINIA.
Elbridge Gerry,	Wm. C. Houston.	Edmund Randolph,
Caleb Strong.		George Mason,
	MARYLAND.	George Wythe,
CONNECTICUT.	John Francis Mercer,	James McClurg.
Oliver Ellsworth.	Luther Martin.	

NEW YORK.	NORTH CAROLINA.	GEORGIA.
John Lansing, Jr.,	Alexander Martin,	Wm. Pierce,
Roberts Yates.	Wm. R. Davie.	Wm. Houston.

Of the 63 delegates originally appointed, ten did not attend, two of which vacancies were filled. Of those attending, 39 signed and 16 did not.

The Constitution was adopted by the Convention on the 17th of September, 1787, appointed in pursuance of the Resolution of the Congress of the Confederation of the 21st of February, 1787, and ratified by the Conventions of the several States, as follows:

Delaware, December 7th, 1787, unanimously.
Pennsylvania, December 12th, 1787, by a vote of 46 to 23
New Jersey, December 18th, 1787, unanimously.
Georgia, January 2d, 1788, unanimously.
Connecticut, January 9th, 1788, by a vote of 128 to 40.

Massachusetts, February 6th, 1788, by a vote of 187 to 168.
Maryland, April 28th, 1788, by a vote of 63 to 12.
South Carolina, May 23d, 1788, by a vote of 149 to 73.
New Hampshire, June 21st, 1788, by a vote of 57 to 47.
Virginia, June 25th, 1788, by a vote of 89 to 79.
New York, July 26th, 1788, by a vote of 30 to 25.
North Carolina, November 21st, 1789, by a vote of 193 to 75.
Rhode Island, May 29th, 1790, by a majority of 2.
Vermont, January 10th, 1791, by a vote of 105 to 4.

Declared ratified by resolution of the Congress, September 13th, 1788. The first Congress under its provisions was to have met at New York, March 4th, 1789, but on that day no quorum was present in either House. The House of Representatives organized on the 1st of April, and the Senate secured a quorum on the 6th of April, 1789.

AMENDMENTS TO THE CONSTITUTION.*

ARTICLE I.

Congress shall make no law respecting an establishment of religion, or prohibiting the free exercise thereof ; or abridging the freedom of speech, or of the press ; or the right of the people peaceably to assemble, and to petition the government for a redress of grievances.

ARTICLE II.

A well-regulated militia, being necessary to the security of a free state, the right of the people to keep and bear arms, shall not be infringed.

ARTICLE III.

No soldier shall, in time of peace, be quartered in any house, without the consent of the owner, nor in time of war, but in a manner to be prescribed by law.

ARTICLE IV.

The right of the people to be secure in their persons, houses, papers, and effects, against unreasonable searches and seizures, shall not be violated, and no warrants

---

* Twelve Constitutional Amendments were proposed by the first Congress, at its first session, September 25th, 1789. The first two were rejected, the last ten were adopted, which are the ten first printed above, and were proclaimed to be in force December 15th, 1791.

The two rejected Articles were as follows :

I. After the first enumeration required by the First Article of the Constitution there shall be one Representative for every 30,000 persons, until the number shall amount to one hundred ; after which, the proportion shall be so regulated by Congress, that there shall not be less than one hundred Representatives for every 40,000 persons, until the number of Representatives shall amount to two hundred ; after which the proportion shall be so regulated by Congress, that there shall be not less than two hundred Representatives, nor more than one Representative for every 50,000 persons.

II. No law varying the compensation for the services of the Senators and Representatives shall take effect until an election of Representatives shall have intervened.

The twelve proposed Amendments were acted upon by the States as follows :

All ratified by Vermont, November 3d, 1791 ; Maryland, December 19th, 1789 ; New Jersey, November 20th, 1789 ; North Carolina, December 22d, 1789 ; South Carolina, January 19th, 1790 ; Virginia and Kentucky, December 15th, 1791—7.

All, excepting Art. I., ratified by Delaware, January 28th, 1790—1.

All, excepting Art. II. ratified by Pennsylvania, March 10th, 1790—1.

All, excepting Arts. I. and II., ratified by New Hampshire, January 25th, 1790 ; New York, March 27th, 1790 ; and Rhode Island, June 15th, 1790—3.

All rejected by Massachusetts, Connecticut and Georgia—3.

shall issue but upon probable cause, supported by oath or affirmation, and particularly describing the place to be searched, and the persons or things to be seized.

ARTICLE V.

No person shall be held to answer for a capital, or otherwise infamous crime, unless on a presentment or indictment of a grand jury, except in cases arising in the land or naval forces, or in the militia, when in actual service in time of war or public danger ; nor shall any person be subject for the same offence to be twice put in jeopardy of life or limb ; nor shall be compelled in any criminal case to be a witness against himself ; nor be deprived of life, liberty, or property, without due process of law ; nor shall private property be taken for public use, without just compensation.

ARTICLE VI.

In all criminal prosecutions, the accused shall enjoy the right to a speedy and public trial, by an impartial jury of the State and district wherein the crime shall have been committed, which district shall have been previously ascertained by law, and to be informed of the nature and cause of the accusation ; to be confronted with the witnesses against him ; to have compulsory process for obtaining witnesses in his favor, and to have the assistance of counsel for his defence.

ARTICLE VII.

In suits at common law, where the value in controversy shall exceed twenty dollars, the right of trial by jury shall be preserved, and no fact tried by a jury shall be otherwise re-examined in any court of the United States, than according to the rules of the common law.

ARTICLE VIII.

Excessive bail shall not be required, nor excessive fines imposed, nor cruel and unusual punishments inflicted.

ARTICLE IX.

The enumeration in the Constitution, of certain rights, shall not be construed to deny or disparage others retained by the people.

ARTICLE X.

The powers not delegated to the United States by the Constitution, nor prohibited by it to the States, are reserved to the States respectively, or to the people.

ARTICLE XI.

[Proposed by Congress March 5th, 1794, and declared in force January 8th, 1798.]

The judicial power of the United States shall not be construed to extend to any suit in law or equity, commenced or prosecuted against one of the United States by citizens of another State, or by citizens or subjects of any foreign state.

ARTICLE XII.

[Proposed December 12th, 1803, in the first session of the Eighth Congress, and declared in force September 25th, 1804.]

The electors shall meet in their respective States, and vote by ballot for President and Vice-President, one of whom, at least, shall not be an inhabitant of the same State with themselves ; they shall name in their ballots the person voted for as President, and in distinct ballots the person voted for as Vice-President, and they shall make distinct lists of all persons voted for as President, and of all persons voted for as Vice-President, and of the number of votes for each, which lists they shall sign and certify, and transmit sealed to the seat of the government of the

United States, directed to the President of the Senate ;—The President of the Senate shall, in the presence of the Senate and House of Representatives, open all the certificates and the votes shall then be counted ;—the person having the greatest number of votes for President, shall be the President, if such number be a majority of the whole number of electors appointed ; and if no person have such majority, then from the persons having the highest numbers not exceeding three on the list of those voted for as President, the House of Representatives shall choose immediately, by ballot, the President. But in choosing the President, the votes shall be taken by States, the representation from each State having one vote ; a quorum for this purpose shall consist of a member or members from two thirds of the States, and a majority of all the States shall be necessary to a choice. And if the House of Representatives shall not choose a President whenever the right of choice shall devolve upon them, before the fourth day of March next following, then the Vice-President shall act as President, as in the case of the death or other constitutional disability of the President. The person having the greatest number of votes as Vice-President, shall be the Vice-President, if such number be a majority of the whole number of electors appointed, and if no person have a majority, then from the two highest numbers on the list the Senate shall choose the Vice-President ; a quorum for the purpose shall consist of two thirds of the whole number of senators, and a majority of the whole number shall be necessary to a choice. But no person constitutionally ineligible to the office of President shall be eligible to that of Vice-President of the United States.

ARTICLE XIII.

[Proposed by Congress February 1st, 1865, and declared in force December 18th, 1865.

Ratified by Arkansas, California, Connecticut, Florida, Georgia, Illinois, Indiana, Iowa, Kansas, Louisiana, Maine, Maryland, Massachusetts, Michigan, Minnesota, Missouri, Nevada, New Hampshire, New Jersey, New York, North Carolina, Ohio, Oregon, Pennsylvania, Rhode Island, South Carolina, Tennessee, Vermont, Virginia, West Virginia, and Wisconsin—32 States out of 36. Ratified conditionally by Alabama and Mississippi. Rejected by Delaware and Kentucky—2. Not acted upon by Texas.]

SEC. 1. Neither slavery nor involuntary servitude, except as a punishment for crime whereof the party shall have been duly convicted, shall exist within the United States, or any place subject to their jurisdiction.

SEC. 2. Congress shall have power to enforce this Article by appropriate legislation.

ARTICLE XIV.

[Proposed by Congress June 16th, 1866, and declared in force, July 28th, 1868.

Ratified by Alabama, Arkansas, Connecticut, Florida, Georgia, Illinois, Indiana, Iowa, Kansas, Louisiana, Maine, Massachusetts, Michigan, Minnesota, Mississippi, Missouri, Nebraska, Nevada, New Hampshire, New Jersey, New York, North Carolina, Ohio, Oregon, Pennsylvania, Rhode Island, South Carolina, Tennessee, Texas, Vermont, Virginia, West Virginia, and Wisconsin—33 States out of 37.

Of the above, Arkansas, Florida, Georgia, Louisiana, Mississippi, North Carolina, South Carolina, Texas, and Virginia (9), first rejected the amendment, but finally ratified it. New Jersey and Ohio (2) rescinded their ratification.

Rejected by Delaware, Kentucky, and Maryland—3.

No final action was taken by California—1.]

SEC. 1. All persons born or naturalized in the United States, and subject to the jurisdiction thereof, are citizens of the United States, and of the State wherein they reside. No State shall make or enforce any law which shall abridge the privileges or immunities of citizens of the United States ; nor shall any State deprive any person of life, liberty, or property, without due process of law ; nor deny to any person within its jurisdiction the equal protection of the laws.

SEC. 2. Representatives shall be apportioned among the several States according to their respective numbers, counting the whole number of persons in each State, excluding Indians not taxed. But when the right to vote at any election for the choice of electors for President and Vice-President of the United States, representatives in Congress, the executive and judicial officers of a State, or the members of the legislature thereof, is denied to any of the male inhabitants of such State, being twenty-one years of age, and citizens of the United States, or in any way abridged, except for participation in rebellion, or other crime, the basis of representation therein shall be reduced in the proportion which the number of such male citizens shall bear to the whole number of male citizens twenty-one years of age in such State.

SEC. 3. No person shall be a senator or representative in Congress, or elector of President and Vice-President, or hold any office, civil or military, under the United States, or under any State, who, having previously taken an oath as a member of Congress, or as an officer of the United States, or as a member of any State legislature, or as an executive or judicial officer of any State, to support the Constitution of the United States, shall have engaged in insurrection or rebellion against the same, or given aid or comfort to the enemies thereof. But Congress may, by a vote of two thirds of each house, remove such disability.

SEC. 4. The validity of the public debt of the United States, authorized by law, including debts incurred for payment of pensions and bounties for services in suppressing insurrection or rebellion, shall not be questioned. But neither the United States nor any State shall assume or pay any debt or obligation incurred in aid of insurrection or rebellion against the United States, or any claim for the loss or emancipation of any slave ; but all such debts, obligations and claims shall be held illegal and void.

SEC. 5. The Congress shall have power to enforce, by appropriate legislation, the provisions of this Article.

ARTICLE XV.

[Proposed by Congress February 26th, 1869, and declared in force March 30th, 1870.

Ratified by Alabama, Arkansas, Connecticut, Florida, Georgia, Illinois, Indiana, Iowa, Kansas, Louisiana, Maine, Massachusetts, Michigan, Minnesota, Mississippi, Missouri, Nebraska, Nevada, New Hampshire, New York, North Carolina, Ohio, Pennsylvania, Rhode Island, South Carolina, Texas, Vermont, Virginia, West Virginia, and Wisconsin—30 States out of 37.

Of the above, Georgia and Ohio at first rejected but finally ratified. New York rescinded its ratification.

Rejected by California, Delaware, Kentucky, Maryland, New Jersey, and Oregon—6.

No final action was taken by Tennessee—1.]

SEC. 1. The right of citizens of the United States to vote shall not be denied or abridged by the United States or by any State on account of race, color, or previous condition of servitude.

SEC. 2. The Congress shall have power to enforce this Article by appropriate legislation.

NOTE.—Another proposed amendment, styled Article XIII., was proposed by Congress to the State legislatures at the second session of the 36th Congress, March 2d, 1861 :

" ART. XIII.—No amendment shall be made to the Constitution which will authorize or give to Congress the power to abolish or interfere within any State with the domestic institutions thereof, including that of persons held to labor or service by the laws of said State."

It was not acted upon by a majority of the States.

AMOUNT OF REVENUE FROM

[From the Annual Reports of the

	1863.	1864.	1865.	1866.	1867.
	$	$	$	$	$
Income over $600, and not over $10,000, a...............	172,770	7,944,154	9,607,247	....	....
Over $10,000, a...............	277,462	6,855,160	9,362,339	....	....
From property of citizens residing abroad, a............	1,872	58,675	169,024	....	....
From interest on United States securities, a.........	3,637	73,374	133,403	....	....
Over $600, and not over $5000,b	....	....	539,143	26,046,760	31,492,694
Over $5000, b.................	....	....	801,942	34,501,123	25,547,947
Over $1000, c.............	....	....	....	....	....
Over $2000, d.................	....	....	....	....	....
From bank dividends and additions to surplus..........	766,606	1,577,011	3,991,211	4,193,071	3,278,323
From bank profits, not divided or added to surplus......	....	....	25,511	47,503	496,632
From canal companies' dividends, etc.................	4,210	92,121	386,223	206,234	195,362
From insurance companies' dividends, etc.............	225,483	445,366	708,771	783,882	568,474
From railroad companies' dividends, etc...............	338,533	927,893	2,471,914	2,205,632	3,379,202
From railroad companies' interest on bonds...........	253,999	596,830	847,684	1,255,917	....
From turnpike companies' dividends, etc..............	1,101	17,493	28,213	27,833	30,708
From salaries of United States officers and employés......	696,181	1,705,125	2,896,492	3,717,395	1,029,992
Total..................	2,741,857	20,294,733	32,050,017	72,969,160	66,014,499

a, Act of July 1, 1862.   b, Act of March 3, 1865.

NOTE.—For the history of the successive changes in the laws imposing an article, that the last taxes levied under the Income-Tax law were paid during the it. Income taxes assessed and due for 1871, and also for some preceding years, 1873, while some arrears are still in process of collection.

INCOME-TAX DURING EACH YEAR.

Commissioner of Internal Revenue.]

1868.	1869.	1870.	1871.	1872.	1873.	1874 to 1877 (4 yrs.)	TOTAL.
$	$	$	$	$	$	$	$
....	....	....	....	....	....	....	17,814,171
....	....	....	....	....	....	....	16,494,961
....	....	....	....	....	....	....	230,471
....	....	....	....	... .	....	....	212,414
....	....	....	....	....	....	....	58,078,597
....	....	....	....	....	....	....	60,851,011
32,027,611	25,025,069	27,115,046	10,680,967	....	....	....	94,848,092
....	....	....	3,753,983	8,416,686	3,927,253	....	16,097,921
2,914,841	3,769,186	3,573,272	1,542,668	2,162,564	85,271	....	27,854,024
709,934	....	....	....	....	....	....	1,279,690
215,230	280,608	251,049	47,043	136,052	24,615	....	1,785,612
605,490	847,668	986,519	243,205	270,531	8,678	....	5,680,070
2,630,174	2,831,140	2,806,802	1,121,440	1,851,296	760,930	....	21,416,739
1,250,156	1,503,847	1,869,369	974,343	1,291,027	135,643	....	9,967,845
49,552	22,381	32,289	11,738	14,140	2,389	....	237,325
1,043,561	561,963	1,109,526	787,263	294,565	117,542	140,391	14,029,995
41,455,599	34,791,857	37,775,872	19,162,652	14,436,861	5,062,312	140,391	346,908,738

c, Act of March 2, 1867.   d, Act of July 14, 1870.

Income-Tax and their final repeal, see page 67. The statement made in that year 1871, is correct as to the levy of the tax, though not as to all payments under continued to be collected, as seen in the above table, to large amounts in 1872 and

SUMMARY OF INTERNAL REVENUE RECEIPTS, FROM ALL SOURCES, FOR FIFTEEN YEARS, 1863-1877.

[From the Annual Reports of the Commissioner of Internal Revenue.]

	Spirits.	Tobacco.	Fermented Liquors.	Banks and Bankers.	Penalties,etc.	Adhesive Stamps.	Articles and occupations formerly taxed, but now exempt.
	$	$	$	$	$	$	$
1863	5,176,530	3,097,620	1,628,934	....	27,170	4,140,175	26,982,763
1864	30,329,150	8,592,099	2,290,000	2,837,720	193,600	5,894,945	67,006,225
1865	18,731,422	11,401,373	3,734,928	4,940,871	520,363	11,102,392	160,638,160
1866	33,268,172	16,531,008	5,220,553	3,463,988	1,142,853	15,044,373	236,236,037
1867	33,542,952	19,765,148	6,057,501	2,046,562	1,459,171	16,094,718	186,954,423
1868	18,655,531	18,730,095	5,955,869	1,866,746	1,256,882	14,852,252	129,863,090
1869	45,071,231	23,430,708	6,099,880	2,196,054	877,069	16,420,710	65,943,673
1870	55,606,094	31,350,708	6,319,127	3,020,064	827,905	16,544,043	71,567,908
1871	46,281,848	33,578,907	7,389,502	3,644,242	636,980	15,342,739	37,136,958
1872	49,475,516	33,736,171	8,258,498	4,628,229	442,205	10,177,821	19,033,007
1873	52,099,372	34,386,303	9,324,938	3,771,031	461,053	7,702,377	6,329,782
1874	49,444,090	33,242,876	9,304,680	3,387,161	364,216	6,136,845	764,880
1875	52,081,991	37,303,462	9,144,004	4,006,698	281,108	6,557,230	1,080,111
1876	56,426,365	39,795,340	9,571,281	4,006,698	409,284	6,518,488	509,631
1877	57,469,430	41,106,547	9,480,789	3,829,729	419,999	6,450,429	238,261
Total in 15 years.	603,659,694	386,048,363	99,780,492	47,736,363	9,320,478	165,039,037	1,010,256,929

[Extract from the Annual Report of the Commissioner of Internal Revenue, Dec., 1877.]

AMOUNTS COLLECTED AND COST OF COLLECTION.

It will be observed that the collections for the past fiscal year [ending June 30th, 1877] were $118,995,184. The accounts for making said collections have not yet been closed, but I am able to state that the expenses will not exceed the following amounts :

For salaries and expenses of collectors, which includes the pay of deputy collectors and clerks, house-rent, fuel, lights, and advertising, $1,865,523

For salaries and expenses of agents, surveyors, gaugers, storekeepers, and miscellaneous expenses..................................... .   1,570,000

For dies, paper, and stamps   402,600

For detecting and bringing to trial and punishment persons guilty of violating the internal revenue laws...........   61,000

For salaries of Internal Revenue Bureau............................   272,372

Total.. $4,171,495

Being scarcely more than three and a half per cent upon the whole amount collected.

When we consider the vast territory over which the internal revenue system extends, the large number of persons engaged in the manufacture and sale of taxable articles, and the amount of watchful care and *surveillance* necessary to be maintained for the purpose of collecting the taxes and preventing frauds, this exhibit must be regarded as exceedingly gratifying in respect to the small percentage the expenses bear to the amount collected.

AGGREGATE RECEIPTS FROM INTERNAL REVENUE (BY STATES) FOR FIFTEEN YEARS, 1863-1877.

[From the Annual Reports of the Commissioner of Internal Revenue.]

FISCAL YEARS ENDED JUNE 30.

STATES AND TERRITORIES.	1863.	1864.	1865.	1866.	1867.
	$	$	$	$	$
1 Alabama				4,132,311	4,119,130
2 Arizona					2,065
3 Arkansas				250,147	1,752,157
4 California	631,832	1,676,388	3,944,052	4,928,899	6,757,132
5 Colorado	21,079	41,160	132,392	150,614	151,687
6 Connecticut	1,552,615	3,272,516	6,576,004	9,636,688	7,582,971
7 Dakota					1,900
8 Delaware	167,468	391,025	819,902	1,013,723	785,967
9 Dist. of Columbia	45,340	365,964	748,632	766,826	704,202
10 Florida				98,215	557,989
11 Georgia				4,308,577	4,487,441
12 Idaho				79,519	81,237
13 Illinois	2,012,592	9,807,071	9,523,722	15,397,464	12,112,986
14 Indiana	924,904	3,398,210	4,821,243	5,417,336	4,122,863
15 Iowa	285,963	632,337	1,746,754	2,715,331	2,074,052
16 Kansas	38,906	65,440	215,319	359,364	367,543
17 Kentucky	1,382,772	3,946,093	4,857,134	5,922,122	5,415,134
18 Louisiana	154,341	2,274,543	1,714,502	6,197,813	6,226,789
19 Maine	514,636	1,294,094	2,618,823	2,822,863	2,826,380
20 Maryland	961,406	3,010,823	5,422,764	7,758,672	6,162,178
21 Massachusetts	4,830,501	12,173,222	25,250,362	34,989,208	28,088,078
22 Michigan	344,419	1,201,087	2,602,438	3,480,832	3,112,070
23 Minnesota	59,561	87,701	256,725	381,911	452,104
24 Mississippi				781,261	4,583,183
25 Missouri	1,194,326	3,307,451	5,480,304	7,490,908	6,404,096
26 Montana			36,023	113,280	77,431
27 Nebraska	12,338	26,796	57,419	100,875	107,975
28 Nevada	22,905	79,784	288,042	283,406	290,174
29 New Hampshire	483,692	1,074,267	2,544,782	3,480,349	2,882,147
30 New Jersey	1,227,444	3,116,358	7,580,310	10,191,967	7,800,263
31 New Mexico	9,318	10,941	49,043	71,358	64,365
32 New York	9,241,039	27,215,721	53,708,375	71,922,529	58,825,159
33 North Carolina				414,407	1,648,752
34 Ohio	3,217,481	12,224,450	16,022,925	25,732,500	19,902,523
35 Oregon	61,304	104,028	159,209	279,445	351,450
36 Pennsylvania	5,226,486	14,029,529	30,289,241	39,941,599	27,580,633
37 Rhode Island	826,950	1,984,969	4,312,781	6,121,938	5,049,974
38 South Carolina				966,486	1,816,804
39 Tennessee		602,706	1,605,263	3,381,841	3,349,460
40 Texas				1,573,290	3,211,864
41 Utah	6,141	13,748	41,728	62,008	64,296
42 Vermont	202,336	463,052	897,587	1,202,404	986,279
43 Virginia	738	137,514	221,273	1,175,447	1,966,722
44 Washington	8,263	22,395	76,741	48,081	78,912
45 West Virginia	90,358	351,957	635,759	1,020,565	944,524
46 Wisconsin	409,307	1,032,511	1,845,755	2,741,765	2,513,025
47 Wyoming					
Aggregate receipts each year	36,158,782	109,526,663	197,112,392	289,931,797	248,124,750
Adhesive stamps	4,140,175	5,804,945	11,162,392	15,044,373	16,094,718
Salaries	606,182	1,705,125	2,896,833	3,717,395	1,029,992
Passports, through Department of State	8,043	10,515	25,675	29,750	27,101
Fines, penalties, collections, etc		8,376	2,735	2,184,342	643,902
Aggregate receipts from all sources	41,003,272	117,145,624	211,129,920	310,906,666	265,920,263

AGGREGATE RECEIPTS FROM INTERNAL REVENUE (BY STATES) FOR FIFTEEN YEARS, 1863-1877.

[From the Annual Reports of the Commissioner of Internal Revenue.]

FISCAL YEARS ENDED JUNE 30.

STATES AND TERRITORIES.	1868.	1869.	1870.	1871.	1872.
	$	$	$	$	$
1 Alabama....	4,279,606	472,316	595,700	363,758	228,160
2 Arizona	13,901	11,315	15,615	16,889	15,579
3 Arkansas.............	844,390	144,965	369,284	130,524	94,201
4 California.......... ...	6,552,526	4,529,547	4,602,439	3,606,922	3,053,517
5 Colorado	119,222	60,999	73,010	69,994	63,272
6 Connecticut..........	4,400,398	2,340,506	2,564,477	1,426,871	1,204,615
7 Dakota...............	10,210	10,900	8,716	7,130	5,986
8 Delaware	588,254	425.106	451,986	444.018	400,101
9 Dist. of Columbia.....	485,366	446,045	514,482	267,809	217,000
10 Florida..............	402,746	71,099	106,318	121,031	99,456
11 Georgia........	6,146,965	1,010,282	1,144,241	736,944	583,160
12 Idaho.................	95,414	78,106	65,424	53,011	23,974
13 Illinois..............	7,564,687	13,063,257	18,364,367	15,119,609	15,799 667
14 Indiana.....	2,342,327	3,869,758	5,045,024	4,798,469	5,441,893
15 Iowa.................	1,182,230	1,558,265	1,377,981	1,081,841	1,067,797
16 Kansas....'..........	253,938	244,764	343,231	236,766	161,372
17 Kentucky.............	4,139,414	7,547,270	9,887,624	6,514,141	5,847,468
18 Louisiana............	3,826,416	1,902,116	2,981,524	1,912,755	1,627,782
19 Maine	1,594.080	669,906	807,224	412,096	302,123
20 Maryland.....	4.281,053	4,547,593	5,438,473	3,708,835	3,791,270
21 Massachusetts........	17,751,223	9,272.435	10,684.090	6,801,075	6,329,061
22 Michigan.............	2,757,816	2,642,514	2,918,987	2,639,670	2,399,972
23 Minnesota...........	368,391	363,338	467,879	252,583	248,979
24 Mississippi...........	3,751,872	194,129	284,793	238,257	133,675
25 Missouri...	4,913,361	5,295,805	6,004,278	5,005,076	4,618,219
26 Montana.............	108,284	64,336	103,556	82,105	28,955
27 Nebraska.............	127,735	161,388	308,502	224,369	195,699
28 Nevada..............	308,970	229,577	188,027	103,634	77,359
29 New Hampshire......	1,941,498	651,348	632,407	896,927	304,236
30 New Jersey..........	5,695,200	3,792,362	4,075,360	2,458,600	2,401,434
31 New Mexico..........	57,435	43,615	46,927	34,811	23,756
32 New York...........	39,395,788	35,716,423	36,361,550	28,870,402	23,468,729
33 North Carolina.......	1,977,286	750,537	1,398,720	1,362,268	1,103,525
34 Ohio................	12,224,617	16,116,548	19,568,744	15,149,489	14,905,229
35 Oregon	350,828	171,898	829,212	156,548	125,542
36 Pennsylvania........	18,269,446	15,470,400	16,748,704	12,535,522	9,227,091
37 Rhode Island........	2,852,575	1,280,395	1,282,377	672,408	636,927
38 South Carolina.......	2,634,801	353,860	412,040	258,720	190,191
39 Tennessee	3,717,010	1,255,781	1,470,800	874,222	766,840
40 Texas...............	1,802,023	483,218	390,954	350,680	322,359
41 Utah.................	48,685	67,071	46,206	39,926	39,481
42 Vermont.............	622,274	318,673	332,317	279,333	158,847
43 Virginia.............	1,783,320	2,744,144	5,496,351	5,319,273	4,939,064
44 Washington..........	70,101	49,367	83,273	36,753	23,840
45 West Virginia........	792.160	563,043	756,907	627,321	465,605
46 Wisconsin............	1,811,415	1,959,041	2,363,015	1,977,704	2,600,227
47 Wyoming.............	....	5,106	25,880	10,845	6,727
Aggregate receipts each year........	175,257,261	143,097,877	167,560,195	127,873,141	113,291,159
Adhesive stamps......	14,852,252	16,420,710	16,544,043	15,342,730	16,177,821
Salaries.............	1,043,561	561,903	1,100,326	787,263	294,565
Passports, through Department of State...	27,500	28,683	22,191	8,065	....
Aggregate receipts from all sources..	191,180,825	160,039,233	185,225,962	144,011,287	131,773,105

AGGREGATE RECEIPTS FROM INTERNAL REVENUE (BY STATES) FOR FIFTEEN YEARS, 1863-1877.

[From the Annual Reports of Commissioner of Internal Revenue.]

FISCAL YEARS ENDED JUNE 30.

STATES AND TERRITORIES	1873.	1874.	1875.	1876.	1877.	Total, 15 Years.
	$	$	$	$	$	$
1 Alabama...	152,493	135,793	115,689	109,341	108,010	14,822,308
2 Arizona....	13,563	10,043	10,263	11.976	15,520	137,329
3 Arkansas...	88,861	68,877	75,377	68,201	85,850	3,978,056
4 California..	2,367,911	2,481,841	2,988,033	3,095,040	2,749,504	53,965,675
5 Colorado...	75,740	64,855	70,532	72,669	75,775	1,243,903
6 Connecticut	873,985	580,379	627,718	658,115	691,420	43,959,337
7 Dakota.....	7,597	11,944	10,040	12,156	22,396	108,976
8 Delaware...	429,393	357,651	360,331	417,593	470,175	7,522,696
9 Dist. of Col.	183,425	115,574	112,227	114,599	26,018	5,063,537
10 Florida.....	158,142	133,675	184,778	174,258	165,891	2,274,197
11 Georgia	477,960	384,623	388,227	362,726	278,279	20,310,024
12 Idaho	19,276	18,882	19,136	16,994	16,562	567,485
13 Illinois.....	16,493,169	15,419,721	17,634,627	23,730,694	21,870,203	214,004,935
14 Indiana	5,678,053	4,823,496	4,653,789	5,579,126	6,037,220	66,953,721
15 Iowa.......	1,012,907	933,261	1,040,218	1,212,618	1,810,400	18,732,043
16 Kansas.....	161,470	149,758	133,686	150,604	130,763	3,021,921
17 Kentucky...	5,456,628	6,950,279	9,025,588	7,705,593	9,534,425	94,131,685
18 Louisiana...	1,339,607	982,465	606,264	529,788	626,440	32,903,145
19 Maine......	214,696	123,069	107,473	90,656	79,621	13,982,763
20 Maryland ..	2,653,802	2,351,107	2,760,737	2,577,570	2,705,246	58,126,557
21 Massachu'ts	3,761,005	2,792,303	2,708,014	2,752,216	2,668,727	170,851,520
22 Michigan...	2,205,721	1,789,080	1,931,285	2,066,164	1,821,882	33,912,938
23 Minnesota..	231,405	227,356	228,862	248,776	239,462	4,114,533
24 Mississippi.	128,079	107,619	96,968	85,165	78,683	10,463,066
25 Missouri ...	4,259,320	4,325,486	4,594,875	2,981,942	4,460,063	70,504,513
26 Montana...	24,018	29,023	23,066	20,983	20,730	734,393
27 Nebraska...	242,962	276,387	292,472	502,398	602,743	3,240,056
28 Nevada	72,305	52,549	58,803	67,923	58,312	2,191,774
29 N. Hamps'e	325,455	218,670	290,390	260,261	234,990	15,760,433
30 New Jersey	2,567,442	1,725,627	2,363,464	3,779,940	4,987,961	63,952,747
31 N. Mexico..	23,238	18,418	22,066	22,162	17,711	515,164
32 New York..	19,219,505	15,182,863	15,238,882	14,616,724	14,452,179	463,450,377
33 N. Carolina.	1,408,322	1,485,731	1,630,424	1,671,138	1,775,846	16,631,957
34 Ohio........	14,851,309	14,985,411	14,662,720	16,587,909	15,474,690	231,626,589
35 Oregon	73,544	46,773	47,930	49,573	53,100	2,359,894
36 Pennsylv'a.	7,826,276	6,373,672	6,157,960	5,973,432	6,270,046	221,929,037
37 Rhode Isl'd	324,552	233,165	231,978	222,673	233,165	26,272,911
38 S. Carolina.	167,214	108,581	122,278	105,804	105,633	7,271,491
39 Tennessee..	644,481	664,717	861,645	596,714	897,182	20,688,711
40 Texas......	272,326	272,638	258,297	245,700	237,049	9,421,317
41 Utah	40,786	41,684	31,800	33,332	28,438	596,792
42 Vermont...	75,860	56,317	58,582	47,125	50,003	5,771,079
43 Virginia....	7,343,799	6,308,665	7,660,921	7,314,394	7,932,221	60,343,830
44 Washingt'n	15,699	17,999	21,147	20,411	21,373	594,353
45 W. Virginia.	449,662	516,119	508,868	430,978	461,031	8,614,918
46 Wisconsin .	1,881,821	2,369,564	2,722,077	3,308,770	2,867,440	29,222,436
47 Wyoming ..	10,633	11,233	11,912	15,063	15,204	114,654
Aggregate receipts each year..	106,255,519	96,368,422	103,771,723	110,718,683	112,544,637	2,149,529,663
Adhesive stamps......	7,702,377	6,136,845	6,557,230	6,518,488	6,450,429	33,365,369
Salaries	117,542	130,472	233	568	98	257,834
Collections under Act of May 8, 1872..	....	....	216,027	....	....	216,027
Aggregate receipts from all sources ..	114,075,838	102,644,749	110,546,876	117,237,770	118,995,184	2,183,363,893

BANK OF ENGLAND RATES OF DISCOUNT.

From 1694, *the year of its Foundation*, *to* 1877.

NOTE.—It is to be understood in all cases that the discount rate against any given date was the rate charged until the next succeeding date. For example, April 20th, 1876, the Directors fixed the minimum rate of discount on first-class bills at 2 per cent, which continued until May 2d, 1877, when it was raised to 3 per cent. Oct. 17th, 1877, it was raised to 5 per cent, at which rate it long continued.

1694	Aug. 8	6
	" 30	4½
	Oct. 24	6
1695	Jan. 16	6
	" 16	4½
	" 16	3
	May 19	3
1704	Feb. 28	4
	" 28	5
1710	June 22	5
1716	July 26	4
1719	April 30	5
1720	Oct. 27	5
1722	Aug. 23	4
1742	Oct. 18	5
	" 18	4
1745	Dec. 12	5
1746	May 1	4
	" 5	5
1773	" 13	5
1822	June 20	4
1825	Dec. 13	5
1827	July 5	4
1836	July 21	4½
	Sept. 1	5
1833	Feb. 15	4
1839	May 16	5
	June 20	5½
	Aug. 1	6
1840	Jan. 23	5
	Oct. 15	5
1841	June 3	5
1842	April 7	4
1844	Sept. 5	2½
	" 5	3
1845	March 13	2½
	Oct. 16	3
	Nov. 6	3½
1846	Aug. 27	3
1847	Jan. 14	3½
	" 21	4
	April 8	5
	" 15	5
	Aug. 5	5½
	Oct. 25	8
	Nov. 27	7
	Dec. 2	6
	" 23	5
1848	Jan. 27	4
	June 15	3½
	Nov. 2	3
1849	Nov. 22	3½
1850	Dec. 26	3
1852	Jan. 1	2½
	April 22	2
1853	Jan. 6	2½
	" 20	3
	June 2	3½
	Sept. 1	4
	" 15	4½
	" 29	5
1854	May 11	5½
	Aug. 3	5
1855	April 5	4½
	May 3	4
	June 14	3½
	Sept. 6	4
	" 13	4½
	" 27	5
	Oct. 4	5½
	" 13	6
	" 18	7
1856	May 22	6
	May 29	5
	June 26	4½
	Oct. 1	5
	" 6	6
	" 6	7
	Nov. 13	7
	Dec. 4	6½
	" 18	6
1857	April 2	6½
	June 18	6
	July 16	5½
	Oct. 8	6
	" 12	7
	" 19	8
	Nov. 5	9
	" 9	10
	Dec. 24	8
1858	Jan. 7	6
	" 14	5
	" 28	4
	Feb. 4	3½
	" 11	3
	Dec. 9	2½
1859	April 28	3½
	May 5	4½
	June 2	3½
	" 9	3
	July 14	2½
1860	Jan. 19	3
	" 31	4
	March 29	4½
	April 12	5
	May 10	4½
	" 24	4
	Nov. 8	4½
	" 13	5
	" 15	6
	" 29	5
	Dec. 31	6
1861	Jan. 7	7
	Feb. 14	8
	March 21	7
	April 4	6
	" 11	5
	May 16	6
	Aug. 1	5
	" 15	4½
	" 29	4
	Sept. 19	3½
	Nov. 7	3
1862	Jan. 9	2½
	May 22	3
	July 10	2½
	" 24	2
	Oct. 30	3
1863	Jan. 15	4
	" 23	5
	Feb. 19	4
	April 23	3½
	" 30	3
	May 16	3½
	" 21	4
	Nov. 2	5
	" 5	6
	Dec. 2	7
	" 3	8
	" 24	7
1864	Jan. 20	8
	Feb. 11	7
	" 25	6
	April 16	7
	May 2	8
	" 5	9
	May 19	8
	" 26	7
	June 16	6
	July 25	7
	Aug. 4	8
	Sept. 8	9
	Nov. 10	8
	" 24	7
	Dec. 15	6
1865	Jan. 12	5½
	" 26	5
	March 2	4½
	" 30	4
	May 4	4½
	" 25	4
	June 1	3½
	" 15	3
	July 27	3½
	Aug. 3	4
	Sept 28	4½
	Oct. 2	5
	" 5	6
	" 7	7
	Nov. 23	6
	Dec. 28	7
1866	Jan. 4	8
	Feb. 22	7
	March 15	6
	May 3	7
	" 8	8
	" 11	9
	" 12	10
	Aug. 16	8
	" 23	7
	" 30	6
	Sept. 6	5
	" 27	4½
	Nov. 8	4
	Dec. 20	3½
1867	Feb. 7	3
	May 30	2½
	July 25	2
1868	Nov. 19	2½
	Dec. 3	3
1869	April 1	4
	May 6	4½
	June 10	4
	" 24	3½
	July 15	3
	Aug. 19	2½
	Nov. 4	3
1870	July 21	3½
	" 23	4
	" 28	5
	Aug. 4	6
	" 11	5½
	" 18	4½
	" 25	4
	Sept. 1	3½
	" 15	3
	" 29	2½
1871	March 2	3
	April 13	2½
	June 15	2½
	July 13	2
	Sept. 21	3
	" 28	4
	Oct. 7	5
	Nov. 16	4
	" 30	3½
	Dec. 14	3
1872	April 4	3½
	" 11	4
	May 9	5
	" 30	4
	June 13	3½
	" 20	3
	July 18	3½
	Sept. 19	4
	" 26	4½
	Oct. 3	5
	" 10	6
	Nov. 9	7
	" 28	6
	Dec. 12	5
1873	Jan. 9	4½
	" 23	4
	" 30	3½
	March 26	4
	May 7	4½
	" 10	5
	" 17	6
	June 4	7
	" 12	6
	July 10	5
	" 17	4½
	" 24	4
	" 31	3½
	Aug. 21	3
	Sept. 25	4
	" 29	5
	Oct. 14	6
	" 18	7
	Nov. 1	8
	" 7	9
	" 20	8
	" 27	6
	Dec. 4	5
	" 11	4½
1874	Jan. 8	4
	" 15	3½
	April 30	4
	May 28	3½
	June 4	3
	" 18	2½
	July 30	3
	Aug. 6	4
	" 20	3½
	" 27	3
	Oct. 15	4
	Nov. 16	5
	" 30	6
1875	Jan. 7	5
	" 14	4
	" 28	3
	Feb. 18	3½
	July 8	3
	" 29	2½
	Aug. 12	2
	Oct. 7	2½
	" 14	3½
	" 21	4
	Nov. 18	3
	Dec. 30	4
1876	Jan. 6	5
	" 27	4
	March 23	3½
	April 6	3
	" 20	2
1877	May 2	3
	July 4	2½
	" 11	2
	Sept. 5	3
	Oct. 10	4
	" 17	5

[From Crump's Key to the London Money Market, 6th ed., 1877.]

Population of all Cities and Towns in the United States having a Population of over 10,000 in 1870, with Population by State or Local Census of Later Date.

CITIES	STATES	Population 1870	Population 1875	CITIES	STATES	Population 1870	Population 1875
Adams	Mass...	12,090	15,760	Evansville	Ind....	21,830	
Akron	O	10,006		Fall River	Mass...	26,766	45,340
Albany	N.Y	76,216	86,013	Fitchburg	Mass...	11,260	12,289
Alexandria	Va	13,570		Fond du Lac	Wis....	12,764	15,308
Allegheny	Penn...	53,180		Fort Wayne	Ind....	17,718	
Allentown	Penn...	13,884		Galesburg	Ill.....	10,158	
Altoona	Penn...	10,610		Galveston	Tex...	13,818	
Atlanta	Ga.....	21,789		Georgetown	D.C...	11,384	
Auburn	N.Y....	17,225	18,359	Gloucester	Mass...	15,389	16,754
Augusta	Ga. ...	15,389		*Grand Rapids	Mich...	16,507	25,923
Aurora	Ill. ...	11,162		Greenburgh	N.Y...	10,790	10,997
Baltimore	Md....	267,354		Hamilton	O.....	11,081	
Bangor	Me....	18,289		Hannibal	Mo....	10,125	
*Bay City	Mich...	7,064	13,690	Harrisburg	Penn..	23,104	
Biddeford	Me....	10,282		Hartford	Conn...	37,180	
Binghamton	N.Y....	12,692	15,550	Haverhill	Mass..	13,092	14,628
Bloomington	Ill.....	14,590		Hoboken	N.J...	20,297	24,766
Boston	Mass..	250,526	341,919	Holyoke	Mass...	10,733	16,260
Bridgeport	Conn..	18,969		Indianapolis	Ind. ..	48,244	
Brookhaven	N.Y..	10,159	11,451	*Jackson	Mich...	11,447	13,859
Brooklyn	N.Y..	396,099	484,616	Janesville	Wis....	8,789	10,115
Buffalo	N.Y..	117,714	134,573	Jersey City	N.J...	82,546	109,227
Burlington	Iowa..	14,930	19,987	†Kansas City	Mo....	82,260	32,736
Burlington	Vt.....	14,387		Keokuk	Iowa...	12,766	11,841
Cambridge	Mass...	39,634	47,838	Kingston City	N.Y...	[new]	20,474
Camden	N.J...	20,045	33,832	La Crosse	Wis....	7,785	11,102
Charleston	S.C...	48,956		Lafayette	Ind....	13,506	
Charlestown	Mass..	28,323	[Bost'n]	Lancaster	Penn..	20,233	
Chelsea	Mass..	18,547	20,737	Lawrence	Mass...	28,921	34,916
Chicago	Ill.....	298,977		Leavenworth	Kan...	17,873	
Chicopee	Mass..	9,607	10,335	Lewiston	Me.....	13,600	
Cincinnati	O.....	216,239		Lexington	Ky.....	14,801	
Cleveland	O.....	92,829		Little Rock	Ark....	12,380	
Cohoes	N.Y..	15,357	17,516	Lockport	N.Y...	12,426	12,624
Columbus	O.....	31,274		Logansport	Ind....	12,191	
Concord	N.H..	12,241		Long Isl'd City	N.Y...	[new]	15,609
Council Bluffs	Iowa..	10,020	9,287	Louisville	Ky.....	100,753	
Covington	Ky.....	24,505		Lowell	Mass...	40,928	49,688
Davenport	Iowa..	20,038	21,234	Lynn	Mass...	28,233	32,600
Dayton	O.....	30,473		Macon	Ga....	10,810	
Des Moines	Iowa..	12,035	14,443	Madison	Ind....	10,709	
*Detroit	Mich..	79,577	101,255	Malden	Mass...		10,843
Dubuque	Iowa..	18,434	23,605	Manchester	N.H..	23,536	
Easton	Penn..	10,987		Memphis	Tenn..	40,226	
*East Saginaw	Mich..	11,350	17,804	Meriden	Conn..	10,495	
Elizabeth	N.J...	20,832	25,923	Milwaukee	Wis...	71,440	100,775
Elmira	N.Y...	15,863	20,538	Minneapolis	Minn...	13,066	32,721
Erie	Penn...	19,646		Mobile	Ala....	32,034	

* Census of 1874.   † Census of 1876.

POPULATION OF CITIES AND TOWNS IN THE U. S.—(Continued).

Cities.	States	Population. 1870.	Population. 1875.	Cities.	States	Population. 1870.	Population. 1875.
Montgomery...	Ala.....	10,588	....	Rockford......	Ill.....	11,049	....
*Morrisania...	N. Y ...	19,609	....	Rome..........	N. Y...	11,000	11,992
Nashville.....	Tenn...	25,865	....	Rondout.......	N. Y...	10,114	[Kingst'n]
Nashua........	N. H...	10,543	....	Sacramento....	Cal.....	16,283	....
New Albany..	Ind.....	15,396	....	†St. Joseph....	Mo.....	19,565	23,099
Newark.......	N. J...	105,059	123,310	†St. Louis.....	Mo.....	310,864	498,182
New Bedford..	Mass...	21,320	25,805	St. Paul.......	Minn...	20,030	33,178
N. Brunswick.	N. J...	15,058	16,660	Salem.........	Mass..	24,117	25,958
Newburgh.....	N. Y...	17,014	17,327	Salt Lake City.	Utah T.	12,854	....
Newburyport..	Mass...	12,595	13,323	San Antonio...	Tex....	12,256	....
New Haven...	Conn..	50,840	....	Sandusky.....	O.......	13,000	....
New Orleans ..	La.	191,418	....	San Francisco.	Cal.....	149,473	....
Newport.......	Ky.....	15,087	....	Saratoga Spr's.	N. Y...	8,537	10,775
Newport......	R. I ...	12,521	14,028	Savannah......	Ga.....	28,235	....
Newton.......	Mass...	12,825	16,105	Schenectady...	N. Y...	11,026	12,748
New York.....	N. Y...	942,292	1,046,037	Scranton	Penn...	35,092	....
Norfolk.......	Va	19,229	....	Somerville....	Mass...	14,685	11,868
Norristown....	Penn...	10,753	....	Springfield ...	Ill.....	17,364	....
Northampton..	Mass...	10,160	11,108	Springfield ...	Mass...	26,703	31,053
Norwich.......	Conn..	16,653	....	Springfield ...	O.......	12,652	....
Norwalk......	Conn..	12,119	....	Stockton	Cal.....	10,066	....
Oakland... ...	Cal.....	10,500	....	Syracuse	N. Y...	43,051	48,315
Ogdensburg...	N. Y...	10,076	13,204	Taunton.......	Mass...	18,629	20,445
Omaha........	Neb....	16.083	....	Terre Haute...	Ind....	16,103	....
Oshkosh......	Wis ..	12,663	17,015	Toledo........	O.......	31,584	....
Oswego.......	N. Y...	20,910	22,455	Trenton.......	N. J...	22,874	25,081
Paterson.....	N. J...	33,579	38,814	Troy..........	N. Y...	46,465	48,821
Pawtucket....	R. I ...	6,619	16,620	Utica..........	N. Y...	28,804	32,070
Peoria........	Ill.....	22,849	....	Vicksburg....	Miss...	12.443	....
Petersburg ...	Va	18,950	....	Washington...	D. C...	109 199	....
†Philadelphia .	Penn...	674,022	817,448	Waterbury....	Conn...	10,826	....
Pittsburg.....	Penn...	86,076	....	Watertown....	N. Y...	9,336	10,041
Pittsfield.....	Mass...	11,112	12,267	West Troy.....	N. Y...	10,693	....
Portland......	Me.....	31,413	....	Wheeling.....	W. Va..	19,280	....
Portsmouth ..	O.......	10,592	....	Wilkesbarre...	Penn...	10,174	....
Portsmouth ...	Va	10,492	....	Williamsport..	Penn..	16,080	....
Pottsville.....	Ill.....	12,384	....	Wilmington...	Del....	30,841	....
Poughkeepsie.	N. Y...	20,080	19,859	Wilmington...	N. C...	13,446	....
Providence....	R. I ...	68,904	100,675	Winona.......	Minn...	7,192	10,737
Quincy.......	Ill	24,052	....	Woonsocket...	R. I ...	11,527	13,168
Racine........	Wis....	9,880	13,274	Worcester.....	Mass...	41,105	49 317
Reading......	Penn...	33,930	....	Yonkers........	N. Y...	12,733	17,269
Richmond.....	Va... .	51,038	....	York..........	Penn...	11,003	....
Rochester.....	N. Y...	62,386	81,673	Zanesville.....	O.......	10,011	....

* Annexed to New York City in 1873. † Census of 1876.

Classification of the Landholders of Great Britain.

	Owners. No.	Extent of Lands. Acres.	Gross Estimated Rental.
Owners of less than 1 acre.................	816,294	179,348	£34,927,723
" between 1 and 10 acres...	131,454	608,006	7,971,480
" " 10 " 50 " ..	76,109	1,827,698	7,392,761
" " 50 " 100 " ..	27,052	1,878,088	4,692,847
" " 100 " 500 " ..	84,664	7,383,719	13,355,583
" " 500 " 1,000 " ..	5,623	3,900,419	7,991,073
" " 1,000 " 2,000 " ..	3,310	4,634,849	9,094,127
" " 2,000 " 5,000 " ..	2,402	7,372,568	11,524,816
" " 5,000 " 10,000 " ..	831	5,701,593	6,566,179
" " 10,000 " 20,000 " ..	382	5,243,785	5,302,180
" " 20,000 " 50,000 " ..	169	4,986,804	3,277,217
" " 50,000 " 100,000 " ..	47	3,220,554	777,634
" " 100,000 acres and upwards........	25	5,113,500	785,022
No Areas stated.........................	6,945	....	2,942,192
No Rentals stated.......................	124	2,570	....
Totals...............	1,164,967	51,960,898	£113,061,103

OCCUPATIONS OF THE PEOPLE OF THE UNITED STATES.

THE tables of the Census of 1870 exhibit interesting statistics on the employments which divide the industry of our people. The population of the United States over ten years of age was shown to amount to 28,228,945, of which number 14,258,866 were males. There were returned as engaged in all classes of occupations a total of 12,505,923, of which number 10,669,635 were males, and 1,836,288 females. In the census of occupations it will be seen that by far the greater number of inhabitants over ten years of age were returned as engaged in some class of labor. Grouping the results of the more detailed table of diversified occupations to be found below, it is shown that they were distributed in the following four great classes of occupations, namely :

Engaged in Agriculture.. 5,922,471
Engaged in Manufactures and Mechanical and Mining Industries. 2,707,421
Engaged in Professional and Personal Services.................... 2,684,793
Engaged in Trade and Transportation............................. 1,191,238

Total..12,505,923

It will be seen that the pursuits of agriculture occupy 46.31 per cent, or something less than half the population ; manufacturing industries, 21.64 per cent of all classes of occupations ; professional and personal services, 21.46 per cent ; and trade and transportation 9.53 per cent of the whole, or less than one tenth.

I.—OCCUPATIONS OF THE PEOPLE OF THE UNITED STATES.

[From the Returns of the United States Census, 1870.]

WHOLE POPULATION, TEN YEARS AND OVER......... 28,228,945	**Professional and Personal Services :**
	Actors 2,053
	Apprentices to learned professions. 396
All occupations (persons engaged in), 10 years and over. 12,505,923	Apprentices to barbers 859
	Apprentices to dentists....... 166
	Architects.................. 2,017
	Artists (not specified)........ 2,948
Engaged in Agriculture :	Auctioneers................. 2,266
	Authors and lecturers 458
Agricultural laborers......... 2,885,996	Barbers and hairdressers...... 23,935
Apiarists..................... 136	Bath-house keepers.......... 94
Dairymen and dairywomen... 3,550	Billiard and bowling saloon
Farm and plantation overseers 3,609	keepers.................... 1,220
Farmers and planters......... 2,977,711	Bill-posters................. 434
Florists 1,085	Boarding and lodging house
Gardeners and nurserymen... 31,435	keepers.................... 12,785
Stock-drovers................ 3,181	Boot-blacks................. 587
Stock-herders 5,590	Card-writers................ 33
Stock-raisers................ 6,588	Chemists (practising)........ 608
Turpentine farmers.......... 861	Chimney-sweeps............. 78
Turpentine laborers.......... 2,117	Chiropodists 65
Vinegrowers 1,112	Claim agents............... 693
	Clergymen... 43,874
Total engaged in Agriculture....... 5,922,471	Clerks and copyists.......... 6,138
	Clerks in Government offices . 8,672

OCCUPATIONS OF THE PEOPLE OF THE UNITED STATES—(*Continued*).

Professional and Personal Services— (Continued).

Clerks in hotels & restaurants	5,243
Dentists	7,839
Designers and draughtsmen	934
Domestic servants	975,734
Employés of companies (n. s.)	848
Employés of Government	14,407
Employés of hotels & restaur's	23,438
Engineers (civil)	4,703
Hostlers	17,586
Hotel-keepers	26,394
Hunters and trappers	940
Indian scouts, guides and interpreters	171
Intelligence-office keepers	191
Inventors	352
Janitors	1,769
Journalists	5,286
Laborers (not specified)	1,031,666
Lamp-lighters	276
Land-surveyors	2,671
Launderers and laundresses	60,906
Lawyers	40,736
Librarians	213
Livery-stable keepers	8,504
Marines (United States)	477
Messengers	8,717
Metallurgists	164
Midwives	1,186
Musicians (professional)	6,519
Naturalists	287
Nurses	10,976
Officers of the Army and Navy	2,286
Officials of companies	8,410
Officials of Government	44,743
Painters	775
Physicians and surgeons	62,383
Restaurant-keepers	35,185
Sailors (United States Navy)	780
Scavengers	801
Sculptors	250
Sextons	1,151
Short-hand writers	154
Showmen and showwomen	1,177
Soldiers (United States Army)	22,081
Teachers (not specified)	126,822
Teachers of dancing	149
Teachers of drawing & paint'g	108
Teachers of music	9,491
Translators	21
Veterinary surgeons	1,163
Whitewashers	2,873
Total Professional and Personal Services	**2,684,793**

Manufactures and Mining:

Agricult'l-implement makers	8,811
Artificial-flower makers	1,169
Apprentices (not specified)	15,342
Bag-makers	856
Bakers	27,680
Basket-makers	3,297
Bell-founders	169
Belting-factory operatives	296
Blacksmiths	141,774
Bleachers, dyers, and scourers	4,901

Manufactures and Mining—(Continued).

Blind, door, and sash makers	5,155
Boat-makers	2,101
Bone and ivory workers	208
Bookbinders and finishers	9,104
Boot and shoe makers	171,127
Box-factory operatives	6,090
Brass founders and workers	4,694
Brewers and maltsters	11,246
Brick and tile makers	26,070
Bridge builders & contractors	1,029
Britannia and japanned ware makers	1,092
Broom and brush makers	5,816
Bronze workers	79
Builders and contractors	7,511
Butchers	44,854
Button-factory operatives	1,272
Cabinetmakers	42,835
Candle, soap, & tallow makers	1,942
Card and fancy-paper makers	339
Car-makers	2,228
Carpenters and joiners	344,596
Carpet-bag and satchel makers	202
Carpet-makers	15,669
Carriage and wagon makers	42,464
Charcoal and lime burners	3,831
Cheese-makers	3,534
Cigar-makers	29,286
Clerks and book-keepers	5,861
Clock-makers	1,779
Comb-makers	603
Confectioners	8,219
Coopers	41,789
Copper-workers	2,122
Cotton-mill operatives	111,606
Curriers, tanners, finishers of leather	28,702
Die-sinkers and stamp-makers	479
Distillers and rectifiers	2,874
Employés (not specified)	20,242
Engineers and firemen	34,233
Engravers	4,226
Fertilizer-establ't operatives	316
File makers, cutters,& grinders	1,413
Fireworks-makers	101
Fishermen and oystermen	27,106
Flax-dressers	1,046
Fur-workers	1,191
Galloon, gimp, & tassel makers	569
Gas-works employés	2,090
Gilders	1,534
Glass-works operatives	9,518
Glove-makers	2,329
Glue-makers	241
Gold and silver workers	18,508
Gun and lock smiths	8,184
Hair cleaners and dressers	1,026
Harness and saddle makers	32,817
Hat and cap makers	12,625
Hoop-skirt makers	962
Hose-makers (leather & other)	249
House-builders & contractors	899
Ice-cutters	142
Ink-makers	78
Iron and steel works and shops operatives	22,141
Iron-foundry operatives	34,345
Iron-furnace operatives	7,452

OCCUPATIONS OF THE PEOPLE OF THE UNITED STATES—(*Continued*).

Manufactures and Mining—(Continued).

Iron & steel rolling-mill operatives	17,249
Knitting & hosiery mill operatives	3,653
Linen-mill operatives	706
Lumbermen and raftsmen	17,752
Macaroni & vermicelli makers	20
Machinists	54,755
Manufacturers	42,877
Marble and stone cutters	25,831
Masons, brick and stone	89,710
Mast, spar, oar, & block makers	653
Mattress-makers	875
Meat and fruit preserving employés	770
Meat packers, curers, & picklers	1,164
Mechanics (not specified)	16,514
Mill & factory operatives (n.s.)	41,619
Millers	41,582
Milliners, dress and mantua makers	92,084
Mineral-water makers	458
Miners	152,107
Mirror & picture frame makers	970
Morocco-dressers	1,729
Musical-instrument makers	377
Needle-makers	164
Officials of manuf'g companies	2,144
Officials of mining companies	576
Oil-cloth makers	454
Oil-refinery operatives	1,747
Oil-well operators and laborers	3,803
Organ-makers	667
Oyster-packers	443
Painters and varnishers	85,123
Paper-hangers	2,490
Paper-mill operatives	12,469
Patent-medicine makers	409
Pattern-makers	3,970
Perfumers	248
Photographers, etc	7,558
Piano-forte makers	2,535
Plasterers	23,577
Plaster-moulders	223
Plate-printers	231
Plumbers and gasfitters	11,143
Potters	5,060
Powder-makers	575
Printers	39,860
Print-works operatives	3,738
Publishers	1,577
Pump-makers	1,672
Quarrymen	13,589
Quartz & stamp mill laborers	617
Rag-pickers	436
Railroad builders & contract's	1,292
Reed and shuttle makers	200
Roofers and slaters	2,750
Rope and cordage makers	2,673
Rubber-factory operatives	3,886
Sail and awning makers	2,309
Salt-makers	1,721
Saw-mill operatives	47,296
Sawyers	6,939
Scale and rule makers	416
Screw-makers	790
Sewing-machine fact'y oper's	3,681
Sewing-machine operators	3,043

Manufactures and Mining—(Continued).

Shingle and lath makers	3,788
Ship-carpenters	15,900
Ship-smiths	396
Ship-caulkers	3,068
Ship-riggers	1,057
Shirt, cuff, and collar makers	4,080
Shot, cartridge, & fusé makers	186
Silk-mill operatives	3,256
Spring and axle makers	301
Starch-makers	229
Stave, shook, & heading m'k'rs	1,858
Steam-boiler makers	6,958
Steam-engine makers	4,172
Stereotypers	333
Stove, furnace, & grate makers	1,543
Straw-workers	2,029
Sugar makers and refiners	1,609
Tailors and seamstresses	161,820
Tinners	30,521
Tool and cutlery makers	5,351
Trunk and valise makers	1,843
Tobacco-factory operatives	11,985
Truss-makers	74
Type founders and cutters	649
Umbrella and parasol makers	1,439
Upholsterers	5,736
Wheelwrights	20,942
Whip-makers	609
Window-shade makers	243
Wire makers and workers	1,831
Woodchoppers	8,338
Wood turners and carvers	7,947
Woollen-mill operatives	58,836
Total Manufactures and Mining	2,707,421

Trade and Transportation:

Agents	10,490
Apprentices in stores	678
Bankers and brokers	10,631
Barkeepers	14,362
Boatmen and watermen	21,332
Book-keepers in stores	31,177
Canalmen	7,338
Clerks in stores	222,504
Clerks & book-keep's in banks	7,103
Clerks and book-keepers in express companies	767
Clerks and book-keepers in insurance offices	1,568
Clerks and book-keepers in railroad offices	7,374
Clerks and book-keepers in telegraph offices	191
Commercial travellers	7,262
Draymen, hackmen, teamsters, etc	120,756
Employés of trading and transportation companies	4,152
Employés of banks (not clerks)	424
Employés of express companies (not clerks)	8,554
Employés of insurance companies (not clerks)	11,611

Trade and Transportation—(Continued).	
Employés of railroad companies (not clerks).........	154,027
Employés of street railroad companies (not clerks).....	5,103
Employés of telegraph companies (not clerks).........	8,316
Hucksters.....................	17,362
Laborers......................	14,882
Milkmen and milkwomen....	3,728
Mule-packers.................	473
Newspaper criers & carriers,.	2,002
Officials of trading and transportation companies........	976
Officials of banks.............	2,738
Officials of express companies	75
Officials of insurance compan's	762
Officials of railroad companies	1,902
Officials of street railroad companies...................	88
Officials of telegraph comp'es	72
Packers......................	1,421
Pawnbrokers.................	384
Pedlers.	16,075
Pilots........................	3,649
Porters in stores and warch's.	16,631
Sailors...	56,663
Salesmen and saleswomen....	14,203
Shippers and freighters......	3,567
Steamboat men and women..	7,975
Stewards and stewardesses...	1,245
Toll-gate and bridge keepers.	2,253
Traders & dealers (not speci'd)	100,406
" in agricultural implem's.	1,939
" in books and stationery.	8,892
" in boots and shoes......	7,019
" in cabinetware.........	4,067
" in cigars and tobacco....	8,234
" in clothing..............	7,595

Trade and Transportation—(Continued).	
Traders and dealers in cloths and textile fabrics...	1,163
" in coal..................	4,143
" in coal and wood........	2,493
" in cotton...............	1,701
" in crockery, china, and stoneware...........	1,765
" in drugs and medicines.	17,319
" in dry-goods...........	89,790
" in gold and silver ware and jewelry..........	6,402
" in groceries.............	74,410
" in hats and caps........	8,875
" in ice..................	1,464
" in iron, tin, and copper wares................	9,003
" in leather hides, & skins	2,261
" in lime.................	310
" in liquors and wines....	11,718
" in live stock...........	7,723
" in lumber..............	9,440
" in machinery (not spec.)	254
" in music and musical instruments...........	848
" in newsp'rs & periodicals	1,455
" in oils,paints,& turpent'e	986
" in optical instruments..	301
" in produce	11,809
" in provisions	7,528
" in real estate...........	8,933
" in sewing-machines.....	3,132
Undertakers.................	1,996
Weighers,gaugers,& measur's	926
Wreckers.....................	98
Total Trade and Transportation....	1,191,238

OCCUPATIONS OF THE PEOPLE IN GREAT BRITAIN.

In England and Wales, out of 22,712,266 persons aged 20 and upwards, at the last census, in 1871, there was the following distribution of the occupations of the people :

Professional Classes—Under Government.......	242,777
Other Professions........	441,325
Commercial Classes...........................	538,260
Agricultural Classes....	1,656,938
Domestic Classes.............................	1,638,514
Industrial Classes........	6,140,202
Persons of Independent Means.................	169,695
Total................................	10,811,911

II.—OCCUPATIONS IN THE UNITED STATES: NUMBER OF PERSONS
ENGAGED IN EACH CLASS, BY STATES AND TERRITORIES—1870.

[From the Official Returns of the Ninth Census, 1870.]

STATES AND TERRITORIES.	Whole populat'n 10 years and over.	Engaged in all kinds of occupations.	Engaged in agriculture.	Engaged in profes-sional and personal service.	Engaged in trade & transpor-tation.	Engaged in manu-factures, mec'anic'l trades and mining.
The U. S.	28,228,945	12,505,923	5,922,471	2,684,793	1,191,238	2,707,421
Alabama	706,802	365,258	291,628	42,125	14,435	17,070
Arizona	8,237	6,030	1,285	3,115	591	1,039
Arkansas	341,737	135,949	109,310	14,877	5,491	6,271
California	430,444	238,648	47,863	76,112	33,165	81,508
Colorado	30,349	17,583	6,462	3,625	2,815	4,681
Connecticut	425,896	193,421	43,653	38,704	24,720	86,344
Dakota	10,640	5,867	2,522	2,704	204	457
Delaware	92.586	40,313	15,973	11,389	3.437	9,514
District Columbia	100,453	49,041	1,365	29,845	6,126	11.705
Florida	131,119	60,703	42,492	10,897	3,023	4,291
Georgia	835,929	444,678	336,145	64,083	17,410	27,040
Idaho	13,189	10,879	1,462	1,423	721	7,273
Illinois	1,809,606	742,015	376,441	151,931	80,422	133,221
Indiana	1,197,936	459,369	266,777	80,018	36,517	76,057
Iowa	837,459	344,276	210,263	58,484	28,210	47,319
Kansas	258,051	121,852	78,228	20,736	11,762	18,126
Kentucky	930,186	414,593	261,080	84,024	25,292	44,197
Louisiana	526,392	256,452	141,467	65,347	23,831	25,807
Maine	493,847	208,225	82,011	36,092	28,115	62,007
Maryland	575,439	258,543	80,449	70,226	35,542	63,326
Massachusetts	1,160,666	579,844	72,810	131,291	83,078	292.665
Michigan	873,763	404,164	187,211	104,728	29,588	82,637
Minnesota	305,568	132,657	75,157	28,330	10,582	18,588
Mississippi	581,206	318,850	259,199	40,522	9,148	9,981
Missouri	1,205,568	505,556	263,918	106,903	54.835	79,850
Montana	18,170	14,048	2,111	2,674	1,233	8,030
Nebraska	89,265	43,837	23,115	10,331	4,628	5,763
Nevada	36,655	26,911	2,070	7,431	3,621	13,789
New Hampshire	260,426	120,168	46,573	18,523	8,514	46,553
New Jersey	630,687	296,036	63,128	83,380	46,206	103,322
New Mexico	66,464	29,361	18,668	7,535	863	2,295
New York	3,378,959	1,491,018	374,323	405,339	234,581	476,775
North Carolina	769,629	351,299	269,238	51,290	10,179	20,592
Ohio	1,953,374	840,889	397,024	168,308	78,547	197,010
Oregon	64,685	30,651	13,248	6,090	2,610	8,694
Pennsylvania	2,597,809	1,020,544	260,051	283,000	121,253	356,240
Rhode Island	173,751	68,574	11,780	19,679	10,103	47,007
South Carolina	503,763	263,301	206,654	34,383	8,470	13,794
Tennessee	890,872	367,987	267,020	54,396	17,510	29,061
Texas	571,075	237,126	166,753	40,882	13,612	15,879
Utah	56,515	21,517	10,428	5,317	1,665	4,107
Vermont	258,731	109,763	57,983	21,032	7,132	22,616
Virginia	890,056	412,665	244,550	98,521	20,181	49,413
Washington	17,334	9,760	3,771	2,207	1,129	2,653
West Virginia	308,424	115,299	73,960	16,699	6,897	17,673
Wisconsin	751,704	292,808	159,687	58,070	21,534	53,517
Wyoming	8,059	6,645	165	3,170	1,646	1,664
Total	28,228,945	12,505,923	5,922,471	2,684,793	1,191,238	2,707,421

STATISTICS OF CHURCHES IN THE UNITED STATES.

I.—BY STATES.

[From the Returns of the U. S. Census, 1870.]

STATES AND TERRITORIES.	Aggregate Population.	Church Organizations.	Church Edifices.	Church Sittings.	Church Property.
The United States.	38,558,371	72,459	63,082	21,665,062	$354,483,551
1 Alabama	996,992	2,095	1,958	510,810	$2,414,515
2 Arizona	9,658	4	4	2,400	24,000
3 Arkansas	484,471	1,371	1,141	264,225	854,975
4 California	560,247	643	532	195,558	7,404,235
5 Colorado	39,864	55	47	17,495	207,230
6 Connecticut	537,454	826	902	838,735	13,428,109
7 Dakota	14,181	17	10	2,800	16,300
8 Delaware	125,015	267	252	87,899	1,823,950
9 District of Columbia	131,700	111	112	63,655	3,393,100
10 Florida	187,748	420	390	78,920	426,520
11 Georgia	1,184,109	2,673	2,698	801,148	3,561,955
12 Idaho	14,999	15	12	2,150	18,200
13 Illinois	2,539,891	4,298	3,459	1,201,403	22,664,283
14 Indiana	1,680,637	3,698	3,106	1,008,380	11,942,227
15 Iowa	1,194,020	2,763	1,446	431,709	5,730,352
16 Kansas	364,399	530	301	102,135	1,722,700
17 Kentucky	1,321,011	2,969	2,696	878,039	9,824,465
18 Louisiana	726,915	638	599	213,955	4,048,525
19 Maine	626,915	1,328	1,104	376,733	5,200,833
20 Maryland	780,894	1,420	1,389	499,770	12,038,650
21 Massachusetts	1,457,351	1,848	1,764	882,317	24,488,385
22 Michigan	1,184,059	2,239	1,415	456,226	9,133,816
23 Minnesota	439,706	877	582	158,266	2,401,750
24 Mississippi	827,922	1,829	1,800	485,398	2,360,800
25 Missouri	1,721,295	3,220	2,082	691,590	9,709,358
26 Montana	20,595	15	11	3,850	09,300
27 Nebraska	122,993	181	108	32,210	386,000
28 Nevada	42,491	32	19	8,000	212,000
29 New Hampshire	318,300	633	624	210,090	3,303,780
30 New Jersey	906,096	1,402	1,384	573,303	18,347,150
31 New Mexico	91,874	158	152	81,560	322,621
32 New York	4,382,759	5,627	5,474	2,282,870	66,073,755
33 North Carolina	1,071,361	2,683	2,497	718,310	2,487,877
34 Ohio	2,665,260	6,488	6,284	2,085,586	25,554,785
35 Oregon	90,923	220	135	39,425	471,100
36 Pennsylvania	3,521,951	5,984	5,668	2,332,288	52,758,384
37 Rhode Island	217,353	295	283	125,183	4,117,260
38 South Carolina	705,606	1,457	1,308	491,425	3,376,982
39 Tennessee	1,258,520	3,180	2,842	878,584	4,607,675
40 Texas	818,579	843	647	199,100	1,085,430
41 Utah	86,786	165	164	86,110	674,600
42 Vermont	330,551	699	744	270,614	3,713,530
43 Virginia	1,225,163	2,582	2,405	765,127	5,277,368
44 Washington	23,955	47	36	6,000	62,450
45 West Virginia	442,014	1,529	1,018	207,315	1,835,720
46 Wisconsin	1,054,670	1,864	1,466	423,015	4,890,781
47 Wyoming	9,118	12	12	3,500	46,000

STATISTICS OF CHURCHES IN THE UNITED STATES.

II.—By Denominations.

[From the Returns of the U. S. Census, 1870.]

DENOMINATIONS	Church Organizations.	Church Edifices.	Church Sittings.	Church Property.
TOTAL—ALL DENOMINATIONS..	72,459	63,082	21,665,062	$354,483,581
1 Baptist (regular)................	14,474	12,857	3,997,116	$39,229,221
2 Baptist (other)..................	1,355	1,105	363,019	2,978,977
3 Christian...................... ...	3,578	2,822	865,602	6,425,137
4 Congregational..................	2,887	2,715	1,117,212	25,069,698
5 Episcopal (Protestant)..	2,835	2,601	991,051	36,514,549
6 Evangelical Association..........	815	641	193,796	2,301,650
7 Friends	692	662	224,664	3,939,560
8 Jewish.........................	189	152	73,265	5,155,234
9 Lutheran.......................	3,032	2,776	977,332	14,917,747
10 Methodist......................	25,278	21,337	6,528,209	69,854,121
11 Miscellaneous..................	27	17	6,935	135,650
12 Moravian (Unitas Fratrum)......	72	67	25,700	709,100
13 Mormon	189	171	87,833	656,750
14 New Jerusalem (Swedenborgian).	90	61	18,755	869,700
15 Presbyterian (regular).......... .	6,262	5,683	2,198,900	47,828,732
16 Presbyterian (other).............	1,562	1,388	499,344	5,436,524
17 Reformed Church in America (late Dutch Reformed)...............	471	468	227,228	10,359,255
18 Reformed Church in the U. S. (late German Reformed)........	1,256	1,145	431,700	5,775,215
19 Roman Catholic.................	4,127	3,806	1,990,514	60,985,566
20 Second Advent....	225	140	34,555	306,240
21 Shaker........................	18	18	8,850	86,900
22 Spiritualist....................	95	22	6,970	100,150
23 Unitarian	331	310	155,471	6,282,675
24 United Brethren in Christ........	1,445	937	265,025	1,819,810
25 Universalist.............	719	602	210,884	5,692,325
26 Unknown (Local Missions).......	26	27	11,925	687,800
27 Unknown (Union)........	409	552	153,202	965,295

NOTE.—"Baptist (other)," consists of *Free-will, German* (also called Dunkers or Tunkers—styling themselves "Brethren"), *Mennonite, Seventh-day, Six-Principle,* and *Winebrenarian.* "Presbyterian (other)," consists of *Cumberland, Reformed* (Synod of the United States), *Reformed* (General Synod of the United States), *Associated Reformed,* and *United.*

Extract from the Report of the Superintendent of the Ninth Census, regarding the accuracy of the Statistics of Churches therein embodied :

"The principal inquiry, under the head of religion, in the schedule of the census law, viz.: 'Number of churches,' is, unfortunately, ambiguous. As the censuses of 1850 and 1860 were taken, it is impossible to feel any assurance, in any particular case, whether church organizations or church edifices are returned in answer to the inquiry, 'Number of Churches.' In preparation for the Ninth Census (1870), this inquiry was divided into 'Number of church organizations. Number of church edifices.'"

IMPORTS INTO THE UNITED STATES.
LAST TWO YEARS.

From the Official Report of the Bureau of Statistics. Corrected to August 23, 1877.	Twelve Months ended June 30.	
	1876.	1877.
FREE OF DUTY.	VALUES.	VALUES.
Argols...	$1,050,396	$1,277,836
Arucles, the produce or manufacture of the United States brought back...	2,007,834	2,780,544
BARKS :		
Medicinal : Peruvian, calisaya, Lima, etc...	1,293,400	564,488
Barks used for tanning...	184,826	311,258
Cork bark and wood, unmanufactured...	606,169	419,114
Bolting cloths...	179,826	193,740
Books...	319,360	265,214
Camphor, crude...	35,542	153,229
Chemicals, drugs, dyes, and medicines...	3,881,290	3,944,796
Chloride of lime, or bleaching-powder...	850,215	711,600
Cocoa, crude, and leaves and shells of...	521,422	597,847
Cochineal...	496,704	649,325
Coffee...	56,788,997	53,634,591
Cotton, raw...	381,723	413,503
Cutch, or catechu, and terra-japonica, or gambier...	782,663	910,479
Dye-woods, in sticks...	1,594,896	1,175,289
Eggs...	630,393	617,622
FISH, NOT OF AMERICAN FISHERIES :		
Fresh, of all kinds...	271,597	236,098
Herring, pickled...	306,555	210.786
Mackerel, pickled...	695,412	372,260
All other...	501,154	581,592
Fur-skins, undressed...	1,497,802	1,561,666
GOLD AND SILVER :		
Gold bullion...	1,204,965	2,119,570
Silver bullion...	1,058,177	4,693,253
Gold coin...	6,787,741	24,126,064
Silver coin...	6,885,795	9,834,927
Guano (except from bonded islands)...	705,782	873,390
Gums...	1,877,322	1,387,310
Gypsum, or plaster of Paris, unground...	126,587	105,635
HAIR, UNMANUFACTURED:		
Horse-hair, used for weaving...	298,461	215,239
Hair of all kinds, not specified...	499,354	296,398
Hides and skins, other than furs...	13,035,707	14,903,701
Household and personal effects and wearing apparel, old and in use, of persons arriving from foreign countries,	1,296,330	1,152,755
India-rubber and gutta-percha, crude...	4,063,659	5,542,166
Indigo...	794,990	1,301,058
Madder, not including the extract of...	151,005	144,213
OILS : Whale or fish, not of American fisheries...	62,435	84,668
Vegetable, fixed or expressed...	390,429	564,813
Volatile, or essential...	396,183	341,486
Paintings, statuary, and other works of art of American artists...	308,189	228,182
PAPER MATERIALS :		
Rags of cotton or linen...	2,485,088	2,587,217
Other materials...	1,368,058	1,329,582
Seeds...	439,149	491,630
Silk, raw...	5,491,408	6,792,947
Soda, nitrate of...	1,055,860	1,325.547
Sulphur or brimstone, crude...	1,473,678	1,242,788
Tea...	19,534,166	10,181,467
Tin in bars, blocks, and pigs...	1,816,289	1,798,613
Wood, unmanufactured...	1,406,681	1,237,518
Articles imported from Hawaiian Islands under reciprocity treaty...	....	2,277,354
All other free articles...	6,623,584	6,770,929
Total imports free of duty...	$156,298,594	$181,562,866

IMPORTS INTO THE UNITED STATES—(*Continued*).

From the Official Report of the Bureau of Statistics. Corrected to August 23, 1877.	Twelve Months ended June 30.	
	1876.	1877.
DUTIABLE.	VALUES.	VALUES.
Animals, living...	$1,749,395	$1,648,465
Beer, ale, porter, and other malt liquors.................	1,161,467	756,850
Books, pamphlets, engravings, and other publications...	2,119,478	1,627,375
Bra-s, and manufactures of...........................	264,431	247,820
BREADSTUFFS AND OTHER FARINACEOUS FOOD :		
Barley..	7,887,886	5,099,326
Barley-malt..	252,622	247,724
Bread and biscuit..................................	39,763	30,713
Indian corn, or maize.............................	46,652	25,046
Oats...	52,995	19,461
Rice...	1,693,547	1,439,767
Rye..	161,247	72,922
Wheat...	1,023,849	372,693
Wheat-flour.......................................	101,081	50,873
Meal or flour made from oats, Indian corn, rye, and buckwheat....................................	130,992	99,866
Pease, beans, and other seeds of leguminous plants, bushels..	672,696	574,419
All other farinaceous food, and preparations of, including arrow-root, pearl or hulled barley, etc....	302,654	208,575
Bristles...	622,178	536,460
Buttons of all kinds, including button materials partly fitted for buttons exclusively.................	2,072,656	2,273,420
Chemicals, drugs, dyes, and medicines.................	4,310,024	4,672,008
Chicory, ground or prepared, and root...............	126,012	139,360
CLOTHING (except when of silk, and except hosiery, etc., of cotton or wool) :		
Cut and sewed together...........................	563,539	228,715
Articles of wear..................................	1,086,159	961,236
Coal, bituminous......................................	1,607,891	1,775,667
Cocoa, manufactured, not including chocolate..........	8,189	9,182
COPPER, AND MANUFACTURES OF :		
Ore..	71,180	2,475
Pigs, bars, ingots, old and other, unmanufactured..	271,266	254,696
Manufactures of...................................	243,902	330,016
Cordage, rope, and twine, of all kinds.................	81,075	67,650
COTTON, MANUFACTURES OF :		
Bleached and unbleached..........................	1,845,653	1,237,312
Printed, painted, or colored......................	2,074,944	1,415,112
Hosiery, shirts, and drawers......................	4,682,871	3,804,520
Jeans, denims, drillings, etc......................	182,257	86,919
Other manufactures of, not specified..............	13,939,873	12,379,751
Earthen, stone, and China ware......................	4,301,808	3,709,542
Fancy-goods...	4,577,097	3,828,302
FISH, NOT OF AMERICAN FISHERIES :		
Herring..	186,535	189,615
Mackerel..	48	148
Sardines and anchovies, preserved in oil or otherwise	595,901	773,331
All other, not specified...........................	96,046	91,634
FLAX, AND MANUFACTURES OF :		
Flax, raw..	1,060,487	1,243,064
Manufactures of, by yard..........................	12,237,936	11,509,894
Other manufactures of.............................	2,218,110	2,402,496
Fruits of all kinds, including nuts....................	11,912,240	9,336,779
Furs and dressed fur-skins............................	8,053,570	2,401,778
GLASS AND GLASS WARE :		
Cylinder, crown, or common window..............	1,292,020	1,006,456
Cylinder and crown, polished	5,448	8,482
Fluted, rolled, or rough plate.....................	29,069	14,405
Cast polished plate, not silvered..................	1,358,881	1,263,864
Cast polished plate, silvered......................	773,423	552,899
Other manufactures of.............................	1,348,107	1,090,680
HAIR (excepting that of the alpaca, goat, and other like animals) AND MANUFACTURES OF :		
Hair, human, and manufactures of.................	144,894	77,075
Hair, other, and manufactures of..................	232,676	102,590
HEMP, AND MANUFACTURES OF :		
Raw..	2,247,549	1,852,489

IMPORTS INTO THE UNITED STATES—(*Continued*).

From the Official Report of the Bureau of Statistics. Corrected to August 23, 1877.	Twelve Months ended June 30.	
	1876.	1877.
HEMP : DUTIABLE.	VALUES.	VALUES.
Manufactures of, by yard..................	$774	$7,404
Other manufactures of.....	79,860	91,593
India-rubber and gutta-percha, manufactures of..........	428,575	325,113
IRON AND STEEL, AND MANUFACTURES OF :		
Pig-iron..	1,918,547	1,556,415
Castings....	3,711	3,044
Bar-iron..... ......•.......................	1,563,819	1,515,691
Boiler-iron.........	1,833	1,182
Band, hoop, and scroll-iron......................	18,743	12,659
Railroad bars or rails, of iron...............	6,738	....
Sheet-iron......................................	732,730	, 103,283
Old and scrap-iron	400,355	148,201
Hardware....	133,326	96,527
Anchors, cables, and chains of all kinds...........	219,695	156,799
Machinery..	705,953	730,020
Muskets, pistols, rifles, and sporting-guns.........	498,887	318,137
Steel ingots, bars, sheets, and wire..............	1,808,459	1,338,982
Railroad bars or rails, of steel..................	314,282	1,464
Cutlery..	1,068 508	875,276
Files...	219,204	135,585
Saws and tools........................	20,403	13,507
Other manufactures of iron and steel.............	3,536,425	2,563,828
Jewelry, and all manufactures of gold and silver........	605,934	542,838
JUTE AND OTHER GRASSES, AND MANUFACTURES OF :		
Raw..	2,384,881	2,351,778
Manufactures of, by yard...............	626	629
Gunny-cloth and gunny-bags, and manufactures of, used for bagging....	197,016	162,286
Other manufactures of, not specified..............	1,963,095	2,213,694
LEAD, AND MANUFACTURES OF :		
Pigs, bars, and old...........................	589,546	702,240
Manufactures of........................	12,720	46,442
LEATHER, AND MANUFACTURES OF :		
Leather of all kinds.......................	3,996,881	4,589,713
Gloves of kid, and all other, of skin or leather, doz. pairs...............................	3,739,061	3,128,919
Other manufactures of.......................	667,982	587,014
Marble and stone, and manufactures of........	1,216,796	865,133
Metals, metal compositions, and manufactures of........	1,039,407	847,041
Musical instruments...........................	773,811	564,530
OILS : Coal and other mineral oils..................	104	376,563
Whale and fish, not of American fisheries..........	63,286	44,015
Olive, salad........	328,357	376,731
Olive, not salad.....................	60,687	114,650
All other vegetable, fixed..................	228,769	169,316
Volatile, or essential..................	238,502	231,533
Opium, and extract of....................	1,805,906	1,788,347
Paintings, chromo-lithographs, photographs, and statuary	1,635,601	998,691
PAINTS :		
White lead.......................	168,070	173,006
Red lead and litharge....................	56,482	27,080
Whiting and Paris white....................	12,863	11,270
Other paints and painters' colors..................	791,239	715,747
PAPER, AND MANUFACTURES OF :		
Printing paper	3,205	413
Writing paper	15,675	8,944
Paper-hangings, and other paper...............	185,549	100,131
Papier-maché, and other manufactures of paper not specified, including parchment...	1,075,692	1,080,612
Perfumery and cosmetics	384,672	331,822
Potatoes...	130,361	1,652,963
Precious stones....	2,480,214	2,114,704
Provisions (meats, poultry, lard, butter, cheese, etc.), not including vegetables....................	958,219	724,252
Salt..	1,773,445	1,659,521
Saltpetre (nitrate of potash).................	216,843	512,327
SEEDS :		
Flaxseed, or linseed...........	3,859,496	1,916,549
All other, not specified...................	609,299	378,121

IMPORTS INTO THE UNITED STATES—(*Continued*).

From the Official Report of the Bureau of Statistics. Corrected to August 23, 1877.	Twelve Months ended June 30.	
	1876.	1877.
DUTIABLE.	VALUES.	VALUES.
SILK, MANUFACTURES OF:		
Dress and piece goods.............................	$17,620,575	$16,750,826
Hosiery...	77,776	78,940
Other manufactures of.............................	6,047,616	5,000,893
SODA, AND SALTS OF:		
Bicarbonate..	131,699	107,169
Carbonate, including sal-soda and soda-ash........	3,174,645	3,441,432
Caustic soda.......................................	1,064,705	1,114,045
Acetate, sulphate, phosphate, and all other salts of soda...	11,395	8,906
Spices of all kinds; also ginger (ground), pepper, and mustard..	1,930,159	1,437,995
Straw and palm-leaf, manufactures of..............	1,850,674	1,679,731
SUGAR AND MOLASSES:		
Brown sugar..	55,702,903	81,187.504
Refined sugar......................................	1,683	29.043
Molasses...	8.157.470	7,808,257
Melado and sirup of sugar-cane..........'.........	2,415,995	1,654.165
Candy and confectionery...........................	18,500	5,857
Sulphur, refined....................................	5,668	48,963
TIN, AND MANUFACTURES OF:		
In plates....................................	10,003,799	9,751,327
Other manufactures of.............................	92,514	39,332
TOBACCO, AND MANUFACTURES OF:		
Leaf...	3,710,490	3,728,619
Cigars...	2,371,157	2,002,347
Other manufactures of.............................	76,901	81,231
Watches and watch movements and materials.........	1,456,809	772,432
WINES, SPIRITS, AND CORDIALS:		
Spirits and cordials in casks......................	1,427,120	1,461,652
Spirits and cordials in bottles....................	413,321	473.085
Wine in casks.....................................	2,084,385	1,899,871
Wine in bottles........................	2,660,725	2,236,889
WOOD, AND MANUFACTURES OF.		
Cabinet-ware, house-furniture, and all manufactures of wood, not otherwise specified...........	1,155,231	798,175
Boards, deals, planks, joists, and scantling........	3,672,105	3,146,093
Shingles...	86,255	69,189
Timber, sawed or hewed, wholly or in part........	30,508	7,170
Other lumber......................................	224,883	224,679
WOOL, SHEEP'S (and hair of the alpaca, goat, and other like animals), AND MANUFACTURES OF:		
Unmanufactured...................................	8,247,617	7,156,944
Cloths and cassimeres..............................	9,838,449	6,624,909
Woollen rags, shoddy, mungo, waste, and flocks..	45,322	33,265
Shawls...	1,453,336	1,208,189
Blankets...	28,739	9,939
Carpets..	1,521,092	674,011
Dress goods..	14,216,291	12,549,867
Hosiery, shirts, and drawers.......................	671,593	559,941
Other manufactures of.............................	5,435,086	3,948,239
ZINC, SPELTER, OR TUTENAG, AND MANUFACTURES OF:		
In blocks or pigs	27,354	64,956
In sheets..	301,026	77,713
All other dutiable articles..........................	3,805,815	4,007,484
Total value of dutiable commodities..........	$320,379,277	$310,527,510
Total value of commodities free of duty......	156,298,594	181,562,866
	$476,677,871	$492,090,406
Total value of coin and bullion.................	$15,936,681	$40,774,414
Total value of merchandise...................	460,741,190	451,315,992
Total imports.........................	$476,677,871	$492,090,406
Brought in American vessels.................	$143,389,704	$151,826,933
Brought in foreign vessels..................	321,139,500	329,565,833
Brought in cars and other land vehicles.......	12,148,667	10,697,640

EXPORTS FROM THE UNITED STATES.

LAST TWO YEARS.

From the Official Report of the Bureau of Statistics. Corrected to August 23, 1877.	Twelve Months ended June 30.	
	1876.	1877.
OF DOMESTIC PRODUCTION.	VALUES.	VALUES.
Acids...	$50,300	$74,930
AGRICULTURAL IMPLEMENTS :		
Fanning-mills...................................	2,949	10,554
Horse-powers...................................	32,284	24,297
Mowers and reapers...........................	1,225,935	765,249
Ploughs and cultivators.......................	146,487	129,235
All other, not specified.......................	843,794	886,538
ANIMALS, LIVING :		
Hogs..	670,042	699,180
Horned cattle..................................	1,110,703	1,593,080
Horses..	234,964	301,134
Mules...	224,860	478,434
Sheep...	171,101	234,480
All other, and fowls...........................	24,617	18,895
Ashes, pot and pearl................................	75,597	53,170
Bark, for tanning...................................	223,276	67,176
BEER, ALE, PORTER, AND CIDER :		
In bottles......................................	13,007	51,077
In casks..	29,657	40,138
Bells and bell and bronze metal...................	13,941	12,366
Billiard-tables and apparatus......................	51,596	33,903
Blacking..	81,401	101,880
Bones and bone-dust...............................	69,159	121,493
Bone-black, ivory-black, and lamp-black...........	29,271	22,876
Books, pamphlets, maps, and other publications...	512,175	634,345
Brass, and manufactures of........................	256,974	327,817
BREAD AND BREADSTUFFS :		
Barley..	210,586	708,541
Bread and biscuit..............................	632,580	626,034
Indian corn....................................	33,265,290	41,621,245
Indian-corn meal..............................	1,305,027	1,511,152
Oats..	588,583	1,150,686
Rye...	480,083	1,822,766
Rye flour......................................	39,054	39,672
Wheat..	68,382,899	47,135,562
Wheat flour....................................	24,433,470	21,663,947
Other small grain and pulse...................	1,136,515	876,665
Maizena, farina, and all other preparations of bread-stuffs used as food.................	707,478	650.206
Bricks ..	18,035	25,571
Brooms and brushes of all kinds...................	198,914	172,000
Candles, tallow and other.........................	229,311	233,634
Carriages, carts, and parts of....................	734,624	860,018
Cars, railroad, passenger and freight.............	413,339	538,997
Clocks, and parts of..............................	967,591	1,025,586
Coffee, cocoa, and spices, including ginger, pepper, and mustard	$5,239	41,264
COAL :		
Bituminous.....................................	850,711	1,024,711
Other...	1,869,434	1,891,351
Combs...	4,185	8,959

EXPORTS FROM THE UNITED STATES—(*Continued*).

From the Official Report of the Bureau of Statistics. Corrected to August 23, 1877.	Twelve Months ended June 30.	
	1876.	1877.
	VALUES.	VALUES.
COPPER, AND MANUFACTURES OF:		
Ore....	$84,471	$109,451
In pigs, bars, sheets, and old....	3,098,395	2,718,213
Other manufactures of...	343,544	195,730
Cordage, rope, and twine of all kinds....	271,090	323,888
COTTON, AND MANUFACTURES OF:		
Sea-island....	941,803	1,084,509
Other, unmanufactured....	191,717,459	170,033,999
Colored manufactures....	1,455,462	2,484,131
Uncolored "	5,314,738	6,437,223
All other manufactures of....	952,778	1,314,489
Drugs, chemicals, and medicines....	2,471,195	1,979,957
Dye-stuffs....	869,793	628,209
Earthen and stone ware....	73.846	87,355
Fancy articles....	293,559	335,310
FRUITS:		
Apples, dried....	67,915	920,292
Apples, green or ripe....	221,764	986,112
Other fruit, green, ripe, or dried....	210,177	268,282
Preserved, in cans or otherwise....	327,422	762,344
Furs and fur-skins....	4,398,883	3,788,802
Gas-fixtures and chandeliers....	27,952	26,899
Ginseng....	646,954	562,268
Glass and glass-ware....	628,121	658,061
Glue....	5,798	16,069
GOLD AND SILVER, AND MANUFACTURES OF:		
Gold bullion....	1,888,896	1,084,536
Gold coin	27,542,861	21,274,565
Silver bullion....	15,240,344	11,483,894
Silver coin.. { Fractional....		620,147
{ Trade-dollars....	5,366,590	8,672,506
Gold and silver leaf	744	141
Jewelry, and other manufactures of gold and silver.	76,397	132,499
HAIR:		
Unmanufactured....	310,761	333,467
Manufactures of	6,254	9,886
HATS, CAPS AND BONNETS:		
Of wool, fur, and silk....	198,618	262,271
Of palm-leaf, straw, etc....	48,737	43,599
Hay....	134,017	116,926
HEMP, AND MANUFACTURES OF:		
Unmanufactured....	8,318	12,182
Cables and cordage....	147,009	175,750
All other manufactures of....	737,042	695,625
Hides and skins, other than fur....	2,905,921	2,480,427
Hoop-skirts	22	....
Hops....	1,384,521	2,305,355
Ice....	176,561	214,084
INDIA-RUBBER AND GUTTA-PERCHA MANUFACTURES:		
Boots and shoes....	19,471	27,445
Other manufactures....	109,345	192,037
IRON AND STEEL, AND MANUFACTURES OF:		
Pig....	181,663	89,029
Bar....	607,921	194,775
Boiler-plate	5,370	14,205
Railroad bars or rails	57,109	243,811
Sheet, band, and hoop....	5,004	21,518
Castings, not otherwise specified....	269,322	218,279
Car-wheels....	132,930	122,039
Stoves, and parts of....	128,660	113,321
Steam-engines, locomotive....	561,559	568,802
Steam-engines, stationary....	74,363	54,038
Boilers for steam-engines, when separate from the engines	103,429	70,018
Machinery, not otherwise specified....	2,709,439	2,698,363

EXPORTS FROM THE UNITED STATES—(Continued).

From the Official Report of the Bureau of Statistics. Corrected to August 23, 1877.	Twelve Months ended June 30.	
	1876.	1877.
IRON AND STEEL, AND MANUFACTURES OF (Continued):	VALUES.	VALUES.
Nails and spikes	$381,236	$319,584
All other manufactures of iron	3,619,889	3,361,767
Steel, and manufactures of:		
Ingots, bars, sheets, and wire	13,208	15,601
Cutlery	43,766	38,714
Edge-tools	628,681	721,012
Files and saws	37,282	36,309
Muskets, pistols, rifles, and sporting guns	3,667,050	5,259.813
Manufactures of steel, not specified	226,633	306,981
Junk (old) and oakum	39,875	37,413
Lamps	188,838	243,373
Lead, and manufactures of	102,726	49,835
LEATHER, AND MANUFACTURES OF:		
Boots and shoes	368,633	414,030
Leather of all kinds, not specified	8,394,590	6,016,873
Morocco, and other fine	948,980	1,280,225
Saddlery and harness	87,730	94,065
Manufactures of, not otherwise specified	200,062	361,988
Lime and cement	77,568	97,923
MANURES:		
Guano	4,859	41,530
Substances used expressly for manures	917,362	1,076,602
MARBLE AND STONE:		
Marble and stone, rough	95,480	131,716
Marble and stone manufactures	236,255	917,037
Matches	153,680	173,812
Mathematical, philosophical, and optical instruments	47,744	48,848
MUSICAL INSTRUMENTS:		
Organs, melodeons, etc	632.949	578,864
Piano-fortes	276,594	330,156
All other	6,390	12,659
NAVAL STORES:		
Rosin and turpentine	2,188,623	2,384,878
Tar and pitch	164,647	160,410
Oil-cake	5,774,585	4,816,145
OILS:		
Mineral, crude	2,220,268	3,756,729
Mineral, refined or manufactured:		
Naphthas, benzine, gasoline, etc	1,442,811	1,816,682
Illuminating	28,755,638	55,401,132
Lubricating, heavy paraffine, etc	303,863	497,540
Residuum	193,206	317,355
Animal: Lard	149,156	281,551
Neat's-foot and other animal	24,498	19,720
Sperm	1,366,246	879,865
Whale and other fish	436,072	442,165
Vegetable: Cotton-seed	146,135	842,348
Linseed	23,770	43,435
Volatile, or essential	248,270	401,829
ORDNANCE-STORES:		
Cannon	24,050	11,538
Cannon and gun-carriages and accoutrements	10,270	
Cartridges and fuses	549,859	2,325,570
Gunpowder	67,887	346,925
Shot and shell	510,823	2,161,866
Ore, argentiferous, or silver bearing	131,211	44,950
Paints and painters' colors	179,822	186,050
Paintings and engravings	206,631	196,518
Paper and stationery	795,176	938,218
Perfumery	875,011	269,785
Plated ware of silver or other metal	94,568	149,772
Printing-presses and type	119,749	159,746
PROVISIONS:		
Bacon and hams	39,864,456	49,512,412
Beef { Fresh		4,552,523
{ Salted or cured	3,186,304	2,950,952

EXPORTS FROM THE UNITED STATES—(*Continued*).

From the Official Report of the Bureau of Statistics. Corrected to August 23, 1877.	Twelve Months ended June 30.	
	1876.	1877.
PROVISIONS—(*Continued*):	VALUES.	VALUES.
Butter..	$1,109,496	$4,424,616
Cheese...	12,270,083	12,700,627
Condensed milk...........................	118,549	123,801
Eggs................................	8,300	8,429
Fish, dried or smoked............................	900,306	791,785
Fish, fresh.	80,879	114,338
Fish, pickled.......................................	417,231	486,738
Fish, other, cured.................	2,102,522	2,486,225
Lard	22,429,485	25.562,665
Meats, preserved...................................	998,052	3,939,977
Mutton, fresh.......................................	....	36,480
Oysters..	214,196	260,620
Pickles and sauces.................................	19,086	45,361
Pork..	5,744,022	6,296.414
Onions...	54,015	48,081
Potatoes.....	431,443	533.187
Other vegetables...................................	119,386	90,536
Vegetables, prepared or preserved.................	13,886	25,982
Quicksilver...	1,740,293	1,767,266
RAGS :		
Cotton and linen..................................	8,675	5,719
Woollen..	25,374	1,140
Rice.......................................	30,918	78,112
Salt..	13.378	20,133
Scales and balances............................. ..	154,931	159,231
SEEDS :		
Cotton...	69,605	130,062
Flaxseed or linseed...........	257	8
Clover, timothy, garden, and all other ....·	1,348,750	3,403,685
Sewing-machines, and parts of......................	1,700,798	1,632,437
SOAP :		
Perfumed, and all toilet...	11.007	11,549
Other...	673,732	627,403
Spermaceti...	35,915	41,037
SPIRITS, DISTILLED :		
From grain.............................. ....|	93,666	489,174
From molasses ....|	457,259	235,979
From other materials......... ....|	766	5,311
Spirits of turpentine............................. ..	1,672.068	2,274,639
Starch..	524,956	434,282
Steam and other fire-engines and apparatus	19,854	61,535
SUGAR and MOLASSES :		
Sugar, brown..........	2,354	6,618
Sugar, refined...........................	5,552,587	4,586,698
Molasses	1,158,585	594,547
Candy and confectionery	32,345	37,636
Tallow	6,734.878	7,883,616
Tin, and manufactures of..........................	48,144	87,057
TOBACCO, AND MANUFACTURES OF :		
Leaf.... ....|	22,737,383	28,825,521
Cigars..... ....|	23,407	38,161
Snuff	4,793	1,988
Other manufactures	2,834.935	3,154,561
Trunks and valises...................................	133,591	131,082
Umbrellas, parasols, and sun-shades..................	1.972	2,492
Varnish	54,906	61,178
VESSELS SOLD TO FOREIGNERS :		
Steamers,..................................... ...|	100,000	9,000
Sailing-vessels................................ ....|	165,484	186,802
Vinegar ....|	6,133	5,858
Watches and parts of................................	65,944	77,857
Wax..	69,127	84,461
Wearing-apparel.....................................	579,595	509,028
Whalebone...	215,327	160,666
Wine	33,480	40,682

EXPORTS FROM THE UNITED STATES—*(Continued)*.

From the Official Report of the Bureau of Statistics. Corrected to August 23, 1877.	Twelve Months ended June 30.	
	1876.	1877.
	VALUES.	VALUES.
WOOD, AND MANUFACTURES OF:		
Boards, clapboards, deals, planks, joists, and scantling	$3,862,793	$5,434,922
Laths, palings, pickets, curtain-sticks, broom-handles, and bed-slats	16,501	16,800
Shingles	130,847	126,632
Box-shooks	105,796	305,201
Other shooks, staves, and headings	4,322,252	3,948,739
Hogsheads and barrels, empty	349,456	255,911
All other lumber	321,790	846,410
Fire-wood	9,029	9,518
Hop, hoop, telegraph, and other poles	476,312	413,321
Logs, masts, spars, and other whole timber	616,197	499,822
Timber, sawed and hewed	3,463,352	3,124,412
All other timber	138,553	60,059
Household furniture	1,574,935	1,700,412
Wooden ware	342,860	328,839
All other manufactures of wood	1,565,602	1,373,039
WOOL, AND MANUFACTURES OF:		
Wool, raw and fleece	13,845	26,446
Carpets	6,586	16,377
Other manufactures of	329,803	275,460
ZINC, AND MANUFACTURES OF:		
Ore or oxide	66,259	34,468
Plates, sheets, pigs, or bars	11,651	115,122
ALL ARTICLES NOT ENUMERATED:		
All other unmanufactured articles	795,450	792,297
All other manufactured articles	1,322,955	2,152,628
Total Domestic Exports	$644,956,406	$676,115,818

Total value of merchandise   1876.   1877.
(*mixed values*)............$594,917,715 $632,980,080
Total value of coin and bullion   50,038,691   43,135,738— $644,956,406 $676,115,818

Gold value of merchandise	$525,562,247	$589,669,400
Shipped in American vessels	160,562,954	156,031,514
Shipped in foreign vessels	480,002,627	515,104,208
Shipped in cars and other land vehicles	4,390,825	4,980,096
	$644,956,406	$676,115,818

II.—EXPORTS FROM THE UNITED STATES OF FOREIGN PRODUCTIONS, LAST TWO YEARS.

Total value of merchandise	$14,802,424	$12,804,996
Total value of coin and bullion	6,467,611	13,027,499
Total foreign exports	$21,270,035	$25,832,495
Add total domestic exports	644,956,406	676,115,818
Gross exports	$666,226,441	$701,948,313

Total value of merchandise....   1876.   1877.
                   $609,720,139 $645,785,076
Total value of coin and bullion.   56,506,302   56,163,237

Gross exports...........$666,226,441 $701,948,313

SAVINGS BANKS AND POSTAL SAVINGS INSTITUTIONS.

[Compiled from a History of Savings Banks by Emerson W. Keyes, and from official documents.]

SAVINGS BANKS were originally institutions devised by philanthropists for safely investing small sums saved from the wages of labor, and paying interest on the same, and returning the principal at short notice. The purpose of a Savings Bank is thus in the highest degree laudable, conducing, as it does, to habits of economy and thrift, and to that wise provision for the future which belongs to man in the best state of civilization. The fact that these institutions, founded for the benefit and profit of the poor man, have been sometimes so mismanaged as to become the means of robbing instead of enriching him, ought not to discredit the system itself, or those prudently managed Savings Banks which conform to all the laws of safety as well as of honesty in their conduct.

The Savings Bank is of very recent origin. The earliest scheme of the modern Savings Bank ever proposed was made by Jeremy Bentham, in 1787, who put forth the idea of "frugal banks," to be instituted and managed by the government, as a part of its system for the care of the poor. His plan failed of adoption by Parliament. In 1803, Malthus advocated a system of county banks to encourage the saving of small sums. In 1806, Patrick Colquhoun drew up a bill which was offered in Parliament for a "fund and insurance office," for investing the funds of the poor. This was to be in fact a national Savings Bank, but it was too early in the field for success. Meanwhile, private benevolence founded the first actual Savings Bank in 1801, Mrs. Priscilla Wakefield, of Tottenham, receiving deposits from women and children only, which was soon followed by others of the same class, purely local institutions. Dr. Henry Duncan, of Ruthwell, Scotland, organized the first complete Savings Bank in his own parish in 1810. Its success was marked and decisive; and Dr. Duncan has even been called the father of Savings Banks.

These institutions kept on growing until they were encouraged and regulated by Act of Parliament. All of the private or trustees' Savings Banks in Great Britain are required to invest their deposits

in 3 per cent government annuities, and the trustees are prohibited by law from deriving any profit from the operations of the banks. The interest paid depositors is limited to £3 0s. 10d. per cent. as a maximum, and in practice varies from this limit, fixed by law, to as low a rate as £2 10s. per cent. The savings of the rich are kept out of these banks by another limitation, fixing the maximum deposits on one account at £30 a year, or 150 pounds in all, and prohibiting depositors from keeping accounts in more than one Savings Bank.

The British Post-Office Savings Banks were first established in 1863. Certain post-offices throughout the kingdom are designated to receive deposits of not less than one shilling, for transmission to the central office in London. The same limitations as to amount are made as indicated in the case of Savings Banks under trustees. The moneys thus received are invested in the public funds, and depositors of one pound, or upward, receive interest at the rate of 2½ per cent per annum. The depositor may apply to any Post-Office Savings Bank in the kingdom to withdraw his money, which he must be paid with interest, in ten days at farthest after his demand. Starting with 301 Postal Savings Banks in England in 1863, the system has since extended over Ireland and Scotland, and the number of Postal Savings Banks was in 1876, 5448, having accounts with 1,702,-374 depositors, who have on deposit an aggregate of £26,996,550. The proportion of depositors to the whole population was 1 in 19. Average amount to credit of each depositor was £15 17s.

The competition of Post-Office Savings Banks had the effect to diminish for several years the deposits of independent Savings Banks, managed by trustees, but the latter have recently recovered, aggregating in 1876 deposits to the amount of £43,283,570, while the Post-Office Savings Banks have deposits to the amount of £26,966,550.

In the United States, the first Savings Bank was started in Philadelphia in 1816. Others went into operation in New York, Boston, Baltimore, and many New England towns, during the three following years. State legislatures were quick to recognize their benefits, and to throw around them the sanctions and regulations of law. The half-dozen Savings Banks first organized in this country sixty years ago are still in existence, and doing a safe and responsible business. Their management varies in different States, but they are chiefly managed by elective trustees, though in Maryland and Pennsylvania both the mutual and stock systems prevail. The funds of the depositor are invested variously, the best approved securities being stocks of the United States, or of State governments in undoubted credit, the bonds of cities and counties, and mortgages on real estate. The management of Savings Banks has in many cases been far from prudent, resulting in numerous suspensions, either temporary or permanent, of these institutions, chiefly during the last two years. A number of mushroom concerns, which grew up during the inflation

era ensuing upon the war of 1861–65, were managed with criminal recklessness of the interests of depositors. Investments in doubtful railway and other bonds, and in over-valued real estate, were made to heavy amounts, and the assets locked up in securities which it was impossible to sell at their pledged value in times of shrinkage. Expenditures were increased to an extravagant amount, and some institutions devoured in salaries and other misappropriations the hard earnings of depositors. More stringent legislation and government inspection are needed as a safeguard against such mismanagement, and for the protection of the community.

The absence of State regulation or of any authoritative statistics whatever of Savings Banks in the majority of our States, prevents any full knowledge of their aggregate business. It may be safely stated, however, from the returns which do exist, that the amount of deposits in Savings Banks throughout the United States reaches, if it does not exceed, $1,000,000,000 (one thousand millions), held by about 2,800,000 depositors, while the amount of annual interest, or dividends, paid by Savings Banks exceeds $45,000,000. In the State of New York alone, it is over $16,000,000 *per annum*. The following table shows the statistics of the Savings Banks in the six New England States and in New York, from 1830 to 1876, inclusive :

Growth of the Savings Banks in New England and New York, as shown by their Deposits from 1830 to 1876.

Years.	Maine.	New Hampshire.	Vermont.	Massachusetts.	Rhode Island.	Connecticut.	New York.
1830..		$250,000		$2,500,000	$200,000	$350,000	$2,623,304
1840..		750,000		5,819,534	500,000	1,500,000	5,431,906
1850..		1,641,543	$199,376	13,660,024	1,495,545	5,466,444	20,832,972
1851..		1,776,768	282,217	15,554,089	1,907,233	6,698,158	24,006,590
1852..		2,009,617	407,188	18,401,308	2,474,109	8,135,016	27,541,923
1853..		2,507,909	704,990	23,370,102	3,308,769	8,883,397	32,824,177
1854..		3,222,261	901,789	25,936,858	4,104,091	10,006,131	33,453,781
1855..	$867,131	3,341,256	897,407	27,296,217	4,834,312	10,844,983	26,012,713
1856..	919,571	3,537,363	897,432	30,373,447	5,797,857	12,162,136	41,699,502
1857..	968,325	3,748,285	875,909	33,015,757	6,079,053	12,562,594	41,422,672
1858..	963,194	3,588,658	819,650	33,914,972	6,349,621	14,052,181	48,194,847
1859..	923,397	4,138,822	940,846	39,424,419	7,765,771	16,565,294	58,178,160
1860..	1,539,257	4,860,624	1,111,532	45,054,286	9,163,760	19,377,670	67,440,397
1861..	1,708,961	5,590,652	1,231,940	44,785,439	9,282,879	19,983,959	64,083,119
1862..	1,876,165	5,653,585	1,348,833	50,403,674	9,560,441	23,146,936	76,588,183
1863..	2,641,476	6,560,306	1,678,261	56,883,828	11,128,713	26,954,802	93,786,384
1864..	3,672,975	7,661,738	1,952,500	62,557,604	12,815,097	29,142,288	111,737,763
1865..	3,336,828	7,831,335	1,706,531	59,036,482	13,533,062	27,319,013	115,472,566
1866..	3,946,433	7,857,601	1,589,354	67,732,264	17,751,718	31,234,464	131,769,074
1867..	5,598,600	10,463,418	1,815,662	80,431,583	21,413,647	36,283,460	151,127,562
1868..	8,032,246	13,541,584	2,046,321	94,833,336	24,408,635	41,803,681	169,808,678
1869..	10,839,955	16,379,857	2,601,940	112,119,016	27,067,072	47,904,834	194,360,217
1870..	16,597,888	18,759,461	2,745,779	135,745,097	30,708,501	55,297,705	230,749,408
1871..	22,787,802	21,472,120	3,172,525	163,704,077	36,289,010	66,717,814	267,905,826
1872..	26,151,333	24,700,774	3,836,224	184,797,313	42,583,533	68,523,397	285,286,621
1873..	29,556,523	29,671,114	4,478,842	202,195,343	46,617,183	70,769,407	285,520,085
1874..	31,051,963	28,829,376	5,011,831	217,452,120	48,771,501	73,783,802	303,935,649
1875..	30,757,651	30,214,585	6,004,694	234,974,601	51,311,331	76,875,049	319,260,202
1876..	32,169,371	29,081,777	8,058,553	240,645,045	50,511,979	78,524,172	316,677,285

Table of the Aggregate Deposits of Savings Banks in Twelve
States, with the Number of their Depositors and the Average
Amount due to each in 1875 and 1876.

[From the Report of the Comptroller of the Currency for 1876.]

STATES.	1874–75.			1875–76.		
	Number of depositors.	Amount of deposits.	Average to each depositor.	Number of depositors.	Amount of deposits.	Aver'ge to each depositor.
Maine.............	96,799	$20,612,221	$305 91	101,326	$32,063,314	$316 00
New Hampshire..	96,938	30,214,585	311 69	100,191	31,198,064	326 01
Vermont........	22,972	6,004,694	261 39	25,060	6,653,540	265 50
Massachusetts....	702,099	217,452,121	322 87	720,639	234,974,691	326 06
Rhode Island.....	98,359	48,771,502	493 85	101,635	51,311,331	504 85
Connecticut......	206,874	73,783,802	357 52	208,030	76,489,310	367 69
New York........	872,498	303,935,649	348 35	859,738	319,260,202	371 00
New Jersey	93,800	30,954,877	330 00	*93,000	32,450,313	348 92
Pennsylvania.....	64,452	17,825,812	276 57	*64,000	16,627,820	259 79
Maryland	49,500	18,338,104	370 46	*49.000	19,077,026	389 34
Minnesota........	458	119,163	260 18	*400	90,839	227 09
California........	91,933	72,569,103	789 36	91,933	72,569,103	789 36
Totals..........	2,396,182	$849,581,633	$354 56	2,414,952	$892,785,553	$369 09

* Estimated.

Since the panic of 1873, and the recent closing of many savings
banks, an agitation in behalf of Government or Postal Savings institutions has sprung up. It is claimed that Postal Savings Banks, if
established in all cities or large towns, would afford an entirely safe
and convenient means of protecting the savings of the people, while
yielding them sure and moderate interest; that the government may
thus become the holder of a large and permanent loan at low interest,
convenient to the public credit; that the losses flowing from careless,
irresponsible, or dishonest private and corporate management would
thus be avoided; and that habits of economy and thrift, as well as of
attachment to the government and its solvency and permanence, would
be largely promoted, were Postal Savings institutions to be established
in the United States.

On the other hand, it is urged by opponents of the scheme, that
it is utterly beyond the legitimate sphere of a republican government
with limited powers, if not directly unconstitutional; that it would
make a banker of every postmaster, complicating the government
business with the care of large funds, extending the field of tempta-
tion to dishonesty, and liable to produce a large crop of defalcations;
that it would transgress the sound principle that the government
should not interfere at any point in the domain of private business or
corporate enterprise; that all of the advantages to the people, of
security for their savings, with remunerative interest, could be better

reached by an authorized issue of government bonds in small denominations, as low as $10 or even $5, bearing 3.65 or 4 per cent interest, thus bringing into the government coffers an enormous amount of the people's savings; and that the scheme of Postal or Government Savings Banks, while it might be justified in case of a paternal government, is out of place in a republic, and might lead to great abuses and corruptions. Various bills have been offered in Congress for the establishment of Postal Savings Institutions, and the plan was recommended by a former Postmaster-General. The present Secretary of the Treasury, in his Annual Report of December, 1877, recommended the plan only in a modified form, authorizing the deposit of small sums with any postal money-order office, and the issue therefor of Government certificates convertible into the 4 per cent bonds of the United States.

BRITISH SAVINGS BANKS.

CAPITAL OR DEPOSITS IN POST-OFFICE AND OTHER SAVINGS BANKS IN THE UNITED KINGDOM FOR 14 YEARS, 1863–1876.

[From the (Official) Statistical Abstract of the United Kingdom, 1877.]

	Post-Office Banks.	Trustees' Banks.	Total, Trustees' and Post-Office.		
	£	£	£		£
1863........	3,376,828	40,951,505	44,328,333	....	
1864........	4,993,124	39,520,336	44,513,460	Increase....	185,127
1865........	6,526,400	38,745,298	45,271,608	"	758,238
1866........	8,121,175	36,382,116	44,503,201	Decrease....	768,407
1867........	9,749,929	36,533,203	46,283,132	Increase....	1,779,841
1868........	11,666,655	36,867,457	48,534,112	"	2,250,980
1869........	13,524,209	37,553,746	51,077,955	"	2,543,843
1870........	15,099,104	37,958,549	53,057,653	"	1,979,698
1871	17,025,004	38,819,663	55,844,667	"	2,787,614
1872.......	19,318,399	40,088,348	59,406,687	"	3,562,020
1873........	21,167,749	40,500,135	61,667,884	"	2,261,197
1874........	23,157,469	41,505,919	64,663,418	"	2,995,534
1875........	25,187,345	42,407,769	67,595,114	"	2,931,696
1876........	26,996,550	43,283,570	70,280,120	" ...	2,685,006

NOTE.—It will be seen that this form of investment for savings has by no means reached so extensive a development in Great Britain as in this country. Only about $351,000,000 of deposits in all the British Savings Banks, both postal and independent, are recorded, or an average of less than $12 per head of population; while in the United States, $893,000,000 are deposited at the Savings Banks of only 12 States, indicating an average of over $25 per head to the whole population. This may be partly accounted for by the stringent limitation of deposits in the English law to one person, while our States have few or no limitations of the amount of individual deposits.

PRINCIPAL IMPORTS INTO THE UNITED STATES, WITH RATES OF DUTY THEREON.*

Table showing Quantities, Values, Total Duties, Rates of Duty and Average Duty, ad valorem, on all imported Commodities paying $100,000 or upwards into the Treasury, in the year 1876.

[Compiled from the Official Report on Commerce and Navigation of the U. S. for 1876.]

COMMODITIES.	Quantities.	Values.	Rate of Duty.	Total Duties.	Average Duty, ad valorem, per cent.
Ale, porter, and beer : In bottles............gallons	856,931	$ 857,810	35 c. per gall.	$ 300,314	34.96
" In casks..........gallons	627,629	274,138	25 c. per gall.	125,673	45.73
Aniline dyes or colors..lbs.	165,753	415,434	{ 50 c. per lb. & 35 p. c. }	228,374	54.94
Animals, living : Cattle, hogs,horses,sheep,etc..No.	347,665	1,729,992	20 per cent.	346,192	20.00
Barley ....bushels	9,327,629	7,102,027	15 c. per bush.	1,399,144	19.70
Books and other printed matter.....................		2,003,858	25 per cent.	501,039	25.00
Braids of straw....;.......		691,171	30 per cent.	208,753	30.00
Brushes...................		281,181	40 per cent.	112,516	40.00
Buttons...................		1,564,942	30 per cent.	469,486	30.00
Cheese.............lbs.	2,994,726	536,216	4 c. per lb.	119,789	22.34
China, porcelain and parian ware, plain, white, and not decorated in any manner......................		409,539	45 per cent.	184,340	45.00
" Gilded, ornamented, or decorated in any manner..		718,155	50 per cent.	359,237	50.00
" Other earthen, stone, or crockery ware, white, glazed, edged, printed, painted, or dipped, or cream colored...........		2,948,516	40 per cent.	1,179,978	40.00
Coal,bitumin. and shale.tons	400,631	1,592,846	75 c. per ton.	300,474	18.86
Corsets and corset-cloth, valued at $6 per dozen, or less................dozen	58,171	299,219	$2 per doz.	116,367	38.88
" val. over $6 per doz...doz.	46,312	386,369	35 per cent.	135,941	35.00
Cotton, manufactures of : Plain bleached, value 20 cents or less per square yard........square yards	12,751,429	1,610,522	5¼ c. per sq.yd.	701,329	43.55
" Printed or colored, value 25 cents or less per square yard.... ......square yards	6,194,471	935,593	{ 5¼c. per sq. yd.& 20p.c. }	858,655	56.88
" Hosiery...................		4,708,125	35 per cent.	1,647,880	35.00
" Laces,cords, braids, gimps, galloons, and cotton laces, colored and insertings....		2,689,653	35 per cent.	941,513	35.00
" Thread-yarn, warps, or warp-yarn not wound on spools, valued at over 60 and not exceeding 80 cents per pound. ....lbs.	622,902	456,939	{ 30 c. per lb. & 20 p. c. }	273,909	60.88

* For greater condensation, fractions are omitted, and the figures are therefore approximate, except as to rates and percentages of duty, which are the figures of the Bureau of Statistics.

PRINCIPAL IMPORTS INTO THE UNITED STATES, WITH RATES OF DUTY THEREON—(Continued).

COMMODITIES.	Quantities.	Values.	Rate of Duty.	Total Duties.	Average Duty, ad valorem, per cent.
Cotton, valued at over 80 cts. per pound..............lbs.	1,511,879	$ 1,903,077	{ 40 c. per lb. } { & 20 p. c. }	$ 997,367	50.81
" Velvet, velveteens, velvet bindings, ribbons, and vestings	....	673,733	35 per cent.	235,807	35.00
Currants, Zante, or other.lbs.	20,911,061	850,426	1 c. per lb.	209,111	24.42
Diamonds (cut), cameos, mosaics, gems, pearls, rubies, and other precious stones, not set............	....	2,409,516	10 per cent.	240.952	10.00
Dolls......................	....	421,756	35 per cent.	147,615	35.00
Embroideries, of cotton or wool..................	....	2,341,531	35 per cent.	819,536	35.00
Fans......................	....	449,107	35 per cent.	157,359	35.00
Feathers, ostrich, cock, and other ornamental	....	766,593	25 per cent.	191,649	25.00
Feathers and flowers, artificial and ornamental, not otherwise provided for ...	....	1,229,648	50 per cent.	614,824	50.00
Figs........lbs.	5,056,779	361,836	2½ c. per lb.	126,419	34.91
Fire-crackers, in boxes of 40 packs, not exceeding 80 to the pack.... ....boxes	221,815	175,166	$1 per box.	221,817	126.63
Flax linens, valued at 30 cents or less per square yd.	....	7,870,360	35 per cent.	2,756,436	35.00
" valued at above 30 cents per square yard.......... ...	....	1,012,174	40 per cent.	805,115	40.00
" Burlaps, and like manufactures of flax, jute, or hemp, of which either shall be the component of chief value (except bagging for cotton)	....	2,093,171	30 per cent.	628,015	30.00
" Duck, canvas, paddings, cot-bottoms, diapers, crash, huckabacks, handkerchiefs (not hemmed), lawns, or other manufactures of flax, jute, or hemp, valued at 30 cents or less per square yard........	....	957,739	35 per cent.	335,360	35.00
" valued at above 30 cents per square yard..........	....	600,791	40 per cent.	243,528	40.00
" Thread, twine, and pack-thread...................	....	731,094	40 per cent.	288,773	40.00
" All other manufactures of flax not otherwise provided for	....	299,398	40 per cent.	119,760	40.00
Fruits and nuts : Almonds, not shelled............lbs.	2,298,041	283,828	6 c. per lb.	138,291	48.56
" Shelled. ....lbs.	1,028,654	180,279	10 c. per lb.	102,865	57.05
" Filberts and walnuts..lbs.	4,317,841	235,703	3 c. per lb.	129,535	55.00
" Prunes................lbs.	55,358,764	2,333,716	1 c. per lb.	533,588	23.72
" Raisins. ....lbs.	32,241,005	2,424,277	2½ c. per lb.	805,530	33.21
Furs, and manufactures of...	....	2,717,502	20 per cent.	543,619	20.00
Glass-ware : Porcelain, Bohemian, cut, engraved, painted, colored, printed, stained, silvered, or gilded. not including plate-glass, silvered, or looking-glass plates.....	....	555,311	40 per cent.	222,132	40.00

PRINCIPAL IMPORTS INTO THE UNITED STATES, WITH RATES OF
DUTY THEREON—(*Continued*).

COMMODITIES.	Quantities.	Values.	Rate of Duty.	Total Duties.	Average Duty, ad valorem, per cent.
Glass-ware: Plate-glass, cast, polished, not silvered, above 24 by 30, and not above 24 by 60 ....square feet	438,049	$ 337,745	25 c. per sq. ft.	$ 109,512	32.43
" Above 24 by 60 in....sq. ft.	1,015,348	936,478	50 c. per sq. ft.	507,674	54.21
" Window-glass, cylinder, crown, or common, unpolished, above 10 by 15 and not above 16 by 24..lbs.	7,263,678	293,216	2 c. per lb.	145,274	49.54
" Above 16 by 24 and not above 24 by 30........lbs.	7,687,693	357,034	2¼ c. per lb.	192,217	53.84
" Above 24 by 30 in.....lbs.	6,632,243	407,992	3 c. per lb.	198,964	48.77
" Manufactures of, not otherwise specified.............	....	605,550	40 per cent.	242,382	40.00
Hats, bonnets, and hoods, straw....................	....	544,232	40 per cent.	217,693	40.00
Hemp, jute, and other fibre : Bags, cotton-bags, and bagging (except bagging for cotton).............	....	771,584	40 per cent.	308,774	40.00
Hemp : Jute, and sunn-hemp ....cwt.	162,674	494,255	$15 per ton.	123,047	24.68
" Jute butts	860,620	1,278,109	$6 per ton.	262,613	20.20
" Manila, India, and other like substitutes for hemp.................cwt.	379,170	2,462,552	$25 per ton.	473,963	19.21
India Rubber, manufactures of : Braces, webbing, etc...	....	333,276	35 per cent.	116,647	35.00
Iron and steel, manufactures of: In slabs, blooms, loops, etc..............lbs.	31,073,774	979,480	35 per cent.	342,818	35.00
" Pig-iron.............cwt.	1,453,097	1,729,036	$7 per ton.	508,584	29.41
" Scrap-iron, old, wro't.cwt.	435,444	386,536	$8 per ton.	174,194	45.06
" Manufactures of iron not otherwise provided for....	....	1,904,928	35 per cent.	682,190	36.00
" Steel, and manufactures of: Pen-knives, jack-knives, and pocket-knives........	....	701,919	50 per cent.	350,960	50.00
" All other cutlery, including sword blades.........	....	360,911	35 per cent.	126,322	35.00
" In ingots, bars, coils, sheets, and steel-wire, not less than ¼ inch diameter, valued at 7 cents per pound or less................lbs.	10,450,250	536,152	2¼ c. per lb.	235,131	43.83
" Valued at above 7 cents and not over 11 cents per pound................lbs.	7,454,403	717,046	3 c. per lb.	223,632	29.91
" Muskets, rifles, and other firearms	....	444,845	35 per cent.	155,699	35.00
" Railway bar, or rails, wholly of steel.......lbs.	11,008,562	347,772	1¼ c. per lb.	137,607	39.57
" Manufactures of steel, not otherwise provided for....	....	846,619	45 per cent.	380,985	45.00
Jewelry of gold, silver, or other metal, or imitations of........................	....	492,849	25 per cent.	123,213	25.00
Lead, and manufactures of : Pigs and bars, and molten................lbs.	12,695,662	507,009	2 c. per lb.	249,913	41.86

PRINCIPAL IMPORTS INTO THE UNITED STATES, WITH RATES OF
DUTY THEREON—(*Continued*).

Commodities.	Quantities.	Values.	Rate of Duty.	Total Duties.	Average Duty, ad valorem, per cent.
Leather, and manufactures of: Calf-skins, tanned, or tanned and dressed......	....	$ 2,489,099	25 per cent.	$ 622,275	25.00
" Gloves, of kid or leather, of all descriptions.........	....	3,755,842	50 per cent.	1,877,935	50.00
" Upper leather of all kinds, and skins, dressed and finished, of all kinds, not otherwise provided for....	....	1,776,034	20 per cent.	355,201	20.00
" Manufactures of, and articles of leather, or of which leather shall be a component part, not otherwise provided for........	....	417,391	35 per cent.	146,087	35.00
Lemons and oranges........	....	3,412,027	20 per cent.	682,469	20.00
Marble, and manufactures of: Veined and all other, in block, roughed or squared, not otherwise specified..................cub. ft.	479,944	529,126	{ 50 c.per cu. ft.& 20 p.c. per cu. ft. }	345,391	65.35
Mats of cocoa-nut, china, and all other floor-matting, of flags, jute, or grass.....	....	349,724	30 per cent.	104,917	30.00
Metal, manufactures of, not otherwise provided for....	....	579,126	35 per cent.	202,704	35.00
Musical instruments........	....	711,472	30 per cent.	213,522	30.00
Oils, olive, salad, in bottles or flasks..........gallons	171,251	320,619	$1 per gall.	171,320	53.41
Opium.............. ...lbs.	228,742	913,078	$1 per lb.	232,415	25.05
Opium prepared for smoking...... ....lbs.	53,190	507,299	$6 per lb.	319,136	55.23
Paintings and statuary, not by American artists.......	....	1,044,362	10 per cent.	103,441	10.00
Papier-maché, manufactures, articles, and wares of......	....	1,119,787	35 per cent.	391,973	35.00
Pickles, sauces, and capers..	....	332,332	35 per cent.	116,437	35.00
Rice, cleaned...........lbs.	49,174,443	1,208,310	2½ c. per lb.	1,241,140	101.74
Salt, in bags, sacks, barrels, or other packages.....lbs.	332,266,140	1,153,480	12 c.per 100 lbs.	395,770	34.46
" in bulk.............. lbs.	389,478,218	462,105	8 c. per 100 lbs.	303,772	65.69
Sardines and anchovies, packed in oil or otherwise.......quarter boxes	6,297,945	503,150	4 c. per box.	251,918	49.77
Seeds: Flaxseed or linseed (56 lbs. to the bushel)..bushels	2,737,906	3,891,082	20 c. per bush.	547,582	14.07
Silk: Braids, laces, fringes, galloons, buttons, and ornaments, dress and piece goods...............	....	14,932,867	60 per cent.	8,959,864	60.00
" Velvets...................	....	1,267,152	60 per cent.	760,891	60.00
" Ribbons..................	....	2,058,813	60 per cent.	1,235,368	60.00
" Ribbons (edge of cotton)..	....	516,726	50 per cent.	258,591	50.00
" Silk manufactures not otherwise provided for, made of silk, or of which silk is the component or chief value..............	....	1,540,202	60 per cent.	924,353	60.00

PRINCIPAL IMPORTS INTO THE UNITED STATES, WITH RATES OF
DUTY THEREON—(*Continued*).

COMMODITIES.	Quantities.	Values.	Rate of Duty.	Total Duties.	Average Duty, ad valorem, per cent.
Silk: Manufactures of, which have as a component thereof 25 per centum, or over, in value of cotton, flax, wool, or worsted.....	....	$ 2,850,165	50 per cent.	$ 1,425,178	50.00
Soda caustic.... ....lbs.	31,093,791	1,107,200	1½ c. per lb.	481,405	43.48
Soda ash................lbs.	165,502,907	2,967,372	¼ c. per lb.	413,757	13.94
Spices: Cassia, and Cassia Vera...............lbs.	1,629,795	181,901	10 c. per lb.	163,554	89.05
" Nutmegs.............lbs.	775,013	530,161	20 c. per lb.	156,721	29.23
" Pepper: black and white, grain................lbs.	7,826,355	783,417	5 c. per lb.	392,288	49.95
Spirits and wines: Brandy, proof.............gallons	661,951	1,269,436	$2 per gall.	1,333,063	104.45
" Cordials, liqueurs, arrack, absinthe, kirschwasser, ratafia...........gallons	56,560	90,166	$2 per gall.	113,545	125.45
" Spirits, other, manufactured or distilled from grain.............gallons	524,341	322,080	$2 per gall.	1,052,068	325.59
" Spirits, other (except brandy), manufactured or distilled from other materials...............gallons	221,058	143,031	$2 per gall.	443,616	309.12
" Cologne-water and other perfumery, of which alcohol forms the principal ingredient.........gallons	10,791	185,268	$3 pr. gall. & 50 per c. per gall.	125,028	67.47
Sugar and molasses: Molasses.............gallons	38,937,426	8,656,268	5 c. plus 25 per cent per lb.	2,434,839	28.13
" Molasses concent'ed, tank-bottoms, sirup of sugar-cane, and melado......lbs.	96,553,303	3,143,735	1½ c. plus 25 c. per lb.	1,810,874	57.58
Sugar: All not above No. 7, Dutch standard........lbs.	524,582,040	19,900,450	1¾ c. plus 25 p.c.p.lb.	11,475,232	57.40
" Above No. 7 and not above No. 10.......lbs.	846,021,062	35,644,815	2 c. plus 25 p. c. per lb.	21,165,542	50.38
" Above No. 7 and not above No. 10................lbs.	23,163,925	948,964	2 c. per lb.	463,322	48.89
" Above No. 13 and not above No. 16..............lbs.	5,684,481	296,932	2¾ c. plus 25 p. c. per lb.	195,404	65.79
Tartar, cream of........lbs.	1,186,553	278,838	10 c. per lb.	118,655	42.55
Tartar, argols, other than crude................lbs.	2,582,651	576,293	6 c. per lb.	154,959	26.88
Tin, plates or sheets.....lbs.	196,863,621	10,163,368	1⅒ c. per lb.	2,166,074	21.30
Tobacco, and manufactures of: Leaf, unmanufactured and not stemmed......lbs.	7,067,066	3,848,984	35 c. per lb.	2,476,016	64.30
" Cigars, cigarettes and cheroots................lbs.	629,325	2,289,712	$2.50 pr. lb. & 25 p. c. per lb.	2,140,132	93.71
Toys, wooden and other....	....	437,398	50 per cent.	218,745	50.00
Watches, of gold or silver...	....	1,315,743	25 per cent.	328,730	25.00
Wines, Champagne, and all other sparkling, in bottles, containing not more than 1 pint each and more than ½ pint...........dozen	110,686	690,444	$3 per dozen.	323,114	48.00

PRINCIPAL IMPORTS INTO THE UNITED STATES, WITH RATES OF
DUTY THEREON—(Continued).

COMMODITIES.	Quantities.	Values.	Rate of Duty.	Total Duties.	Average Duty, ad valorem, per cent.
		$		$	
Wines, Champagne, and all other sparkling, in bottles, containing not more than 1 quart and more than 1 pint..............dozens	102,061	1.203,910	$6 per doz.	612,886	50.86
" Still wines, in casks..galls.	4,431,898	2,123,273	40 c. per gall.	1,775,955	83.49
" in bottles, containing each not more than 1 quart and more than 1 pint.doz.bots.	157,076	652,032	$1.60 per doz.	251,029	38.54
Wood: Boards, planks,deals, and other lumber.....M ft.	259,149	3,204,890	$2 per M. ft.	578,678	18.04
" Manufactures of, not otherwise provided for....	....	678,985	35 per cent.	237,740	35.00
Wools, hair of the alpaca, goat, etc.: Raw and manufactured, Class No. 1, clothing wool, value 32 cents or less per lb....lbs.	4,756,911	1,109,456	{ 10 c. per lb. & 11 p. c. }	597,731	53.88
" Value 32 cents or less per pound.................lbs.	3,093,767	734,738	{ 10 c. p.lb.& 11 p.c., less 10 per c. }	356,156	45.38
" Value over 32 cents per pound........... .....lbs.	707,501	261,747	{ 12 c. pr. lb. & 10 p. c. }	122,176	42.63
" Class No. 2, value over 32 cents per pound.......lbs.	2,631,333	939,952	{ 12 c. per lb. & 10 p. c. }	415,755	41.58
" Class No. 3, carpet and other similar wools, valued at 12 cents or less per pound.................lbs.	14,431,527	1,747,975	3 c. per lb.	448,814	22.77
" value over 12 cents per pound............. ...lbs.	11,903,130	2,501,185	6 c. per lb.	714,186	28.55
" Carpets and carpetings of all kinds,Aubusson andAxminster, and carpets woven whole for rooms...sq. yds.	122,550	291,816	50 per cent.	145,997	50.09
" Brussels carpet wrought by Jacquard machine..sq. yd.	244,367	347,271	{ 44 c.per sq. yd.&35 p.c. }	229,067	65.96
" Brussels tapestry, printed on the warp or otherwise................sq. yds.	438,184	394,993	{ 28 c.per sq. yd.&35 p.c. }	261,373	65.80
" Patent velvet and tapestry velvet, printed on the warp or otherwise..sq. yds.	134,305	210,158	{ 40 c. per sq. yd.&35 p.c. }	127,327	60.56
" Dress goods, women and children's, and real or imitation Italian cloths, valued at not exceeding 20 cents per sq. yd...sq. yds.	20,781,789	3,655,851	{ 6 c. per sq. yd.&35 p.c. }	2,520,455	68.81
" Valued at above 20 cents per square yard.. sq. yds.	32,541,034	10,364,038	{ 8 c. per sq. yd.&40 p.c. }	6,749,445	65.12
" Dress goods, women and children's, and real or imitation Italian cloths, weighing 4 ounces and over per square yard...lbs.	1,103,504	1,698,486	{ 50 c. per lb. & 35 p. c. }	1,146,264	67.48
" Hosiery, valued at above 80 cents per pound.......lbs.	210,177	556,099	{ 50 c. per lb. & 35 p. c. }	302,723	54.43
" Manufactures not otherwise specified, valued at above 80 cents per lb..lbs.	1,290,266	1,701,709	{ 50 c. p. lb. & 35 p. c. }	1,240,722	72.91

PRINCIPAL IMPORTS INTO THE UNITED STATES, WITH RATES OF
DUTY THEREON—(*Continued*).

COMMODITIES.	Quantities.	Values.	Rate of Duty.	Total Duties.	Average Duty, ad valorem, per cent.
		$		$	
Wool Cloths............lbs.	5,568,356	8,636,762	{ 50 c. p. lb. } { & 35 p. c. }	5,807,035	67.24
" Cloths................lbs.	197,441	267,672	{ 50 c. p. lb. } { & 35 p. c., } { less 10 p. c. }	173,684	64.69
" Clothing—articles of wear..................lbs.	101,638	370,637	{ 50 c. p. lb. } { & 40 p. c. }	199,112	53.71
" Clothing—ready-made.lbs.	153,879	444,148	{ 50 c. p. lb. } { & 40 p. c. }	254,599	57.32
Wool, manufactures wholly or in part of, not otherwise provided for......lbs.	185,970	314,000	{ 50 c. p. lb. } { & 35 p. c. }	202,836	64.59
" Shawls, woollen......lbs.	70,550	203,883	{ 50 c. p. lb. } { & 35 p. c. }	108,222	52.80
" Worsted, etc., not otherwise provided for.....lbs.	400,604	1,272,235	{ 50 c. p. lb. } { & 40 p. c. }	728,974	55.98
" Webbings, beltings, bindings, braids, galloons, fringes, cords, buttons, etc..................lbs.	452,282	1,385,092	{ 50 c. p. lb. } { & 50 p. c. }	918,688	66.33
" Yarns, valued at above 80 cents per pound.......lbs.	321,949	415,399	{ 50 c. p. lb. } { & 50 p. c. }	306,364	73.75
Zinc, in sheets..............	4,460,077	288,589	2¼ c. per lb.	100,352	34.77
Average duty on all dutiable commodities................................44.74					

TRANSACTIONS OF THE NEW YORK CLEARING HOUSE.

For Twenty-four Years, from its Establishment in 1853 to January 1, 1877.

YEAR.	AMOUNT OF CLEARANCES.	YEAR.	AMOUNT OF CLEARANCES.
1853 (3 months).....	$1,376,096,627 40	1865.............	$26,891,344,853 95
1854.......	6,093,669,425 91	1866.............	32,601,878,591 69
1855................	5,973,026,298 80	1867.......	26,886,692,870 35
1856........:.....	7,689,926,013 49	1868.........	34,351,891,941 45
1857................	7,543,771,620 63	1869.	36,602,776,490 44
1858................	5,712,796,028 49	1870....	28,127,961,006 98
1859................	6,963,415,589 12	1871......... ...	31,906,309,467 00
1860................	7,779,910,699 33	1872.............	37,876,153,125 90
1861.......	5,873,560,990 84	1873.............	31,199,131,468 75
1862................	8,695,252,485 69	1874.............	25,807,149,917 55
1863................	18,160,578,352 98	1875.............	25,708,112,647 83
1864............. ..	26,562,489,714 48	1876.........	22,783,800,312 75

DIVIDENDS OF NEW ENGLAND MANUFACTURING COMPANIES FOR SEVEN YEARS, 1870-1876.

[From J. G. Martin's Stock Fluctuations, Boston, 1871-77.]

Manufacturing Companies.	Capital, Jan., 1877.	Par.	1870.	1871.	1872.	1873.	1874.	1875.	1876.
Amoskeag	3,000,000	1,000	10	13	18	14	14	9	9
Androscoggin	1,000,000	100	8	5	10	10	10	9	6
Appleton	600,000	1,000	9	14	12	9	3	0	0
Atlantic	1,000,000	100	3	8	8	8	0	3	0
Bartlett	350,000	100	....	....	3½	7	2½	0	0
Bates	1,500,000	100	6	4	10	8	8	*0	3
Boott	1,200,000	1,000	11	20	20	16	12½	8	8
Boston	800,000	1,000	10	11	12	8	6	6	6
Boston Duck	350,000	700	33	10	11	10	10	8	6
Cabot	600,000	500	....	8	10	10	10	5	0
Chicopee	1,000,000	100	18	70	50	30	10	5	7
Cocheco	1,000,000	500	13	20	20	20	20	15	5
Continental	1,500,000	100	0	0	8	8	4	0	0
Dwight	1,200,000	500	0	0	5	10	6	0	0
Everett	800,000	100	0	3	9	0	3	0	3
Franklin	1,000,000	100	3	0	8	8	8	3	0
Great Falls	1,500,000	100	8	9	10	10	3	0	0
Hamilton Cotton	1,200,000	1,000	3	6½	9	8	8	7	3
" Woollen	600,000	100	15	15	20	15	10	10	10
Hill	1,000,000	100	9	11	16	11	10	7	0
Jackson	600,000	1,000	12	20	18	14	12	6	3
Kearsarge	600,000	100	....	0	0	7	3	0	2
Laconia	1,000,000	400	3	3	11	12	7	0	0
Lancaster	800,000	400	20	20	20	22½	20	20	15
Lawrence	1,500,000	1,000	3	6	6	6	6	6	6
Lowell	2,000,000	690	90	140	70	50	45	40	20
" Bleachery	300,000	200	20	20	20	20	18	10	8
" Machine Shop	600,000	500	12	12	12	12	12	12	12
Lyman	1,470,000	100	6	8	10	8	6	3	0
Manchester	2,000,000	100	0	0	0	0	115*	7	8
Massachusetts	1,800,000	1,000	6	10	16	12	8	3	6
Merrimack	2,500,000	1,000	7	18	18	13	10	4	5
Middlesex	750,000	100	15	17	13	9	14	9	10
Nashua	1,000,000	500	8	16	16	12	11	8	6
Naumkeag	1,500,000	100	7	0	15	8	7	6	3
Newmarket	600,000	500	9	8	14	14	8	3	0
New England Glass	500,000	500	8	8	3	0	4	6	0
Otis	800,000	1,000	20	20	15	10	10	10	9
Pacific	2,500,000	1,000	12	16	22	20	20	20	16
Pepperell	1,200,000	500	20	5	11	12	12	12	11
Salisbury	1,000,000	100	10	13½	12½	0	0	0	0
Salmon Falls	600,000	300	7	9	10	9	3	0	0
Sandwich Glass	400,000	80	6	8	7	4	0	0	0
Stark Mills	1,200,000	1,000	7	10	13	11	11	7	3
Tremont and Suffolk	1,200,000	100	0	0	9	9	8	8	8
Thorndike	450,000	1,000	0	6	8½	10	9	6	6
Washington	1,650,000	100	4	5	10	0	0	0	6
York Mills	1,200,000	1,000	18	20	20	18	11	9	8

* Dividend in liquidation. The new Manchester Mills organized 1875.

UNITED STATES PUBLIC LANDS—WHERE THEY LIE.

Statement Showing the Number of Acres of Public Lands Surveyed in the Land States and Territories up to June 30, 1877; also, the total Area of the Public Domain remaining Unsurveyed.

[From the Report of the Commissioner of the General Land Office, 1877.]

LAND STATES AND TERRITORIES.	Total Areas of Lands in 29 States & Territories in which Public Lands have been situated.		Number of Acres of Public Lands Surveyed.			Total Area of Public and Indian Lands remaining Unsurveyed and Unoffered to June 30, 1877.
	In Acres.	In Square Miles.	Prior to June 30, 1876, not heretofore reported.	Within the Fiscal Year ending June 30, 1877.	Total Acres Surveyed up to June 30, 1877.	
1 Alabama	82,462,080	50,722	....	....	32,462,080	....
2 Alaska.......	369,529,600	577,390				
3 Arizona......	72,906,304	113,916	120,242	496,496	4,666,883	68,239,421
4 Arkansas	33,406,720	52,198	....	....	33,406,720	....
5 California....	100,992,640	157,801	296,212	1,258,395	44,972,349	56,020,391
6 Colorado.....	66,880,000	104,500	....	1,581,058	20,999,022	45,880,098
7 Dakota.......	96,595,840	150,982	....	1,488,807	20,520,214	76,075,626
8 Florida	37,931,520	59,268	75,556	....	30,103,706	7,827,514
9 Idaho	55,228,160	86,294	62,720	200,683	6,193,013	49,035,147
10 Illinois	35,462,400	55,410			35,462,400	
11 Indian Terr'y.	44,154,240	68,991	....	....	27,003,990	17,150,250
12 Indiana.......	21,637,760	33,809			21,637,760	
13 Iowa.........	35,228,800	55,045			35,228,800	
14 Kansas.......	51,769,976	80,891			51,770,940	
15 Louisiana....	26,461,440	41,346	2,456	....	25,232,044	1,220,396
16 Michigan.....	36,128,640	56,451			36,128,640	
17 Minnesota....	53,459,840	83,531	79,418	527,679	38,765,710	14,694,130
18 Mississippi...	30,179,840	47,156			30,179,840	
19 Missouri......	41,824,000	65,350			41,824,000	
20 Montana.....	92,016,640	143,776	....	796,594	9,918,986	82,097,654
21 Nebraska....	48,686,800	75,995	....	1,338,188	39,234,402	9,402,398
22 Nevada.......	71,737,741	112,090	....	322,932	11,254,087	60,483,654
23 New Mexico..	77,568,640	121,201	....	630,072	7,920,750	69,647,890
24 Ohio	25,576,960	39,964			25,576,960	
25 Oregon.......	60,975,300	95,274	....	645,363	19,928,816	41,051,534
26 Utah.........	54,065,075	84,476	....	724,497	8,374,534	45,690,541
27 Washington..	44,796,160	69,994	27,175	360,756	12,508,568	32,287,592
28 Wisconsin....	34,511,360	53,924	....	....	34,511,360	....
29 Wyoming...	62,645,120	97,883	....	359,330	7,731,061	54,914,059
Total	1,814,769,656	2,835,578	665,759	10,731,759	693,572,735	*731,687,283

* Or, adding Alaska, 1,101,216,883 acres.

STATISTICS OF LAND GRANTS.

Land Grants by Acts of Congress to States and Corporations for Railroad Purposes, from the First Grant in 1850 to June 30, 1877.

[Compiled from Reports of the Commissioner of the General Land Office.]

NOTE.—Fractions of acres are omitted.

STATES.	Date of Acts.	Name of Road.	Estimated quantity embraced in the Grant.	No. of acres certified for year ending June 30, 1877.	Number of acres certified up to June 30, 1877.
			Acres.		
Illinois	Sep. 20, 1850	Illinois Central	} 2,595,053		2,595,053
"	" "	Mobile and Chicago			
Mississippi	" "	Mobile and Ohio River	1,004,640		737,130
"	Aug. 11,1856	Vicksburg & Meridian	404,800		198,027
"	" "	Gulf and Ship Island	652,800		
Alabama	Sep. 20, 1850	Mobile and Ohio River	230,400		419.528
"	May 17, 1856	Alabama and Florida	419,520		394,522
"	{ June 3, 1856 { May 23, 1872	Selma, Rome & Dalton	481,920		457,407
"	June 3, 1856	Coosa and Tennessee	132,480		67,784
"	" "	Mobile and Girard	840,880		504,145
"	Apr. 10, 1860	} Alabama & Chattanooga	897,920		552,199
"	{ June 3, 1856 { Mar. 3, 1871	South & North Alabama	576,000		436,720
Florida	May 17, 1856	Florida Railroad	442,542		281,984
"	" "	Florida and Alabama	165,689		165,688
"	" "	Pensacola and Georgia	1,568,729		1,275,212
"	" "	Fla.,Atlantic & Gulf Cen.	183,153		37,583
Louisiana	June 3, 1856	Vicksburg & Shreveport	610,880		353,211
"	{ " " { July 14, 1870	{ New Orleans, Ope- { lousas & Gt.West.	967,840		719,193
Arkansas	{ Feb. 9, 1853 { July 28, 1866 { May 6, 1870	} Cairo and Fulton	1,160,667 1,040,000	} } .... {	1,115,408 194,534
"	{ Feb. 9, 1853 { July 28, 1866	} Memphis & Little Rock.	{ 438,646 { 365,539		127,238 14,606
"	{ Feb. 9, 1853 { July 28, 1866 { Apr. 10, 1869 { Mar. 8, 1870	{ Little Rock and Fort { Smith	{ 550,525 { 458,771		550,520 366,196
"	July 4, 1866	Iron Mountain	864,000		
Missouri	June 10,1852	Hannibal & St. Joseph.	781,944		599,031
"	" "	Pacific & S. West Branch	1,161,235		1,161,204
"	{ Feb. 9, 1853 { July 28, 1866	} Cairo and Fulton	{ 219,202 { 182,718		64,017
"	July 4, 1866	St. Louis & Iron Mount.	640,000	7,635	7,635
Iowa	{ May 15, 1856 { June 2, 1864 { Feb. 10, 1866	} Burlington & Mo. River.	948,643		{ 292,080 { 97,227
"	{ May 15, 1856 { June 2, 1864 { Jan. 31, 1873	{ Chicago,Rock Island { and Pacific	1,261,181		{ 482,254 { 161,372
"	{ May 15, 1856 { June 2, 1864	{ Cedar Rapids and { Missouri River	1,298,739	10,214	{ 782,250 { 359,110
"	May 15, 1856	Iowa Falls & Sioux City.	1,226,163		683,023
"	{ " " { June 2, 1864 { Mar. 2, 1868	} Dubuque and Sioux City		1,273	474,879

STATISTICS OF LAND GRANTS—(Continued).

States.	Date of Acts.	Name of Road.	Estimated quantity embraced in the Grant.	No. of acres certified for year ending June 30, 1877.	Number of acres certified up to June 30, 1877.
			Acres.		
Iowa.........	May 12, 1864..	McGregor & Mo. River.	1,536,000	....	137.572
"	" "	Sioux City and St. Paul.	524,800	160	396.993
Michigan.....	June 3, 1856..	Detroit and Milwaukee..	355,420	....	30.958
"	" "	Port Huron and Milwau.	312,384	....	6,428
" ...	June 3, 1856 / July 3, 1866 / Mar. 2, 1867 / Mar. 3, 1871	Jackson, Lansing & Sag.	1,052,469	....	742,940
" ...	June 3, 1856 / Feb. 17, 1865 / July 3, 1866 / Mar. 3, 1871	Flint & Pere Marquette.	586,828	....	512,529
" ...	June 3, 1856 / June 7, 1864 / Mar. 3, 1865	Grand Rapids & Indiana	{ 629,182 { 531,200	 6,456	699.182 223,890
" ...	June 3, 1856 / Mar. 3, 1865 / May 20, 1868 / Apr. 20, 1871	{ Marquette, Hough- { ton & Ontonagon. }	552,515	....	432,707
" ...	Mar. 3, 1865..	Bay de Noquet & Marq'te	128,000	....	128,000
" (Res.)	July 5, 1862 / Mar. 3, 1865 / May 23, 1872	Chicago & Northwest'n.	564,480	....	517,908
Wisconsin..	June 3, 1856 / May 5, 1864 / Mar. 3, 1873	West Wisconsin........	999,983 534,714	2,984	799,896
" ..	June 3, 1856 / May 5, 1864 / June 3, 1856	{ St. Croix & L. Supe- { rior & Br. to Bayfield }	318,737 350,000 215,000	}	{ 524,718 { 318,740
" ..	Apr. 25, 1862 / Mar. 3, 1855 / Mar. 3, 1869	Chicago & Northwest'n.	600,000	200	546,522
" ..	May 5, 1864 / June 21,1866	Wisconsin Central......	750,000	45,825	444,690
" ..	June 3, 1856 / July 27, 1868	{ Wisconsin R.R.Farm { Mortgage Land Co. }	....	120	40,049
Minnesota..	Mar. 3, 1857 / Mar. 3, 1865 / Mar. 3, 1873	St. Paul and Pacific.....	1,248,638	6,145	1,243,589
" ..	Mar. 3, 1857 / Mar. 3, 1865 / July 12, 1862	Branch St. Paul & Pacific	1,475,000	....	522.925
" ..	Mar. 3, 1871 / Mar. 3, 1873	{ St.Vincent Extens'n { St. Paul & Pacific. }	2,000,000	....	780,291
" ..	Mar. 3, 1857 / Mar. 3, 1865	Minnesota Central......	643,403	....	179,058
" ..	Mar. 3, 1857 / Mar. 3, 1865 / July 13, 1866 / Jan. 13, 1873	Winona and St. Peter...	1,410,000	11,737	162.485
" ..	Mar. 3, 1857 / May 12, 1864 / July 13, 1866	St. Paul and Sioux City.	1,010,000	15,892	945.458
" ..	May 5, 1864 / July 13, 1866	Lake Superior & Missis.	920,000	....	743,241
"	July 4, 1866..	Southern Minnesota	735,000	5,067	270.461
" "	Hastings and Dakota...	550,000	320	170,231
Kansas	Mar. 3, 1863 / July 1, 1864 / Apr. 19, 1871	{ Leavenworth, Law- { rence & Galveston }	800,000	120	259,950
"	Mar. 3, 1863 / July 1, 1864	Missouri, Kansas & Tex.	1,520,000	4,088	982,012

STATISTICS OF LAND GRANTS—(Continued).

STATES AND CORPORATIONS.	Date of Acts.	Name of Road.	Estimated quantity embraced in the Grant.	No. of acres certified for year ending June 30, 1877.	Number of acres certified up to June 30, 1877.
			Acres.		
Kansas......	Mar. 3, 1863	Atchison,Top.&SantaFé	3,000,000	....	2,274,686
"	July 23, 1866..	St. Joseph & DenverCity	1,700,000	....	441,158
"	July 25, 1866..	Mo.Riv.,Ft.Scott & Gulf	2,350,000	....	22,527
Corporations.	July 1, 1862 / July 2, 1864 / July 3, 1866 / July 26, 1866 / Apr. 10, 1869 / May 6, 1870	Union Pacific...........	12,000,000	39,372	1,883,669
"	July 1, 1862 / July 2, 1864	Cent. Branch Union Pac.	245,166	....	186,453
"	July 1, 1862 / July 2, 1864 / July 3, 1866 / May 7, 1866 / Mar. 3, 1869	Kansas Pacific..........	6,000,000	32,285	538,840
"	" "	Denver Pacific..........	1,000,100	....	49,811
"	July 1, 1862 / July 2, 1864	Central Pacific	8,000,000	352,663	739,040
"	July 1, 1862 / July 2, 1864 / Mar. 3, 1865 / July 13, 1866 / May 21, 1866 / May 6, 1870	Central Pacific, successor by consolidation with Western Pacific........	1,100,100	2,639	330,319
"	July 2, 1864 / May 6, 1870	Burlington & Mo. River	2,441,600	....	2,374,090
"	July 2, 1864..	Sioux City and Pacific..	60,000	162	40,758
"	May 7, 1866 / July 1, 1868 / Mar. 1, 1869 / Apr. 10, 1869 / May 31, 1870	Northern Pacific........	47,000,000	....	630,717
"	July 13, 1866..	Placerv'le & Sacram.Val.	200,000	....	....
"	July 25, 1866 / June 25, 1868 / Apr. 10, 1869	Oregon Branch of the Central Pac...	3,000,000	45,841	539,890
"	July 25, 1866 / June 25, 1868 / Apr. 10, 1869	Oregon and California..	3,500,000	86,623	323,148
"	July 27, 1866 / Apr. 30, 1871	Atlantic and Pacific.....	42,000,000	....	504,478
"	July 27, 1866 / Mar. 3, 1871	Southern Pacific......	6,000,000 / 3,520,000	22,920	709,030 ....
"	Mar. 2, 1867..	Stockton & Copperopolis	320,000		
"	May 4, 1870..	Oregon Central.	1,200,000		

NOTE.—It is proper to state that the first column of figures above given, "Estimated quantity embraced in the Grant," although from official Reports of the General Land Office at Washington, published in 1873, is not regarded as an accurate statement of the amount of public lands to which the railways will be entitled under the various acts, and has been omitted from recent tabular statements issued by the Commissioner of Public Lands.

ASSESSED VALUE AND ESTIMATED TRUE VALUE OF PROPERTY IN THE UNITED STATES IN 1870.

[From the Returns of the Ninth Census, 1870.]

STATES AND TERRITORIES.	ASSESSED VALUE.			TRUE VALUE.
	Total.	Real Estate	Personal Estate.	Real and Personal Estate.
	$	$	$	$
The United States..	14,178,986,732	9,914,780,825	4,264,205,907	30,068,518,507
1 Alabama	155,582,595	117,223,043	38,359,552	201,855,841
2 Arkansas............	94,528,843	63,102,304	31,426,539	156,394,691
3 California...........	269,644,068	176,527,160	93,116,908	638,767,017
4 Connecticut.........	425,433,237	204,110,509	221,322,728	774,631,524
5 Delaware	64,787,223	48,744,783	16,042,440	97,180,838
6 Florida	32,480,843	20,197,691	12,283,152	44,163,655
7 Georgia	227,219,519	143,948,216	83,271,303	268,169,207
8 Illinois..............	482,899,575	348,433,906	134,465,669	2,121,680,579
9 Indiana	663,455,044	460,120,974	203,334,070	1,268,180,543
10 Iowa.................	302,515,418	226,610,638	75,904,780	717,644,750
11 Kansas..............	92,125,861	65,499,365	26,626,496	188,892,014
12 Kentucky...........	409,544,294	311,479,694	98,064,600	604,318,552
13 Louisiana	253,371,890	191,343,376	62,028,514	323,125,666
14 Maine	204,253,780	134,580,157	69,673,623	348,155,671
15 Maryland	423,834,918	286,910,332	136,924,586	643,748,976
16 Massachusetts...	1,591,983,112	901,037,841	690,945,271	2,132,148,741
17 Michigan............	272,242,917	224,663,667	47,579,250	719,208,118
18 Minnesota .	84,135,332	62,079,587	22,055,745	228,909,590
19 Mississippi..........	177,278,690	118,278,460	59,000,430	209,197,345
20 Missouri............	556,129,960	418,527,535	137,602,434	1,284,992,897
21 Nebraska	54,584,616	38,365,999	16,218,617	69,277,483
22 Nevada	25,740,973	14,594,722	11,146,251	31,134,012
23 New Hampshire......	149,065,290	85,231,288	63,834,002	252,624,112
24 New Jersey.........	624,868,971	448,832,127	176,036,844	940,976,064
25 New York	1,967,001,185	1,532,790,907	434,290,278	6,500,841,264
26 North Carolina......	130,378,622	83,322,012	47,056,610	260,757,244
27 Ohio	1,167,731,697	707,846,836	459,884,861	2,235,430,300
28 Oregon	31,798,510	17,674,202	14,124,308	51,558,932
29 Pennsylvania........	1,313,236,042	1,071,680,934	241,555,108	3,808,340,112
30 Rhode Island.......	244,278,854	132,876,581	111,402,273	296,965,646
31 South Carolina......	183,913,337	119,494,675	64,418,662	208,146,989
32 Tennessee...........	253,752,161	223,035,375	30,746,786	498,237,724
33 Texas	149,732,929	97,186,568	52,546,361	159,052,542
34 Vermont............	102,548,528	80,993,100	21,555,428	235,349,553
35 Virginia	365,439,917	279,116,017	86,323,900	409,588,133
36 West Virginia.......	140,538,273	95,924,774	44,613,499	190,651,491
37 Wisconsin	333,209,838	252,322,107	80,887,731	702,307,320
The States.	14,021,297,071	9,804,637,462	4,216,659,609	29,822,525,140
1 Arizona............	1,410,295	538,355	871,940	3,440,791
2 Colorado	17,353,101	8,840,811	8,497,290	20,243,308
3 Dakota	2,924,489	1,695,723	1,228,766	5,599,753
4 District of Columbia.	74,271,693	71,437,468	2,834,225	126,873,618
5 Idaho	5,292,205	1,926,565	3,365,640	6,552,681
6 Montana	9,943,411	2,728,129	7,215,283	15,184,523
7 New Mexico	17,784,014	9,917,991	7,866,023	31,349,793
8 Utah....	12,565,842	7,047,881	5,517,961	16,159,995
9 Washington	10,642,863	5,146,776	5,496,087	13,562,164
10 Wyoming	5,516,748	863,665	4,653,083	7,016,748
The Territories.. ..	157,689,661	110,143,363	47,546,298	245,983,367
Total—The U. S...	14,178,986,732	9,914,780,825	4,264,205,907	30,068,518,507

PUBLIC INDEBTEDNESS OF THE STATES IN 1870.

[From the Official Report of the Ninth Census, 1870.]

STATES AND TERRITORIES.	Total.	State.	County.	Town, City, etc.
	$	$	$	$
The United States...........	868,676,758	352,866,698	187,565,540	328,244,520
Alabama....................	13,277,154	8,477,018	1,704,173	3,094,963
Arkansas..................	4,151,152	3,459,557	536,649	154,946
California	18,089,082	3,429,027	13,807,741	842,344
Connecticut............	17,088,906	7,275,000	7,003	9,806,903
Delaware	526,125	....	139,875	386,250
Florida....................	2,185,838	1,278,697	443,041	454,100
Georgia....................	21,753,712	6,544,500	561,735	14,647,477
Illinois	42,191,869	4,890,937	12,817,922	24,483,010
Indiana...................	7,818,710	4,167,507	1,127,269	2,528,934
Iowa......................	8,043,133	534,498	3,732,929	3,774,706
Kansas....................	6,442,282	1,593,306	3,736,901	1,112,075
Kentucky..................	18,953,484	3,892,480	7,173,644	7,897,360
Louisiana....	53,087,441	25,021,734	1,326,635	26,739,072
Maine	16,624,624	8,067,900	274,153	8,282,571
Maryland....	29,032,577	13,317,475	1,565,779	14,149,323
Massachusetts.	69,211,538	28,270,881	680,123	40,233,534
Michigan	6,725,231	2,385,028	1,275,479	3,064,724
Minnesota.................	2,788,797	350,000	472,694	1,966,103
Mississippi	2,594,415	1,796,230	655,585	141,600
Missouri..................	46,909,865	17,866,000	11,819,012	17,224,853
Nebraska..................	2,089,264	244,300	1,769,564	70,600
Nevada...................	1,986,093	642,894	987,423	355,776
New Hampshire	11,153,373	2,817,869	745,070	7,590,434
New Jersey................	22,554,304	2,996,200	6,935,315	12,922,789
New York................ ...	159,808,234	32,409,144	50,679,784	76,719,306
North Carolina.............	32,474,036	29,900,045	1,732,773	841,218
Ohio......................	22,241,988	9,732,078	4,337,543	8,272,367
Oregon	218,486	106,583	105,903	6,000
Pennsylvania..............	89,027,131	31,111,662	49,173,840	8,741,619
Rhode Island............. .	5,938,642	2,913,500	....	3,025,142
South Carolina.........	13,075,229	7,665,909	97,112	5,312,208
Tennessee.................	43,827,191	33,539,802	2,729,659	7,557,730
Texas.....................	1,613,907	508,641	426,866	678,400
Vermont.	3,594,700	1,002,500	8,042	2,584,148
Virginia..................	55,921,255	47,290,839	1,365,766	7,164,650
West Virginia..	561,767	(a)	329,833	231,954
Wisconsin.................	5,908,532	2,252,057	1,077,328	2,574,247
The States................	864,785,067	352,866,698	186,297,043	325,621,326
Arizona....	10,500	....	10,500	....
Colorado...................	681,158	....	708,829	2,329
Dakota.	5,761	....	5,671	90
District of Columbia	2,596,545	....	....	2,596,545
Idaho.....................	222,621	....	218,522	4,699
Montana...................	278,719	....	276,219	2,500
New Mexico................	7,560	.. ..	7,560	....
Utah......................	....	....	....	....
Washington................	88,827	....	71,196	17,630
Wyoming..................	....	....	....	....
The Territories...	3,891,691	....	1,268,497	2,623,194
The United States..........	868,676,758	352,866,698	187,565,540	328,244,520

(a) Included in Virginia.

RECEIPTS OF THE UNITED STATES FROM MARCH 4, 1789, TO JUNE 30, 1877.

Years.	Customs.	Internal Revenue.	Direct Tax.	Public Lands.
1789–1791.........	$4,399,473 09			
1792.............	3,443,070 85	$208,942 81		
1793.............	4,255,306 56	337,705 70		
1794.......	4,801,065 28	274,089 62		
1795.............	5,588,461 26	337,755 36		
1796.............	6,567,987 94	475,289 60		$4,836 13
1797.............	7,549,649 65	575,491 45		83,540 60
1798.............	7,106,061 93	644,357 95		11,963 11
1799.............	6,610,449 31	779,136 44		
1800.............	9,080,932 73	809,396 55	$734,223 97	443 75
1801.............	10,750,778 93	1,048,033 43	534,343 38	167,726 06
1802.............	12,438,235 74	621,898 89	206,565 44	188,628 02
1803.............	10,479,417 61	215,179 69	71,879 20	165,675 69
1804.............	11,098,565 33	50,941 29	50,196 44	487,526 79
1805.............	12,936,487 04	21,747 15	21,882 91	540,193 80
1806.............	14,667,698 17	20,101 45	55,763 86	765,245 73
1807.............	15,845,521 61	13,051 40	34,732 56	466,163 27
1808.............	16,363,550 58	8,190 23	19,159 21	647,939 06
1809.......	7,257,506 02	4,084 29	7,517 31	442,252 33
1810.............	8,583,309 31	7,430 63	12,448 68	696,548 82
1811.............	13,313,222 73	2,295 95	7,666 66	1,040,237 53
1812.............	8,958,777 53	4,903 06	859 22	710,427 78
1813.............	13,224,623 25	4,735 04	3,805 52	835,655 14
1814.............	5,998,772 08	1,662,984 82	2,219,497 36	1,135,971 09
1815.............	7,282,942 22	4,678,059 07	2,162,673 41	1,287,959 28
1816.............	36,306,874 88	5,124,708 31	4,253,635 09	1,717,985 03
1817.............	26,283,348 49	2,678,100 77	1,834,187 04	1,991,226 06
1818.............	17,176,385 00	955,270 20	264,333 36	2,606,564 77
1819.............	20,283,608 76	229,593 63	83,650 78	3,274,422 78
1820.............	15,005,612 15	106,260 53	31,586 82	1,635,871 61
1821.............	13,004,447 15	69,027 63	29,349 05	1,212,966 46
1822.............	17,589,761 94	67,665 71	20,961 56	1,803,581 54
1823.............	19,088,433 44	34,242 17	10,337 71	916,523 10
1824.............	17,878,325 71	34,863 37	6,201 96	984,418 15
1825.............	20,098,713 45	25,771 35	2,330 85	1,216,090 56
1826.............	23,341,331 77	21,589 93	6,638 76	1,393,785 09
1827.............	19,712,283 29	19,885 68	2,626 90	1,495,845 26
1828.............	23,205,523 64	17,451 54	2,218 81	1,018,308 75
1829.............	22,681,965 91	14,502 74	11,335 05	1,517,175 13
1830.............	21,922,391 39	12,160 62	16,980 59	2,329,356 14
1831.............	24,224,441 77	6,933 51	10,506 01	3,210,815 48
1832.......	28,465,237 24	11,530 65	6,791 13	2,623,381 03
1833.............	29,032,508 91	2,759 00	394 12	3,967,682 55
1834.............	16,214,957 15	4,196 09	19 80	4,857,600 69
1835.............	19,391,310 59	10,459 48	4,263 33	14,757,600 75
1836.............	23,409,940 53	370 00	728 79	24,877,179 86
1837.............	11,169,290 39	5,493 84	1,697 70	6,776,236 52
1838.............	16,158,800 36	2,467 27		3,730,945 66
1839.............	23,137,924 81	2,553 32	755 22	7,361,576 40
1840.............	13,499,502 17	1,082 25		3,411,818 63
1841.............	14,487,216 74	3,261 36		1,365,627 42
1842.............	18,187,008 76	495 00		1,335,797 52
1843.............	7,046,843 91	103 25		898,158 18
1844.............	26,183,570 94	1,777 34		2,059,039 80
1845.............	27,528,112 70	8,517 12		2,077,022 30
1846.............	26,712,667 87	2,897 26		2,694,452 48
1847.............	23,747,864 66	375 00		2,498,355 20
1848.............	31,757,070 96	375 00		3,328,642 56
1849.............	28,346,738 82			1,688,959 55
1850.............	59,669,686 42			1,859,894 25
1851.............	49,017,567 92			2,352,305 30
1852.............	47,339,326 62			2,043,239 58

RECEIPTS OF THE UNITED STATES FROM MARCH 4, 1789, TO JUNE 30, 1877.

Years.	Premiums.	Interest.	Dividends.	Miscellaneous Receipts.	Total Net Ordinary Receipts, excluding Loans.
1789–1791..				$10,478 10	$4,409,951 19
1792......			$8,028 00	9,918 65	3,669,960 31
1793......			38,500 00	21,410 88	4,652,923 14
1794......			303,472 00	53,277 97	5,431,904 87
1795.....		$4,800 00	160,000 00	28,317 97	6,114,534 59
1796......		42,800 00	160,000 00	1,169,415 98	8,377,529 65
1797......			80,960 00	399,139 29	8,688,780 99
1798......		78,675 00	79,920 00	58,192 81	7,900,495 80
1799......			71,040 00	86,187 56	7,546,813 31
1800......			71,040 00	152,712 10	10,848,749 10
1801......		10,125 00	88,800 00	345,649 15	12,935,330 95
1802......			39,960 00	1,500,505 86	14,995,793 95
1803......				131,945 44	11,064,097 63
1804......				139,075 53	11,826,307 38
1805......				40,382 30	13,560,693 20
1806......				51,121 86	15,559,931 07
1807......				38,550 42	16,398,019 26
1808......				21,822 85	17,060,661 93
1809......				62,162 57	7,773,473 12
1810......				84,476 84	9,384,214 28
1811......				59,211 22	14,422,634 09
1812......				126,165 17	9,801,132 76
1813......		800 00		271,571 00	14,340,409 95
1814......		85 79		164,399 81	11,181,625 16
1815......	$32,107 64	11,541 74		285,282 84	15,696,916 82
1816......	686 09	68,665 16		273,782 35	47,676,985 66
1817......		267,819 14	203,496 30	100,761 08	33,099,049 74
1818......		412 62	525,000 00	57,617 71	21,585,171 04
1819......			675,000 00	57,098 42	24,603,374 37
1820......	40,000 00		1,000,000 00	61,338 44	17,840,669 55
1821......			105,000 00	152,589 43	14,573,379 72
1822......			297,500 00	452,957 19	20,232,427 94
1823......			350,000 00	141,129 84	20,540,666 26
1824......			850,000 00	127,603 60	19,381,212 79
1825......			367,500 00	130,451 81	21,840,858 02
1826......			402,500 00	94,589 66	25,260,434 21
1827......			420,000 00	1,315,722 83	22,966,363 96
1828......			455,000 00	65,126 49	24,763,029 23
1829......			490,000 00	112,648 55	24,827,627 38
1830......			490,000 00	73,227 77	24,844,116 51
1831......			490,000 00	584,124 05	28,526,820 82
1832......			490,000 00	270,410 61	31,867,450 66
1833......			474,985 00	470,096 67	33,948,426 25
1834......			234,349 50	480,812 32	21,791,935 55
1835......			506,480 82	759,972 13	35,430,087 10
1836......			292,674 67	2,245,902 23	50,826,796 08
1837......				7,001,444 59	24,954,153 04
1838......				6,410,348 45	26,302,561 74
1839......				979,939 86	31,482,749 61
1840......				2,567,112 28	19,480,115 33
1841......				1,004,054 75	16,860,160 27
1842......				451,995 97	19,976,197 25
1843......	71,700 83			285,895 92	8,231,001 26
1844......	666 60			1,075,419 70	29,320,707 78
1845......				361,453 68	29,970,105 80
1846......				289,950 13	29,699,967 74
1847......	28,365 91			220,808 30	26,467,403 16
1848......	37,080 00			612,610 69	35,698,699 21
1849......	487,065 48			685,379 13	30,721,077 50
1850......	10,550 00			2,064,308 21	43,592,888 88
1851......	4,264 92			1,185,166 11	52,555,039 33
1852......				464,249 40	49,846,815 60

RECEIPTS OF THE UNITED STATES FROM MARCH 4, 1789, TO JUNE
30, 1877—(Continued).

Years.	Customs.	Internal Revenue	Direct Tax.	Public Lands.
1853	$58,931,865 52			$1,667,064 99
1854	64,224,190 27			8,470,798 39
1855	53,025,794 21			11,497,049 07
1856	64,022,863 50			8,917,644 93
1857	63,875,905 05			3,829,486 64
1858	41,789,620 96			3,513,715 87
1859	49,565,824 38			1,756,687 30
1860	53,187,511 87			1,778,557 71
1861	39,582,125 64			870,658 54
1862	49,056,397 62		$1,795,331 73	152,203 77
1863	69,059,642 40	$37,640,787 95	1,485,103 61	167,617 17
1864	102,316,152 99	109,741,134 10	475,648 96	588,333 29
1865	84,928,260 60	209,464,215 25	1,200,573 03	996,553 31
1866	179,046,651 58	309,226,813 42	1,974,754 12	665,081 03
1867	176,417,810 88	266,027,537 43	4,200,233 70	1,163,575 76
1868	164,464,599 56	191,087,589 41	1,788,445 85	1,348,715 41
1869	180,048,426 63	158,356,460 86	765,685 61	4,020,344 34
1870	194,538,374 44	184,899,756 49	229,102 88	3,350,481 76
1871	206,270,408 05	143,096,153 63	580,355 37	2,388,646 68
1872	216,370,286 77	130,642,177 72		2,575,714 19
1873	188,089,522 70	113,729,314 14	315,254 51	2,882,312 38
1874	163,103,833 69	102,409,784 90		1,852,428 93
1875	157,167,722 35	110,007,493 58		1,413,640 17
1876	148,071,984 61	116,700,732 03	93,798 80	1,129,466 95
1877	130,956,493 07	118,630,407 83		976,253 68
Total	$3,985,020,634 90	$2,323,940,371 53	$27,646,725 73	$202,543,268 38

EXPENDITURES OF THE UNITED STATES FROM MARCH
4, 1789, TO JUNE 30, 1877.

Years.	Civil and Miscellaneous.	War.	Navy.	Indians.
1789-1791	$1,083,971 61	$632,804 03		$27,000 00
1792	4,672,664 38	1,100,702 09		13,648 85
1793	511,451 01	1,130,249 08		27,282 83
1794	750,350 74	2,639,097 59	$61,408 97	13,042 46
1795	1,378,920 66	2,480,910 13	410,562 03	23,475 68
1796	801,847 58	1,260,203 84	274,784 04	113,563 99
1797	1,259,422 62	1,039,402 46	382,631 89	62,396 58
1798	1,139,524 94	2,009,522 30	1,381,347 76	16,470 09
1799	1,039,391 68	2,466,946 98	2,858,081 84	20,302 13
1800	1,337,613 22	2,560,878 77	3,448,716 03	31 22
1801	1,114,768 45	1,672,944 08	2,111,424 00	9,000 00
1802	1,462,929 40	1,179,148 25	915,561 87	94,000 00
1803	1,842,635 76	822,055 85	1,215,230 53	60,000 00
1804	2,191,009 43	875,423 93	1,189,832 75	116,500 00
1805	3,768,598 75	712,781 28	1,597,500 00	196,500 00
1806	2,890,137 01	1,224,355 38	1,649,641 44	234,200 00
1807	1,697,897 51	1,296,685 91	1,722,064 47	205,425 00
1808	1,423,285 61	2,900,834 40	1,884,067 80	213,575 00
1809	1,215,803 79	3,345,772 17	2,427,758 80	337,508 84
1810	1,101,144 98	2,294,323 94	1,654,244 20	177,625 00
1811	1,367,291 40	2,032,828 19	1,965,566 39	151,875 00
1812	1,683,088 21	11,817,798 24	3,959,365 15	277,845 00

RECEIPTS OF THE UNITED STATES FROM MARCH 4, 1789, TO JUNE 30, 1877—(Continued).

Years.	Premiums.	Interest.	Dividends.	Miscellaneous Receipts.	Total Net Ordinary Receipts, excluding Loans.
1853......	$24 50			$988,081 17	$61,587,031 68
1854......				1,105,352 74	73,800,341 40
1855......				827,731 40	65,350,574 68
1856..				1,116,190 81	74,056,699 24
1857......				1,259,920 88	68,965,312 57
1858......				1,352,029 13	46,655,365 96
1859......	709,357 72			1,454,596 24	52,777,107 92
1860......	10,008 00			1,088,530 25	56,054,599 83
1861......	33,630 90			1,023,515 31	41,476,299 49
1862......	68,400 00			915,327 97	51,919,261 09
1863......	602,345 44			3,741,794 38	112,094,945 51
1864......	21,174,101 01			30,291,701 86	243,412,971 20
1865......	11,683,446 89			25,441,556 00	322,031,158 19
1866......	38,083,055 68			29,036,314 23	519,949,564 38
1867......	27,787,830 35			15,037,522 15	462,846,679 92
1868......	29,208,629 50			17,745,403 59	376,434,453 82
1869......	13,755,491 12			13,997,338 65	357,188,256 09
1870......	15,295,643 76			12,942,118 30	395,959,833 87
1871......	8,892,839 95			22,093,541 21	374,431,104 94
1872......	9,412,637 65			15,106,051 23	364,694,229 91
1873......	11,560,530 89			17,161,270 05	322,177,673 78
1874......	5,037,665 22			32,575,043 32	299,941,090 84
1875......	3,979,279 69			15,431,915 31	284,020,771 41
1876......	4,029,280 58			24,070,602 81	290,066,584 70
1877......	405,776 58			18,031,655 46	269,000,586 62
Total...	$202,436,960 90	$485,224 45	$9,720,136 29	$343,843,577 47	$6,892,122,509 88

Note.—The receipts for 1843 are for the half-year from January 1st to June 30th, 1843. After this date, the fiscal year was changed so as to run from June 30th to June 30th, instead of from January 1st to December 31st. Each fiscal year is designated by the year in which it closes. Thus, the fiscal year 1877 denotes the year beginning July 1st, 1876, and ending June 30th, 1877.

EXPENDITURES OF THE UNITED STATES FROM MARCH 4, 1789, TO JUNE 30, 1877.

Years.	Pensions.	Premiums.	Interest.	Total Net Ordinary Expenditures, excluding Interest.
1789-1791.......	$175,813 88		$1,177,863 63	$1,919,589 52
1792..........	109,243 15		2,373,611 28	5,896,258 47
1793........ ...	80,087 81		2,097,859 17	1,740,070 73
1794..........	81,399 24		2,752,523 04	3,545,299 00
1795..........	68,673 22		2,947,059 06	4,362,541 72
1796..........	100,843 71		3,239,347 68	2,551,303 15
1797..........	92,256 97		3,172,516 73	2,836,110 52
1798..........	104,845 33		2,955,875 90	4,651,710 42
1799..........	95,444 03		2,815,651 41	6,480,166 72
1800..........	64,130 73		3,402,601 04	7,411,369 97
1801....	73,533 37		4,411,830 06	4,981,669 90
1802..........	85,440 39		4,239,172 16	3,737,079 91
1803..........	62,902 10		3,949,462 36	4,002,824 24
1804..........	80,092 80		4,185,048 74	4,452,858 91
1805..........	81,854 59		2,657,114 22	6,357,234 62
1806..........	81,875 53		3,368,968 26	6,080,209 36
1807..........	70,500 00		3,369,578 48	4,984,572 89
1808..........	82,576 04		2,557,074 23	6,504,338 85
1809..........	87,833 54		2,866,074 90	7,414,672 14
1810..........	83,744 16		3,163,671 00	5,311,082 28
1811..........	75,043 88		2,585,435 57	5,592,604 86
1812..........	91,402 10		2,451,272 57	17,829,498 70

EXPENDITURES OF THE UNITED STATES FROM MARCH 4, 1789, TO
JUNE 30, 1877—(*Continued*).

Years.	Civil and Miscellaneous.	War.	Navy.	Indians.
1813..........	$1,729,435 61	$19,652,013 02	$6,446,600 10	$167,358 28
1814..........	2,208,029 70	20,350,806 86	7,311,290 60	167,394 86
1815..........	2,898,870 47	14,794,294 22	8,660,000 25	530,750 00
1816..........	2,989,741 17	16,012,096 80	3,908,278 30	274,512 16
1817..........	3,518,936 76	8,004,236 53	3,314,598 49	319,463 71
1818..........	3,835,839 51	5,622,715 10	2,953,605 00	505,704 27
1819..........	3,067,211 41	6,506,300 37	3,847,640 42	463,181 39
1820..........	2,592,021 94	2,630,392 31	4,387,990 00	315,750 01
1821..........	2,223,121 54	4,461,291 78	3,319,243 06	477,005 44
1822..........	1,967,996 24	3,111,981 48	2,224,458 98	575,007 41
1823..........	2,022,093 99	3,096,924 43	2,503,765 83	380,781 82
1824..........	7,155,308 81	3,340 939 65	2,904,581 56	429,987 90
1825..........	2,748,544 89	3,659,914 18	3,049,083 86	724,106 44
1826..........	2,600,177 79	3,943,194 37	4,218,902 45	743,447 83
1827..........	2,713,476 58	3,948,977 88	4,263,877 45	750,624 88
1828..........	3,676,052 64	4,145,544 56	3,918,786 44	705,084 24
1829..........	3,082,234 65	4,724,291 07	3,308,745 47	576,344 74
1830..........	3,237,416 04	4,767,128 88	3,239,428 63	622,262 47
1831..........	3,064,646 10	4,841,835 55	3,856,183 07	930,738 04
1832..........	4,577,141 45	5,446,034 88	3,956,370 29	1,352,419 75
1833..........	5,716,245 93	6,704,019 10	3,901,356 75	1,802,980 98
1834..........	4,404,728 95	5,696,189 38	3,956,260 42	1,003,953 20
1835..........	4,229,698 53	5,759,156 89	3,864,939 06	1,706,444 48
1836..........	5,393,279 72	11,747,345 25	5,807,718 23	5,037,022 88
1837..........	9,893,370 27	13,682,730 80	6,646,914 53	4,348,036 19
1838..........	7,160,664 76	12,897,224 16	6,131,580 53	5,504,191 34
1839..........	5,725,990 89	8,916,995 80	6,182,294 25	2,528,917 28
1840..........	5,995,398 96	7,095,267 23	6,113,896 89	2,331,794 86
1841..........	6,490,881 45	8,801,610 24	6,001,076 97	2,514,837 12
1842..........	6,775,624 61	6,610,438 02	8,397,242 95	1,199,099 68
1843..........	3,202,713 00	2,908,671 95	3,727,711 53	578,371 00
1844..........	5,645,183 86	5,218,183 66	6,498,199 11	1,256,532 39
1845..........	5,911,760 98	5,746,291 28	6,297,177 89	1,539,351 85
1846..........	6,711,283 89	10,413,370 58	6,455,013 92	1,027,693 64
1847..........	6,885,608 35	35,840,030 33	7,900,635 76	1,430,411 30
1848..........	5,650,851 25	27,688,334 21	9,408,476 02	1,252,296 81
1849..........	12,885,334 24	14,558,473 26	9,786,705 92	1,374,161 55
1850..........	16,043,763 36	9,687,024 58	7,904,724 66	1,663,591 47
1851..........	17,888,992 18	12,161,965 11	8,880,581 38	2,829,801 77
1852..........	17,504,171 45	8,521,506 19	8,918,842 10	3,043,576 04
1853..........	17,463,068 01	9,910,498 49	11,067,789 53	3,880,494 12
1854..........	26,672,144 68	11,722,282 87	10,790,096 32	1,550,339 55
1855..........	21,090,425 43	14,648,074 07	13,327,095 11	2,772,990 73
1856..........	31,794,088 87	16,963,160 51	14,074,834 64	2,644,263 97
1857..........	28,565,498 77	19,159,150 87	12,651,694 61	4,354,418 87
1858..........	26,400,016 42	25,679,121 63	14,053,264 64	4,978,266 18
1859..........	23,797,544 40	23,154,720 53	14,690,927 90	3,490,534 53
1860..........	27,997,978 30	16,472,202 72	11,514,649 83	2,991,121 54
1861..........	23,327,287 69	23,001,530 67	12,387,156 52	2,865,481 17
1862..........	21,385,862 59	389,173,562 29	42,640,353 09	2,827,048 37
1863..........	23,198,382 37	603,214,411 82	63,261,235 31	3,152,062 70
1864..........	27,572,216 87	690,391,048 66	85,704,963 74	2,099,975 97
1865..........	42,989,360 10	1,030,690,400 06	122,617,434 07	5,059,360 71
1866..........	40,613,114 17	283,154,670 06	43,285,662 00	3,295,729 32
1867..........	51,110,223 72	95,224,415 63	31,034,011 04	4,642,531 77
1868..........	53,009,867 67	123,246,648 62	25,775,502 72	4,100,682 32
1869..........	56,474,061 53	78,501,990 61	20,000,757 97	7,042,923 06
1870..........	53,237,461 56	57,655,675 40	21,780,229 87	3,407,938 15
1871..........	60,481,916 23	35,799,991 82	19,431,027 21	7,426,997 44
1872..........	60,984,757 42	35,372,157 20	21,249,809 99	7,061,728 82
1873..........	73,328,110 06	46,323,138 31	23,526,256 79	7,951,704 88
1874..........	*85,141,593 61	42,313,927 22	30,932,587 42	6,692,462 09
1875..........	71,070,702 98	41,120,645 98	21,497,626 27	8,384,656 86
1876..........	73,599,661 04	38,070,888 64	18,963,300 82	5,966,558 17
1877..........	56,252,066 60	37,082,735 90	14,959,935 36	5,277,007 22
Total........	$1,339,013,746 27	$4,202,972,307 68	$966,780,863 02	$171,377,689 77

* In this amount is included $15,500,000 expended under Geneva award.

EXPENDITURES OF THE UNITED STATES FROM MARCH 4, 1789, TO JUNE 30, 1877—(*Continued*).

Years.	Pensions.	Premiums.	Interest.	Total Net Ordinary Expenditures, excluding Interest.
1813	$86,989 91		$3,599,455 22	$28,082,396 92
1814	90,164 36		4,593,239 04	30,127,686 38
1815	69,656 06		5,990,090 24	26,953,571 00
1816	188,804 15		7,822,923 34	23,373,432 58
1817	297,374 43		4,536,282 55	15,454,609 92
1818	890,719 90		6,209,954 03	13,808,673 78
1819	2,415,939 85		5,211,730 56	16,300,273 44
1820	3,208,376 31		5,151,004 32	13,134,530 57
1821	242,817 25		5,126,073 79	10,723,479 07
1822	1,948,199 40		5,172,788 79	9,827,643 51
1823	1,780,588 52		4,922,475 40	9,784,154 59
1824	1,499,326 59		4,943,557 93	15,330,144 71
1825	1,308,810 57		4,366,757 40	11,490,459 94
1826	1,556,593 83		3,975,542 95	13,062,316 27
1827	976,138 86		3,486,071 51	12,653,095 65
1828	850,573 57		3,098,800 60	13,296,041 45
1829	949,594 47		2,542,843 23	12,641,210 40
1830	1,363,297 31		1,912,574 93	13,229,533 33
1831	1,170,665 14		1,373,748 74	13,664,067 00
1832	1,184,422 40		772,561 50	16,516,388 77
1833	4,589,152 40		303,796 87	22,713,755 11
1834	3,364,285 30		202,152 98	18,425,417 25
1835	1,954,711 32		57,863 08	17,514,950 28
1836	2,882,797 96			30,868,164 04
1837	2,672,162 45			37,243,214 24
1838	2,156,057 29		14,996 48	33,849,718 08
1839	3,142,750 51		399,833 89	26,496,948 73
1840	2,603,562 17		174,598 08	24,139,920 11
1841	2,398,434 51		284,977 55	26,196,840 20
1842	1,378,931 33		773,549 85	24,361,336 59
1843	839,041 12		523,583 91	11,256,508 60
1844	2,032,008 99		1,833,452 13	20,650,108 01
1845	2,400,788 11	$13,231 43	1,040,458 18	21,895,369 61
1846	1,811,097 56		842,723 27	26,418,459 59
1847	1,744,883 63		1,119,214 72	53,801,569 37
1848	1,227,496 48		2,390,765 88	45,227,454 77
1849	1,328,867 64	82,865 81	3,565,535 78	39,933,542 61
1850	1,866,886 02		3,782,393 03	37,165,990 09
1851	2,293,377 22	69,713 19	3,696,760 75	44,054,717 66
1852	2,401,858 78	170,063 42	4,000,297 80	40,389,954 56
1853	1,756,806 20	420,498 64	3,665,832 74	44,078,156 35
1854	1,232,665 00	2,877,818 69	3,070,926 69	51,967,528 42
1855	1,477,612 33	672,017 39	2,314,464 99	56,316,197 72
1856	1,296,229 65	385,372 90	1,953,822 37	66,772,527 64
1857	1,310,380 58	303,572 39	1,593,265 23	66,041,143 70
1858	1,219,768 30	574,443 08	1,652,055 67	72,330,437 17
1859	1,222,222 71		2,637,649 70	66,355,950 07
1860	1,100,802 32		3,144,120 94	60,056,754 71
1861	1,034,599 73		4,034,157 30	62,616,055 78
1862	852,170 47		13,190,344 84	456,379,896 81
1863	1,078,513 36		24,729,700 62	694,004,575 56
1864	4,985,473 90		53,685,421 69	811,283,679 14
1865	16,347,621 34	1,717,900 11	77,395,090 30	1,217,704,199 28
1866	15,605,549 88	58,476 51	133,067,724 91	385,954,731 43
1867	20,936,551 71	10,813,349 38	143,781,591 91	202,947,733 87
1868	23,782,386 78	7,001,151 04	140,424,045 71	229,915,088 11
1869	28,476,621 78	1,674,680 05	130,694,242 80	190,496,354 95
1870	28,340,202 17	15,996,555 60	129,235,498 00	164,421,507 15
1871	34,443,894 88	9,016,794 74	125,576,565 93	157,583,827 58
1872	28,533,402 76	6,958,266 76	117,357,839 72	153,201,856 19
1873	29,359,426 86	5,105,919 99	104,750,688 44	180,488,636 90
1874	29,038,414 66	1,395,073 55	107,119,815 21	194,118,985 00
1875	29,456,216 22		103,093,544 57	171,529,848 27
1876	28,257,395 69		100,243,271 23	164,857,813 36
1877	27,963,752 27		97,124,511 58	141,535,497 35
Total	$423,205,659 06	$65,573,794 67	$1,802,044,022 85	$7,108,850,265 40

FIRE-INSURANCE COMPANIES OF OTHER STATES DOING BUSINESS IN NEW YORK, 1877.

[From the Insurance Year-Book, August, 1877.]

NAME OF COMPANY.	Cash Capital.	Gross Assets, Jan. 1, 1877.	Total Fire Losses Paid in 1876.	Total Liabilities, including Re-insurance, Profit Scrip and Capital.	Surplus over all Liabilities, including Re-insurance, Capital and Profit Scrip.
	$	$	$	$	$
Ætna, Hartford...... ..	3,000,000	7,115,624	1,729,855	5,170,388	1,945,236
Allemannia, Pittsburgh.	200,000	348,272	117,924	309,931	38,341
Amazon, Cincinnati....	500,000	935,163	390,471	916,551	18,612
American, Boston......	300,000	560,315	3,025	430,371	129,914
American, Chicago.....	200,000	882,028	284,997	650,385	231,643
American, Philadelphia	400,000	1,280,976	221,734	909,916	371,060
Amer. Central, St. Louis	300,000	747,468	217,933	544,623	202,845
American, Newark.... .	632,435	1,377,108	40,299	767,283	609,825
- Atlantic F. & M., Prov.	200,000	267,247	35,506	250,064	17,183
Atlas, Hartford	200,000	442,133	323,687	432,634	9,499
Bangor, Bangor	201,520	375,395	181,542	357,207	18,183
Boylston Mut., Bost., P.	557,2 0	962,390	36,439	915,288	47,102
Citizens',Newark......	200,000	521,807	331,925	512,109	9,693
Citizens', St. Louis.....	200,000	433,146	132,173	311,043	122,103
Connecticut, Hartford..	1,000,000	1,362,844	132,325	1,178,870	183,974
Commonwealth, Boston	300,000	435,834	34,148	380,604	55,230
Detroit F. & M., Detroit	250,000	481,906	46,293	322,434	162,472
Eliot, Boston	200,000	399,510	25,433	268,512	130,998
Equitable F.& M.. Prov.	200,000	345,369	40,989	271,883	73,486
Equitable, Nashville....	220,000	314,724	74,840	308,222	6,502
Fairfield, S. Norwalk...	200,000	305,315	98,766	270,390	34,925
Faneuil Hall, Boston...	400,000	519,902	106,972	517,636	2,263
Farmers', York	Mutual.	368,082	226,551	239,673	128,409
Fireman's Fd.,SanFran.	300,000	703,622	246,201	601,430	102,192
Firemen's Fire, Boston.	300,000	669,407	57,642	445,680	223,719
Firemen's, Dayton	250,000	423,252	40,479	346,465	76,737
Firemen's, Newark, P..	400,000	977,438	74,457	551,764	429,053
Fire Association, Phila.	600,000	3,778,651	551,559	2,773,672	1,004,979
First Nat., Worcester ..	100,000	242,540	52,948	167,453	75,087
Franklin, Boston..	200,000	268,275	57,803	250,785	17,490
Franklin, Philadelphia..	400,000	3,352,865	467,127	2,586,135	766,730
German, Baltimore.....	300,000	655,884	27,460	375,064	280,820
Germania, Newark......	225,000	802,283	52,950	296,240	6,034
Girard F. & M., Phila..	300,000	1,112,277	107,901	691,789	420,488
Granite, Richmond.....	200,000	242,630	23,453	232,516	10,114
Hartford, Hartford.....	1,000,000	3,273,869	844,780	2,173,319	1,100,550
Home, Columbus......	250,000	481,922	151,102	370,852	114,070
Home, Newark.........	200,000	255,836	22,178	241,564	14,272
Ins.Co. of N.Am.,Phila.	2,000,000	6,601,884	681,522	4,235,511	2,366,373
Ins.Co.St'e of Pa.,Phila.	200,000	621,474	66,094	440,388	181,049
Jefferson, St. Louis . ..	200,000	269,535	13,157	240,298	29,242
Lancaster, Lancaster...	200,000	323,455	139,388	263,308	60,147
Lycoming, Muncy.	Mutual.	5,338,977	503,506	390,212	4,918,705
Manayunk, Phila.......	200,000	246,252	28,103	235,721	10,531
Manufr's' F. & M., Bost.	500,000	1,100,058	112,730	931,024	169,034
Manufacturers',Newark	200,000	308,986	61,314	237,987	21,001
Mercantile, Cleveland..	200,000	379,380	47,605	267,056	112,324
Mercantile Marine,Bost.	300,000	706,284	4,780	403,349	302,935
Meriden, Meriden......	200,000	321,689	104,762	291,533	30,156
Merchants', Providence.	200,000	398,829	100,397	315,613	83,216

P, Participation or Scrip Companies.

FIRE-INSURANCE COMPANIES OF OTHER STATES DOING BUSINESS IN NEW YORK, 1877—(*Continued*).

NAME OF COMPANY.	Cash Capital.	Gross Assets, Jan. 1, 1877.	Total Fire Losses Paid in 1876.	Total Liabilities, including Re-insurance, Profit Scrip, and Capital.	Surplus over all Liabilities, including Re-insurance, Capital and Profit Scrip.
	$	$	$	$	$
Merchants', Newark....	200,000	1,003,084	177,313	600,726	402,358
Mobile Fire Dept., Mob.	200,000	293,941	64,420	282,812	11,129
National, Hartford	500,000	1,040,524	140,547	715,247	325,277
Neptune F. & M., Bost..	300,000	638,771	29,354	510,483	123,288
Newark City, Newark..	200,000	326.215	68,384	284,316	41,899
Newark Mut., New'k,P.	Mutual.	642.749	22,513	323,017	319,732
N. Hampshire, Manch'r	250,000	453,195	96,779	358,270	94,925
N. American, Boston..	200,000	329,655	13,192	245,582	84,123
N.W. Nat'l, Milwaukee.	600,000	877,193	145,812	806,681	70,512
Orient, Hartford.......	500,000	776,179	145,920	672,642	103,537
Paterson, Paterson.....	200,000	373,827	140,525	355,008	18,819
People's, Newark, P....	200,000	430,733	139,464	337,355	93,378
People's, Trenton......	300,000	622,911	91,971	445,482	177,429
Pennsylvania, Phila....	400,000	1,675,694	267,443	1,162,911	512,783
Phœnix, Hartford......	1,000,000	2.407,531	637,473	1,875.280	532,251
Philadelphia, Phila.....	200,000	272,422	37,317	264,731	7,691
Prescott, Boston........	200,000	385,804	68,764	300,811	84,993
Prov.Washingt'n, Prov.	400,000	601,556	83,884	561,639	39,917
Roger Williams, Prov..	200,000	393,226	144,201	388,100	5,117
Reading, Reading.	200,000	308,905	30,035	262,222	41,683
Revere, Boston....	200,000	268,375	10,254	248,671	19,704
Security, New Haven ..	200 000	384,059	75,795	333,265	50,794
Phawmut, Boston	500,000	580,150	64,866	596,349	—16,199
Shoe & Leather, Boston	300,000	642,033	43,133	510,696	131,337
Springf'd F.& M.Sp'gf'd	750,000	1,515,672	271,598	1,263,538	252,134
St. Louis, St. Louis	240,000	347,001	127,104	345,853	1,148
St.Paul F. & M., St. P'l.	400,000	943,661	280,046	725,665	217,996
St.Joseph F.&M.,St.Jos	220,000	420,245	75,767	313,465	106,780
Standard, Trenton......	200.000	324,902	117,041	322,241	2,601
Sun, Philadelphia	200,000	280,301	37,040	261,239	19,062
Teutonia, Philadelphia.	200,000	275,315	5,855	233,094	42,221
Toledo F. & M., Toledo	200,000	252,392	40,111	243,796	8,596
Traders, Chicago.......	500,000	827,359	126,319	645,408	181,951
Union M. & F.,Galve-'n	200,000	255,217	39,839	238,273	16,944
Virginia F.& M., Rich'd	250,000	584,697	81,942	447,305	137,392
Virginia State, Richm'd.	200.000	271,204	14,406	235,402	35,802
Wash'n F. & M., Bost..	400,000	879,604	34,623	667,147	212,457
87 Companies........	30,196,155	77,047,416	13,470,522	55,027,439	22,039,555

P, Participation or Scrip Companies.

THE JOINT-STOCK FIRE-INSURANCE COMPANIES OF NEW YORK STATE IN 1877.

[From the Insurance Year-Book, August, 1877.]

NAME OF COMPANY.	Cash Capital.	Gross Assets, Jan. 1, 1877.	Total Fire Losses Paid in 1876.	Total Liabilities, including Re-insurance, Profit Scrip and Capital.	Surplus over all Liabilities, including Re-insurance, Capital and Profit Scrip.
	$	$	$	$	$
Ætna	200,000	293,050	52,077	236,943	56,107
Adriatic	200,000	304,391	71,433	264,040	40,351
Agricultural, Watertown	200,000	1,095,310	265,807	905,985	189,325
Albany	200,000	405,881	36,077	237,504	168,377
American, P	400,000	1,079,644	48,521	819,315	260,329
American Exchange	200,000	301,922	9,725	224,726	77,196
Amity	200,000	231,717	32,608	236,471	5,246
Arctic	200,000	244,667	22,157	232,882	11,785
Atlantic	200,000	457,966	266,650	348,780	109,186
Brewers and Maltsters'	200,000	282,949	37,212	254,143	28,806
Broadway	200,000	538,595	14,149	231,685	306,910
Brooklyn	153,000	406,408	7,135	177,157	229,251
Buffalo, Buffalo	200,000	320,188	50,540	253,070	67,118
Buffalo German, Buffalo	200,000	684,799	110,280	346,730	338,069
Capital City, Albany	150,000	179,253	32,083	170,495	8,758
Citizens'	300,000	923,201	61,600	431,192	489,009
City	210,000	433,059	26,666	241,799	191,160
Clinton	250,000	473,149	49,198	300,830	172,319
Columbia	300,000	359,050	54,268	346,843	12,207
Commerce, Albany	200,000	421,239	34,252	254,735	166,504
Commerce	200,000	240,161	32 521	226,785	13,376
Commercial	200,000	537,615	187,809	367,430	170,185
Continental, P	1,000,000	3,040,085	664,892	2,216,070	824,015
Eagle	300,000	887,122	60,991	876,800	510,322
Empire City	200,000	347,206	59,008	233,198	114,008
Emporium	200,000	245,883	35,378	239,479	6,404
Exchange	200,010	398,547	79,405	265,088	133,439
Farragut	200,000	440,921	43,865	281,669	159,232
Farmers' J'nt St'k, Mer.	100,000	233,848	61,471	229,728	4,120
Firemen's	201,000	250,722	17,802	242,258	108,464
Firemen's Fund	150,000	209,689	46,144	193,036	16,653
Fireman's Trust	150,000	291,187	27,188	186,186	105,001
Franklin	200,000	252,018	10,855	246,761	5,257
Gebhard	200,000	222,858	10,338	218,001	4,857
German-American	1,000,000	2,226,553	368,227	1,574,715	651,838
Germania	500,000	1,717,848	285,783	1,023,048	694,800
Glenn's Falls	200,000	821,709	144,131	509,694	312,015
Globe	200,000	384,957	46,061	249,915	135,042
Greenwich	200,000	644,211	58,700	326,572	317,639
Guaranty	200,000	280,939	68,484	269,455	11,484
Guardian	200,000	302,940	31,414	245,277	57,663
Hamilton	150,000	346,180	33,263	203,883	142,297
Hanover	500,000	1,642,883	403,206	1,133,489	509,394
Hoffman	200,000	387,993	110,037	282,307	105,686
Holland Purch., Batavia.	100,000	228,936	57,782	210,478	18,458
Home	3,000,000	6,101,651	1,581,382	5,101,867	1,002,784
Homestead, Watertown	200,000	272,619	72,169	260,529	12,090
Hope	150,000	211,546	30,167	171,248	40,303
Howard	500,000	793,913	56,484	603,290	190,623
Importers and Traders'.	200,000	351,096	24,851	240,495	110,091
Irving	200,000	310,339	35,635	249,234	61,105

P. Participation or Scrip Companies.

THE JOINT-STOCK FIRE-INSURANCE COMPANIES OF NEW YORK
STATE IN 1877—(Continued).

NAME OF COMPANY.	Cash Capital.	Gross Assets, Jan. 1, 1877.	Total Fire Losses Paid in 1876.	Total Liabilities, including Re-insurance, Profit Scrip and Capital.	Surplus over all Liabilities, including Re-insurance, Capital and Profit Scrip.
	$	$	$	$	$
Jefferson	200,010	566,449	25,834	248,870	317,579
Kings Connty..........	150,000	411,363	56,855	206,527	204,836
Knickerbocker....... ..	280,000	372,878	13,336	306,285	66,593
Lafayette..............	150,000	383,776	49,049	222,275	161,503
Lamar........	200,000	411,269	72,171	278,496	132,773
Lenox............	150,000	248,129	26,101	174,954	73,175
Long Island, P.........	200,000	536,190	8,643	379,172	157,018
Lorillard................	300,000	476,287	55,621	365,959	110,328
Manhattan.............	250,000	850,658	362,788	543,516	307,142
Manuf's and Builders'.	200,000	424,429	18,734	238,961	185,468
Mechanics'	150,000	387,652	45,312	203,408	184,244
Mechanics and Traders'	200,000	620,338	116,834	304,431	315,907
Mercantile.............	200,000	297,553	19,331	231,837	65,716
Merchants'........	200,000	511,704	60,273	322,850	188,854
Montauk...............	200,000	369,654	28,983	244,243	125,411
Nassau	200,000	465,921	18,373	236,281	229,640
National	200,000	425,685	78,411	293,343	132,342
New York and Boston..	200,000	213,003	410	212,991	12
New York Bowery......	300,000	788,937	60,698	363,465	425,472
New York Central......	100,000	262,081	129,485	246,461	15,620
New York Equitable....	210,000	589,518	20,035	248,283	341,235
New York Fire.........	200,000	459,585	54,564	258,936	200,649
N. Y. Produce Exchange	200,000	235,157	18,696	221,866	13,291
New York City...... ...	200,000	965,767	47,994	943,137	22,630
Niagara................	500,000	1,442,445	359,408	935,508	506,937
North River..........	350,000	503,812	4,859	371,098	132,714
Northern, Watertown...	250,000	369,243	56,662	322,901	46,342
Pacific.................	200,000	703,792	69,603	293,715	410,077
Park..................	200,000	372,722	26,860	233,637	139,085
People's..............	150,000	301,959	27,653	179,376	122,583
Peter Cooper...........	150,000	390,497	3,235	171,167	219,330
Phœnix................	1,000,000	2,792,903	471,014	1,906,557	886,346
Relief................	200,000	349,533	72,966	261,546	87,987
Republic, P...........	300,000	487,229	54,772	405,279	81,950
Resolute..............	200,000	248,341	44,958	245,071	3,270
Ridgewood............	200,000	331,199	81,263	250,218	80,981
Rochester German, R..	200,000	367,185	117,870	310,118	57,067
Rutgers	200,000	459,026	19,130	239,592	219,434
Safeguard.............	200,000	411,660	69,054	261,110	150,550
Standard..............	200,000	427,132	27,261	258,882	168,250
Star................	200,000	450,713	47,600	292,715	157,998
Sterling	200,000	305,602	29,861	228,145	77,457
St. Nicholas..........	200,000	329,537	55,579	269,279	59,558
Stuyvesant............	200,000	386,060	26,422	229,797	156,263
Tradesmen's..........	150,000	396,830	37,338	156,241	192,769
Union, Buffalo........	100,000	133,578	11,273	120,012	13,566
United States.........	250,000	596,729	11,599	275,191	251,538
Watertown............	200,000	725,819	200,137	661,064	64,755
Westchester...	300,000	861,409	442,930	659,909	201,500
Williamsburgh City....	250,000	848,511	147,806	441,687	406,824
101 Companies........	26,957,020	59,661,955	9,884,224	41,263,192	18,398,063

P, Participation or Scrip Companies.

NEW YORK FIRE-INSURANCE STOCKS AND DIVIDENDS.

[From the Insurance Year-Book, August, 1877.]

Name of Company.	Capital.	Par Value	Annual Dividend—Per Cent. 1862.	1863.	1864.	1865.	1866.	1867.	1868.	1869.	1870.	1871.	1872.	1873.	1874.	1875.	1876.	1877.	Latest sales, 1877, Per $100.
Ætna	$200,000	100	......	......	......	......	......	......	......	......	......	......	5	......	10	14	25	15	$100½
Adriatic	200,000	25	4	4	8	......	......	......	......	......	10	......	10	3½	10	10	10	10	74
Agricultural	200,000	5	......	......	20	10	15	20	20	25	30	30	20	20	10	10	10	10	175
Albany	200,000	30	18	......	......	15	6	12	13½	13½	20	6⅝	10	12	18	16½	17½	......	......
American	400,000	50	10½	12½	13½	16	14	17½	14½	17	18	17	14	14	14	15	15	15	151
American Exchange	200,000	100	......	......	......	5	7½	10	10	10	13	12	6	10	10	10	10	10	101
Amity	200,000	100	......	......	......	......	......	......	......	......	......	......	......	......	7½	8	8	4	85
Arctic	200,000	20	......	10	10	5	......	......	10	10	10	10	10	5	10	10	10	5	73
Atlantic	200,000	50	......	......	......	......	......	......	......	......	......	......	......	10	10	10	10	15	110
Brewers and Maltsters'	200,000	100	......	......	......	......	......	......	......	......	......	......	......	......	5	5	10	10	95
Broadway	200,000	25	13	10	11	12	10	12	16	16	16	14	18	20	20	20	20	20	217
Brooklyn	153,000	17	20	20	20	20	20	20	20	20	20	10	20	20	30	30	20	20	209
Buffalo	200,000	100	......	......	......	......	......	......	......	......	......	......	......	......	......	10	10	15	110
Buffalo German	200,000	100	......	......	......	......	......	......	6	7	5	6½	10	10	15	15	15	10	150
Capital City	150,000	100	......	......	......	......	......	9	10	10	10	10	......	9	10	10	5	5	......
Citizens'	300,000	20	25	25	25	20	20	15	20	20	33½	16½	17½	10	20½	23½	23½	20	185
City	210,000	70	13½	11½	12	10½	12	15	14	14	14	15	20	14	20	20	20	20	161
Clinton	250,000	100	12	11	11	10	5	11	10	13	14	14	17	10½	17	20	20	18	153½
Columbia	300,000	30	8	9	5	......	......	......	10	10	10	10	10	......	10	10	10	5	65
Commerce, Albany	200,000	25	8	8	4	10	8	8	8	10	10	20	5	10	10	14	16	8	130
Commerce	200,000	100	4	4	10	10	10	10	10	10	11	10	10	5	10	10	10	5	85
Commercial	200,000	50	12	10	10	10	10	10	10	10	10	10	11	5	13	20	25	25	151
Continental	1,000,000	100	13	13	14	14	14	14	15	16	18	10	8	8½	10	9¾	11½	12½	135
Eagle	300,000	40	20	15	17½	12½	10	10	5	20	20	20	20	20	30	30	30	20	204½
Empire City	200,000	100	14	14	17	14	12	7	14	10	11	10	10	10	10	14	14	14	125
Emporium	200,000	100	......	......	......	......	......	......	......	......	......	......	......	......	10	10	10	3	108½
Exchange	200,000	30	......	......	......	......	......	......	......	......	4	......	7½	10	10	15	20	15	122
Farragut	200,000	50	......	......	......	......	......	......	......	......	......	......	3½	10	10	12½	15	15	138
Firemen's	204,000	17	11	10	5	10	10	10	17	20	20	10	5	5	13	13⅓	15	12	120½
Firemen's Fund	150,000	10	3½	7	8½	......	3½	......	......	......	......	......	......	......	10	10	10	10	68½
Firemen's Trust	150,000	10	10	10	5	5	......	5	10	10	10	10	10	10	10	12	12	12	115
Franklin	200,000	100	......	......	......	......	......	......	......	......	......	......	......	......	......	......	......	......	100
Gebhard	200,000	100	4	9	5	5	11	10	10	10	10	10	10	5	10	10	10	......	75
German American	1,000,000	100	......	......	......	......	......	......	......	......	......	......	......	4	10	10	10	10	118¾
Germania	500,000	50	5	10	10	10	10	7	10	10	10	10	10	10	10	10	30	15	192
Glenn's Falls	200,000	10	......	......	......	......	......	5	10	10	10	5	10	10	10	10	10	15	......
Globe	200,000	50	......	......	5	10	5	5	10	10	20	11	12½	12½	15	18	20	20	133
Greenwich	200,000	25	10	13	14	14	10	12	20	20	20	22	28	29	50	55	40	40	309
Guaranty	200,000	100	......	......	......	......	......	......	......	......	......	......	......	......	......	......	......	5	85
Guardian	200,000	100	......	......	......	......	......	......	5	5	10	10	8½	......	10	10	10	10	93
Hamilton	150,000	15	8	8	8	8	8	10	10	10	16	10	17½	20	20	20	15	20	192
Hanover	500,000	50	12	11	12	12	10	10	10	10	10	8½	10	10	10	10	10	10	134
Hoffman	200,000	50	......	......	......	......	5	......	......	......	......	......	10	......	10	10	10	10	99½
Holland Purchase	100,000	100	......	......	......	......	......	......	7	7	......	10	7	7	7	11	8	......	......

Home
Homestead
Hope
Howard
Importers and Traders'
Irving
Jefferson
Kings County
Knickerbocker
Lafayette
Lamar
Lenox
Long Island
Lorillard
Manhattan
Manufacturers and builders'
Mechanics
Mechanics and Traders'
Mercantile
Merchants'
Montauk
Nassau
National
New York and Boston
New York Bowery
New York Central
New York Equitable
New York Fire
New York Produce Exchange
New York City
Niagara
North River
Northern
Pacific
Park
People's
Peter Cooper
Phenix
Relief
Republic
Resolute
Ridgewood
Rochester German
Rutgers
Safeguard
Standard
Star
Sterling
Mt. Nicholas
Stuyvesant
Tradesmen's
Union
United States
Watertown
Westchester
Williamsburgh City

THE AMERICAN BUSINESS OF THE FOREIGN INSURANCE COMPANIES, 1877.

[From the Insurance Year-Book, August, 1877.]

COMPANY.	Total Assets in the United States.	Fire Premium Receipts in 1876.	Fire Losses paid in 1876.	Risks Written in 1876.	Risks in Force, Jan. 1, 1877.
	$	$	$	$	$
British America.........	660,080	882,137	157,038	36,973,942	27,382,110
Commercial Union	813,390	596,877	296,213	61,336,141	50,917,107
Guardian....	773,305	102,678	40,090	23,254,410	11,298,234
Hamburg-Bremen.......	667,787	325,004	136,091	26,412,664	27,516,635
Imperial................	903,529	319,313	162,581	34,434,365	31,505,818
La Caisse Générale.....	315,540	136,548	77,343	11,884,198	10,715,847
Lancashire..............	495,109	499,660	301,757	54,410,495	32,672,252
Liverp'l & Lond. & Globe	3,652,063	2,123,709	904,218	278,663,358	195,981,879
London Assurance......	905,878	349,438	143,910	49,947,238	44,808,526
N. British and Mercantile	1,767,277	1,193,830	650,553	126,314,195	103,510,074
Northern...............	561,308	318,605	73,950	34,434,365	24,359,066
Queen	1,422,571	923,788	446,964	85,928,835	65,461,544
Royal Canadian.........	833,629	807,692	463,983	91,540,976	60,304,896
Royal...	2,552,304	1,570,476	717,517	168,330,556	145,707,675
Scottish Commercial....	661,294	229,820	154,432	37,210,326	31,515,724
Western................	671,684	397,854	177,459	38,504,003	22,849,847
16 Companies..........	17,670,748	10,377,429	4,904,099	1,168,380,067	896,457,834

Cost of Collection of the Revenue of Great Britain and Management of Revenue Departments, in each Fiscal Year ended 31st March, from 1861-1877.

Years ended 31st March.	Customs.		Inland Revenue (Excise, Stamps, Taxes, and Income Tax).		Post Office (Including the Telegraph Service, from 1st January, 1870).		Total.	
	Gross Revenue.	Charges of Collection issued out of the Exchequer.	Gross Revenue.	Charges of Collection issued out of the Exchequer.	Gross Revenue.	Expenses and Charges of Department (Including Packet Service).	Revenue from Customs, Inland Revenue, Post Office, and Telegraph Service.	Charges of Collection of Revenue.
	£	£	£	£	£	£	£	£
1861	23,305,776	1,025,848	41,834,029	1,512,589	3,422,229	2,088,789	68,762,231	5,557,226
1862	23,674,000	1,006,527	40,447,945	1,514,675	3,552,805	3,070,299	67,674,750	5,591,501
1863	24,034,000	990,927	39,866,000	1,487,930	3,730,540	2,995,191	67,630,540	5,474,048
1864	23,232,000	976,601	39,826,000	1,476,632	3,874,869	2,996,281	66,932,869	5,419,514
1865	22,572,000	936,394	40,388,000	1,483,528	4,134,576	3,007,252	67,044,576	5,477,141
1866	21,276,000	988,265	39,088,000	1,511,338	4,273,842	2,947,737	64,637,842	5,447,340
1867	22,303,000	1,000,465	39,258,000	1,480,471	4,470,000	3,159,015	66,031,000	5,659,951
1868	22,650,000	989,925	39,389,000	1,491,227	4,651,804	3,210,569	66,690,804	5,691,721
1869	22,424,000	994,360	41,792,000	1,581,795	4,944,600	3,541,476	69,160,000	6,117,640
1870	21,529,000	979,915	43,555,000	1,577,884	4,996,210	3,597,552	72,080,210	6,155,354
1871	20,191,000	967,184	40,870,000	1,605,914	5,421,415	3,919,422	66,482,415	5,892,550
1872	20,324,000	998,761	44,514,000	1,579,432	5,669,627	4,048,869	70,507,627	6,094,962
1873	21,033,000	972,510	45,560,000	1,621,792	6,008,807	4,608,951	72,610,807	7,203,256
1874	20,330,000	1,007,652	45,737,000	1,669,363	7,329,994	4,934,767	73,405,994	7,610,782
1875	19,349,000	1,022,534	44,681,000	1,672,374	6,884,841	5,076,983	70,854,841	7,771,801
1876	20,030,000	991,504	45,233,000	1,699,899	7,250,069	4,888,054	72,503,069	7,582,447
1877	19,922,000	988,283	46,439,000	1,777,997	7,767,458	5,151,107	74,127,458	7,917,367

NEWSPAPERS AND PERIODICALS IN THE UNITED STATES, 1850-1877.

[From the Official Returns of the U. S. Census for 1850, 1860, and 1870, and from Rowell's Newspaper Directory for 1877.]

STATES AND TERRITORIES.	1850.		1860.		1870.		1877.
	No.	Circulation.	No.	Circulation.	No.	Circulation.	No. of Periodicals.
1 Alabama	60	34,282	96	93,595	89	91,165	86
2 Arizona					1	280	4
3 Arkansas	9	7,250	37	39,812	56	29,830	65
4 California	7	4,619	121	229,898	201	491,903	250
5 Colorado					14	12,750	49
6 Connecticut	46	52,670	55	95,536	71	203,725	111
7 Dakota					3	1,652	17
8 Delaware	10	7,500	14	16,144	17	20,860	23
9 Dist. of Columbia	18	100,073	13	69,510	22	81,400	26
10 Florida	10	5,750	22	15,500	23	10,545	30
11 Georgia	51	64,155	105	180,972	110	150,987	137
12 Idaho					6	2,750	9
13 Illinois	107	88,050	286	356,150	505	1,722,541	709
14 Indiana	107	63,138	186	159,381	293	363,542	357
15 Iowa	29	22,500	130	89,240	233	219,090	401
16 Kansas			27	21,920	97	96,803	170
17 Kentucky	62	79,868	77	179,597	89	197,130	184
18 Louisiana	55	80,288	81	120,650	92	84,165	86
19 Maine	49	63,430	70	126,169	65	170,690	86
20 Maryland	68	124,779	57	122,244	88	235,450	110
21 Massachusetts	209	718,221	222	1,368,960	259	1,692,124	329
22 Michigan	58	52,690	118	128,848	211	253,774	306
23 Minnesota			49	32,554	95	110,778	146
24 Mississippi	50	30,535	73	88,737	111	71,868	92
25 Missouri	61	70,235	173	354,007	279	522,866	370
26 Montana					10	19,580	10
27 Nebraska			14	9,750	42	31,600	109
28 Nevada					12	11,300	24
29 New Hampshire	38	60,226	20	19,700	51	173,919	66
30 New Jersey	51	44,521	90	162,016	122	205,500	173
31 New Mexico	2	1,150	2	1,150	5	1,525	7
32 New York	428	1,624,756	542	6,034,636	835	7,561,497	1,043
33 North Carolina	51	35,252	74	79,874	64	64,820	89
34 Ohio	261	339,463	340	1,121,682	395	1,388,367	584
35 Oregon	2	1,134	16	27,620	35	45,750	44
36 Pennsylvania	310	984,777	367	1,432,695	540	3,419,765	704
37 Rhode Island	19	24,472	26	49,600	82	82,050	29
38 South Carolina	46	53,743	45	53,870	55	80,900	72
39 Tennessee	50	67,672	83	176,008	91	225,952	134
40 Texas	34	18,205	89	108,038	112	55,250	181
41 Utah			2	6,300	10	14,250	9
42 Vermont	35	45,061	31	47,415	47	71,390	63
43 Virginia (a)	87	87,768	139	301,622	114	143,840	125
44 Washington			4	2,350	14	6,785	18
45 West Virginia (a)					59	54,432	81
46 Wisconsin	46	33,015	155	139,145	190	243,385	268
47 Wyoming					6	1,950	5
Total	2,526	5,142,177	4,051	13,663,409	5,871	20,842,475	7,941

(a) In 1850 and 1860 Virginia included West Virginia.

POPULATION OF THE UNITED STATES

STATES AND TERRITORIES.	1790.		1800.		1810.		1820.	
The United States...		3,929,214		5,306,483		7,239,881		9,633,822
The States		3,929,214		5,294,390		7,215,858		9,600,783
1 Alabama...............							19	127,901
2 Arkansas.............							25	14,255
3 California............								
4 Connecticut...........	8	237,946	8	251,002	9	261,942	14	275,148
5 Delaware.............	16	59,096	17	64,273	19	72,674	22	72,749
6 Florida...								
7 Georgia..............	13	82,548	12	162,686	11	252,433	11	340,985
8 Illinois					23	12,282	24	55,162
9 Indiana..............			20	5,641	21	24,520	18	147,178
10 Iowa.................								
11 Kansas......								
12 Kentucky	14	73,677	9	220,955	7	406,511	6	564,135
13 Louisiana............					18	76,556	17	152,923
14 Maine...............	11	96,540	14	151,719	14	228,705	12	298,269
15 Maryland............	6	319,728	7	341,548	8	380,546	10	407,350
16 Massachusetts........	4	378,787	5	422,845	5	472,040	7	523,159
17 Michigan.............					24	4,762	26	8,765
18 Minnesota............								
19 Mississippi...........			19	8,850	20	40,352	21	75,448
20 Missouri.............					22	20,845	23	66,557
21 Nebraska..								
22 Nevada...............								
23 New Hampshire.......	10	141,885	11	183,858	16	214,460	15	244,022
24 New Jersey...........	9	184,139	10	211,149	12	245,562	13	277,426
25 New York............	5	340,120	3	589,051	2	959,049	1	1,372,111
26 North Carolina.......	3	393,751	4	478,103	4	555,500	4	638,829
27 Ohio.................			18	45,365	13	230,760	5	581,295
28 Oregon...............								
29 Pennsylvania	2	434,373	2	602,365	3	810,091	3	1,047,507
30 Rhode Island........ .	15	68,825	16	69,122	17	76,931	20	83,015
31 South Carolina........	7	249,073	6	345,591	6	415,115	8	502,741
32 Tennessee............	17	35,691	15	105,602	10	261,727	9	422,771
33 Texas								
34 Vermont...	12	85,425	13	154,465	15	217,895	16	235,966
35 Virginia	1	747,610	1	880,200	1	974,600	2	1,065,116
36 West Virginia....								
37 Wisconsin............								
The States.........		3,929,214		5,294,390		7,215,858		9,600,783
1 Arizona...............								
2 Colorado.............								
3 Dakota..								
4 District of Columbia..			1	14,093	1	24,023	1	33,039
5 Idaho.................								
6 Montana.............								
7 New Mexico..........								
8 Utah.................								
9 Washington..........								
10 Wyoming.............								
The Territories.....				14,093		24,023		33,039
Total population....		3,929,214		5,306,483		7,239,881		9,633,822
				Increase per cent, 1790-1800, 35.10		Increase per cent, 1801 10, 56.38		Increase per cent, 1810-20, 33.06

NOTE.—The narrow column under each censu* year shows the order of the

AT EACH CENSUS, 1790-1870.

STATES AND TERRITORIES.	1830.	1840.	1850.	1860.	1870.
The United States	12,866,020	17,069,453	23,191,876	31,443,321	38,558,371
The States........	12,820,868	17,019,641	23,067,262	31,183,744	38,115,641
Alabama............	15	309,527 12	590,756 12	771,623 13	964,201 16	996,092
Arkansas	27	30,388 25	97,574 26	209,897 25	435,450 26	484,471
California..........	..	29	92,597 26	379,994 24	560,247
Connecticut........	16	297,675 20	300,078 21	370,792 24	460,147 25	537,454
Delaware...........	24	76,748 36	78,085 30	91,532 32	112,216 34	125,015
Florida............	25	34,730 27	54,477 31	87,445 31	140,424 33	187,748
Georgia	10	516,823 9	691,392 9	906,185 11	1,057,286 12	1,184,109
Illinois............	20	157,445 14	476,183 11	851,470 4	1,711,951 4	2,589,891
Indiana............	13	343,031 10	685,866 7	988,416 6	1,350,428 6	1,680,637
Iowa..............	..	 28	43,112 27	192,214 20	674,913 11	1,194,020
Kansas............				33	107,206 29	364,399
Kentucky..........	6	687,917 6	779,828 8	982,405 9	1,155,684 8	1,321,011
Louisiana.........	19	215,739 19	352,411 18	517,762 17	708,002 21	726,915
Maine	12	399,455 13	501,793 16	583,169 22	628,279 23	626,915
Maryland..	11	447,040 15	470,019 17	583,034 19	687,049 20	780,894
Massachusetts......	8	610,408 8	737,699 6	994,514 7	1,231,066 7	1,457,351
Michigan	26	31,639 23	212,267 20	397,654 16	749,113 13	1,184,059
Minnesota.........	..			33	6,077 30	172,023 28	439,706
Mississippi........	22	136,621 17	375,651 15	606,526 14	791,305 18	827,922
Missouri	21	140,455 16	383,702 13	682,044 8	1,182,012 5	1,721,205
Nebraska..........					35	28,841 35	122,993
Nevada............					36	6,857 37	42,491
New Hampshire....	18	269,328 22	284,574 22	317,976 27	326,073 31	318,300
New Jersey........	14	320,823 18	373,306 19	489,555 21	672,035 17	906,096
New York..........	1	1,918,608 1	2,428,921 1	3,097,394 1	3,880,735 1	4,382,759
North Carolina.....	5	737,987 7	753,419 10	869,039 12	992,622 14	1,071,361
Ohio..............	4	937,903 3	1,519,467 3	1,980,359 3	2,339,511 3	2,665,260
Oregon............	..			32	13,294 34	52,465 36	90,923
Pennsylvania.......	2	1,348,233 2	1,724,033 2	2,311,786 2	2,906,215 2	3,521,951
Rhode Island......	23	97,199 24	108,830 28	147,545 29	174,620 32	217,353
South Carolina.....	9	581,185 11	594,398 14	668,507 18	703,706 22	705,606
Tennessee.........	7	681,904 5	829,210 5	1,002,717 10	1,109,801 9	1,258,520
Texas.............	..			25	212,592 23	604,215 19	818,579
Vermont...........	17	280,652 21	291,948 23	314,120 28	315,098 30	330,551
Virginia	3	1,211,405 4	1,239,797 4	1,421,661 5	1,596,318 10	1,225,163
West Virginia.....	..	....				27	442,014
Wisconsin	..	29	30,945 24	305,391 15	775,881 15	1,054,670
The States.......	12,820,868	17,019,641	23,067,262	31,183,744	38,115,641
Arizona...........					9	9,658
Colorado..........				4	34,277 4	39,864
Dakota............				6	4,837 8	14,181
Dist. of Columbia...	1	39,834 1	43,712 2	51,687 2	75,080 1	131,700
Idaho.............					7	14,999
Montana...........					6	20,595
New Mexico.			1	61,547 1	93,516 2	91,874
Utah..............			3	11,380 3	40,273 3	86,786
Washington........				5	11,594 5	23,955
Wyoming..........					10	9,118
The Territories ..	39,834	43,712	124,614	259,577	442,730
Total population.	12,866,020	17,069,453	23,191,876	31,443,321	28,558,371
	Increase per cent, 1820-30, 32.51	Increase per cent. 1830-40, 83.52	Increase per cent, 1840-50, 35.83	Increase per cent, 1850-60, 35.11	Increase per cent, 1860-70, 22.65

States and Territories when arranged according to magnitude of population.

POPULATION OF THE UNITED STATES IN 1870.

[From the Official Returns of the Ninth Census.]

STATES AND TERRITORIES.	AGGREGATE	WHITE.	COLORED.	CHINESE.	INDIANS (ESTIMATED).
1 Alabama	996,992	521,384	475,510		93
2 Arkansas	484,471	362,115	122,169	98	89
3 California	582,031	499,424	4,272	49,310	29,025
4 Connecticut	537,454	527,549	9,668	2	235
5 Delaware	125,015	102,221	22,794		
6 Florida	188,248	96,057	91,689		502
7 Georgia	1,184,109	638,926	545,142	1	40
8 Illinois	2,539,891	2,511,096	28,762	1	32
9 Indiana	1,680,637	1,655,837	24,560		240
10 Iowa	1,194,320	1,188,207	5,762	3	348
11 Kansas	373,399	346,377	17,108		9,814
12 Kentucky	1,321,011	1,098,692	222,210	1	108
13 Louisiana	726,915	362,065	364,210	71	569
14 Maine	626,915	624,809	1,606	1	499
15 Maryland	780,894	605,497	175,391	2	4
16 Massachusetts	1,457,351	1,443,156	13,947	97	151
17 Michigan	1,187,234	1,167,282	11,849	2	8,101
18 Minnesota	446,056	438,257	759		7,040
19 Mississippi	827,922	382,896	444,201	16	800
20 Missouri	1,721,295	1,603,146	118,071	3	75
21 Nebraska	129,322	122,117	789		6,416
22 Nevada	59,711	38,959	357	3,152	16,243
23 New Hampshire	318,300	317,697	580		23
24 New Jersey	906,096	875,407	30,658	15	16
25 New York	4,337,464	4,330,210	52,081	29	5,144
26 North Carolina	1,071,361	678,470	391,650		1,241
27 Ohio	2,665,260	2,601,946	63,213	1	100
28 Oregon	101,883	86,929	346	3,330	11,378
29 Pennsylvania	3,522,050	3,456,609	65,294	14	133
30 Rhode Island	217,353	212,219	4,980		154
31 South Carolina	705,606	289,667	415,814	1	124
32 Tennessee	1,258,520	936,119	322,331		70
33 Texas	818,899	564,700	253,475	25	699
34 Vermont	330,551	329,613	924		14
35 Virginia	1,225,163	712,089	512,841	4	229
36 West Virginia	442,014	424,033	17,980		1
37 Wisconsin	1,064,985	1,051,351	2,113		11,521
The States	38,205,598	33,203,128	4,835,106	56,179	111,185
1 Alaska	70,461	461			70,000
2 Arizona	41,710	9,581	26	20	32,033
3 Colorado	47,164	39,221	456	7	7,480
4 Dakota	40,501	12,887	94		27,520
5 District of Columbia	131,700	88,278	43,404	3	15
6 Idaho	20,593	10,618	60	4,274	5,631
7 Indian Country	68,152	2,407	6,378		59,367
8 Montana	39,895	18,306	183	1,919	19,457
9 New Mexico	111,303	90,393	172		20,733
10 Utah	99,551	86,044	118	445	12,974
11 Washington	37,432	22,195	207	231	14,793
12 Wyoming	11,518	8,726	183	143	2,466
The Territories	720,000	389,117	51,281	7,075	272,527
Total in United States	38,925,598	33,592,345	4,886,387	63,254	383,712

NOTE.—The above figures of population vary from other tables given in the Census of 1870 by including in the aggregate the population of Alaska (estimated), and the Indian population (partly estimated and partly enumerated). No provision is made by law for taking the census of Indians not taxed, and the Superintendent of the Census therefore caused careful estimates to be made throughout the Indian agencies, and the result has been added to the enumerated population. This increases the aggregate population of the United States in 1870 from 38,558,371 (as in most of the tables) to 38,925,598.

POPULATION OF THE UNITED STATES, AS NATIVE, FOREIGN-BORN, AND OF FOREIGN PARENTAGE.

[From the Official Returns of the United States Census of 1870.]

STATES AND TERRITORIES.	TOTAL POPULATION.	NATIVE.	FOREIGN-BORN.	HAVING ONE OR BOTH PARENTS FOREIGN-BORN.
1 Alabama....................	996,992	987,030	9,962	21,844
2 Arkansas............	484,471	479,445	5,026	10,617
3 California	560,247	350,416	209,831	323,507
4 Connecticut................	537,454	423,815	113,639	203,650
5 Delaware	125,015	115,879	9,136	20,361
6 Florida	187,748	182,781	4,967	9,295
7 Georgia........	1,184,109	1,172,982	11,127	23,814
8 Illinois................	2,539,891	2,024,093	515,198	986,035
9 Indiana................	1,680,637	1,539,163	141,474	341,001
10 Iowa.....	1,194,020	989,328	204,692	416,139
11 Kansas	364,399	316,007	48,392	87,211
12 Kentucky................	1,321,011	1,257,613	63,398	142,720
13 Louisiana................	726,915	665,088	61,827	132,011
14 Maine	626,915	578,034	48,881	91,651
15 Maryland................	780,894	697,482	83,412	181,362
16 Massachusetts..............	1,457,351	1,104,032	353,319	626,211
17 Michigan..................	1,184,059	916,049	268,010	488,159
18 Minnesota	439,706	279,009	160,697	285,516
19 Mississippi..................	827,922	816,731	11,191	18,756
20 Missouri	1,721,295	1,499,028	222,267	465,125
21 Nebraska..................	122,993	92,245	30,748	50,017
22 Nevada....................	42,491	23,690	18,801	25,117
23 New Hampshire.............	318,300	288,689	29,611	41,592
24 New Jersey.................	906,096	717,153	188,943	350,316
25 New York................	4,382,759	3,244,406	1,138,353	2,225,627
26 North Carolina.............	1,071,361	1,068,332	3,029	6,464
27 Ohio....	2,665,260	2,292,767	372,493	849,815
28 Oregon.....................	90,923	79,323	11,600	20,705
29 Pennsylvania..............	3,521,951	2,976,642	545,309	1,151,208
30 Rhode Island..............	217,353	161,957	55,396	95,000
31 South Carolina............	705,606	697,532	8,074	16,449
32 Tennessee..................	1,258,520	1,239,204	19,316	36,326
33 Texas	818,579	756,168	62,411	107,327
34 Vermont................	330,551	283,396	47,155	83,615
35 Virginia.................	1,225,163	1,211,409	13,754	80,794
36 West Virginia..............	442,014	424,923	17,091	46,204
37 Wisconsin	1,054,670	690,171	364,499	717,832
The States...............	38,115,641	32,642,612	5,473,029	10,732,483
1 Arizona.......	9,658	3,849	5,809	6,766
2 Colorado....................	39,864	33,265	6,599	10,707
3 Dakota....................	14,181	9,366	4,815	7,319
4 District of Columbia.......	131,700	115,446	16,254	34,106
5 Idaho.....................	14,909	7,114	7,895	9,305
6 Montana	20,595	12,616	7,979	10,246
7 New Mexico.................	91,874	86,254	5,620	8,677
8 Utah.......................	86,786	56,084	30,702	59,024
9 Washington	23,955	18,931	5,024	8,382
10 Wyoming....................	9,118	5,605	3,513	5,000
The Territories..........	442,730	348,530	94,200	159,533
Total Population	38,558,371	32,991,142	5,567,229	10,892,015

THE NATURAL MILITIA, WITH THE TOTAL MALE POPULATION—1870.

[From the Official Returns of the United States Census, 1870.]

STATES AND TERRITORIES.	TOTAL MALE.	18 TO 45—MALE.				
		All Classes.	Native.	Foreign-born.	White.	Colored.
The United States.	19,493,565	7,570,487	5,697,085	1,873,402	6,655,811	861,164
1 Alabama	483,738	168,986	165,045	3,941	88,175	80,794
2 Arizona	6,887	5,157	2,051	3,106	5,115	17
3 Arkansas	248,261	94,873	92,037	2,836	70,253	24,507
4 California	349,479	194,935	77,828	117,107	154,200	1,264
5 Colorado	24,820	15,166	10,955	4,211	14,936	204
6 Connecticut	265,270	109,881	71,349	38,532	107,631	2,207
7 Dakota	8,878	5,301	2,808	2,493	5,071	32
8 Delaware	62,628	24,018	21,097	2,921	19,593	4,425
9 Dist. of Columbia	62,192	26,824	21,681	5,143	18,486	8,323
10 Florida	94,548	34,539	32,704	1,835	17,900	16,633
11 Georgia	578,955	202,573	198,265	4,308	108,711	93,832
12 Idaho	12,184	9,431	3,288	6,143	5,679	34
13 Illinois	1,316,537	525,873	346,564	179,309	518,924	6,911
14 Indiana	857,994	319,658	274,648	45,010	314,329	5,294
15 Iowa	625,917	240,769	173,060	67,709	239,331	1,425
16 Kansas	202,224	95,002	73,067	21,935	91,258	3,569
17 Kentucky	665,075	239,483	217,834	21,649	202,093	37,379
18 Louisiana	362,165	136,753	115,851	20,902	70,401	66,158
19 Maine	313,103	118,940	105,023	13,917	118,403	433
20 Maryland	384,984	144,695	121,004	23,691	112,613	32,079
21 Massachusetts	703,779	298,767	191,788	106,979	295,275	3,435
22 Michigan	617,745	252,821	165,088	87,733	249,300	2,640
23 Minnesota	235,290	94,238	40,808	53,430	93,848	258
24 Mississippi	413,421	149,698	144,574	5,124	72,505	77,069
25 Missouri	896,347	352,998	267,450	85,539	331,304	21,680
26 Montana	16,771	12,418	6,935	5,483	11,531	101
27 Nebraska	70,425	35,677	22,257	13,420	35,365	302
28 Nevada	32,379	24,762	11,109	13,653	22,082	154
29 New Hampshire	155,640	60,684	51,732	8,952	60,504	175
30 New Jersey	419,072	180,987	118,871	62,116	174,066	6,307
31 New Mexico	47,185	20,070	17,300	2,764	19,876	83
32 New York	2,163,229	881,500	527,820	353,680	869,403	11,988
33 North Carolina	518,704	174,825	173,610	1,215	110,085	64,534
34 Ohio	1,337,550	501,750	387,360	114,390	488,547	13,180
35 Oregon	53,131	23,959	16,837	7,122	20,964	119
36 Pennsylvania	1,758,499	679,506	506,438	173,068	665,704	13,791
37 Rhode Island	104,756	44,377	28,648	15,729	43,187	1,165
38 South Carolina	343,902	120,151	117,545	2,606	49,721	70,407
39 Tennessee	623,347	222,903	214,698	8,210	167,454	55,430
40 Texas	423,557	158,765	136,894	21,871	113,756	44,894
41 Utah	44,121	14,608	5,971	8,632	14,173	33
42 Vermont	165,721	62,459	48,479	13,980	62,206	248
43 Virginia	597,058	206,658	202,072	4,586	123,194	83,484
44 Washington	14,990	7,835	4,701	3,134	7,350	62
45 West Virginia	222,843	76,832	71,967	4,865	73,492	3,340
46 Wisconsin	544,880	192,331	86,593	105,738	191,521	603
47 Wyoming	7,219	6,056	3,371	2,685	5,816	109
Totals	19,493,565	7,570,487	5,697,085	1,873,402	6,655,811	861,164

NOTE.—There are included in "all classes" of males from the age of 18 to 45 inclusive, 49,663 Chinese and 4916 Indians.

CITIZENSHIP, WITH THE TOTAL MALE POPULATION— 1870.

[From the Official Returns of the United States Census, 1870.]

STATES AND TERRITORIES.	TOTAL MALE.	MALES 21 YEARS AND UPWARD.					21 AND UPWARD
		All Classes.	White.	Colored.	Chinese.	Indian.	Male Citizens.
The United States	19,493,565	9,439,206	8,353,719	1,082,475	47,531	5,481	8,425,941
1 Alabama	488,738	203,315	105,474	97,823	.....	18	202,046
2 Arizona	6,897	5,353	5,311	18	19	5	3,397
3 Arkansas	248,261	104,083	77,195	26,789	63	16	100,408
4 California	349,479	227,256	186,823	1,731	36,890	1,812	145,802
5 Colorado	24,820	16,294	16,083	197	6	8	15,515
6 Connecticut	265,270	150,415	147,659	2,700	.....	56	127,490
7 Dakota	8,878	5,724	5,496	28	.....	200	5,234
8 Delaware	62,628	30,035	24,811	5,224	.....	.....	28,207
9 Dist. of Columbia	62,192	33,320	23,178	10,143	1	7	31,622
10 Florida	94,548	39,907	21,064	18,842	.....	1	38,854
11 Georgia	578,955	237,640	129,665	107,962	1	12	234,919
12 Idaho	12,184	10,313	6,501	38	3,766	8	5,557
13 Illinois	1,316,537	625,139	617,435	7,694	1	9	542,883
14 Indiana	857,904	388,231	382,070	6,113	.....	48	376,780
15 Iowa	625,917	290,717	289,162	1,542	1	11	255,802
16 Kansas	202,224	105,671	101,480	3,985	.....	206	99,069
17 Kentucky	665,675	289,471	245,133	44,321	.....	17	282,305
18 Louisiana	362,105	174,187	87,066	86,913	68	140	159,001
19 Maine	313,103	169,821	169,192	497	1	131	153,160
20 Maryland	384,984	184,742	145,619	39,120	1	2	169,845
21 Massachusetts	703,779	398,157	394,031	4,073	20	33	312,770
22 Michigan	617,745	315,937	311,712	3,130	2	1,093	274,459
23 Minnesota	235,299	114,739	114,344	246	.....	149	75,274
24 Mississippi	413,421	174,845	84,784	89,926	15	120	169,737
25 Missouri	896,347	408,206	384,314	23,882	2	8	380,235
26 Montana	16,771	13,424	12,545	108	742	29	11,523
27 Nebraska	70,425	39,080	38,782	290	.....	8	36,169
28 Nevada	32,379	26,920	24,245	203	2,467	5	18,652
29 New Hampshire	155,640	91,016	90,834	176	.....	6	83,361
30 New Jersey	449,672	231,862	223,983	7,870	5	4	194,100
31 New Mexico	47,135	23,332	23,176	85	.....	71	22,442
32 New York	2,163,229	1,158,901	1,144,165	14,586	23	127	961,587
33 North Carolina	518,704	217,813	139,535	78,019	.....	250	214,224
34 Ohio	1,337,550	640,820	625,176	15,614	1	29	592,850
35 Oregon	53,131	28,616	25,640	143	2,789	44	24,608
36 Pennsylvania	1,758,499	865,883	848,790	17,072	9	12	776,345
37 Rhode Island	104,756	58,752	57,312	1,404	.....	36	43,096
38 South Carolina	343,902	148,052	62,547	85,475	1	29	146,614
39 Tennessee	623,347	263,200	199,056	64,131	.....	13	259,016
40 Texas	423,557	184,004	132,390	51,575	14	115	169,215
41 Utah	44,121	18,042	17,654	36	316	36	10,147
42 Vermont	165,721	90,806	90,522	278	.....	6	74,867
43 Virginia	507,058	269,242	161,500	107,691	4	47	266,680
44 Washington	14,990	9,241	8,750	67	185	239	7,902
45 West Virginia	222,843	95,317	91,345	3,972	.....	.....	93,435
46 Wisconsin	544,896	255,159	254,262	642	.....	255	203,077
47 Wyoming	7,219	6,107	5,908	101	97	1	5,297
Totals	19,493,565	9,439,206	8,353,719	1,082,475	47,531	5,481	8,425,941

NOTE.—The last column on the right indicates the total number of citizens under the Constitution, born or naturalized in the United States, who have reached the age qualifying them for the right of suffrage.

ILLITERACY BY STATES AND TERRITORIES: DISTINGUISHED INTO WHITE AND COLORED, NATIVE AND FOREIGN-BORN.

[Compiled from the Census of the United States for 1870.]

STATES AND TERRITORIES.	TOTAL POPULATION, 1870.	CANNOT WRITE.					CANNOT READ.
		White. 10 years and upward.	Colored. 10 years and upward.	Native. 10 years and upward.	Foreign Born. 10 years and upward.	Total. 10 years and upward.	Total. 10 years and upward.
1 Alabama........	996,992	92,059	290,898	382,142	870	383,012	349,771
2 Arkansas........	484,471	64,095	68,533	133,043	296	133,339	111,790
3 California.......	560,247	26,158	586	9,520	22,196	31,716	24,877
4 Connecticut......	537,454	27,913	1,675	5,678	23,938	29,616	19,680
5 Delaware........	125,015	11,280	11,820	20,631	2,469	23,100	19,356
6 Florida..........	187,748	18,904	52,894	71,235	568	71,803	66,238
7 Georgia.........	1,184,109	124,939	333,637	467,503	1,090	468,593	418,553
8 Illinois..........	2,539,891	123,624	9,950	90,595	42,989	133,584	86,368
9 Indiana.........	1,680,637	120,761	8,258	113,185	13,939	127,124	76,634
10 Iowa	1,191,792	44,145	1,524	24,979	20,602	45,671	24,115
11 Kansas	364,399	16,978	7,213	20,449	4,101	24,550	16,369
12 Kentucky.......	1,321,011	201,077	131,050	324,945	7,231	332,176	249,567
13 Louisiana	726,915	50,749	224,993	268,773	7,385	276,158	257,184
14 Maine...........	626,915	18,754	171	7,986	11,066	19,052	13,486
15 Maryland.......	730,894	46,792	88,703	126,907	8,592	135,499	114,100
16 Massachusetts...	1,457,351	95,576	2,148	7,912	89,830	97,742	74,935
17 Michigan	1,184,059	48,649	2,655	22,547	30,580	53,127	34,613
18 Minnesota......	439,706	23,941	102	5,558	18,855	24,413	12,747
19 Mississippi......	827,922	48,028	264,902	312,483	827	313,310	291,718
20 Missouri.........	1,721,295	161,763	60,622	206,827	15,584	222,411	146,771
21 Nebraska	122,993	4,630	205	3,552	1,309	4,861	2,365
22 Nevada	42,491	653	21	98	774	872	727
23 New Hampshire.	318,300	10,131	95	1,992	7,934	9,926	7,618
24 New Jersey.....	906,096	46,386	8,297	29,726	24,961	54,687	37,057
25 New York......	4,382,759	228,424	10,730	70,702	168,569	239,271	163,501
26 North Carolina..	1,071,361	166,397	230,606	397,573	117	397,690	339,789
27 Ohio............	2,665,260	142,383	20,766	134,102	39,070	173,172	92,720
28 Oregon	90,923	2,411	96	3,003	1,424	4,427	2,609
29 Pennsylvania.. .	3,521,791	206,458	15,893	126,803	95,553	222,356	131,728
30 Rhode Island....	217,353	20,031	870	4,444	17,477	21,921	15,416
31 South Carolina......	705,606	55,167	235,164	289,726	653	290,379	265,892
32 Tennessee......	1,258,520	178,727	185,952	362,935	1,742	364,697	290,549
33 Texas...........	818,579	70,895	150,617	203,334	18,369	221,703	199,423
34 Vermont........	330,551	17,584	116	3,902	13,804	17,706	15,185
35 Virginia	1,225,163	123,538	322,236	444,623	1,270	445,898	390,913
36 West Virginia...	442,014	71,493	9,997	78,389	3,101	81,490	48,802
37 Wisconsin.......	1,054,670	54,845	460	14,113	41,328	55,441	35,031
The States.....	38,115,641	776,158	2,765,370	4,791,935	760,553	5,552,488	4,438,206
1 Arizona.........	9,658	2,729	1	262	2,491	2,753	2,690
2 Colorado.	39,864	6,564	146	6,568	255	6,823	6,297
3 Dakota	14,181	914	31	758	805	1,563	1,249
4 Dist. of Columbia	131,700	4,876	23,843	26,501	2,218	28,719	22,845
5 Idaho...........	14,999	486	16	138	3,250	3,388	3,293
6 Montana	20,595	643	68	394	524	918	667
7 New Mexico.....	91,874	51,130	109	49,311	2,900	52,220	49,836
8 Utah............	86,786	7,097	22	3,334	4,029	7,363	2,513
9 Washington	23,955	823	34	804	503	1,307	1,018
10 Wyoming.......	9,118	481	49	266	336	602	453
The Territories	412,730	75,753	24,319	88,336	17,320	105,656	89,873
Total in the U.S.	38,558,371	2,851,911	2,780,689	4,880,271	777,873	5,658,144	4,528,081

NOTE.—The second column shows the white population of ten years and over who are unable to write, in each State and Territory, and for the whole United States; the sixth column sums up all classes and nativities over ten years who are unable to write; and the last column shows the aggregate of all classes and nativities over ten years who are unable to read.

TABLE OF THE INSANE, IDIOTIC, DEAF AND DUMB, AND BLIND, IN THE UNITED STATES, IN 1870.

STATES AND TERRITORIES.	Insane.	Idiotic.	Deaf and Dumb.	Blind.
The United States................	37,432	24,527	16,205	20,320
1 Alabama...........................	555	721	401	611
2 Arkansas..........................	161	289	265	333
3 California.........................	1,146	87	141	179
4 Connecticut.......................	772	341	475	252
5 Delaware..........................	65	69	61	68
6 Florida............................	20	100	48	88
7 Georgia...........................	634	871	326	740
8 Illinois............................	1,625	1,244	833	1,042
9 Indiana...........................	1,504	1,360	872	991
10 Iowa..............................	742	533	549	465
11 Kansas...........................	131	109	121	128
12 Kentucky.........................	1,245	1,141	723	978
13 Louisiana.........................	451	296	197	447
14 Maine............................	792	628	299	324
15 Maryland.........................	733	362	384	427
16 Massachusetts....................	2,662	778	538	761
17 Michigan..........................	814	613	455	418
18 Minnesota........................	302	134	166	103
19 Mississippi.......................	245	485	245	474
20 Missouri..........................	1,263	779	790	904
21 Nebraska.........................	28	25	55	22
22 Nevada...........................	2	2	4	4
23 New Hampshire..................	548	325	170	206
24 New Jersey.......................	918	436	231	317
25 New York.........................	6,353	2,486	1,783	2,213
26 North Carolina...................	779	976	619	835
27 Ohio..............................	3,414	2,338	1,339	1,306
28 Oregon...........................	122	55	23	35
29 Pennsylvania.....................	3,895	2,250	1,433	1,767
30 Rhode Island.....................	312	123	64	121
31 South Carolina...................	333	465	212	451
32 Tennessee........................	925	1,091	570	876
33 Texas............................	270	451	232	404
34 Vermont..........................	721	325	148	189
35 Virginia..........................	1,125	1,130	534	895
36 West Virginia....................	374	427	218	168
37 Wisconsin........................	846	560	459	400
1 Arizona...........................	1	....	....	1
2 Colorado..........................	12	3	4	26
3 Dakota............................	3	3	4	5
4 District of Columbia..............	479	50	134	78
5 Idaho.............................	1	1	1	4
6 Montana..........................	2	1	5	....
7 New Mexico.......................	50	46	48	159
8 Utah..............................	25	23	18	29
9 Washington.......................	23	5	6	5
10 Wyoming.........................	....	....	2	2
The United States................	37,432	24,527	16,205	20,320

THE ARMY OF THE UNITED STATES.

THE following facts are summarized from the Annual Report of the General of the Army, General W. T. Sherman, for the year 1877. The following is given as the "Return or actual strength" of the army up to the 12th of October, 1877, showing that at that date the regular army was composed of—

General officers, 11; general staff officers, 566; hospital stewards, 186; engineer battalion, 193; ordnance enlisted men, 346; enlisted men of staff corps, 731.

Ten regiments of cavalry: Officers, 430; enlisted men, 7,911—total cavalry, 8,350.

Five regiments of artillery: Officers, 284; enlisted men, 2,321—total, 2,605.

Twenty-five regiments of infantry: Officers, 877; enlisted men, 8,778—total infantry, 9,655.

Besides which there are reported as non-commissioned staff unattached to regiments, military academy, recruits unassigned, Indian scouts and prison-guard, amounting to 1,877 men; signal corps, 404; retired officers, 301; and captain of United States army by Act of Congress, 1. Aggregating officers and men, 24,501, of which the force available for war is made up of the cavalry, artillery, and infantry regiments, amounting to **20,610** officers and men, to which should be added the eleven general officers and the officers of the general staff serving with them, together with 570 Indian scouts.

For convenience and to fix responsibility, the country is divided into ten military departments, each of which is commanded by a brigadier-general, or by the senior colonel serving in the department, especially empowered by the President of the United States.

These departments are grouped into three geographical divisions, commanded by the lieutenant-general and by two of the major-generals.

There is also the Department of West Point, commanded by Major-General Schofield, which is somewhat exceptional in its nature, designed to give due importance to the Military Academy, and to vest the commanding general thereof with power to exercise all the functions necessary to insure perfect discipline and thorough administration.

		Entered the Army.
General of the Army	William T. Sherman	1840
Lieutenant-General	Philip H. Sheridan	1853
Major-Generals (limited by law to three)	Winfield S. Hancock	1844
	John M. Schofield	1853
	Irvin McDowell	1838
Brigadier-Generals (limited by law to six)	John Pope	1842
	Oliver O. Howard	1854
	Alfred H. Terry	1865
	Edward O. C. Ord	1839
	Christopher C. Augur	1843
	George Crook	1852
*Adjutant-General of the Army	Edward D. Townsend	1837
*Judge Advocate-General	William McKee Dunn	1864
*Quartermaster-General	Montgomery C. Meigs	1836
*Commissary-General	Robert Macfeely	1850
*Surgeon-General	Joseph K. Barnes	1840
*Paymaster-General	Benjamin Alvord	1833
*Chief of Engineers	Andrew A. Humphreys	1831
*Chief of Ordnance	Stephen V. Benét	1849
†Inspector-General	Randolph B. Marcy	1832
†Chief Signal Officer	Albert J. Myer	1854

NOTE.—The officers marked thus (*) have each the rank and pay of a brigadier-general; those marked thus (†) have the rank and pay of colonels.

PAY OF THE ARMY OF THE UNITED STATES.

[From the Official Army Register, 1877.]

GRADE.	Pay of Officers in Active Service. Yearly Pay.					Pay of Retired Officers. Yearly Pay.				
	First 5 years' service.	After 5 yrs' service.	After 10yrs' service.	After 15 yrs' service.	After 20yrs' service.	First 5 yrs' service.	After 5 yrs' service.	After 10yrs' service.	After 15yrs' service.	After 20yrs' service.
		10p.c.	20p.c.	30p.c.	40p.c.					
General	$13,500	......	......	......	......	......	......	......	......	......
Lieutenant-General	11,000	......	......	......	......	......	......	......	......	......
Major-General	7,500	......	......	......	......	$5,625	......	......	......	......
Brigadier-General	5,500	......	......	......	......	4,125	......	......	......	......
Colonel	3,500	$3,850	$4,200	*$4,500	*4,500	2,625	$2,887	$3,150	$3,375	$3,375
Lieutenant-Colonel	3,000	3,300	3,600	3,900	*4,000	2,250	2,475	2,700	2,925	3,000
Major	2,500	2,750	3,000	3,250	3,500	1,875	2,062	2,250	2,437	2,625
Captain, mounted	2,000	2,200	2,400	2,600	2,800	1,500	1,650	1,800	1,950	2,100
Captain, not mounted	1,800	1,980	2,160	2,340	2,520	1,350	1,485	1,620	1,755	1,890
Regimental Adjutant	1,800	1,980	2,160	2,340	2,520	......	......	......	......	......
Regimental Quartermast'r	1,800	1,980	2,160	2,340	2,520	......	......	......	......	......
1st Lieutenant, mounted	1,600	1,760	1,920	2,080	2,240	1,200	1,320	1,440	1,560	1,680
1st Lieutenant, not m't'd.	1,500	1,650	1,800	1,950	2,100	1,125	1,237	1,350	1,462	1,575
2d Lieutenant, mounted	1,500	1,650	1,800	1,950	2,100	1,125	1,237	1,350	1,462	1,575
2d Lieutenant, not m't'd.	1,400	1,540	1,680	1,820	1,960	1,050	1,155	1,260	1,365	1,470
Chaplain	1,500	1,650	1,800	1,950	2,100	1,350	1,485	1,620	1,755	1,890

* The maximum pay of colonels is limited to $4,500, and of lieutenant-colonels to $4,000.

QUARTERS, FUEL, AND FORAGE ALLOWED TO ARMY OFFICERS.

GRADE.	Rooms.		Cords of wood per month.		No. of Horses for which forage is allowed	Increased allowance from September to April, inclusive.		
	As quarters.	As kitchen.	May 1 to Sep. 1.	Sep. 1 to May 1.		Betw'n 36° and 43° N. Lat., one fourth.	North of 43° N. Lat., one third.	
General	......	......	......	......	$50 p.m.	....	....	$300 per month for quart'rs and fuel.
Lieutenant-General	5	1	1	5	$50 p.m.	1¼	1⅔	
Major-General	5	1	1	5	5	1¼	1⅔	
Brigadier-General	4	1	1	4	4	1	1⅓	
Colonel	4	1	1	4	2	1	1⅓	
Lieut.-Col. or Major	3	1	1	3½	2	⅞	1⅙	
Captain or Chaplain	2	1	¾	3	2	¾	1	
1st or 2d Lieutenant, mounted	1	1	½	2	2	½	⅔	
1st or 2d Lieutenant, not mounted	1	1	½	2	....	½	⅔	

NOTE.—The law provides that no allowances shall be made to officers in addition to their pay, except fuel, quarters, and forage furnished in kind.

Mileage at the rate of eight cents per mile is allowed for travel under orders.

The pay of cadets at the U. S. Military Academy, West Point, was placed at $540 per annum, by Act of Aug. 7th, 1876, instead of $500 and one ration *per diem* (equivalent to $609.50), by former laws.

The pay of privates runs from $156 ($13 a month and rations) for first two years, to $21 a month after twenty years, service.

UNITED STATES INTERNAL REVENUE TAXES.

[From the Revised Statutes of the United States, as amended in 1875.]

Ale, per bbl. of 31 gallons $1 00
Banks, on average amount of deposits, each month................... ₁/₂₄ of 1 per ct.
Banks, deposits, savings, etc., having no capital stock, per six months, ¼ of 1 per ct.
Banks, on capital, beyond the average amount invested in United States
  bonds, each month .... ₁/₂₄ of 1 per ct.
Banks, on average amount of circulation, each month................. ₁/₁₂ of 1 per ct.
Banks, on average amount of circulation, beyond 90 per cent of the capital,
  an additional tax each month .... ⅙ of 1 per ct.
Banks, on amount of notes of any person, State bank, or State banking
  association, used and paid out as circulation...........................10 per ct.
Beer, per bbl. of 31 gallons.. $1 00
Brandy, made from grapes, per gallon... 70
Brewers, special tax on.. .... 100 00
Cigars, manufacturers of, special tax.. 10 00
Cigars, of all descriptions, made of tobacco or any substitute therefor, per
  1000 .... 6 00
Cigars, imported, in addition to import duty to pay same as above.
Cigarettes, not weighing more than 3 lbs. per 1000, per 1000.................. 1 75
Cigarettes, weight exceeding 3 lbs. per 1000, per 1000........................ 6 00
Distillers, producing 100 bbls. or less (40 gallons of proof spirit to bbl.) per
  annum.......................... .... 400 00
Distillers, for each bbl. in excess of 100 bbls........... .... 4 00
Distillers, on each bbl. of 40 gallons in warehouse when act took effect, and
  when withdrawn.. 4 00
Distillers of brandy from grapes, peaches, and apples exclusively, producing
  less than 150 bbls. annually, special tax $50, and $4 per bbl. of 40 gallons.
Distillery, having aggregate capacity for mashing, etc., 20 bushels of grain
  per day, or less per day. 2 00
Distillery, in excess of 20 bushels of grain per day, for every 20 bushels, per
  day 2 00
Gas, coal, illuminating, product not above 200,000 cubic feet per month, per
  1000 cubic feet... 10
Gas, coal, when product exceeds 200,000, and does not exceed 500,000 cubic
  feet per month, per 1000 cubic feet. 15
Gas, coal, when product exceeds 500,000, and does not exceed 5,000,000 cubic
  feet per month, per 1000 cubic feet... 20
Gas, coal, when product exceeds 5,000,000 feet per month, per 1000 cubic feet 25
Lager beer, per bbl. of 31 gallons.. 1 00
Liquors, fermented, per bbl... 1 00
Liquors, distilled, per proof gallon... 90
Liquor dealers (wholesale) 100 00
Malt liquor dealers (wholesale) 50 00
Liquor dealers (retail), special tax... 25 00
Malt liquor dealers (retail)... 20 00
Liquors, dealers in, whose sales, including sales of all other merchandise,
  shall exceed $25,000, an additional tax for every $100 on sales of liquors
  in excess of such $25,000.. 1 00
Manufacturers of stills.. 50 00
Manufacturers of stills, for each still or worm made........................... 20 00
Porter, per bbl. of 31 gallons... 1 00
Rectifiers, special tax.. 200 00
Snuff, manufactured of tobacco, or any substitute, when prepared for use,
  per lb... 32
Snuff-flour, sold or removed, for use, per lb..................... 32
Spirits, distilled, per proof gallon... 90
Stamps, distillers', other than tax-paid stamps charged to collector, each.... 10
Tobacco, dealers in 5 00
Tobacco, manufacturers of... 10 00
Tobacco, dealers in leaf, wholesale 25 00
Tobacco, dealers in leaf, retail.................................... .... 500 00
Tobacco, dealers in leaf, for sales in excess of $1000, per dollar of excess .. 50

Tobacco, chewing, smoking, fine cut, cavendish, plug or twist, and twisted
by hand, or reduced from leaf, to be consumed, without the use of machine or instrument, and not pressed or sweetened, per lb................ $0 24
Tobacco, all other kinds not provided for, per lb.....   21
Tobacco pedlers, travelling with more than two horses, mules, or other ani-
mals (first class)........ ....   50 00
Tobacco pedlers, travelling with two horses, mules, or other animals
(second class)........ ....   25 00
Tobacco pedlers, travelling with one horse, mule, or other animal (third
class)... .. ..   15 00
Tobacco pedlers, travelling on foot, or by public conveyance (fourth class)..   10 00
Tobacco, snuff, and cigars, for immediate export, stamps for, each   10
Whiskey, per proof gallon...   90
Wines and champagne (imitation), not made from grapes, currants, rhu-
barb, or berries, grown in the United States, rectified or mixed, to be
sold as wine or any other name, per dozen bottles of more than a pint
and not more than a quart........... ....   2 40
Imitation wines, containing not more than one pint, per dozen bottles....   1 20

STAMP DUTIES.

Bank check, draft, or order for the payment of any sum of money whatsoever, drawn upon any bank, banker, or trust company, or for any sum exceeding $10, drawn upon any other person or persons, companies or cor-
porations, at sight, or on demand...2 cents.

MEDICINES OR PREPARATIONS.

Every packet, box, bottle, pot, vial, or other inclosure, containing any pills,
powders, tinctures, troches, or lozenges, syrups, cordials, bitters, ano-
dynes, tonics, plasters, liniments, salves, ointments, pastes, drops, waters,
essences, spirits, oils, or other preparations or compositions whatsoever,
made and sold, or removed for consumption and sale, by any person or
persons whatever, wherein the person making or preparing the same has,
or claims to have, any private formula or occult secret or art for the making or preparing the same, or has, or claims to have, any exclusive right
or title to the making or preparing the same, or which are prepared, ut-
tered, vended or exposed for sale under any letters-patent, or held out or
recommended to the public by the makers, venders, or proprietors thereof
as proprietary medicines, or as remedies or specifics for any disease, diseases, or affections whatever affecting the human or animal body, as follows : where such packet, box, bottle, vial, or other inclosure, with its
contents, shall not exceed, at the retail price or value, the sum of twenty-
five cents, one cent ....1 cent.
Where such packet, box, bottle, etc., with its contents, shall exceed the
retail price of 25 cents, and not exceed the retail price or value of 50
cents, two cents..2 cents.
Where such packet, box, bottle, etc., with its contents, shall exceed the
retail price of 50 cents, and shall not exceed the retail price of 75 cents,
three cents...3 cents.
Where such packet, box, bottle, etc., with its contents, shall exceed the
retail price of 75 cents, and shall not exceed the retail price or value of
$1, four cents... .... 4 cents.
Where such packet, box, bottle. etc., with its contents, shall exceed the
retail price of $1, for each and every 50 cents or fractional part thereof
over and above the $1, as before mentioned, an additional two cents.....2 cents.

PERFUMERY, COSMETICS, MATCHES, ETC.

Every packet, box, bottle, pot, vial, or other inclosure, containing any
essence, extract, toilet water, cosmetic, hair oil, pomade, hair dressing,
hair restorative, hair dye, tooth wash, dentifrice, tooth paste, aromatic
cachous, or any similar articles, by whatsoever name the same have been,
now are, or may hereafter be called, known, or distinguished, used or
applied, or to be used or applied as perfumes or applications to the hair,

UNITED STATES INTERNAL REVENUE TAXES—(Continued).

mouth, or skin, made, prepared, and sold or removed for consumption and sale in the United States, where such packet, box, bottle, pot, vial, or other inclosure, with its contents, shall not exceed, at retail price, the sum of 25 cents, one cent ....1 cent.
Where such packet, bottle, box, etc., with its contents, shall exceed the retail price of 25 cents, and shall not exceed the retail price of 50 cents, two cents........... ....2 cents.
Where such packet, box, bottle, etc., shall exceed the retail price of 50 cents, and shall not exceed the retail price or value of 75 cents, three cents ....3 cents.
Where such packet, box, bottle, etc., shall exceed the retail price of 75 cents, and shall not exceed the retail price or value of $1, four cents............4 cents.
Where such packet, box, bottle, etc., shall exceed the retail price of $1, for each and every 50 cents or fractional part thereof over and above the $1, as before mentioned, an additional two cents........... ....2 cents.
Friction matches, or lucifer matches, or other articles made in part of wood, and used for like purposes, in parcels or packages containing 100 matches or less, for each parcel or package, one cent................. ....1 cent.
When in parcels or packages containing more than 100 and not more than 200 matches, for each parcel or package, two cents...... ....2 cents.
And for every additional 100 matches, or fractional parts thereof, one cent.1 cent.
For wax tapers, double the rates upon friction or lucifer matches ; on cigar lights, made in part of wood, wax, glass, paper, or other materials, in parcels or packages containing 25 lights or less in each parcel or package, one cent............ ....1 cent.
When in parcels or packages containing more than 25 and not more than 50 lights, two cents...... ....2 cents.
For every additional 25 lights or fractional part of that number, one cent additional ....1 cent.

Note to Statistics of Manufactures in the United States, on p. 269.

The Superintendent of the Census of 1870 accompanied the tables of statistics relating to manufacturing industry with a statement as to their untrustworthy character, from which the following are extracts :

"The census returns of capital invested in manufactures are entirely untrustworthy and delusive. The inquiry is one of which it is not too much to say, that it ought never to be embraced in the schedules of the census ; not merely for the reason that the results are, and must remain, wholly worthless, but, also, because the inquiry in respect to capital creates more prejudice and arouses more opposition to the progress of the enumeration than all the other inquiries of the manufacturing schedule united. It is, in fact, the one question which manufacturers resent as needlessly obtrusive, while, at the same time, it is perhaps the one question in respect to their business which manufacturers, certainly the majority of them, could not answer to their own satisfaction, even if disposed. No man in business knows what he is worth—far less can say what portion of his estate is to be treated as capital.
"The aggregate amount of capital invested in manufactures in the United States as returned is $2,118,208,769. It is doubtful whether this sum represents one fourth of the capital actually contributing to the annual gross product of $4,232,325,442. It is a pity, and may almost be said to be a shame, that statistical information, in many respects, of high authority and accuracy, should be discredited by association with statements so flagrantly false, even to the least critical eye ; yet, as the manufacturing schedule annexed to the Act of 1850 requires this return, and as there is a vague popular notion that the statement of capital in this connection is of real and great importance (instead of being, as it is, at the best, of the least consequence), the Superintendent does not feel at liberty to withhold the results from publication ; but he feels not only authorized, but required by the facts of the case to brand them as he has here done, in order that no one may be deceived by the show of authority they present. Outgrown and ineffective as is the census law of 1850 in almost all particulars, it is nowhere so painfully and almost ludicrously inadequate as in the canvass of the national industry."

MANUFACTURES IN THE UNITED STATES IN 1870.

[Compiled from the Tables of the Ninth Census.]

STATES AND TERRITORIES.	No. of Establishments.	No. of Hands Employed	Capital Invested. Dollars.	Wages Paid. Dollars.	Value of Products. Dollars.
The United States.	252,148	2,053,996	2,118,208,769	775,584,343	4,232,325,442
1 Alabama.............	2,188	8,248	5,714,032	2,227,968	13,040,644
2 Arizona....	18	84	150,700	45,580	185,410
3 Arkansas.............	1,079	3,206	1,782,913	673,963	4,629,234
4 California............	3,984	25,392	39,728,202	13,136,722	66,594,556
5 Colorado...	256	876	2,835,605	528,221	2,852,820
6 Connecticut	5,128	69,523	95,281,278	38,987,187	161,065,474
7 Dakota..............	17	91	79,200	21,106	178,570
8 Delaware.............	800	9,710	10,839,093	3,692,195	16,791,382
9 District of Columbia.	952	4,685	5,021,925	2,007,600	9,292,173
10 Florida..............	659	2,749	1,679,930	989,592	4,685,403
11 Georgia.............	3,836	17,871	13,930,125	4,844,508	31,196,115
12 Idaho...............	101	265	742,300	112,372	1,047,624
13 Illinois.............	12,597	82,979	94,368,057	31,100,244	205,620,672
14 Indiana....	11,847	58,852	52,052,425	18,366,780	108,617,278
15 Iowa...............	6,566	25,032	22,420,183	6,803,292	46,534,322
16 Kansas	1,477	6,844	4,319,060	2,377,511	11,775,833
17 Kentucky....	5,390	30,636	29,277,809	9,444,524	54,625,809
18 Louisiana...........	2,557	30,071	18,313,974	4,593,470	24,161,005
19 Maine..............	5,550	49,180	39,796,190	14,282,205	79,497,521
20 Maryland...........	5,812	44,860	36,438,729	12,682,817	76,593,613
21 Massachusetts.......	13,212	279,380	231,677,862	118,051,896	553,912,508
22 Michigan...........	9,455	63,694	71,712,283	21,205,355	118,394,676
23 Minnesota..........	2,270	11,290	11,993,729	4,052,837	23,110,700
24 Mississippi.........	1,731	5,941	4,501,714	1,547,428	8,154,758
25 Missouri.......... ..	11,871	65,354	80,257,244	31,055,445	206,213,429
26 Montana...........	201	701	1,794,300	870,843	2,494,511
27 Nebraska...........	670	2,005	2,169,963	1,429,913	5,738,512
28 Nevada.............	330	2,859	5,127,790	2,498,473	15,870,539
29 New Hampshire.....	3,342	40,783	36,023,743	13,823,001	71,038,249
30 New Jersey.........	6,636	75,552	79,606,719	32,648,409	169,237,732
31 New Mexico....... ...	182	427	1,450,695	167,281	1,489,868
32 New York...........	36,206	351,800	366,994,320	142,466,758	785,194,651
33 North Carolina.....	3,642	13,622	8,140,473	2,195,711	19,021,827
34 Ohio................	22,773	137,202	141,923,964	49,066,488	269,713,610
35 Oregon....	969	2,884	4,376,849	1,120,173	6,877,387
36 Pennsylvania.......	37,200	319,487	406,821,845	127,976,594	711,894,344
37 Rhode Island........	1,850	49,417	66,557,322	19,354,256	111,418,354
38 South Carolina......	1,584	8,141	5,400,418	1,543,715	9,858,981
39 Tennessee..........	5,317	19,412	15,595,295	5,390,630	34,362,636
40 Texas..............	2,399	7,927	5,284,110	1,787,835	11,517,302
41 Utah...............	533	1,534	1,391,898	395,365	2,343,019
42 Vermont............	3,270	18,686	20,329,637	6,264,581	32,184,606
43 Virginia............	5,933	26,974	18,455,400	5,343,009	38,364,322
44 Washington.........	269	1,026	1,893,674	674,936	2,851,052
45 West Virginia.......	2,444	11,672	11,081,520	4,322,164	24,102,201
46 Wisconsin..........	7,013	43,910	41,981,872	13,575,642	77,214,326
47 Wyoming	32	502	889,400	347,578	765,424
Total—United States	252,148	2,053,996	2,118,208,769	775,584,343	4,232,325,442

PRINCIPAL CEREAL PRODUCTIONS OF THE UNITED STATES, 1870.

[From the Official Report of the Ninth Census, 1870.]

STATES AND TERRITORIES.	Wheat.	Indian Corn.	Oats.	Barley.	Rye.	Buckwheat.
	Bushels.	Bushels.	Bushels.	Bushels.	Bushels.	Bushels.
The U. S...	287,745,626	760,944,549	282,107,157	29,761,305	16,918,795	9,821,721
1 Alabama.........	1,055 048	16,977,948	770,866	5,174	18,977	141
2 Arizona..........	27,052	32,041	25	53,077	....	.....
3 Arkansas	741,736	13,382,145	522,777	1,921	27.645	226
4 California.........	16,676,702	1,221,222	1,757,507	8,783,490	26.275	21,928
5 Colorado.........	238,474	231,903	332,940	35,141	5,235	178
6 Connecticut......	33,144	1,570,364	1,114,595	26,458	289,057	148,155
7 Dakota....	170,662	183,140	114,327	4,118	....	179
8 Delaware	845,477	3,010,390	554,388	1,799	10.222	1,349
9 Dist. of Columbia.	3,782	28,020	8,500	....	3.724	7
10 Florida...	....	2,225,056	114,204	12	545	....
11 Georgia..........	2,127,017	17,646,459	1,904,601	5,640	82,519	403
12 Idaho....	75,640	5,750	100,119	72,316	1.756	....
13 Illinois...........	30,128,405	129,921,305	42,780,851	2,490,400	2,456,578	168,862
14 Indiana..........	27,747,222	51,094,533	8,590,409	356,902	437,468	80,231
15 Iowa.............	29,435,692	68,935,065	21,005,142	1,960,779	505,807	109,452
16 Kansas..........	2,391,198	17,025,525	4,097,925	98,405	85,207	27,826
17 Kentucky.........	5,723,704	50,091,006	6,620,103	238,496	1,108,933	3,443
18 Louisiana........	9,906	7,596,628	17,782	1,226	984	260
19 Maine...........	278,793	1,089,883	2,351,354	638,816	34.113	466,635
20 Maryland........	5,774,503	11,701,817	3,221,643	11.315	307.089	77,867
21 Massachusetts	31,618	1,397,807	797,664	133,071	239,227	58,049
22 Michigan........	16,265,773	14,086,238	8,954,466	834,558	144,509	436,755
23 Minnesota.......	18,866,073	4,743,117	10,678,261	1,032,034	78,088	52,438
24 Mississippi......	274,479	15,637,316	414,586	3,973	14,852	1,619
25 Missouri.........	14,315,926	66,034,075	16,578,313	269,240	559,532	36,252
26 Montana.........	181,184	390	149,367	85,756	1,141	998
27 Nebraska........	2,125,086	4,736,710	1,477,562	216,481	13,532	3,471
28 Nevada..........	223,866	9,660	55,916	295,452	310	935
29 New Hampshire ..	193,621	1,277,768	1,146,451	105,822	47,420	100,084
30 New Jersey......	2,301,433	8,745,384	4,000,830	8,283	566,775	353,933
31 New Mexico......	352,823	640,823	67,660	3,676	42	10
32 New York........	12,178,472	16,462,825	35,293,625	7,434,621	2,473,125	3,901,030
33 North Carolina...	2,859,879	18,454,215	3,220,105	3,186	352,006	20,109
34 Ohio.............	27,882,159	67,501,144	25,347,549	1,715,221	846,800	190,311
35 Oregon	2,340,746	72,138	2,029,909	210,736	8,890	1,645
36 Pennsylvania.....	19,672,967	34,702,006	36,478,585	529,562	3,577,641	2,532,173
37 Rhode Island.	784	311,957	157,010	33,559	20,214	1,444
38 South Carolina....	783,610	7,614.207	613,593	4,752	36,163	312
39 Tennessee	6,188,916	41,343,614	4,513,315	75,068	223,335	77,437
40 Texas........	415.112	20,554,538	762,663	41,351	28,521	44
41 Utah.............	558.473	95,557	65,630	49,117	1,312	178
42 Vermont..........	454,703	1,639,882	3,602,490	117.333	73,846	415,086
43 Virginia	7,398,787	17,649,304	6,857,555	7,259	582,261	43,075
44 Washington.......	217,043	21,781	255.169	55,787	4.153	316
45 West Virginia.....	2,483,543	8,197,865	2,413,749	50,363	277,746	82,916
46 Wisconsin	25,606,344	15,033,998	20,180,016	1,645,019	1,325,294	408,897
47 Wyoming.....	....	....	....	....	....	....
Total—U. S......	287,745,626	760,944,549	282,107,157	29,761,305	16,918,795	9,821,721

NOTE.—The production of the six cereals above named, at the two preceding censuses, was as follows :

	Wheat.	Indian Corn.	Oats.	Barley.	Rye.	Buckwheat.
	Bushels.	Bushels.	Bushels.	Bushels.	Bushels.	Bushels.
Census of 1850......	100,485,944	592,071,104	146,584,179	5,167,015	14,188,813	8,956,912
Census of 1860......	173,104,924	838,792,742	172,643,185	15,825,898	21,101,380	17,571,818

PRINCIPAL FIBROUS PRODUCTIONS OF THE UNITED STATES, 1870.

[From the Tables of the Ninth Census.]

STATES AND TERRITORIES.	Cotton.	Flax.	Hemp.	Silk Cocoons.	Wool.
	Bales.*	Pounds.	Tons.	Pounds.	Pounds.
The United States..	3,011,996	27,133,034	12,746	3,937	100,102,387
1 Alabama............	429,482	37			381,253
2 Arizona.............					679
3 Arkansas	247,068	420			214,784
4 California...........	34	31,740	200	3,587	11,391,743
5 Colorado					204,925
6 Connecticut.........		300			254,129
7 Dakota					8,810
8 Delaware...........		678			58,316
9 District of Columbia..					
10 Florida	29,780				37,562
11 Georgia.............	473,934	983		14	816,947
12 Idaho					3,415
13 Illinois.........	465	2,204,606	174		5,739,249
14 Indiana..............	3	37,771	21		5,029,023
15 Iowa................		695,518	4		2,967,043
16 Kansas.............	7	1,040	35		335,003
17 Kentucky...........	1,080	237,268	7,777	45	2,234,450
18 Louisiana...........	350,832			1	140,429
19 Maine		5,435			1,774,168
20 Maryland		30,760			435,213
21 Massachusetts		930	2		306,659
22 Michigan............		240,110			8,726,145
23 Minnesota...........		122,571			401,185
24 Mississippi..........	564,938	100	3	81	288,285
25 Missouri............	1,246	16,613	2,816	3	3,649,390
26 Montana......					100
27 Nebraska............		54			74,655
28 Nevada............ ..	106				27,029
29 New Hampshire.....		177			1,129,442
30 New Jersey.........		234,061	5		336,600
31 New Mexico.........					684,930
32 New York		3,670,818	6		10,599,225
33 North Carolina.......	144,935	59,552		95	799,667
34 Ohio		17,830,624	25		20,539,643
35 Oregon......		40,474			1,080,638
36 Pennsylvania........		815,906	571	1	6,561,722
37 Rhode Island........					77,328
38 South Carolina......	224,500				156,314
39 Tennessee..	181,842	90,930	1,033	158	1,389,762
40 Texas...............	350,628	25	5		1,251,328
41 Utah	22	10			109,018
42 Vermont		12,899			3,102,137
43 Virginia.............	133	130,750	31	7	877,110
44 Washington..........					162,713
45 West Virginia........	2	82,276	37		1,598,541
46 Wisconsin...........		497,398			4,090,670
47 Wyoming......					30,000
Total—United States	3,011,996	27,133,034	12,746	3,937	100,102,387

* Four hundred pounds each.

HAY, HOPS, RICE, AND TOBACCO CROPS IN 1870.

[From the Returns of the Ninth Census.]

STATES AND TERRITORIES.	Hay.	Hops.	Rice.	Tobacco.
	Tons.	*Pounds.*	*Pounds.*	*Pounds.*
The United States..........	27,316,048	25,456,669	73,635,021	262,735,341
1 Alabama.......................	10,613	32	222,945	152,742
2 Arizona	105	......	....	100
3 Arkansas.....................	6,839	25	73,021	504,886
4 California	551,773	625,064	....	63,809
5 Colorado	19,787	......	....	890
6 Connecticut..................	563,323	1,004	....	6,328,798
7 Dakota.......................	13,347	......	....	....
8 Delaware	41,890	800	....	250
9 District of Columbia.........	2,019	......	....	....
10 Florida	17	......	401.687	157,405
11 Georgia	10,518	2	22,277,380	283,596
12 Idaho.......................	6,985	21	....	....
13 Illinois.....................	2,747,339	104,032	....	5,249,274
14 Indiana	1,076,768	63,884	....	9,325,392
15 Iowa........................	1,777,339	171,113	....	71,792
16 Kansas......................	490,289	396	....	83,241
17 Kentucky....................	204,399	947	....	105,305,869
18 Louisiana....................	8,776	......	15,854,012	15,541
19 Maine.......................	1,053,415	236,850	....	15
20 Maryland....................	223,119	2,800	....	15,785,339
21 Massachusetts...............	597,455	61,910	....	7,312,885
22 Michigan....................	1,290,923	828,260	....	5,385
23 Minnesota	695,053	222,065	....	8,247
24 Mississippi..................	8,324	......	374,627	61,012
25 Missouri....................	615,611	19,297	....	12,820,493
26 Montana.	18,727	......	....	600
27 Nebraska....	189,354	100	.....	5,968
28 Nevada......................	33,855	......	....	25
29 New Hampshire..............	612,648	99,469	....	155,334
30 New Jersey..................	521,975	19,033	....	40,871
31 New Mexico.................	4,209	......	....	8,587
32 New York...................	5,614,205	17,538,681	....	2,349,798
33 North Carolina..............	83,540	238	2,059,281	11,150.087
34 Ohio........................	2,289,565	101,236	....	18,741,973
35 Oregon......................	75,357	9,745	....	3,847
36 Pennsylvania...........	2,848,219	90,688	....	3,467,539
37 Rhode Island................	89,045	249	....	796
38 South Carolina..............	10,665	1,507	32,304,825	34,805
39 Tennessee...................	116,582	565	8,399	21,465,452
40 Texas.......................	18,982	51	63,841	59,706
41 Utah........................	27,305	322	....	....
42 Vermont	1,020,660	527,927	....	72,671
43 Virginia....................	190,883	10,099	....	37,086,364
44 Washington	30,233	6,162	....	1,682
45 West Virginia...............	224,164	1,031	....	2,046,432
46 Wisconsin	1,237,651	4,639,155	....	960,813
47 Wyoming....................	3,180	......	....	....
Total—United States.......	27,316,048	25,456,669	73,635,021	262,735,341

NOTE.—The production of the above-named staples was as follows in the census of 1850 and 1860, respectively:

	Hay, tons.	Hops, lbs.	Rice, lbs.	Tobacco, lbs.
1850	13,838,642	3,497,029	215,313,497	199,752,655
1860	19,083,896	10,991,996	187,167,032	434,209,461

UNITED STATES PENSION STATISTICS.

Aggregate of Pensions paid by the United States, 1789-1877.

1791	$175,813 88	1821	$242,817 25	1851	$2,293,377 22
1792	109,243 15	1822	1,948,199 40	1852	2,401,858 78
1793	80,087 81	1823	1,780,588 52	1853	1,756,306 20
1794	81,399 24	1824	1,409,326 59	1854	1,232,665 00
1795	68,673 22	1825	1,308,810 57	1855	1,477,612 33
1796	100,843 71	1826	1,556,593 83	1856	1,296,229 65
1797	92,256 97	1827	976,138 86	1857	1,310,380 58
1798	104,845 33	1828	850,573 57	1858	1,219,768 30
1799	95,441 03	1829	949,504 47	1859	1,222,222 71
1800	64,130 73	1830	1,363,297 31	1860	1,100,802 32
1801	73,583 37	1831	1,170,665 14	1861	1,034,599 73
1802	85,440 89	1832	1,184,422 40	1862	852,170 47
1803	62,902 10	1833	4,589,152 40	1863	1,078,513 36
1804	80,002 80	1834	3,364,285 30	1864	4,985,473 90
1805	81,854 59	1835	1,954,711 32	1865	16,347,621 84
1806	81,875 53	1836	2,882,797 96	1866	15,615,287 75
1807	70,500 00	1837	2,672,162 45	1867	20,936,551 71
1808	82,576 04	1838	2,156,057 29	1868	23,782,386 78
1809	87,833 54	1839	3,142,730 51	1869	28,476,621 78
1810	83,744 10	1840	2,603,562 17	1870	28,340,202 17
1811	75,043 88	1841	2,388,434 51	1871	34,443,894 88
1812	91,402 10	1842	1,378,931 33	1872	28,533,402 76
1813	86,989 91	1843	839,041 12	1873	29,359,426 86
1814	90,164 36	1844	2,032,008 99	1874	29,038,414 66
1815	69,656 06	1845	2,400,788 11	1875	29,456,216 22
1816	188,804 15	1846	1,811,097 56	1876	28,257,395 60
1817	297,374 43	1847	1,744,883 63	1877	27,963,752 27
1818	890,719 90	1848	1,227,496 48		
1819	2,415,939 85	1849	1,328,867 64	Total	$428,205,659 66
1820	3,208,376 31	1850	1,866,886 02		

Statement of the Rates of Pension, and the Number Pensioned to each Rate, of the Army and Navy Invalids on the Rolls June 30, 1877.

Annual Pension.	Number of Pensioners.	Annual Pension.	Number of Pensioners.	Annual Pension.	Number of Pensioners.	Annual Pension.	Number of Pensioners.
$600 00	714	$195 00	2	$127 44	6	$67 44	6
480 00	1	192 00	542	126 00	4	66 00	2
402 00	1	189 00	7	123 00	1	63 96	1,230
432 00	9	187 44	2	122 40	1	63 60	2
375 00	338	180 00	1,194	120 00	3,585	60 00	2,206
360 00	207	178 20	2	117 00	5	57 60	....
319 92	1	177 00	1	114 00	4	54 00	4
315 00	2	174 00	2	112 44	4	51 00	149
312 00	1	171 00	5	108 00	47	48 00	27,687
309 00	1	168 00	1,530	105 00	3	45 00	135
300 00	157	165 00	3	102 00	602	42 00	2
288 00	6,300	162 00	6	99 96	5	40 80	1
270 00	6	159 96	43	99 00	3	39 96	1
247 00	46	159 00	11	96 00	18,196	38 40	4
254 00	1	156 00	86	93 00	1	37 92	1
240 00	747	153 00	261	90 00	484	36 00	4,165
234 00	1	150 00	125	87 00	1	31 92	1,520
231 00	1	147 00	2	84 00	483	30 00	10
228 00	2	144 00	4,036	82 80	1	27 00	6
225 00	54	141 00	2	81 00	3	24 00	9,334
222 00	2	139 92	2	79 92	62	22 44	2
219 00	3	138 00	9	78 00	3	19 20	4
216 00	11,170	135 96	63	76 44	3	18 00	1
210 00	2	135 00	151	75 00	25	15 96	8
204 00	572	132 00	15	72 00	17,005	12 00	385
201 00	2	129 00	15	69 00	3		
199 92	16	127 92	1	67 92	59		

NOTE.—The above table includes invalid pensioners, July 1, 1877, but does not include pensions paid to widows, etc.

PENSIONS PAID BY THE UNITED STATES IN 1877.

From the Annual Report of the Commissioner of Pensions, 1877.

	Whole Amount Paid for Pensions during Year.	Whole Number of Pensioners.	Yearly Value of Pensions.	Added to Roll since June 30, 1876.	Reductions in Roll since June 30, 1876.
Army :					
Invalid.............	$12,955,544 15	114,199	$11,891,649 36	5,800	....
Widows, etc........	13,348,383 57	97,055	11,328,251 74	....	4,112
Navy :					
Invalid...........	190,619 40	1,722	195,748 33	79	....
Widows, etc........	322,920 63	1,717	283,010 00	....	27
War of 1812 :					
Survivors...	934,657 82	12,802	1,228,992 00	....	1,404
Widows........ ...	361,548 91	4,609	442,464 00	......	378
Total..............	$28,122,683 48	232,104	$25,371,215 43	5,888	5,921
Total Reduction in Roll					33

NUMBER OF PENSIONERS ON THE ROLL AT THE TERMINATION OF EACH FISCAL YEAR SINCE 1861.

FOR THE YEAR ENDING JUNE 30.	ARMY AND NAVY.				
	Invalids.	Widows, etc.	Total.	Addition.	Reduction.
1861...........................	4,337	4,299	8,636	....	......
1862...........................	4,841	3,818	8,109	....	467
1863...........................	7,821	6,970	14,791	6,682	......
1864	23,479	27,656	41,135	26,344	......
1865...........................	35,880	50,106	85,986	44,851	......
1866...........................	55,652	71,070	126,722	40,736	......
1867...........................	69,565	83,618	153,184	26,402	......
1868...........................	75,957	93,686	169,643	16,459	......
1869...........................	82,859	105,104	187,963	18,320	......
1870...........................	87,521	111,165	198,686	10,723	......
1871...........................	93,394	114,101	207,495	8,809	......
1872...........................	113,954	118,275	232,229	24,734	......
1873...........................	119,500	118,911	238,411	6,182	......
1874...........................	121,628	114,613	236,241	....	2,170
1875...........................	122,989	111,832	234,821	....	1,400
1876...........................	124,239	107,898	232,137	....	2,084
1877...........................	128,723	103,881	232,104	....	33

In the above are included those pensioned for service in the War of 1812, 12,802 ; also the widows of the soldiers and sailors of that war, 4609.

PENSION AGENCY DISTRICTS AND PENSION AGENTS.

1. **Boston, Mass.**—D. W. Gooch.
   The States of Massachusetts, Connecticut and Rhode Island.
2. **Canandaigua, N. Y.**—L. M. Drury.
   Counties of New York State not in New York City District.
3. **Chicago, Ill.**—Ada C. Sweet.
   The State of Illinois.
4. **Columbus, Ohio.**—A. T. Wikoff.
   The State of Ohio.
5. **Concord, N. H.**—E. L. Whitford.
   The States of Maine, New Hampshire and Vermont.
6. **Des Moines, Iowa.**—B. F. Gue.
   The States of Iowa and Nebraska.
7. **Detroit, Mich.**—Samuel Post.
   The State of Michigan.
8. **Indianapolis, Ind.**—Fred. Knefler.
   The State of Indiana.
9. **Knoxville, Tenn.**—D. T. Boynton.
   The States of Virginia, West Virginia, North Carolina and Tennessee.
10. **Louisville, Ky.**—R. M. Kelly.
    The State of Kentucky.
11. **Milwaukee, Wis.**—E. Ferguson.
    The States of Wisconsin and Minnesota, and the Territories of Dakota, Montana and Wyoming.
12. **New Orleans, La.**—W. L. McMillen.
    The States of Arkansas, Mississippi, Texas, Louisiana, Alabama, Georgia, Florida, South Carolina, and the Indian Territory.
13. **New York City, N. Y.**—F. E. Howe.
    The Counties of Albany, Clinton, Columbia, Delaware, Dutchess, Essex, Greene, Kings, Queens, New York, Orange, Putnam, Richmond, Rensselaer, Rockland, Saratoga, Schenectady, Sullivan, Suffolk, Ulster, Warren, Washington and Westchester.
14. **Philadelphia, Pa.**—H. G. Sickel.
    The Counties of Berks, Bradford, Bucks, Carbon, Chester, Columbia, Dauphin, Delaware, Lancaster, Lebanon, Lehigh, Lucerne, Monroe, Montgomery, Montour, Northampton, Northumberland, Philadelphia, Pike, Schuylkill, Sullivan, Susquehanna, Wayne, Wyoming and York.
15. **Pittsburgh, Pa.**—J. McGregor.
    The remaining Counties of Pennsylvania.
16. **St. Louis, Mo.**—R. Campion.
    The States of Missouri, Kansas and Colorado, and the Territory of New Mexico.
17. **San Francisco, Cal.**—A. Hart.
    The States of California, Nevada and Oregon, and the Territories of Idaho, Washington, Arizona and Utah.
18. **Washington, D. C.**—D. C. Cox.
    The States of New Jersey, Delaware, Maryland, the District of Columbia, and all the National Home and Foreign Pensioners.

Note.—May 7th, 1877, an Executive order was issued by the President, reducing the number of agencies for the payment of pensions from 58 to 18, by the consolidation of districts. The consolidation saves to the Government, in salaries of the agents, $142,000 per annum, according to the Report of the Commissioner of Pensions. The salaries of pension agents under existing laws are 2 per cent on disbursements, but such percentage not to exceed $4000 salary. An extra allowance or perquisite of 25 cents for each pension voucher is, however, still in force.

TOTAL REVENUE OF GREAT BRITAIN, 1861-1877.

AMOUNT OF THE GROSS PUBLIC REVENUE OF THE UNITED KINGDOM, DISTINGUISHING THE PRINCIPAL BRANCHES THEREOF.

Years ended 31st March.	Customs.	Excise, Licenses, etc.	Stamps.	Taxes.	Property and Income Tax.	Post-Office.	Telegraph Service.	Crown Lands. (Net Receipts.)	Miscellaneous.	Total Gross Revenue.
1861	£23,305,177	£19,435,000	£8,948,412	£3,127,000	£10,923,817	£3,400,000		£290,568	£1,657,511	£70,388,085
1862	23,674,000	18,332,000	8,590,915	3,160,000	10,365,000	3,510,000		295,000	1,938,112	69,865,057
1863	24,031,000	17,155,000	8,994,000	3,150,000	10,567,000	3,650,000		300,000	2,754,562	70,604,562
1864	23,232,000	18,207,000	9,317,000	3,218,000	9,064,000	3,810,000		305,000	3,086,065	70,209,065
1865	22,572,000	19,556,000	9,530,000	3,292,000	7,958,000	4,100,000		310,000	2,993,787	70,313,787
1866	21,270,000	19,786,000	9,560,000	3,350,000	6,380,000	4,250,000		320,000	2,878,292	67,812,292
1867	22,303,000	20,070,000	9,420,000	3,468,000	5,700,000	4,470,000		330,000	3,073,568	68,434,568
1868	22,650,000	20,162,000	9,541,000	3,309,000	6,177,000	4,630,000		345,000	2,586,218	69,600,218
1869	22,434,000	20,408,000	9,218,000	3,494,000	8,615,000	4,640,003		360,000	3,355,992	72,591,992
1870	21,525,000	21,703,000	9,243,000	4,500,000	10,044,000	4,670,000	£100,000	375,000	3,201,252	75,434,252
1871	21,191,000	22,798,000	9,007,000	2,725,040	6,350,000	4,770,000	500,000	385,000	3,329,320	69,945,220
1872	20,396,000	23,826,000	9,772,000	2,339,000	9,064,000	4,690,000	755,000	375,000	4,060,814	74,708,314
1873	21,033,000	25,785,000	9,947,000	2,887,000	7,560,000	4,820,000	1,015,000	375,000	3,796,770	76,606,770
1874	20,399,000	27,172,000	10,650,000	2,884,000	5,691,000	5,792,000	1,210,000	275,000	3,582,657	77,385,657
1875	19,249,000	27,305,000	10,540,000	2,440,000	4,506,000	5,500,000	1,120,000	385,000	3,770,873	74,021,873
1876	20,020,000	27,095,000	11,003,010	2,496,000	4,109,000	5,950,000	1,245,000	395,000	4,288,693	77,131,693
1877	19,982,000	27,736,000	10,890,000	2,332,000	5,280,000	6,000,000	1,305,000	410,000	4,400,036	78,565,036

NOTE.—On Incomes from £100 to £150 ......6d. in the pound. 1861-63.
" of and above £150......9d.

On Incomes of and above £100, with abatement of £80 on Incomes under £200...... { 1864-65. 6d. | 1866-67. 4d. | 1867-68. 5d. | 1868-69. 6d. | 1869-70. 5d. | 1870-71. 4d. | 1871-72. 0d. }

With an abatement of £80 on Incomes under £300 ...... { 1872-73. 4d. | 1873-74. 3d. | 1874-76. 2d. }

TOTAL EXPENDITURE OF GREAT BRITAIN, 1861-1877.

AMOUNT OF THE GROSS PUBLIC EXPENDITURE OF THE UNITED KINGDOM, DISTINGUISHING THE PRINCIPAL BRANCHES THEREOF.

Years ended 31st March.	New Sinking Fund.	Total Interest on Debt.	Interest on Loans for Local Purposes.	Civil List and Civil Charges of all kinds.	Army.	Navy.	Charges of Collection of Revenue.	Total Gross Expenditure.
1861		£26,985,114		£10,739,020	£14,970,000	£18,331,066	£4,487,448	£72,800,155
1862		26,380,094		10,821,056	15,570,809	12,598,042	4,069,581	71,804,568
1863		26,831,657		10,881,512	16,264,700	11,970,588	4,553,461	69,802,004
1864		26,911,701		10,771,490	14,639,051	10,821,506	4,527,433	67,050,296
1865		26,389,994		10,205,412	14,892,072	10,808,253	4,001,472	66,462,397
1866		26,253,298		10,250,065	13,804,450	10,259,788	4,001,087	65,914,357
1867		26,041,778		10,523,010	14,675,540	10,676,101	4,823,068	66,730,806
1868		26,571,750		11,193,738	15,418,683	11,108,949	4,883,903	71,290,242
1869		26,018,386		11,066,643	15,000,000	11,366,545	5,021,902	74,072,816
1870		27,053,560		12,254,700	13,565,400	9,757,259	4,833,692	68,904,752
1871		26,929,437		13,170,659	13,430,400	9,450,041	5,308,402	69,548,539
1872		26,689,601		13,296,093	£15,221,580	9,900,480	5,488,963	71,490,090
1873		26,804,853		12,985,197	14,729,700 / £940,000	9,543,000	5,070,194	70,714,444
1874		26,706,736		17,067,600	14,489,900 / 683,500	10,279,900	5,471,311	76,400,510
1875		27,094,480		14,523,716	14,519,434 / 713,974 / 570,115	10,080,404	5,709,891	74,328,040
1876	290,150	Permanent Charge of Debt 27,400,000	£43,750	15,637,074	14,577,400 / 500,000 / 300,000 / 501,658	11,053,440	6,698,388	76,621,777
1877	624,750	27,700,000	222,831	15,779,779	15,251,355 / 170,000 / 408,302	11,364,383	7,066,498	78,123,228

PRICES OF COMMODITIES FOR FIFTY-THREE YEARS—1825-1877.

Showing the Average Price of the Articles named in the New York Market in the Month of January of each year.

[Compiled from the Finance Report of 1863, the Bankers' Almanac, and the Commercial and Financial Chronicle.]

Year	Beef, Mess.	Butter.	Cheese	Coal, Anthracite.	Coffee, Brazil.	Corn.	Cotton, Upland	Flour, West.	Hams.	Hops	Iron, Bar.	Iron, Scotch Pig.
	Bbl.	lb.	lb.	Ton.	lb.	Bush.	lb.	Bbl.	lb.	lb.	Ton.	Ton.
1825	8 78	15	7¼	10 00	16½	42	14	5 13	9¼	14	87 50	42 50
1826	9 10	15¼	8	12 00	16½	74	13½	4 80	9½	24½	97 50	65 00
1827	9 02	17½	7¼	12 00	14½	70	9½	5 14	10½	18	92 50	50 00
1828	9 14	15½	6⅛	11 50	14½	57	9	5 58	9½	7½	82 50	51 00
1829	9 21	13¾	6¼	11 50	12½	59	10	6 45	9⅛	9	80 00	52 50
1830	8 99	13½	6¾	12 00	12	54	9½	4 98½	9¾	10½	73 75	45 00
1831	8 50	14¾	6	7 50	10	58½	10	5 71	10¾	16	76 25	42 50
1832	9 46	15½	6	12 50	13	75	8½	5 76½	9½	13	72 00	43 75
1833	9 38	15½	6	9 25	13	81½	10½	5 56½	9½	34	75 00	42 50
1834	9 17	14	6¾	6 00	11½	59½	11	4 98	9¼	19	75 00	42 75
1835	11 08	17½	7¼	6 00	11½	74	16½	5 86½	9¾	12½	68 75	40 25
1836	10 97	19½	8¼	8 00	11½	90½	15	7 40½	12¾	14½	75 00	40 25
1837	13 49	19	9⅓	10 50	11	1 06	16	9 14	12½	8½	98 75	65 00
1838	14 70	20	8	9 00	10½	86	11½	7 96	12¼	5½	87 50	52 50
1839	14 81	19	9	8 25	10½	92	14	7 30	11¾	16½	88 75	38 75
1840	13 02	17½	6¾	7 50	10	59½	8½	5 29½	10	19	82 50	38 75
1841	9 01	11½	5¾	8 00	10½	52	9½	5 58½	7¾	37½	73 75	36 25
1842	7 39	11¼	7	8 50	9	67	8½	5 57	6¼	15	61 25	34 50
1843	7 15	8½	5¼	5 75	8½	59½	7	4 85½	8	11	58 75	27 25
1844	5 62	10¼	4 27/32	5 25	6½	43	8	4 67	9	7½	57 50	32 00
1845	8 21	13½	6⅞	5 50	6½	51½	5	4 93½	6	14½	68 75	30 50
1846	7 54	13	7	5 50	7½	74	6½	5 06	6½	27½	78 75	39 00
1847	11 44	16	6¾	6 50	7½	80	10	6 68½	10¾	10	76 25	33 50
1848	9 88	16	6¾	5 75	7	77	7½	5 96	7¾	6½	70 00	36 25
1849	11 68	15	6	5 25	5½	64½	6	5 51	8½	9½	50 00	25 50
1850	9 08	15⅛	6¼	5 75	11½	61	11	5 55	8	17½	43 75	23 50
1851	8 86	14¼	5¾	6 75	10½	64½	13½	4 52	8	31½	40 50	22 25
1852	10 72	18¾	6¾	5 25	8½	70½	8	5 00	9⅛	33½	34 50	20 15
1853	8 87	18	8½	5 25	8½	68½	9½	5 78	8¾	23½	67 50	31 00
1854	10 94	19½	9½	6 75	11½	82½	10	8 89½	7½	45	67 50	38 00
1855	11 47	22¼	9½	7 25	9	1 01	7	8 76	8¾	34	58 25	28 75
1856	8 57	22½	8½	5 95	10½	93	9	6 42	9	11	60 50	32 50
1857	12 87	22½	9½	6 50	8½	73½	13	5 78½	10½	10½	56 25	30 50
1858	10 48	18½	6¼	5 50	7½	61	9	4 29½	8¼	9¼	53 75	26 50
1859	7 59	19	8½	5 25	13½	80½	11	4 11	8¾	11	46 50	26 50
1860	9 00	16	11	5 50	15	91½	11	4 30	9¼	11½	42 25	24 50
1861	6 00	14	10	5 75	28½	73	12	5 35	8	11½	41 25	20 50
1862	5 50	15	7	4 75	19½	67	37	5 50	6	18½	53 00	24 00
1863	12 00	22	12	8 50	21½	75	66½	6 05	8	29½	78 75	33 00
1864	14 00	24	15½	9 75	31	1 26	75	7 00	11	31	105 00	44 00
1865	20 50	45	20	10 00	44	1 95	70	10 00	20	42½	125 00	50 00
1866	20 00	30	18½	8 50	45	95½	51½	8 75	16½	20½	94 00	51 50
1867	18 00	30	17½	5 50	18¼	1 10½	29	11 00	12¾	55	90 00	47 00
1868	32 00	45	15	5 00	11½	1 20	16	9 55	12	60	85 00	36 00
1869	28 00	40	19½	5 50	11	90	26	6 60	15¼	20	85 00	40 50
1870	27 00	30	17½	5 50	10½	1 12	25⅜	4 85	15	25	75 00	33 00
1871	27 00	20	16¼	0 00	12	80	15¼	6 25	11	12	73 00	34 00
1872	21 00	15	13¾	4 50	16	78	20	6 40	9¾	60	105 00	34 00
1873	21 00	16	14¼	6 00	17¼	66	20½	6 25	9½	55	110 00	48 00
1874	22 00	27	14¾	0 00	19	84	16¼	0 00	10	40	160 00	42 00
1875	21 00	29	15¾	5 25	19	97	14¼	4 50	11	48	135 00	38 00
1876	23 00	26	13¼	5 50	18	71	13¼	4 35	12½	15	133 00	32 00
1877	20 00	28	14¼	3 00	20	59	12½	5 50	10½	28	131 00	27 50

PRICES OF COMMODITIES FOR FIFTY-THREE YEARS—1825-1877.

Showing the Average Price of the Articles named in the New York Market in the Month of January of each year.

[Compiled from the Finance Report of 1863, the Bankers' Almanac, and the Commercial and Financial Chronicle.]

Year	Lard	Leather, Hem.	Mackerel, No. 1.	Molasses, N. O.	Oats.	Pork, Mess.	Rice.	Salt, Liv. Sack.	Sugar, Raw	Tobacco.	Wheat.	Whiskey.	Wool
	lb.	lb.	Bbl.	Gal.	Bush.	Bbl.	100lbs		lb.	lb.	Bush.	Gal.	lb.
1825	8⅛	23¾	5 33½	31	27½	13 37	2 59½	2 65	8¾	15¾	1 01	26½	32½
1826	7¾	21	5 19½	33⅛	45½	11 75	2 87½	2 31½	9	12½	90	29	34
1827	8⅜	19½	5 33½	31	56	11 87½	3 27	2 24	8	11½	93	29½	25
1828	7	21	5 35½	35	34	14 12½	3 15	2 56½	8	11½	1 15	22½	25
1829	5⅛	20⅛	5 51	32	30½	12 25	3 00	2 30½	8	11½	1 63	23⅛	22½
1830	8	20	5 83	29	32	11 50	2 67	1 99	7½	10½	1 04	25¼	21½
1831	9	21¾	6 80	33⅛	31½	13 87	3 11	1 91	6	10¾	1 25	31½	25
1832	8⅛	20⅜	5 64½	28⅛	50	13 50	3 35	2 00	5½	10½	1 26	30½	27½
1833	8⅛	17½	6 62	38	49½	13 25	3 22	1 83½	7	10½	1 19¾	30¾	32½
1834	7¾	16¼	6 24½	31	44	14 50	2 91	1 56	7½	12	1 06	25	32⅛
1835	9½	17	7 15	27⅛	40	13 75	3 49	1 77½	6½	13	1 05	33½	27½
1836	14⅛	18½	9 61½	33½	56½	18 25	3 64	1 91	9½	15⅝	1 78	37	37½
1837	10½	19	9 83	43	57	23 50	4 01	1 99½	7½	16	1 77½	36½	45
1838	10¾	18¾	11 33½	42½	42½	21 50	4 35	1 95½	6½	15¾	1 92	36	30
1839	11¾	21½	13 52	32½	55	23 25	4 37	1 74½	6½	21	1 24½	36½	38½
1840	10	18½	12 82	27½	33½	14 25	3 38	1 52½	5½	13¼	1 06	25	32½
1841	7½	20⅜	13 55	27	52	13 25	3 46	1 59	6	13½	1 09	21½	27½
1842	6¼	17	10 55	25	49	9 62½	2 85	1 67	6	11½	1 25	18½	20
1843	6¼	16¼	9 25	19½	33½	8 87½	2 64	1 46½	4	12½	88½	22	19
1844	5⅜	15½	10 78½	29	48	10 12½	3 03	1 40½	6½	12½	1 00	23¾	26½
1845	7¼	14⅛	12 56½	24½	51¼	9 31½	3 81	1 37	4	12½	1 02½	23	29
1846	6¾	13	10 64½	26¼	47½	13 56	3 65½	1 34	6	12½	1 31	21⅜	27
1847	9½	15¾	9 97	34½	40½	10 25	3 12½	1 35½	6½	13	1 02½	28¼	23
1848	7⅛	13⅜	8 41½	28	50½	11 00	3 17	1 39	5	13½	1 25	24	29
1849	6⅛	15⅛	10 55½	28	41	14 18	2 97	1 29	4½	14	1 22½	24	26
1850	6¼	15¾	10 79½	26½	43½	11 81	3 18½	1 36½	4½	21	1 25	25¼	31
1851	8⅛	14½	9 04	31	48½	12 18	3 02½	1 34	5½	25½	1 20	23½	34½
1852	10	15⅛	10 06	27½	47½	14 68	3 71	1 20	5	19½	1 09	22½	31
1853	10½	18⅛	13 45½	30	51½	19 62	3 93½	1 34½	5	20¼	1 32	24½	30
1854	9⅛	21	16 91½	27½	49½	13 43	4 39	1 59½	4½	18½	2 04	32¼	30
1855	10½	22½	20 10	25½	55½	12 62	4 52½	1 03½	4½	19½	2 57	37¾	25½
1856	11½	25⅛	20 87½	48½	46½	17 37	4 16½	91½	8½	22	2 14	32½	32
1857	13½	26⅛	20 50	76	47	19 67	4 32	79¾	10	27¾	1 75	27	35
1858	10¼	22¾	11 68	34½	42½	15 75	3 24	65½	6½	24	1 37	22¼	29½
1859	10¾	24½	15 93	36½	50½	17 57	3 66½	83	6½	23	1 40	26½	38
1860	10½	21⅛	16 72	53½	46½	16 18	4 20	89½	7½	19¾	1 45	26	39
1861	10⅜	19⅛	11 63½	34½	38	16 12	4 00	73	5½	24	1 44	19¾	32
1862	8⅜	20½	15 32	52½	40½	12 25	7 00	1 10½	8½	42½	1 38	20½	47
1863	10	27	19 00	53	70½	14 43	8 75	1 25	9	20	1 53	39	63½
1864	13	30	18 00	67½	89½	19 87	10 00	1 85	13¼	30	1 82½	94	28½
1865	23	42	16 00	1 00	1 03	35 25	13 00	2 27	19⅝	25	1 85	2 24	55
1866	19	36	18 50	1 20	1 20	29 12	12 50	2 00	11¾	20	1 87½	2 27½	70
1867	10	32	18 50	80	80	19 12	9 25	2 00	10	16	3 00	2 38	60
1868	12⅝	25½	22 50	85	85	21 00	8 87	2 00	11½	16½	2 45	..	48
1869	17½	29	29 00	75	75	28 00	9 25	2 10	11½	12½	1 70	93	57
1870	17⅛	30	27 00	78	78	29 75	7 25	1 70	10⅝	11	1 30	98	61
1871	12⅜	27	25 00	75	75	19 75	7 00	1 50	11⅛	8	1 42	94½	49
1872	9½	26	15 00	54	54	14 50	8 50	1 45	11	9	1 50	93	70
1873	7¾	28	22 00	68	68	13 25	8 25	1 50	9¾	7½	1 67	99	70
1874	13	28	17 00	77	77	16 50	8 25	1 25	7¾	6	1 65	97½	53
1875	13⅝	27	11 50	65	65	20 50	7 62	1 25	8	12	1 25	99	56
1876	12⅜	23	19 00	59	59	20 75	7 00	1 10	8	8	1 30	1 14½	49
1877	11¼	28	20 00	55	55	17 50	6 00	1 10	9⅝	8	1 47	1 13	48

FAMILIES, DWELLINGS, AND POPULATION IN FIFTY PRINCIPAL CITIES OF THE UNITED STATES—1870.

[From the Official Report of the Ninth Census, 1870.]

CITIES.	Size.*	FAMILIES. Number.	Persons to Family.	DWELLINGS. Number.	Persons to Dwelling.	Population.	Native.	Foreign-born.	White.	Colored.
Albany, N. Y.	20	14,105	4.92	8,748	7.94	69,422	47,215	22,207	68,658	764
Allegheny, Pa.	23	10,147	5.24	8,347	6.37	53,180	37,872	15,308	52,018	1,162
Baltimore, Md.	6	49,929	5.35	40,350	6.63	267,354	210,870	56,484	227,794	39,558
Boston, Mass.	7	48,188	5.20	29,623	8.46	250,526	102,540	87,966	247,013	3,496
Brooklyn, N. Y.	3	80,066	4.95	45,834	8.64	396,099	251,381	144,718	391,142	4,944
Buffalo, N. Y.	11	22,325	5.27	18,285	6.44	117,714	71,477	46,237	117,018	696
Cambridge, Mass.	33	7,897	5.02	6,348	6.24	39,634	27,579	12,055	38,785	849
Charleston, S. C.	26	9,098	5.38	6,861	7.14	48,956	44,064	4,892	22,749	26,173
Charlestown, Mass.	47	6,155	4.60	4,396	6.44	28,323	21,399	6,921	28,196	127
Chicago, Ill.	5	59,497	5.03	44,620	6.70	298,977	154,420	144,557	295,281	3,691
Cincinnati, Ohio	8	42,937	5.01	24,550	8.81	216,230	136,627	79,612	210,385	5,900
Cleveland, Ohio	15	18,411	5.04	16,692	5.56	92,829	54,014	38,815	91,535	1,293
Columbus, Ohio	42	5,790	5.40	5,011	6.24	31,274	23,663	7,611	29,427	1,847
Dayton, Ohio	44	6,109	4.99	5,611	5.43	30,473	23,050	7,423	29,925	548
Detroit, Mich.	18	15,636	5.09	14,688	5.42	79,577	44,196	35,381	77,368	2,235
Fall River, Mass.	50	5,216	5.13	2,687	9.96	26,766	15,288	11,478	26,635	100
Hartford, Conn.	34	7,427	5.01	6,688	5.54	37,180	26,363	10,817	36,232	946
Indianapolis, Ind.	27	9,200	5.24	7,820	6.17	48,244	37,587	10,657	45,309	2,931
Jersey City, N. J.	17	16,687	4.95	9,867	8.37	82,546	50,711	31,835	81,840	705
Kansas City, Mo.	38	5,585	5.78	5,424	5.95	32,260	24,581	7,679	28,464	3,770
Lawrence, Mass.	45	5,287	5.47	3,443	8.40	28,921	16,204	12,717	28,814	100
Louisville, Ky.	14	19,177	5.25	14,670	6.87	100,418	142,943	25,668	85,706	14,956
Lowell, Mass.	31	7,649	5.35	6,302	6.43	40,928	26,493	14,435	40,815	111
Lynn, Mass.	49	6,100	4.63	4,625	6.10	28,223	23,298	4,935	27,862	371
Memphis, Tenn.	32	7,824	5.14	6,408	6.28	40,226	33,446	6,780	24,755	15,671
Milwaukee, Wis.	19	14,226	5.02	13,048	5.48	71,440	37,667	23,773	71,263	176
Mobile, Ala.	31	6,301	5.08	5,738	5.58	32,034	27,795	4,239	18,115	13,919
Newark, N. J.	13	21,631	4.86	14,350	7.32	105,059	69,175	35,884	103,267	1,789
New Haven, Conn.	25	10,482	4.85	8,100	6.28	50,840	36,484	14,356	49,090	1,749
New Orleans, La.	9	39,130	4.89	33,656	5.69	191,418	142,943	48,475	140,928	50,456
New York, N. Y.	1	185,789	5.07	64,044	14.72	942,292	523,198	419,094	929,199	13,072
Paterson, N. J.	37	7,645	4.76	4,653	7.22	33,579	20,711	12,868	33,218	361
Philadelphia, Pa.	2	127,740	5.28	112,366	6.01	674,022	490,398	183,624	651,954	22,147
Pittsburgh, Pa.	16	16,182	5.32	14,224	6.05	86,076	58,254	27,822	84,061	2,015
Portland, Me.	41	6,682	4.74	4,836	6.50	31,413	24,401	7,012	31,079	334
Providence, R. I.	21	14,775	4.66	9,277	7.46	68,904	51,727	17,177	66,320	2,559
Reading, Pa.	36	6,932	4.89	6,294	5.39	33,930	30,059	8,871	33,611	311
Richmond, Va.	24	9,792	5.21	8,033	6.35	51,038	47,260	3,778	27,928	23,110
Rochester, N. Y.	22	12,213	5.11	11,649	5.36	62,386	41,202	21,184	61,959	427
San Francisco, Cal.	10	30,553	4.89	25,905	5.77	149,473	75,754	73,719	186,059	†1,330
Savannah, Ga.	48	5,013	5.68	4,561	6.19	28,235	24,564	3,671	15,166	13,068
Scranton, Pa.	35	6,042	5.26	5,646	6.21	35,092	19,205	15,887	35,043	49
St. Louis, Mo.	4	59,431	5.23	39,675	7.84	310,864	198,615	112,249	288,737	22,088
Syracuse, N. Y.	29	8,677	4.96	7,088	6.07	43,051	29,061	13,990	42,616	435
Toledo, Ohio	40	6,457	4.89	6,069	5.20	31,584	20,485	11,009	30,972	612
Troy, N. Y.	28	9,302	5.00	8,933	7.88	46,465	30,246	16,219	46,047	418
Utica, N. Y.	46	5,793	4.97	4,799	6.00	28,804	18,955	9,849	28,683	219
Washington, D. C.	12	21,343	5.12	19,545	5.59	109,199	95,442	13,757	73,731	35,455
Wilmington, Del.	43	5,808	5.31	5,898	5.71	30,841	25,689	5,152	27,630	3,211
Worcester, Mass.	30	8,658	4.74	4,922	8.35	41,105	29,159	11,946	40,588	513

* This column expresses the relative size of the cities in regard to population.

† San Francisco had also 12,000 Chinese population in 1870.

AREAS, DENSITY OF POPULATION, FAMILIES, AND DWELLINGS IN THE UNITED STATES, 1870.

[From the Official Report of the Ninth Census, 1870.]

STATES AND TERRITORIES.	AREAS.		FAMILIES.		DWELLINGS.	
	Square Miles.	Persons to a Square Mile.	Number.	Persons to a Family.	Number.	Persons to a Dwelling.
The United States.	3,603,884	10.70	7,579,363	5.09	7,042,833	5.47
1 Alabama	50,722	19.66	202,704	4.92	198,327	5.03
2 Arkansas	52,198	9.30	96,135	5.04	93,195	5.20
3 California	188,981	2.29	128,752	4.35	126,307	4.44
4 Connecticut	4,750	113.15	114,981	4.67	96,880	5.55
5 Delaware	2,120	58.97	22,900	5.46	22,577	5.54
6 Florida	59,268	3.17	39,394	4.77	41,047	4.57
7 Georgia	58,000	20.42	237,850	4.98	236,436	5.01
8 Illinois	55,410	45.84	474,533	5.35	464,155	5.47
9 Indiana	33,809	49.71	320,160	5.25	318,469	5.28
10 Iowa	55,045	21.69	222,430	5.37	219,846	5.41
11 Kansas	81,318	4.48	72,493	5.03	71,071	5.13
12 Kentucky	37,680	35.33	232,797	5.67	224,969	5.87
13 Louisiana	41,346	17.58	158,099	4.60	150,427	4.83
14 Maine	35,000	17.91	131,017	4.78	121,953	5.14
15 Maryland	11,124	70.20	140,078	5.57	129,620	6.02
16 Massachusetts	7,800	186.84	305,534	4.77	236,473	6.16
17 Michigan	56,451	20.97	241,006	4.91	237,036	5.00
18 Minnesota	83,531	5.26	82,471	5.33	81,140	5.42
19 Mississippi	47,156	17.56	166,828	4.96	164,150	5.04
20 Missouri	65,350	26.34	316,917	5.43	292,769	5.87
21 Nebraska	75,995	1.62	25,075	4.91	25,144	4.89
22 Nevada	104,125	0.41	9,880	4.30	12,990	3.27
23 New Hampshire.	9,280	34.30	72,144	4.41	67,046	4.75
24 New Jersey	8,320	108.91	183,043	4.95	155,936	5.81
25 New York	47,000	93.25	898,772	4.88	688,559	6.37
26 North Carolina	50,704	21.13	203,970	5.20	202,504	5.29
27 Ohio	39,964	66.69	521,931	5.11	495,667	5.38
28 Oregon	95,274	0.95	18,504	4.91	19,372	4.69
29 Pennsylvania	46,000	76.56	675,408	5.21	635,680	5.54
30 Rhode Island	1,306	166.43	46,133	4.71	34,828	6.24
31 South Carolina	34,000	20.75	151,105	4.67	148,485	4.92
32 Tennessee	45,600	27.60	231,365	5.44	224,816	5.60
33 Texas	274,356	2.98	154,483	5.30	111,685	5.78
34 Vermont	10,212	32.37	70,462	4.69	66,145	5.00
35 Virginia	38,348	31.95	231,574	5.20	224,947	5.45
36 West Virginia	23,000	19.22	78,474	5.63	78,854	5.61
37 Wisconsin	53,924	19.56	200,155	5.27	197,098	5.35
The States	1,984,467	19.21	7,481,607	5.09	6,941,603	5.49
1 Alaska (unorganized)	577,390					
2 Arizona	113,916	0.08	2,290	4.22	2,822	3.42
3 Colorado	104,500	0.88	9,358	4.26	10,009	3.98
4 Dakota	150,932	0.09	8,090	4.59	3,231	4.39
5 Dist. of Columbia	64	2,057.81	25,276	5.21	23,308	5.65
6 Idaho	86,294	0.17	4,104	3.65	4,622	3.25
7 Indian Country	68,991					
8 Montana	143,776	0.14	7,058	2.92	9,450	2.18
9 New Mexico	131,201	0.76	21,419	4.28	21,053	4.36
10 Utah	84,476	1.03	17,210	5.04	18,290	4.75
11 Washington	69,994	0.34	5,673	4.22	6,006	3.95
12 Wyoming	97,883	0.09	2,243	4.06	2,379	3.83
The Territories	1,619,417	0.27	97,756	4.48	101,230	4.87
Total in the United States	3,603,884	10.70	7,579,363	5.09	7,042,833	5.47

NATIVITY OF THE FOREIGN-BORN POPULATION OF THE UNITED STATES IN 1870.

[Selected from the Official Returns of the Ninth Census.]

Living in.	All Foreign Countries	Austria.	Bohemia	British America.	China.	Denmark.	France.	Germany.
The U. S..	5,567,229	30,508	40,289	493,464	63,042	30,107	116,402	1,690,533
Alabama ...	9,962	90	29	183	1	80	594	2,482
Arkansas...	5,026	41	21	342	93	55	237	1,563
California..	209,831	1,078	90	10,660	48,826	1,837	8,068	29,701
Connecticut	113,639	154	95	10,861	11	116	821	12,443
Delaware...	9,136	8	1	112	....	8	127	1,142
Florida. ...	4,967	17	3	174	1	41	126	597
Georgia....	11,127	34	23	247	4	42	312	2,761
Illinois.....	515,198	2,099	7,350	32,550	8	3,711	10,911	203,758
Indiana	141,474	443	141	4,765	6	315	6,363	78,060
Iowa......	204,692	2,691	6,766	17,907	3	2,827	3,130	66,162
Kansas	48,392	448	105	5,324	....	503	1,274	12,775
Kentucky ..	63,398	146	40	1,082	8	53	2,057	30,318
Louisiana ..	61,827	435	23	714	79	291	12,341	18,933
Maine... ..	48,881	10	1	26,788	4	102	137	508
Maryland...	83,412	266	789	644	6	107	649	47,045
Massach'tts	353,319	255	110	70,055	115	267	1,629	13,072
Michigan...	268,010	795	1,179	89,590	4	1,354	3,121	64,143
Minnesota..	160,697	2,647	2,166	16,698	6	1,910	1,749	41,864
Mississippi.	11,191	85	9	375	16	193	630	2,960
Missouri ...	222,267	1,493	3,517	8,448	4	665	6,293	113,618
Nebraska ..	30,748	299	1,770	2,635	2	1,129	340	10,954
Nevada.....	18,801	157	7	2,365	3,146	208	414	2,181
N. H'pshire	29,611	9	4	12,955	5	11	60	436
New Jersey	188,943	686	271	2,474	30	510	3,130	54,001
New York..	1,138,353	3,928	2,071	79,042	17 7	1,701	22,302	316,902
N. Carolina.	3,020	13	5	171	4	8	51	904
Ohio	372,493	3,090	1,429	12,968	12	284	12,781	182,897
Oregon	11,600	53	36	1,187	3,327	87	308	1,875
Pennsylv'a.	545,309	1,536	580	10,022	32	561	8,695	160,146
Rhode Isl'd	55,396	19	19	10,242	....	24	167	1,201
S. Carolina.	8,074	10	1	77	6	50	143	2,754
Tennessee..	19,316	112	37	587	4	88	562	4,530
Texas......	62,411	1,748	781	597	20	159	2,232	23,985
Vermont...	47,155	2	....	28,544	1	21	93	370
Virginia...	13,754	56	31	327	6	23	369	4,050
W. Virginia	17,091	59	1	207	....	21	228	6,232
Wisconsin..	364,499	4,486	10,570	23,666	....	5,212	2,704	162,314
The States	5,473,829	30,116	40,071	487,605	55,974	24,574	115,140	1,679,146
Arizona....	5,809	24	2	142	21	19	69	379
Colorado...	6,599	51	15	753	7	77	209	1,456
Dakota	4,815	171	153	906	....	115	57	563
District of Columbia	16,254	26	9	290	4	29	233	4,920
Idaho.......	7,885	26	1	334	4,268	88	144	599
Montana....	7,979	36	23	1,172	1,043	95	193	1,233
New Mexico	5,620	10	2	125	....	15	134	582
Utah	30,702	4	3	687	446	4,957	63	854
Washington	5,624	19	2	1,121	236	84	113	615
Wyoming...	3,513	25	8	329	143	54	57	632
Territories	94,200	392	218	5,850	7,068	5,523	1,262	11,387
Total, United States	5,567,229	30,508	40,289	493,464	63,042	30,107	116,402	1,690,533

NATIVITY OF THE FOREIGN-BORN POPULATION OF THE UNITED STATES IN 1870.

[Selected from the Official Returns of the Ninth Census.]

Living in.	Eng-land.	Ireland.	Scot-land.	Wales	Hol-land.	Italy.	Mexi-co.	Nor-way.	Swe-den.	Swit-zer-land.
The U. S..	550,994	1,855,827	140,835	74,583	46,802	17,157	42,435	114,246	97,332	75,153
Alabama...	1,041	3,893	458	30	14	118	13	21	105	168
Arkansas ..	526	1,429	156	24	71	30	14	19	135	104
California..	17,699	54,421	4,949	1,517	432	4,660	9,339	1,000	1,944	2,927
Connecticut	13,001	70,630	3,238	288	90	117	5	72	323	492
Delaware...	1,421	5,907	229	43	10	5			9	33
Florida.....	399	737	144	6	7	56	41	16	30	14
Georgia....	1,068	5,043	420	61	42	50	9	14	35	103
Illinois.....	53,871	120,162	15,737	3,146	4,180	761	73	11,880	29,979	8,980
Indiana....	9,945	28,698	2,507	556	873	95	17	123	2,180	4,287
Iowa	16,660	40,124	5,248	1,967	4,513	54	14	17,556	10,796	3,937
Kansas.....	6,161	10,940	1,531	1,021	300	55	63	588	4,954	1,328
Kentucky..	4,173	21,642	1,019	347	270	325	31	16	112	1,147
Louisiana...	2,811	17,068	814	114	232	1,889	409	76	358	873
Maine. ...	3,650	15,745	998	279	26	48	4	58	91	9
Maryland ..	4,855	23,630	2,432	994	236	210	19	18	100	297
Massachu'ts	34,099	216,120	9,008	576	490	454	20	302	1,386	491
Michigan..	35,051	42,013	8,552	658	12,559	110	25	1,516	2,406	2,116
Minnesota..	5,670	21,746	2,194	944	1,855	40	5	35,940	20,987	2,162
Mississippi.	1,088	3,359	434	25	35	147	32	78	970	263
Missouri....	14,314	54,983	3,283	1,524	1,167	936	90	297	2,302	6,597
Nebraska...	3,603	4,999	792	220	189	44	11	506	2,352	593
Nevada	2,540	5,035	630	301	44	199	226	80	217	247
N. H'pshire	2,679	12,190	892	27	5	9	1	55	42	11
New Jersey	20,614	86,794	5,710	804	2,914	257	46	90	554	2,061
New York .	110,071	528,806	27,282	7,857	6,426	3,592	127	975	5,522	7,916
N Carolina	490	677	420	10	13	19	2	5	38	60
Ohio........	26,561	82,674	7,819	12,980	2,018	564	41	64	252	12,727
Oregon.....	1 317	1,967	394	63	39	31	51	76	203	160
Pennsylv'ia	69,665	235,798	16,846	27,633	819	734	86	115	2,266	5,765
Rhode Isl'd	9,291	31,534	1,948	56	45	58	2	22	106	74
S. Carolina.	617	3,262	310	15	32	63	2		61	45
Tennessee..	2,085	8,048	555	314	100	483	17	37	349	802
Texas......	2,037	4,081	621	55	54	186	23,020	403	364	599
Vermont...	1,946	14,080	1,240	565	20	17	5	34	83	19
Virginia....	1,939	5,191	705	148	231	162	13	17	30	148
W. Virginia	1,811	6,523	746	321	174	34		1	5	325
Wisconsin .	28,192	48,479	6,590	6,550	5,990	104	47	40,046	2,790	6,069
The States	523,999	1,838,726	136,846	74,607	46,561	16,766	33,920	112,116	94,447	73,972
Arizona ..	134	495	54	3	11	12	4,318	7	7	23
Colorado...	1,358	1,685	188	165	17	16	129	40	180	140
Dakota.....	248	898	77	3	8	4	6	1,179	380	33
District of }Columbia }	1,422	8,218	352	29	23	182	17	5	22	175
Idaho.......	540	986	114	335	9	11	46	61	91	52
Montana ...	692	1,635	208	197	18	34	31	88	141	97
N. Mexico.	120	543	36	9	3	25	3,913	5	6	42
Utah	16,073	502	2,391	1,783	122	74	8	613	1,790	509
Washington	791	1,047	309	44	25	24	13	104	159	50
Wyoming ..	556	1,102	200	58	5	9	4	28	109	60
Territories	21,934	17,101	3,980	2,630	241	391	8,515	2,130	2,895	1,181
Total, Uni-ted States	550,924	1,855,827	140,835	74,533	46,802	17,157	42,435	114,246	97,332	75,153

THE BANK OF FRANCE.

[From Crump's English Manual of Banking, London, 1877, and from the Economist, and the Bankers' Magazine, London, 1877.]

THE Bank of France was founded by Napoleon I. at the beginning of this century, and an institution then existing, and called "Caisse d'escompte," which was established in 1776, was amalgamated with it. The capital of the Bank of France was at first 30,000,000 francs, divided into 30,000 name shares of 1000 francs each. The bank commenced business on the 20th of February, 1800, and was presided over by a committee of fifteen members. Its operations consisted of discounting and collecting bills, opening of current accounts, issuing notes payable to bearer on demand, and receiving deposits, on which it paid interest.

In 1803, the bank was granted for fifteen years the monopoly of issuing notes, the capital being raised at the same time to 45 millions. Since that time provincial banks have not been able to issue notes except under government license.

In 1805, the bullion reserve of the bank was very small, and the government ordered the bank to encash only 600,000 francs of notes per diem, the total amount of notes issued, which, moreover, had fallen to a discount of ten per cent to fifteen per cent, being 70,000,000 francs. This state of affairs continued till the beginning of 1806.

In 1808, the monopoly of the bank, which was to expire in 1818, was extended to 1843, and the capital of the institution was doubled. From this time the bank, which had retained the character of a private company, became essentially a government institution, with private commandite partners. The management was confined to a governor and two sub-governors, named by the government, and to fifteen regents and three censors, who are nominated by the shareholders, and who form the general council.

In consequence of the political events of 1848, the bank asked the government to be allowed to suspend payment. The government granted this request, and decreed the forced currency of the bank-notes, on condition that the whole issue of notes should not exceed 350,000,000 francs. In consequence of this decree, the notes, which had been at a discount of five per cent, rose to par. This maximum was raised to 525,000,000 francs in 1849, and in August, 1850, the maximum was done away with altogether, and the notes were again convertible.

In 1857, the monopoly of the bank was continued until 1897, and the capital was doubled to 182,500 shares, or $36,500,000, the new shares being issued at 1100 francs.

In consequence of the Franco-German war, the notes of the Bank of France were declared legal tender, and became a forced currency on the 12th August, 1870, and the limit of the circulation was fixed at 1,800,000 francs. This limit was raised to 2,400,000 francs in December, 1870 ; to 2,800,000 francs in December, 1871; and to 3,200,000 francs in July, 1872. The notes remain still inconvertible, but are at par with gold.

In July, 1870, when the war began, the circulation of the Bank of France was $251,000,000, and the specie in hand $229,000,000, or about 90 per cent. The first bank statement after the peace, June, 1871, showed a paper circulation of $442,000,-000, and a specie reserve of $110,000,000, or about 25 per cent. The highest point attained by the paper-money emissions was in November, 1873, $622,000,000, with a metallic reserve of $146,000,000, or 24 per cent. The largest depreciation of bank-notes was 2¼ per cent as compared with gold, in November, 1871.

Since 1848, the Bank of France has had the sole right of issuing notes in France, and paid, up to 1871, ⅓ per mille, and since 25th August, 1871, 1 per mille stamp duty on its issue to the government.

If the rate of discount rises above six per cent, the extra profit goes to the reserve.

As long as the notes had not a forced currency, no limit was prescribed to the amount of the circulation, or to the proportion of the specie kept as cover for the notes ; all this was left to the discretion of the management.

The Bank of France has eighty-nine branches.

The official report of M. Rouland, governor, and the censors of the Bank of France, January 25th, 1877, represents a considerable decrease in transactions. This decrease was in discounts of commercial paper and bills by the bank and branches, as follows (stated in dollars) :

Discounts in 1875	$1,924,050,100
" " 1876	1,472,400,480
Decrease	$451,649,620

The decrease of discounts is attributed to the general depression of business in

France, and in part to the steady raising of the stamp duty on commercial paper, diminishing the number of commercial bills which can afford to pay so heavy a tax. The metallic reserves were stated as follows:

Specie, December 27th, 1875... ....$334,420,000
"   "   23d, 1876.............................. 436,580,000

The statement adds that over $100,000,000 of specie, proceeding from abroad, has been put into the bank, the rate of exchange being steadily favorable to France. This aggregate specie was composed of $93,200,000 in gold and $8,980,000 in silver. The report adds that the metallic reserves are so much the greater, as the country, strong in its confidence in the note circulation of the Bank of France, continues more than ever to prefer its notes to gold and silver. It is urged that the true interests of France require speedy resumption in specie, a paper circulation being only supplementary to specie. It is added that the Bank of France is in a very strong condition for resumption, which is to take place, under existing laws, on the 1st of January, 1878.

The total circulation of notes issued by the bank and branches is given as follows:

Circulation, December 27th, 1875........................$404,903,760
"   November 30th, 1876........................... 520,430,040
"   November 15th, 1877................ 491,110,950

This circulation is nearly half made up of notes of one hundred francs, or twenty dollars. The smallest notes issued are for five francs, of which, however, there are only 257,724 in circulation, representing only a quarter of a million dollars out of about five hundred million. The maximum limit of note circulation is fixed by law at $640,000,000.

The liabilities of the French public treasury toward the bank have been diminished by more than one half. It owed on the 24th of January, 1876, $111,275,000. On the 25th of January, 1877, the state owed the bank only $67,500,000. On November 15th, 1877, the debt of the government was still further reduced to $62,135,000.

As to the relative proportions of gold and silver in the large specie reserve of the Bank of France, it was stated July 15th, 1877, as follows:

Gold................ ......1,386,780,000 francs.
Silver............................... 823,930,000   "

Of this heavy amount of silver coin, all but about 50,000,000 francs was in five-franc pieces, which are a legal tender in France to any amount for all debts, public and private. There was thus over $150,000,000 in silver money of full-valued currency in the Bank of France, besides $277,000,000 in gold coin.

STATEMENT OF THE CONDITION OF THE BANK OF FRANCE, Nov. 15, 1877.

DEBTOR.	Francs.	CREDITOR.	Francs.
Capital of the bank..............	182,500,000	Cash in hand and in branch banks	2,111,646,057
Profits in addition to capital	5,002,313	Commercial bills over-due.......	91,637
Reserve of the bank and its		" " discounted, not	
branches.....................	22,105,750	yet due...................	258,051,832
Reserve of landed property.....	4,000,000	Treasury bonds..............	310,775,000
Special reserve................	12,000,000	Commercial bills, branch banks..	319,520,013
Notes in circulation.............	2,455,554,750	Advances on deposits of bullion.	22,206,500
Bank-notes to order, receipts payable at sight...................	62,595,371	" in branch banks.......	4,741,600
Treasury account-current, creditor	233,465,121	" on French public securities...............	40,409,800
Current accounts, Paris..........	394,527,251	" by branch banks......	29,208,900
" " branch banks.	39,054,413	" on railway shares and	
Dividends payable.............	1,346,726	debentures.........	21,819,300
Interest on securities transferred or deposited...................	4,278,030	" by branch banks.......	17,316,800
Discounts and sundry interests ..	5,269,817	" on Credit Foncier bonds	1,547,700
Re-discounted the last six months	1,271,342	" in branches...........	1,000,100
Bills not disposable.............	2,761,699	" to the state (convention	
Reserve for eventual losses on		June 10th, 1857)....	60,000,000
prolonged bills................	6,897,164	Government stock reserve......	12,980,750
Sundries......................	16,715,598	" " disposable	81,988,823
		Rentes Immobilisées (Law of June 9th, 1857)...............	100,000,000
		Hotel and furniture of the bank and landed property branches.	9,249,423
		Expenses of management......	4,134,304
		Employ of the special reserve....	12,000,000
		Sundries......................	34,657,591
Total...............3,453,345,375		Total...............3,453,345,375	

DISTILLERIES IN THE UNITED STATES, 1877.

The following Statement shows the Number of Distilleries Registered and Operated during the Fiscal Year ended June 30, 1877.

[From the Annual Report of the Commissioner of Internal Revenue, 1877.]

STATES AND TERRITORIES.	GRAIN.		MOLASSES.		FRUIT.		Total Number Registered.	Total Number Operated.
	Number Registered.	Number Operated.	Number Registered.	Number Operated.	Number Registered.	Number Operated.		
Alabama	4	3			85	73	89	76
Arizona								
Arkansas	15	14			12	7	27	21
California	3	3			398	231	401	234
Colorado								
Connecticut	4	4			185	128	189	132
Dakota								
Delaware					73	73	73	73
District of Columbia								
Florida								
Georgia	23	22			277	228	300	250
Idaho	1	1					1	1
Illinois	34	33			41	40	75	73
Indiana	17	16			103	103	120	119
Iowa	2	1			22	20	24	21
Kansas	1				3	3	4	3
Kentucky	221	190			533	517	734	707
Louisiana	1	1					1	1
Maine								
Maryland	12	12			20	20	32	32
Massachusetts	2	2	6	6	31	30	39	28
Michigan	1	1					1	1
Minnesota								
Mississippi					2	2	2	2
Missouri	19	19			45	43	64	62
Montana								
Nebraska	1	1					1	1
Nevada								
New Hampshire			1	1	1	1	2	2
New Jersey	2	1			156	156	158	157
New Mexico					5	5	5	5
New York	8	8			103	96	111	104
North Carolina	78	63			947	930	1,025	993
Ohio	41	36			65	59	106	95
Oregon					3	3	3	3
Pennsylvania	67	63			73	73	140	136
Rhode Island								
South Carolina	5	3			16	1	21	4
Tennessee	65	65			410	402	475	467
Texas	10	8			2	2	12	10
Utah								
Vermont					8	8	8	8
Virginia	31	30			485	483	516	513
Washington								
West Virginia					164	158	164	158
Wisconsin	9	8					9	8
Wyoming								
Total	677	608	7	7	4,263	3,895	4,952	4,510

INTEREST LAWS IN THE UNITED STATES.

[Compiled from Hubbell's Legal Directory, 1877.]

Laws of each State and Territory regarding Rates of Interest and Penalties for Usury.

STATES AND TERRITORIES.	Legal Rate of Interest, per cent.	Rate Allowed by Contract, per cent.	PENALTIES FOR USURY.
Alabama	8	8	Forfeiture of entire interest.
Arizona	10	Any rate.	None.
Arkansas	6	10	Forft. of principal and interest.
California	10	Any rate.	None.
Colorado	10	Any rate.	None, except of excess.
Connecticut	6	6	Forfeiture of excess of interest.
Dakota	7	12	Forfeiture of interest.
Delaware	6	6	Forfeiture of principal.
District of Columbia	6	10	Forfeiture of entire interest.
Florida	8	Any rate.	None.
Georgia	7	12	Forfeiture of excess of interest.
Idaho	10	24	Fine of $300 or imprisonment.
Illinois	6	10	Forfeiture of excess of interest.
Indiana	6	10	Forfeiture of excess of interest.
Iowa	6	10	Forfeiture of excess of interest.
Kansas	7	12	Forfeiture of excess of interest.
Kentucky	6	8	Forfeiture of entire interest.
Louisiana	5	8	Forfeiture of entire interest.
Maine	6	Any rate.	None.
Maryland	6	6	Forfeiture of excess of interest.
Massachusetts	6	Any rate.	None.
Michigan	7	10	Forfeiture of excess of interest.
Minnesota	7	12	Forfeiture of excess over 12 p.c.
Mississippi	6	Any rate.	None.
Missouri	6	10	Forfeiture of entire interest.
Montana	10	Any rate.	None.
Nebraska	10	12	Forfeiture of interest and costs.
Nevada	10	Any rate.	None.
New Hampshire	6	6	Forfeiture of thrice the excess.
New Jersey	7	7	Forfeiture of entire interest.
New Mexico	6	Any rate.	None.
New York	7	7	Forfeiture of contract.
North Carolina	6	8	Forfeiture of entire interest.
Ohio	6	8	Forfeiture of excess above 6 p.c.
Oregon	10	12	Forfeiture of principal and int.
Pennsylvania	6	Any rate.	None.
Rhode Island	6	Any rate.	None.
South Carolina	7	Any rate.	None.
Tennessee	6	10	Forfeiture of excess of interest.
Texas	8	Any rate.	None.
Utah	10	Any rate.	None.
Vermont	6	6	Forfeiture of excess of interest.
Virginia	6	6	Forfeiture of entire interest.
Washington Territory	10	Any rate.	None.
West Virginia	6	6	Forfeiture of excess of interest.
Wisconsin	7	10	Forfeiture of entire interest.
Wyoming	12	Any rate.	None.

THE CUSTOMS TARIFF OF GREAT BRITAIN.

No protective duties are now levied on goods imported, Customs duties being charged solely for the sake of revenue. Formerly the articles subject to duty numbered nearly a thousand ; now they are only twenty-two, the chief being to-bacco, spirits, tea, and wine. The following is a complete list:

Articles.	Duty.	Articles.	Duty.
	£ s. d.		£ s. d.
Ale or beer, spec. gravity not exceeding 1065°, per bbl....	0 8 0	Naphtha, purified, gallon......	0 10 5
		Pickles, in vinegar, gallon	0 0 1
Ale or beer, spec. grav. not exceeding 1090°, per bbl......	0 11 0	Plate, gold, ounce......	0 17 0
		Plate, silver, ounce...........	0 1 6
Ale or beer, spec. gravity exceeding 1090°, per bbl......	0 16 0	Spirits, brandy, Geneva, rum, etc., gallon.................	0 10 5
Beer, Mum, per bbl...........	1 1 0	Spirits, rum,from British Colonies, gallon	0 10 2
Beer, spruce, spec. gravity not exceeding 1190°, per bbl.....	1 1 0	Spirits, cologne water, gallon.	0 16 6
Beer, spruce, exceeding 1190°, per barrel..................	1 4 0	Tea, pound	0 0 6
		Tobacco, unmanufactured, lb.	0 3 1½
Cards, playing, per doz. packs	0 3 9	Tobacco, containing less than ten per cent of moisture, lb.	0 3 6
Chicory (raw or kiln dried),cwt.	0 13 3		
Chicory (roasted or ground),lb.	0 0 2	Cavendish or Negro-head....	0 4 6
Chloral hydrate, pound.......	0 1 3	Other manufactured tobacco..	0 4 0
Chloroform, pound	0 3 0	Snuff, containing more than 13 per cent of moisture, lb...	0 3 9
Cocoa, pound................	0 0 1		
Cocoa, cwt , husks and shells.	0 2 0	Snuff, less than 13 per cent of moisture, lb...............	0 4 6
Cocoa paste and chocolate, pound	0 0 2	Tobacco, cigars, pound......	0 5 0
Coffee, raw, cwt..............	0 14 0	Varnish, containing alcohol, gallon....................	0 12 0
Coffee, kiln-dried, roasted, or ground, pound.............	0 0 2	Vinegar, gallon................	0 0 3
Collodion, gallon............	0 1 4	Wine, containing less than 26° proof spirit, gallon........	0 1 0
Essence of spruce, 10 per cent ad valorem...		Wine,containing more than 26° and less than 42° spirit,gallon	0 2 6
Ethyl, iodide of, gallon......	0 13 0		
Ether, gallon	0 1 5	Wine, for each additional degree of strength beyond 42°, gallon	0 0 3
Fruit, dried, cwt..............	0 7 0		
Malt, per quarter.............	1 4 0		

POPULATION OF GREAT BRITAIN AND IRELAND AT EACH DECENNIAL CENSUS FROM 1801 TO 1871.

	1801.	1811.	1821.	1831.	1841.	1851.	1861.	1871.
Eng. and Wales	9,156,171	10,454,529	12,172,664	14,051,986	16,035,198	18,054,170	20,228,417	22,712,266
Scotland.......	1,679,452	1,884,044	2,137,325	2,405,610	2,652,379	2,922,302	3,096,805	3,360,018
Ireland*.......	5,319,867	*6,084,996	6,869,544	7,828,347	8,222,664	6,683,968	5,880,309	5,411,416
Islands*.......	82,810	*85,547	92,654	106,542	126,249	143,435	145,674	144,638
Army, Navy, & Merchant Seamen abroad..	....	....	....	....	202,951	212,194	250,356	229,000
Unit. Kingdom	16,237,900	18,509,116	21,272,187	24,392,485	27,239,484	27,958,143	29,571,644	31,857,388

* The population of Ireland and that of the Channel Islands in the British Seas for 1801 and 1811 are given by estimate, no census having been taken before 1821.

THE COMMERCIAL CRISES OF THE CENTURY IN ENGLAND.

Compiled mainly from Levi's History of British Commerce.

ALTHOUGH what are known as commercial crises may occur in countries where the currency consists mainly of gold and silver, or where there is a mixed currency of specie and of paper based directly on the precious metals, yet the distress and ruin caused by these panics are greatly increased wherever the amount of paper money is largest, or where there is seen the greatest inflation of credit in some other form. If the reader will look carefully into the facts attending all the panics of the present century, he will find abundant evidence of the truth of this statement.

In the commercial distress and panic of 1816, in England, which closely ensued upon the restoration of peace after the protracted wars of the French Revolution, there was an enormous expansion of credit in all directions. The manufacturers of England rushed into over-production, in the hope of reaping heavy profits from the reopened markets of the Continent. In this hope they were disappointed, because of the exhaustion of the means of purchase on the part of the European populations. At the same time agricultural production, stimulated to an unnatural extent by the prodigious tax levied upon imported grain through the corn laws, carried up the price of wheat to about double its normal value. The shipping interest, which had been stimulated by hope of great gain, was compelled to feel the pressure of hard times. And the aggregate circulation of paper money, which rose to its maximum in 1814, was only half a million less in 1816. The depreciation of the paper money, which had been twenty-five per cent in the former year, stood at nearly seventeen per cent in 1815 and 1816. This redundant currency, stimulating commercial, manufacturing, and speculative enterprises, was the chief cause of the panic that soon ensued, carrying wide-spread distress throughout the United Kingdom.

The great panic of 1825–6 was directly caused by the expansion that ensued from the postponement of specie payments by Parliament

in 1823.   An act was then passed which suspended the operations of
the cash-payment act as regarded one and two pound notes for the
period of eleven years.   The effects of this respite were most disastrous.   The bankers universally put out their paper again, as if that
state of things was to last forever.   The result was seen in the stimu-
lation of all kinds of joint-stock companies and speculative enterprises.   The plethora of small notes led to an immense speculation in
goods.   Prices rose, and dealings in every commodity rose with them.
Foreign loans were put upon the London market, and eagerly gobbled
up by investors in South American securities, and all sorts of irresponsible mining and commercial companies.   The country banks,
no longer restricted by act of Parliament, instead of preparing for
specie payments by a curtailment of their issues, put forth an almost
unlimited circulation of their notes.   At last the crisis came.   In
December, 1825, the private banking houses of London began to
tumble.   Credit, which had been pushed to its utmost tension, was
unable to stand the strain.   The ruin of many commercial firms, and
the terrible struggle of others to keep their position, led to the dark-
est depression in the community.   The total number of bankruptcies
in 1825 was about 1100 ; in 1826 the number rose to 2600.   The
destruction of credit, growing out of its excessive previous expansion,
paralyzed industry, and led to the greatest distress among the working population.   Employment diminished and wages fell.   In the
financial world borrowers and lenders were involved in almost equal
ruin.   It was a bitter lesson, taught by inflation, which Parliament
improved in the following session by passing a stringent act for the
gradual withdrawal from circulation of the one and two pound bank-
note currency, and substituting a metallic currency in their room.
With this measure prosperity gradually returned to England.

    The next commercial excitement broke forth in 1836.   There had
been abundant harvests for two or three years previous, and the country was thought to be in a state of great prosperity.   Partly in consequence of this, many projects for profitable speculations were set on
foot.   Joint-stock banks, a new idea in the metropolis and elsewhere,
were started with great success.   Many projects for new lines of railway, and for all sorts of joint-stock companies, gathered around the
share market the commercial spirit of the nation, and rendered it vastly
more attractive than the markets for produce and manufactures.   Mining companies became a favorite branch of investment.   Coal, copper,
slate, lead, and silver mine companies were formed in all directions,
involving the people in great monetary obligations.   Many loans, too,
were contracted.   The stocks of foreign nations and companies rose
to a fictitious value.   In the year 1837–38, not less than four hundred
different companies were organized, with capital amounting to one
hundred million pounds.   While things were in this critical condition, news arrived of the great bank panic, and suspension of specie

payments in the United States. This was the spark which exploded the magazine, already stored with inflammable material to a dangerous extent. Additional trouble and distress were felt by many houses with American connections, who were forced to suspend. Great gloom gathered over commerce. A panic set in in earnest, and bankruptcies, stoppage of business, a fall in the value of merchandise and securities, with a chronic prostration of trade, ensued.

Ten years later came on the great English panic of 1847. This was not, like the preceding one, accompanied with a commercial crisis in the United States, but it arose, like the former one, from an inflated use of credit, though in a new and different form. Capital had become abundant in England, and profitable methods of investment were eagerly sought for. The railway, then a comparatively new means of transport, was assuming great prominence. In 1846, railway acts were passed, involving an expenditure of about £15,000,000. In 1845 the rage for railway speculation reached a most extraordinary height. The prices of shares, both of railways in operation and of merely projected lines, rose enormously. Great Western shares were quoted at £156 in January, and at £228 in September. The Midland, which in January was at £114 a share, rose in September to £188. Fortunes were made and lost, and people became wild with a market so excited. New railway enterprises by the score, and finally by the hundred, were thrust before the public, the London *Gazette* on a single day containing as many as three hundred columns of official railway advertising. Of course multitudes of abortive schemes, unreal enterprises, and fraudulent shares were foisted upon credulous investors. The frenzy soon brought about its own retribution. A partial crop failure came in, the rate of interest began to rise, money was no longer procurable on easy terms, and the value of railway shares fell fearfully.· Heavy losses ensued to all who held them. Alarm and anxiety spread by degrees from the share market to the various branches of trade. The grain merchants lost heavily from the great fall in prices. A speculation in pig-iron, which had been largely sold for future delivery (another trick of inflation times), led to the ruin of many. The price of iron went down from £5 to £3 per ton. Several banks succumbed ; consols fell to eighty-five, and everything appeared to portend an approaching national bankruptcy. Parliament not being in session, the Ministry urged upon the Bank of England to enlarge their discounts for the relief of the community, and promised a bill of indemnity if the Bank Restriction Act should be infringed. This assurance that additional relief might be obtained produced the same effect as if the Bank of England had made an issue, because it brought out the hoards of notes which the destruction of confidence had hidden away, and they went into circulation. Thus the cause of the panic was gradually removed. A parliamentary report by a committee of investigation attributed this commercial

crisis to the diversion of capital from its legitimate employment in commercial transactions, to the too rapid construction of railways, to the undue expansion of credit, and to the exaggerated expectations of extended trade.

The crisis of 1857 was accompanied by the stoppage of many banks and commercial houses. Just before this there had been a steady drain of specie from England for export to the East for a large expenditure in railways. A great amount of specie had also gone abroad for silks and other imported articles, while the war in the Crimea caused a large remittance of money for the payment of troops. At the same time, the banks of London and other cities had been long loaning upon all sorts of securities to the utmost extent of their means. "The chief failures of 1857 did not arise so much from the panic," says Levi, in his "History of British Commerce," "as from the effect of a system of acceptances and open credits, or from trading on fictitious credit, then largely prevalent." This state of things was charged by an investigating committee of the House of Commons as the principal cause of the panic. Said the report:

"It is impossible for your committee to attribute the failure of such establishments to any other cause than to their inherent unsoundness, the natural, the inevitable result of their own misconduct. Thus we have traced a system under which extensive fictitious credits have been created, by means of accommodation bills and open credits, great facilities for which have been offered by the practice of joint-stock country banks discounting such bills and rediscounting them with the bill brokers in the London market, upon the credit of the bank alone, without reference to the quality of the bills otherwise."

The British commercial crisis of 1866 sprang primarily out of the undue extension of credit in the formation of multitudes of joint-stock companies. These companies, based upon the_ leading idea of the French Credit Mobilier—which was, to limit the liability of all the shareholders to the amount of capital each contributed—led to an enormous expansion of these corporations. From 1855, when limited liability companies were for the first time admitted in the English law, to 1866, there were organized 7000 limited companies, involving a nominal investment to the amount of £893,000,000. These companies adopted not a few of the objectionable features of the Credit Mobilier of Paris. One of these illegitimate abuses of credit was the indorsement of the bills of the projectors of public works. No sooner was a project started, involving investments of millions, at home or abroad, than these finance companies indorsed the debentures, bonds, stocks, and shares, which were created and circulated in the community, producing all the risks and evils of an irredeemable paper currency. These bills were founded, not on solid security or completed enterprises, still less upon gold and silver, but they represented, like irredeemable paper, no real value. Says the London *Economist :*

"Such securities were a powerful speculation on the future, and a speculation subject to all kinds of casualties. An unfinished railway or dock has no value whatever."

We have no space to detail the sad story of this inflation. The disgraceful failure of Overend, Gurney & Co., Limited, one of those inflation houses which did a business of some thirty millions of dollars on fictitious securities, is a part of the history of that time. Two thirds of the speculative corporations ceased to exist, and out of £504,000,000 in shares, supposed to have been invested by these great companies, two thirds disappeared—some through bankruptcy, some through winding up, and some by a sudden disappearance from the market.

THE NATIONAL DEBT OF GREAT BRITAIN.

Compiled from Fenn's Compendium of Funds, 12th ed., 1874; the Financial Reform Almanac, 1877 ; and The Stock Exchange Year-Book, 1877.

THIS fiscal monster, which has swallowed upwards of TWO THOUSAND MILLIONS during the present century, owes its origin to Indirect Taxation, the Funding—*i.e.*, *Mortgaging* system, and "the Balance of Power." From the Norman Conquest to the accession of Charles II., this country contrived to fight and pay its way, without contracting a farthing of debt, because its revenue was derived from lands reserved to the Crown, lands allotted on conditions of feudal service, and feudal payments from the allottees, strictly in the nature of rent ; with occasional direct levies on the community generally, duties on commodities being almost entirely unknown. As a condition of his restoration, probably, Charles II. did away with these feudal obligations and payments, and his Parliament of Land*holders*, converting themselves into Land*owners*, gave His Majesty and his successors Excise duties on Beer, etc., payable by the people, "in compensation" for what they and their predecessors had been bound to pay as tenants of the Crown. The "Merry Monarch" contrived to overrun his means to the extent of upwards of half a million, but the debt was called "the King's," not that of the Nation. It was somewhat increased by his successor; but with William III. came the notion that it was the function of this country to maintain "The Balance of Power in Europe ;" and hence arose the Funding System, which was a mortgaging of taxes ; a conversion of the "King's Debt" into the "National Debt ;" and a very rapid growth of the latter.

The National Debt, at the period of the Revolution in 1688, amounted to about £664,000.

It was during the war with France in which this country engaged at the time of the Revolution, and which continued for a period of nearly ten years, that the foundation of the present National Debt was laid. At the close of this war in 1697, the debt was found to amount to nearly £15,000,000, and the revenue was deficient the sum of £5,000,000. At this time, also, from the irregularity with which the interest upon the floating debt was paid, Exchequer tallies and orders were at a discount of 40 per cent : and government, to redeem the credit of the nation, as well as to provide for the deficiency of the revenue, was obliged to contract a further debt, and to fund a portion of the floating securities.

At the close of the reign of Queen Anne, in 1714, the public debt had increased to about £36,175,460, bearing an annual charge for interest and annuities of £3,063,135.

In the year 1718, the interest on a part of the permanent debt, £3,775,028, was reduced from 6 to 5 per cent, the creditors having the option of taking the reduced interest or accepting payment of their principal in full, and a regular sinking fund was provided by act of Parliament for the redemption of the permanent debt. The National Debt, at the close of the reign of George I., amounted to upwards of £52,000,000. The annual charge was considerably diminished by the reduction of interest in 1717, and by a further reduction from 5 per cent to 4 per cent in 1727.

From the year 1739, the National Debt received vast additions annually for several years. The debt in 1748, after the Treaty of Peace at Aix-la-Chapelle, amounted to nearly £76,000,000, being an increase during the war of about £29,000,000.

The return of peace in 1749 having lowered the current rate of interest, and the 3 per cents, in consequence, rising to par, whilst the 4 per cents were at 107, the scheme for reducing the interest of the whole public debt to 3 per cent was revived, and carried into effect by several resolutions of the House of Commons. On the 29th of November, 1749, the act passed for this purpose, stipulating that the interest should be reduced on all the public debt redeemable by law, then bearing 4 per cent interest, including the sums due to the Bank and East India Company, and the South Sea Annuities, amounting together to £57,703,475.

The companies and the proprietors of 4 per cent stock, upon signifying their consent to the reduction on or before the 28th of February, 1750, were to receive 4 per cent to the 25th of December following; from that time to the 25th of December, 1757, 3½ per cent; after which they could receive only 3 per cent, and no part of these debts, except that due to the East India Company, to be liable to be redeemed till after the 25th of December, 1757. The time for receiving the assents to this measure was extended to the 30th of May, 1750, on condition that the interest on the further loans subscribed should be reduced from 3½ to 3 per cent, on the 25th of December, 1755. At the expiration of this second extension of time, there remained still unsubscribed the sum of £3,351,499 (of which £2,325,023 consisted of old and new South Sea Annuities). A loan of £2,100,000 was raised at 3 per cent, and the Bank advanced the remainder to pay off the above amount. Thus the interest on the entire British debt was "scaled" or reduced to 3 per cent in 1749-53 (at which it has ever since remained), by simply paying off old loans bearing higher rates with the proceeds of new loans at 3 per cent. Practically, however, the holders were in most cases glad to become themselves the purchasers. Various stocks were consolidated in 1751 into one fund, this being the origin of the present consolidated annuities.

The principal portion of the debt of Great Britain is not in the form of bonds, but of annuities. Strictly speaking, the government of Great Britain has no bonded debt. It is all a funded debt, and the practice of the government is to sell annuities; that is, upon paying £100 into the treasury, the subscriber receives a government promise to pay so much per annum during a certain time, but without any promise to return the sum paid in. The 3 per cent consolidated annuities, familiarly known as consols, practically make the funded debt of Great Britain consist of never-ending annuities, unless redeemed at the option of the government. It has never been the British practice to sell the government bonds payable at a certain time, or option, and bearing a certain interest, at a fixed price, or to the highest bidder, as in France and the United States.

The war with France, which broke out in 1756, though it continued but seven years, added nearly £60,000,000 to the public debt, which at the conclusion of the war in 1763 amounted to £133,000,000. During the twelve years of tranquillity which succeeded the Peace of Paris, about £6,000,000 of the debt was discharged; so that at the commencement of the American War, in 1775, the debt amounted to £126,842,811. During the seven years in which this country was engaged in war with the United States, the National Debt was more than doubled; for although the independence of America was acknowledged in 1782, yet loans were raised in several subsequent years in order to defray the remaining expenses of the war;

and it was not until 1786 that the revenue was found to be sufficient for the expenditure. In that year, the debt amounted to £245,466,855.

Early in the year 1793, the war with France commenced, which continued, with only a very short interruption, until 1815, a period of 22 years. This long contest brought with it an immense increase in the expenditure of the country, and a consequent augmentation of the public debt; stock to the amount of upwards of £613,000,000 was added to the National Debt during this contest, and about £23,000,000 to the annual charges.

The following table shows the progress of the National Debt, funded and unfunded, from its commencement to the close of the war in 1815, and its decrease since:

	PRINCIPAL.	INTEREST.
National Debt at the Revolution in 1688.............	£664,263	£39,855
Increase during William III.'s reign................	12,102,902	1,175,469
Debt at the accession of Queen Anne, 1702..........	£12,767,225	£1,215,324
Increase during her reign	23,408,235	1,847,811
At the accession of George I., 1714.................	£36,175,460	£3,063,185
Increase during his reign	16,675,337	323,507
At the accession of George II., 1727.................	£52,850,797	£2,739,628
Decrease during 12 years' peace, ending 1739.......	6,236,914	708,744
At the commencement of the Spanish War, 1739.....	£46,613,883	£2,030,884
Increase during the war..............................	29,195,249	1,134,881
At the end of the Spanish War, 1748.................	£75,812,132	£3,165,765
Decrease during 8 years' peace......................	1,237,107	412,199
At the commencement of the Seven Years' War, 1756.	£74,575,025	£2,753,566
Increase during the war..............................	52,219,912	1,994,283
At the Peace of 1762.................................	£126,794,937	£4,747,849
Increase during 13 years' peace.............	367,476	44,330
At the commencement of the American War, 1775...	£127,162,413	£4,703,519
Increase during the war..............................	104,681,218	4,362,066
At the end of the American War, 1783...............	£231,843,631	£9,065,585
Increase during 10 years' peace.....................	16,031,203	645,653
At the commencement of the French War, 1793.....	£247,874,434	£9,711,238
Increase during 9 years' war........................	289,778,574	10,557,313
At the Peace of Amiens, 1802.......................	£537,653,008	£20,268,551
Increase during 13 years' war......................	323,386,041	12,377,067
Debt at the Peace of Paris, in September, 1815.......	£861,039,049	£32,645,618
Decrease to March 31, 1835........................ ..	55,627,359	4,669,036
Debt in March, 1835...............................	£805,411,690	£27,976,592
Increase during 2 years of the Russian War........	30,264,564	809,226
Debt in March, 1857...............................	£835,676,254	£28,785,808
Decrease during the past 20 years..................	59,802,541	1,085,808
Debt in March, 1877...............................	£775,873,713	£27,700,000

Since the conclusion of the long war in 1815, the National Debt of the Empire has thus declined from £861,039,049 to £775,873,713, or about 10 per cent, in something over half a century, notwithstanding the additions in 1835, when slavery was

abolished in the Colonies; in 1847, to supply food to Ireland; in 1855–56, on account of the Russian War ; and in 1870 for the purchase of the telegraphs.   The annual interest on the debt has fallen from £32,645,618 to £27,700,000 in the same period, or about 18 per cent.   In the same interval both the population and the wealth of the Empire have materially increased, thus rendering the individual burden far less onerous now than fifty years ago.   The following outline will convey some idea of the comparative drain entailed by the National Debt upon individual resources and national wealth :

Years.	Population of Great Britain and Ireland.	Amount of National Debt.	Average Debt per Head.	Annual Charge on Debt.	Rate of Annual Charge per Head.
1815...	20,000,000	£861,000,000	£43	£32,600,000	£1.63 or 32s. 7d.
1855...	28,200,000	805,000,000	28½	28,000,000	1.00 or 20 0
1860...	29,300,000	822,000,000	28	28,700,000	0.98 or 19 7
1865...	30,300,000	812,000,000	26¾	26,400,000	0.88 or 17 7
1870...	31,500,000	800,000,000	25⅓	27,000,000	0.86 or 17 2
1877...	33,100,000	776,000,000	23½	27,700,000	0.84 or 16 9

There is, therefore, now a very much smaller tax upon each individual inhabitant of the British Islands on account of the National Debt than there was half a century ago.

It must, however, be noted that Great Britain has seldom been able to borrow large sums at par for its 3 per cent obligations.   It was one part of Mr. PITT's vicious system of finance during the great wars of the French Revolution, to pretend that the government could always get money at 3 per cent, when, in point of fact, it could not borrow at any such rate.   The operation was about this : A £100 annuity at 3 per cent was sold, and if the money market was also at 3 per cent, the purchaser would pay £100 for it ; but if interest was higher, at 5 per cent, for example, he would only pay £60 for it.   If the market rate was 4 per cent, the government would sell its £100 annuity at £75.   British consols sold at 90 (which is rather above than below the average price) represent an interest of 3⅓ per cent, and if redeemed require the government to pay £100 for every £90 received.   In this way the great National Debt as it now exists was largely contracted.   The money was borrowed nominally at 3 per cent, but really at 4 to 5 per cent, with the obligation to return more than was actually received for the annuity, by one tenth to one half.   Sir Archibald Alison, in his History of Modern Europe, estimates, that when Great Britain pays off its whole debt, it will have to pay about £250,000,000, or upwards of one thousand millions of dollars, more than it received.

The public debt, in January, 1816, amounted to £863,601,190, which represented its maximum at any period.   From that date to the Russian war there was a considerable decrease ; but that conflict caused an increase from 805¼ millions to more than 835¼ millions.   Since then, we have, in obedience to an increasing public feeling on the subject, met all special outlays out of revenue (the most recent being the Abyssinian War, the purchase of the telegraphs, and the Geneva Award), and have at the same time materially reduced both the volume and the relative annual charge of the debt.   The total is now, including terminable annuities, taken at their capital value, £773,348,686.   By act of Parliament passed in 1875, a sum of £27,400,000 was to be used in the service of the debt for the year 1875–76; £27,800,000 for 1876–77; and thereafter £28,000,000 per annum.   Whatever remains after paying the interest on the debt is to be used in reducing the amount of the debt.   At present the surplus is unimportant ; but in 1885 annuities amounting to £4,354,719 fall in, and

there will then be a large margin for sinking-fund purposes, supposing that the arrangement is not interfered with in the meantime. The several public stocks stood as follows on March 31st, 1876 :

Consols, £394,551,674. Interest at the rate of 3 per cent per annum, due the 5th of January and July.
Reduced 3 per cents, £94,896,607. Interest due the 5th of April and October.
New 3 per cents, £207,265,708. Interest due the 5th of April and October.
New 3½ per cents, £225,746. Interest due the 5th of January and July, and the principal January, 1894.
New 2½ per cents, £3,794,426. Interest due the 5th of January and July, and the principal January, 1894.
Annuities expiring 1855, to the amount of £4,354,719 a year, due the 5th of April and October.
Annuities (Red Sea Telegraph) expiring August, 1908, to the amount of £36,000 a year, due the 4th of February and August.
Annuities expiring at various periods amounting to £782,935 per annum.
Exchequer bills are issued for periods of six months, and there are two classes always in the market, namely, those on which interest is due the 11th of March and September, and those on which it is due the 11th of June and December. They bear a rate of interest fixed at the time of issue, and in the month preceding their maturity the Treasury gives notice of the rate at which they may be renewed. This rate harmonizes necessarily with the current value of money. The amount of Exchequer bills afloat on March 31st, 1876, was only £4,239,300 ; but in 1871 the amount was close upon fifty-seven millions.

This list of public stocks does not represent the entire National Debt, the most important amounts excluded being the £11,015,100 due to the Bank of England, and £2,630,739 due to the Bank of Ireland, on which 3 per cent interest is paid. There are also Exchequer bonds to the amount of about a million and a half. The Government debt is managed by the Bank of England and the Bank of Ireland, as regards Great Britain and Ireland, respectively.

THE SINKING FUND.

Many schemes have been proposed for the extinction of the National Debt. One of the most plausible, and which even now has its advocates, is that which was first proposed by Sir Robert Walpole, and afterwards elaborated by Mr. Pitt. The proposal was that a sum of money be raised every year, and put by at compound interest, and, allowing this money to accumulate, it would eventually reach a sum as large as the debt itself, and thus extinguish it. The advocates of this scheme did not see that by annually paying off such an amount as that proposed to be put by, the same result would be arrived at by a less costly process. Accordingly, for many years, it has been customary to apply surplus income for this purpose, and the Commissioners for the Reduction of the National Debt, every quarter, when there is a surplus, lay out the amount in stock, and cancel it ; thus, by purchasing consols at the market price of 92¼, the sum of £92,250 would enable them to cancel debt to the nominal amount of £100,000. Another plan, one which found favor both with Mr. Gladstone and Mr. Lowe, was in creating annuities for various terms of years, as shown above. By this means the sum of £5,364,487, paid annually, is the means of extinguishing debt to the amount of £51,911,227. Lord Beaconsfield has now made a systematic attempt to cancel the National Debt, by the simple, old-fashioned plan of paying off some amount every year. In 1876 the sum of £280,150 was thus paid off.

TOTAL AMOUNT OF THE NATIONAL DEBT AT THE END OF EACH
FINANCIAL YEAR, FROM 1861 TO 1877, INCLUSIVE.

From the (official) Statistical Abstract of the United Kingdom for 1877.

Financial Years ended 31st March.	Funded Debt.			Amount of Unfunded Debt.	Total Amount of National Debt, inclusive of Unclaimed Stock and Dividends.
	Capital of Unredeemed Funded Debt, inclusive of Unclaimed Stock and Dividends.	Estimated Capital of Terminable Annuities (computed in 3 per cent Stock).			
1861............	£788,970,719	£18,947,740		£16,689,000	£824,607,459
1862............	788,229,618	19,388,876		16,517,900	824,136,394
1863............	787,422,928	20,716,727		16,495,400	824,635,055
1864............	781,712,401	26,442,428		13,136,000	821,290,829
1865............	780,202,104	25,408,370		10,742,500	816,352,974
1866............	773,941,190	25,435,034		8,187,700	807,563,924
1867............	770,188,625	27,521,513		7,956,800	805,666,938
1868............	741,844,981	56,816,803		7,911,100	806,572,884
1869............	741,112,640	55,471,424		8,896,100	805,480,164
1870............	741,514,681	53,130,380		6,761,500	801,406,561
1871............	732,043,270	57,969,885		6,091,000	796,104,155
1872............	731,756,962	55,749,070		5,155,100	792,661,132
1873............	727,374,082	53,558,580		4,829,100	785,761,762
1874............	728,514,005	51,289,640		4,479,600	779,283,245
1875............	714,797,715	55,311,671		5,239,000	775,348,386
1876............	713,657,517	51,911.227		11,401,800	776,970,544
1877............	712,621,355	49,308,558		13,943,800	775,873,713

STATISTICS OF BRITISH EMIGRATION AND IMMIGRATION.

OFFICIAL reports of the emigration from and immigration into the United Kingdom during the year 1876, show that the total number of emigrants and immigrants of British and Irish origin from and into the United Kingdom during the year was as follows: To the United States, 34,554 ; from the United States, 54,697 ; excess of immigrants from the United States, 143. To Canada, 9335 ; from Canada, 6629 ; excess of emigrants, 2706. To Australia, 32,196 ; from Australia, 2579 ; excess of emigrants, 29,617. To all other places, 13,384 ; from all other places, 7499 ; excess of emigrants, 5888. Total emigration, 109,469 ; total immigration, 71,404 ; excess of emigrants, 38,065. The total emigration of all nationalities was 138,222 ; total immigration of all nationalities, 91,647 ; excess of emigration of all nationalities, 45,575.

Great stress is laid in these reports upon the almost total cessation of Irish emigration to the United States (the favorite land of the Irish emigrants in the past), and the great decline in Irish emigration in general.

The following statistics concerning Irish emigration are given in these reports : The total number of emigrants (natives of Ireland) who left Ireland from May 1st, 1851 (the date at which these official returns commenced), to December 31st, 1876 (irrespective of the Irish who sailed from England and Scotland), was 2,414,978. Nineteen-twentieths of those emigrants found homes in the United States. The total Irish emigration, from Irish ports to the United States, during the year 1876, was 14,887 ; the Irish immigrants returned from the United States during the same year numbered 11,140.

Total emigration from the United Kingdom during the year 1876 : English, 73,396 ; Irish, 25,076 ; Scotch, 10,097 ; foreigners, 28,753. The total number of emigrants from the United Kingdom (British and Irish) from 1853 to 1876, inclusive, is given as 8,963,518 ; to the United States, 2,667,043 (67 per cent of the whole) ; to Canada, 874,469 ; to Australia, 804,272 ; to all other places, 117,733.

FOREIGN TRADE OF GREAT BRITAIN, 1861-1876.

From the Statistical Abstract of the United Kingdom, 1877.

VALUE OF THE TOTAL IMPORTS AND EXPORTS OF MERCHANDISE INTO AND FROM THE UNITED KINGDOM, WITH PROPORTION THEREOF PER HEAD OF TOTAL POPULATION.

Years	IMPORTS.		EXPORTS.					TOTAL OF IMPORTS AND EXPORTS.	
	Total Value.	Proportion per Head of Population United Kingdom	British Produce.		Foreign and Colonial Produce.	Total Value of British and Foreign and Colonial Produce.	Total Value.		Proportion per Head of Population United Kingdom
			Total Value.	Proportion per Head of Population United Kingdom					
	£	£ s. d.	£	£ s. d	£	£	£		£ s. d.
1861..	217,485,024	7 10 2	125,102,814	4 6 5	34,529,684	159,632,498	377,117,522		13 0 5
1862..	225,716,976	7 14 7	123,999,264	4 5 7	42,175,870	166,168,134	391,885,110		13 8 5
1863..	248,919,020	8 9 5	146,602,342	5 0 0	50,300,067	196,902,400	445,821,429		15 3 5
1864..	274,952,172	9 5 7	160,449,053	5 8 4	52,170,561	212,619,614	487,571,786		16 9 0
1865..	271,072,285	9 1 7	165,835,725	5 11 1	52,995,851	218,831,576	489,903,861		16 8 2
1866..	295,290,274	9 16 4	188,917,536	6 5 7	49,988,146	238,905,682	534,195,956		17 15 2
1867..	275,183,137	9 1 5	180,961,923	5 19 4	44,840,606	225,802,529	500,985,666		16 1 3
1868..	294,693,608	9 12 10	179,677,812	5 17 4	48,100,642	227,778,454	522,472,062		17 1 3
1869..	295,460,214	9 11 2	189,953,957	6 2 7	47,061,095	237,015,052	532,475,266		17 4 6
1870..	303,257,493	9 14 4	190,586,322	6 7 11	44,493,755	244,080,577	547,838,070		17 10 10
1871..	331,015,480	10 10 1	223,066,162	7 1 7	60,508,538	283,574,700	614,590,180		19 10 1
1872..	354,693,694	11 2 6	251,257,347	8 1 0	59,331,497	314,588,834	669,282,458		21 0 6
1873..	371,287,372	11 11 2	255,161,603	7 18 10	55,840,162	311,004,765	682,292,137		21 4 6
1874..	370,082,701	11 8 3	239,558,121	7 7 9	58,092,343	297,650,464	667,733,165		20 11 10
1875..	373,939,577	11 8 5	223,465,963	6 16 6	53,146,360	281,612,323	655,551,900		20 0 4
1876..	375,154,703	11 6 8	200,639,204	6 1 3	56,137,398	256,776,602	631,931,306		19 1 11

From the Statistical Abstract of the United Kingdom, 1877.

TONNAGE OF BRITISH AND FOREIGN VESSELS (Sailing and Steam) ENTERED AND CLEARED AT PORTS IN THE UNITED KINGDOM, FROM AND TO FOREIGN COUNTRIES AND BRITISH POSSESSIONS.

Years	ENTERED.			CLEARED.			TOTAL.		
	British.	Foreign.	Total.	British.	Foreign.	Total.	British.	Foreign.	Total.
	Tons.	Tons.	Tons.	Tons.	Tons.	Tons.	Tons.	Tons.	Tons.
1861	7,721,035	5,458,554	13,179,589	7,699,497	5,716,553	13,416,052	15,420,582	11,175,109	26,595,641
1862	7,856,539	5,234,451	13,091,090	8,090,221	5,354,128	13,444,349	15,946,660	10,588,579	26,535,439
1863	8,430,146	4,825,917	13,256,063	8,569,346	4,893,494	13,482,670	17,019,392	9,719,341	26,738,733
1864	9,028,100	4,486,911	13,515,011	9,173,575	4,515,923	13,689,498	18,201,675	9,002,834	27,204,509
1865	9,623,432	4,694,454	14,317,886	9,735,523	4,843,683	14,579,206	19,358,965	9,538,137	28,897,092
1866	10,692,102	4,920,068	15,612,170	10,563,694	5,086,556	15,650,280	21,255,726	10,006,724	31,262,450
1867	11,197,865	5,140,952	16,338,817	11,172,203	5,245,090	16,417,295	22,370,070	10,386,042	32,756,112
1868	11,225,917	5,396,758	16,622,675	11,434,507	5,623,797	17,058,304	22,660,424	11,020,555	33,680,979
1869	11,721,697	5,476,427	17,198,924	12,067,270	5,644,687	17,711,957	23,789,167	11,121,114	34,910,281
1870	12,980,390	5,732,974	18,113,364	12,691,790	5,835,028	18,526,818	25,072,180	11,568,002	36,640,182
1871	13,857,638	6,622,259	20,479,897	14,177,110	6,890,871	21,067,981	28,034,748	13,513,130	41,547,878
1872	14,173,289	6,842,126	21,015,415	14,545,801	6,939,809	21,485,610	28,719,090	13,781,935	42,501,025
1873	14,541,028	7,323,929	21,864,957	15,106,316	7,468,713	22,575,029	29,647,344	14,792,642	44,439,986
1874	14,833,644	7,534,966	22,368,510	15,434,507	7,804,408	23,088,683	30,089,683	15,339,274	45,428,957
1875	15,190,991	7,502,172	22,693,163	15,753,753	7,829,922	23,583,675	30,944,744	15,332,094	46,276,638
1876	16,511,951	8,555,313	25,067,264	16,930,026	8,787,610	25,717,636	33,441,973	17,342,923	50,784,902

WHERE ENGLAND BUYS HER COTTON.—QUANTITIES OF RAW COTTON IMPORTED INTO THE UNITED KINGDOM FROM VARIOUS COUNTRIES.

From the Statistical Abstract of Great Britain, 1877.

Years.	The United States.	Mexico.	British West India Islands and British Guiana.	New Granada and Venezuela.	Brazil.	The Mediterranean, exclusive of Egypt.	Egypt.	British Possessions in the East Indies.	China.	Japan.	Other Countries.	Total Imported.
	Lbs.	Lbs.	Lbs.	Lbs.	Lbs.	Lbs.	Lbs.	Lbs.	Lbs.	Lbs.	Lbs.	Lbs.
1861	819,500,528	......	486,304	154,896	17,290,336	587,104	40,892,096	369,040,448	......	......	9,083,024	1,256,984,736
1862	18,524,224	3,131,520	5,563,376	1,170,736	23,339,008	6,225,856	50,012,464	392,654,528	1,766,016	......	17,585,844	523,973,296
1863	6,994,080	19,278,112	25,181,856	2,623,600	22,603,168	13,806,576	93,559,368	434,420,784	30,856,336	224	20,655,824	670,061,128
1864	14,199,656	25,539,024	28,738,992	6,600,968	38,017,504	21,755,216	125,493,648	506,527,992	86,187,008	711,424	33,770,240	894,102,894
1865	135,832,440	36,661,890	16,536,912	14,059,328	65,403,152	27,239,072	176,838,144	445,947,600	35,855,792	9,404,904	30,501,744	973,502,000
1866	590,001,136	352,240	11,589,392	11,369,342	68,524,400	11,510,688	118,260,800	615,302,240	5,837,440	2,988,896	22,419,376	1,377,514,096
1867	598,199,800	2,464	4,810,288	9,713,872	70,430,080	6,780,480	126,295,264	498,317,008	527,184	46,082	17,802,464	1,202,885,904
1868	574,478,016	......	2,725,856	4,906,160	94,796,768	6,702,304	129,182,928	498,706,640	......	......	18,939,440	1,326,761,616
1869	457,358,944	40,544	1,095,568	8,045,728	79,417,948	13,506,640	160,450,290	481,440,176	448	21,504	19,574,936	1,221,571,232
1870	716,348,848	2,016	2,314,256	4,767,056	64,234,688	11,510,912	143,710,448	341,596,608	10,528	......	55,031,760	1,339,367,190
1871	1,088,677,920	......	2,671,536	6,582,240	86,158,800	3,777,424	176,166,480	431,209,744	102,144	......	82,795,468	1,778,139,776
1872	625,600,080	31,136	1,450,960	7,960,624	112,509,624	8,081,744	177,581,712	443,294,736	252,112	......	32,184,544	1,406,837,472
1873	832,573,616	28,448	1,070,160	3,973,096	72,480,800	8,670,816	204,977,196	367,649,744	1,016,848	......	35,155,568	1,527,596,224
1874	874,196,864	16,464	592,768	6,391,952	70,501,408	2,195,312	172,317,498	412,025,040	396,832	......	18,598,301	1,566,864,432
1875	841,333,472	......	662,928	4,195,632	71,859,536	5,835,760	163,912,336	385,645,552	543,520	......	18,982,432	1,492,351,168
1876	932,800,176	45,094	752,192	2,029,498	53,369,341	434,672	199,245,312	275,856,336	350,176	224	22,471,904	1,467,858,846

Note.—The above statistics represent, in each case, the amount of cotton imported into the United Kingdom during each fiscal year. The fiscal year of Great Britain closes March 31st.

HOW THE FRENCH PAID THE THOUSAND MILLIONS.

No event of modern times has excited more wide and genuine surprise than the ease with which the French people paid off the heavy war indemnity of $1,000,000,000 to Germany. It has been a puzzle alike to financiers, to statesmen, and to political economists, how a nation but just emerged from a most costly (though brief) military struggle, and whose annual expenditures exceeded its income, could raise so enormous a sum in cash in less than two years' time. National pride, it was widely said, had much to do with it ; but no amount of national pride could have raised a thousand millions of dollars in a nation where the conditions of great accumulated wealth and general prosperity did not pre-exist. National pride had not availed to save French honor from condign and overwhelming defeat in war, nor to avert the humiliating aspect of her capital in the hands of a foreign foe, nor to redeem her arms from the reproach of ill-prepared and undisciplined forces, and badly organized campaigns.

Another theory of this rapid payment of the stupendous fine of five milliards of francs was that France was the holder of about ten milliards ($2,000,000,000) of foreign securities, which were sold out, and the proceeds invested in the new *rentes*, or government bonds issued at five per cent interest, to raise money for meeting the German indemnity. For, be it mentioned, Bismarck had exacted not only cash payment, without credit, but also payment in gold and silver. The whole sum of $1,100,000,000 (including 200,000,000 francs levied on the city of Paris, and other war contributions levied during the progress of hostilities) was paid in specie, excepting only 100,000,000 francs in notes of the Bank of France, which the Prussians consented to take in place of an equal amount of gold. Inquiry into the current of exchanges actually developed the fact that France was exporting securities and importing gold the whole time of the indemnity payments ; but the actual amount to which the flow of the precious metals into France extended on this account could not be accurately learned.

Another explanation of the rapid liquidation by France of this
prodigious levy has been furnished by citing the alleged facts (first
brought out by M. Bonnet, in the *Revue des Deux Mondes*) that the
annual income of France is eighteen milliards, or $3,600,000,000, and
that the payment to Germany took only about one third of this gross
annual earnings of the French people. How much should be
deducted for annual expenditure, was not clearly shown. But there
can be no doubt that to the general character for frugality, and the
accumulated savings of the French people, must be mainly credited
the great financial phenomenon of the nineteenth century. The
enormous loans which the payment of the indemnity compelled the
French Government to put upon the market were all promptly taken,
and the greater portion of the money came from the French people.
Five per cent *rentes* or bonds to the heavy amount of 8,200,000,000
francs, or $1,640,000,000, were all taken, at an average price of eighty-
three per cent, thus making the interest to investors average six
per cent. Not only so, but the second loan, of 1872, was so eagerly
sought for that the subscriptions covered the amount called for, thirteen times over, compelling the government to award the *rentes*
among the subscribers *pro rata*.

All travellers in France in former years as well as in recent times
unite in representing the French people as great economists. With
them, not only does a very little money go a great way in supplying
their wants, but the sums saved, even out of the slenderest incomes,
represent a handsome surplus. Sir Robert Peel used to say that
" in England there is one man in every five who spends all he gets,
but that in France there is not one in forty who spends his income ;
the other thirty-nine lay something by." This observation has been
actually verified by inquiring travellers as regards the agricultural
population throughout France. And while it is not true in so extraordinary a proportion of the artisan population, and especially of
those who earn high wages, the spirit of frugality is far more widely
diffused in France than in any other European nation. That profusion and waste which characterize the use of the means of living
in England, and more conspicuously still in the United States, is
quite unknown among the French people. Of what nine families of
every ten would here throw away, a French family would make a
variety of appetizing dishes ; and it is literally true that French men
and women would live, and live well, on the mere waste of American
families. These habits of economy enable the people to lay up their
little savings year by year, and it is well known that the public
funds are the most favorite means of investment with the peasantry.
The French *rentes* can be had in denominations of one hundred francs
($20) and upwards, and have always been highly popular with the
masses. The principle of popularizing the loans of the government

has worked admirably, and has been borrowed by us to advantage in the issue of United States bonds, which are now to be had in sums as low as fifty dollars, although it might be more widely extended, to the interest of the people and the government, giving the people a ten-dollar bond as a secure investment for small savings.

Here is a fact which speaks volumes in favor of the French system of public loans. So long ago as 1867, the debt of France was held by 1,095,683 persons, who averaged $2000 each. It is now still more widely distributed, till it might be said with almost literal truth, that half the families in France have money in the public funds. In England, on the other hand, her great public debt of $3,850,000,000 is in the hands of only 126,331 persons, thus averaging more than $30,000 to each holder. It is, unfortunately, impossible to ascertain how many persons hold the public debt of the United States, because so large a proportion of it is in the form of coupon bonds, which pass from hand to hand without registration. In France, on the other hand, all the *rentes* are inscribed in the name of the holder on the books of the treasury. To have their names in the *Grand Livre* of the public debt is an honor eagerly sought after by the masses of the people. The recent reports of the French Savings Banks prove that a very large withdrawal of deposits has taken place from these savings institutions for the purpose of putting them into *rentes*.

This wide diffusion of the evidences of credit of the government has another most wholesome effect which must not be overlooked. During all the recent enormous drain upon her resources, which has nearly doubled her national debt, there has not been heard anywhere among the French people the slightest hint of repudiation. That which demagogues are continually preaching to the laboring classes in England and in this country is practically unknown, even as an idea, in France, and, if it were broached, would be met with an almost unanimous cry of reprobation from one end of the land to the other. The French people look upon their public debt as an obligation sacredly due ; and it is due in the larger part to themselves.

Another striking feature of the prosperity of France which aids in enabling her to bear the extraordinary fiscal burdens imposed upon her, is the fact of the wide distribution of real estate among the citizens. Statistics establish the fact that there are six millions of houses in France, and the majority of them are homesteads belonging to their tenants. Three fifths of the entire population are inhabitants of the rural districts, while in England the proportion is only one fifth, four fifths being residents of towns. The extraordinarily large proportion of Frenchmen who live on their own land has long excited the attention of observing travellers.

Finally, one conspicuous element in that national prosperity which has brought the world to a wondering recognition of the vast

resources of France is the recent development of her commerce. Since 1855 the foreign commerce of France has been considerably more than doubled. Her mastery of the finer mechanic arts and the perfection to which the processes of manufacture have been carried, are well known the world over. The frugality of her people is only matched by their industry. The whole country teems with productiveness. French fabrics are found in almost endless profusion and variety in all the markets of the globe. It is this constantly growing fertility of production, joined with the causes previously enumerated, which has enabled the French people to bear with such marvellous ease a burden which it was almost universally predicted would crush and overwhelm them.

THE LATIN UNION AND THE SILVER QUESTION.

From the Paris Correspondence of The Economist, November, 1877.

THE time is approaching for the annual meeting of the delegates of the Latin Union, unless the five Powers should conclude among themselves by their diplomatic agents, as on the last occasion, some arrangement to postpone any reopening of the discussion on the silver question. In January, 1876, the delegates fixed the total coinage of silver five-franc pieces for that year at a total sum of 120 millions of francs, in which was, however, comprised a sum of 8,400,000 francs for Greece, in addition to her proportional contingent. During the year the subject lost much of its interest, in France at least, from M. Leon Say's bill, passed in August, 1876, to suspend all coinage of silver for private individuals. As the government alone preserved the right to coin even the sum of silver fixed for France, all speculation in silver ceased. The price of silver having besides recovered, the government apparently thought it unnecessary to assemble the delegates in January last, and a verbal convention was agreed to, that each of the five powers should limit its coinage in 1877 to one half of the sum fixed for 1876. According to that arrangement, the share of each of the powers would be—Switzerland, 3,600,000 fr. ; Belgium, 5,400,000 fr. ; France, 27,000,000 fr.; Italy, 18,000,000 fr.; Greece, 1,800,000 fr.; together, 55,800,000 fr. In what measure each of the powers has exercised its right of coining silver during the last two years is not known, as no official information has been given since the publication of the report by the Swiss delegates to their government last year. According to that document, the Swiss Government, in 1875, although empowered by the convention to coin to the amount of ten millions in that year, did not exercise the right. France also, since the coinage has become a government monopoly, may have abstained from adding to the already enormous stock of silver in the country, at least so long as M. Leon Say was at the Ministry of Finance; for although he opposed the demonetization of silver, he was not insensible to the inconveniences of the double standard, and is likely to have stopped the further production of legal-tender silver coin. The resumption of specie payments in January next—if it takes place—can produce no effect on the market value of silver, so long as the law of August, 1876, suspending the coinage of silver for private individuals, remains unrepealed.

The law according to which the Bank of France was to resume specie payments on the 1st of January next, was passed two or three years ago, and the subject has not since been mentioned in the Chambers. The freedom of converting bullion into coin is a necessary corollary to the resumption of specie payments by the Bank of France.

With respect to Belgium, I am informed that no silver has been coined in the mint there this year. Italy has probably exercised her right to the full, but it will be found that the total coinage of the countries forming the Latin Union in 1877 has been considerably within the limit of 55,000,000 francs, at which it was fixed.

VALUE OF FOREIGN COINS IN UNITED STATES MONEY,

AS PROCLAIMED BY THE TREASURY DEPARTMENT,

January 1, 1877.

COUNTRY.	MONETARY UNIT.	STANDARD.	VALUE IN U. S. MONEY.	STANDARD COIN.
Austria........	Florin...	Silver..	$0.45 3	Florin.
Belgium	Franc..........	G. & S.	.19 3	5, 10, and 20 francs.
Bolivia	Dollar..........	G. & S.	.06 5	Escudo, ½ bolivar and bolivar.
Brazil..........	Milreis of 1,000 reis	Gold...	.54 5	None.
British Possessions in North America	Dollar..........	Gold...	1.00	
Bogota..........	Peso.......... ..	Gold...	.96 5	
Cent'l America.	Dollar..........	Silver..	.91 8	Dollar.
Chili........ .	Peso.......... ..	Gold...	.91 2	Condor, doubloon, and escudo.
Denmark..... ..	Crown..........	Gold ..	.26 8	10 and 20 crowns.
Ecuador......	Dollar..........	Silver..	.91 8	Dollar.
Egypt..........	Pound of 100 piasters......	Gold...	4.97 4	5, 10, 25, and 50 piasters.
France..... ...	Franc..........	G. & S.	.19 3	5, 10, and 20 francs.
Great Britain...	Pound sterling.	Gold...	4.86 6½	½ sovereign and sovereign.
Greece	Drachma.......	G. & S.	.19 3	5, 10, 20, 50, and 100 drachmas.
German Empire	Mark...........	Gold...	.23 8	5, 10, and 20 marks.
Japan....... ..	Yen...........	Gold...	.99 7	1, 2, 5, 10, and 20 yen.
India..........	Rupee of 16 annas...........	Silver..	.43 6	
Italy....	Lira..........	G. & S.	.19 3	5, 10, 20, 50, and 100 lire.
Liberia	Dollar..........	Gold...	1.00	
Mexico.........	Dollar..........	Silver..	.99 8	Peso or dol..5,10,25, & 50 centavo.
Netherlands....	Florin..........	G. & S.	.38 5	Florin ; 10 guldens, gold ($4.01,9).
Norway........	Crown	Gold...	.26 8	10 and 20 crowns.
Peru.	Dollar..........	Silver..	.91 8	
Portugal........	Milreis of 1,000 reis	Gold...	1.08	2, 5, and 10 milreis.
Russia..........	Rouble of 100 copecks......	Silver..	.73 4	¼, ½, and 1 rouble.
Sandwich Isl'ds	Dollar..	Gold...	1.00	
Spain...........	Peseta of 100 centimes.....	G. & S.	.19 3	5, 10, 20, 50, and 100 pesetas.
Sweden.........	Crown..........	Gold...	.26 8	10 and 20 crowns.
Switzerland....	Franc..........	G. & S.	.19 3	5, 10, and 20 francs.
Tripoli.........	Mahbub of 20 piasters......	Silver..	.82 9	
Tunis..........	Piaster of 16 caroubs	Silver..	.11 8	
Turkey	Piaster....... ...	Gold...	.04 3	25, 50, 100, 250, and 500 piasters.
United States of Colombia..	Peso	Silver..	.91 8	

The above table exhibits the values in United States money of account, of the pure gold or silver representing, respectively, the monetary units and standard coins of foreign countries, in compliance with the Act of Congress of March 3, 1873, which provides " that the value of foreign coin, as expressed in the money of account of the United States, shall be that of the pure metal of such coin of standard value," and that " the values of the standard coins in circulation of the various nations of the world shall be estimated annually by the Director of the Mint, and be proclaimed on the first day of January by the Secretary of the Treasury."

The estimate of values contained in the above table has been made by the Director of the Mint, and proclaimed in compliance with the above stated provisions of law.

COINAGE OF THE UNITED STATES FROM THE ORGANI-
ZATION OF THE MINT TO JUNE 30, 1877.

From the Official Report of the Director of the Mint.

Gold Coinage.

Period.	Double-eagles.	Eagles.	Half-eagles.	Quarter-eagles.	Three dollars.	Dollars.
	$	$	$	$	$	$
1793 to 1795	....	27,950	43,535			
1796	....	69,340	30,980	2,407 50		
1797	....	83,230	18,045	2,147 50		
1798	....	79,740	124,335	1,585 00		
1799	....	174,830	37,255	1,200 00		
1800	....	259,650	58,110			
1801	....	292,540	130,030			
1802	....	150,900	265,880	6,530 00		
1803	....	89,790	167,530	1,057 50		
1804	....	97,950	152,875	8,317 50		
1805	....	....	165,915	4,452 50		
1806	....	....	320,465	4,040 00		
1807	....	....	420,465	17,030 00		
1808	....	....	277,890	6,775 00		
1809	....	....	169,375			
1810	....	....	501,435			
1811	....	....	497,905			
1812	....	....	290,435			
1813	....	....	477,140			
1814	....	....	77,270			
1815	....	....	3,175			
1816	....	....	....			
1817	....	....	....			
1818	....	....	242,940			
1819	....	....	258,615			
1820	....	....	1,319,030			
1821	....	....	173,205	16,120 00		
1822	....	....	88,980			
1823	....	....	72,425			
1824	....	....	86,700	6,500 00		
1825	....	....	145,300	11,085 00		
1826	....	....	90,345	1,900 00		
1827	....	....	124,565	7,000 00		
1828	....	....	140,145			
1829	....	....	287,210	8,507 50		
1830	....	....	631,755	11,350 00		
1831	....	....	702,970	11,300 00		
1832	....	....	787,435	11,000 00		
1833	....	....	968,150	10,400 00		
1834	....	....	3,660,845	293,425 00		
1835	....	....	1,857,670	328,505 00		
1836	....	....	2,765,735	1,369,965 00		
1837	....	....	1,035,605	112,700 00		
1838	....	72,000	1,600,285	137,310 00		
1839	....	382,480	802,745	170,660 00		
1840	....	473,380	1,048,360	153,502 50		
1841	....	656,310	380,725	54,562 50		
1842	....	1,089,070	655,330	89,770 00		
1843	....	2,506,240	4,275,425	1,327,132 50		
1844	....	1,250,610	4,068,275	89,345 00		
1845	....	736,530	2,743,640	270,277 50		
1846	....	1,018,750	2,736,155	279,272 50		
1847	....	14,337,040	5,401,685	482,060 00		
1848	....	1,813,340	1,863,560	98,612 50		
1849	....	6,775,180	1,184,643	111,147 50		936,789
1850	26,225,220	3,489,510	860,160	895,547 50		511,301
1851	48,043,100	4,393,280	2,651,955	8,867,377 50		3,658,820
1852	44,860,520	2,811,060	3,689,635	3,283,827 50		2,901,145
1853	26,646,520	2,522,530	2,305,095	8,519,615 00		4,384,149
1854	18,052,340	2,805,760	1,513,195	1,896,397 50	401,214	1,657,012

COINAGE OF THE UNITED STATES—GOLD COINAGE—(Continued).

Period.	Double-eagles.	Eagles.	Half-eagles.	Quarter-eagles.	Three dollars.	Dollars.
	$	$	$	$	$	$
1855	24,636,820	1,497,010	1,257,030	600,700 00	171,465	824,833
1856	30,277,560	1,484,900	1,751,005	1,213,117 50	181,530	1,783,996
1857	14,056,300	129,160	673,610	320,465 00	38,496	593,531
1858	23,039,880	629,900	772,775	515,632 50	66,177	230,301
1859	16,236,720	148,000	406,710	213,010 00	34,572	259,065
1860	15,458,800	342,130	361,145	128,980 00	61,206	93,215
1861	59,316,420	552,050	452,590	338,440 00	18,216	15,521
1862	36,247,500	972,990	3,287,160	3,208,122 50	17,355	1,799,259
1863	20,337,720	126,580	117,010	62,475 00	117	1,950
1864	21,465,640	85,800	61,500	23,185 00	16,470	6,750
1865	24,879,000	93,750	86,075	30,502 50	10,005	7,225
1866	27,494,900	876,100	300,750	122,975 00	12,090	7,130
1867	27,925,400	51,150	154,475	73,062 50	7,875	5,225
1868	17,705,800	155,590	153,750	74,125 00	14,700	10,550
1869	21,270,500	209 850	228,925	105,862 50	7,575	5,925
1870	22,018,480	89,130	94,625	35,137 50	10,605	9,335
1871	20,919,240	163,250	158,625	53,400 00	4,020	3,940
1872	19,798,500	254,600	243,700	72,575 00	6,090	1,030
1873	31,765,500	204,650	237,525	39,062 50	75	2,525
1874	48,283,900	333,480	809,780	516,150 00	125,460	323,920
1875	32,748,140	599,840	203,655	2,250 00	60	20
1876	37,896,720	153,610	71,800	53,052 50	135	3,645
1877	43,941,700	56,200	67,835	5,780 00	4,464	2,220
Total	809,508,440	56,707,220	63,412,815	26,795,750 00	1,300,032	10,345,438

Silver Coinage.

Period.	Dollars.	Half-dollars.	Quarter-dollars.	Dimes.	Half-dimes.	Three-cents.
	$	$	$	$	$	$
1793 to 1795	204,791	161,572 00	....	....	4,320 80	....
1796	72,920	1,959 00	1,473 50	2,213 50	511 50	....
1797	7,776	....	63 00	2,536 10	2,226 35	....
1798	327,536	....	....	2,755 00	....	....
1799	423,515	....	....	....	....	....
1800	220,920	....	....	2,176 00	1,200 00	....
1801	54,454	15,144 50	....	3,464 00	1,695 50	....
1802	41,650	14,945 00	....	1,097 50	650 50	....
1803	66,064	15,857 50	....	3,304 00	1,892 50	....
1804	19,570	78,259 50	1,684 50	825 50	....	....
1805	321	105,861 00	30,348 50	12,078 00	780 00	....
1806	....	419.788 00	51,531 00	....	....	....
1807	....	525.788 00	55,160 75	16,500 00	....	....
1808	....	684,300 00	....	....	....	....
1809	....	702,905 00	....	4,471 00	....	....
1810	....	638,138 00	....	635 50	....	....
1811	....	601,822 00	....	6,518 00	....	....
1812	....	814,029 50	....	....	....	....
1813	....	620,951 50	....	....	....	....
1814	....	519,537 50	....	42,150 00	....	....
1815	....	....	17,308 00	....	....	....
1816	....	23,575 00	5,000 75	....	....	....
1817	....	607,783 50	....	....	....	....
1818	....	989,161 00	90,293 50	....	....	....
1819	....	1,104,000 00	36,000 00	....	....	....
1820	....	375,561 00	31,861 00	94,258 70	....	....
1821	....	652,898 50	54,212 75	118,651 20	....	....

COINAGE OF THE UNITED STATES—SILVER COINAGE—(*Continued*).

Period.	Dollars.	Half-dollars.	Quarter-dollars.	Dimes.	Half-dimes.	Three-cents.
	$	$	$	$	$	$
1822......		779,786 50	16,020 00	10,000 00		
1823.....		847,100 00	4,450 00	44,000 00		
1824.....		1,752,477 00				
1825.....		1,471,583 00	42,000 00	51,000 00		
1826.....		2,002,090 00				
1827......		2,746,700 00	1,000 00	121,500 00		
1828......		1,537,600 00	25,500 00	12,500 00		
1829......		1,856,078 00		77,000 00	61,500 00	
1830......		2,382,400 00		51,000 00	62,000 00	
1831......		2,996,830 00	99,500 00	77,135 00	62,135 00	
1832......		2,398,500 00	80,000 00	52,250 00	48,250 00	
1833......		2,603,000 00	39,000 00	48,500 00	68,500 00	
1834......		3,206,002 00	71,500 00	63,500 00	74,000 00	
1835......		2,676,003 00	488,000 00	141,000 00	138,000 00	
1836......	1,000	3,273,100 00	118,000 00	119,000 00	95,000 00	
1837......		1,814,910 00	63,100 00	104,200 00	113,800 00	
1838......		1,773,000 00	206,000 00	239,493 00	112,750 00	
1839......	300	1,717,280 50	122,786 50	229,471 50	106,457 50	
1840......	61,005	1,145,054 00	153,331 75	253,358 00	113,954 25	
1841......	173,000	355,500 00	143,000 00	363,000 00	98,250 00	
1842......	184,618	1,484,882 00	214,250 00	390,750 00	58,250 00	
1843......	165,100	3,056,000 00	403,400 00	152,000 00	58,250 00	
1844......	20,000	1,885,500 00	290,300 00	7,250 00	32,500 00	
1845......	24,500	1,341,500 00	230,500 00	196,500 00	78,200 00	
1846......	169,600	2,257,000 00	127,500 00	3,130 00	1,350 00	
1847......	140,750	1,870,000 00	280,500 00	24,500 00	63,700 00	
1848......	15,000	1,880,000 00	36,500 00	45,150 00	63,400 00	
1849......	62,600	1,781,000 00	85,000 00	113,900 00	72,450 00	
1850......	47,500	1,341,500 00	150,700 00	244,150 00	82,250 00	
1851......	1,300	301,375 00	62,000 00	142,650 00	82,050 00	185,022 00
1852......	1,100	110,565 00	68,265 00	196,550 00	63,025 00	559,905 00
1853......	46,110	2,430,354 00	4,146,555 00	1,327,301 00	785,251 00	342,000 00
1854......	33,140	4,111,000 00	3,466,000 00	624,000 00	365,000 00	20,130 00
1855......	26,000	2,284,725 00	861,350 00	207,500 00	117,500 00	4,170 00
1856......	63,500	1,903,500 00	2,129,500 00	696,000 00	299,000 00	43,740 00
1857......	94,000	114,000 00	583,000 00	489,000 00	197,000 00	
1858......		4,430,000 00	3,019,750 00	236,000 00	327,000 00	37,980 00
1859......	288,500	4,005,500 00	1,428,000 00	229,000 00	195,000 00	41,400 00
1860......	600,590	1,627,400 00	330,450 00	98,600 00	96,500 00	16,440 00
1861......	559,900	959,650 00	771,550 00	167,300 00	139,350 00	7,950 00
1862......	1,750	1,785,425 00	730,937 50	158,405 00	117,627 50	18,256 50
1863......	31,400	983,600 00	113,965 00	34,071 00	8,223 00	2,803 80
1864......	23,170	483,985 00	22,492 50	14,037 00	4,518 50	11 10
1865......	32,900	553,100 00	27,650 00	17,160 00	4,880 90	618 00
1866......	58,550	579,525 00	9,712 50	21,065 00	10,732 50	679 50
1867......	57,000	897,450 00	18,175 00	13,670 00	435 00	141 00
1868......	54,800	946,750 00	37,475 00	73,315 00	24,290 00	120 00
1869......	231,350	561,075 00	23,137 50	23,905 00	527 50	151 50
1870......	588,308	1,009,375 00	23,047 50	98,185 00	48,222 50	115 50
1871......	657,929	1,242,771 00	29,971 75	10,707 50	14,396 25	129 75
1872......	1,112,961	1,496,492 50	55,096 25	222,471 50	152,751 75	61 05
1873......	977,150	1,199,775 00	174,362 50	419,040 00	175,442 50	25 50
1874......		1,438,980 00	458,515 50	497,255 80		
1875......		2,853,500 00	623,050 00	889,560 00		
1876......		4,985,525 00	4,106,262 50	3,699,105 00		
1877... ...		9,746,350 00	7,584,175 00	2,055,070 00		
Total...	8,043,828	118,869,540 50	34,774,121 50	16,141,786 30	4,906,946 90	1,281,850 20

NOTE.—Besides the above there were coined Trade-dollars for exportation, under act of February 12, 1873, as follows : 1874, $3,588,900 ; 1875, $5,697,500 ; 1876, $6,192,-050 ; 1877, $9,162,900—total, $24,581,350 ; and of Twenty-cent pieces, under act of March 3, 1875, as follows : 1875, $5,858 ; 1876, $263,560 ; 1877, $1,440—total, $270,858.

TOTAL COINAGE OF THE UNITED STATES MINT, 1793 to 1877, INCLUSIVE.

From the Official Report of the Director of the Mint.

	Gold.	Silver.	Minor.	Total.
1793 to 1795..	$71,485 00	$370,683 80	$11,373 00	$453,541 80
1796.........	102,727 50	79,077 50	10,324 40	192,129 40
1797	103,422 70	12,591 45	9,510 34	125,524 29
1798.........	205,610 00	330,291 00	9,797 00	545,698 00
1799.........	213,285 00	423,515 00	9,106 68	645,906 68
1800.........	317,760 00	224,296 00	29,279 40	571,335 40
1801.........	422,570 00	74,758 00	13,628 37	510,956 37
1802.........	423,310 00	58,343 00	31,422 83	516,075 83
1803.........	258,377 50	87,118 00	25,203 03	370,698 53
1804.........	258,642 50	100,310 50	12,844 94	371,827 94
1805.........	170,367 50	149,388 50	13,483 48	333,239 48
1806.........	324,505 00	471,319 00	5,260 00	801,084 00
1807...	437,495 00	597,448 75	9,652 21	1,044,595 96
1808..... ...	284,645 00	684,300 00	13,090 00	982,055 00
1809.........	169,375 00	707,376 00	8,001 53	884,752 53
1810.........	501,435 00	638,773 50	15,660 00	1,155,868 50
1811.........	497,905 00	658,340 00	2,495 95	1,108,740 95
1812.........	290,435 00	814,029 50	10,755 00	1,115,219 50
1813.........	477,140 00	620,951 50	4,180 00	1,102,271 50
1814.........	77,270 00	561,687 50	3,578 30	642,535 80
1815.........	3,175 00	17,308 00	....	20,483 00
1816.........	....	28,575 75	28,209 82	56,785 57
1817..	....	607,783 50	39,484 00	647,267 50
1818.........	242,940 00	1,070,454 50	31,670 00	1,345,064 50
1819.........	258,615 00	1,140,000 00	26,710 00	1,425,325 00
1820.........	319,030 00	501,680 70	44,075 50	1,864,786 20
1821.........	189,325 00	825,762 45	3,890 00	1,018,977 45
1822.........	88,980 00	805,806 50	20,723 39	915,509 89
1823.........	72,425 00	895,550 00	....	967,975 00
1824.........	93,200 00	1,752,477 00	12,620 00	1,858,297 00
1825.........	156,385 00	1,564,583 00	14,926 00	1,735,894 00
1826.........	92,245 00	2,002,090 00	16,344 25	2,110,679 25
1827.........	131,565 00	2,869,200 00	23,577 32	3,024,342 32
1828.........	140,145 00	1,575,600 00	25,636 24	1,741,381 24
1829.........	295,717 50	1,994,578 00	16,580 00	2,306,875 50
1830.........	643,105 00	2,495,400 00	17,115 00	3,155,620 00
1831.........	714,270 00	3,175,600 00	33,603 60	3,923,473 60
1832.........	798,435 00	2,579,000 00	23,620 00	3,401,055 00
1833.	978,550 00	2,759,000 00	28,160 00	3,765,710 00
1834.........	954,270 00	3,415,002 00	19,151 00	7,388,423 00
1835.........	186,175 00	3,443,003 00	39,489 00	5,668,667 00
1836.........	185,700 00	3,606,100 00	23,100 00	7,764,900 00
1837.........	148,305 00	2,096,010 00	55,583 00	3,299,898 00
1838.........	809,595 00	2,333,243 00	63,702 00	4,206,540 00
1839.........	1,355,885 00	2,176,296 00	31,286 61	3,563,467 61
1840.........	1,675,302 50	1,726,703 00	24,627 00	3,426,632 50
1841.........	1,091,597 50	1,132,750 00	15,973 67	2,240,321 17
1842.........	1,834,170 00	2,332,750 00	23,833 90	4,190,753 90
1843.........	8,108,797 50	3,834,750 00	24,283 20	11,967,830 70
1844.........	5,428,230 00	2,235,550 00	23,987 52	7,687,767 52
1845.........	3,756,447 50	1,873,200 00	38,948 04	5,668,595 54
1846.........	4,034,177 50	2,558,580 00	41,208 00	6,633,965 50
1847..-.....	20,221,385 00	2,379,450 00	61,836 69	22,662,671 69
1848.........	3,775,512 50	2,040,050 00	64,157 99	5,879,720 49
1849.........	9,007,761 50	2,114,950 00	41,984 32	11,164,695 82

TOTAL COINAGE OF THE UNITED STATES MINT 1793 TO 1877, IN-
CLUSIVE—(Continued).

	Gold.	Silver.	Minor.	Total.
1850........	$31,981,738 50	$1,866,100 00	$44,467 50	$33,892,306 00
1851........	62,614,492 50	774.397 00	99,635 43	63,488,524 93
1852........	56,846,187 50	909,410 00	50,630 94	57,896,228 44
1853........	39,377,909 00	9,077,571 00	67,059 78	48,522,539 78
1854........	25,915,918 50	8,619,270 00	42,638 35	34,577,826 85
1855........	28,977,968 00	3,501,245 00	16,030 79	32,495,243 79
1856........	36,697,768 50	5,135,240 00	27,106 78	41,860,115 28
1857...	15,811,563 00	1,477,000 00	63,510 46	17,352,073 46
1858........	30,253,725 50	8,040,730 00	234,000 00	38,528,455 50
1859........	17,296,077 00	6,187,400 00	307,000 00	23,790,477 00
1860........	16,445,476 00	2,769,920 00	342,000 00	19,557,396 00
1861	60,692,237 00	2,605,700 00	101,660 00	63,400,597 00
1862........	45,532,386 50	2,812,401 50	116,000 00	48,460,788 00
1863........	20,695,852 00	1,174,092 80	478,450 00	22,348,394 80
1864	21,649,345 00	548,214 10	463,800 00	22,661,359 10
1865........	25,107,217 50	636,308 00	1,183,330 00	26,926,855 50
1866........	28,313,945 00	680,264 50	646,570 00	29,640,779 50
1867........	28,217,187 50	986,871 00	1,879,540 00	31,083,598 50
1868........	18,114,425 00	1,136,750 00	1,713,385 00	20,964,560 00
1869........	21,828,637 50	840,746 50	1,279,035 00	23,948,439 00
1870........	22,257,312 50	1,767,253 50	611,445 00	24,636,011 00
1871........	21,302,475 00	1,955,905 25	283,760 00	23,542,140 25
1872........	20,376,495 00	3,029,834 05	123,020 00	23,529,349 05
1873	35,249,337 50	2,945,795 50	494,050 00	38,699,183 00
1874.....,....	50,442,690 00	5,983,601 30	411,925 00	56,838,216 30
1875....' ...	33,553,965 00	10,070,368 00	230,375 00	43,854,708 00
1876........	38,178,962 50	19,126,502 50	260,350 00	57,565,815 00
1877........	44,078,199 00	28,549,935 00	62,165 00	72,690,299 00
Total......	$983,159,695 00	$206,872,291 40	$12,884,703 55	$1,205,916,689 95

INVESTMENTS OF SAVINGS BANKS, ETC., IN U. S. BONDS.

*Statement of Average Capital and Deposits of Savings Banks, and the Capital of
Bankers, and Banks other than National Banks, invested in United States
Bonds, for the Years ended May 31, 1876 and 1877.*
From the Annual Report of the Comptroller of the Currency, December, 1877.

	1876.	1877.
Capital of Savings Banks...........................	$590,135	$362,095
Capital of Banks and Bankers.......................	25,574,003	33,027,436
Deposits of Savings Banks....	95,245,863	102,859,674

*Statement of the Gross Amount of Average Capital and Deposits of Savings Banks,
Bankers, and Banks other than National Banks, for the Years ended May 31,
1876 and 1877.*
From the Report of the Comptroller of the Currency, December, 1877.

	1876.	1877.
Capital of Savings Banks........................... .	$5,016,659	$4,965,500
Capital of Banks and Bankers.....................•.	211,634,586	217,215,388
Deposits of Savings Banks having Capital............	33,207,891	38,055,540
Deposits of Savings Banks having no Capital.........	845,109,217	855,057,027
Deposits of Banks and Bankers.....................	483,458,342	475,790,064
Totals........	$1,583,426,595	$1,591,083,519

COINS OF THE UNITED STATES, AUTHORITY FOR COIN- ING, AND CHANGES IN WEIGHT AND FINENESS.

From the Report of the Director of the Mint, 1877.

GOLD COINS.

Double-eagle = $20.

Authorized to be coined, Act of March 3, 1849.
Weight, 516 grains ; fineness, 900.
Total amount coined to June 30, 1877, $314,598,440.

Eagle = $10.

Authorized to be coined, Act of April 2, 1792.
Weight, 270 grains ; fineness, 916⅔.
Weight changed, Act of June 28, 1834, to 258 grains.
Fineness changed, Act of June 28, 1834, to 899.225.
Fineness changed, Act of January 18, 1837, to 900.
Total amount coined to June 30, 1877, $56,707,230.

Half-eagle = $5.

Authorized to be coined, Act of April 2, 1792.
Weight, 135 grains ; fineness, 916⅔.
Weight changed, Act of June 28, 1834, to 129 grains.
Fineness changed, Act of June 28, 1834, to 899.225.
Fineness changed, Act of January 18, 1837, to 900.
Total amount coined to June 30, 1877, $300,412,815.

Quarter-eagle = $2.50.

Authorized to be coined, Act of April 2, 1792.
Weight, 67.5 grains ; fineness, 916⅔.
Weight changed, Act of June 28, 1834, to 64.5 grains.
Fineness changed, Act of June 28, 1834, to 899.225.
Fineness changed, Act of January 18, 1837, to 900.
Total amount coined to June 30, 1877, $26,793,750.

Three-dollar piece.

Authorized to be coined, Act of Febru- ary 21, 1853.
Weight, 77.4 grains ; fineness, 900.
Total amount coined to June 30, 1877, $1,300,032.

One-dollar.

Authorized to be coined, Act of March 3, 1849.
Weight, 25.8 grains ; fineness, 900.
Total amount coined to June 30, 1877, $19,345,438.

SILVER COINS.

Silver Dollar.

Authorized to be coined, Act of April 2, 1792.
Weight, 416 grains ; fineness, 892.4.
Weight changed, Act of January 18, 1837, to 412½ grains.
Fineness changed, Act of January 18, 1837, to 900.
Coinage discontinued, Act of February 12, 1873.
Total amount coined, $8,045,838.

Trade-dollar.

Authorized to be coined, Act of Febru- ary 12, 1873.
Weight, 420 grains ; fineness, 900.
Total amount coined to June 30, 1877, $34,581,350.

Half-dollar.

Authorized to be coined, Act of April 2, 1792.
Weight, 208 grains ; fineness, 892.4.
Weight changed, Act of January 18, 1837, to 206½ grains.
Fineness changed, Act of January 18, 1837, to 900.
Weight changed, Act of February 21, 1853, to 192 grains.
Weight changed, Act of February 12, 1873, to 12½ grams, or 192.9 grains.
Total amount coined to June 30, 1877, $118,869,540.50.

Quarter-dollar.

Authorized to be coined, Act of April 2, 1792.
Weight, 104 grains ; fineness, 892.4.
Weight changed, Act of January 18, 1837, to 103½ grains.
Fineness changed, Act of January 18, 1837, to 900.
Weight changed, Act of February 21, 1853, to 96 grains.
Weight changed, Act of February 12, 1873, to 6¼ grams, or 96.45 grains.
Total amount coined to June 30, 1877, $34,774,121.50.

COINS OF THE UNITED STATES, AUTHORITY FOR COINING, AND CHANGES IN WEIGHT AND FINENESS—(Continued).

Twenty-cent piece.

Authorized to be coined, Act of March 3, 1875.
Weight, 5 grams, or 77.16 grains; fineness, 900.
Total amount coined to June 30, 1877, $209,418.

Dime.

Authorized to be coined, Act of April 2, 1792.
Weight, 41.6 grains, fineness, 892.4.
Weight changed, Act of January 18, 1837, to 41¼ grains.
Fineness changed, Act of January 18, 1837, to 900.
Weight changed, Act of February 21, 1853, to 38.4 grains.
Weight changed, Act of February 12, 1873, to 2½ grams, or 38.58 grains.
Total amount coined to June 30, 1877, $16,141,786.30.

Half-dime.

Authorized to be coined, Act of April 2, 1792.
Weight, 20.8 grains; fineness, 892.4.
Weight changed, Act of January 18, 1837, to 20⅝ grains.
Fineness changed, Act of January 18, 1837, to 900.
Weight changed, Act of February 21, 1853, to 19.2 grains.
Coinage discontinued, Act of February 12, 1873.
Total amount coined, $4,906,946.90.

Three-cent piece.

Authorized to be coined, Act of March 3, 1851.
Weight, 12⅜ grains; fineness, 750.
Weight changed, Act of March 3, 1853, to 11.52 grains.
Fineness changed, Act of March 3, 1853, to 900.
Coinage discontinued, Act of February 12, 1873.
Total amount coined, $1,281,850.20.

MINOR COINS.

Five-cent (nickel).

Authorized to be coined, Act of May 16, 1866.
Weight, 77.16 grains, composed of 75 per cent copper and 25 per cent nickel.
Total amount coined to June 30, 1877, $5,773,090.

Three-cent (nickel).

Authorized to be coined, Act of March 3, 1865.
Weight, 30 grains, composed of 75 per cent copper and 25 per cent nickel.
Total amount coined to June 30, 1877, $855,090.

Two-cent (bronze).

Authorized to be coined, Act of April 22, 1864.
Weight, 96 grains, composed of 95 per cent copper and 5 per cent tin and zinc.
Coinage discontinued, Act of February 12, 1873.
Total amount coined, $912,020.

Cent (copper).

Authorized to be coined, Act of April 2, 1792.
Weight, 264 grains.
Weight changed, Act of January 14, 1793, to 208 grains.
Weight changed by proclamation of the President, January 26, 1796, in conformity with Act of March 3, 1795, to 168 grains.
Coinage discontinued, Act of February 21, 1857.
Total amount coined, $1,562,887.44.

Cent (nickel).

Authorized to be coined, Act of February 21, 1857.
Weight, 72 grains, composed of 88 per cent copper and 12 per cent nickel.
Coinage discontinued, Act of April 22, 1864.
Total amount coined, $2,007,720.

Cent (bronze).

Coinage authorized, Act of April 22, 1864.
Weight, 48 grains, composed of 95 per cent copper and 5 per cent tin and zinc.
Total amount coined to June 30, 1877, $1,733,980.

Half-cent (copper).

Authorized to be coined, Act of April 2, 1792.
Weight, 132 grains.
Weight changed, Act of January 14, 1793, to 104 grains.
Weight changed by proclamation of the President, January 26, 1796, in conformity with Act of March 3, 1795, to 84 grains.
Coinage discontinued, Act of February 21, 1857.
Total amount coined, $39,926.10.

The World's Annual Production of GOLD and SILVER since 1852.

From the Journal des Economistes.

DATE.	ESTIMATED PRODUCT.		
	Gold.	Silver.	Total.
1852	$182,500,000	$40,500,000	$223,000,000
1853	155,000,000	40,500,000	195,500,000
1854	127,000,000	40,500,000	167,500,000
1855	135,000,000	40,500,000	175,500,000
1856	147,500,000	40,500,000	188,000,000
1857	133,000,000	40,500,000	173,500,000
1858	124,500,000	40,500,000	165,000,000
1859	124,500,000	40,500,000	165,000,000
1860	119,000,000	40,500,000	159,500,000
1861	114,000,000	42,500,000	156,500,000
1862	107,500,000	45,000,000	152,500,000
1863	107,000,000	49,000,000	156,000,000
1864	113,000,000	51,500,000	164,500,000
1865	120,000,000	52,000,000	172,000,000
1866	121,000,000	50,500,000	171,500,000
1867	116,000,000	54,000,000	170,000,000
1868	120,000,000	50,000,000	170,000,000
1869	121,000,000	47,500,000	168,500,000
1870	116,000,000	51,500,000	167,500,000
1871	116,500,000	61,000,000	177,500,000
1872	101,500,000	65,000,000	166,500,000
1873	103,500,000	70,000,000	173,500,000
1874	90,500,000	71,500,000	162,000,000
1875	97,500,000	62,000,000	159,500,000
Total	$2,913,000,000	$1,187,500,000	$4,100,500,000

Estimate of the World's Product of GOLD, from 1849 to 1876, inclusive, and of Gold and Silver Combined.

Year.	United States.	Australia.	Mexico and S.America	Russia.	Other Countries,	Total Gold Product.	Total Gold and Silver Product.
1849	$40,000,000		$5,000,000	$14,000,000	$2,500,000	$61,500,000	$102,000,000
1850	50,000,000		5,000,000	13,000,000	2,500,000	70,500,000	111,000,000
1851	55,000,000	$7,000,000	5,000,000	12,000,000	2,500,000	81,500,000	122,000,000
1852	60,000,000	80,000,000	5,000,000	12,000,000	2,500,000	159,500,000	200,200,000
1853	65,000,000	70,500,000	5,000,000	12,000,000	2,500,000	155,000,000	195,700,000
1854	60,000,000	47,500,000	5,000,000	12,000,000	2,500,000	127,000,000	167,700,000
1855	55,000,000	60,500,000	5,000,000	12,000,000	2,500,000	135,000,000	175,700,000
1856	55,000,000	71,500,000	5,000,000	13,500,000	2,500,000	147,500,000	188,200,000
1857	55,000,000	57,000,000	5,000,000	13,500,000	2,500,000	133,000,000	173,700,000
1858	50,000,000	53,500,000	5,000,000	13,500,000	2,500,000	124,500,000	165,200,000
1859	50,000,000	54,000,000	4,500,000	13,500,000	2,500,000	124,500,000	165,200,000
1860	46,000,000	52,500,000	4,500,000	13,500,000	2,500,000	119,000,000	160,500,000
1861	43,000,000	49,000,000	4,500,000	15,000,000	2,500,000	114,000,000	156,000,000
1862	39,000,000	46,500,000	4,500,000	15,000,000	2,500,000	107,500,000	151,000,000
1863	40,000,000	44,500,000	4,500,000	15,500,000	2,500,000	107,000,000	154,500,000
1864	46,000,000	45,500,000	4,000,000	15,000,000	2,500,000	113,000,000	163,500,000
1865	53,000,000	44,000,000	4,000,000	16,500,000	2,500,000	120,000,000	171,500,000
1866	53,500,000	44,000,000	4,000,000	17,000,000	2,500,000	121,000,000	171,500,000
1867	51,500,000	41,500,000	3,500,000	17,000,000	2,500,000	116,000,000	169,500,000
1868	48,000,000	48,500,000	3,000,000	18,000,000	2,500,000	120,000,000	170,000,000
1869	49,500,000	46,500,000	2,500,000	20,000,000	2,500,000	121,000,000	168,500,000
1870	50,000,000	38,500,000	2,500,000	22,500,000	2,500,000	116,000,000	167,500,000
1871	35,898,000	43,000,000	3,500,000	24,000,000	2,500,000	108,898,000	167,184,000
1872	39,459,459	36,500,000	3,500,000	23,000,000	2,500,000	104,959,459	161,986,959
1873	40,456,593	39,000,000	3,500,000	22,500,000	2,500,000	107,956,593	170,808,693
1874	40,103,045	29,500,000	4,000,000	22,500,000	2,500,000	98,603,045	164,601,045
1875	41,745,147	28,000,000	4,000,000	22,500,000	2,500,000	99,745,147	168,789,057
1876	44,328,501	28,000,000	4,000,000	22,500,000	2,500,000	101,328,501	178,335,173
	1,356,490,745	1,207,000,000	118,500,000	463,000,000	70,000,000	3,214,990,745	4,589,304,927

Table showing the estimated Production of SILVER in the Western World (America, Europe, and Africa), annually, since the commencement of the Nineteenth Century.

From the Report of the U. S. Monetary Commission, 1877.

THE figures for the years 1800 to 1829 inclusive are constructed on the following basis: The amounts coined at all the legal mints of Mexico, brought to the royal mint of Potosi, and raised in and exported from Coquimbo, are put together, and to the quotient ten million dollars are added each year for the conjectured production of all other countries in Europe and America. This conjecture is warranted by Sir Hector Hay, and employed in his tables of production.

The figures for the years 1830 to 1851 inclusive are from various compilations, indicated in the foot-notes. When not otherwise indicated, they are from Danson's compilation, *London Statistical Journal*, xiv. 23.

The figures for the years 1852 to 1874 inclusive are from Sir Hector Hay.

The figures for 1875 and 1876 are compiled by the present writer, and for 1877 estimated.

Sums in millions of dollars.

Years.	Production.	Years.	Production.	Years.	Production.
1800	32.8	1830	22.0	1852	40.6
1801	30.9	1831	22.0	1853	40 6
1802	31.4	1832	21.0	1854	40.6
1803	35.8	1833	21.0	1855	40.6
1804	39 5	1834	21.0	1856	40.7
1805	39.2	1835	20.0	1857	40.7
1806	36.8	1836	20.0	1858	40.7
1807	34.4	1837	20.0	1859	40.8
1808	33.4	1838	20.0	1860	40.8
1809	37.5	1839	22.0	1861	42.7
1810	31.4	1840	24.0	1862	45.2
1811	26.4	1841	25.0	1863	47.2
1812	21.3	1842	25.5	1864	50.7
1813	22.7	1843	28.0	1865	52.0
1814	22.7	1844	32.0	1866	50.7
1815	18.6	1845	30.0	1867	54.2
1816	21.3	1846	31.5	1868	50.2
1817	20.8	1847	34.0	1869	47.8
1818	24.1	1848	39.0	1870	51.6
1819	24.4	1849	38.0	1871	61.0
1820	22.6	1850	43.9	1872	65.2
1821	19 5	1851	40.5	1873	70.2
1822	22.7			1874	71.5
1823	21.0	Total, 22 years.	600.4	1875	70.0
1824	21.3			1876	76.0
1825	20.5			1877	70 0
1826	20.2				
1827	21.6			Total, 26 years.	1,841.8
1828	21.5				
1829	22.8				
Total, 30 years.	799.1	Grand total, 78 years, 1800-1877, $2,741,300,000.			

ESTIMATE OF THE WORLD'S PRODUCTION OF GOLD AND SILVER, BY EPOCHS, SINCE 1848.

From a Report by Edward Young, Chief of the Bureau of Statistics, in Senate Document No. 64, First Session, 44th Congress, May, 1876.

Epochs.	No. of Years.	AGGREGATE.			ANNUAL AVERAGE.		
		Gold.	Silver.	Gold and Silver.	Gold.	Silver.	Gold and Silver.
		Million dollars.	*Million dollars.*	*Million dollars.*	*Million dollars.*	*Million dollars.*	*Million dollars.*
1849–'51.	3	171.1	129.8	300.9	57.03	43.3	100.80
1852–'56.	5	674.2	213.2	887.4	134.85	42.6	177.45
1857–'61.	5	558.0	252.1	810.1	111.60	50.5	162.00
1862–'66.	5	502.2	327.5	829.7	100.40	65.5	165.90
1867–'71.	5	491.8	349.3	841.1	98.40	69.9	168.20
1872–'75.	4	364.4	302.0	666.4	91.10	75.5	166.60
1849–'75.	27	2,761.7	1,573.9	4,335.6	102.29	58.29	160.58

Estimated Aggregate Production of the Precious Metals during the Twenty-seven Years from 1849 to 1875, inclusive.

COUNTRIES.	Gold.	Silver.	Gold and Silver.
	Million dollars.	*Million dollars.*	*Million dollars.*
Entire World	2,761.7	1,573.9	4,335.6
United States	1,351.6	*265.55	1,617.15
Other Countries	1,410.1	1,308.35	2,718.45

* Seventeen years, 1859 to 1875. The silver mines of the United States were first discovered in 1859.

Annual Average Production of the Precious Metals in the World, also in the United States of America, since 1848, the Year of the Discovery of the Gold-fields of California.

COUNTRIES.	EPOCHS.	No. of Years.	Gold.	Silver.	Gold and Silver.
			Million dollars.	*Million dollars.*	*Million dollars.*
Entire World	1849–'75	27	102.29	58.29	160.53
United States	1849–'75	27	50.06	....	59.89
" "	1859–'75	17	....	15.62	....
Other Countries	1849–'75	27	52.23	49.94	102.17

THE ESTIMATED GOLD AND SILVER YIELD OF 1877.

The following estimate of the product of gold and silver mines in the United States for the year 1877 is based upon the returns for nine months, from January to October, and is from the *Banker's Magazine:*

Gold.		
Comstock Lode	$16,000,000	
California	15,500,000	
All other	540,000	
		$32,040,000
Silver.		
Comstock Lode	$19,000,000	
Outside Comstock	11,480,000	
Arizona	1,200,000	
		$31,680,000
Total		$63,720,000

Note.—The Director of the Mint, in his Annual Report, December, 1877, estimates the United States gold and silver product of 1877 at $84,050,000.

Estimate of the World's Product of SILVER, Lowest and Highest Price in London, in Pence, per Standard Ounce, and Exports from Great Britain to India, China, etc., from 1849 to 1876, inclusive.

Year.	United States.	Mexico and South America.	Russia.	Other Countries.	Total.	Lowest.	Highest.	*Amount Exported.
	$	$	$	$	$	d.	d.	$
1849	....	30,000,000	500,000	10,000,000	40,500,000	59 1/2	60 1/8	....
1850	....	30,000,000	500,000	10,000,000	40,500,000	59 1/2	61 1/2	....
1851	....	30,000,000	500,000	10,000,000	40,500,000	60	61 5/8	8,575,000
1852	200,000	30,000,000	500,000	10,000,000	40,700,000	59 7/8	61 7/8	12,235,000
1853	200,000	30,000,000	500,000	10,000,000	40,700,000	60 5/8	62 1/8	15,585,000
1854	200,000	30,000,000	500,000	10,000,000	40,700,000	60 7/8	61 7/8	15,475,000
1855	200,000	30,000,000	500,000	10,000,000	40,700,000	60	61 5/8	32,155,000
1856	200,000	30,000,000	500,000	10,000,000	40,700,000	60 1/2	62 1/4	60,565,000
1857	200,000	30,000,000	500,000	10,000,000	40,700,000	61	62 3/8	83,655,000
1858	200,000	30,000,000	500,000	10,000,000	40,700,000	60 3/4	61 7/8	23,765,000
1859	200,000	30,000,000	500,000	10,000,000	40,700,000	61 3/4	62 3/4	74,140,000
1860	1,000,000	30,000,000	500,000	10,000,000	41,500,000	61 1/4	62 3/8	42,890,000
1861	1,500,000	30,000,000	500,000	10,000,000	42,000,000	60 1/8	61 3/8	34,120,000
1862	3,000,000	30,000,000	500,000	10,000,000	43,500,000	61	62 1/8	50,435,000
1863	7,000,000	30,000,000	500,000	10,000,000	47,500,000	61	61 3/4	41,815,000
1864	10,000,000	30,000,000	500,000	10,000,000	50,500,000	60 5/8	62 1/4	31,270,000
1865	11,000,000	30,000,000	500,000	10,000,000	51,500,000	60 1/2	61 5/8	17,990,000
1866	10,000,000	30,000,000	500,000	10,000,000	50,500,000	60 3/8	62 1/4	11,825,000
1867	13,000,000	30,000,000	500,000	10,000,000	53,500,000	60 3/8	61 1/4	† 8,210,000
1868	12,000,000	27,500,000	500,000	10,000,000	50,000,000	60 1/8	61 1/8	8,175,000
1869	12,000,000	25,000,000	500,000	10,000,000	47,500,000	60	61	11,810,000
1870	16,000,000	25,000,000	500,000	10,000,000	51,500,000	60 1/4	62	7,895,000
1871	20,286,000	27,500,000	500,000	10,000,000	58,286,000	60 1/4	61	18,580,000
1872	20,527,500	26,000,000	500,000	10,000,000	57,027,500	59 1/4	61 1/8	28,270,000
1873	28,352,100	21,000,000	500,000	10,000,000	62,852,100	57 7/8	59 15/16	12,485,000
1874	30,498,000	25,000,000	500,000	10,000,000	65,998,000	57 1/4	59 1/2	35,460,000
1875	34,043,910	25,000,000	500,000	10,000,000	69,543,910	55 1/2	57 5/8	18,570,000
1876	41,506,672	25,000,000	500,000	10,000,000	77,006,672	46 3/4	58 1/2	47,500,000
	273,314,182	800,000,000	14,000,000	280,000,000	1,367,314,182	....	....	747,450,000

* Amount exported from Southampton to India, China, etc.

Amount of Precious Metals Produced in the States and Territories West of the Missouri River, during the Year 1876.

By J. J. VALENTINE, of Wells, Fargo & Co.'s Express, San Francisco.

States and Territories.	Gold Dust and Bullion by Express.	Gold Dust and Bullion by other Conveyances.	Silver Bullion by Express.	Ores and Base Bullion by Freight.	Total.
California	$14,635,963	$1,463,596	$796,308	$1,719,940	$18,615,807
Nevada	230,803	22,080	44,725,802	4,312,079	49,290,764
Oregon	919,257	229,814			1,149,071
Washington	54,702	5,670			62,372
Idaho	1,182,222	236,444	220,605	35,000	1,674,361
Montana	1,956,553	195,655	274,824	350,000	2,777,032
Utah	47,705	4,779	781,263	4,373,682	5,207,519
Colorado	2,829,877		2,796,661	1,364,109	6,990,647
New Mexico	76,392		255,281	18,621	350,294
Arizona	103,528		336,564	671,900	1,111,992
Mexico	51,880		1,020,656	541,212	2,213,748
British Columbia	1,310,515	181,051			1,441,566
	$23,391,487	$2,289,089	$51,808,051	$13,386,543	$90,875,173

The method and form of the foregoing is exactly similar to that of statements, which we have compiled since 1870, wherein no attempt was made to show the amount of gold contained in silver or doré bullion, or the lead and copper in base bullion, but the violent fluctuation of silver as compared to gold, during the present year, renders an analysis desirable, and we have spared no pains to arrive at a correct conclusion, and the results are as follows: In round figures, of $37,-000,000 produced from the Comstock Lode this year, $17,125,000, or quite 46 per cent, was gold; of the whole product of Nevada, 33 per cent was gold, and of the total silver product, so called, $18,647,825, or 31 per cent, was gold. The gross yield is constituted as follows: Gold, $44,328,501; Silver, $41,506,672; Lead and Copper, $5,040,000 = $90,875,173.

Estimate of the Production of Gold and Silver in the United States in 1877, by H. R. Linderman, Director of the Mint.

From the Report of the Director of the Mint, December, 1877.

State or Territory.	Gold.	Silver.	Total.
California	$15,000,000	$1,000,000	$16,000,000
Nevada	18,000,000	26,000,000	44,000,000
Montana	3,200,000	750,000	3,950,000
Idaho	1,500,000	250,000	1,750,000
Utah	350,000	5,075,000	5,425,000
Colorado	3,000,000	4,500,000	7,500,000
Arizona	300,000	500,000	800,000
New Mexico	175,000	500,000	675,000
Oregon	1,000,000	100,000	1,100,000
Washington	300,000	50,000	350,000
Dakota	2,000,000		2,000,000
Lake Superior		200,000	200,000
Virginia	50,000		50,000
North Carolina	100,000		100,000
Georgia	100,000		100,000
Other sources	25,000	25,000	50,000
Total	$45,100,000	$39,950,000	$84,050,000

ESTIMATE OF GOLD AND SILVER PRODUCED IN THE UNITED STATES FROM 1845 TO 1876, INCLUSIVE.

From an Official Report by H. R. Linderman, Director of the U. S. Mint.

DATE.	ESTIMATED PRODUCT.		
	Gold.	Silver.	Total.
		From 1849 to 1858.*	
1845................................	$1,008,327	....	$1,008,327
1846................................	1,139,857	....	1,139,357
1847................................	889,085	....	889,085
1848................................	10,000,000	....	10,000,000
1849................................	40,000,000	....	40,000,000
1850................................	50,000,000	....	50,000,000
1851................................	55,000,000	....	55,000,000
1852................................	60,000,000	....	60,000,000
1853................................	65,000,000	....	65,000,000
1854................................	60,000,000	....	60,000,000
1855................................	55,000,000	....	55,000,000
1856................................	55,000,000	....	55,000,000
1857................................	55,000,000	....	55,000,000
1858................................	50,000,000	$500,000	50,500,000
1859................................	50,000,000	100,000	50,100,000
1860................................	46,000,000	150,000	46,150,000
1861................................	43,000,000	2,000,000	45,000,000
1862................................	39,200,000	4,500,000	43,700,000
1863................................	40,000,000	8,500,000	48,500,000
1864................................	46,100,000	11,000,000	57,100,000
1865................................	53,225,000	11,250,000	64,475,000
1866................................	53,500,000	10,000,000	63,500,000
1867................................	51,725,000	13,500,000	65,225,000
1868................................	48,000,000	12,000,000	60,000,000
1869................................	49,500,000	12,000,000	61,500,000
1870................................	50,000,000	16,000,000	66,000,000
1871................................	43,500,000	23,000,000	66,500,000
1872................................	36,000,000	28,750,000	64,750,000
1873................................	36,000,000	35,750,000	71,750,000
1874................................	40,000,000	32,000,000	72,000,000
1875................................	40,000,000	32,000,000	72,000,000
1876................................	44,300,000	41,500,000	85,700,000
Total.....................	$1,367,986,769	$294,500,000	$1,661,486,769

The Director of the Mint says, concerning the future of the yield of the precious metals :

"It is impossible to state with any degree of accuracy how long this large rate of production will be maintained. A gradual increase may be expected in Montana and Arizona, and there is nothing to indicate a decrease in any bullion-producing State or Territory, except in the State of Nevada, and that depends upon contingencies which to a great extent must be a matter of conjecture only. Several mines in different localities in that State have within the last year or two been opened, and are producing considerable bullion. But whether they, and others which in the meantime may be discovered, will yield sufficient to make up the decrease, which, unless other ore-bodies on the Comstock shall be found, must sooner or later take place, is somewhat doubtful."

NOTE.—The actual production of all the Nevada mines for the fiscal year ended June 30th, 1877, was $42,460,177.

* The annual silver product from 1849 to 1858 has been estimated at $50,000.

Production of Gold and Silver in the United States from tho Discovery of the Mines—that is, for Gold from 1849, and for Silver from 1859, to 1876, inclusive.

From a Table prepared by E. B. Elliott, of the U. S. Bureau of Statistics.

YEARS AND PERIODS.	Gold.	Silver.	Gold and Silver.
	Million Dollars.	Million Dollars.	Million Dollars.
1849...................................	14.0	....	14.0
1850...................................	32.4	....	32.4
1851...................................	47.6	....	47.6
1849-1851, 3 years.....................	94.0	....	94.0
Annual average.......................	31.33	....	31.33
1852...................................	60.5	....	60.5
1853...................................	68.8	....	68.8
1854...................................	74.7	....	74.7
1855...................................	74.0	....	74.0
1856...................................	72.8	....	72.8
1852-1856, 5 years.....................	350.8	....	350.8
Annual average.......................	70.16	....	70.16
1857...................................	67.1	....	67.1
1858...................................	64.8	....	64.8
1857-1858, 2 years.....................	131.9	....	131.9
Annual average.......................	65.95	....	65.95
1859...................................	61.8	0.07	61.87
1860...................................	56.6	0.13	56.73
1861...................................	52.5	2.50	55.00
1862...................................	49.6	6.00	55.60
1863...................................	47.7	9.60	57.30
1859-1863, 5 years.....................	268.3	18.30	286.60
Annual average.......................	53.66	3.66	57.32
1864...................................	45.3	10.9	56.2
1865...................................	40.9	12.3	53.2
1866...................................	39.0	13.8	52.8
1867...................................	39.6	15.3	54.9
1868...................................	42.6	17.0	59.6
1864-1868, 5 years.....................	207.4	69.3	276.7
Annual average.......................	41.48	13.86	55.34
1869...................................	43.0	18.7	61.7
1870...................................	43.1	20.1	63.2
1871...................................	43.2	22.0	65.2
1872...................................	43.0	24.4	67.4
1873...................................	42.7	27.3	70.0
1869-1873, 5 years.....................	215.0	112.5	327.5
Annual average	43.0	22.5	65.5
1874...................................	42.3	31.1	73.4
1875...................................	41.7	34.3	76.0
1876...................................	44.3	41.5	85 8
1874-1876, 3 years...	128.3	106.9	235.2
Annual average.......................	42.8	35.6	78.4
Entire period.............	1,395.7	307.0	1,702.7
Annual average....	*49.85	† 16.5	* 60.8

* Average of 28 years, 1849-1876.   † Average of 18 years, 1859-1876.

WHERE OUR GOLD AND SILVER COME FROM.

From the Report of the Director of the Mint, December, 1877.

Gold and Silver of Domestic Production Deposited at the Mints and Assay Offices, from their Organization to the Close of the Fiscal Year ended June 30, 1877.

LOCALITY.	Gold.	Silver.	Total.
Alabama	$215,469 71		$215,469 71
Alaska	19,777 49		19,777 49
Arizona	1,737,927 45	$340,845 49	2,078,772 94
California	677,843,687 90	1,100,550 42	678,944,238 41
Colorado	27,496,039 69	11,644,134 63	39,140,174 32
Dakota	469,828 75		469,828 75
Georgia	7,451,591 83	403 83	7,451,995 66
Idaho	21,956,462 61	424,353 60	22,380,816 21
Iowa	192 58	408 00	660 58
Kansas	956,859 10		956,859 10
Lake Superior		2,455,607 19	2,455,607 19
Maryland	402 12		402 12
Massachusetts		917 56	917 56
Michigan		1,196 87	1,196 87
Montana	43,051,085 74	1,132,354 82	44,183,440 56
Nebraska	37,084 25	749,730 71	786,814 96
Nevada	10,605,058 75	49,048,914 00	59,653,972 75
New Hampshire	10,299 00		10,299 00
New Mexico	1,288,703 96	1,114,300 54	2,403,004 50
North Carolina	10,370,492 18	44,743 33	10,415,235 51
Oregon	13,785,872 17	3,232 12	13,789,104 29
South Carolina	1,382,455 74	2 93	1,382,458 67
Tennessee	80,252 43		80,252 43
Utah	291,922 52	5,323,537 22	5,615,459 74
Vermont	10,800 41		10,800 41
Virginia	1,641,343 89		1,641,343 89
Washington	126,713 15		126,713 15
Wyoming	619,466 90	11,793 86	631,260 76
Refined gold	135,958,026 10		135,958,026 10
Parted from silver	9,772,931 55		9,772,931 55
Contained in silver	9,302,132 36		9,302,132 36
Refined silver		26,860,370 61	26,860,370 61
Parted from gold		6,225,872 58	6,225,872 58
Contained in gold		502,816 17	502,816 17
Other sources	9,990,000 46	2,572,785 18	12,563,775 64
Total	$986,473,870 88	$109,558,931 66	$1,096,032,802 54

Profit of the Government on Silver Coinage under the Existing Laws regulating the Mint.

From the Annual Report of the Director of the Mint, December, 1877.

THE total purchases of silver bullion made by the government from January, 1875, to October 31st, 1877, inclusive, were 28,707.634.57 fine ounces, at a total cost of $34,118,973.26, or an average cost of 118 8/10 cents per ounce fine. During that period the London rate averaged 54.7656 pence, or $1.20,05 per ounce fine. The purchases were therefore obtained by the government at 1 3/10 cents lower than the equivalent of the average London rate.

The total bullion purchased, 28,707,634.57 fine, or 31,807,371.73 standard ounces, costing $34,118,973.26, will produce, at the coining rate of $1.24.4168 per standard ounce, fractional silver coins to the amount of $39,685,688, and give a seigniorage or gain of $5,566,714.74.

HOW MUCH GOLD AND SILVER MONEY HAVE WE?

Two estimates of the aggregate of gold and silver money in the United States were published May 19th, 1876, in Senate Document No. 64, 44th Congress, 1st Session. One of these estimates was as follows :

The amount of gold and silver coin and bullion in the United States at the present time is estimated to be about $145,000,000, of which about $20,000,000 consists of silver coin and bullion.
H. R. LINDERMAN,
Director of the Mint.

Another estimate in the same Document, by Edward Young, Chief of the Bureau of Statistics, was as follows :

"The value of the imports of the precious metals in the 55 fiscal years from September 30th, 1820, to June 30th, 1875, was $535,237,227. From inspection of the tables it will be seen that the excess of the exports over the imports of the precious metals during the 27 fiscal years from June 30th, 1848, to June 30th, 1875, is $1,211,-480,000, which, subtracted from the product above given, to wit, $1,167,150,000, for the same period, leaves $105,670,000 as the net increase of our stock of precious metals. The stock of precious metals in the United States in 1848 may be estimated at $4,000,000. Assuming an expenditure of $150,000,000 in the arts and manufactures during this period of 27 years, and also an unregistered excess of exports of coin and bullion of $35,000,000 from the whole country during this period of 27 years, leaves $279,670,000 as the present stock of precious metals in the United States for monetary purposes, of which it is roughly estimated that about one fourth, or $70,-000,000, is silver, and the remaining three fourths, about $210,000,000, gold."

The Annual Report of the Director of the Mint for 1877 estimates the aggregate gold and silver coin and bullion in the United States on the 31st of October, 1877, as follows :

Gold Coin and Bullion.............................. $207,459,095
Silver Coin and Bullion........................... . 53,492,656

Total Coin and Bullion........................... $260,951,751

Table showing the average annual ratio of value between gold and silver—expressed, as is customary, in quantities of pure silver to one of gold—in the London market from 1760 to 1876, inclusive. Up to 1829, from Ex. Doc. 117, first session Twenty-first Congress ; from 1833 to 1875, from Pixley & Abell's London circulars ; for 1876, from the weekly gold averages for standard silver in the London Economist.
From the Report of the U. S. Monetary Commission, 1877.

Year	Ratio	Year	Ratio	Year	Ratio	Year	Ratio
1760	14.29	1790	15.01	1819	15.82	1848	15.83
1761	13.94	1791	14.95	1820	15.71	1849	15.78
1762	14.63	1792	14.43	1821	15.98	1850	15.70
1763	14.71	1793	15.01	1822	15.91	1851	15.46
1764	14.91	1794	15.33	1823	15.91	1852	15.58
1765	14.69	1795	14.77	1824	15.64	1853	15.33
1766	14.41	1796	14.77	1825	15.09	1854	15.33
1767	14.45	1797	15.45	1826	15.69	1855	15.38
1768	14.58	1798	15.45	1827	15.77	1856	15.38
1769	14.45	1799	14.29	1828	15.77	1857	15.27
1770	14.35	1800	14.81	1829	15.95	1858	15 38
1771	14.36	1801	14.47	1830	15.73	1859	15.19
1772	14.19	1802	15.23	1831	15.73	1860	15.23
1773	14 73	1803	14.47	1832	15.73	1861	15.50
1774	15.05	1804	14.67	1833	15.93	1862	15.35
1775	14.62	1805	15.14	1834	15.73	1863	15.36
1776	14.34	1806	14.25	1835	15.79	1864	15.36
1777	14.04	1807	14.46	1836	15.71	1865	15.44
1778	14.34	1808	14.79	1837	15.83	1866	15.43
1779	11.89	1809	16.25	1838	15.85	1867	15.57
1780	14.43	1810	16.15	1839	15.61	1868	15.58
1781	13.33	1811	15.72	1840	15.61	1869	15.60
1782	13.54	1812	15.04	1841	15.70	1870	15.57
1783	13.73	1813	14.53	1842	15.86	1871	15.58
1784	14.90	1814	15.85	1843	15.93	1872	15.63
1785	15.21	1815	16.30	1844	15.85	1873	15 92
1786	14.89	1816	13.64	1845	15.91	1874	16.16
1787	14.83	1817	15.58	1846	15.89	1875	16.69
1788	14.71	1818	15.42	1847	15.79	1876	17.83
1789	14.89						

Weekly Fluctuations in the Gold Value of Fine Bar Silver, etc., during the Fiscal Year ended June 30, 1877 (prepared from Quotations furnished by Pixley & Abell, London).

DATE.	Price per ounce British standard 925 thousandths fine.	Price per ounce fine in U.S gold coin.	Gold value of the old silver dollar of 412½ grains.	Relative value of gold to silver.	DATE.	Price per ounce British standard 925 thousandths fine.	Price per ounce fine in U.S. gold coin.	Gold value of the old silver dollar of 412½ grains.	Relative value of gold to silver.
1876.	*Pence*	*doll. cts.*	*cents.*		1877.	*Pence.*	*doll. cts.*	*cents.*	
July 6.	47¾	1 04.67	80.96	1 to 19.74	Jan. 4.	57¼	1 25.50	97.06	1 to 16.47
July 13.	46¾	1 02.48	79.26	1 to 20.17	Jan. 11.	57¼	1 25.50	97.06	1 to 16.47
July 20.	48¼	1 05.77	81.80	1 to 19.54	Jan. 18.	58	1 27.14	98.33	1 to 16.20
July 27.	51	1 11.80	86.47	1 to 18.49	Jan. 25.	58⅛	1 27.42	98.55	1 to 16.22
Aug. 3.	51⅜	1 12.89	87.31	1 to 18.31	Feb. 1.	57⅜	1 26.04	97.48	1 to 16.40
Aug. 10.	51¾	1 13.44	87.74	1 to 18.22	Feb. 8.	57	1 24.95	96.64	1 to 15.61
Aug. 17.	53¾	1 17.82	91.12	1 to 17.54	Feb. 5.	57	1 24.95	96.64	1 to 16.61
Aug. 24.	52	1 13.99	88.16	1 to 18.13	Feb. 22.	56	1 22.76	94.94	1 to 16.84
Aug. 31.	51⅝	1 13.17	87.52	1 to 18.26	Mar. 1.	56⅛	1 23.03	95.15	1 to 16.80
Sept. 7.	51¼	1 12.35	86.89	1 to 18.40	Mar. 8.	56⅛	1 23.03	95.15	1 to 16.80
Sept. 14.	51¼	1 12.35	86.89	1 to 18.40	Mar. 15.	55	1 20.57	93.25	1 to 17.14
Sept. 21.	51⅝	1 13.17	87.52	1 to 18.26	Mar. 22.	53½	1 17.28	90.70	1 to 17.62
Sept. 28.	52 9/16	1 15.22	89.11	1 to 17.94	Mar. 28.	54⅜	1 19.20	92.19	1 to 17.34
Oct. 5.	52	1 13.99	88.16	1 to 18.13	Apr. 5.	53¾	1 17.82	91.12	1 to 17.54
Oct. 12.	52⅛	1 14.26	88.37	1 to 18.09	Apr. 12.	54¼	1 18.92	91.98	1 to 17.38
Oct. 19.	52½	1 15.09	88.85	1 to 17.96	Apr. 19.	55	1 20.57	93.25	1 to 17.14
Oct. 26.	53⅛	1 17.28	90.70	1 to 17.62	Apr. 26.	54¼	1 18.92	91.98	1 to 17.38
Nov. 2.	53⅛	1 16.45	90.07	1 to 17.73	May 3.	53¾	1 17.82	91.12	1 to 17.54
Nov. 9.	53¾	1 17.82	91.12	1 to 17.54	May 10.	54⅝	1 19.74	92.61	1 to 17.26
Nov. 16.	54	1 18.37	91.55	1 to 17.46	May 17.	54½	1 19.47	92.40	1 to 17.30
Nov. 23.	54½	1 19.47	92.40	1 to 17.30	May 24.	54⅛	1 18.65	91.76	1 to 17.42
Nov. 30.	55	1 20.57	93.25	1 to 17.14	May 31.	53⅝	1 17.55	90.92	1 to 17.58
Dec. 7.	56	1 22.76	94.94	1 to 16.84	June 7.	53⅝	1 17.55	90.92	1 to 17.58
Dec. 14.	58½	1 28.24	99.19	1 to 16.11	June 14.	53¾	1 17.82	91.12	1 to 17.54
Dec. 21.	56⅜	1 23.58	95.58	1 to 16.72	June 21.	53½	1 17.28	90.70	1 to 17.62
Dec. 28.	56½	1 23.85	95.79	1 to 16.69	June 28.	54	1 18.37	91.55	1 to 17.46
					Av. for year..	53 11/16	1 18.24	91.45	1 to 17.48

NOTE by the Director of the Mint:

The lowest point touched by silver during the year 1876 was 46¾ pence per ounce .925 fine (British standard), the weekly quotation for July 13th. At this rate the relative valne of gold to silver was as 1 to 20.17, and the old silver dollar of 412½ grains would have been worth 79¼ cents. Five months afterward, December 14th, the highest price during the year was realized, 58½ pence, at which rate the relative value to gold was as 1 to 16.11, and the silver dollar would have been worth 99¼ cents. This was the highest point reached by silver since July, 1874.

Summary of the Operations of the General Land Office.

FOR THE FISCAL YEAR ENDING JUNE 30, 1877.

	Acres.
Disposal of Public Lands by Cash Sales	740.696
Military Bounty Land Warrant Locations	97,480
Homestead Entries	2,178,098
Timber Culture Entries	520,673
Agricultural College Scrip Locations	1,290
Approved to States as Swamp Lands	320,985
Certified to Railroads	700,792
Certified for Wagon Roads	61,543
Certified for Agricultural Colleges	63.443
Certified for Common Schools	27,974
Certified for Universities	3,236
Internal Improvement Selections	50,985
Sioux Half-breed Scrip Locations	2,655
Chippewa " " "	5,423
Special Scrip Entries	60,460
Entries under the Mining Laws	14,103
Total acres	4,849,767

SPECIE IN BANKS, 1868-1877.

From the Annual Report of the Comptroller of the Currency, 1877.

THE table below exhibits the amount of specie held by the national banks at the dates of their reports for the last nine years; the coin, coin-certificates, and checks payable in coin held by the New York City banks being stated separately.

Dates.	Held by National Banks in New York City.				Held by other National Banks.	Aggregate Specie.
	Coin.	U. S. Coin-certificates.	Checks Payable in Coin.	Total.		
Oct. 5, 1868	$1,608,623	$6,390,140	$1,536,354	$9,625,117	$3,378,596	$13,003,713
Jan. 4, 1869	1,902,760	18,038,520	2,348,140	22,289,430	7,337,320	29,626,750
Apr. 17, 1869	1,632,575	3,720,040	1,489,827	6,842,442	3,102,090	9,944,532
June 12, 1869	2,542,534	11,953,680	975,016	15,471,230	2,983,861	18,455,091
Oct. 9, 1869	1,792,741	16,897,900	1,013,949	19,704,590	3,297,816	23,002,406
Jan. 22, 1870	6,196,036	28,501,460	2,190,645	36,888,141	11,457,243	48,345,384
Mar. 24, 1870	2,647,908	21,872,480	1,069,094	25,589,483	11,507,061	37,006,544
June 9, 1870	2,942,400	18,660,920	1,163,906	22,767,226	8,332,212	31,099,438
Oct. 8, 1870	1,607,743	7,533,900	3,994,006	13,135,649	5,324,362	18,460,011
Dec. 28, 1870	2,268,582	14,063,540	3,748,127	20,080,249	6,227,003	26,307,252
Mar. 18, 1871	2,982,156	13,099,720	3,829,882	19,911,758	5,857,409	25,769,167
Apr. 29, 1871	2,047,931	9,845,080	4,382,107	16,275,118	6,456,909	22,732,027
June 10, 1871	2,249,408	9,161,160	3,690,855	15,091,423	4,833,532	19,924,955
Oct. 2, 1871	1,121,860	7,500,960	1,163,628	9,875,758	3,377,240	13,252,998
Dec. 16, 1871	1,454,931	17,354,740	4,255,631	23,065,302	6,520,997	29,595,299
Feb. 27, 1872	1,490,418	12,341,060	3,117,101	16,948,579	8,559,247	25,507,826
Apr. 19, 1872	1,828,660	10,102,400	4,715,364	16,646,424	7,787,475	24,433,899
June 10, 1872	3,782,910	11,412,160	4,219,420	19,414,490	4,842,155	24,256,644
Oct. 3, 1872	930,767	5,454,580	....	6,375,347	3,854,409	10,229,750
Dec. 27, 1872	1,306,091	12,471,940	....	13,778,031	5,269,305	19,047,336
Feb. 28, 1873	1,938,770	11,539,780	....	13,498,550	4,279,124	17,777,674
Apr. 25, 1873	1,344,951	11,743,320	....	13,088,251	3,780,558	16,868,809
June 13, 1873	1,442,098	22,139,080	....	23,581,178	4,368,909	27,950,087
Sept. 12, 1873	1,063,211	13,522,600	....	14,585,811	5,282,659	19,868,470
Dec. 26, 1873	1,376,171	18,325,760	....	19,701,931	7,205,107	26,907,038
Feb. 27, 1874	1,167,620	23,518,040	....	24,686,460	8,679,403	33,365,864
May 1, 1874	1,530,282	23,454,660	....	24,984,942	7,585,027	32,569,969
June 26, 1874	1,842,525	13,671,660	....	15,514,185	6,812,022	22,326,207
Oct. 2, 1874	1,291,787	13,114,480	....	14,406,267	6,834,679	21,240,946
Dec. 31, 1874	1,443,215	14,410,940	....	15,854,155	6,582,606	22,436,761
Mar. 1, 1875	1,064,556	10,642,160	....	11,706,716	4,960,391	16,667,107
May 1, 1875	930,106	5,753,220	....	6,683,326	3,937,036	10,620,362
June 30, 1875	1,023,016	12,642,180	....	13,665,196	5,294,386	18,959,582
Oct. 1, 1875	753,905	4,201,720	....	4,955,625	3,094,705	8,050,330
Dec. 17, 1875	869,437	12,532,810	....	13,402,247	3,668,659	17,070,906
Mar. 10, 1876	3,261,131	19,086,920	....	22,348,051	6,729,294	29,077,345
May 12, 1876	832,314	15,183,760	....	16,016,074	5,698,521	21,714,595
June 30, 1876	1,214,523	16,872,780	....	18,087,303	7,131,167	25,218,470
Oct. 2, 1876	1,129,814	13,446,760	....	14,576,574	6,785,080	21,361,654
Dec. 22, 1876	1,434,702	21,602,900	....	23,037,602	9,962,046	32,999,649
Jan. 20, 1877	1,669,285	33,629,660	....	35,298,945	14,410,323	49,709,268
Apr. 14, 1877	1,930,726	13,899,180	....	15,829,906	11,240,132	27,070,038
June 22, 1877	1,423,258	10,324,320	....	11,747,578	9,588,418	21,335,996
Oct. 1, 1877	1,533,486	11,409,920	....	12,943,403	9,710,414	22,653,820

AMOUNT OF PAPER MONEY IN THE UNITED STATES.

From the Report of the Comptroller of the Currency, December, 1877.

THE subjoined table exhibits, by denominations, the amount of national-bank and legal-tender notes outstanding on November 1, 1877:

DENOMINATIONS.	Amount of National-bank Notes.	Amount of Legal-tenders.	Total.
Ones........................	$3,800,456	$24,806,459	$28,606,915
Twos	2,282,884	24,600,544	26,883,428
Fives	93,504,900	52,932,148	146,437,048
Tens.......................	98,312,850	63,146,861	161,459,711
Twenties.......	65,454,500	60,836,495	126,290,995
Fifties........................	22,255,100	30,108,715	52,363,815
One hundreds.................	28,800,000	30,176,670	58,976,670
Five hundreds.................	1,203,500	34,752,500	35,956,000
One thousands................	257,000	34,123,500	34,380,500
	*10,800	†1,000,000	1,010,800
	$315,881,990	$356,483,892	$672,365,882

Section 5175 of the Revised Statutes provides "that not more than one-sixth part of the notes furnished to any association shall be of a less denomination than five dollars, and that after specie payments are resumed no association shall be furnished with notes of a less denomination than five dollars."

AMOUNT OF PAPER CURRENCY RETIRED, 1875-1877.

THE following summary exhibits concisely the operations of the acts of June 20, 1874, and of January 14, 1875, down to December 1, 1877:

National-bank notes outstanding, June 20, 1874............		$349,894,182
Amount of same issued from June 20, 1874, to Jan. 14, 1875..	$4,734,500	
Amount redeemed and retired between same dates..........	2,767,252	
Increase from June 20, 1874, to January 14, 1875................		1,967,263
Total amount outstanding, January 14, 1875..........................		$351,861,450
Amount redeemed and retired from Jan. 14, 1875, to date...	$61,728,384	
Amount surrendered between same dates...................	9,238,107	
Total redeemed and surrendered.....................	$70,966,491	
Amount issued between same dates.....	38,324,640	
Decrease from January 14, 1875, to date........................		32,641,851
National-bank notes outstanding at date..... ....'.....		$319,219,599
Greenbacks on deposit June 20, 1874, to retire notes of closed banks...		$3,813,675
Deposited from June 20, 1874, to date, to retire national-bank notes....		72,669,145
Total deposits......		$76,482,820
Circulation redeemed by Treas'r between same dates without reissue.		64,495,616
Greenbacks on deposit at date......................		$11,987,204
Greenbacks retired under act of January 14, 1875....		$30,659,712
Greenbacks outstanding at date................................... ...		351,340,288

* Fractions of notes.   † Destroyed in Chicago fire.

AMOUNTS OF LEGAL-TENDER NOTES AND NATIONAL-BANK NOTES OUTSTANDING AT THE DATES NAMED FROM 1865 TO NOVEMBER 1, 1877.

From the Annual Report of the Comptroller of the Currency, 1877.

DATE.	UNITED STATES ISSUES. Legal-tender Notes.	Old Demand Notes.	Fractional Currency.	Total United States Currency.	Notes of National Banks, Including Gold Notes.	Aggregate Paper Currency.	Currency Price of $100 Gold.	Gold Price of $100 Currency.
August 31, 1865	$432,757,004	$402,965	$26,344,742	$459,505,311	$176,213,955	$635,719,266	$144.25	$69.32
January 1, 1866	425,839,319	392,070	26,000,420	452,231,809	296,588,410	750,820,228	144.50	69.31
January 1, 1867	380,276,160	321,082	28,732,812	409,250,654	299,846,206	709,076,860	133.00	75.18
January 1, 1868	356,000,000	159,127	31,597,583	387,756,710	299,747,569	687,504,279	133.25	75.04
January 1, 1869	356,492,075	128,044	34,215,715	390,296,788	299,620,322	689,866,110	135.00	74.07
January 1, 1870	356,000,000	113,094	39,762,664	395,875,762	299,004,029	695,779,791	120.00	83.33
January 1, 1871	356,000,000	101,086	39,995,089	396,096,175	306,307,672	702,403,847	110.75	90.29
January 1, 1872	357,500,000	92,901	40,767,877	398,360,678	328,465,431	726,826,109	109.50	91.32
January 1, 1873	358,557,007	84,387	45,722,061	404,364,355	344,582,812	748,947,167	112.00	89.28
January 1, 1874	378,401,702	79,037	48,544,792	427,026,181	350,848,236	777,874,367	110.25	90.70
January 1, 1875	382,000,000	72,817	46,390,598	428,462,015	354,128,250	782,591,165	112.50	88.89
January 1, 1876	371,827,220	69,642	44,147,072	416,043,934	346,479,756	762,523,690	112.75	88.69
January 1, 1877	366,055,084	65,402	26,348,200	392,468,732	321,595,606	714,064,358	107.00	93.40
November 1, 1877	354,490,802	63,702	18,358,575	372,907,160	318,307,231	691,114,400	102.75	97.32

Statement Showing Aggregate Circulation of Paper Currency and Circulation per capita for the Years named.

From a Table prepared by Edward Young, Chief of the Bureau of Statistics, November, 1877.

Year.	Circulation of Bank of United States.	Circulation of State Banks.	Aggregate Paper Money.	Population.	Paper Circulation per capita.
1811.......	$5,400,000	$28,100,000	$33,500,000	$7,453,000	$4 49
1815.......	....	45,500,000	45,500,000	8,369,000	5 43
1816.......	....	68,000,000	68,000,000	8,614,000	7 89
1820.......	3,589,481	44,863,344	48,452,825	*9,658,453	5 02
1830.......	12,924,145	61,323,898	74,248,043	*12,866,020	5 77
1834.......	19,208,379	94,839,570	114,047,949	14,373,000	7 95
1835.......	17,339,797	103,692,495	121,032,292	14,786,000	8 19
1836.......	23,075,422	140,301,038	163,376,460	15,213,000	10 74
1837.......	11,447,968	149,185,890	160,633,858	15,655,000	10 26
1838.......	6,768,067	116,138,910	122,906,977	16,112,000	7 62
1839.......	5,982,621	135,170,995	141,153,616	16,584,000	8 51
1840.......	6,695,861	106,968,572	113,664,433	*17,069,453	6 66
1851.......	....	155,165,251	155,165,251	23,995,000	6 47
1860.......	....	207,102,477	207,102,477	*31,443,321	6 59
			Greenbacks, National Bank Notes, and other Paper Money.		
1861.......			$202,205,000	32,064,000	$6 31
1862.......			332,794,000	32,704,000	10 17
1863.......			297,736,000	33,365,000	8 92
1864.......			502,072,000	34,046,000	14 74
1865.......			628,692,000	34,748,000	18 09
1866.......			708,061,000	35,469,000	19 95
1867.......			693,090,000	36,211,000	19 14
1868.......			678,745,000	36,973,000	18 36
1869.......			676,508,000	37,756,000	17 92
1870.......			683,878,000	*38,558,371	17 73
1871.......			721,582,000	39,555,000	18 24
1872.......			731,355,000	40,604,000	18 01
1873.......			740,799,000	41,704,000	17 75
1874.......			777,538,000	42,856,000	18 14
1875.......			769,840,119	44,060,000	17 47
1876.......			717,241,912	45,316,000	15 82
1877.......			689,618,578	46,624,000	14 79

PAPER MONEY AND COIN OF GREAT BRITAIN.

The following is the estimate of the Deputy-master of the Mint, in an official communication :

Estimated value of the GOLD COIN in circulation in the United Kingdom December 31, 1875..	£118,560,000
Gold bullion December 31, 1875......................................	14,908,000
	£133,468,000

Estimated value of the SILVER COIN in circulation in the United Kingdom December 31, 1875..................................... £19,000,000

Estimated value of the PAPER CURRENCY in circulation in the United Kingdom December 31, 1875 :

Notes of Bank of England..	£29,041,000
Notes of English banks..	4,728,000
Notes of Scotch and Irish banks..................................	13,529,000
Total paper money...............................	£46,298,000
Total currency of Great Britain, specie and paper................	£198,766,000

* Enumerated ; for all other years the population is estimated.

NATIONAL BANK CIRCULATION, NOVEMBER, 1877.

From the Report of the Comptroller of the Currency, December, 1877.

STATES AND TERRITORIES.	BANKS	CAPITAL. Capital paid in.	BONDS. Bonds on deposit.	CIRCULATION. Issued.	Redeemed.	Outstanding.
Maine	72	$10,660,000	$9,459,250	$19,239,520	$10,569,631	$8,669,889
New Hampshire..	46	5,740,000	5,769,000	11,401,455	6,198,638	5,202,817
Vermont.........	46	8,768,700	7,635,500	17,350,960	10,150,370	7,200,590
Massachusetts ...	237	97,147,000	69,556,850	153,671,580	92,252,113	61,419,467
Rhode Island	61	20,079,800	14,053,900	32,447,825	19,629,985	12,817,840
Connecticut......	81	25,548,120	19,731,200	43,955,140	26,587,407	17,367,733
Totals, Eastern States	543	167,943,620	126,205,700	278,066,480	165,388,144	112,678,336
New York........	282	95,199,691	54,619,950	156,836,355	107,103,027	49,733,328
New Jersey......	69	14,178,350	12,549,350	27,288,720	16,061,668	11,227,052
Pennsylvania	232	56,014,340	44,954,300	101,154,415	59,664,955	41,489,460
Delaware	13	1,663,985	1,484,200	3,149,315	1,784,115	1,365,200
Maryland........	32	13,298,685	8,145,000	21,118,700	13,161,270	7,957,430
Totals, Middle States	628	180,355,051	121,752,800	309,547,505	197,775,035	111,772,470
Dist. of Columbia	6	1,432,000	1,038,000	3,296,300	2,258,857	1,039,443
Virginia	19	3,485,000	2,719,850	6,889,990	4,373,967	2,516,023
West Virginia....	15	1,846,000	1,548,250	4,743,240	3,115,568	1,627,672
North Carolina...	15	2,601,000	1,399,000	3,409,550	1,914,760	1,494,790
South Carolina...	12	2,870,700	1,470,000	3,367,185	1,968,825	1,398,350
Georgia	12	2,141,000	1,809,000	4,451,260	2,611,125	1,840,135
Florida	1	50,000	50,000	52,400	8,000	44,400
Alabama........	10	1,658,000	1,521,000	2,736,750	1,271,267	1,465,483
Mississippi......				66,000	64,479	1,521
Louisiana..	7	3,900,000	920,000	5,664,760	4,120,698	1,544,002
Texas	12	1,125,000	684,000	1,608,430	1,039,487	568,943
Arkansas........	2	205,000	205,000	473,700	220,765	252,935
Kentucky........	46	9,986,500	8,357,350	16,618,055	8,341,797	8,276,258
Tennessee.......	25	3,040,300	2,624,500	5,930,520	3,430,066	2,500,454
Missouri.........	30	7,735,000	2,270,000	10,607,405	7,889,811	2,717,594
Totals, Southern and Southwestern States...	212	42,115,500	26,705,950	69,917,545	42,629,482	27,288,063
Ohio............	164	28,471,000	23,627,250	53,122,830	30,939,539	22,183,291
Indiana	99	16,180,500	13,281,700	32,253,385	19,695,761	12,557,624
Illinois........ ..	144	18,461,000	10,413,000	31,895,265	21,233,462	10,661,803
Michigan	81	9,844,500	6,267,100	14,990,120	9,117,897	5,872,223
Wisconsin	40	3,500,000	2,295,500	6,777,140	4,382,428	2,394,712
Iowa............	78	6,137,000	4,475,500	11,447,880	7,148,096	4,299,784
Minnesota........	31	4,628,700	2,694,400	6,638,580	3,960,462	2,678,118
Kansas..........	15	1,065,000	940,000	2,676,260	1,637,988	1,038,272
Nebraska	10	1,000,000	824,000	1,746,860	955,900	790,960
Totals, Western States	662	89,288,500	64,818,450	161,548,320	99,071,533	62,476,787
Nevada..........				131,700	127,877	3,823
Oregon..........	1	250,000	250,000	460,400	235,400	225,000
Colorado........	13	1,235,000	732,000	1,417,620	729,137	688,483
Utah............	1	200,000	50,000	602,230	519,162	83,068
Idaho...........	1	100,000	100,000	186,040	103,339	82,701
Montana	5	350,000	236,000	464,420	249,351	215,069
Wyoming........	2	125,000	60,000	103,200	47,060	56,140
New Mexico.....	2	300,000	300,000	543,260	275,210	268,050
Dakota..........	1	50,000	50,000	90,930	46,930	44,000
Totals, Pacific States and Territories........	26	2,610,000	1,778,000	3,999,800	2,333,466	1,666,334
Due banks for mutilated notes retired						893,121
Grand totals....	2,071	482,312,771	341,260,900	823,079,650	507,197,660	316,775,111

NATIONAL BANKS OF THE UNITED STATES IN 1877.

From the Report of the Comptroller of the Currency, December, 1877.

THE following table exhibits the resources and liabilities of all the national banks at the close of business on the first day of October, 1877—the date of their last report :

	New York City.	Boston, Philadelphia and Baltimore.	Other Banks.	Aggregate.
	47 banks.	99 banks.	1,934 banks.	2,080 banks.
RESOURCES.	$	$	$	$
Loans and discounts........			465,250,106	888,243,290
On U. S. bonds on demand........	4,763,448	1,213,512	377,400	....
On other stocks, bonds, etc., on demand........................	48,376,033	18,058,413	8,680,788	....
Payable in gold...................	4,319,014	661	2,958,481	....
On single-name paper, without other security.................	15,800,540	10,588,072	7,054,807	....
All other loans...................	95,902,756	134,750,212	70,148,447	....
Overdrafts......................	108,894	39,899	3,528,510	3,677,303
Bonds for circulation..............	19,058,500	47,719,200	270,033,250	336,810,950
Bonds for deposits...............	780,000	600,000	13,523,000	14,903,000
U. S. bonds on hand..............	11,388,050	4,272,900	14,427,750	30,088,700
Other stocks and bonds..........	9,218,526	3,776,317	21,441,152	34,435,995
Due from reserve agents	... ...	13,195,086	60,089,047	73,284,133
Due from other national banks.....	14,900,901	8,850,609	21,465,737	45,217,247
Due from other banks and bankers.	2,421,599	969,836	8,024,416	11,415,761
Real estate, furniture, and fixtures..	9,389,268	6,746,895	29,093,820	45,229,983
Current expenses.................	1,048,806	684,391	4,982,595	6,915,792
Premiums.......................	1,722,001	1,138,738	6,358,436	9,219,175
Checks and other cash items.......	1,947,341	880,331	8,846,916	11,674,588
Exchanges for clearing-house......	53,814,891	15,838,971	4,841,354	74,595,216
Bills of other national banks.......	1,469,304	2,361,129	11,701,034	15,531,467
Fractional currency...............	75,933	80,059	744,814	900,806
Specie.........................	12,948,406	3,984,687	5,725,727	22,658,820
Legal-tender notes	15,236,845	8,476,998	43,206,841	66,920,684
U. S. certificates of deposit........	19,075,000	10,015,000	4,320,000	33,410,000
Five-per-cent redemption fund	797,278	2,045,718	11,651,638	14,494,634
Due from U. S. Treasury..........	187,807	250,195	1,089,117	1,527,119
Totals...................	344,781,651	296,737,829	1,099,565,183	1,741,084,663
LIABILITIES.				
Capital stock........	57,400,000	80,034,985	342,032,786	479,467,771
Surplus fund...	16,566,847	21,625,952	84,583,322	122,776,121
Undivided profits.............	9,241,772	4,176,195	31,154,712	44,572,679
National-bank notes outstanding....	15,395,257	40,445,791	236,033,188	291,874,236
State-bank notes outstanding......	77,279	91,513	312,946	481,738
Dividends unpaid.................	221,211	1,344,090	2,056,373	3,621,704
Individual deposits...............	162,400,317	112,321,118	341,682,552	616,408,947
U. S. deposits....................	302,086	303,090	7,366,649	7,972,715
Deposits of U. S. disbursing officers	129,775	11,186	2,236,022	2,376,983
Due to national banks.............	61,459,374	27,634,739	25,934,841	115,028,954
Due to other banks and bankers...	21,586,763	7,563,677	17,426,999	46,577,499
Notes and bills rediscounted.......	....	....	3,791,219	3,791,219
Bills payable.....................		1,185,503	4,951,614	6,137,117
Totals...................	344,781,651	296,737,829	1,099,565,183	1,741,084,663

CONDITION OF THE UNITED STATES NATIONAL BANKS, 1871-1877.

From the Report of the Comptroller of the Currency, December, 1877.

THE following table exhibits the resources and liabilities of the national banks in operation at corresponding dates for the last six years:

	Oct. 2, 1871.	Oct. 3, 1872.	Sept. 12, 1873.	Oct. 2, 1874.	Oct. 1, 1875.	Oct. 2, 1876.	Oct. 1, 1877.
	1,767 banks.	1,919 banks.	1,976 banks.	2,004 banks.	2,087 banks.	2,089 banks.	2,080 banks.
RESOURCES.	*Millions.*	*Millions.*	*Millions.*	*Millions.*	*Millions.*	*Millions.*	*Millions.*
Loans.................	831.6	877.2	944.2	954.4	984.7	931.3	891.9
Bonds for circulation..	364.5	392.0	389.3	383.3	370.3	337.2	336.8
Other U. S. bonds.....	45.8	27.6	23.6	29.0	28.1	47.8	45.0
Other stocks, bonds, etc.	21.5	23.5	23.7	27.8	33.5	31.4	34.5
Due from other banks.	143.2	128.2	149.5	131.8	144.7	146.9	129.9
Real estate.............	30.1	32.3	34.7	36.1	42.4	43.1	45.2
Specie	13.2	10.2	19.9	21.2	8.1	21.4	22.7
Legal-tender notes. ..	107.0	102.1	92.4	80.0	76 5	84.2	66.9
National-bank notes...	14.3	15.8	16.1	18.5	18.5	15.9	15.6
Clearing-house exchanges.........	115.2	125.0	100.3	109.7	87.9	100.0	74.5
U. S. certificates of deposit.................	....	6.7	20.6	43.8	48.8	29.2	33.4
Due from U. S. Treasurer...............	......	....	....	20.3	19.6	16.7	16.0
Other resources.......	41.2	25.2	17.3	18.9	19.1	19.1	28.7
Totals..........	1,730.6	1,755.8	1,830.6	1,877.2	1,882.2	1,827.2	1,741.1
LIABILITIES.							
Capital stock..........	458.3	479.6	491.0	493.8	504 8	499.8	479.5
Surplus fund	101.1	110.3	120.3	129.0	134.4	132.2	122.8
Undivided profits......	48.0	46.6	54.5	51.5	53 0	46.4	44.5
Circulation	317.4	335.1	340.3	334.2	319.1	292.2	291.9
Due to depositors.....	631.4	623.9	640.0	683 8	679 4	666.2	631.4
Due to other banks...	171.9	143.8	173.0	175.8	179.7	179.8	161.6
Other liabilities,......	8.5	11.5	11.5	9.1	11.8	10.6	10.4
Totals..........	1,730.6	1,755.8	1,830.6	1,877.2	1,882.2	1,827.2	1,741.1

Average Circulation, Deposits and Reserve Funds of the National Banks in New York City, in the other Principal Cities, and in the Remainder of the Country, separately, and the Average of the whole for the Last Eight Years.

CITIES AND STATES.	No. of Banks.	Circulation.	Net Deposits	Legal-tender Funds.	Due from Reserve Agents and Redemption Fund.	Total Reserve Funds.	Ratios of Legal-tender Funds to— Circulation.	Ratios of Legal-tender Funds to— Circulation and Deposits.	Ratio of Reserve Funds to Circ. and Deposits.
		$ Millions.	*$ Millions.*	*$ Millions.*	*$ Millions.*	*$ Millions.*	*Per cent.*	*Per cent.*	*Per cent.*
N. Y. City ..	49	24 03	176.86	53.92	50.00	54.43	224.4	26.8	27.1
Other cities..	181	69.81	191.43	41.34	27.94	69.28	59.2	15.8	26.5
States & Ter.	1,724	221.42	270.62	40.43	56.92	97.36	18.3	8.2	19.8
Averages...	1,954	315.26	638.93	135.70	85.37	221.08	43.0	14.2	23.2

It will be seen from the tables given, that the average strength of the national banks for the last eight years is fully equal to that of the State banks during periods of suspension and redemption in former times : and, if resumption is to take place upon any fixed date, the national banks will be certain, as a matter of precaution, to strengthen their reserves beyond the averages here given. It cannot be doubted, therefore, that the national banks will be prepared to redeem their circulating notes at any date of resumption which may be fixed upon.

THE SILVER MONEY QUESTION.

DURING the past two or three years, questions relating to the coinage, to the kind and amount of metallic money in circulation, and to
the monetary standard have assumed an unprecedented public interest. From utter inattention or obliviousness, the public mind has
been suddenly aroused to an eager and intense discussion of the most
abstruse questions of financial science. The journals of two hemi-
spheres have teemed for more than two years with articles, communications, and statistics bearing upon the relative uses and abuses of
gold and silver as mediums of exchange. Parties have formed or are
forming upon the issue whether silver money shall be a legal tender,
or shall be so far discredited as to be used only to a very limited
amount as subsidiary coinage. The silver problem, which was made
the subject of monetary conventions in Europe as early as 1867, and
which in 1873, when the great German Empire determined to demonetize silver, became still more prominently a question of public
interest abroad, has since, owing to the impending resumption
of specie payments in this country, taken a still stronger hold upon
the public mind in the United States. So far from the position
and rank of silver in our currency system having been settled by the
legislation of 1873, it is now apparent that the question of what is
or what is to be the currency of the United States was never more
unsettled than at the present time.

It is urged by the advocates of the single gold standard, that the
attempt to maintain two metals side by side as equal legal tenders
is neither philosophical, practicable, nor desirable; that the money
measure cannot be based upon two unequal units, any more than the
measure of length upon two yard-sticks of different lengths; that
the attempt to measure values by two standards is as absurd as to
set up two varying standards of measure, or of weight; that gold is
commended as the universal money measure, as well by its scarcity and
consequent inherent value as by the superior convenience of making
heavy payments in coins of that metal; that it is further recommended
as the sole monetary standard by its adoption and use for more than
sixty years past by Great Britain, whose capital is the most important

financial centre of the world; that the subsequent adoption of the single gold standard by Spain, Portugal, Sweden, Norway, Denmark, and finally by Germany, has greatly extended the reasons why gold should become the standard of all commercial nations; that to maintain silver money as full legal tender is an attempt to fly in the face of existing facts as to the commercial exchanges of the world; that, in point of fact, no payments to any considerable amount are made in silver, even in countries maintaining the double standard; that all such payments are made either by the transfer of gold, or by credits in the form of checks, drafts, or bills of exchange; that the attempt to keep a silver currency of full value in circulation as legal tender would give the people a heavy, burdensome, and inconvenient medium of exchange; that the wear of silver coins by abrasion in constant use would be a heavy loss to the people; that its intrinsic qualities render gold more permanent in value than silver; that the immense superiority of gold to silver secures it a permanent demand that guards against its depreciation; that the double standard subjects business to the fluctuations of two metals instead of one; that to give debtors the right of paying in the cheaper metal is a great wrong to the creditor; that the fluctuations under the double standard give a harvest of profit to money changers and brokers; that the creation of an international money standard must necessarily lead to the adoption of one metal, and that standard can only be gold; that the gold standard gives certainty and stability to commercial transactions; that it would be the wisest plan for all nations to agree upon gold as the monetary standard; that, pending such a general agreement, it becomes every government to shape its policy and legislation toward the establishing of the unitary system of gold coinage; and that the nations which persist in maintaining the double standard will thereby become unwilling holders on a falling market of the rejected silver of other countries, subjecting them not only to enormous pecuniary losses, but to predestined failure in attempting to maintain silver.

On the other hand, the advocates of the double or optional standard of gold and silver maintain that silver is entitled to rank side by side with gold as a full-valued money of payment and legal tender; that its monetary uses, as shown in the history of all nations, have been so widespread and beneficent as to call for its continuance; that at the present day nearly three fourths of the nations of the world, and more than three fourths of the populations, have silver money in actual circulation as a full legal tender for all debts; that silver has incontestable advantages over gold as a circulating medium for small payments, it being intrinsically a harder metal, and much less liable to abrasion and consequent loss to the community by use; that while gold coins of small amount (like the American gold dollar) are extremely inconvenient and liable to loss and speedy wearing out, besides being very difficult to count and to handle, the silver dollar and

half-dollar, on the contrary, are found to last half a century even with constant handling ; that the objection to silver money, founded on its great bulk and weight, is answered by the statement that nearly all modern exchanges are effected, not by transfer of any metal, but by credits in the familiar form of checks and bills of exchange ; that, therefore, the argument from inconvenience has little or no more weight as against silver than it has against gold ; that there is no gold coin which can take the place that the five-franc piece and the piaster, or dollar, have so long and so well occupied ; that the claim of the depreciation of silver where it is demonetized simply marks the measure of the wrong done to the people in depriving them of one of the precious metals, and throwing the loss upon all holders ; that governments have no right to confiscate property, or to add to the burdens of debt by degrading a metal which they themselves have stamped and coined as money of full value; that the gold standard necessitates the restriction of silver to a debased token money, which pays the wages of labor in a depreciated currency, while the profits of capital are reaped in gold ; that gold is subject to much greater fluctuations of demand and supply, and can readily be cornered or made artificially scarce, while if commerce has two metals to fall back upon, this liability is diminished by one half; that the history of the single gold standard in England proves that great commercial and monetary panics are more liable to occur under the mono-metallic than under the double standard ; that when either metal is available as a substitute for the other, the local fluctuations of supply and demand for either inevitably bring out the other to restore equilibrium ; that the double standard system thus secures more stable value to money, and the interest thereon, than is attainable under the single standard ; that the analogy drawn from standards of measure has no application to the standard of value or to economic science, as has been shown by the ablest political economists; that the withdrawal from current use as money of any considerable body of the coinage, by demonetizing it, is a violent contraction of the circulating medium, entailing great stringency, inconvenience, and loss upon the people where it is withdrawn ; that the demonetizing of silver by Germany in 1873, though not fully carried out, produced a financial panic of the severest kind in that country, from which France, on the other hand (which continued to maintain the double standard), was wholly free ; that the example of France disproves the claim that silver cannot be maintained side by side with gold, as a full legal-tender; that the effect of the demonetization of silver is logically admitted by the advocates of the single gold standard; that any attempt to bring all nations to gold as the only full-valued metallic money would result in an enormous shrinkage in the volume of the currency, a fearful depression in the prices of all commodities and securities, in enormous losses of property, in universal commercial

and financial embarrassment, and in widespread bankruptcy and ruin ; that this violent monetary contraction, while it would carry down the price of the discredited silver to the great loss of all nations holding that form of currency, would raise in an equal ratio the value of gold, which would become so scarce and dear as to be at times unobtainable ; that the best statistics procurable show the amount of the world's silver coinage to be nearly, if not quite, equal to that of the gold coinage in circulation ; and that thus to demonetize or virtually to abolish silver as a legal tender would have the effect of a contraction of almost fifty per cent in the circulating medium ; that this contraction of the legal currency would become a fearful creator of panics and monetary crises ; that the rejection of silver from its former high place as a received money measure and standard of value would be a great wrong to all individuals and nations owing debts at the time the change was made ; that such a contraction would require all debts which before it were payable in either gold or silver, to be paid in gold alone ; that this enhancement of the value of money, which would become dearer and dearer in proportion as the demonetization extended, would practically bankrupt that large portion of the community in debt, while it would unduly enrich the fortunate possessors of ready money ; that consequently the attempt to establish the single gold standard everywhere is a movement in the interest of the few as against the many, and that a just regard for vested rights, for the vast interests engaged in commerce and industry, for the convenience of the common people, and even for national solvency, requires the maintenance of both gold and silver as money of payment in all countries now using them, if indeed it does not demand the restoration of the double standard in countries which have discarded it.

In addition to these general considerations urged by the advocates of both sides on the silver question, there is another branch of the argument based upon considerations peculiar to the United States. It is alleged by the advocates of the double standard, that this country had the silver dollar as a full-valued currency and legal tender to any amount, until the year 1873; that for nearly eighty years the silver dollar of 371¼ grains of pure silver (412½ grains standard silver) went side by side with the Mexican dollar of equal value and weight, as the real monetary unit; that though this dollar was never coined to any great amount, it was none the less the standard measure, while half-dollars of equal proportional value were coined to the amount of $109,000,000, and were everywhere in circulation; that the legislation of 1873, under the guise of amending the mint statutes, prohibited the coinage of the silver dollar, and limited the legal-tender power of other silver coins to five dollars in any one payment; that this act, while it did not take away the value of the existing dollar coinage, practically effected demonetiza-

tion by prohibiting the further coinage of the silver dollar; that
the demonetization was actually completed by the revision of
the whole statute law enacted in bulk June 22d, 1874, in which it
was provided, in section 3586, that the silver coins of the United States
should be a legal tender to the amount of five dollars only in any
one payment—these silver coins, by section 3513, having been speci-
fied so as expressly to exclude the silver dollar; that this legislation
was effected without any public discussion in the country, with very
brief debate in either House or Senate; that it was during a suspension of specie payments, and before the Resumption Act of 1875 was
passed, when there was no silver coin in circulation, and public attention was not drawn to questions of coinage or of currency; that the
act thus passed, revolutionizing the entire metallic money system of
the country, was in effect without the consent of the people, and
ought to be rescinded; that its effect was, coupled with the subsequent legislation for resumption of specie payments, to change the
measure of all obligations, public and private, to make debts before
payable in gold or silver at option, payable in gold alone; that thus
an enormous enhancement of indebtedness was effected, alike unjust
to the debtor class while unduly favoring that of the creditor, and
prejudicial to public policy and to private welfare; that the United
States is, of all nations, the one most interested in maintaining the
value of silver as money, being the largest producer of silver metal;
that upon the market for this one of the precious metals depends a
very large share of our national prosperity; that the present as well
as the prospective value of our silver mines closely approaches, if it
does not exceed, that of our gold mines; that the discrediting of silver,
and its banishment from use as legal-tender currency, implies nothing
less than the almost entire destruction of the market for American
silver; that for us to enter into the designs of those who would make
the gold standard universal, would be to enhance not only all public
and private obligations, but to throw away one of our most efficient
sources of national wealth; and that Congress is bound, by considerations of public equity, as well as by those of national interest, to restore the money measure to what it was before the legislation of 1873,
as perfected by the enactment of the Revised Statutes. It is added by
some of the advocates of this view, that the only hope of the United
States for returning to successful and permanent specie payments lies
in the remonetization of silver, and its availability as a part of the
lawful circulating medium; and that specie resumption, if attempted
in gold alone, will have to be postponed for many years, or will
prove a failure, while, if undertaken on the solid basis of two metals,
it may be expected to prove a speedy and permanent success.

On the other hand, the opponents of the restoration of the double
standard in this country maintain that adequate notice was given of
the proposed demonetization of silver in 1873; that the demone-

tizing of silver could not have been part of a scheme to raise all debts to the gold standard, because silver was actually worth 3 per cent more than gold at the time; that as early as 1869, the proposition was made in Congress to adopt the single gold standard; that bills were brought forward at repeated sessions of Congress, from 1869 to 1873, embodying that revision of the coinage which finally became a law; that the reason assigned on the floor of the House for stopping the coinage of silver dollars—namely, that such coins were worth three per cent more than their face, so that they were at once exported, or went into the melting pot—was a sufficient reason for rejecting silver as a money measure, as the much greater depreciation of that metal below gold is a sufficient reason now ; that facts beyond controversy show the impossibility of fixing the value of silver by legislation, while gold is virtually the one money of payment employed by the leading nations ; that even when the silver dollar was legal tender to any amount, it was practically out of circulation, only about $8,000,000 in that denomination having been coined in the United States from first to last; that the public faith has been solemnly pledged by repeated acts of Congress to the payment of the national debt, and the outstanding legal-tender currency, in coin of the United States, of full value ; that this pledge of the public credit can never be redeemed by payment in depreciated silver; that the attempt to remonetize silver now, by undoing the legislation of 1873, and authorizing the coinage of silver dollars as an unlimited legal tender, would be to flood the country with a depreciated and depreciating currency ; that the attempt to pay off the national debt, or the interest thereon, by such a coinage of silver dollars, would be an act of bad faith, highly injurious to the national credit, and productive in the end of far greater losses than the percentage which would be saved by paying in the cheaper metal ; that the tendency of commercial nations in Europe to the adoption of the single gold standard is too powerful to be successfully resisted ; that if the United States should remonetize silver as full legal tender, it would stand almost alone in the quixotic enterprise, opposed to great commercial laws and to the spirit of the age ; that were our laws so changed as to make silver once more a legal tender, the United States would become a market for the cast-off silver of other nations, in addition to the product of our own mines, until silver would become a drug which everybody would be anxious to get rid of ; and that resumption of specie payments, if attempted in gold and silver, would break down by the double load it would have to carry, and result in the worst blow to our national credit which it has ever yet sustained.

Amid so wide a conflict of opinion, it is important to recapitulate the leading historical facts in the revolution or threatened revolution impending, as to the relative use of the precious metals as currency.

On the 23d of December, 1865, the four governments of France
Belgium, Italy, and Switzerland entered into a monetary convention,
which established an identity in the weight and fineness of the silver
and gold coins of those countries. This convention, which is commonly known as the Latin Monetary League (from the fact that the
nations participating were of Latin origin chiefly), is still in force.
Greece was afterwards admitted as a member of the convention, and
officially appointed agents from these five Powers were empowered to
hold an annual conference, at which the amount and proportions of
the coinage for the succeeding year by each member of the League
are fixed. As the double standard is still maintained among the
countries of the Latin League, the demonetizing of silver by Germany
so far discredited that metal, leading to an abrupt decline in its value
as measured by gold, that the League has since greatly restricted the
coinage of silver. The original motive for forming the convention
grew out of the great change in the relative value of the precious
metals, which had been occasioned by the influx of gold to Europe
from the newly discovered mines of California and Australia. The
disturbing effect thereby created upon the currency of those countries which had the double standard brought them to devise some
means of maintaining a more fixed relation of value between silver
and gold in the proportion legalized in France ever since 1803, of $15\frac{1}{2}$
of silver to 1 of gold.

The Paris Convention of December 23d, 1865, by the four Powers
named, fixed the proportion of pure metal in gold coins of twenty
francs, ten francs, and five francs, and also of the silver coin of five
francs, at $\frac{9}{10}$ of pure metal with $\frac{1}{10}$ alloy. It also reduced the proportion of lightness in the silver coins below five francs from $\frac{900}{1000}$ to
$\frac{835}{1000}$. At the same time, these subsidiary coins were made legal tender only to an amount not exceeding fifty francs.*

An International Conference on weights, measures, and coins was
held in Paris, in June, 1867, followed by an International Monetary
Conference in the same city, June 21st to July 9th, 1867. These con-
ferences grew out of the International Exhibition of that year, and

---

* By the terms of the monetary league between France, Belgium, Italy, and
Switzerland, no government has the power to demonetize silver, or to change the
common monetary unit (the five-franc piece) before the year 1880. The following
table exhibits the maximum amount of silver money to be coined for each of the
nations which are parties to the league in 1877 :

	Francs.	
France	27,000,000	or $5,400,000
Italy	18,000,000	" 3,600,000
Belgium	5,400,000	" 1,080,000
Switzerland	3,600,000	" 720,000
Greece	1,800,000	" 360,000

55,800,000 or $11,160,000

The meeting of the conference of the representatives of the contracting Powers, which was to have been held in January, 1877, was postponed, by agreement
between the governments, until the close of that year.

were composed chiefly of commissioners at that exhibition, with other persons eminent in science and in commerce. Among them were the Baron de Hock for Austria, Feer-Herzog for Switzerland, Raymond de Segary for Spain, Samuel D. Ruggles for the United States, Leone Levi for Great Britain, M. de Jacobi for Russia, and Messrs. Becquerel, Bevuderilla, Michel Chevalier, and M. Wolowski for France. The Prince Napoleon presided over the monetary conference, and a report in favor of uniform coinage for all nations, styled the Unification Money, was agreed upon. The series of gold coins now in use in France being adopted by the greater part of the population in Europe, was recommended as a basis for the uniform system, and it was urged that all governments adopt a similar unit in the issue of their gold coins, and make them everywhere of the same fineness, $\frac{9}{10}$ fine. It was also resolved to be desirable that the system of the double monetary standards be abandoned wherever it yet exists. M. Wolowski opposed the abandonment of the double standard, which was a problem on which public opinion was divided, and which each nation should resolve for itself. He thought it inexpedient to take the full legal-tender power from silver, which would diminish by half the mass of the precious metals in circulation. The forced circulation of paper money must cease one day in Austria, Russia, and America, and then a new demand for a metal for coinage would take place, which it would be necessary to meet with silver; otherwise the value of the only metal having legal course would increase so much as to turn all contracts against the debtors. Baron de Hock argued in behalf of the gold standard, insisting that it was more steady than either the double standard or the silver. The report in favor of the gold standard was adopted by a large majority.

The Paris Conference of 1867 was, it was understood, semi-officially supported by the French Government, which was anxious that other governments, represented (however unofficially) to the number of twenty, should prosecute the scheme of the monetary unification to a successful issue.

Out of the representations of the British deputies to the Paris Conference grew the Royal Commission on International Coinage, constituted by an order of the queen, July 18th, 1868. This commission took testimony from financiers, statisticians, and monetary experts, and brought in a report, July 25th, 1868, of 394 folio pages, including evidence. In this report, the recommendation of the Paris Monetary Conference of a single gold standard is held as an adoption of the British law and custom on the subject, and the arguments in favor of gold as of superior steadiness of value, and of economy as a medium of exchange, are urged, together with the uncertainty and inconvenience arising from a double or alternative standard. The report enters into detail regarding the history of coinage regulations, and closes with opposing the adoption by England of a gold coin of

the value of 25 francs in the place of the sovereign, while favoring the other recommendations of the Paris Monetary Conference.

Let us now turn to the first steps taken in the United States toward the demonetization of silver. On the 6th of January, 1868, Hon. John Sherman, a member of the Committee of the Senate on Finance, introduced a bill, the first three sections of which were as follows :

A Bill in Relation to the Coinage of Gold and Silver.

Be it enacted by the Senate and House of Representatives of the United States of America in Congress assembled, That, with a view to promote a uniform currency among the nations, the gold coin of five dollars shall be one hundred and twenty-four and nine twentieths troy grains, so that it shall agree with a French coin of twenty-five francs, and with the rate of thirty-one hundred francs to the kilogram ; and the other sizes or denominations shall be in due proportion of weight, and the fineness shall be nine tenths or nine hundred parts fine in one thousand.

SEC. 2. And be it further enacted, That, in order to conform the silver coinage to this rate, and to the French valuation, the weight of the half-dollar shall be one hundred and seventy-nine grains, equivalent to one hundred and sixteen decigrams ; and the lesser coins shall be in due proportion, and the fineness shall be nine tenths. But the coinage of silver pieces of one dollar, five cents, and three cents shall be discontinued.

SEC. 3. And be it further enacted, That the gold coins to be issued under this act shall be a legal tender in all payments to any amount, and the silver coins shall be a legal tender to an amount not exceeding ten dollars in any one payment.

This bill was referred to the Committee on Finance, and reported back June 9th, 1868, with certain amendments. One of these amended Section 3 to read as follows :

SEC. 3. And be it further enacted, That the gold coins to be issued under this act shall be a legal tender for all payments to any amount, *except for such existing bonds of the United States as are payable in coin ;* and the silver coins shall be a legal tender to an amount not exceeding ten dollars in any one payment.

March 3d, 1868, Senator Frelinghuysen brought in a bill to promote uniform coinage, the leading feature of which provided that the amount of pure gold in an eagle or five-dollar gold piece should hereafter be 113 grains troy weight, to correspond to the amount of gold contained in an English pound sterling. The Committee on Finance, to whom these bills were referred, together with the proceedings of the International Monetary Conference of 1867, and the report of Mr. Ruggles, delegate from the United States to that conference, reported June 9th, 1868, through Mr. Sherman, that the bill first named be reported with amendments, supported by a report from Mr. Sherman ; and that Hon. E. D. Morgan, of the same committee, be authorized to submit a report adverse to the bill ; that these reports be printed and the bill be postponed, with a view to elicit full discussion of the several questions embraced.

Mr. Sherman's report dwelt upon the importance of a common monetary standard among all nations, the inconvenience of the different standards of value, the history of the efforts towards unification of coinage, and gave a statement of the result arrived at by the Paris Monetary Conference of the preceding year (1867). It urged as a reason why the United States should now adopt the single gold standard, that this nation is the great gold-producing country of the

world ; that gold with us is like cotton—a raw product; that every
obstruction to its free use diminishes its value, and that loss falls
upon the United States, the country of production; that the United
States, being a debtor nation, should place itself in harmony with
the money units of the creditor nations, and thus promote the ease of
borrowing money and payment of debts, without loss of recoinage or
of exchange—always paid by the debtor ; that the single standard of
gold is an American idea, yielded reluctantly by France and other
countries, where silver is the chief standard of value ; that to maintain two standards of value is an impossible attempt, and has given
rise to nearly all the debasement of coinage of the last two centuries ;
that the opportunity is now offered to the United States to secure a
common international standard in the metal most available, best
adapted for coinage, and mainly the product of our own country, and
in conformity with a policy now agreed to by the oldest and wealthi-
est nations of the world. The report of the committee further stated
that the Secretary of the Treasury and the Director of the Mint had
been consulted, and the result of this conference was the bill herewith
reported (the most important provisions of which are given above),
discontinuing the coinage of the silver dollar, and limiting the legal-
tender power of the subsidiary silver coin to ten dollars. The report
adds :

"The provisions in regard to silver coinage are urged by the Director of the
Mint, to secure harmony between the present market value of gold and silver; but
this coinage can be regulated hereafter by the varying values of the two metals,
and without disturbing the sole legal standard of value for large sums."

On the subject of existing contracts as affected by the proposed
change in the monetary system, the report held :

"All private contracts are made in view of the power of Congress to regulate
the value of coins. This power has been repeatedly exercised by Congress, and in
no case was any provision made for enforcing existing contracts in the old rather
than the new standard. All property and contracts may be affected by legislation,
but it is not presumed that in the exercise of its legislative power Congress will be
controlled by either the debtor or the creditor, but only by the general good.
. . . . All contracts are now on the legal-tender basis. Every private creditor
would now take the new coin, and would be largely benefited by the changed
medium of payment. The small relief of the debtor by the slightly diminished
standard of coin will tend to that degree to lessen the unavoidable hardship to him
of a return to specie payment. . . . Your committee therefore conclude, that
as to all private debts or contracts, the only provision necessary in this bill is to
postpone the operation of its legal-tender clause for a reasonable time after the passage of the act."

On the subject of public debts the report holds the following language :

" As to public debts, the contract of loan is the only law that ought to affect the
creditor until his debt is fully discharged. Congress, as the authorized agent of the
American people, is one party to the contract, and it may no more vary the contract
by subsequent acts than any other debtor may vary his contract. As to the public
creditor, no legislative power stands between him and the exact performance of his
contract. Public faith holds the scales between him and the United States, and the
penalties for a breach of this faith are far more severe and disastrous to the nation
than courts, constables, and sheriffs can be to the private debtor. . . . The public
debt is so large, that a change of three and one half per cent in the value of our coin
is a reduction of the public debt of $90,000,000. So much of this debt as exists in

the form of legal-tender notes will be received and disbursed as money, and as its value for some time will be less than the new coin, no provision need be made for it; but for so much of the debt as is payable, principal or interest, in coin of a specific weight and value, provision ought to be made for its exact discharge in that coin or its equivalent in the new. Your committee, therefore, propose an amendment to that effect."

The minority report of the Finance Committee, presented by Hon. E. D. Morgan, opposed the adoption of the single gold standard for the following reasons:

"A change in our national coinage so grave as that proposed by the bill should be made only after the most mature deliberation. The circulating medium is a matter that directly concerns the affairs of everyday life, affecting not only the varied, intricate, and multiform interests of the people at home, to the minutest detail, but the relations of the nation with all other countries as well. The United States has a peculiar interest in such a question. It is a principal producer of the precious metals. . . .

"Antecedent to any action by Congress on this subject we should carefully consider—

"I. The effect which the present abundant production of the precious metals, especially of gold, and the probable great increase in the supply, as mining facilities are improved and more generally applied, will have upon the purchasing power of these metals.

"II. The question of preserving such a relation between gold and silver as will retain the latter metal in free circulation, and continuance of the coinage of such denominations of silver as will serve to encourage American commerce with Mexico and with South American and Asiatic nations."

It is further urged, that there should be opportunity for further popular discussion of the subject, so that the business public would fully understand on what grounds so important a change in the value of our monetary unit, the dollar, is based.

On the silver question, the report of Mr. Morgan says:

"The American continent, too, produces four fifths of the silver of commerce. The mines of Nevada have already taken high rank, and Mexico alone supplies more than half the world's grand total. Our relations with the silver-producing people, geographically most favorable, are otherwise intimate.

"These two streams of the precious metals, poured into the current of commerce in full volume, will produce perturbations marked and important. Other countries will be affected, but the United States will feel the effect first and more directly than any other.

"The Pacific Railway will open to us the trade of China, Japan, India, and other Oriental countries, of whose prepossessions we must not lose sight. For years, silver, for reasons not fully understood, has been the object of unusual demand among these Asiatic nations, and now forms the almost universal medium of circulation, absorbing rapidly the silver coinage. The silver dollar, a favorite coin of the native Indian and distant Asiatic, has well-nigh disappeared from domestic circulation, to reappear among the Eastern peoples with whom we more than ever seek close intimacy. As they prefer this piece, we would do well to increase rather than discontinue its coinage, for we must not deprive ourselves of the advantages which its agency will afford.

"Mr. Ruggles says that nearly all the silver coined in the United States prior to 1853 has disappeared. A remedy is not to be found in the adoption of a system that undervalues this metal, for that commodity, like any other, shuns the market where not taken at its full value, to find the more favorable one. It is a favorite metal, entering into all transactions of daily life, and deserves proper recognition in any monetary system."

The report proceeds to urge that, independently of all other considerations, Congress may very properly decline to act until the leading nations represented at the Paris Monetary Conference should adopt a plan of unification:

"To be acceptable, a change in our coinage must be a thing of clearly obvious advantage, and proceed from the people. There has, however, been no popular expression in favor of the proposed plan, nor, indeed, any voluntary action in that direction whatever on the part of financial men, either in this country or elsewhere.

If there has been any complaint in regard to our monetary system, the fact has not come to the knowledge of your committee. . . . Our coinage is believed to be the simplest of any in circulation, and every way satisfactory for purposes of domestic commerce ; it possesses special merits of everyday value, and should not for light reasons be exchanged where the advantages sought to be gained are mainly theoretical, engaging more properly the attention of the philosopher than the practical man. . . .

"Unification of the coinage, like all similar questions, should be taken up without bias, and considered on the broad ground of national interest. At the proper time, when the country is restored to a normal financial condition, and the public ask a change in this regard, it may be well to appoint a commission of experts carefully to consider the question in its various bearings. Reflection and further observation here and elsewhere may suggest the foundations for a better and more enduring system than the one now proposed, which in the nature of things is but a provisional one. Permanency is equally important with uniformity in our coinage."

No action was taken by the Senate upon either of these reports, and the whole question went over to the following years. Late in 1869 there was prepared at the Treasury Department, under the supervision of J. J. Knox, then Deputy Comptroller of the Currency, a revision of all laws existing relative to the mint and coinage of the United States. This revision, put into the form of a bill for the consideration of Congress, and accompanied by a report in favor of its adoption, substantially embodied those changes in the laws regulating the coinage of the United States, subsequently adopted by the legislation of 1873.* This bill and report in favor of changing the coinage were transmitted to the Finance Committee of the Senate, April 25th, 1870, by Secretary Boutwell, recommending the passage of the bill. The accompanying report stated that the provisions of the bill had been submitted to all the different mints and assay offices, to the leading officers of the Treasury Department, and to other gentlemen intelligent upon the subject of the coinage, to receive suggestions of improvement. The report summarized the many changes and reforms proposed in the manufacture of coin, and contained the following paragraph:

"The coinage of the silver-dollar piece, the history of which is here given, is discontinued in the proposed bill. It is by law the dollar unit, and, assuming the value of gold to be fifteen and one half times that of silver, being about the mean ratio for the past six years, is worth in gold a premium of about three per cent (its value being $103.12) and intrinsically more than seven per cent premium in our other silver coin, its value thus being $107.42. The present laws consequently authorize both a gold-dollar unit and a silver-dollar unit, differing from each other in intrinsic value. The present gold-dollar piece is made the dollar unit in the proposed bill, and the silver-dollar piece is discontinued. If, however, such a coin is authorized, it should be issued only as a commercial dollar, not as a standard unit of account, and of the exact value of the Mexican dollar, which is the favorite for circulation in China and Japan and other Oriental countries."

Two months after the submission of this report and bill to the Senate, the Secretary of the Treasury sent to the House of Representatives a letter of Deputy Comptroller Knox, with copies of the correspondence relating to the bill and report previously submitted. This correspondence was printed by order of the House,† and contained, among many other letters, one from Dr. H. R. Linderman,

---

* Senate Misc. Doc. No. 132, 41st Congress, 2d Session, 1870.

† H. R. Ex. Doc. No. 307, 41st Congress, 2d Session, June, 1870.

now Director of the Mint, urging the discontinuance of the silver dollar, stating that the gold dollar is really the legal unit and measure of value, and that the silver dollar, having a higher value as bullion than its nominal value, long ago ceased to be a coin of circulation, and being of no practical use whatever, its issue should be discontinued.   On the other hand, Mr. J. R. Snowden, formerly Director of the Mint, said :

"I see that it is proposed to demonetize the silver dollar. This I think unadvisable. Silver coins below the dollar are now not money in a proper sense, but only tokens. I do not like the idea of reducing the silver dollar to that level. It is quite true that the silver dollar, being more valuable than two half-dollars or four quarter-dollars, will not be used as a circulating medium, but only for cabinets, and perhaps to supply some occasional or local demand ; yet I think there is no necessity for so considerable a piece as a dollar to be struck from metal which is only worth ninety-four cents. When we speak of dollars, let it be known that we speak of dollars not demonetized and reduced below their intrinsic value, and thus avoid the introduction of contradictory and loose ideas of the standards of value."

The bill was favorably reported by the Finance Committee of the Senate, December 19th, 1870, and having been printed with amendments, was, after discussion, passed by the Senate on the 10th of January, 1871, yeas 36, nays 14.   On the 13th of January, the Senate bill was ordered to be printed in the House and referred to the Committee on Coinage.   On the 25th of February, 1871, Hon. W. D. Kelley, chairman of that committee, reported the bill back with a substitute, which was again printed and recommitted.   The session expired without action, however, and the bill was reintroduced March 9th, 1871, by Mr. Kelley, and ordered to be printed.

The next year, January 9th, 1872, the bill was reported by Mr. Kelley, Chairman of the Coinage Committee, with a recommendation that it pass.   After discussion, the bill was recommitted.   On February 13th, 1872, the bill was reported back by Mr. Samuel Hooper, of Massachusetts, with amendments, which were printed, and on the 9th of April the bill came up for discussion, when Mr. Hooper said :

"Section 16 re-enacts the provisions of the existing laws defining the silver coins and their weights, respectively, in relation to the silver dollar, which is reduced in weight from 412½ to 384 grains, thus making it a subsidiary coin in harmony with the silver coins of less denomination, to secure its concurrent circulation with them. The silver dollar of 412½ grains, by reason of its bullion or intrinsic value being greater than its nominal value, long since ceased to be a coin of circulation, and is melted by manufacturers of silverware. It does not circulate now in commercial transactions with any country, and the convenience of these manufacturers in this respect can better be met by supplying small stamped bars of the same standard, avoiding the useless expense of coining the dollar for that purpose."

Mr. Clarkson N. Potter, of New York, said :

"This bill provides for the making of changes in the legal-tender coin of the country, and for substituting as legal tender, coin of only one metal instead as heretofore of two. I think myself this would be a wise provision, and that legal-tender coins, except subsidiary coin, should be of gold alone; but why should we legislate on this now, when we are not using either of those metals as a circulating medium ?
"The bill provides also for a change in respect of the weight and value of the silver dollar, which I think is a subject which, when we come to require legislation about it at all, will demand at our hands very serious consideration, and which, as we are not using such coins for circulation now, seems at this time to be an unnecessary subject about which to legislate." (Congressional Globe, vol. 102, page 2310.)

Mr. Kelley said, in reply :

"I wish to ask the gentleman who has just spoken (Mr. Potter) if he knows of any government in the world which makes its subsidiary coinage of full value. The silver coin of England is ten per cent below the value of gold coin.

"It is impossible to retain the double standard. The values of gold and silver continually fluctuate. You cannot determine this year what will be the relative values of gold and silver next year. They were 15 to 1 a short time ago ; they are 16 to 1 now.

"Hence all experience has shown that you must have one standard coin which shall be a legal tender for all others, and then you may promote your domestic convenience by having a subsidiary coinage of silver, which shall circulate in all parts of your country as legal tender for a limited amount, and be redeemable at its face value by your government. But, sir, I again call the attention of the House to the fact that the gentlemen who oppose this bill insist upon maintaining a silver dollar worth three and one half cents more than the gold dollar, and worth seven cents more than two half-dollars, and that so long as those provisions remain you cannot keep silver coin in the country."

On the 27th of May, 1872, the bill passed the House by a vote of yeas 110, nays 13.

Two days later, the bill was again reported in the Senate by the Committee on Finance, but no action was taken until the following December, when it was reported back, and ordered to be printed with amendments. On the 17th of January, 1873, the bill passed the Senate, after a discussion, in the course of which Senator Sherman said :

"This bill proposes a silver coinage exactly the same as the French, and what are called the associated nations of Europe, who have adopted the international standard of silver coinage ; that is, the dollar (two half-dollars) provided for by this bill is the precise equivalent of a five-franc piece. It contains the same number of grains of silver, and we have adopted the international gram instead of the grain for the standard of our silver coinage. The trade-dollar has been adopted mainly for the benefit of the people of California and others engaged in trade with China."

The bill then went to the House for concurrence, January 21st, 1873. It was again printed with amendments, and the differences between the two houses were adjusted by a committee of conference, whose report was agreed to. The bill was signed by President Grant, and became a law on February 12th, 1873.

The bill as finally passed differed radically, as regards the silver dollar, from the bill originally prepared at the Treasury, as well as from the bill first passed by the House of Representatives. The bill prepared at the Treasury wholly omitted the silver-dollar piece, and as first passed by the Senate in 1871, no silver-dollar coinage whatever was authorized. The bill passed by the House, May 27th, 1872, provided for a new silver dollar of a reduced value of 384 grains of standard silver, equal in weight to two half-dollars already in circulation. The Senate substituted for this a trade-dollar weighing 420 grains of standard silver, in accordance (as was said) with the wishes of the dealers in bullion on the Pacific Coast, that being considered by them the most advantageous weight for a coin to be used for shipment to China and Japan.

In his Annual Report for 1872, the Secretary of the Treasury, in again calling the attention of Congress to the Mint Bill, used the following language :

"In the last ten years the commercial value of silver has depreciated about three per cent as compared with gold, and its use as a currency has been discontinued by

Germany and by some other countries. The financial condition of the United States has prevented the use of silver as currency for more than ten years, and I am of opinion that upon grounds of public policy no attempt should be made to introduce it, but that the coinage should be limited to commercial purposes, and designed exclusively for commercial uses with other nations.

"The intrinsic value of a metallic currency should correspond to its commercial value, or metal should be used for the coinage of tokens redeemable by the government at their nominal value. As the depreciation of silver is likely to continue, it is impossible to issue coin redeemable in gold without ultimate loss to the government; for when the difference becomes considerable the holders will present the silver for redemption and leave it in the hands of the government, to be disposed of subsequently at a loss.

"Therefore, in renewing the recommendations heretofore made for the passage of the Mint Bill, I suggest such alterations as will prohibit the coinage of silver for circulation in this country, but that authority be given for the coinage of a silver dollar that shall be as valuable as the Mexican dollar, and to be furnished at its actual cost."

The act of February 12th, 1873, did not directly demonetize the silver dollar ; it simply prohibited its further coinage by the following provision :

"That no coins, either of gold, silver, or minor coinage, shall hereafter be issued from the mint other than those of the denominations, standards, and weights herein set forth."

A previous section had fixed the silver coins, thereafter to be issued, as follows :

"That the silver coins of the United States shall be a trade-dollar, a half-dollar or fifty-cent piece ; and the weight of the trade-dollar shall be four hundred and twenty grains troy ; the weight of the half-dollar shall be twelve grammes and one half of a gramme ; the quarter-dollar and the dime shall be, respectively, one half and one fifth the weight of said half-dollar ; and said coins shall be a legal tender at their nominal value for any amount not exceeding five dollars in any one payment."

It is carefully to be noted, that neither in these sections nor in any other part of the act of 1873 is the quality of legal tender taken away from the silver dollars already coined. Their demonetization was accomplished by the Revised Statutes enacted by Congress June 22d, 1874, in which all the then existing body of laws of the United States were codified and reduced into one volume. In this revision, after repeating the above provision as to what should constitute the silver coins of the United States (Revised Statutes, Section 3513), the prohibition of issuing other coins already cited followed (Section 3516), and the demonetizing of silver was perfected by the sections regarding legal tender, which are as follows:

"The gold coins of the United States shall be a legal tender in all payments at their nominal value. . . . . The silver coins of the United States shall be a legal tender at their nominal value for any amount not exceeding five dollars in any one payment." (Revised Statutes of the U. S., Sections 3585, 3586.)

General public attention was not drawn to the radical change effected in the laws regulating the silver coinage of the United States until after the passage by Congress of the act to provide for the resumption of specie payments in 1879, which became a law January 14th, 1875. Within one year from the passage of this act, financial questions became great and leading issues, and in Ohio and other States the policy and expediency of returning to specie payments,

of withdrawing the current greenback paper money, of perpetuating the bank-note system, or substituting for it United States legal-tender notes, became topics of universal discussion. Congress was agitated by a multitude of influences, and at the very next session following the passage of the resumption act there came a great flood of bills proposing new financial legislation.

At this session of Congress an enlarged coinage of subsidiary silver money was authorized, consisting of half-dollars, quarters, twenty-cent and ten-cent coins. The act of April 17th, 1876, provided for this issue of minor silver coin in redemption of an equal amount of paper fractional currency; while another act, approved July 22d, 1876, authorized the issue of silver coin to the amount of ten million dollars in exchange for an equal amount of legal-tender notes (not fractional), and increased the coinage of subsidiary silver authorized to be issued in redemption of fractional currency to the aggregate of $50,000,000.

The passage of these acts was due in part to the increasing scarcity and unsatisfactory character of the fractional paper currency. This subsidiary legal tender, the first issues of which were authorized during the war, by act of July 17th, 1862, proved to be so quickly worn out and defaced in use as to entail considerable loss upon the people. This fact, with the increasing scarcity of change, from its rapid deterioration, and the strong agitation in favor of a better coinage which set in upon the further discovery that silver had been demonetized, led to the passage through Congress by large majorities of these acts authorizing the coinage of fifty millions of small silver.

The House of Representatives passed, December 13th, 1876, what was known as the Bland Silver Bill, the direct object of which was to remonetize the silver dollar, and to make it a legal tender to any amount, for all debts, public and private. This measure, however, failed to pass the Senate. A bill for the repeal of the resumption act, long pending in the House in the summer of 1876, also failed to pass. But on the 15th of August, 1876, a joint resolution became a law creating a Monetary Commission, to consist of three Senators, three Representatives, and experts not exceeding three in number to be selected by them, whose duty it should be to inquire—

"*First.* Into the change which has taken place in the relative value of gold and silver; the causes thereof, whether permanent or otherwise; the effects thereof upon trade, commerce, finance, and the productive interests of the country, and upon the standard (of) value in this and foreign countries;

"*Second.* Into the policy of the restoration of the double standard in this country; and, if restored, what the legal relation between the two coins, silver and gold, should be;

"*Third.* Into the policy of continuing legal-tender notes concurrently with the metallic standards, and the effects thereof upon the labor, industries, and wealth of the country; and

"*Fourth.* Into the best means for providing for facilitating the resumption of specie payments."

The commission as organized consisted of Senators John P. Jones,

Louis V. Bogy, and George S. Boutwell; Messrs. Randall L. Gibson, Richard P. Bland, and George Willard, of the House of Representatives; William S. Groesbeck, of Ohio; and Francis Bowen, of Massachusetts.

This commission held many meetings in New York City and in Washington, and instituted correspondence with bankers, publicists, and commercial men in the United States, as well as with eminent financial authorities in Europe.

The report of this commission, although agreed to as early as March, 1877, did not appear in print until about the first of November. The majority of the commission, consisting of Messrs. Jones, Bogy, Willard, Bland, and Groesbeck, concurred in the following general conclusions:

"The true and only cause of the stagnation in industry and commerce now everywhere felt is the fact everywhere existing of falling prices, caused by a shrinkage in the volume of money. This is in part the misfortune of mankind, as the mines have failed for several years, under energetic working, to yield the precious metals in quantity sufficient to keep pace with the increasing needs of the world for money. But it is in part due to the folly of mankind in throwing away a benefaction of nature by discarding one of the precious metals. Existing evils date with that folly, which precipitated and now enormously aggravates them."

The commission recommended, by a majority of five to three, the remonetizing of silver in the United States. Three of the majority of the committee, Messrs. Jones, Bogy, and Willard, further recommended the adoption of the ratio between silver and gold of 15½ to 1, instead of remonetizing the old silver dollar, which would give a relation between the metals of 15.98 to 1. Messrs. Groesbeck and Bland of the majority non-concurred in this recommendation of 15½ as the standard, but urged the recoinage of the old silver dollar, so as simply to undo the recent legislation for demonetizing silver, and restore the dollar to its exact former position as legal-tender currency.

The minority of the committee, Senator Boutwell, Professor Francis Bowen, and Hon. R. L. Gibson, made dissenting reports. Mr. Boutwell, while deeming it desirable to secure the use of the two metals by concurrent action of commercial nations, was of the opinion that the United States should adhere to existing legislation; that the public creditor was entitled to receive gold coin in payment of the interest and principal of the public debt; that the recoinage of silver dollars would lead to a flow to the United States of the demonetized and discredited silver of every other country, largely depreciating its value; and that the adoption of silver as the standard would be followed by a loss in the depreciation of the public credit far greater than any gain to the government by the payment of the interest and principal of the public debt in a coin less valuable than gold.

Mr. Bowen, in his report, concurred in by Mr. Gibson, held that every attempt to establish the so-called double standard has been a

failure ; that though the law may declare either of the two commodities legal tender, only one of them, and that the cheaper one, is actually adopted as the medium of payment ; that while France had silver for her only standard from 1803 to the gold discoveries about 1850, gold had been actually made the only standard ever since ; that in the United States, Congress had several times been under the necessity of tinkering the so-called double standard of currency through the fluctuations in price ; that the best thing for the United States to do would be to take a further step toward assimilating our metallic currency to that of England, and the commercial world generally ; that this should be done by diminishing the quantity of gold in the dollar three fifths of one grain, so that the half-eagle, or $5 piece, would become almost the equivalent of the pound sterling, and would differ only by a fraction from the gold twenty-five-franc piece of France, and the twenty gold marks of Germany.

Congress adjourned August 15th, 1876, in the midst of the agitation and preparation attendant upon a coming Presidential election, leaving financial questions substantially *in statu quo*, with the exception of the authorized coinage of fifty millions in subsidiary silver. Its next session, December, 1876, to March, 1877, was almost wholly absorbed in the settlement of a disputed Presidential election, and bills for the repeal of the resumption act, for the remonetizing of silver, for the substitution of greenbacks for the National-bank circulation, and many other financial measures, failed to become laws.

At the extraordinary session convened October 15th, 1877, to provide for the support of the army, the financial issues before the country came up again with renewed force. Out of a multitude of bills proposed for the amendment or repeal of the existing monetary legislation, the bill for remonetizing the silver dollar of 412½ grains of standard silver, and making it a legal tender for all debts, public and private, passed the House on the 5th day of November, 1877, by a vote of 164 ayes to 34 noes.

The bill to repeal the resumption act, or so much thereof as provided for the redemption in coin of the United States legal-tender notes on the 1st of January, 1879, passed the House on the 23d day of November, 1877, by the close vote of 133 yeas to 120 nays. Neither of these bills, however, was acted upon in the Senate prior to the holiday recess of Congress, terminating with the 10th of January, 1878.

DIPLOMATIC SERVICE OF THE UNITED STATES.

From the Register of the Department of State, December, 1877.

Name and Rank.	Resi-dence.	Whence Appointed.	Date of Commis-sion.	Salary.
Argentine Rep.. Thomas O. Osborn, Min. Res.	BuenosA.	Ill....	Feb. 10, '74	$7,500
Aust'ia-H'ngary John A. Kasson,* E.E. & M.P.	Vienna...	Iowa.	June 11, '77	12,000
John F. Delaplaine, Sec. Leg.	Vienna...	N. Y.	June 1, '69	1,800
Belgium........	Brussels.			7,500
Brazil..........	Rio de J..			12,000
W. Hayden Edwards, Sec.Leg.	Rio de J..	D. C..		1,800
CentralAmeri-can States : Costa Rica Guatemala Honduras Nicaragua Salvador.. } George Williamson, Min. Res.	Guatemal.	La....	May 17, '73	10,000
Chili .... Thos. A. Osborn, E. E. & M.P.	Santiago..	Kans.	May 31, '77	10,000
China .... Geo. F. Seward, E. E. & M. P.	Peking...	Cal...	Jan. 7, '76	12,000
Chest. Holcomb, S. Leg. & Int.	Peking....		Aug. 15, '76	5,000
Denmark.... .. Mich. J. Cramer, Chargé d'Af.	Copenh'n	Ky...	Aug. 15, '76	5,000
France........ Edw. F. Noyes, E. E. & M. P.	Paris.....	Ohio..	July 1, '77	17,500
Robert R. Hitt, Sec. of Leg...	Paris.....	Ill....	Dec. 15, '74	2,625
Henri Vignaud, 2d Sec. of Leg.	Paris.....	La....	Dec. 14, '75	2,000
Germany.......				17,500
H. Sidney Everett, Sec. of Leg. and Chargé d'Af.ad interim.	Berlin....	Mass.	Aug. 1, '77	2,625
Chapman Coleman, 2d S. Leg.	Berlin....	Md ..	May 8, '74	2,000
Great Britain.. John Welsh, E. E. & M. P....	London...	Pa...	Oct. 9, '77	17,500
Wm. J. Hoppin, Sec. of Leg..	London ..	N. Y.	June 22, '76	2,625
E. S. Nadal, 2d Sec. of Leg..	London...	N. J.	June 8, '77	2,000
Greece......... John Meredith Read, Ch.d'Af.	Athens...		Aug. 15, '76	5,000
Hawaiian Isl'ds. James M. Comly, Min. Res..	Honolulu.	Ohio.	July 1, '77	7,500
Hayti.......... John M. Langston,M.R.&C.G.	Port au P.	D. C.	Sept. 28, '77	7,500
Italy........... Geo. P. Marsh, E. E. & M. P.	Rome....	Vt...	Mar. 20, '61	12,000
Geo. W. Wurts, Sec. of Leg..	Rome....	Pa...	April 16, '69	1,800
Japan.......... John A.Bingham, E.E. & M.P.	Yedo.....	Ohio.	May 31, '73	12,000
Durham W. Stevens, Sec. Leg.	Yedo.....	D. C .	Aug. 6, '73	2,500
David Thompson, Interpreter.	Yedo.....	Ohio.	Nov. 18, '74	2,500
Liberia .... J. Milton Turner, M.R.& C.G.	Monrovia	Mo...	Mar. 1, '71	4,000
Mexico........ John W. Foster, E. E. & M. P.	Mexico...	Ind ..	Mar. 17, '73	12,000
Daniel S. Richardson,Sec.Leg.	Mexico...	Cal...	July 28, '73	1,800
Netherlands ... James Birney, Min. Res......	TheHague	Mich.	Jan. 10, '76	7,500
Paraguay and Uruguay...... John C. Caldwell, Ch. d'Aff..	Montevid.	Me...	Aug. 15, '76	5,000
Peru .... Richard Gibbs, E. E. & M. P.	Lima.....	N. Y.	April 9, '75	10,000
Portugal....... Benj. Moran, Chargé d'Aff...	Lisbon...		Aug. 16, '76	5,000
Russia......... E. W. Stoughton, E E. & M.P.	St.Peters.	N. Y.	Oct. 30, '77	17,500
Wickham Hoffman, Sec. Leg.	St.Peters.	N. Y.	May 31, '77	2,625
Spain.. .... James R. Lowell, E.E. & M. P.	Madrid...	Mass.	June 11, '77	12,000
Dwight T. Reed, Sec. of Leg..	Madrid...	N. Y.	July 9, '77	1,800
Sweden,Norway John L. Stevens, Min. Res...	Stockhol.	Me...	Aug. 28, '77	7,500
Switzerland.... Nicholas Fish, Chargé d'Aff..	Berne....	N. Y.	June 20, '77	5,000
Turkey........ Horace Maynard, Min. Res...	Constanti.	Tenn.	Mar. 9, '75	7,500
Eugene Schuyler, Sec. of Leg. and Consul-General.	Constanti.	N. Y.	Jan. 17, '76	3,000
A. A. Gargiulo, Interpreter...	Constanti.		July 1, '77	3,000
Venezuela...... Thomas Russell, Min. Res....	Caracas...	Mass.	April 20, '74	7,500

* Envoy Extraordinary and Minister Plenipotentiary.

UNITED STATES CONSULAR SERVICE.

THE following table includes all consuls, consuls-general, and commercial agents of the United States, the amount of whose compensation reaches $1000, or upwards, annually. By the act of June 1st, 1874, the salaried consulates are divided into seven classes, besides other subdivisions, with specific fixed salaries for each, as follows :

Five consulates at	$6,000	Twenty-one consulates at	$3,000
Two " at	5,000	Sixteen " at	2,500
One consulate at	4,500	Thirty-seven " at	2,000
Six consulates at	4,000	Forty-seven " at	1,500
Eight " at	3,500	Eighteen " at	1,000

By law, all consuls receiving a fixed salary are required to pay into the Treasury, without reduction, all fees received by virtue of their offices. At other consulates and consular agencies the fees collected form the sole compensation of the incumbent, which, however, is limited in the case of consular agents to a maximum of $1000, and such agents are usually allowed to transact business. Consuls whose salaries do not exceed $1500, and from whose consulates without the agencies fees are paid into the Treasury to the amount of $3000 a year, are compensated at $2000 a year. The compensation of the feed consuls is limited to $2500. If the fees exceed that sum, such consuls can pay clerk-hire from the fees received at the consulate when specially authorized, but not otherwise. The column of fees shows the amount of fees received at each consulate and agency from which returns have been made for the year ending December 31st, 1876.

From the Register of the Department of State, December, 1877.

CONSULS OF THE UNITED STATES.

C.A. means Commercial Agent ; C.G., Consul-General ; C.C., Consular Clerk.

PLACE.	NAME.	STATE.	Date Appointed.	Salary.	Fees in 1876.
Argentine Republic.					
Buenos Ayres	Edward L. Baker....	Ill.....	Jan. 8, '74	$3,000	$2,334 44
Austria-Hungary.					
Prague..	Charles A. Phelps...	Mass...	Feb. 22, '77	2,000	2,652 22
Trieste.........	Alex. W. Thayer....	N. Y...	Nov. 1, '64	2,000	2,159 25
Vienna..............	P. Sidney Post..C.G.	Ill	June 17, '74	3,000	4,781 00
Barbary States.					
Tangier.............	Felix A. Mathews...	Cal.....	July 9, '70	3,000	No rep't.
Tunis...............	G. H. Heap	Pa......	Mar. 14, '67	3,000	14 00
Belgium.					
Antwerp............	James Riley Weaver	W. Va..	Mar. 17, '70	2,500	2,901 40
Brussels............	John Wilson.........	Pa......	Jan. 18, '72	2,500	No rep't.
Verviers............	George C. Tanner...	S. C....	June 13, '77	1,500	568 50
Brazil.					
Bahia.........	Richard A. Edes....	D. C...	June 12, '65	1,500	921 81
Para...............	Andrew Cone.......	Pa	April 12, '76	1,000	1,485 62
Pernambuco	Joseph W. Stryker..	N. Y...	April 6, '71	2,000	989 00
Rio Grande	Charles E. Merry....		Feb. 22, '77	1,000	453 08
Rio de Janeiro......	Joseph M. Hinds.C.G.	Ala	June 17, '74	6,000	....
Chili.					
Talcahuano.........	William Crosby.....	Ohio ...	Mar. 11, '75	1,000	No rep't.
Valparaiso.........	David J. Williamson	Cal.....	May 13, '74	3,000	1,661 12

UNITED STATES CONSULAR SERVICE—(Continued).

PLACE.	NAME.	STATE.	Date Appointed.	Salary.	Fees in 1876.
China.					
Amoy..............	Joseph J.Henderson.	Oregon.	April 13, '73	$3,500	$2,009 13
"	...............Marshal	....	.... {	1,000 and fees. }	....
Canton.............	Charles P. Lincoln...	Miss ...	May 28, '75	3,500	701 89
Chin-Kiang........				3,500	580 79
Foo-Chow..........	M. M. DeLano......	Col.....	April 20, '69	3,500	830 27
"	K.B. Lee.Interpreter	....	June 8, '75	1,500	....
Hankow............	Isaac F. Shepard....	Mo.....	Nov. 3, '76	3,500	No rep't.
"	Nelson E. Bryant...Marshal. }		Dec.17,'75 {	1,000 and fees. }	
Ningpo...	Edward C. Lord	N. Y...	Mar. 18, '67	3,500	234 18
Shanghai..........	.............C. G.	Miss ...	June 23, '77	5,000	8,321 64
"	O. B. Bradford..C.C.	Pa....	May 27, '67	1,200	
"	Richard Phoenix...Marshal. }		Dec.12,'76 {	1,000 and fees. }	....
"	D. B. McCartec.,Int.	....	Aug. 9, '77	2,000	
Tien-Tsin...	Owen N. Denny....	Oregon.	May 1, '77	3,500	262 28
"	Ernest Lösch...Marshal. }		Apr.14,'75 {	1,000 and fees. }	....
"	Wm. N. Pethick.Int.	....	June 8, '75	2,000	....
Colombia, United States of.					
Aspinwall..........	James Thorington...	Iowa...	May 27, '73	3,000	3,465 32
Panama	Owen M. Long......	Ill	April 7, '69	3,000	1,528 90
Sabanilla..........	Elias P. Pellet.......	N. Y...	June 17, '74	1,000	2,732 54
Denmark and Dominions.					
Copenhagen.......	Henry B. Ryder.....	....	April 7, '74	1,500	274 25
St. Thomas........	Volney V. Smith....	Ark....	April 12, '75	2,500	1,552 65
Ecuador.					
Guayaquil.........	Phanor M. Eder	Nevada.	Aug. 15, '76	1,000	No rep't.
France and Dominions.					
Algiers............				Fees.	....
"	C. F. Thirion...C.C.	D. C ...	Jan. 8, '70	1,200	....
Bordeaux	Benj. Gerrish, Jr....	N. H...	Oct. 24, '73	2,500	7,001 80
Guadaloupe.......	H. Thionville........	Guad...	May 18, '64	Fees.	1,128 40
Havre.............	John A. Bridgland..	Ind	Oct. 7, '73	8,000	6,448 77
Lyons........	A. J. DeZeyk...C.C.	....	Feb. 7, '66	1,200	....
"	H.O.Wagoner,Jr,C.C	Col.....	Nov. 14, '73	1,000	......
Marseilles..........	Frank W. Potter....	N. J ...	Mar. 14, '73	2,500	2,669 57
Martinique.........	Walter H. Garfield..	Mass...	Nov. 13, '77	1,500	1,557 54
Nice	William H. Vesey...	D. C...	Oct. 1, '70	1,500	477 00
Paris	A. T.A. Torbert.C.G.	Del	Nov. 7, '73	6,000	39,692 50
Rheims	A. Gouverneur Gill.	N. Y...	March 1, '67	Fees.	1,559 50
Friendly and Navigators' Islands.					
Apia..............	Gilderoy W. Griffin.	Ky.....	June 2, '76	1,000	57 34
Germany.					
Barmen...........	Edgar Stanton......	Ill	Jan. 13, '73	2,000	7,052 00
Berlin.............	H. Kreismann..C.G.	Ill	June 17, '74	4,000	5,079 50
"	Edw.P.McLean.C.C.	N. Y...	Nov. 18, '70	1,200	....
Bremen...........	Wilson King........	Pa....	Feb. 25, '76	2,500	8,680 00
Brunswick.........	Williams C. Fox....	Mo	Mar. 28, '76	Fees.	1,840 50
Chemnitz..........	Nathan K. Griggs...	Nebr...	Aug. 5, '76	2,000	6,830 00
Cologne........ ...	Emory P.Beauchamp	Ind	Mar. 24, '76	2,000	1,582 50
Crefeld............	Fred'k Wansleben..	....	Dec. 28, '71	....	3,067 50
Dresden...........	Joseph T. Mason ...	Va.....	March 8, '76	2,500	3,077 00
Frankfort........ ..	Alfred E. Lee ..C.G.	Ohio...	April 5, '77	3,000	2,551 00
Geestemunde.......	Fayette G. Day.....	N. Y...	Aug. 21, '77	....	2,375 08
Hamburg..........	John M. Wilson.....	Ohio...	Feb. 25, '76	2,500	6,584 65
Harburg...........	J. D. Westedt.......	....	Nov. 20, '69	....	1,648 50
Leipzig...........	John H. Steuart	Pa....	Sept. 9, '70	2,000	5,334 00

UNITED STATES CONSULAR SERVICE—(Continued).

PLACE.	NAME.	STATE.	Date Appointed.	Salary.	Fees in 1876.
Mannheim.........	Edward M. Smith ..	N. Y....	Jan. 17, '76	$1,500	$2,380 95
Mayence...........	August Heidelberger	....	July 24, '77	....	2,125 00
Munich	G.Henry Horstmaun	Pa ...	April 19, '69	1,500	1,394 50
Nuremberg	James M. Wilson...	Mo ..	Mar. 31, '71	2,000	4,350 50
Sonneberg	Henry J. Winser....	N. J ..	April 16, '69	2,000	3,844 50
Stuttgart........	Joseph S. Potter....	Mass...	Mar. 11, '75	1,500	1,964 25
Great Britain and Dominions.					
Aberdeen	John Ramsay...Agt.	....	May 19, '76	....	1,095 88
Auckland	....	....	June 17, '74	1,500	582 98
Barbadoes	Robert Y. Holly....	Vt....	Dec. 23, '74	1,500	2,843 37
Belfast	James M. Donnan..	Va.....	May 12, '73	2,500	8,470 78
Belleville, Canada..	William D. Fuller...	....	Dec. 4, '76	..	1,038 00
Bermuda...........	Chas. M. Allen.....	N. Y..	Aug. 7, '61	1,500	1,765 60
Birmingham.......	John B. Gould	Me...	May 12, '69	2,500	5,060 00
Bradford..........	Charles O. Shepard.	N. Y..	June 6, '77	3,000	10,869 00
Bristol...........	Theodore Canisius..	Ill	Jan. 13, '75	1,500	1,082 99
Calcutta	A. C. Litchfield.C.G.	Mich...	May 23, '71	5,000	5,148 46
Cape Town........	W. W. Edgecomb...	Me ..	April 19, '71	1,500	431 90
Cardiff...........	William Wirt Sikes.	N. Y...	June 8, '76	2,000	2,543 78
Ceylon...........	William Morey.....	Me...	Aug. 9, '77	1,000	330 04
Charlottet'n, P. E. I.	David M. Dunn.....	Ind ...	Mar. 15, '71	1,500	921 12
Chatham, Canada..	W. McCutchen.Agt.	....	Sept. 11, '76	....	1,000 50
Clifton...........	Robert S. Chilton...	D. C .	Feb. 2, '71	1,500	1,159 00
Coaticook.........	Edwin Vaughan....	N. H..	April 16, '69	2,000	1,904 00
Cork.............	Lewis Richmond....	R. I...	May 17, '75	2,000	1,054 62
Demerara.	Philip Figyelmesy..	D. C .	Jan. 30, '65	3,000	2,047 55
Dublin	Ben. H. Barrows....	Nebr...	Feb. 25, '76	2,000	1,914 98
Dundee	M. McDougall.......	N. Y..	Aug. 2, '71	2,000	6,523 11
Dunfermline.......				Fees.	1,737 50
"	G. H. Scidmore.C.C.	....	May 6, '76	1,000	....
Fort Erie,........	Andrew C. Phillips..	Mo ...	April 16, '69	1,500	1,040 00
Gaspé Basin.......	George H. Holt	N. Y..	April 17, '71	1,000	No fees.
Gibraltar,.........	Horatio J. Sprague..	Mass..	May 12, '48	1,500	1,011 04
Glasgow..........	Samuel F. Cooper...	Iowa...	Aug. 5, '76	3,000	No rep't.
Guelph, Canada ...	M. O. Macgregor....	....	Oct. 27, '73	....	1,508 50
Halifax...........	Mortimer M.Jackson	Wis...	Aug. 1, '61	2,000	2,219 95
Hamilton, Canada..	Robert H. Knox	Ala...	Sept. 4, '77	2,000	1,180 25
Hong-Kong	David H. Bailey.....	Ohio..	Aug. 5, '70	4,000	12,756 72
Huddersfield.......	C. W. Whitman.....	....	Feb. 7, '77	....	1,857 50
Hull.............	Joseph Atkinson....	....	Dec. 23, '73	....	1,583 28
Kingston, Canada..	James M. True.....	Ill	Feb. 20, '74	1,500	536 50
Kingston, Jamaica.	George E. Hoskinson	Wis....	Dec. 20, '75	2,000	3,529 43
Lauthala, F. I.....	............C.A.	....	....	1,000	74 25
Leeds	Alfred V. Dockery..	N. C ..	June 20, '77	2,000	1,077 50
Leicester..........	J.Barber Haxby.Agt.	....	Nov. 16, '69	....	1,367 50
Leith.............	John T. Robeson ...	Tenn ..	July 9, '70	2,000	1,980 80
Liverpool.........	Lucius Fairchild....	Wis....	Oct. 17, '72	6,000	42,174 67
London	Adam Badeau..C.G.	N. Y...	April 28, '70	6,000	36,990 67
London, Canada...	Wm. F. Blake......	....	April 18, '72	....	1,415 00
Mahé (Seychelles)..	Thomas T. Prentis..	Vt	Dec. 19, '71	1,500	154 86
Manchester	....	....	....	3,000	14,885 50
Melbourne.........	T. Adamson,Jr.C.G.	Pa	June 17, '74	3,500	2,320 41
Montreal..........	John Q. Smith.C.G.	Ohio...	Sept. 27, '77	4,000	2,850 65
Nassau...........	T. J. McLain, Jr....	....	....	2,000	1,453 78
Newcastle.........	Evan R. Jones......	Wis....	April 16, '69	1,500	1,622 04
Newcastle, N. S. W.	George Mitchell.....	....	July 23, '67	....	1,052 37
Nottingham.......	Jasper Smith...C.A.	D. C ..	May 23, '77	Fees.	5,820 00
Paris, Canada.....	Geo. C. Baker......	....	Dec. 18, '69	....	1,092 50
Port Louis........	John J. Turtle......	Del ...	April 12, '76	2,000	404 40
Port Sarnia, Canada	Samuel D. Pace.....	Mich...	April 19, '69	1,500	1,149 00
Port Stanley, F. I..	George Gerard......	Pa	June 17, '74	1,500	26 48
Prescott...........	Clifford S. Sims.....	Ark....	April 21, '69	1,500	577 50
Quebec............	Wm. C. Howells....	Ohio...	June 2, '74	1,500	536 43
Redditch..........	H. C. Browning.Agt.	....	June 22, '71	....	1,127 50
Sheffield..........	Claudius B. Webster	Conn ..	July 11, '70	2,500	4,604 00
Singapore..........	Adolph G. Studer...	Iowa...	May 23, '71	2,500	1,538 68
St. Helena.........	James W. Siler	Ark....	Feb. 16, '77	1,500	833 01
St. Helen's.......	John Hammill	....	Oct. 19, '65	....	2,917 22
St. John's, N. B......	Darius B. Warner...	Ohio....	May 4, '66	2,000	2,805 11

UNITED STATES CONSULAR SERVICE—(Continued).

PLACE.	NAME.	STATE.	Date Appointed.	Salary.	Fees in 1876.
St. John's, N. F....	Thos. N. Molloy....	N. Y....	Mar. 18, '67	Fees.	$1,343 32
St. John's, Quebec..	Robert J. Saxe......	Vt	Dec. 17, '74	$1,500	1,053 50
Sydney............	James H. Williams..	Me.....	Feb. 1, '76	Fees.	1,748 04
Toronto............	Albert D. Shaw....	N. Y...	April 19, '69	2,000	3,006 50
"	De Witt C. Baker...		April 12, '76		
Trinidad............	Fulton Paul........	N. Y...	May 27, '74	Fees.	1,659 28
Tunstall...........	Josiah M. Lucas....	Ill	June 16, '71	2,500	5,827 50
Victoria...........	Allen Francis.......	Oregon.	June 13, '77	Fees.	3,232 05
Windsor, Canada...	John H. Jenks.C.A.	Ill	Sept. 15, '77	....	No rep't.
Winnipeg..........	James W. Taylor...	Minn...	Sept. 14, '70	1,500	634 56
Hawaiian Islands.					
Honolulu...........	James Scott........	Ohio...	Aug. 23, '74	4,000	4,356 73
"	F. P. Hastings..C.C.	....	June 11, '77	1,000	....
Hayti.					
Aux Cayes.........	Thomas Dutton....	....	Feb. 27, '77	....	1,089 02
Cape Haytien......	Stanislas Gontier...	Pa	July 9, '70	1,000	541 42
Port au Prince......	J. M. Langston.C.G.	D. C...	Sept. 28, '77	7,500	1,784 88
Honduras.					
Omoa and Truxillo.	Frank E. Frye......	Me.....	April 24, '74	1,000	640 10
Italy.					
Florence...........	J. Schuyler Crosby.	N. Y...	Aug. 15, '76	1,500	1,727 70
Genoa.............	O. M. Spencer......	Iowa...	Mar. 21, '66	1.500	1,908 21
Leghorn...........				1,500	2,014 28
Messina...........	George H. Owen....	Vt	July 12, '75	1,500	2,308 52
Naples	B. Odell Duncan....	S. C...	June 1, '69	1,500	1,457 41
Palermo...........	Sampson P. Bayly..	Va.....	Aug. 31, '76	1,500	5,515 53
Rome.............	Chas. McMillan.C.G.	N. Y...	April 10, '76	3,000	712 50
"	Chas. M. Wood.C.C.	Vt	Mar. 24, '73	1,000	....
Japan.					
Kanagawa.........	T. B. Van Buren.C.G.	N. J...	June 17, '74	4,000	6,460 28
"	George E. Rice...... Marshal.		Mar. 24, '76	1,000 and fees.	....
"	H. W. Denison..Int.	....	Oct. 8, '75	2,000	....
gasaki...........	Willie P. Mangum...	N. C...	Mar. 18, '65	3,000	357 62
"	Rodney H. Powers. Marshal.		Sep. 22, '73	1,000 and fees.	....
Osaka and Hiogo...	Julius Stahel........	N. Y...	Aug. 13, '77	3,000	2,181 14
Liberia.					
Monrovia	J. Milton Turner.C.G.	Mo	March 1, '71	4,000	....
Madagascar.					
Tamatave..........	Wm. W. Robinson..	Wis....	Mar. 16, '75	2,000	52 08
Mexico.					
Acapulco..........	John A. Sutter, Jr...	Cal. ...	July 13, '70	2,000	908 28
Guaymas..........	Alexander Willard..	Cal.....	Sept. 16, '67	1,000	635 09
Matamoras........	Thomas F. Wilson..	Pa	April 4, '70	2,000	683 19
Mazatlan..........	Edward G. Kelton..	Mar. 11, '73	Fees.	1,123 50
Mexico...........	Jul. A. Skilton.C.G.	La	June 10, '72	2,000	132 80
Santa Cruz Point...	Geo. W. Miller..Agt.	....	Mar. 28, '77	....	1,434 00
Tampico	Edmund Johnson...	Va	June 10, '72	1,500	558 16
Vera Cruz.........	S. T. Trowbridge...	Ill	April 19, '69	3,000	1,591 08
Muscat.					
Zanzibar..........	William H. Hathorne	Mass...	Aug. 2, '76	1,000	196 69
Netherlands and Dominions.					
Amsterdam	Charles Mueller.....	Ohio...	June 26, '66	1,500	997 31
Batavia...........	Pliny M. Nickerson.	Mass...	April 19, '71	1,000	1,179 55
Curaçoa...........	Wm. H. Faxon.....	Conn ..	April 28, '70	Fees.	1,127 95
Rotterdam.........	John F. Winter.....	Ill	Aug. 3, '77	2,000	2,677 08
Schiedam......... .	W.H.C.Tansen.Agt.	....	April 22, '70	....	1,385 50
Nicaragua.					
San Juan del Norte and Punta Arenas	Wm. E. Sibell..C.A.	Nic	Jan. 15, '77	1,000	500 85

UNITED STATES CONSULAR SERVICE—(Continued).

Place.	Name.	State.	Date Appointed.	Salary.	Fees in 1876.
Peru.					
Callao..............	Robert T. Clayton..	Ga.....	June 12, '77	$3,500	$1,632 67
Portugal and Dominions.					
Fayal..............	Samuel W. Dabney.	Mass...	July 23, '72	1,500	670 04
Funchal............	Thomas B. Reid....	Me.....	July 5, '77	1,500	376 12
Lisbon	Henry W. Diman...	R. I....	July 12, '70	2,000	808 98
Santiago,CapeVerde	Thomas M. Terry...	Mich...	Aug. 15, '76	1,000	No rep't.
Setnbal............	Joaquim T. O'Neill.	....	Aug. 27, '74	....	1,085 00
St. Paul de Loanda.	Joseph E. Jackson..	Mich...	Aug. 3, '77	1,000	23 71
Russia.					
Odessa	Leander E. Dyer....	Tenn...	April 13, '75	2,000	194 25
St. Petersburg......	George Pomutz.C.G.	Iowa...	June 17, '74	2,000	460 00
San Domingo.					
San Domingo.......	Paul Jones.........	Ohio...	June 17, '74	1,500	1,026 30
Siam.					
Bangkok...........	David B. Sickles....	Ark....	Aug. 15, '76	3,000	732 63
Society Islands.					
Tahiti..............	Dorence Atwater...	Conn...	July 11, '70	1,000	486 01
Spain and Dominions.					
Baracoa............	Jos. R. Puente..Agt.	....	Mar. 26, '77	....	1,228 38
Barcelona.	Fred'k H. Scheuch.	Ind	Mar. 24, '74	1,500	340 67
Cadiz	Alfred N. Duffié....	R. I...	April 21, '69	1,500	1,146 98
Cardenas...........	J.H.Washington.Agt	....	Feb. 10, '75	....	4,799 37
Cienfuegos	De Witte Stearns...	Miss ...	Aug. 15, '76	2,500	2,340 60
Havana............	Henry C. Hall..C.G.	....	Nov. 7, '73	6,000	No rep't.
"	Jos.A.Springer.C.C.	Cuba...	Jan. 8, '70	1,200	....
"	Jos. A. Raphel..C.C.	Md.....	Feb. 14, '72	1,200	....
Malaga............	John F. Quarles	Ga.....	June 13, '77	1,500	1,758 95
Manila............	Frederick G. Heron.	N. Y...	Feb. 22, '77	Fees.	1,880 82
Matanzas..........	James W. Steele....	Kan ...	Mar. 19, '74	3,000	4,132 03
Mayaguez..........	G. E. Hubbard .Agt.	....	March 2, '75	....	1,282 38
Ponce.............	Wm. Russell...C.A.	....	Sept. 29, '77	Fees.	1,210 08
Sagua la Grande....	John S. Harris..Agt.	....	Nov. 4, '76	....	2,358 60
Santiago de Cuba...	John C. Landreau...	La.....	Dec. 12, '76	2,500	928 61
Switzerland.					
Basle..............	John A. Campbell..	Wyom..	........187..	2,000	1,712 50
Geneva............	J. E. Montgomery..	N. Y...	June 25, '77	1,500	760 75
Olten.............	H. Salathe........Agt.	....	Oct. 18, '66	....	1,696 50
St. Gallen	Emile Myer....Agt.	....	Mar. 26, '73	....	3,257 50
Zurich.............	Samuel H. M. Byers.	Iowa...	May 25, '69	2,000	4,701 00
Turkey and Dominions.					
Beirut	John T. Edgar......	Neb....	Mar. 11, '75	2,000	127 26
Cairo..............	E. E. Farman...Agt. and C.G.	} N. Y.	Mar. 27, '76	4,000	194 50
"	E. A. Van Dyck.C.C.	Mich...	May 12, '73	1,000	....
Constantinople.....	Eug. Schuyler..C.G.	....	Jan. 17, '76	3,000	385 75
"	James Maynard.... Marshal.	} Tenn.	Jan.19,'76 }	1,000 and fees.	} ....
Jerusalem..........	Joseph G. Willson..	Iowa...	Aug. 1, '77	1,500	No rep't.
Smyrna	E. J. Smithers.....	D. C...	Mar. 11, 67	2,000	1,397 94
Tripoli............	Cuthbert B. Jones..	La.....	Aug. 15, '76	3,000	....
Uruguay.					
Montevideo........	Frederick Crocker..	....	Aug. 15, '76	2,000	1,806 22
Venezuela.					
Laguayra..........	Almont Barnes.C.A.	Vt	Aug. 6, '77	1,500	1,990 05

354 AN AMERICAN ALMANAC FOR 1878.

FOREIGN LEGATIONS IN THE UNITED STATES.
From the Register of the Department of State, December, 1877.

COUNTRY, AND DATE OF PRESENTATION.	NAME.	RANK.
ARGENTINE REPUBLIC. March 16, 1869.	Señor Don Manuel R. Garcia...	*E. E. and M. P.
AUSTRIA-HUNGARY .... October 26, 1875.	Count Ladislas Hoyos..........	E. E. and M. P.
BELGIUM .... May 21, 1873.	Mr. Maurice Delfossc..........	E. E. and M. P.
BRAZIL............... October 9, 1871.	Councillor A. P. de Carvalho Borges.	E. E. and M. P.
CHILI	Señor Don Eduardo Vijil Zan-artu.	Secretary of Legation and Chargé d'Affaires ad interim.
COSTA RICA............ March 21, 1876.	Señor Don Manuel Peralta......	Minister Resident.
DENMARK......... December 8, 1875.	Mr. J. H. de Hegermann-Lin-dencrone.	Minister Resident.
FRANCE............... February 23, 1877.	Maxime Outrey...............	E. E. and M. P.
GERMANY. .... August 1, 1871.	Mr. Kurd Von Schlözer........	E. E. and M. P.
GREAT BRITAIN........ February 7, 1868.	The Right Honorable Sir Edward Thornton, K.C.B.	E. E. and M. P.
GUATEMALA .... October 25, 1872.	Señor Don Vicente Dardon.....	E. E. and M. P.
HAWAII................. January 14, 1870.	Mr. Elisha H. Allen...........	E. E. and M. P.
HAYTI. .... February 18, 1873.	Mr. Stephen Preston...........	E. E. and M. P.
HONDURAS............ October 2, 1874.	Señor Don Vicente Dardon.....	Minister Resident.
ITALY........ November 12, 1875.	Baron Albert Blanc...........	E. E. and M. P.
JAPAN................. December 18, 1874.	Jushie Yoshida Kiyonari........	E. E. and M. P.
MEXICO .... June 26, 1877.	Señor Don José T. de Cuellar ..	Chargé d'Affaires ad interim.
NETHERLANDS .... April 27, 1875.	Mr. de Pestel.................	Minister Resident.
PARAGUAY............ June 9, 1876.	Señor Don José Machain.......	E. E. and M. P.
PERU .... October 27, 1876.	Coronel Don Manuel Freyre....	E. E. and M. P.
RUSSIA................ October 29, 1875.	Mr. Nicholas Shishkin..........	E. E. and M. P.
SALVADOR .... February 13, 1874.	Señor Don Vicente Dardon.....	M. P.
SPAIN................ September 15, 1874.	Señor Don Antonio Mantilla de los Rios.	E. E. and M. P.
SWEDEN AND NORWAY. May 8, 1876.	Count Carl Lewenhaupt........	E. E. and M. P.
TURKEY............... October 14, 1873.	Gregoire Aristarchi Bey........	E. E. and M. P.
VENEZUELA........... June 5, 1874.	Señor Don Juan B. Dalla Costa.	E. E. and M. P.

* Envoy Extraordinary and Minister Plenipotentiary.

Summary of Electors, or Those having the Right of Suffrage in Great Britain.
From the Financial Reform Almanac, 1877.

Eng-land.	Pop.	Wales.	Pop.	Scot-land.	Pop.	Ire-land.	Pop.	Total.	Total Pop.
Voters. 2,211,470	21,495,531	Voters. 129,393	1,217,135	Voters 295,420	3,360,018	Voters. 230,773	5,411,016	2,866,956	31,483,700

NOTE.—The political complexion of the present House of Commons stands as follows: Conservative, 350 ; Liberal, 299. Conservative majority, 51.

STATEMENT OF MILES OF RAILROAD IN EACH STATE AND TERRITORY FROM 1867 TO JANUARY 1, 1877.

From Poor's Manual of the Railroads of the United States, 1877-78.

Miles of R.R. in..	1867.	1868.	1869.	1870.	1871.	1872.	1873.	1874.	1875.	1876.
1 Alabama	851	953	916	1,157	1,496	1,628	1,722	1,722	1,732	1,738
2 Arkansas	38	86	128	256	258	450	700	700	740	788
3 California	383	468	702	925	1,013	1,042	1,208	1,328	1,503	1,919
4 Colorado	...	...	...	157	338	483	603	682	807	957
5 Connecticut	637	637	602	742	820	868	897	897	918	918
6 Dakota	...	...	...	...	65	234	275	275	275	275
7 Delaware	165	165	210	224	227	254	264	280	285	285
8 Florida	437	437	446	446	466	466	466	484	484	484
9 Georgia	1,548	1,575	1,652	1,845	2,108	2,160	2,260	2,260	2,264	2,306
10 Illinois	3,224	3,440	4,081	4,823	5,904	6,361	6,589	6,759	7,109	7,285
11 Indiana	2,506	2,600	2,863	3,177	3,529	3,649	3,714	3,890	3,963	4,003
12 Indian Territory	...	...	...	...	92	279	279	279	279	279
13 Iowa	1,283	1,523	2,095	2,683	3,160	3,643	3,728	3,765	3,850	3,939
14 Kansas	491	648	931	1,501	1,760	2,063	2,100	2,150	2,150	2,238
15 Kentucky	635	813	832	1,017	1,123	1,266	1,320	1,326	1,326	1,475
16 Louisiana	335	335	375	479	539	539	539	539	539	539
17 Maine	521	560	580	786	871	871	905	957	980	1,000
18 Maryland and D.C.	527	535	588	671	820	1,012	1,016	1,060	1,077	1,107
19 Massachusetts	1,401	1,425	1,480	1,480	1,606	1,658	1,755	1,786	1,817	1,837
20 Michigan	1,163	1,199	1,325	1,638	2,116	2,976	3,253	3,315	3,346	3,395
21 Minnesota	482	572	795	1,092	1,612	1,906	1,950	1,990	1,990	2,020
22 Mississippi	898	898	990	990	990	990	990	1,018	1,018	1,044
23 Missouri	1,085	1,351	1,712	2,000	2,580	2,673	2,858	2,880	2,905	3,146
24 Nebraska	473	473	473	705	943	1,051	1,107	1,107	1,127	1,150
25 Nevada	30	472	402	593	593	611	629	650	650	680
26 New Hampshire	667	667	702	786	790	810	877	918	934	940
27 New Jersey	942	973	1,011	1,125	1,265	1,378	1,418	1,488	1,511	1,601
28 New York	3,245	3,829	3,658	3,928	4,470	4,925	5,165	5,250	5,423	5,525
29 North Carolina	1,042	1,097	1,130	1,178	1,190	1,250	1,265	1,315	1,528	1,570
30 Ohio	3,396	3,898	3,449	3,538	3,740	4,108	4,258	4,398	4,461	4,687
31 Oregon	19	19	60	159	241	241	251	251	251	251
32 Pennsylvania	4,311	4,809	4,598	4,636	5,113	5,369	5,550	5,687	5,868	5,983
33 Rhode Island	125	125	125	136	136	136	159	173	179	189
34 South Carolina	1,007	1,076	1,101	1,139	1,291	1,290	1,320	1,320	1,335	1,353
35 Tennessee	1,359	1,436	1,451	1,432	1,520	1,520	1,620	1,630	1,630	1,645
36 Texas	513	513	583	711	865	1,078	1,578	1,650	1,685	2,085
37 Utah	...	...	257	257	257	349	372	453	515	515
38 Vermont	587	605	614	614	675	710	721	778	810	810
39 Virginia	1,464	1,464	1,483	1,486	1,490	1,537	1,573	1,638	1,638	1,649
40 Washington Terr.	...	...	...	...	25	65	105	110	110	110
41 West Virginia	365	365	387	387	485	561	576	576	576	584
42 Wisconsin	1,036	1,235	1,512	1,525	1,725	1,878	2,360	2,546	2,566	2,707
43 Wyoming	82	447	447	459	459	459	459	459	459	459

RECAPITULATION.

STATES.	1867.	1868.	1869.	1870.	1871.	1872.	1873.	1874.	1875.	1876.
New England States.	3,938	4,019	4,301	4,494	4,898	5,053	5,344	5,509	5,638	5,694
Middle States	9,555	9,765	10,752	10,991	12,380	13,499	14,019	14,291	14,740	15,065
Western States	15,226	16,889	19,884	23,540	28,269	32,112	33,905	34,954	35,802	37,055
Southern States	10,126	10,683	11,107	12,196	13,246	14,112	15,353	15,602	15,919	16,676
Pacific States	431	689	1,164	1,677	1,765	1,959	2,193	2,339	2,514	2,960
Grand Total	39,276	42,255	47,208	52,898	60,565	66,735	70,784	72,695	74,613	77,470

Table showing the Mileage, Gross and Net Earnings, Freight and Passenger Earnings, and Dividends of the Railroads of the United States for Four Years, 1873-76, arranged by Geographical Divisions.

From Poor's Manual of the Railroads of the United States, 1877-78.

	1873.	1874.	1875.	1876.
NEW ENGLAND.				
Miles of railroad...............	5,303	5,617	5,732	5,783
	$	$	$	$
Earnings from passengers.......	22,358,645	22,111,787	21,776,893	20,516,215
" " freight, etc......	29,310,043	27,952,987	26,552,029	25,244,778
" " all sources.......	51,676,688	50,064,774	48,328,922	45,760,993
Net earnings....................	15,061,777	16,713,183	15,324,654	15,379,072
Dividends....................	9,004,488	8,511,971	8,788,040	7,607,973
MIDDLE STATES.				
Miles of railroad	12,441	12,874	13,173	13,647
	$	$	$	$
Earnings from passengers.......	42,355,230	41,699,871	40,772,967	47,483,865
" " freight, etc......	151,697,072	144,798,567	134,904,451	130,129,542
" " all sources.......	194,052,302	186,498,438	175,677,418	177,613,407
Net earnings	69,280,585	90,188,972	65,609,418	69,382,517
Dividends....................	36,531,343	37,600,154	39,357,196	33,690,111
WESTERN STATES.				
Miles of railroad	32,973	35,639	36,058	36,753
	$	$	$	$
Earnings from passengers.......	51,620,779	56,783,466	54,993,064	43,362,211
" " freight, etc......	160,097,002	158,086,011	151,224,570	142,880,621
" " all sources.......	211,717,781	214,869,477	206,217,654	186,942,832
Net earnings....................	72,464,212	75,546,695	75,604,104	63,912,968
Dividends	19,055,247	16,605,832	19,230,511	17,394,532
SOUTHERN STATES.				
Miles of railroad...............	13,908	13,505	13,522	13,948
	$	$	$	$
Earnings from passengers.......	15,310,989	14,131,291	13,864,915	11,877,901
" " freight, etc......	38,385,420	38,127,950	36,534,312	38,865,747
" " all sources.......	53,696,409	52,259,241	50,399,227	50,743,648
Net earnings	18,133,349	17,269,332	16,741,060	17.119,081
Dividends.......	901,396	1,068,455	1,496,906	1,860,351
PACIFIC STATES.				
Miles of railroad	390	417	1,023	1,126
	$	$	$	$
Earnings from passengers.......	1,175,193	1,223,248	1,843,207	1,727,911
" " freight, etc......	1,237,603	1,316,124	3.737,239	4,136,405
" " all sources.......	2,412,796	2,539,372	5,580,446	5,864,316
Net earnings....................	1,263,097	1,395,790	2,687,069	2,331,825
Dividends....................	....	....	....	187,701
PACIFIC RAILROADS.				
Miles of railroad...............	2,251	2,251	2,251	2,251
	$	$	$	$
Earnings from passengers.......	8,641,013	9,002,276	10,243,956	10,216,424
" " freight, etc......	15,568,931	15,792,318	18,770,892	20,817,379
" " all sources.......	24,209,944	24,794,594	29,014,848	31,033,803
Net earnings..................	13,648,195	14,374,742	16,614,855	17,033,517
Dividends....................	1,628,265	3,256,590	7,632,250	7,299,000

Miles of New Railroad Constructed in each State and Territory in 1872, 1873, 1874, 1875 and 1876.

NAME OF STATE OR TERRITORY.	No. Miles Built in 1872.	No. Miles Built in 1873.	No. Miles Built in 1874.	No. Miles Built in 1875.	No. Miles Built in 1876.
Alabama	132	94	0	10	6
Alaska	0	0	0	0	0
Arizona	0	0	0	0	0
Arkansas	192	250	0	40	48
California	29	166	120	175	416
Colorado	155	120	79	125	150
Connecticut	48	29	0	21	0
Dakota	169	41	0	0	0
Delaware	27	10	16	5	0
Florida	0	0	18	0	0
Georgia	52	100	0	4	42
Idaho	0	0	0	0	0
Illinois	457	228	170	350	176
Indiana	120	56	176	73	40
Indian Territory	187	0	0	0	0
Iowa	483	85	37	53	89
Kansas	303	37	50	0	88
Kentucky	143	54	6	0	149
Louisiana	0	0	0	0	0
Maine	0	34	52	23	20
Maryland and D. C.	192	34	14	17	30
Massachusetts	52	97	33	31	20
Michigan	860	277	62	31	49
Minnesota	214	44	40	0	30
Mississippi	0	0	28	0	26
Missouri	93	185	22	25	241
Montana	0	0	0	0	0
Nebraska	108	56	0	20	23
Nevada	18	18	21	0	30
New Hampshire	20	67	41	16	6
New Jersey	103	40	20	73	90
New Mexico	0	0	0	0	0
New York	455	240	85	173	102
North Carolina	60	15	50	213	42
Ohio	368	150	140	63	26
Oregon	0	10	0	0	0
Pennsylvania	256	181	137	181	115
Rhode Island	0	23	11	6	10
South Carolina	80	30	0	15	18
Tennessee	0	100	10	0	15
Texas	213	500	72	35	400
Utah	97	23	87	56	0
Vermont	35	11	57	32	0
Virginia	47	36	65	0	11
Washington	35	40	5	0	0
West Virginia	76	15	0	0	8
Wisconsin	153	482	186	20	141
Wyoming	0	0	0	0	0
Totals	6,032	3,978	1,910	1,891	2,657

RAILROADS OF THE WORLD.

Statement Exhibiting the Aggregate of the Railroads of each Country and State, and the Relations thereof to Area and Population, at the Close of 1876.

From Poor's Manual of the Railroads of the United States, 1877-78.

COUNTRIES AND STATES.	AREA. English Sq. Miles.	POPULA-TION. Census or Estimate.	RAIL-ROADS. Miles in Operation.	RAILROAD MILE TO— Square Miles of Area.	RAILROAD MILE TO— Numbers of Inhabitants.	Population to Sq. Mile.
NORTH AMERICA.						
United States.	3,026,504	44,672,918	77,470	39.1	576.6	14.66
Dominion of Canada..	686,353	5,169,789	5,219	131.5	990.6	7.53
Mexico...............	829,916	8,133,719	378	2,195.6	21,517.8	9.80
Total, North America	4,542,773	57,976,426	83,067	54.7	697.9	12.96
CENTRAL AMERICA AND WEST INDIES.						
Honduras.............	47,100	351,800	66	713.6	5,330.6	7.47
Costa Rica...........	21,510	165,000	29	741.4	5,689.6	7.67
Panama..............	27,346	226,000	49	558.1	4,612.2	8.26
Cuba................	48,489	1,370,211	459	105.6	2,985.2	28.26
Porto Rico...........	3,965	452,916	21	184.0	21,567.4	117.15
Jamaica	6,400	401,817	34	188.3	11,803.5	62.70
Barbadoes............	166	31,719	6	27.7	5,286.5	19.11
Total, Central America and West Indies	154,866	2,998,963	664	233.2	4,516.5	19.87
SOUTH AMERICA.						
Colombia.............	495,700	2,572,000	43	11,529.5	59,813.9	5.19
Venezuela............	426,800	1,379,500	39	10,944.2	35,371.8	8.23
Guiana (British)......	76,000	152,700	68	1,117.6	2,245.6	2.01
Brazil	3,956,000	10,278,000	1,357	2,915.3	7,574.1	2.50
Paraguay.............	72,000	1,000,000	47	1,531.8	21,276.5	13.89
Uruguay.............	73,500	600,000	231	318.2	2,597.4	8.16
Argentine Republic....	542,800	2,500,000	1,466	370.2	1,705.1	4.61
Peru	520,600	3,000,000	1,238	420.5	2,422.1	5.78
Bolivia..............	473,500	1,600,000	38	12,467.3	42,105.3	3.38
Chili	249,900	2,250,000	691	361.6	3,256.1	9.00
Total, South America	6,886,860	25,332,200	5,218	1,319.7	4,854.7	3.68
EUROPE.						
Gt. Britain and Ireland	122,520	32,103,972	17,263	7.1	1,859.6	262.08
France..............	207,149	36,391,702	12,722	16.3	2,860.5	175.68
Spain...............	182,713	16,681,719	4,112	44.4	4,056.9	91.80
Portugal.............	36,869	4,008,703	902	40.8	4,441.2	108.73
Italy...	121,718	27,311,410	5,028	24.2	5,431.9	224.38
Switzerland	15,261	2,708,801	1,211	12.6	2,286.8	181.40
⎰ Austria............	171,215	29,832,511	6,931	24.7	4,303.9	174.34
⎱ Hungary	69,391	10,409,839	4,023	17.2	2,592.4	150.30
Germany............	234,370	42,783,415	18,229	12.3	2,346.9	190.70
Belgium.............	11,313	5,201,718	2,278	5.0	2,283.5	459.80
⎰ Holland............	13,890	3,739,846	1,091	12.7	3,427.9	269.24
⎱ Luxemburg	990	200,178	169	5.9	1,184.5	202.20
Denmark	21,856	2,013,257	898	24.4	2,254.6	92.11
⎰ Sweden	170,100	4,001,218	2,597	65.5	1,540.7	28.52
⎱ Norway	123,228	1,642,827	369	333.9	4,455.9	13 33
Russia...............	2,120,897	72,140,396	13,702	154.9	5,265.6	34.02
Roumania.	65,363	3,621,749	891	73.4	4,064.8	55.41
Turkey..............	189,230	12,791,715	997	189.8	12,830.2	67.90
Greece..............	19,250	1,461,201	7	2,750.0	208,743.0	75.91
Total, Europe........	3,886,813	309,133,628	93,415	41.6	3,309.2	79.53

RAILROADS OF THE WORLD—(*Continued*).

COUNTRIES AND STATES.	AREA. English Sq. Miles.	POPULA-TION. Census or Estimate.	RAIL-ROADS. Miles in Opera-tion.	RAILROAD MILE TO— Square Miles of Area.	Numbers of Inhabi-tants.	Popu-lation to Sq. Mile.
ASIA.						
Turkey (Asia Minor)...	673,744	13,636,315	279	2,414.9	49,054.9	20.31
India (British).......	943,810	193,111,917	7,152	131.9	27,001.1	204.61
Ceylon	24,700	2,405,289	209	118.2	11,508.6	98.13
Philippine Islands....	120,000	5 000,000	279	430.1	17,921.2	41.66
Java	51,336	13,019,108	296	173.4	43,983.5	253.65
China	1,298,000	338,719,000	10	129,800.0	33,871,960.0	260.96
Japan..............	152 004	33,110,503	41	3,727.0	807,573.2	216.97
Total, Asia..........	3,264,194	599,052,732	8,266	394.9	72,471.9	183 52
AFRICA.						
Egypt.....	520,800	8,442,000	1,013	520.0	8,333.6	16.02
Tunis................	72,500	2,000,000	92	799.0	21,739.1	27.56
Algeria....	161,800	2,600,000	401	402.2	6,483.8	16.12
Cape Colony..........	119,328	1,000,000	136	877.4	7,352.9	8.38
Mauritius	708	300,000	66	10.7	4,545.4	423.73
Total, Africa.......	880,636	14,342,000	1,708	515.6	8,396.9	16 28
AUSTRALASIA.						
Victoria	86,800	862,917	697	124.5	1,238.1	9.94
New South Wales.....	323,500	586,322	501	645.7	1,170.3	1.81
Queensland	678,000	179,448	452	1,500.0	397.0	0.26
South Australia	383,300	222,711	301	1,273.4	739.9	0.58
Western Australia	800,000	36,191	69	11,594.2	524.5	0.04
Tasmania	26,200	131,319	45	582.2	2,918.2	5.01
New Zealand..........	106,300	350,696	412	258.0	872.9	3.38
Tahiti	2,000	10,000	21	97.2	476.2	5.00
Total, Australasia...	2,406,100	2,388,534	2,498	963.2	956.2	0.99

RECAPITULATION BY GRAND DIVISIONS.

North America........	4,542,773	57,976,426	83,067	54.7	697.9	12.96
Central America and West Indies.........	154,866	2,998,963	664	233.2	4,516.5	19.37
South America........	6,886,860	25,332,200	5,218	1,480.1	5,444.2	3.03
Total, America......	11,584,499	86,297,589	88,949	130.31	977.07	7.49
Europe................	3,896,813	309,133,623	93,415	41.6	3,309.2	79.53
Asia..................	3,264,194	599,052,732	8,266	394.9	72,471.9	183.52
Africa................	880,636	14,342,000	1,708	515.6	8,396.9	16.28
Australasia...........	2,406,100	2,388,534	2,498	963.2	956.2	0.99
Total of the World....	22,022,242	1,011,214,478	194,836	113.1	5,191.4	45.92
World without the Railroad	29,313,268	401,719,205	....	....	....	13 70
WORLD in the Aggre-gate................	51,335,510	1,412,933,693	194,836	263.5	7,253.7	27.52

RAILWAY DIVIDENDS AND INTEREST IN 1876.

STATEMENT showing amounts of STOCKS and BONDS issued by Railroad Companies and existing at the close of 1876, distinguishing the dividend and interest paying, and giving the amounts paid thereon in the year then ended, and exhibiting the relations such amounts bear to the *Total* and the *Paying* issues respectively.

From Poor's Railroad Manual, 1877-78.

STOCK ISSUES.

STATES, ETC.	AMOUNTS OF STOCKS.			DIVIDENDS.		
	TOTAL ISSUES.	PAYING.		AMOUNT PAID.	AVERAGE RATE.	
		Issues.	Proportion.		Total.	Paying.
	$	$	p. ct.	$	p. ct.	p. ct.
New England..............	195,942,115	98,057,272	52.59	7,607,973	3.88	7.70
Middle States..............	696,490,076	447,889,077	64.31	33,690,111	4.83	7.52
Southern and S. W. States...	287,223,474	34,214,113	11.76	1,860,351	0.64	5.44
Western States..............	919,399,210	264,326,910	28.75	17,394,532	1.89	6.59
Pacific States............. ...	58,125,400	1,300,000	2.24	187,701	0.32	14 14
	2,157,120,675	845,787,372	34.57	60,740,668	2.81	7.18
Pacific Railroads............	91,237,500	91,237,500	100.00	7,299,000	8.00	8.00
United States	2,248,358,375	937,024,872	41.69	68,039,668	3.03	7.20

BOND ISSUES.

STATES, ETC.	AMOUNTS OF BONDS.			INTEREST.		
	TOTAL ISSUES.	PAYING.		AMOUNT PAID.	AVERAGE RATE.	
		Issues.	Proportion.		Total.	Paying.
	$	$	p. ct.	$	p. ct.	p. ct.
New England..............	110,146,245	81,970,905	74.71	4,740,465	4.28	5.76
Middle States	676,529,727	629,923,941	93.11	38,326,579	5.66	6.08
Southern and S. W. States...	313,788,119	171,582,990	54.58	9,544,823	3.08	5.64
Western States..............	909,078,277	500,280,185	54.93	32,774,828	3.59	6.55
Pacific States	48,438,000	32,217,500	66.51	1,580,563	3.26	4.91
	2,058,580,368	1,415,975,527	68.78	86,946,758	4.22	6.14
Pacific Railroads............	106,561,000	106,561,000	100.00	6,612,815	6.21	6.21
United States...............	2,165,141,368	1,522,536,527	70.32	93,559,573	4.32	6.15

Statement showing the Number of Miles of Railroad constructed each Year in the United States, from 1830 to the close of 1876, inclusive.

From Poor's Railway Manual for 1877-78.

Year.	Miles in Operation.	Annual Increase of Mileage.	Year.	Miles in Operation.	Annual Increase of Mileage.	Year.	Miles in Operation.	Annual Increase of Mileage.
1830 ...	23	....	1846....	4,930	297	1862..	32,120	834
1831....	95	72	1847....	5,598	668	1863..	33,170	1,050
1832...	229	134	1848....	5,996	393	1864..	33,908	738
1833....	380	151	1849....	7,365	1,369	1865..	35,085	1,177
1834....	633	253	1850....	9,021	1,656	1866..	36,827	1,742
1835....	1,098	465	1851....	10,982	1,961	1867..	39,276	2,449
1836....	1,273	175	1852....	12,908	1,926	1868..	42,255	2,979
1837....	1,497	224	1853....	15,360	2,452	1869..	47,208	4,953
1838....	1,913	416	1854....	16,720	1,360	1870..	52,898	5,690
1839....	2,302	389	1855....	18,374	1,654	1871..	60,568	7,670
1840....	2,818	516	1856....	22,016	3,647	1872..	66,735	6,167
1841....	3,535	717	1857....	24,503	2,647	1873..	70,784	4,049
1842 ...	4,026	491	1858....	26,968	2,465	1874..	72,695	1,911
1843....	4,185	159	1859....	28,789	1,821	1875..	74,614	1,919
1844....	4,377	192	1860....	30,635	1,846	1876..	77,470	2,856
1845....	4,633	256	1861....	31,286	651			

LAW SCHOOLS IN THE UNITED STATES.

From the Report of the Commissioner of Education for 1876.

STATES.	Number in each State.	Corps of Instruction.	Number of Students.	Graduates at the Commencement of 1876.	Volumes in Libraries.	Value of Grounds and Buildings.	Amount of Productive Funds.	Income from Productive Funds.	Receipts for last year from Tuition Fees.
Alabama.....	2	6	15	8	....	....	....	....	....
Connecticut..	1	12	65	34	8,000	....	$10,000	$700	....
Georgia......	2	7	11	6	600	....	....	....	....
Illinois......	4	45	202	67	....	....	....	....	$6,515
Indiana......	1	2	40	20	700	....	....	....	....
Iowa.........	2	14	111	80	1,860	....	....	....	3,30
Kentucky....	2	8	27	12	....	....	....	....	900
Louisiana....	1	4	23	7	....	$15,000	....	....	2,500
Maryland	1	3	39	29	30	0	0	0	4,690
Massachu'tts.	2	20	327	53	18,000	....	51,614	11,668	20,950
Michigan	1	5	309	....	3,500	....	....	....	....
Missouri.....	2	14	98	23	3,750	....	....	....	5,120
New York...	4	17	711	130	12,300	....	....	....	4,800
N'th Carolina	2	2	18	4	....	....	....	....	....
Ohio.........	2	6	83	37	1,125	....	....	....	3,045
Pennsylvania	2	10	90	16	300	....	....	....	4,840
S'th Carolina.	1	1	12	9	....	....	0	0	0
Tennessee ...	3	9	68	54	650	....	10,000	....	6,600
Virginia	2	10	109	28	3,640	....	....	....	6,000
Wisconsin ...	1	7	18	25	430	....	....	3,500	1,400
Dist. of Col..	4	16	289	95	301	25,000	10,000	600	7,581
Total	42	218	2,664	742	55,186	$40,000	$81,614	$16,468	$78,301

SCHOOL STATISTICS OF THE UNITED STATES IN 1876.
From the Annual Report of the Commissioner of Education for 1876.

STATES AND TERRITORIES.	School Age.	School Population.	Number from Six to Sixteen Years.	Number Enrolled in Public Schools.	Average Daily Attendance.	Average School Days in Year.
Alabama.	5-21	405,226	*283,659	126,893	....	80
Arkansas.	6-21	189,130	*141,848	15,890	....	....
California......	5-17	184,787	*166,309	140,468	83,391	141.8
Colorado......	6-21	21,962	*16,472	14,364	8,043	100
Connecticut....	4-16	135,189	b112,657	119,106	70,495	178.1
Delaware......	5-21	a39,807	*33,836	21,587	....	....
Florida........	4-21	74,828	*48,639	26,052	16,720	....
Georgia........	6-18	394,037	*354,633	179,405	115,121	....
Illinois........	6-21	973,589	*730,192	667,446	....	....
Indiana	6-21	679,230	*509,423	516,270	314,168	129
Iowa..........	5-21	553,920	b354,424	398,825	229,315	136.5
Kansas........	5-21	212,977	127,502	147,224	89,896	108.5
Kentucky......	6-20	498,744	*398,995	228,000	156,000	110
Louisiana......	6-21	274,688	*206,016	74,307	52,315	97
Maine	4-21	218,490	*142,019	156,148	102,451	118
Maryland	5-20	276,120	*207,090	146,198	73,069	182
Massachusetts .	5-15	300,834	*300,834	305,776	218,903	176
Michigan......	5-20	459,847	*344,885	314,956	200,000	156
Minnesota.....	5-21	228,362	*159,853	151,866	....	100
Mississippi....	5-21	355,919	*249,143	166,204	....	100
Missouri........	6-20	725,728	*580,582	394,848	b182,000	60
Nebraska	5-21	86,191	*60,333	59,966	....	95.8
Nevada	6-18	8,475	*7,628	5,521	3,832	142.8
New Hampshire	4-21	74,747	55,565	66,599	48,857	93.7
New Jersey....	5-18	314,826	*267,602	196,252	103,520	192
New York......	5-21	1,585,601	*1,109,921	1,067,199	541,610	176
North Carolina.	6-21	348,603	*261,452	146,737	97,830	50
Ohio	6-21	1,025,635	763,976	722,963	447,139	155
Oregon	4-20	48,473	*33,931	27,426	15,565	82.4
Pennsylvania...	6-21	1,200,000	*900,000	902,345	578,718	150
Rhode Island...	5-15	53,316	b48,321	39,328	27,021	180
South Carolina.	6-16	237,971	237,971	123,085	....	90
Tennessee	6-18	434,131	*390,718	194,180	125,908	71.9
Texas.....	6-18	313,061	*281,754	b184,705	b125,224	78
Vermont.......	5-20	92,577	*69,432	71,325	....	....
Virginia.......	5-21	482,789	307,230	199,856	115,243	113
West Virginia..	6-21	184,760	*138,570	123,504	72,278	95.04
Wisconsin......	4-20	474,811	*332,368	282,186	....	152.5
Total	....	14,169,381	10,735,773	8,755,010	4,214,630	....
Arizona........	6-21	2,955	*2,216	1,213	900	....
Dakota........	5-21	6,396	*7,277	5,410	....	....
District of Col..	6-17	31,671	29,133	19,029	14,907	191
Idaho........ ...	5-18	2,777	*2,360	2,724	....	....
Montana.......	4-21	4,238	*2,755	2,734	2,000	100
New Mexico ...	7-18	a29,312	*24,016	5,151	....	132
Utah..........	6-16	30,900	30,900	19,886	13,608	143
Washington....	4-20	11,000	*7,700	7,500	....	104
Wyoming	5-20	*6,000	*4,500	1,222	....	....
Indian :						
Cherokees....	7-21	4,041	*3,233	2,800	1,500	200
Creeks	10-18	716	*787	616	448	....
Choctaws.....	6-20	2,300	*1,840	1,133	745	168
Seminoles....	....	471	....	157	108	180
Total......	....	136,777	117,617	70,175	34,216	....
Grand Total	....	14,306,158	10,853,390	8,825,185	4,248,849	....

* Estimated by the Bureau.   (a) United States Census of 1870.
(b) Estimate of State Superintendent.

UNIVERSITIES AND COLLEGES IN THE UNITED STATES.

From the Report of the Commissioner of Education for 1876.

States and Territories	No. of Colleges.	Preparatory Department.		Collegiate Department.		Income from Productive Funds.	Receipts Last Year from Tuition.	Volumes in College Libraries.	Value of Grounds, Buildings, and Apparatus.
		No. of Instructors.	No. of Students.	No. of Instructors.	No. of Students.	$	$		$
Alabama	4	2	71	41	316	25,600	55,560	12,100	410,000
Arkans..	4	4	169	20	104	2,600	3,000	660	139,600
Califor'a	12	18	809	163	831	15,100	110,950	34,054	1,429,000
Colorado	1								
Conn'cut	8			57	856	37,203	68,008	125,000	570,000
Delaw're	1	0	0	7	40	5,000	1,000	6,000	75,000
Georgia.	7	7	268	50	488	33,935	7,750	25,550	540,000
Illinois..	28	62	3,906	244	1,530	116,358	87,552	86,052	2,905,906
Indiana..	17	42	1,444	131	1,307	54,580	26.822	72,785	1,233,300
Iowa. ...	18	35	2,348	144	954	56,722	39,232	34,783	981,000
Kansas..	8	5	809	48	167	5,213	17,200	19,700	560,000
Kent'ky.	15	18	930	94	902	20,176	67,168	25,497	926,000
Louis'na	6	9	387	34	54		25,931	21,650	310,035
Maine ..	3			30	360	36,045	22,675	85,278	330,000
Maryl'd.	8	12	196	98	644	180,000	9,445	43,550	253,000
Mass'tts.	7	10	200	113	1,668	82,396	131,915	249,455	1,400,000
Michig'n	9	17	1,239	114	811	81,818	6,335	40,898	1,153,250
Min'sota	6	13	412	48	154	23,021	5,648	14,440	472,143
Missi'pi.	4	6	200	21	189	7,125	6,220	7,640	375,903
Missouri	18	32	1,279	171	921	113,967	112,055	71,200	1,292,000
Nebr..sk.	2		250	13	92	2,000	700	2,250	180,000
Nevada .	1	1	31						
N.Hamp.	1			16	219	25,000	15,000	48,000	160,000
N.Jersey	4		18	58	712	82,748	39,581	47,000	1,370,000
N. York.	26	71	2,644	419	3,015	472,128	378,894	219,402	7,315,443
N.Car'na	8	7	784	54	383	8,000	34,985	26,200	422,000
Ohio	32	47	2,568	230	2,230	161,390	161,487	112,459	2,908,973
Oregon..	6	9	307	21	210	17,490	7,189	5,812	137,000
Penn'via	29	46	2,064	345	2,242	143,925	245,698	130,795	5,314,500
Rhode 1.	1			16	219	46,091	27,629	46,000	1,500,000
S. Car'na	6	4	211	38	351	30,500	3,640	50,500	750,000
Tenn'see	23	33	1,723	157	1,029	56,468	63,171	39,404	1,327,000
Texas...	9	17	939	65	457	1,600	41,400	7,250	255,000
Vermont	3			23	160	13,755	3,857	31,827	389,100
Virginia.	8	3	162	80	998	23,650	41,255	89,580	1,265,000
West Va.	3	5	55	25	164	9,800	4,200	7,074	290,000
Wisc'sin	10	23	1,041	89	689	55,775	107,603	40,600	965,050
D.of Col.	4	15	254	36	152	10,000	1,200	47,100	1,020,000
Utah....	1		320				2,856	2,553	1,500
Total..	356	563	28,128	3,352	25,647	2,060,182	1,984,811	1,879,103	40,956,724

UNIVERSITIES AND COLLEGES IN THE UNITED STATES, 1872-1876.

The following is a statement of the aggregate number of this class of institutions, with instructors and students, as reported to the Bureau of Education each year, from 1870 to 1876, inclusive:

	1870.	1871.	1872.	1873.	1874.	1875.	1876.
Number of institutions	266	290	298	323	343	355	356
Number of instructors.	2,823	2,962	3,040	3.106	3,783	3,999	3,920
Number of students...	49,163	49,827	45,617	52,053	56,692	58,694	56,481

STATISTICS OF EXPENDITURE FOR PUBLIC SCHOOLS IN THE UNITED STATES IN 1876.

From the Report of the Commissioner of Education for 1876.

STATES.	Salaries of Teachers.	Total Expended.	STATES.	Salaries of Teachers.	Total Expended.
Alabama.......	$316,076	$337,276	South Carolina.	$377,920	$423,572
Arkansas	73,166	119,403	Tennessee	558,518	698,220
California......	1,976,155	2,890,219	Texas.....	630,334	726,236
Colorado......	131,378	233,298	Vermont		
Connecticut....	1,085,290	1,529,181	Virginia	783,025	1,069,679
Delaware	114,027	216,225	West Virginia..	531,545	793,272
Florida	74,628	101,722	Wisconsin	1,462,326	2,126,641
Georgia					
Illinois.........	4,945,194	8,168,539	Total.........	$47,422,489	$83,078,596
Indiana	3,093,559	4,921,085			
Iowa...	2,784,099	4,288,582	TERRITORIES :		
Kansas	743,578	1,198,437	Arizona........	$10,039	$23,744
Kentucky......	1,400.000	1,491,000	Dakota.........		50,002
Louisiana	539,018	776,009	District of Col.	163,646	405,828
Maine..........	897,056	1,248,762	Idaho	14,376	16,590
Maryland	1,045,864	1,623,349	Montana	35,287	50,134
Massachusetts .		6,105,536	New Mexico...	15,432	18,890
Michigan.... ..	2,026,725	3,458,505	Utah	85,716	129,297
Minnesota	821,072	1,530,883	Washington ...	54,720	55,520
Mississippi		417,760	Wyoming.....	16,400	16,400
Missouri		2,374,960	Indian :		
Nebraska	426,921	919,344	Cherokees ...	43,075	110,110
Nevada........	101,016	162,760	Creeks......	11,200	13,000
New Hampshire	450,440	660,020	Choctaws.....	12,000	29,022
New Jersey....	1,511,701	2,154,415	Seminoles....	2,250	3,200
New York.....	7,965,804	11,559,288			
North Carolina.	158,129	191,674	Total	$464,141	$926,737
Ohio	4,936,834	8,462,757			
Oregon	181,902	240,568			
Pennsylvania ..	4,856,889	9,149,653			
Rhode Island ..	422,310	709,466	Grand Total..	$47,886,630	$84,005,333

STATISTICS OF THEOLOGICAL SEMINARIES IN THE UNITED STATES.

From the Report of the Commissioner of Education for 1876.

DENOMINATION.	No. of Seminaries.	No. of Professors.	No. of Students.	DENOMINATION.	No. of Seminaries.	No. of Professors.	No. of Students.
Roman Catholic........	18	112	879	Unsectarian...........	2	10	94
Protestant Episcopal....	17	62	267	Reformed (Dutch).......	2	9	49
Presbyterian............	16	78	624	Universalist...........	2	8	56
Baptist	15	68	702	African Methodist Epis-			
Lutheran...............	14	40	354	copal................	1	3	6
Congregational	8	50	341	Mennonite	1	6	26
Methodist Episcopal....	7	52	370	Methodist...	1	...	....
Christian..............	3	6	82	Moravian.............	1	3	34
Reformed..............	3	8	67	New Jerusalem	1	2	......
United Presbyterian.....	3	11	79	Union Evangelical......	1	5	30
CumberlandPresbyterian	2	7	49	Unitarian	1	7	17
Free Will Baptist.......	2	9	44	United Brethren...	1	3	25
Methodist Episcopal (South)................	2	6	74	Total...............	124	580	4,968

SCHOOLS OF MEDICINE IN THE UNITED STATES.

From the Report of the Commissioner of Education for 1876.

	Number in all the States.	Corps of Instruction.	Number of Students.	Graduates at the Commencement of 1876.	Volumes in Libraries.	Increase in the last School year.	Value of Grounds, Buildings, and Apparatus.	Amount of Productive Funds.	Income from Productive Funds.	Receipts for the last year from Tuition and other fees.
							$	$	$	$
Regular.....	63	896	7,496	2,210	46,942	175	2,711,200	188,315	10,447	228,673
Eclectic.....	4	36	314	129	600	....	199,000	....	....	23,250
Homœo-pathic.	11	133	877	290	8,600	635	427,000	53,000	2,500	59,517
Dental......	11	152	520	177	1,985	90	57,050	....	....	37,289
Pharma-ceutical.	13	54	934	260	6,731	50	104,550	43,000	4,170	19,037
Grand total	102	1,201	10,143	3,066	64,858	950	3,489,800	284,315	17,117	367,766

The following is a comparative statement of the number of schools of medicine, dentistry, and pharmacy reported each year from 1870 to 1876, inclusive, with the number of instructors and students :

	1870.	1871.	1872.	1873.	1874.	1875.	1876.
Number of institutions.	63	82	87	94	99	106	102
Number of instructors.	588	750	726	1,146	1,121	1,172	1,201
Number of students	6,943	7,045	5,995	8,681	9,093	9,971	10,143

Gifts for Education in the United States in 1876.

From the Report of the Commissioner of Education for 1876.

INSTITUTIONS.	Total.	INSTITUTIONS.	Total.
Universities and Colleges	$2,743,248	Schools for Girls	$35,575
Schools of Science...........	48,634	Schools for Boys and Girls..	247,557
Schools of Theology.........	254,584	Libraries...	970,300
Schools of Law.............	2,500	Museums of Natural History.	1,725
Schools of Medicine.........	36,750	Institutions for the Deaf and	
Institutions for the Superior		Dumb................... ..	33,751
Instruction of Women.....	79,950		
Preparatory Schools.........	202,331		
Schools for Boys	85,000	Total....................	$4,691,945

The above summary includes direct donations and bequests to Universities, Colleges, Libraries, and Schools, as reported to the Bureau of Education by the institutions themselves. It is gratifying to record that, notwithstanding the severe financial depression, the amount of these private benefactions to promote the public intelligence is increasing, having been $4,891,645 in 1876, as against $4,136,562 in 1875.

Statistics of Schools for the Unfortunate Classes in the United States.

THE number of institutions for the instruction of the Deaf and Dumb in the United States for 1876 was 42, with 312 instructors, 5209 pupils, and $1,232,858 expenditure for the year.

The number of schools for the Blind in 1876 was 29, with 580 instructors and other employés, 2083 pupils; $736,559 expenditures.

The number of schools for Feeble-Minded Youth (idiots and imbeciles) was 11, having 318 instructors and other employés, 1560 inmates, at an expenditure of $302,686.

The number of Reform Schools in the United States was 51, all located in 19 Northern and Western States, and having 800 teachers, officers, and assistants, with 12,087 inmates, at an annual cost for instruction of $1,404,483, and annual earnings by the inmates of $174,119.

The number of Orphan Asylums in the United States, in 1876, was 188, in 29 States and 2 Territories, having 1530 officers and assistants, 18,759 inmates, maintained at an expenditure of $1,541,444. Of Soldiers' Orphan Homes, there were 20, with 366 officers, etc.; 4146 inmates, and an expenditure of $433,678 in 1876.

Of Industrial Schools there were 36, located in 17 States, employing 495 teachers and assistants, with 13,662 pupils, and an expenditure last year of $342,599.

THE BALANCE OF TRADE FOR 22 YEARS, 1856-1877.

From the Financial Review, 1877, with Additions.

FOR the purpose of showing the total amount of exports and imports of merchandise and the total of specie in each year since 1856, the table below has been compiled. In the columns headed "Excess" are given the differences between exports and imports each year, showing at a glance the "trade balance" of the country.

Gold Value of Imports and Exports of Merchandise and Specie into and from the United States in each Fiscal Year since 1856.

YEAR.	MERCHANDISE.			SPECIE.		
	Imports.	Exports.	Excess.	Imports.	Exports.	Excess.
	$	$	$	$	$	$
1856....	310,432,310	281,219,423	Im. 29,212,887	4,207,632	58,929,651	Ex. 41,537,853
1857....	348,428,342	293,823,760	Im. 54,604,582	12,461,709	74,995,399	Ex. 56,675,128
1858 ...	263,338,654	272,011,274	Ex. 8,672,620	19,274,496	63,067,487	Ex. 33,358,651
1859....	331,333,341	292,901,051	Im. 38,432,290	7,434,789	72,012,276	Ex. 56,453,622
1860....	353,616,119	333,576,057	Im. 20,040,062	8,550,135	66,546,239	Ex. 57,996,104
1861....	289,310,542	219,553,833	Im. 69,756,709	46,339,611	29,791,080	Im. 16,548,531
1862....	189,356,677	190,670,501	Ex. 1,313,824	16,415,052	36,887,640	Ex. 19,972,588
1863....	243,335,815	203,964,097	Im. 39,370,818	9,584,105	64,156,611	Ex. 56,571,956
1864....	316,447,283	158,887,988	Im. 157,559,295	13,115,612	105,396,541	Ex. 92,280,929
1865....	238,745,580	162,013,500	Im. 76,732,082	9,810,072	67,643,226	Ex. 57,833,154
1866....	434,812,066	348,859,522	Im. 85,952,544	10,700,092	86,044,071	Ex. 75,343,979
1867....	395,763,100	297,303,653	Im. 98,459,447	22,070,475	60,868,372	Ex. 38,797,897
1868....	357,436,440	281,952,899	Im. 75,483,541	14,188,368	93,784,102	Ex. 79,595,734
1869....	417,506,379	286,117,697	Im. 131,388,682	19,807,876	57,138,380	Ex. 37,330,504
1870....	435,058,408	392,771,768	Im. 43,180,640	26,419,179	58,155,666	Ex. 31,736,486
1871....	520,223,684	442,820,178	Im. 77,403,500	21,270,024	98,441,968	Ex. 77,171,964
1872....	626,595,077	444,177,586	Im. 182,417,401	13,743,689	79,877,534	Ex. 66,133,845
1873....	642,136,210	522,479,317	Im. 119,656,248	21,480,937	84,608,574	Ex. 63,127,637
1874....	567,406,342	586,283,040	Ex. 18,876,098	28,454,906	56,630,405	Ex. 28,175,499
1875....	533,005,436	513,441,711	Im. 19,563,725	20,900,727	92,132,142	Ex. 71,231,425
1876....	460,741,191	540,384,671	Ex. 70,623,480	15,936,681	56,506,302	Ex. 40,569,621
1877....	451,323,126	602,475,220	Ex. 152,152,094	40,774,414	56,162,237	Ex. 15,387,753

VITAL STATISTICS.—RATE OF MORTALITY.

The Carlisle tables, showing how many persons out of 10,000 will annually die, on the average, until all are deceased; also, the expectation of life at all ages.

Age.	Number Alive.	Deaths each year.	Expectation. Years.	Age.	Number Alive.	Deaths each year.	Expectation. Years.
At Birth.	10,000	1,539	38.72	53	4,211	68	18.97
1	8,461	682	44.68	54	4,143	70	18.28
2	7,779	505	47.54	55	4,073	73	17.60
3	7,274	276	49.81	56	4,000	76	16.90
4	6,998	201	50.75	57	3,924	82	16.20
5	6,797	121	51.24	58	3,842	93	15.54
6	6,676	82	51.16	59	3,749	106	14.91
7	6,594	58	50.80	60	3,633	122	14.33
8	6,536	43	50.24	61	3,521	126	13.81
9	6,493	33	49.57	62	3,395	127	13.31
10	6,460	29	48.82	63	3,268	125	12.80
11	6,431	31	48.03	64	3,143	125	12.20
12	6,400	32	47.27	65	3,018	124	11.80
13	6,368	33	46.50	66	2,894	123	11.30
14	6,335	35	45.74	67	2,771	123	10.74
15	6,300	39	45.00	68	2,648	123	10.22
16	6,261	42	44.27	69	2,525	124	9.70
17	6,219	43	43.57	70	2,401	121	9.14
18	6,176	43	42.87	71	2,277	134	8.64
19	6,133	43	42.16	72	2,143	146	8.15
20	6,090	43	41.45	73	1,997	156	7.71
21	6,047	42	40.74	74	1,841	166	7.33
22	6,005	42	40.03	75	1,675	160	7.00
23	5,963	42	39.30	76	1,515	156	6.70
24	5,921	42	38.59	77	1,359	146	6.40
25	5,879	43	37.85	78	1,213	132	6.11
26	5,836	43	37.13	79	1,081	128	5.80
27	5,793	45	36.40	80	953	116	5.50
28	5,748	50	35.69	81	837	112	5.20
29	5,698	56	35.00	82	725	102	4.93
30	5,642	57	34.33	83	623	94	4.65
31	5,585	57	33.70	84	529	84	4.39
32	5,528	56	33.02	85	445	73	4.12
33	5,472	55	32.35	86	367	71	3.90
34	5,417	55	31.68	87	296	64	3.70
35	5,362	55	31.00	88	232	51	3.39
36	5,307	56	30.31	89	181	39	3.40
37	5,251	57	29.63	90	142	37	3.29
38	5,194	58	28.95	91	105	30	3.27
39	5,136	61	28.27	92	75	21	3.37
40	5,075	66	27.60	93	54	14	3.50
41	5,009	69	26.97	94	40	10	3.52
42	4,940	71	26.33	95	30	7	3.53
43	4,869	71	25.71	96	23	5	3.45
44	4,798	71	25.08	97	18	4	3.27
45	4,727	70	24.45	98	14	3	3.07
46	4,657	69	23.81	99	11	2	2.77
47	4,588	67	23.16	100	9	2	2.27
48	4,521	63	22.50	101	7	2	1.80
49	4,458	61	21.81	102	5	2	1.30
50	4,397	59	21.10	103	3	2	0.83
51	4,338	62	20.39	104	1	1	0.50
52	4,276	65	19.68				

NOTE.—The rate of mortality of males of all ages is 1 in 40, and of females 1 in 42, nearly. The expectation of life is thus reckoned at about 5 per cent longer for women than for men.

PRESIDENTS AND THEIR CABINETS.
PRESIDENTS AND VICE-PRESIDENTS.

		PRESIDENTS.				VICE-PRESIDENTS.	
Term.	No.	Name.	Qualified.		No.	Name.	Qualified.
*1	1	George Washington.	April 30, 1789		1	John Adams	June 3, 1789
2		" "	Mar. 4, 1793			" "	Dec. 2, 1793
3	2	John Adams	Mar. 4, 1797		2	Thomas Jefferson. ...	March 4, 1797
4	3	Thomas Jefferson ..	Mar. 4, 1801		3	Aaron Burr	March 4, 1801
5		" " ..	Mar. 4, 1805		4	George Clinton.......	March 4, 1805
6	4	James Madison....	Mar. 4, 1809			" "	March 4, 1809
7		" "	Mar. 4, 1813		5	Elbridge Gerry........	March 4, 1813
						†John Gaillard........	Nov. 25, 1814
8	5	James Monroe	Mar. 4, 1817		6	Daniel D. Tompkins ..	March 4, 1817
9		" "	Mar. 5, 1821			" "	March 5, 1821
10	6	John Quincy Adams	Mar. 4, 1825		7	John C. Calhoun......	March 4, 1825
11	7	Andrew Jackson....	Mar. 4, 1829			" "	March 4, 1829
12		" "	Mar. 4, 1833		8	Martin Van Buren.....	March 4, 1833
13	8	Martin Van Buren..	Mar. 4, 1837		9	Richard M. Johnson...	March 4, 1837
14	9	Wm.Henry Harrison	Mar. 4, 1841		10	John Tyler....	March 4, 1841
14a	10	John Tyler.........	April 6, 1841			†Samuel L. Southard..	April 6, 1841
						†Willie P. Mangum....	May 31, 1842
15	11	James K. Polk	Mar. 4, 1845		11	George M. Dallas......	March 4, 1845
16	12	Zachary Taylor.....	Mar. 5, 1849		12	Millard Fillmore.......	March 5, 1849
16a	13	Millard Fillmore. ..	July 10, 1850			†William R. King......	July 11, 1850
17	14	Franklin Pierce....	Mar. 4, 1853		13	William R. King......	March 4, 1853
						†David R. Atchison...	April 18, 1853
						†Jesse D. Bright.	Dec. 5, 1854
18	15	James Buchanan...	Mar. 4, 1857		14	John C. Breckinridge..	March 4, 1857
19	16	Abraham Lincoln ..	Mar. 4, 1861		15	Hannibal Hamlin......	March 4, 1861
20		" "	Mar. 4, 1865		16	Andrew Johnson......	March 4, 1865
20a	17	Andrew Johnson...	April 15, 1865			†Lafayette S. Foster...	April 15, 1865
						†Benjamin F. Wade...	March 2, 1867
21	18	Ulysses S. Grant ...	Mar. 4, 1869		17	Schuyler Colfax.......	March 4, 1869
22		" "	Mar. 4, 1873		18	Henry Wilson.........	March 4, 1873
						†Thomas W. Ferry....	Nov. 22, 1875
23	19	Rutherford B.Hayes	Mar. 5, 1877		19	William A. Wheeler...	March 5, 1877

* The heavy-faced figures in this column mark the terms held by the Presidents, and are
referred to in succeeding tables. The smaller figures indicate the numerical order or sequence
of individual officers from the first.
† Acting Vice-President and President *pro tem.* of the Senate.

SECRETARIES OF STATE.

Term.	No.	NAME.	APPOINTED.		Term.	No.	NAME.	APPOINTED.
1	1	Thomas Jefferson..	Sept. 26, 1789		14	14	Daniel Webster ...	Mar. 5, 1841
2		" "	March 4, 1793		14a		" "	... April 6, 1841
	2	Edmund Randolph.	Jan. 2, 1794			15	Hugh S. Legare....	May 24, 1843
	3	Timothy Pickering.	Dec. 10, 1795			16	Abel P. Upshur ...	July 24, 1843
3		" "	March 4, 1797			17	John C. Calhoun...	Mar. 6, 1844
	4	John Marshall.....	May 13, 1800		15	18	James Buchanan...	Mar. 6, 1845
4	5	James Madison....	March 5, 1801		16	19	John M. Clayton...	Mar. 8, 1849
5		" "	March 4, 1805		16a		Daniel Webster ...	July 22, 1850
6	6	Robert Smith......	March 6, 1809			20	Edward Everett...	Nov. 6, 1852
	7	James Monroe.. ..	April 2, 1811		17	21	William L. Marcy.	Mar. 7, 1853
7		" "	March 4, 1813		18	22	Lewis Cass........	Mar. 6, 1857
8	8	John QuincyAdams	March 5, 1817			23	Jeremiah S. Black.	Dec. 17, 1860
9		" "	March 5, 1821		19	24	William H. Seward	Mar. 6, 1861
10	9	Henry Clay........	March 7, 1825		20		" "	Mar. 4, 1865
11	10	Martin Van Buren..	March 6, 1829		20a		" "	April 15, 1865
	11	Edward Livingston.	May 24, 1831			25	E. B. Washburne..	Mar. 5, 1869
12	12	Louis McLane......	May 29, 1833		21	26	Hamilton Fish	Mar. 11, 1869
	13	John Forsyth	June 27, 1834		22		" "	Mar. 4, 1873
13		" "	March 4, 1837		23	27	William M. Evarts.	Mar. 12, 1877

The heavy-faced figures mark the Presidential term in which each Cabinet Officer held his
appointment, as shown by the table of Presidents preceding.

SECRETARIES OF THE TREASURY.

Term	No.	Name	Appointed	Term	No.	Name	Appointed
1	1 Alex. Hamilton.....		Sept. 11, 1789	14a		Thomas Ewing....	April 6, 1841
2		" "	Mar. 4, 1793		15	Walter Forward...	Sept. 13, 1841
	2 Oliver Wolcott......		Feb. 2, 1795		16	John C. Spencer...	March 3, 1843
3		" "	Mar. 4, 1797		17	George M. Bibb...	June 15, 1844
	3 Samuel Dexter.....		Jan. 1, 1801	15	18	Robert J. Walker .	March 6, 1845
4	4 Albert Gallatin.....		May 14, 1801	16	19	Wm. M. Meredith.	March 8, 1849
5		" "	Mar. 4, 1809	16a	20	Thomas Corwin...	July 23, 1850
6		" "	Mar. 4, 1813	17	21	James Guthrie....	March 7, 1853
7	5 Geo. W. Campbell..		Feb. 9, 1814	18	22	Howell Cobb......	March 6, 1857
	6 Alexander J. Dallas.		Oct. 6, 1814		23	Philip F. Thomas .	Dec. 12, 1860
	7 Wm. H. Crawford..		Oct. 22, 1816		24	John A. Dix... ...	Jan. 11, 1861
8		" " ..	Mar. 5, 1817	19	25	Salmon P. Chase..	March 7, 1861
9		" " ..	Mar. 5, 1821		26	Wm.PittFessenden	July 1, 1864
10	8 Richard Rush		Mar. 7, 1825	20	27	Hugh McCulloch..	March 7, 1865
11	9 Samuel D. Ingham..		Mar. 6, 1829	20a		" " ..	April 15, 1865
	10 Louis McLane		Aug. 2, 1831	21	28	George S. Boutwell	March 11, 1869
12	11 William J. Duane..		May 29, 1833	22	29	Wm. A.Richardson	March 17, 1873
	12 Roger B. Taney....		Sept. 23, 1833		30	Benj. H. Bristow..	June 4, 1874
	13 Levi Woodbury.....		June 27, 1834		31	Lot M. Morrill.....	July 7, 1876
13		" "	Mar. 4, 1837	23	32	John Sherman.....	March 8, 1877
14	14 Thomas Ewing.....		Mar. 5, 1841				

SECRETARIES OF WAR.

Term	No.	Name	Appointed	Term	No.	Name	Appointed
1	1 Henry Knox........		Sept. 12, 1789	14a		John Bell..........	April 6, 1841
2		" "	Mar. 4, 1793		19	John C. Spencer...	Oct. 12, 1841
	2 Timothy Pickering.		Jan. 2, 1795		20	James M. Porter ..	March 8, 1843
	3 James McHenry....		Jan. 27, 1796		21	William Wilkins..	Feb. 15, 1844
3		" "	Mar. 4, 1797	15	22	William L. Marcy.	March 6, 1845
	4 Samuel Dexter....		May 13, 1800	16	23	Geo. W. Crawford.	March 8, 1849
	5 Roger Griswold		Feb. 3, 1801	16a	24	Charles M. Conrad	Aug. 15, 1850
4	6 Henry Dearborn....		Mar. 5, 1801	17	25	Jefferson Davis....	March 5, 1853
5		" "	Mar. 4, 1805	18	26	James B. Floyd...	March 6, 1857
6	7 William Eustis.....		Mar. 7, 1809		27	Joseph Holt......	Jan. 18, 1861
	8 John Armstrong....		Jan. 13, 1813	19	28	Simon Cameron...	March 5, 1861
7		" "	Mar. 4, 1813		29	Edwin M. Stanton.	Jan. 15, 1862
	9 James Monroe..		Sept. 27, 1814	20		" "	March 4, 1865
	10 Wm. H. Crawford..		Aug. 1, 1815	20a		" "	April 15, 1865
8	11 George Graham		April 7, 1817			U.S.Grant,ad inter.	Aug. 12, 1867
	12 John C. Calhoun...		Oct. 8, 1817			L. Thomas,"	Feb. 21, 1868
9		" " ...	Mar. 5, 1821		30	John M. Schofield.	May 28, 1868
10	13 James Barbour.....		Mar. 7, 1825	21	31	John A. Rawlins..	March 11, 1869
	14 Peter B. Porter.....		May 26, 1828		32	Wm. W. Belknap .	Oct. 25, 1869
11	15 John H. Eaton.....		Mar. 9, 1829	22		" "	March 4, 1873
	16 Lewis Cass........		Aug. 1, 1831		33	Alphonso Taft	March 8, 1876
12		" "	Mar. 4, 1833		34	James D. Cameron.	May 22, 1876
13	17 Joel R. Poinsett...		Mar. 7, 1837	23	35	Geo. W. McCrary.	March 12, 1877
14	18 John Bell..........		March 5, 1841				

SECRETARIES OF THE NAVY.

Term	No.	Name	Appointed	Term	No.	Name	Appointed
3	1 Benjamin Stoddert.		May 21, 1798	14a		George E. Badger..	April 6, 1841
4		" "	Mar. 4, 1801	14	14	Abel P. Upshur ...	Sept. 13, 1841
	2 Robert Smith		July 15, 1801		15	David Henshaw ...	July 24, 1843
5	3 J. Crowninshield...		Mar. 3, 1805		16	Thomas W. Gilmer	Feb. 15, 1844
6	4 Paul Hamilton.....		Mar. 7, 1809		17	John Y. Mason ...	March 14, 1844
	5 William Jones.....		Jan. 12, 1813	15	18	George Bancroft...	March 10, 1845
7		" "	March 4, 1813			John Y. Mason.....	Sept. 9, 1846
	6 B.W. Crowninshield		Dec. 19, 1814	16	19	William B. Preston	March 8, 1849
8		" "	March 4, 1817	16a	20	William A.Graham	July 22, 1850
	7 Smith Thompson...		Nov. 9, 1818		21	John P. Kennedy .	July 22, 1852
9		" "	Mar. 5, 1821	17	22	James C. Dobbin..	March 7, 1853
	8 Samuel L. Southard		Sept. 16, 1823	18	23	Isaac Toucey	March 6, 1857
10		" "	March 4, 1825	19	24	Gideon Welles	March 5, 1861
11	9 John Branch.......		March 9, 1829	20		" "	March 4, 1865
	10 Levi Woodbury		May 23, 1831	20a		" "	April 15, 1865
12		" "	March 4, 1833	21	25	Adolph E. Borie...	March 5, 1869
	11 Mahlon Dickerson..		June 30, 1834		26	Geo. M. Robeson..	June 25, 1869
13		" "	March 4, 1837	22		" "	March 4, 1873
	12 James K. Paulding.		June 25, 1838	23	27	Rich.W.Thompson	March 12, 1877
14	13 George E. Badger...		March 5, 1841				

SECRETARIES OF THE INTERIOR.

Term.	No.	NAME.	APPOINTED.	Term.	No.	NAME.	APPOINTED.
16	1	Thomas Ewing.....	Mar. 8, 1849		7	James Harlan.....	May 15, 1865
16a	2	Alex. H. H. Stuart.	Sept. 12, 1850		8	O. H. Browning...	July 27, 1866
17	3	Robert McClelland.	Mar. 7, 1853	21	9	Jacob D. Cox.....	March 5, 1869
18	4	Jacob Thompson...	Mar. 6, 1857		10	Columbus Delano.	Nov. 1, 1870
19	5	Caleb B. Smith.....	Mar. 5, 1861	22		" "	March 4, 1873
	6	John P. Usher......	Jan. 8, 1863		11	ZachariahChandler	Oct. 19, 1875
20		" "	Mar. 4, 1865	23	12	Carl Schurz.......	March 12, 1877
20a		" "	April 15, 1865				

POSTMASTERS-GENERAL.

No.	No.	NAME	APPOINTED		No.	NAME	APPOINTED
1	1	Samuel Osgood.....	Sept. 26, 1789	14a		Francis Granger...	April 6, 1841
	2	Timothy Pickering.	Aug. 12, 1791		11	Chas. A. Wickliffe.	Sept. 13, 1841
2		" "	March 4, 1793	15	12	Cave Johnson.....	Mar. 6, 1845
	3	Joseph Habersham.	Feb. 25, 1795	16	13	Jacob Collamer....	Mar. 8, 1849
3		" "	March 4, 1797	16a	14	Nathan K. Hall. ..	July 23, 1850
4		" "	March 4, 1801		15	Sam'l D. Hubbard.	Aug. 31, 1852
	4	Gideon Granger....	Nov. 28, 1801	17	16	James Campbell..	Mar. 5, 1853
5		" "	March 4, 1805	18	17	Aaron V. Brown..	Mar. 6, 1857
6		" "	March 4, 1809		18	Joseph Holt.......	Mar. 14, 1859
7	5	Return J. Meigs, Jr.	March 17, 1814		19	Horatio King......	Feb. 12, 1861
8		" "	March 4, 1817	19	20	Montgomery Blair.	Mar. 5, 1861
9		" "	March 5, 1821		21	William Dennison.	Sept 24, 1864
	6	John McLean......	June 26, 1823	20		" "	Mar. 4, 1865
10		" "	March 4, 1825	20a			April 15, 1865
11	7	William T. Barry...	March 9, 1829		22	Alex. W. Randall	July 25, 1866
12		" "	March 4, 1833	21	23	John A. J.Creswell	Mar. 5, 1869
	8	Amos Kendall......	May 1, 1835	22		" "	Mar. 4, 1873
13		" "	March 4, 1837		24	Marshall Jewell...	Aug. 24, 1874
	9	John M. Niles......	May 25, 1840		25	James N. Tyner...	July 12, 1876
14	10	Francis Granger....	March 6, 1841	23	26	David McK. Key..	Mar. 12, 1877

ATTORNEYS-GENERAL.

No.	No.	NAME	APPOINTED		No.	NAME	APPOINTED
1	1	Edmund Randolph.	Sept. 26, 1789	14a		John J. Crittenden	April 6, 1841
2		" "	March 4, 1793		18	Hugh S. Legare...	Sept. 13, 1841
	2	William Bradford..	Jan. 27, 1794		19	John Nelson.......	July 1, 1843
	3	Charles Lee........	Dec. 10, 1795	15	20	John Y. Mason....	Mar. 6, 1845
3		" "	March 4, 1797		21	Nathan Clifford...	Oct. 17, 1846
	4	Theophilus Parsons	Feb. 20, 1801		22	Isaac Toucey.....	June 21, 1848
4	5	Levi Lincoln.......	March 5, 1801	16	23	Reverdy Johnson..	Mar. 8, 1849
5	6	Robert Smith......	March 3, 1805	16a		John J. Crittenden	July 22, 1850
	7	John Breckinridge.	Aug. 7, 1805	17	24	Caleb Cushing.....	Mar. 7, 1853
	8	Cæsar A. Rodney..	Jan. 28, 1807	18	25	Jeremiah S. Black.	Mar. 6, 1857
6		" "	March 4, 1809		26	Edwin M. Stanton.	Dec. 20, 1860
	9	William Pinkney...	Dec. 11, 1811	19	27	Edward Bates.....	Mar. 5, 1861
7		" "	March 4, 1813			T. J. Coffey, ad int.	June 22, 1863
	10	Richard Rush......	Feb. 10, 1814		28	James Speed......	Dec. 2, 1864
8		" "	March 4, 1817	20		" "	Mar. 4, 1865
	11	William Wirt......	Nov. 13, 1817	20a			April 15, 1865
9		" "	March 5, 1821		29	Henry Stanbery...	July 23, 1866
10		" "	March 4, 1825		30	William M. Evarts.	July 15, 1868
11	12	John M. Berrien...	March 9, 1829	21	31	E. Rockwood Hoar	Mar. 5, 1869
	13	Roger B. Taney....	July 20, 1831		32	Amos T. Akerman.	June 23, 1870
12		" "	March 4, 1833		33	George H. Williams	Dec. 14, 1871
	14	Benjamin F. Butler.	Nov. 15, 1833	22		" "	Mar. 4, 1873
13		" "	March 4, 1837		34	EdwardsPierrepont	April 26, 1875
	15	Felix Grundy......	July 5, 1838		35	Alphonso Taft	May 22, 1876
	16	Henry D. Gilpin....	Jan. 11, 1840	23	36	Charles Devens....	Mar. 12, 1877
14	17	John J. Crittenden.	March 5, 1841				

IMMIGRATION INTO THE UNITED STATES, 1820-1877.

PRIOR to the year 1820, no statistics of immigration were officially kept. By the act of Congress of March 2d, 1819, Collectors of Customs were required to keep a record and make a quarterly return to the Treasury of all passengers arriving in their respective districts from foreign ports; and these reports, published from time to time by the officers of the Treasury Department, constitute the sources of information as to the growth and progress of immigration. The total number of foreign-born passengers arriving at the ports of the United States, in the several years from 1820 to 1870 inclusive, is given below.

Year.	Total Immigration.	Year.	Total Immigration.
1820...................	8,385	1850.....	369,980
1821...	9,127	1851.....................	379,466
1822	6,911	1852.....................	371,603
1823....	6,354	1853.....................	368,645
1824.......	7,912	1854.....................	427,833
1825...	10,199	1855.....................	200,887
1826.....................	10,837	1856.....................	200,436
1827.....................	18,875	1857.....................	251,306
1828.....................	27,382	1858.....................	123,126
1829.....................	22,520	1859.....................	121,282
1830.....................	23,322	1860.....................	153,640
1831.....................	22,633	1861.....................	91,920
1832.....................	60,482	1862.....................	91,987
1833.....................	58,640	1863.....................	176,282
1834...................	65,365	1864.....................	193,416
1835.....................	45,374	1865.....................	249,061
1836.....................	76,242	1866.....................	318,494
1837......	79,340	1867.....................	298,358
1838.....................	38,914	1868.....................	297,215
1839.....................	68,069	1869.....................	395,922
1840.....................	84,066	1870.....................	378,796
1841.....................	80,290	1871.....................	367,789
1842.....................	104,565	1872.....................	449,483
1843.....................	52,496	1873.....................	437,004
1844.....................	78,615	1874.....................	277,593
1845.....................	114,371	1875.....................	209,096
1846.....................	154,416	1876.....................	182,027
1847.....................	234,968	1877 (6 months,Jan. to June)	79,485
1848.....................	266,527		
1849.....................	297,024	Total..............	9,596,292

NOTE.—The above figures, from 1850 to 1877, are for calendar years—January 1st to December 31st. Other statements of immigration vary, being for fiscal years ending June 30th. Another source of variation is that some tables give the total number of aliens arriving in the United States; others what is called the *net* immigration only. As the latter is not ascertainable for all the years, the figures above given represent the total immigration of aliens in each year.

Chinese Immigration into the United States for each Calendar Year from 1855 to 1876, inclusive.

Year.	No.	Year.	No.	Year.	No.
1855...............	3,526	1864...............	2,795	1873...............	18,154
1856...	4,733	1865...............	2,942	1874...............	16,651
1857...............	5,944	1866...............	2,385	1875...............	19,033
1858...............	5,128	1867...............	3,863	1876...............	16,879
1859...............	3,457	1868...............	10,684	1877 (Jan. to June,	
1860...............	5,467	1869...............	14,902	inclusive)........	7,656
1861...............	7,518	1870...............	11,943		
1862...............	3,633	1871...............	6,089	Total 191,118	
1863...............	7,214	1872...............	10,642		

NOTE.—The statement is made that nearly one half of all the Chinese who have arrived in the United States have returned to their native country.

Succession of Justices of the Supreme Court.

CHIEF JUSTICES.	ASSOCIATE JUSTICES.	STATE WHENCE APPOINTED.	TERM OF SERVICE.	YEARS OF SERVICE.	BORN.	DIED.
1 John Jay†		New York..	1789–1795	6	1745	1829
	1 John Rutledge†	S. Carolina.	1780–1791	2	1730	1800
	2 William Cushing...	Mass.......	1789–1810	21	1733	1810
	3 James Wilson......	Penn.......	1789–1798	9	1742	1798
	4 John Blair.........	Virginia....	1789–1796	7	1732	1800
	5 Rob't H. Harrison†	Maryland ..	1789–1790	1	1745	1790
	6 James Iredell	5 N. Carolina.	1790–1799	9	1751	1799
	7 Thomas Johnson†..	1 Maryland ..	1791–1793	2	1732	1819
	8 William Patterson..	7 New Jersey.	1793–1806	13	1745	1806
2 John Rutledge‡		S. Carolina.	1795–1795	....	1739	1811
	9 Samuel Chase......	4 Maryland ..	1796–1811	15	1741	1811
3 Oliver Ellsworth†		Connecticut	1796–1801	5	1745	1807
	10 Bushr'd Washington	8 Virginia....	1798–1829	31	1762	1829
	11 Alfred Moore†	6 N. Carolina.	1799–1804	5	1755	1810
4 John Marshall		Virginia....	1801–1835	34	1755	1835
	12 William Johnson ..	11 S. Carolina.	1804–1834	30	1771	1834
	13 Brockh't Livingston	8 New York..	1806–1823	17	1757	1823
	14 Thomas Todd......	§ Kentucky ..	1807–1826	19	1765	1826
	15 Joseph Story......	2 Mass.......	1811–1845	34	1779	1845
	16 Gabriel Duval†	9 Maryland ..	1811–1836	25	1752	1844
	17 Smith Thompson...	13 New York..	1823–1845	22	1767	1845
	18 Robert Trimble....	14 Kentucky..	1826–1828	2	1777	1828
	19 John McLean.....	18 Ohio.......	1829–1861	32	1785	1861
	20 Henry Baldwin....	10 Penn.......	1830–1846	16	1779	1846
	21 James M. Wayne§.	12 Georgia...	1835–1867	32	1790	1867
5 Roger B. Taney		Maryland...	1836–1864	28	1777	1864
	22 Philip P. Barbour..	16 Virginia. ..	1836–1841	5	1783	1841
	23 John Catron......	§ Tennessee.	1837–1865	29	1778	1865
	24 John McKinley	§ Alabama...	1837–1852	15	1780	1852
	25 Peter V. Daniel	22 Virginia....	1841–1860	19	1785	1860
	26 Samuel Nelson†...	17 New York..	1845–1872	27	1792	1873
	27 Levi Woodbury....	15 New Hamp.	1845–1851	6	1789	1851
	28 Robert C. Grier†..	20 Penn.......	1846–1869	23	1794	1870
	29 Benj. R. Curtis†...	27 Maryland ..	1851–1857	6	1809	1874
	30 James A. Campbell†	24 Alabama...	1853–1861	8	1811	....
	31 Nathan Clifford....	29 Maine......	1857–....	..	1803	....
	32 Noah H. Swayne...	19 Ohio.......	1862–....	....	1805	....
	33 Samuel F. Miller...	25 Iowa.......	1862–....	....	1816	....
	34 David Davis†	30 Illinois.....	1862–1877	15	1815	....
	35 Stephen J. Field...	§ California .	1863–....	....	1816	....
6 Salmon P. Chase		Ohio.......	1864–1873	9	1808	1873
	36 Williar M. Strong.	28 Penn.......	1870–....	....	1808	....
	37 Joseph P. Bradley.	§ New Jersey	1870–....	....	1813	....
	38 Ward Hunt......	26 New York..	1872–....	....	1811	....
7 Morrison R. Waite.		Ohio.......	1874–....	....	1816	....
	39 John M. Harlan....	34 Kentucky..	1877–....	....	1833	....

* The figures before the names of the Associate Justices indicate the order of their appointment. The numbers following refer to the same numbers in the first column, and show the vacancy filled by each appointment.

† Resigned.

‡ Presided one term of the court; appointment not confirmed by the Senate.

§ The Supreme Court, at its first session in 1790, consisted of a Chief Justice and five Associates. The number of Associate Justices was increased to six in 1807 by the appointment of Thomas Todd; increased in 1837 by the appointments of John Catron and John McKinley; increased to nine in 1863 by the appointment of Stephen J. Field; decreased to eight on the death of John Catron in 1865; decreased to seven on the death of James M. Wayne in 1867; and again increased to eight in 1870.

JUDICIARY OF THE UNITED STATES.

Supreme Court of the United States.

	Appointed from	Date of Commission.	Salary.
Mr. Chief Justice Waite	Ohio	Jan. 21, 1874	$10,500
Mr. Justice Clifford	Maine	Jan. 12, 1857	10,000
Mr. Justice Swayne	Ohio	Jan. 24, 1862	10,000
Mr. Justice Miller	Iowa	July 16, 1862	10,000
Mr. Justice Field	California	Mar. 10, 1863	10,000
Mr. Justice Strong	Pennsylvania	Feb. 18, 1870	10,000
Mr. Justice Bradley	New Jersey	Mar. 21, 1870	10,000
Mr. Justice Hunt	New York	Dec. 11, 1872	10,000
Mr. Justice Harlan	Kentucky	Nov. 29, 1877	10,000

OFFICERS OF THE SUPREME COURT.

Clerk.—D. W. Middleton	District of Columbia	1863	Fees.
Marshal.—John G. Nicolay	Illinois	1872	$3,000
Reporter.—William T. Otto	Indiana	1875	2,500

Circuit Courts of the United States.

First Judicial Circuit.—Mr. Justice Clifford, of Portland, Maine. Districts of—

Maine,	Massachusetts,
New Hampshire,	Rhode Island.

Circuit Judge.—George F. Shepley, Portland, Me............ 1869.......$6,000

Second Judicial Circuit.—Mr. Justice Hunt, of Utica, New York. Districts of—

Vermont,	Southern New York,
Connecticut,	Eastern New York.
Northern New York,	

Circuit Judge.—Alexander S. Johnson, New York City..........1875.......$6,000

Third Judicial Circuit.—Mr. Justice Strong, of Philadelphia, Pa. Districts of—

New Jersey,	Western Pennsylvania,
Eastern Pennsylvania,	Delaware.

Circuit Judge.—William McKennan, Washington, Pa..........1869.......$6,000

Fourth Judicial Circuit.—Mr. Chief Justice Waite. Districts of—

Maryland,	North Carolina (Eastern and West-
West Virginia,	ern),
Virginia (Eastern and Western Districts),	South Carolina.

Circuit Judge.—Hugh L. Bond, Baltimore....................1870.......$6,000

Fifth Judicial Circuit.—Mr. Justice Bradley, of Newark, N. J. Districts of—

Georgia (Northern and Southern),	Mississippi (Northern and Southern),
Northern Florida,	Louisiana,
Southern Florida,	Eastern Texas,
Northern, Middle, and Southern Ala-	Western Texas.
bama,	

Circuit Judge.—William B. Woods, Mobile, Ala...............1869.......$6,000

Sixth Judicial Circuit.—Mr. Justice Swayne, of Columbus, Ohio. Districts of—

Northern Ohio,	Kentucky,
Southern Ohio,	Eastern, Middle, and Western Ten-
Eastern Michigan,	nessee.
Western Michigan,	

Circuit Judge.--John Baxter, of Knoxville, Tenn............. 1877.......$6,000

Seventh Judicial Circuit.—Mr. Justice Harlan, of Louisville, Ky. Districts of—

Indiana,	Eastern Wisconsin,
Northern Illinois,	Western Wisconsin.
Southern Illinois,	

Circuit Judge.—Thomas Drummond, Chicago.................1869. ... .$6,000

Eighth Judicial Circuit.—Mr. Justice Miller, of Keokuk, Iowa. Districts of—

Minnesota,	Kansas,
Iowa,	Eastern Arkansas,
Eastern Missouri,	Western Arkansas,
Western Missouri,	Nebraska.

Circuit Judge.—John F. Dillon, Davenport, Iowa..............1869.......$6,000

Ninth Judicial Circuit.—Mr. Justice Field, of San Francisco, Cal. Districts of—

California,	Nevada.
Oregon,	

Circuit Judge.—Lorenzo Sawyer, San Francisco...............1870.......$6,000

United States Court of Claims.

	Appointed from	Date of Commission.	Salary.
Charles D. Drake, Chief Justice	Missouri....	....Dec. 12, 1870	..$4,500
Ebenezer Peck	Illinois	.........May 10, 1963	4,500
Charles C. Nott	New York	......Feb. 22, 1865	4,500
William A. Richardson	Massachusetts	..June 2, 1874	4,500
J. C. Bancroft Davis	New York	.......Jan. 1, 1878	4,500

JUDGES OF THE UNITED STATES ;DISTRICT COURTS.

DISTRICTS.	NAME.	RESIDENCE.	DATE OF COMMISSION.	SALARY.
ALABAMA :				
(Three Districts)..	John Bruce	Montgomery ...	Feb. 28, 1875.	$3,500
ARKANSAS :				
Eastern District..	Henry C. Caldwell	Little Rock	June 30, 1864.	3,500
Western "	Isaac C. Parker	Fort Smith....	Mar. 24, 1875.	3,500
CALIFORNIA	Ogden Hoffman	San Francisco..	Feb. 27, 1851.	5,000
CONNECTICUT	Nathaniel Shipman...	Hartford	April 17, 1873.	3,500
DELAWARE	Edward C. Bradford....	Wilmington ...	Dec. 12, 1871.	3,500
FLORIDA :				
Northern District.	Thomas Settle	Jacksonville...	July 17, 1862.	3,500
Southern "	James W. Locke	Key West	Feb. 1, 1872.	3,500
GEORGIA :				
(Two Districts)...	John Erskine	Atlanta	Jan. 22, 1866.	3,500
ILLINOIS :				
Northern District.	Henry W. Blodgett	Waukegan	Jan. 11, 1870.	4,000
Southern "	Samuel H. Treat	Springfield	Mar. 3, 1855.	3,500
INDIANA	Walter Q. Gresham ...	Indianapolis...	Dec. 21, 1869.	3,500
IOWA	James M. Love	Keokuk	Feb. 21, 1856.	3,500
KANSAS	Cassius G. Foster	Atchison... ...	Mar. 10, 1874.	3,500
KENTUCKY	Bland Ballard	Louisville	Jan. 22, 1862.	3,500
LOUISIANA	Edward C. Billings	New Orleans...	Feb. 10, 1876.	4,500
MAINE	Edward Fox	Portland	May 31, 1866.	3,500
MARYLAND	William F. Giles	Baltimore	Jan. 11, 1854.	4,000
MASSACHUSETTS....	John Lowell	Boston	Mar. 11, 1865.	4,000
MICHIGAN :				
Eastern District..	Henry B. Brown	Detroit	Mar. 19, 1875.	3,500
Western "	Solomon L. Withey ...	Grand Rapids..	Mar. 11, 1863.	3,500
MINNESOTA	Rensselaer R. Nelson...	St. Paul	June 1, 1858.	3,500
MISSISSIPPI :				
(Two Districts)...	Robert A. Hill	Oxford	May 10, 1866.	3,500
MISSOURI :				
Eastern District..	Samuel Treat	St. Louis	Mar. 3, 1857.	3,500
Western "	Arnold Krekel	Jefferson City..	Mar. 31, 1865.	3,500
NEBRASKA	Elmer S. Dundy	Falls City	April 9, 1868.	3,500
NEVADA	Edgar W. Hillyer	Carson City....	Dec. 21, 1869.	3,500
NEW HAMPSHIRE. .	Daniel Clark	Manchester	July 27, 1866.	3,500
NEW JERSEY	John T. Nixon	Trenton	April 28, 1871.	4,000
NEW YORK :				
Northern District.	William J. Wallace	Syracuse	April 7, 1874.	4,000
Southern "	Samuel Blatchford	New York City.	July 16, 1867.	4,000
Eastern "	Charles L. Benedict ...	Brooklyn	Mar. 9, 1865.	4,000
NORTH CAROLINA :				
Eastern District..	George W. Brooks	Elizabeth City..	Jan. 22, 1866.	3,500
Western "	Robert P. Dick	Greensboro	June 7, 1872.	3,500
OHIO :				
Northern District.	Martin Welker	Wooster	Nov. 25, 1873.	3,500
Southern "	Philip B. Swing	Batavia	Mar. 30, 1871.	4,000
OREGON	Matthew P. Deady	Portland	Mar. 9, 1859.	3,500
PENNSYLVANIA :				
Eastern District..	John Cadwalader	Philadelphia ...	April 24, 1858.	4,000
Western "	Winthrop W. Ketcham.	Pittsburgh	June 26, 1876.	4,000
RHODE ISLAND	John P. Knowles	Providence	Jan. 8, 1870.	3,500
SOUTH CAROLINA..	George S. Bryan	Charleston	Mar. 12, 1866.	3,500
TENNESSEE :				
(Three Districts).	Connally F. ,Trigg	Bristol	July 17, 1862.	3,500
TEXAS :				
Eastern District..	Amos Morrill	Galveston.	Feb. 5, 1872.	3,500
Western "	Thomas H. Duval	Austin	Mar. 3, 1857.	3,500
VERMONT	Hoyt H. Wheeler	Burlington	Feb. 3, 1857.	3,500
VIRGINIA :				
Eastern District..	Robert W. Hughes	Norfolk	Jan. 14, 1874.	3,500
Western "	Alexander Rives	Charlottesville..	Feb. 6, 1871.	3,500
WEST VIRGINIA	John J. Jackson, Jr ...	Parkersburg....	Aug. 3, 1861.	3,500
WISCONSIN :				
Eastern District..	Charles E. Dyer	Milwaukee	Feb. 10, 1875.	3.500
Western "	Romanzo E. Bunn	Madison	Dec. 1877.	3.500

SPEAKERS OF THE HOUSE OF REPRESENTATIVES.

	NAME.	State.	Congress.	Term of Service.	Born	Died
1	F. A. Muhlenberg..	Pa....	1st Cong.	April 1, 1789, to Mar. 4, 1791.	1750	1801
2	Jonathan Trumbull	Conn.	2d Cong.	Oct. 24, 1791, to Mar. 4, 1793.	1740	1809
	F. A. Muhlenberg..	Pa....	3d Cong.	Dec. 2, 1793, to Mar. 4, 1795.	.....	....
3	Jonathan Dayton..	N. J..	4th Cong.	Dec. 7, 1795, to Mar. 4, 1797.	1760	1824
	" " ..	"	5th Cong.	May 15, 1797, to Mar. 3, 1799.	....	....
4	Theodore Sedgwick	Mass.	6th Cong.	Dec. 2, 1799, to Mar. 4, 1801.	1746	1813
5	Nathaniel Macon..	N. C..	7th Cong.	Dec. 7, 1801, to Mar. 4, 1803.	1757	1837
	" " ..	" ..	8th Cong.	Oct. 17, 1803, to Mar. 4, 1805.	....	....
	" " ..	" ..	9th Cong.	Dec. 2, 1805, to Mar. 4, 1807.	....	....
6	Joseph B. Varnum.	Mass.	10th Cong.	Oct. 26, 1807, to Mar. 4, 1809.	1750	1821
	" " ..	"	11th Cong.	May 22, 1809, to Mar. 4, 1811.	....	....
7	Henry Clay........	Ky...	12th Cong.	Nov. 4, 1811, to Mar. 4, 1813.	1777	1852
	" " ..	"	13th Cong.	May 24, 1813, to Jan. 19, 1814.	....	....
8	Langdon Cheves .	{ S. C } 2d { Ses. }	13th Cong.	Jan. 19, 1814, to Mar. 4, 1815.	1776	1857
	Henry Clay.......	Ky...	14th Cong.	Dec. 4, 1815, to Mar. 4, 1817.	....	...
	" "	" ..	15th Cong.	Dec. 1, 1817, to Mar. 4, 1819.	....	...
	" "	"	16th Cong.	Dec. 6, 1819, to May 15, 1820.	....	....
9	John W. Taylor .	{ N.Y } 2d { Ses. }	16th Cong.	Nov. 15, 1820, to Mar. 4, 1821.	1784	1854
10	Philip P. Barbour..	Va..	17th Cong.	Dec. 4, 1821, to Mar. 4, 1823.	1783	1841
	Henry Clay.......	Ky..	18th Cong.	Dec. 1, 1823, to Mar. 4, 1825.	....	....
	John W. Taylor ...	N. Y.	19th Cong.	Dec. 5, 1825, to Mar. 4, 1827.	....	....
11	Andrew Stevenson.	Va..	20th Cong.	Dec. 3, 1827, to Mar. 4, 1829.	1784	1857
	" "	" ...	21st Cong.	Dec. 7, 1829, to Mar. 4, 1831.	....	....
	" "	" ..	22d Cong.	Dec. 5, 1831, to Mar. 4, 1833.	....	....
	" "	" ..	23d Cong.	Dec. 2, 1833, to June 2, 1834.	1784	1857
12	John Bell........	{ Ten } 2d { Ses. }	23d Cong.	June 2, 1834, to Mar. 4, 1835.	1797	1869
13	James K. Polk.....	"	24th Cong.	Dec. 7, 1835, to Mar. 4, 1837.	1795	1849
	" "	"	25th Cong.	Sept. 5, 1837, to Mar. 4, 1839.	....	....
14	Rob't M. T. Hunter.	Va...	26th Cong.	Dec. 16, 1839, to Mar. 4, 1841.	1809	....
15	John White........	Ky...	27th Cong.	May 31, 1841, to Mar. 4, 1843.	1805	1845
16	John W. Jones.....	Va...	28th Cong.	Dec. 4, 1843, to Mar. 4, 1845.	1805	1848
17	John W. Davis.....	Ind...	29th Cong.	Dec. 1, 1845, to Mar. 4, 1847.	1799	1850
18	Robert C. Winthrop	Mass.	30th Cong.	Dec. 6, 1847, to Mar. 4, 1849.	1809	....
19	Howell Cobb......	Ga ...	31st Cong.	Dec. 22, 1849, to Mar. 4, 1851.	1815	1868
20	Linn Boyd........	Ky...	32d Cong.	Dec. 1, 1851, to Mar. 4, 1853.	1800	1859
	" "	"	33d Cong.	Dec. 5, 1853, to Mar. 4, 1855.	....	....
21	Nathaniel P. Banks	Mass.	34th Cong.	Feb. 2, 1856, to Mar. 4, 1857.	1816	....
22	James L. Orr	S. C..	35th Cong.	Dec. 7, 1857, to Mar. 4, 1859.	1822	1873
23	Wm. Pennington...	N. J..	36th Cong.	Feb. 1, 1860, to Mar. 4, 1861.	1796	1862
24	Galusha A. Grow..	Pa....	37th Cong.	July 4, 1861, to Mar. 4, 1863.	1823	....
25	Schuyler Colfax...	Ind ..	38th Cong.	Dec. 7, 1863, to Mar. 4, 1865.	1823	....
	" "	"	39th Cong.	Dec. 4, 1865, to Mar. 4, 1867.	....	....
	" "	"	40th Cong.	Mar. 4, 1867, to Mar. 4, 1869.	....	....
26	James G. Blaine...	Me...	41st Cong.	Mar. 4, 1869, to Mar. 4, 1871.	1830	....
	" " ...	" ..	42d Cong.	Mar. 4, 1871, to Mar. 4, 1873.	....	....
	" " ...	" ..	43d Cong.	Dec. 1, 1873, to Mar. 4, 1875.	....	....
27	Michael C. Kerr....	Ind ..	44th Cong.	Dec. 6, 1875, to Aug. 20, 1876.	1827	1876
28	Samuel J. Randall {	{ Pa. } 2d { Ses. }	44th Cong.	Dec. 4, 1876, to Mar. 4, 1877.	1828	....
	" "	" ..	45th Cong.	Oct. 15, 1877, to ——	——	....

NOTE.—Speakers elected *pro tempore* are not included in the above table. The figures prefixed indicate the number of Speakers, not the sequence of their official terms.

EXECUTIVE OFFICERS OF THE UNITED STATES.

EXECUTIVE MANSION.

Office.	Name.	Whence Appointed.	Date of Commission.	Salary.
President of the U. S.....	Rutherford B.Hayes	Ohio.........	March 4, 1877	$50,000
Private Secretary........	W. K. Rogers......	Minnesota ...	March 4, 1877	3,500

DEPARTMENT OF STATE.

Secretary of State........	William M. Evarts..	New York....	March 12, 1877	8,000
Assistant Secretary.......	Fred'k W. Seward..	New York....	March 16, 1877	3,500
Second Assist. Secretary..	William Hunter....	Rhode Island	July 27, 1866	3,500
Chief Clerk....	Sevellon A. Brown..	New York....	Aug. 7, 1873	2,500
Examiner of Claims.......	Henry O'Conner....	Iowa.........	Feb. 9, 1872	3,500

TREASURY DEPARTMENT.

Secretary	John Sherman.....	Ohio	March 8, 1877	8,000
Assistant Secretary.......	John P. Hawley....	Illinois	Dec. 6, 1877	4,500
Assistant Secretary.......	Henry F. French...	Massachus'ts.	Aug. 12, 1876	4,500
Chief Clerk.	J. K. Upton.......	N. Hampshire	May 1, 1877	2,700
Solicitor of the Treasury..	Kenneth Rayner...	N. Carolina ..	June 30, 1877	4,500
Supervising Architect.....	James G. Hill.......	Massachus'ts.	Aug. 11, 1876	4,500
Chief of Bureau of Engraving and Printing........	Edward McPherson	Pennsylvania.	May 1, 1877	4,500
Ch'f of Bureau of Statistics	Edward Young.....	Pennsylvania.	July 1, 1870	2,400
Chief Clerk of Bureau of Statistics..............	E. B. Elliott......	Massachus'ts.	Sept. 1, 1870	2,400
Director of the Mint......	H. R. Linderman...	Pennsylvania.	Dec. 8, 1873	4,500
First Comptroller........	Robert W. Tayler..	Ohio.........	Jan. 14, 1863	5,000
Second Comptroller......	William W. Upton..	Oregon.......	Sept. 26, 1877	5,000
Commissioner of Customs	Henry C. Johnson..	Pennsylvania.	April 8, 1874	4,000
Register of the Treasury..	John Allison.......	Pennsylvania.	April 3, 1869	4,000
First Auditor............	David W. Mahon...	Pennsylvania.	Dec. 19, 1871	3,600
Second Auditor..........	Ezra B. French.....	Maine........	Aug. 3, 1861	3,600
Third Auditor...........	Horace Austin......	Minnesota....	Jan. 7, 1876	3,600
Fourth Auditor..........	Stephen J.W. Tabor	Iowa........	May 19, 1863	3,600
Fifth Auditor............	Jacob H. Ela.......	N. Hampshire	Dec. 19, 1871	3,600
Sixth Auditor...........	Jacob M. McGrew..	Ohio.........	July 1, 1875	3,600
Treasurer of the U. S.....	James Gilfillan.....	Connecticut..	June 6, 1877	6,000
Assistant Treasurer.......	Albert U. Wyman..	Nebraska	June 6, 1877	3,600
Compt'r of the Currency..	John Jay Knox.....	New York....	April 24, 1872	5,000
Com. of Internal Revenue	Green B. Raum....	Illinois	Aug. 2, 1876	6,000
Solic'r of Internal Revenue	Charles Chesley....	N. Hampshire	Oct. 13, 1871	4,500
Chairman of Light-House Board..................	Prof. Joseph Henry	Dist. of Col. .	Oct. 30, 1871	
Supt. of U. S. Coast Survey	Carlile P. Patterson	California....	Feb. 17, 1874	6,000
Assist. in Charge of Office	J. E. Hilgard.......	Illinois.......	April 1, 1873	4,200
Supervising Surgeon-Gen.	John M.Woodworth	Illinois.......	March 13, 1875	4,000

DEPARTMENT OF THE INTERIOR.

Secretary of the Interior..	Carl Schurz........	Missouri......	March 12, 1877	8,000
Assistant Secretary.......	Alonzo Bell........	New York. ..	April 9, 1877	2,500
Chief Clerk..............	Geo. M. Lockwood.	New York....	April 10, 1877	2,500
Asst. Attorney-General...	Edgar M. Marble..	Michigan.....	March 30, 1877	5,000

General Land Office.

Commissioner....	Jas. A. Williamson.	Iowa.........	June 26, 1876	4,000
Chief Clerk..............	Uri J. Baxter.......	Michigan.....	April 1, 1867	2,000

Pension Office.

Commissioner............	John A. Bentley. ..	Wisconsin ...	March 23, 1876	3,600
Chief Clerk..............	O. P. G. Clarke.....	Rhode Island.	July 16, 1875	2,000

DEPARTMENT OF THE INTERIOR—(*Continued*).
Patent Office.

OFFICE.	NAME.	Whence Appointed.	Date of Commission.	Salary.
Commissioner............	Ellis Spear.........	Maine........	Jan. 30, 1877	$4,500
Assistant Commissioner..	W. H. Doolittle	Minnesota ...	July 16, 1873	3,000
Chief Clerk..............	F. A. Seeley........	Pennsylvania.	April 10, 1877	2,250
Examiners-in-chief...... { R. L. B. Clarke. ...	Iowa.........	April 13, 1869	3,000
	V. D. Stockbridge..	Maine	April 13, 1869	3,000
	II. H. Bates........	New York ...	April 28, 1877	3,000
EXAMINERS.				
Chemistry, Class B........	Thomas Antisell....	Dist. of Col..	May 10, 1877	2,500
Sewing Machines and Textile Machinery..........	Wm. H. Appleton..	N. Hampshire	July 16, 1572	2,500
Official Gazette of the Patent Office..............	Frank A. Burr.......	W. Virginia..	1877	2,500
Fine Arts................	William Burke.....	Pennsylvania.	Dec. 1, 1868	2,500
Calorifics — Stoves and Lamps.................	B. R. Catlin..... ...	New York....	May 2, 1871	2,500
Leather - working Machinery and Products...	J. P. Chapman......	Ohio.........	June 1, 1872	2,500
Metal Working, Class A..	J. R. Church........	Dist. of Col..	July 10, 1877	2,500
Metal Working, Class B..	S. W. Stocking.....	New York....	July 9, 1863	2,500
Hydraulics and Pneumatics..................	J. B. Durnall.......	Colorado.....	Oct. 1, 1872	2,500
Chemistry, Class A.......	R. G. Dyrenforth...	Illinois.	May 1, 1871	2,500
Agriculture..............	Oscar C. Fox.......	Ohio.........	May 23, 1870	2,500
Printing and Stationery..	Frank L. Freeman..	Mass	Oct. 1, 1872	2,500
Steam Engineering......	Frank Fowler......	Dist. of Col...	July 1, 1869	2,500
Plastics, Ceramics, etc ...	B. S. Hedrick......	N. Carolina..	April 10, 1861	2,500
Agricultural Products....	J. W. Jayne........	Pennsylvania.	May 21, 1861	2,500
Civil Engineering	B. W. Pond.........	Maine........	Aug. 7, 1877	2,500
Harvesters and Mills.....	Jos. G. Parkinson..	Main	June 1, 1869	2,500
Carriages, Wagons and Cars..................	Henry P. Sanders ..	New York...	May 15, 1867	2,500
Mechanical Engineering..	Albin Schoepf......	Maryland	March 14, 1866	2,500
Household...............	Charles B. Tilden..	Vermont.....	April 26, 1870	2,500
Fire Arms, Navigation, Wood-working, etc.....	W. A. Bartlett......	New York...	Dec. 1, 1875	2,500
Philosophical............	H. C. Townsend....	Maine........	May 9, 1877	2,500
Builders'Hardware,Locks, etc..................	A. G. Wilkinson....	Connecticut..	July 1, 1864	2,500
Examiner of Interferences	Zenas F. Wilber ...	Ohio.........	May 1, 1877	2,500
Trade-Marks and Labels .	James E. M. Bowen.	Dist. of Col..	May 1, 1875	2,250

Indian Office.

Commissioner............	E. A. Hayt.........	New York....	Sept., 1877	3,000
Chief Clerk, Acting..... ..	C. W. Holcomb ..	....	... .1877	2,000

Bureau of Education.

Commissioner of Education....	John Eaton...... ...	Tennessee....	March 16, 1870	3,000
Chief Clerk..............	Charles Warren.....	Illinois........	Oct. 1, 1870	1,800

POST-OFFICE DEPARTMENT.

Postmaster-General	David M. Key......	Tennessee. ..	March 12, 1877	8,000
Chief Clerk..............	W. A. Knapp......	Ohio.........	1876	2,200
First Assistant Postmaster-General..........	James N. Tyner....	Indiana......	March 16, 1877	3,500
Second Assistant Postmaster-General.........	Thomas J. Brady ..	Indiana......	July 24, 1876	3,500
Third Assistant Postmaster-General	Abraham D. Hazen.	Pennsylvania.	June 7, 1877	3,500
Superintendent of Foreign Mails.............	Jos. H. Blackfan...	New Jersey..	1868	3,000
Assistant Attorney-General for Post-Office Department..........	Alfred A. Freeman.	Tennessee....	1877	4,000
Superintendent of Money-Order System..........	Chas. F. Macdonald.	Mass........	1865	3,000

WAR DEPARTMENT.

Office.	Name.	Whence Appointed.	Date of Commission.	Salary.
Secretary of War.........	Geo. W. McCrary ..	Iowa........	March 12, 1877	$8.000
Chief Clerk...............	H. T. Crosby.......	Army.........	....	2,500

NOTE.—For the various Bureaus of the War Department, see under Army of the United States, p. 264.

NAVY DEPARTMENT.

Office.	Name.	Whence Appointed.	Date of Commission.	Salary.
Secretary of the Navy....	R. W. Thompson...	Indiana......	March 12, 1877	$8,000
Chief Clerk	John W. Hogg	Tennessee....	Jan. 1, 1854	2,500
Naval Solicitor	John A. Bolles.....	Mass'chusetts	July 17, 1875	3,500
Chief of Bureau of Yards and Docks.....	Rear-Admiral John C. Howell........	New Jersey..	Sept. 22, 1874	5,000
Chief of Bureau of Navigation	Commodore Daniel Ammen..........	Maryland.....	Oct. 1, 1871	4,000
Chief of Bureau of Ordnance............	Captain William N. Jeffers	District of Columbia	April 10, 1873	3,500
Chief of Bureau of Provisions and Clothing...	P. D. Geo. F. Cutter	Mass'chusetts	Nov. 1, 1877	4,400
Chief of Bureau of Medicine and Surgery	Brigadier - General William Grier....	Maryland.....	March 3, 1871	3,500
Chief of Bureau of Equipment and Recruiting..	Commodore R. W. Shufeldt..........	Connecticut..	Feb. 1, 1875	4,000
Chief of Bureau of Construction and Repair....	Engineer - in - Chief, William H. Shock	Maryland	1877	4,000
Chief of Bureau of Steam-Engineering...	Commodore John C. Febiger	Ohio	1877	4,000
Commandant of Navy Yard, Washington....				

Navy Pay Office.

Office.	Name.	Whence Appointed.	Date of Commission.	Salary.
Pay Inspector	W. W. Williams....	Ohio.........	Oct. 24, 1871	4,400
Commandant Marine Corps	Colonel Charles G. McCawley.......	Louisiana....	Nov. 1, 1876	3,500

Marine Barracks.

In charge...............	Major Charles Heywood...	New York....	 1877	2,500

Naval Observatory.

Superintendent..........	Rear-Admiral John Rodgers	District of Columbia	1877	5,000
Professors.............	Mordecai Yarnall...	Kentucky....	Aug. 14, 1848	3,500
	Asaph Hall.........	Mass'chusetts	May 2, 1863	3,000
	William Harkness..	New York....	Aug. 24, 1863	3,000
	Joseph E. Nouree..	Dist. of Col...	May 21, 1864	2,000
	John R. Eastman...	N. Hampshire	Feb. 17, 1865	3,000
	Edward S. Holden..	Army	March 21, 1873	2,400

Nautical Almanac.

Superintendent..........	Professor Simon Newcomb........	Mass'chusetts	Sept. 21, 1861	3,500

Signal Office.

In charge...............	Commodore John C. Beaumont........	Pennsylvania.	June 14, 1874	4,000

Hydrographic Office.

Hydrographer...........	Commodore R. H. Wyman	New Hampshire.....	July 19, 1872	4,000

DEPARTMENT OF JUSTICE.

Office.	Name.	Whence Appointed.	Date of Commission.	Salary.
Attorney-General.........	Charles Devens.....	Mass'chusetts	March 12, 1877	8,000
Solicitor-General.........	Samuel F. Phillips.	N. Carolina...	Nov. 15, 1872	7,000
Assistant Attorney-Gen'l..	Edwin B. Smith....	Maine........	Aug. 28, 1875	5,000
Assistant Attorney-Gen'l..	Thomas Simons....	New York....	May 28, 1875	5,000
Chief Clerk..............	Aaron R. Dutton ..	Ohio........	July 1, 1875	2,200
Law Clerk......	Alexander J. Bentley	"	June 10, 1867	2,700

DEPARTMENT OF AGRICULTURE.

Office.	Name.	Whence Appointed.	Date of Commission.	Salary.
Commissioner	William G. Le Duc.	Minnesota....	June 30, 1877	3.000
Chief Clerk.............	E. A. Carman......	....	July, 1877	1,900

REDUCTION OF THE NATIONAL DEBT OF THE UNITED STATES, AND OF THE INTEREST THEREON.

From the Monthly Debt Statements of the Treasury, from the first, issued March 1, 1869, to December 1, 1877.

	Debt, including Accrued Interest thereon, less Cash in the Treasury.	Decrease of Debt during the Preceding Month.	Increase of Debt during the Preceding Month.	Total Decrease from March 1, 1869, to Date.	Decrease in Annual Interest Charge.
	$	$	$	$	$
1869.					
March 1.	2,525,463,260 01				
April 1.	2,525,196,461 74	266,798 27			74,694 00
May 1.	2,518,797,391 09	6,399,070 65		6,665,868 92	115,521 00
June 1.	2,505,412,613 12	13,384,777 97		20,050,646 89	304,467 00
July 1.	2,489,002,480 58	16,410,132 54		36,460,779 43	667,467 00
Aug. 1.	2,481,566,736 29	7,435,744 29		43,896,523 72	1,786,725 00
Sept. 1.	2,475,962,501 50	5,604,234 79		49,500,758 51	2,387,325 00
Oct. 1.	2,468,495,072 11	7,467,429 39		56,968,187 90	3,354,345 00
Nov. 1.	2,461,131,189 36	7,363,882 75		64,332,070 65	4,050,705 00
Dec. 1.	2,453,559,735 23	7,571,454 13		71,903,524 78	4,822,041 00
1870.					
Jan. 1.	2,448,746,953 31	4,812,781 92		76,716,306 70	5,651,475 00
Feb. 1.	2,444,813,288 92	3,933,664 39		80,649,971 09	6,119,574 00
March 1.	2,438,328,477 17	6,484,811 75		87,134,782 84	6,301,797 00
April 1.	2,432,562,127 74	5,786,349 43		92,901,132 27	6,601,350 00
May 1.	2,420,864,334 35	11,697,793 39		104,598,925 66	6,908,436 00
June 1.	2,406,562,371 78	14,301,962 57		118,900,888 23	7,268,397 00
July 1.	2,386,358,599 74	20,203,772 04		139,104,660 27	7,747,797 00
Aug. 1.	2,369,324,476 00	17,034,123 74		156,138,784 01	8,133,954 00
Sept. 1.	2,355,921,150 41	13,403,325 59	.⸱.........	169,542,109 60	8,614,470 00
Oct. 1.	2,346,913,652 28	9,007,498 13		178,549,607 73	9,162,270 00
Nov. 1.	2,341,784,355 55	5,129,296 73		183,678,904 46	9,768,311 04
Dec. 1.	2,334,308,494 65	7,475,860 90		191,154,765 36	10,155,576 96
1871.					
Jan. 1.	2,332,067,793 75	2,240,700 90		193,395,466 26	10,661.026 44
Feb. 1.	2,328,026,807 00	4,040,986 75		197,436,453 01	11,064,916 44
March 1.	2,320,708,846 92	7,317,960 08		204,754,413 09	11,537,461 08
April 1.	2,309,697,590 27	11,011,250 65		215,765,663 74	12,062,997 96
May 1.	2,303,573,543 14	6,124,053 13		221,889,716 87	12,870,089 96
June 1.	2,299,134,184 81	4,439,358 33		226,329,075 20	13,489,202 04
July 1.	2,292,306,034 90	7,103,349 91		233,432,425 11	14,440,219 56
Aug. 1.	2,283,328,857 98	8,701,976 92		242,134,402 03	14,761,404 00
Sept. 1.	2,274,122,560 38	9,206,297 60		251,340,609 63	14,950,164 48
Oc' 1.	2,260,663,939 87	13,458,620 51		264,799,320 14	15,413,528 04
Nov. 1.	2,251,713,448 03	8,950,461 84		273,749,811 98	16,368,108 96
Dec. 1.	2,248,251,367 85	3,462,080 18		277,211,892 16	16,741,436 04
1872.					
Jan. 1.	2,243,838,411 14	4,412,956 71		281,624,848 87	17,165,927 52
Feb. 1.	2,238,204,949 50	5,633,461 64		287,258,310 51	17,598,834 48
March 1.	2,225,813,497 98	12,391,451 52		290,649,762 03	18,203,915 04
April 1.	2,210,331,529 34	15,481,968 64		315,131,730 67	20,484,552 00
May 1.	2,197,743,440 72	12,588,088 62		327,719,819 29	21,472,089 00
June 1.	2,193,517,378 94	4,226,061 78		331,945,881 07	22,002,519 00
July 1.	2,191,486,343 62	2,031,035 32		333,976,916 39	22,401,087 00
Aug. 1.	2,188,058,656 44	3,427,687 18		337,404,603 57	22,610,457 00
Sept. 1.	2,177,322,020 55	10,736,635 89		348,141,239 46	23,191,365 00
Oct. 1.	2,166,994,677 46	10,327,343 09		358,468,582 55	23,595,735 00
Nov. 1.	2,161,766,260 14	5,228,417 32		363,696,999 87	24,187,851 00
Dec. 1.	2,160,568,030 32	1,198,229 82		364,895,229 69	24,355,068 00
1873.					
Jan. 1.	2,162,252,338 12		1,684,307 80	363,210,921 89	24,605,616 00
Feb. 1.	2,162,658,581 30		406,243 18	362,804,678 71	24,569,343 00
March 1.	2,157,380,700 53	5,277,880 77		368,082,559 48	24,820,023 00
April 1.	2,155,736,641 56	1,644,058 97		369,726,618 45	25,110,054 00
May 1.	2,153,489,155 96	2,247,485 60		371,974,104 05	25,183,296 00

REDUCTION OF THE NATIONAL DEBT OF THE UNITED STATES, AND OF THE INTEREST THEREON—(Continued).

	Debt, including Accrued Interest thereon, less Cash in the Treasury.	Decrease of Debt during the Preceding Month.	Increase of Debt during the Preceding Month.	Total Decrease from March 1, 1869, to Date.	Decrease in Annual Interest Charge.
	$	$	$	$	$
June 1.	2,149,963,873 46	3,525,282 50		375,499,386 55	25,249,746 00
July 1.	2,147,818,713 57	2,145,150 89		377,644,546 44	28,339,746 00
Aug. 1.	2,147,448,194 62	370,518 05		378,015,065 39	26,798,231 00
Sept. 1.	2,140,695,365 33	6,752,829 29		384,767,894 68	26,522,846 04
Oct. 1.	2,138,793,898 17	1,901,467 16		386,669,361 84	27,414,053 04
Nov. 1.	2,141,833,476 62		3,039,578 45	383,629,783 39	27,432,932 04
Dec. 1.	2,150,862,053 40		9,028,576 84	374,601,206 55	27,921,951 00
1874.					
Jan. 1	2,159,815,326 17		8,453,272 71	366,147,933 84	27,644,801 04
Feb. 1.	2,157,470,114 41	1,845,211 76		367,993,145 60	28,117,688 52
March 1.	2,154,880,066 96	2,590,047 45		370,583,193 05	27,765,763 44
April 1.	2,152,690,728 50	2,189,338 46		372,772,531 51	27,600,468 48
May 1.	2,149,725,277 02	2,965,451 48		375,737,982 99	27,598,247 52
June 1.	2,145,269,438 10	4,456,838 92		380,194,821 91	27,590,406 00
July 1.	2,143,088,241 16	2,130,196 94		382,375,018 85	27,593,545 56
Aug. 1.	2,141,805,375 03	1,282,866 13		383,657,884 98	27,597,487 08
Sept. 1.	2,140,178,614 24	1,626,700 79		385,284,645 77	27,597,487 08
Oct. 1.	2,189,743,196 32	435,417 92		385,720,063 69	27,758,894 04
Nov. 1.	2,139,061,761 82	681,434 50		386,401,498 19	28,085,175 00
Dec. 1.	2,138,938,334 14	123,427 08		386,524,925 87	28,279,688 04
1875.					
Jan. 1.	2,142,598,302 02		3,659,967 88	382,864,957 99	28,691,064 00
Feb. 1.	2,143,996,172 29		1,397,870 27	381,467,087 72	28,416,063 96
March 1.	2,137,315,989 17	6,680,183 12		388,147,270 84	28,215,992 52
April 1.	2,133,634,778 54	3,681,210 63		391,828,481 47	28,281,638 52
May 1.	2,131,309,431 91	2,325,346 63		394,153,828 10	28,979,160 48
June 1.	2,130,119,975 88	1,189,456 03		395,343,284 13	28,519,802 52
July 1.	2,128,688,726 32	1,431,249 56		396,774,533 69	29,533,859 52
Aug. 1.	2,127,393,838 96	1,294,837 36		398,069,421 05	29,500,279 56
Sept. 1.	2,125,808,789 70	1,585,049 26		399,654,470 31	29,638,859 52
Oct. 1.	2,122,466,227 09	3,342,562 61		402,997,032 92	30,091,466 52
Nov. 1.	2,118,397,211 40	4,069,015 69		407,066,048 61	30,507,859 44
Dec. 1.	2,117,917,132 57	480,078 83		407,546,127 44	30,918,319 56
1876.					
Jan. 1.	2,119,832,195 27		1,915,062 70	405,631,064 74	31,393,388 52
Feb. 1.	2,118,233,039 80	1,599,155 47		407,230,220 21	30,812,001 48
March 1.	2,114,960,306 80	3,272,733 00		410,502,953 21	31,975,333 56
April 1.	2,110,719,439 88	4,240,866 92		414,743,820 13	31,367,691 00
May 1.	2,107,938,258 39	2,781,181 49		417,525,001 62	31,367,481 00
June 1.	2,103,320,742 53	4,617,515 84		422,142,517 46	31,367,481 00
July 1.	2,099,439,344 99	3,881,397 56		426,023,915 02	31,285,281 00
Aug. 1.	2,098,301,311 06	1,138,033 93		427,161,948 95	31,285,281 00
Sept. 1.	2,095,181,941 14	3,119,369 92		430,281,318 87	31,253,548 56
Oct. 1.	2,092,266,575 79	2,915,365 35		433,196,684 22	31,253,548 56
Nov. 1.	2,088,878,436 78	3,388,139 01		436,584,823 23	31,253,548 56
Dec. 1.	2,089,336,099 42		457,662 64	436,127,160 59	31,253,548 56
1877.					
Jan. 1.	2,092,921,241 81		3,585,142 39	432,542,018 20	32,147,479 56
Feb. 1.	2,090,851,572 10	2,069,669 71		434,611,687 91	32,673,904 56
March 1.	2,088,781,143 04	2,070,429 06		436,682,116 97	32,405,904 48
April 1.	2,074,674,126 63	14,107,016 41		450,789,133 38	32,463,594 60
May 1.	2,070,358,617 20	4,315,509 43		455,104,642 81	32,770,971 50
June 1.	2,063,377,342 37	6,931,274 83		462,085,917 64	32,849,337 50
July 1.	2,060,158,223 26	3,219,119 11		465,305,036 75	33,228,906 50
Aug. 1.	2,059,339,318 42	818,904 84		466,124,941 59	33,159,702 50
Sept. 1.	2,055,469,779 67	3,869,538 75		469,994,480 34	33,620,751 50
Oct. 1.	2,051,587,254 87	3,882,524 80		473,887,005 14	33,308,601 50
Nov. 1.	2,047,350,700 57	4,236,554 30		478,133,559 44	
Dec. 1.	2,046,027,065 94	1,323,634 63		479,437,194 07	

MUNICIPAL DEBTS IN THE UNITED STATES.

Table showing the Debt, Valuation, and Taxation of One Hundred and Twenty-seven Cities of the United States, for the Years 1866 and 1876, respectively.

From the Galaxy, September, 1877.

Name of City.	Total Debt, 1876.	Total Debt, 1866.	Valuation, 1876.	Valuation, 1866.	Annual Tax, 1876.	Annual Tax, 1866.
	$	$	$	$	$	$
Adams, Mass	347,976	310,000	6,347,234	3,173,617	104,158	62,079
Albany, N. Y	2,762,000	665,500	35,617,154	26,977,000	1,171,530	1,010,011
Alleghany, Pa	1,711,000	593,574	55,020,000	4,804,232	226,916	84,500
Arlington, Mass	350,643	78,065	5,786,482	2,893,241	71,506	35,753
Atlanta, Ga	2,487,000	829,000	20,000,000	5,700,000	384,000	57,000
Augusta, Me	1,751,000	583,333				
Aurora, Ill	40,000	25,000	3,000,000	1,000,000	40,000	25,000
Baltimore, Md	33,343,251	21,928,656	228,816,100	144,926,217	4,089,340	2,316,643
Bangor, Me	587,000	232,700	10,469,156	7,290,525	274,777	238,298
Belleville, Ill	244,726	80,000	2,969,119	1,210,675	58,000	30,000
Beverly, Mass	1,042,490	676,540	8,565,480	4,222,740	125,854	62,927
Bloomington, Ill	222,500	12,865	5,083,039	1,579,840	129,500	23,697
Boston, Mass	43,590,497	13,021,463	748,678,100	415,362,345	9,270,804	5,274,484
Brookline, Mass	1,368,300	473,800	27,490,300	13,745,150	335,382	167,691
Brooklyn, N. Y	35,758,114	9,722,274	227,013,123	186,424,786	4,854,932	1,885,969
Buffalo, N. Y	7,139,291	750,500	111,995,955	34,957,700	1,545,000	532,447
Burlington, Iowa	523,500	645,744	5,091,315	3,012,544	102,980	30,125
Cambridge, Mass	4,741,500	841,092	62,636,453	28,385,700	1,033,717	389,237
Camden, N. J	831,000	277,000				
Charleston, S. C	4,749,793	1,600,000	85,000,000	19,000,000		155,931
Chelsea, Mass	1,611,650	794,400	17,759,530	8,879,766	311,862	
Chicago, Ill	17,831,692	5,397,064	108,038,178	195,953,250	4,046,300	1,719,064
Cincinnati, O	23,334,701	3,203,000	164,493,565	133,672,163	2,856,263	1,210,322
Cleveland, O	7,261,000	2,420,333				
Columbus, O	1,165,000	No debt.	27,147,541	14,935,050	257,903	108,278
Cumberland, Md	349,900	50,000	4,000,000	357,900	71,500	20,000
Davenport, Iowa	296,175	450,000	6,513,535	3,848,900	121,266	30,315
Dayton, O	1,130,500	300,000			241,452	120,726
Decatur, Ill	89,000	33,500	2,857,851	3,929,925	50,000	40,920
Detroit, Mich	2,630,900	451,968	94,570,905	21,373,921	953,649	391,500
Dubuque, Iowa	1,500,000	860,000				
East St. Louis, Ill	270,000	No debt.	6,500,000	2,300,000	93,800	11,700
Elgin, Ill	47,343	15,775	2,550,000	846,293	23,000	13,966
Elizabeth, N. J	5,131,092	1,710,364	16,255,535	8,127,777	328,000	114,000
Elmira, N. Y	294,400	98,133				
Erie, Pa	1,193,692	110,000	16,660,000	1,375,815	182,097	62,230
Evansville, Ind	1,477,489	206,964	18,000,000	8,000,000	300,000	140,000
Fall River, Mass	3,195,032	195,032	48,980,455	24,460,242	629,258	264,689
Fitchburg, Mass	978,045	572,400	11,714,888	5,857,444	200,582	100,291
Fond du Lac, Wis	178,325	179,005	3,736,618	1,093,360	119,003	83,029
Fort Wayne, Ind	667,260	255,753	14,000,000	5,696,420	164,790	72,186
Freeport, Ill	69,000	80,400	4,200,000	3,400,000	27,000	22,000
Galena, Ill	173,091	177,352	824,793	730,977	15,179	12,329
Galesburg, Ill	100,000	28,000	4,800,000	1,200,000	97,000	38,000
Galveston, Texas	1,273,000	493,678				
Hannibal, Mo	298,629	303,271	3,263,125	2,268,973	99,596	32,243
Hartford, Conn	4,256,415	1,517,446	48,982,120	36,948,805	892,221	504,700
Haverhill, Mass	362,217	176,314	10,334,237	5,545,139	181,934	198,261
Hoboken, N. J	370,400	180,000	15,600,000	10,739,135	340,000	157,013
Holyoke, Mass	929,750	222,800	9,637,992	4,818,996	199,200	90,500
Indianapolis, Ind	1,606,000	500,000	60,345,930	23,702,402	844,943	355,556
Jacksonville, Ill	316,400	38,028	3,731,701	377,900	97,336	18,920
Janesville, Wis	39,825	82,500	3,800,000	2,802,000	46,000	80,000
Jersey City, N. J	13,967,450	4,655,816	62,000,000	31,000,000	1,092,175	011,088
Joliet, Ill	120,000	20,000	4,345,234	837,366	79,455	25,970
Kansas City, Mo	1,519,080	506,360	8,923,190	4,451,545	205,243	109,617
Lancaster, Pa	568,572	295,894	11,400,000	3,500,000	68,400	35,000
La Salle, Ill	80,000	15,000	1,800,000	900,000	24,000	18,000
Lawrence, Mass	1,721,498	837,700	23,993,598	13,748,280	463,102	195,272
Leavenworth, Kan	493,498	161,166	7,360,888	3,469,930	112,253	98,456
Leominster, Mass	338,000	47,000	3,930,973	1,990,466	66,923	33,461
Lexington, Ky	82,000	10,666	5,508,944	2,754,472	73,903	34,616
Louisville, Ky	10,600,000	3,533,210	71,849,772	63,933,654	1,406,187	674,398
Lowell, Mass	2,331,000	452,000	39,393,464	21,984,769	543,649	319,633
Lynn, Mass	1,800,505	430,500	25,937,431	14,740,563	452,127	360,397
Malden, Mass	535,744	340,000	9,961,630	4,980,815	155,240	77,480
Manchester, N. H	939,627	380,799	15,309,348	10,050,030	248,900	245,567
Medford, Mass	511,500	300,390	873,745	4,068,726	130,162	65,081
Melrose, Mass	296,666	182,800	4,666,889	2,333,444	62,874	31,457
Memphis, Tenn	5,711,991	2,479,408	22,653,660	30,819,293	583,098	291,844
Milwaukee, Wis	2,194,790	1,003,853	53,676,160	14,428,285	1,069,675	323,674
Minneapolis, Minn	1,050,000	No debt.	21,000,000	1,500,000	291,000	25,000

MUNICIPAL DEBTS IN THE UNITED STATES—(Continued).

NAME OF CITY.	Total Debt, 1876.	Total Debt, 1866.	Valuation, 1876.	Valuation, 1866.	Annual Tax 1876.	Annual Tax, 1866.
Mobile, Ala.........	2,772,800	924,266	18,272,841	9,136,420	233,933	494,924
Nashville, Tenn....	1,671,721	893,446	10,798,435	17,344,750	271,254	297,556
Natick, Mass.......	238,000	60,000	3,725,125	1,962,562	63,821	31,910
Newark, N. J......	8,610,000	253,666	97,116,004	43,558,002	1,657,281	838,691
New Bedford, Mass.	1,178,000	392,100	26,750,202	21,359,100	457,355	340,332
Newburgh, N. Y..	334,600	322,450	11,821,025	8,080,000	81,566	65,838
N. Brunswick, N. J.	113,380	40,000	7,000,000	5,000,000	220,944	96,853
Newburyport, Mass.	407,666	214,725	7,725,617	7,214,200	150,408	161,357
New Haven, Conn..	936,081	175,000	46,000,000	31,932,292	437,000	159,661
New Orleans, La...	22,638,779	13,858,413	119,000,000	126,000,000	1,780,000	1,890,000
Newport, R. I......	962,000	94,500	7,509,860	4,085,152	122,000	47,440
Newton, Mass.......	1,248,000	381,000	28,200,965	14,100,482	392,201	196,101
New York, N. Y...	149,357,557	33,651,683	1,111,054,343	736,989,908	31,109,521	16,950,763
Norfolk, Va.........	2,265,199	1,420,345	10,210,963	5,597,070	246,034	96,967
Northampton, Mass.	617,873	463,906	7,645,300	3,882,650	117,841	58,929
Oshkosh, Wis,......	61,000	170,000	5,146,640	787,604	131,603	68,302
Oswego, N. Y......	1,256	419	7,083,067	3,566,531	373,396	181,648
Paterson, N. J......	1,357,500	450,000	23,329,946	17,500,000	591,246	350,000
Peabody, Mass......	342,000	343,000	6,151,950	5,075,975	91,570	45,755
Peoria, Ill	736,500	454,122	14,300,860	3,400,000	27,500	22,000
Philadelphia, Pa...	66,169,271	35,140,335	595,413,378	162,831,629	11,739,364	6,513,273
Pittsburgh, Pa......	13,772,466	2,854,482	122,942,173	100,116,000	1,108,543	314,879
Portland, Me......	6,073,300	2,473,356	30,660,358	29,004,115	791,876	741,568
Providence, R. I...	9,632,246	989,983	121,065,200	83,443,800	1,753,415	781,418
Quincy, Ill.........	1,666,376	500,000	9,715,140	8,075,503	176,814	76,717
Racine, Wis........	230,000	800,000	4,200,000	2,500,000	125,000	30,000
Rahway, N. J......	1,161,500	387,166				
Reading, Pa........	1,171,446	625,909	35,598,667	4,000,000	161,981	70,000
Richmond, Va......	4,492,195	2,071,642	42,018,077	2,203,509	630,271	320,797
Rochester, N. Y....	5,543,186	1,127,000	55,664,970	11,000,000	1,010,660	349,209
Rockford, Ill.......	265,565	87,000	4,100,000	1,432,797	121,776	53,864
Rock Island, Ill....	263,000	81,481	4,035,000	876,602	42,000	12,757
St. Joseph, Mo.....	1,380,900	460,300	20,000,000	10,000,000		
St. Louis, Mo......	16,318,000	5,671,500	162,444,490	108,565,391	2,783,072	1,222,433
St. Paul, Minn......	1,882,500	508,158	25,694,000	9,000,000	256,940	68,219
Salem, Mass........	1,509,000	1,473,925	26,044,532	13,022,266	403,252	301,626
San Francisco, Cal.	3,893,801	8,831,797	263,532,859	76,206,437	4,309,952	2,379,513
Savannah, Ga......	3,600,640	1,900,313				
Somerville, Mass...	1,571,854	612,063	26,573,400	13,296,700	504,757	232,378
Springfield, Ill....	854,875	309,276	5,693,156	7,592,877	163,774	176,498
Springfield, Mass..	1,981,000	347,160	33,109,456	14,997,020	497,453	221,423
Springfield, O......	103,196	23,700	9,673,976	4,616,080	101,465	46,996
Syracuse, N. Y.....	1,316,000	86,500	35,029,350	10,773,541	480,445	119,112
Taunton, Mass.....	273,250	335,329	16,890,271	8,445,135	243,420	121,626
Toledo, O...........	2,928,754	976,951				
Trenton, N. J.......	493,648	164,649	17,744,072	8,874,536	266,333	125,000
Troy, N. Y.........	846,144	856,289	13,539,700	14,710,081	632,146	360,574
Utica, N. Y........	785,000	750,000	25,888,155	4,375,615	184,752	103,799
Waltham, Mass.....	467,350	190,000	9,526,918	4,763,459	109,840	54,920
Washington, D. C..	23,000,000	8,333,333				
Waukegan, Ill......	No debt.	6,000	800,000	400,000	25,000	30,000
Westfield, Mass....	387,000	174,509	7,544,369	3,772,191	102,761	51,381
Wilmington, Del...	1,078,650	378,333	26,603,383	19,442,000	261,508	113,115
Winchester, Mass..	234,370	36,553	3,752,889	1,876,444	59,818	29,909
Worcester, Mass...	2,939,700	2,623,140	43,919,397	22,599,850	634,672	297,665
Total..............	644,378,663	221,312,000	6,175,082,158	3,451,619,391	112,711,275	64,060,093

Increase of debt, about 200 per cent, average.
Increase of annual taxation, about 83 per cent.
Increase of valuation, about 75 per cent.
Increase of population, about 33 per cent (estimated).
Population and value of property have by no means kept pace with debt.

BANKS IN THE UNITED STATES OTHER THAN NATIONAL.

From the Report of the Comptroller of the Currency, December 1, 1877.

Number of State Banks, Savings Banks, Trust Companies, and Private Bankers, and their Average Capital and Deposits, by States, for the six months ending May 31, 1877.

STATES AND TERRITORIES.	No. of banks	Capital.	Deposits.	STATES AND TERRITORIES.	No. of banks	Capital.	Deposits.
		$	$			$	$
Maine	66	173,905	26,499,219	Ohio	257	6,331,477	16,640,560
N. Hampshire	72	52,333	30,896,234	Cincinnati	23	2,078,549	9,016,478
Vermont	21	335,000	8,107,445	Cleveland	9	836,290	12,767,959
Massachusetts	167	819,339	162,477,183	Indiana	146	5,696,955	11,128,830
Boston	64	3,127,387	88,716,005	Illinois	319	5,483,644	17,299,692
Rhode Island	58	3,894,673	53,031,370	Chicago	42	4,836,153	15,196,791
Connecticut	109	2,869,642	82,893,262	Michigan	145	2,605,763	4,914,596
				Detroit	18	1,240,932	5,870,285
N.E. States	557	11,272,273	452,620,717	Wisconsin	90	1,389,348	8,765,813
				Milwaukee	12	672,065	6,328,969
New York	336	11,061,720	148,889,703	Iowa	279	5,178,643	8,730,477
N. Y. City	466	45,785,796	271,948,412	Minnesota	71	1,168,905	2,508,655
Albany	14	637,000	12,529,737	Missouri	180	3,806,229	11,223,423
New Jersey	65	2,170,838	35,457,184	Saint Louis	46	7,530,583	22,691,281
Pennsylvania	346	12,216,780	39,203,675	Kansas	114	1,725,224	3,116,289
Philadelphia	60	2,091,742	31,884,459	Nebraska	39	465,664	1,184,932
Pittsburg	41	5,018,826	14,616,683				
Delaware	10	717,411	1,780,859	West. States	1,790	50,909,484	152,325,000
Maryland	15	623,378	566,984				
Baltimore	40	4,104,003	25,023,652	Oregon	8	610,724	1,840,112
Dist. of Col	1	5,917	7,008	California	91	12,110,922	41,522,335
Washington	10	595,359	3,657,830	S. Francisco	33	26,902,567	65,865,076
				Colorado	30	588,858	971,936
Mid. States	1,404	85,028,770	585,566,186	Nevada	19	417,039	1,545,409
				Utah	8	179,521	587,894
Virginia	78	3,407,110	6,809,858	New Mexico	4	5,667	36,342
West Virginia	24	1,455,900	3,917,534	Wyoming	4	55,489	98,987
N. Carolina	14	574,451	872,287	Idaho	3	56,507	16,182
S. Carolina	19	1,003,105	1,095,859	Dakota	8	34,167	140,321
Georgia	66	4,392,147	4,363,519	Montana	8	103,037	93,800
Florida	5	47,000	271,057	Washington	4	222,312	317,696
Alabama	20	1,034,733	1,747,031	Arizona	1	10,000	5,000
Mississippi	28	1,264,396	1,413,083				
Louisiana	2	54,000	49,915	Pacif. States and Territo.	226	41,296,810	112,550,090
New Orleans	23	3,558,192	7,310,099				
Texas	107	3,494,002	4,891,428	Totals	4,501	223,503,171	1,351,867,650
Arkansas	15	258,333	376,619				
Kentucky	73	7,279,957	6,626,535				
Louisville	17	5,404,361	6,041,033				
Tennessee	33	1,768,147	3,019,790				
South.States	524	34,995,834	48,805,597				

GERMANY'S DEMONETIZATION OF SILVER.

THE demonetization of silver in Germany was provided for by the mint act on the 23d of May, 1873, providing that on the 1st of October, 1876, the old silver currency should cease to be a legal tender, and fixing the relative value of gold to silver in the conversion (or adoption of the single gold standard) at 15.675 to one. In January, 1876, an act was passed giving the Federal Council power to reduce the remaining silver coinage to the rank of subsidiary or token coins, by limiting the legal-tender power to the amount of twenty marks, or five dollars. This power was exercised in November, 1876, so far as concerned the two-thaler and one-sixth-thaler fractional pieces, which were demonetized after February 15th, 1877. Under this provision, large amounts of silver coins have been withdrawn from circulation in Germany; the total silver shipments to Great Britain were to the amount of $113,000,000 up to November, 1877. But the most important step, the demonetization and withdrawal of the silver thalers, of which a large number, variously estimated at from sixty to one hundred millions of dollars, are still in circulation, remains to be taken. About $93,000,000 of the old silver has been coined into new silver marks, and retained in the country. Late in 1876, a resolution was passed by the *Bundesrath* for increasing the limit of the silver-token coinage, which by the coinage law of 1873 was to be struck at the mint, to fifteen marks per head of the population. Objections, however, were raised by the adherents of the single gold standard, and, owing to the strong feeling in the *Reichsrath* against it, the Imperial Government decided not to submit it to that body.

Mainly from the Journal Télégraphique.

THE SUBMARINE TELEGRAPH CABLES OF THE WORLD IN 1877.

THE first submarine telegraph cable was laid in 1851, between Dover and Calais, and was twenty-five nautical miles in length. From this small commencement the system of submarine telegraphs has grown until at the present time it embraces a total of 569 cables, with a length of 65,190 nautical miles, and 72,462 miles of conductors. Of these, 149 cables, with 59,547 nautical miles length, are owned and operated by private or incorporated companies; and 420 cables, with 5,643 nautical miles length, are owned and operated by government telegraph administrations.

CABLES OWNED BY COMPANIES.	NUMBER OF CABLES.	LENGTH (in nautical miles).	
		OF CABLES.	OF CONDUC-TORS.
1 Submarine Telegraph Company................	13	801	3,717
2 Vereinigte Deutsche Telegraphen-Gesellschaft.......	2	235	900
3 Hamburger-Helgolander Telegraphen-Gesellschaft......	1	32	32
4 Scilly Telegraph Company........................	1	27	27
5 Direct Spanish Telegraph Company..............	3	748	748
6 Mediterranean Extension Telegraph Company..........	3	198	198
7 Black Sea Telegraph Company....................	1	865	2,535
8 Indo-European Telegraph Company...................	1	8	24
9 Great Northern Telegraph Company..................	13	4,107	4,219
10 Eastern Telegraph Company.....................	33	14,503	14,548
11 Eastern Extension, Australasia and China Telegraph Co.	9	7,381	7,381
12 Anglo-American Telegraph Company..............	17	12,315	12,315
13 Direct United States Cable Company..................	2	3,040	3,040
14 Brazilian Submarine Telegraph Company..............	3	3,366	3,866
15 International Ocean Telegraph Company..............	4	490	490
16 Cuba Submarine Telegraph Company..............	3	940	940
17 West India and Panama Telegraph Company....... ...	13	3,970	3,970
18 Central American Telegraph Company.................	2	1,090	1,090
19 Western and Brazilian Telegraph Company............	9	3,750	3,750
20 River Plate Telegraph Company...................	1	32	64
21 West Coast of America Telegraph Company...........	6	1,669	1,669
	149	59,847	65,533

CABLES UNDER GOVERNMENT ADMINISTRATION.	NUMBER OF CABLES.	LENGTH (in nautical miles).	
		OF CABLES.	OF CONDUC-TORS.
1 Austro-Hungary.........................	23	86	97
2 Denmark............................	29	101	883
3 France..............................	26	673	673
4 Germany............................	21	149	267
5 Great Britain and Ireland.............	49	601	1,333
6 Greece..............................	2	4	4
7 Italy...............................	12	218	221
8 Netherlands..........................	13	37	55
9 Norway.............................	123	1,433	1,433
10 Russia..............................	3	63	71
11 Spain..............................	6	233	337
12 Switzerland..........................	4	23	23
13 Turkey.............................	11	143	146
14 British India, Indo-European Telegraph Department....	6	1,721	1,721
15 " " Indian Administration	2	60	60
16 Japan..............................	11	73	73
17 Dutch Indies........................	1	56	56
18 New Zealand.........................	1	20	20
	420	5,643	6,929

	WHEN LAID.	CABLES ACROSS THE ATLANTIC OCEAN.		LENGTH (in miles).	WEIGHT OF CABLE (per mile) Tons.	GREATEST DEPTH (in fathoms).
		FROM	TO			
1*	1858	Ireland	Newfoundland (not now working).	2,036	1.00	2,400
2	1865-6	Ireland	Newfoundland........................	2,196	1.75	2,424
3	1866	Ireland	Newfoundland........................	1,896	1.5	2,424
4	1869	Brest, France	Duxbury, Mass. (via Newfoundl'd)	2,584	1.6	2,760
5	1873	Ireland	Newfoundland........................	1,900	....	....
6	1874-5	Ireland	Rye Beach, N. H. (via Newfound-land). Cost, $6,055,000............	3,060	....	....

TELEGRAPHS OF THE WORLD IN 1877.

	No. of Offices.	Length of Lines, Miles.		No. of Offices.	Length of Lines, Miles.
Argentine Republic.....	182	5,339	India, British..........	225	15,705
Australia and Polynesia.	658	22,039	Italy............	1,408	45,557
Austria-Hungary........	2,924	23,148	Japan	1	1,840
Belgium	613	3,160	Mexico	194	5,700
Bolivia	15	475	Netherlands............	335	2,765
Brazil	89	3,510	Norway	197	4,827
Canada, Dominion of...	830	10,995	Persia................	46	2,458
Chili..................	55	2,650	Peru................	25	6:8
Colombia............ ..	36	1,227	Portugal....	144	2,190
Costa Rica..............	16	220	Roumania........... ..	165	2,487
Denmark	178	1,591	Russia...............	1,691	57,333
Ecuador............. ..	10	210	Spain....	264	7,510
Egypt	78	3,980	Sweden............	628	6,094
France.................	4,406	33,895	Switzerland	1,053	4,015
Germany...............	5,109	24,103	Turkey	401	17,618
Great Britain & Ireland.	5,375	*25,206	United States of America	8,829	*94,714
Greece.................	69	992	Uruguay...............	......	1,300
Guatemala........	42	1,226			

* This does not include the railway lines of telegraph, of which no statement is published.

GROWTH OF THE TELEGRAPH IN THE UNITED STATES.

In 1866, the Western Union Telegraph Company owned and operated 37,380 miles of line, with 2250 telegraph offices. Ten years later, in July, 1877, the company had 76,955 miles of line, with 7503 offices. In 1877, the Atlantic and Pacific Telegraph Company was consolidated with the Western Union, adding its 17,759 miles of line to the former, making 94,714 miles of inland telegraph in the United States, besides private, railway, and government lines, length not given.

PUBLIC DEBT OF THE UNITED STATES, 1791-1877.

Statement of Outstanding Principal of the Public Debt of the United States on the 1st of January of each Year from 1791 to 1842, inclusive; and on the 1st of July of each Year from 1843 to 1877, inclusive.

From the Annual Report of the Secretary of the Treasury on the Finances.

1791......	$75,463,476 52	1820.......	$91,015,566 15	1849......	$63,061,858 69
1792......	77,227,924 66	1821.......	89,987,427 66	1850......	63,452,773 55
1793......	80,352,634 04	1822.......	93,546,676 98	1851......	68,304,796 02
1794......	78,427,404 77	1823.......	90,875,877 28	1852......	66,199,341 71
1795......	80,747,587 39	1824.......	90,269,777 77	1853......	59,803,117 70
1796......	83,762,172 07	1825.......	83,788,432 71	1854......	42,242,222 42
1797......	82,064,479 33	1826.......	81,054,059 99	1855......	35,586,858 56
1798......	79,228,529 12	1827.......	73,987,357 20	1856......	31,972,537 90
1799......	78,408,669 77	1828.......	67,475,043 87	1857......	28,699,831 85
1800......	82,976,294 35	1829.......	58,421,413 67	1858......	44,911,881 03
1801.. ...	83,038,050 80	1830.......	48,565,406 50	1859......	58,496,837 88
1802......	86,712,632 25	1831.......	39,123,191 68	1860......	64,842,287 88
1803......	77,054,686 30	1832.......	24,322,235 18	1861......	90,580,873 72
1804......	86,427,120 88	1833.......	7,001,098 83	1862......	524,176,412 13
1805......	82,312,150 50	1834.......	4,760,082 08	1863......	1,119,772,138 63
1806......	75,723,270 66	1835.......	37,513 05	1864......	1,815,784,370 57
1807......	69,218,398 64	1836.......	336,957 83	1865......	2,680,647,869 74
1808......	65,196,317 97	1837.......	3,308,124 07	1866......	2,773,236,173 69
1809... ..	57,023,192 09	1838.......	10,434,221 14	1867......	2,678,126,103 87
1810......	53,173,217 52	1839.......	3,573,343 82	1868......	2,611,687,851 19
1811......	48,005,587 76	1840.......	5,250,875 54	1869......	2,588,452,213 94
1812......	45,209,737 90	1841.......	13,594,480 73	1870......	2,480,672,427 81
1813......	55,962,827 57	1842.......	20,601,226 28	1871:.....	2,353,211,332 32
1814......	81,487,846 24	1843.......	32,742,922 00	1872......	2,253,251,078 78
1815......	99,833,660 15	1844.......	23,461,652 50	1873	2,234,482,743 20
1816......	127,334,936 74	1845.......	15,925,303 01	1874......	2,251,690,218 43
1817......	123,491,965 16	1846.......	15,550,202 97	1875......	2,232,284,281 95
1818......	103,466,633 83	1847.......	38,826,534 77	1876......	2,180,394,817 15
1819......	95,529,648 28	1848.......	47,044,862 23	1877......	2,060,158,228 26

LENGTH OF SESSIONS OF CONGRESS, 1789-1877.

No. of Congress	No. of Session	Time of Session.	No. of Congress	No. of Session	Time of Session.
1st	1st..March	4, 1789--Sept. 29, 1789	25th	1st..Sept.	4, 1837—Oct. 16, 1837
	2d ..Jan.	4, 1790—Aug. 12, 1790		2d ..Dec.	4, 1837—July 9, 1838
	3d ..Dec.	6, 1790—Mar. 3, 1791		3d ..Dec.	3, 1838—March 3, 1839
2d	1st..Oct.	24, 1791—May 8, 1792	26th	1st..Dec.	2, 1839—July 21, 1840
	2d . Nov.	5, 1792—Mar. 2, 1793		2d ..Dec.	7, 1840—March 3, 1841
3d	1st..Dec.	2, 1793—June 9, 1794	27th	1st. May	31, 1841—Sept. 13, 1841
	2d ..Nov.	3, 1794—March 3, 1795		2d ..Dec.	6, 1841—Aug. 31, 1842
4th	1st..Dec.	7, 1795—June 1, 1796		3d ..Dec.	5, 1842—March 3, 1843
	2d ..Dec.	5, 1796—March 3, 1797	28th	1st..Dec.	4, 1843—June 17, 1844
5th	1st..May	15, 1797—July 10, 1797		2d ..Dec.	2, 1844—March 3, 1845
	2d ..Nov.	13, 1797—July 16, 1798	29th	1st..Dec.	1, 1845—Aug. 10, 1846
	3d ..Dec.	3, 1798—March 3, 1799		2d ..Dec.	7, 1846—March 3, 1847
6th	1st..Dec.	2, 1799—May 14, 1800	30th	1st..Dec.	6, 1847—Aug. 14, 1848
	2d ..Nov.	17, 1800—March 3, 1801		2d ..Dec.	4, 1848—March 3, 1849
7th	1st..Dec.	7, 1801—May 3, 1802	31st	1st..Dec.	3, 1849—Sept. 30, 1850
	2d ..Dec.	6, 1802—March 3, 1803		2d ..Dec.	2, 1850—March 3, 1851
8th	1st..Oct.	17, 1803—Mar. 27, 1804	32d	1st..Dec.	1, 1851—Aug. 31, 1852
	2d ..Nov.	5, 1804—March 3, 1805		2d ..Dec.	6, 1852—March 3, 1853
9th	1st..Dec.	2, 1805—April 21, 1806	33d	1st..Dec.	5, 1853—Aug. 7, 1854
	2d ..Dec.	1, 1806—March 3, 1807		2d ..Dec.	4, 1854—March 3, 1855
10th	1st..Oct.	26, 1807--April 25, 1808	34th	1st..Dec.	3, 1855—Aug. 18, 1856
	2d ..Nov.	7, 1808—March 3, 1809		2d ..Aug.	21, 1856—Aug. 30, 1856
11th	1st..May	22, 1809—June 28, 1809		3d ..Dec.	1, 1856—March 3, 1857
	2d ..Nov.	27, 1809—May 1, 1810	35th	1st..Dec.	7, 1857—June 14, 1858
	3d . Dec.	3, 1810—March 3, 1811		2d ..Dec.	6, 1858—March 3, 1859
12th	1st..Nov.	4, 1811—July 6, 1812	36th	1st..Dec.	5, 1859—June 25, 1860
	2d ..Nov.	2, 1812—March 3, 1813		2d ..Dec.	3, 1860—March 4, 1861
13th	1st..May	24, 1813—Aug. 2, 1813	37th	1st..July	4, 1861—Aug. 6, 1861
	2d ..Dec.	6, 1813—April 18, 1814		2d ..Dec.	2, 1861—July 17, 1862
	3d ..Sept.	19, 1814—March 3, 1815		3d ..Dec.	1, 1862—March 4, 1863
14th	1st..Dec.	4, 1815—April 30, 1816	38th	1st..Dec.	7, 1863—July 4, 1864
	2d ..Dec.	2, 1816—March 3, 1817		2d ..Dec.	5, 1864—March 4, 1865
15th	1st..Dec.	1, 1817—April 20, 1818	39th	1st..Dec.	4, 1865—July 28, 1866
	2d ..Nov.	16, 1818—March 3, 1819		2d ..Dec.	3, 1866—March 4, 1867
16th	1st..Dec.	6, 1819—May 15, 1820	40th	1st..March	4, 1867—Mar. 30, 1867
	2d ..Nov.	13, 1820—March 3, 1821		" ..July	3, 1867—July 20, 1867
17th	1st..Dec.	3, 1821—May 8, 1822		" ..Nov.	21, 1867—Dec. 2, 1867
	2d ..Dec.	2, 1822—March 3, 1823		2d ..Dec.	2, 1867—July 27, 1868
18th	1st. Dec.	1, 1823—May 27, 1824		3d . Dec.	7, 1868—March 4, 1869
	2d ..Dec.	6, 1824—March 3, 1825	41st	1st..March	4, 1869—April 23, 1869
19th	1st..Dec.	5, 1825—May 22, 1826		2d ..Dec.	6, 1869—July 15, 1870
	2d ..Dec.	4, 1826—March 3, 1827		3d ..Dec.	5, 1870—March 4, 1871
20th	1st..Dec.	3, 1827—May 26, 1828	42d	1st..March	4, 1871—April 20, 1871
	2d ..Dec.	1, 1828—March 3, 1829		2d ..Dec.	4, 1871—June 10, 1872
21st	1st..Dec.	7, 1829—May 31, 1830		3d ..Dec.	2, 1872—March 4, 1873
	2d ..Dec.	6, 1830—March 3, 1831	43d	1st..Dec.	1, 1873—June 23, 1874
22d	1st..Dec.	5, 1831—July 16, 1832		2d ..Dec.	7, 1874—March 4, 1875
	2d ..Dec.	3, 1832—March 3, 1833	44th	1st..Dec.	6, 1875—Aug. 15, 1876
23d	1st..Dec.	2, 1833—June 30, 1834		2d ..Dec.	4, 1876—March 4, 1877
	2d ..Dec.	1, 1834—March 3, 1835	45th	1st..Oct.	15, 1877—Dec. 3, 1877
24th	1st..Dec.	7, 1835—July 4, 1836		2d ..Dec.	3, 1877—........ 1878
	2d ..Dec.	5, 1836—March 3, 1837		3d ..Dec.	2, 1878—March 4, 1879

NOTE.—To determine the years covered by a given Congress, double the number of the Congress, and add the product to 1789; the result will be the year in which the Congress closed. Thus, the 35th Congress = 70 + 1789 = 1859, that being the year which terminated the 35th Congress, on the 4th of March. To find the number of a Congress sitting in any given year, subtract 1789 from the year; if the result is an even number, half that number will give the Congress, of which the year in question will be the closing year. If the result is an odd number, add one to it, and half the result will give the Congress, of which the year in question will be the first year.

TABLES OF TEMPERATURE IN AMERICA.

From the Smithsonian Contributions to Knowledge: Tables, Distribution and Variations of the Atmospheric Temperature in the United States; edited by C. A. Schott, Washington, 1876.

I.—THE UNITED STATES.

PLACES.	Lati- tude.	Heig't Fect.	Spri'g	Sum- mer.	Au- tumn.	Win- ter.	Year, Mean.	No.of Years and Mos.
	° ′		°	°	°	°	°	
ALABAMA :								
Green Springs	32 50	500	63.18	78.45	62.35	46.29	62.57	10 0
Huntsville	34 45	600	59.96	75.62	59.80	42.15	59.38	13 0
Mobile	30 41	15	66.87	79.00	66.27	52.43	68.14	10 0
ALASKA :								
Sitka	57 03	20	39.91	53.09	43.90	31.28	42.05	16 11
ARIZONA :								
Camp Goodwin	32 52	......	65.52	84.50	67.89	46.85	66.19	3 10
" Tucson	32 13	... ..	67.49	85.52	71.46	50.24	68.68	4 0
ARKANSAS :								
Little Rock	34 40	... ..	60.76	81.57	64.29	44.21	62.71	2 1
Washington	33 44	660	62.20	78.19	61.20	44.61	61.56	22 1
CALIFORNIA :								
Benicia Barracks	38 03	64	57.73	67.00	61.59	48.75	58.77	15 7
Fort Yuma	32 46	200	73.40	92.07	75.66	57.96	74.77	14 11
San Diego	32 42	150	60.14	69 67	64.53	54.00	62.11	20 10
San Francisco	37 48	130	54.96	58.04	57.81	50.09	55.23	11 2
COLORADO :								
Fort Garland	37 32	8365	42.93	64.39	43.49	20.63	42.86	15 3
CONNECTICUT :								
Hartford	41 46	60	47.89	69.75	51.70	29.89	49.81	16 7
New Haven	41 18	45	46.76	69 63	51.28	28.32	49.00	86 0
DAKOTA :								
Fort Abercrombie	46 27	......	38.66	70.94	43.81	7.05	40.34	10 1
" Randall	43 01	1245	43.28	74.61	49.06	20.93	46.97	12 8
DELAWARE :								
Fort Delaware	39 35	10	51.70	75.23	57.61	34.23	54.09	18 10
Wilmington	39 44	115	52.74	73.56	53.64	31.71	52.91	1 10
DISTRICT OF COLUMBIA :								
Washington	33 51	75	55 77	76.33	56.43	36.11	56.16	12 3
FLORIDA :								
Ft. Barancas (n'r Pensacola)	30 21	20	68.41	81.60	69.58	54.37	68.49	20 2
St. Augustine	29 54	25	68.69	80.36	71.90	58.25	69.80	25 4
Jacksonville	30 20	20	69.27	80.98	70.04	55.62	68.98	12 4
Key West	24 33	10	75.85	83.35	78.55	70.44	77.05	26 6
GEORGIA :								
Athens	33 58	850	61.15	75.74	60.77	46.06	60.93	6 6
Atlanta	33 45	1050	58.27	74.87	58.44	41.86	58.36	5 2
Augusta	33 29	150	64.25	79.49	62.63	46.82	63.80	7 5
Savannah	32 05	42	67.06	80.61	66.81	52.56	66.76	26 1
IDAHO :								
Fort Boisé	43 40	......	52.03	75.04	52.97	29.81	52.46	5 10
ILLINOIS :								
Augusta	40 12	500	50.33	72.83	52.66	27.67	50.87	26 9
Chicago	41 51	600	43.55	66.76	48.82	24.78	45.85	17 3
Highland	38 44	620	56.55	77.60	56.60	34.13	56.24	15 1
Manchester	39 31	683	51.16	73.90	53.34	28.89	51.82	15 6
Ottawa	41 20	500	47.07	72.05	51.22	25.39	48.92	18 9
Peoria	40 43	512	50.63	74.46	52.94	27.40	51.36	14 9
Springfield	39 48	550	48.37	74.02	48.94	27.62	49.74	5 7
INDIANA '								
Aurora	39 04	709	51.98	75.61	53.90	30.98	53.09	5 0
Indianapolis	39 47	698	49.34	72.61	51.96	28.71	50.66	6 5
New Harmony	38 10	350	54.85	75.92	55 87	34.25	55.22	19 5
Richmond	39 50	850	50.02	71.79	52.52	29.16	50.87	12 3
Vevay	38 45	525	54.46	76.41	55.38	32.48	54.68	5 11
INDIAN TERRITORY :								
Fort Gibson	35 48	560	61.08	79.13	61.44	40.25	60.48	29 10
IOWA :								
Council Bluffs	41 16	1327	50.84	75.48	51.46	22.06	49.96	6 0
Davenport	41 30	737	45.86	71.60	49.46	22.42	47.33	9 3
Des Moines City	41 36	780	49.99	71.80	48.59	25.39	48.94	8 10
Dubuque	42 30	680	47.33	71.71	40.16	22.55	47.69	18 10
Keokuk	40 25	600	50.09	74.77	54.05	29.87	52.07	2 5
Muscatine	41 26	596	47.03	69.08	48.81	22.99	46.98	27 6

TABLES OF TEMPERATURE IN AMERICA—(Continued).

PLACES.	Latitude.	Heig't Feet.	Spr'g	Summer.	Autumn.	Winter.	Year, Mean.	No. of years & mos.
KANSAS :	° '		°	°	°	°	°	
Fort Leavenworth	39 21	896	53.69	75.24	54.35	29.35	53.16	39 11
Lawrence.................	38 58	850	53.43	75.82	53.08	31.64	53.49	7 9
Leavenworth City..........	39 15	896	50.87	74.24	52.02	28.69	51.45	7 6
KENTUCKY :								
Danville.................	37 40	900	56.28	75.58	58.56	37.84	57.07	12 7
Louisville................	38 18	450	55.71	73.56	55.79	37.34	55.70	4 6
Newport Barracks..........	39 05	500	53.82	75.06	50.09	34.14	54.78	23 0
Paris......................	38 13	810	51.54	72.75	53.06	32.45	52.45	4 0
LOUISIANA :								
Baton Rouge	30 26	41	68.90	81.36	68.13	54.20	68.15	28 0
Monroe................. ..	32 31	100	71.53	80.95	50.30	43.87	63.91	10 0
New Orleans..............	29 56	25	69.37	81.08	69.80	56.00	69.06	32 9
MAINE :								
Bath......	43 55	50	41.96	65.36	47.62	23.88	44.71	10 7
Brunswick.................	43 54	74	42.26	65.11	47.59	22.63	44.40	51 3
Portland..................	43 39	50	40.11	63.73	46.49	21.69	43.00	37 3
MARYLAND :								
Annapolis.................	38 58	20	52.33	75.71	57.53	35.95	55.38	13 10
Baltimore.................	39 16	36	53.01	75.08	57.04	34.50	54.91	36 0
Frederick City.............	39 24	274	51.10	73.40	54.76	33.11	53.09	15 6
MASSACHUSETTS :								
Amherst (College)..........	42 22	267	44.17	67.58	47.09	24.15	45.97	17 6
Boston.....................	42 21	83	45.61	68.68	51.04	28.08	48.35	38 5
Cambridge.	42 23	60	44.93	69.47	50.45	26.96	47.95	48 5
New Bedford.....	41 39	90	44.80	66.95	52.27	30.21	44.56	58 1
Newburyport	42 48	46	42.45	66.69	49.96	24.91	46.00	6 1
Williamstown (Will.College)	42 43	686	43.44	67.25	47.36	23.28	45.33	36 0
Worcester.................	42 16	528	45.01	68.16	49.96	25.67	47.20	31 9
MICHIGAN :								
Detroit...................	42 20	597	45.46	68.05	48.83	26.61	47.24	30 3
Fort Mackinac.............	45 51	728	37.06	62 26	44 92	19.84	41.02	27 6
Grand Rapids....	43 00	780	44.69	69.75	48.75	24.62	46.90	11 3
Lansing................	42 46	895	45.90	68.43	47.63	24.96	46.55	7 3
MINNESOTA :								
Fort Snelling	41 53	820	43.12	71.05	46.12	15.79	44.52	42 2
Minneapolis...............	44 53	856	40.12	68.34	45.33	12.87	41.67	6 2
St. Paul.	44 56	800	41.29	68.03	44.98	15.09	42.32	8 5
MISSISSIPPI :								
Columbus.................	33 31	227	62.18	78.90	62.16	45.50	62.19	15 9
Jefferson Barracks...	38 28	472	56.37	76.84	56.03	33.96	55.79	32 11
Natchez..................	31 34	264	65.49	79.81	65.46	50.43	65.30	15 5
Vicksburg...........	32 23	350	65.79	80.52	65.54	50.45	65.57	8 11
MISSOURI :								
St. Joseph.................	39 45	......	52.80	74.74	51.12	34.32	53.24	2 1
St. Louis.................	38 37	481	55.09	76.12	55.88	32.90	55.00	41 0
MONTANA :								
Fort Shaw.................	47 30	6000	43.22	67.50	47.74	25.41	46.47	3 4
Helena City....	46 37	4150	33.76	70.28	48.94	19.16	43.04	1 7
NEBRASKA :								
Fort Kearney..............	40 38	2360	46.53	72 41	49.26	21.91	47.53	15 11
Omaha..................	41 15	1300	48.40	74.26	51.10	23.36	49.23	4 0
NEVADA :								
Fort Churchill.............	39 17	4234	52.45	75.18	51.36	31.55	54.13	7 10
NEW HAMPSHIRE :								
Concord...................	43 12	374	43.62	67.52	48.64	22.81	45.65	22 2
Hanover.................	43 42	530	40.87	65.15	44.76	19.17	42.40	20 0
Manchester...............	42 59	300	47.80	70.02	51.14	25.90	48.72	14 1
Portsmouth...............	43 05	38	44.02	66.99	47.88	25.15	46.01	9 11
NEW JERSEY :								
Burlington	41 04	60	49 71	72.01	54.81	31.22	51.94	13 3
Newark...................	40 44	35	47.86	70.35	53 04	30.75	50.50	24 5
Trenton...................	40 14	60	50.46	73.03	54.90	32.66	52.76	11 0
NEW MEXICO :								
Fort Craig................	33 36	4576	61.86	80.10	59.88	39.62	60.37	13 10
Santa Fé..................	35 41	6846	50.06	70.50	51.34	30.23	50.54	18 6
NEW YORK :								
Albany....................	42 39	130	46.54	70.43	49.56	25.26	47.95	45 11
Auburn...................	42 55	650	44.57	68.43	48.80	25.88	46.80	28 0
Buffalo..................	42 53	600	42.92	67.73	50.33	26.58	46.89	12 7
Ithaca....................	42 25	417	46.48	68.29	49.51	28.86	48.29	20 10
Kingston..................	41 55	188	48.70	70.30	51.28	28.29	49.64	19 10
Malone...................	44 50	703	43.17	64.19	44.98	21.31	43.41	3 0
Newburgh.................	41 31	74	47.81	70.67	52.92	28.57	49.99	27 1

TABLES OF TEMPERATURE IN AMERICA—(*Continued*).

PLACES.	Lati-tude.	Heig't Feet.	Spri'g	Summer.	Autumn.	Winter.	Year, Mean.	No. of years & mos.
NEW YORK—(*Continued*):	° '		°	°	°	°	°	
New York	40 50	25	48.26	72.62	54.54	31.93	51.83	21 8
Utica	43 05	473	44 77	67.17	48.33	24.71	46.25	27 2
West Point	41 24	167	40.27	72.24	54.11	30.26	51.47	46 5
NORTH CAROLINA :								
Chapel Hill	35 58	.....	58.85	76.80	60.46	42.92	59.76	20 0
Raleigh	35 48	317	56.92	77.24	59.79	40.14	58.52	3 11
OHIO :								
Cincinnati	39 06	540	54.13	75.24	55.21	34.28	54.72	36 8
Cleveland	41 30	643	46.28	69.68	51.87	28.82	49.99	17 1
Columbus	39 57	834	53.56	74.44	50.95	34.22	53.29	3 0
Hillsboro	39 10	1150	50.01	70.44	51.64	30.52	50.65	32 4
Kelley's Island	41 36	587	45.46	71.33	53.24	28.52	49.64	11 9
Marietta	39 28	670	51.98	71.29	52.85	32.84	52.24	49 10
Oberlin	41 20	800	46.46	70.62	51.59	27.52	49.05	8 5
Steubenville	40 25	670	50.99	72.60	52.52	31.22	51.83	39 11
Toledo	41 40	604	46.90	70.20	50.83	28.88	49.20	13 10
OREGON :								
Astoria	46 11	52	48.72	59.52	52.41	39.35	50.00	18 3
Portland	45 30	45	50.12	67.72	54.85	40.23	53.23	2 0
PENNSYLVANIA :								
Alleghany	40 20	704	50.23	71.69	51.99	20.67	51.19	33 2
Gettysburg	39 49	624	49.83	71.62	51.19	29.88	50.13	24 2
Harrisburg	40 16	375	51.76	75.61	55.38	32.18	53.73	29 3
Philadelphia	39 56	36	50. 7	73. 0	54. 0	30. 5	52. 1	57 0
RHODE ISLAND :								
Newport	41 30	25	44.84	68.12	53.42	31.16	49.39	40 0
Providence	41 50	155	45.27	67.95	51.01	27.41	47.91	34 8
SOUTH CAROLINA .								
Aiken	33 32	565	61.32	77.86	61.96	45.82	61.61	8 8
Beaufort	32 26	14	62.47	80.67	......	48.47	....	1 5
Charleston	32 47	20	65.49	79.55	65.63	51.46	65.53	24 8
Columbia	34 02	315	61.93	77.89	62.79	45.48	62.03	4 11
TENNESSEE :								
Knoxville	35 56	1000	55.80	74.73	58.62	37.82	56.74	6 4
Lookout Mountain	35 00	1626	57.57	77.20	59.73	41.10	58.92	4 5
Memphis	35 08	262	60.86	79.53	60.32	42.12	60.71	11 3
Nashville	36 19	533	59.85	76.32	57.42	39.67	58.34	6 7
TEXAS :								
Austin	30 17	650	67.17	81.68	66.88	51.16	66.72	19 0
Galveston	29 18	30	69.35	83.73	70.92	53.51	69.38	8 1
San Antonio	29 25	600	70.48	83.73	71.56	52.74	69.29	2 4
UTAH :								
Great Salt Lake City	40 46	4260	49.93	73.57	53.56	30.38	51.86	9 0
VERMONT :								
Burlington	44 28	346	41.61	66.66	47.26	20.97	44.12	20 6
Middlebury	44 02	398	42.39	67.20	47.66	21.01	44.57	10 1
Montpelier	44 17	540	38.10	64.02	47.61	21.82	42.76	2 5
VIRGINIA :								
Alexandria	38 48	56	52.42	76.57	56.20	34.23	54.86	6 8
Fortress Monroe	37 00	8	57.84	77.07	61.92	41.77	59.52	45 5
Norfolk	36 51	20	56.50	76.53	61.43	41.57	59.01	25 0
Richmond	37 32	172	56.51	75.56	58.03	40.08	57.53	7 2
Staunton	38 00	1387	51.98	73.60	52.93	37.56	53.79	2 3
WASHINGTON TERRITORY :								
Fort Steilacoom	47 11	250	49.20	63.42	51.83	38.78	50.81	17 7
WEST VIRGINIA :								
Kanawha	38 53	.....	54.38	71.40	54.65	36.66	54.27	7 10
Romney	39 20	573	51.05	73.30	53.79	29.65	51.95	3 1
WISCONSIN :								
Green Bay	44 29	732	40 46	69.10	47.43	18.62	43.65	8 0
Janesville	42 41	780	44.75	70.43	48.25	20.84	46.07	8 6
Madison	43 05	1088	43.47	69.11	48.20	20.81	45.40	9 3
Milwaukee	43 04	604	43.04	67.02	48.96	24.00	45.75	26 7
WYOMING :								
Fort Bridger	41 20	6656	38.75	62.98	42.56	20.81	41.27	10 6
Fort Laramie	42 12	4472	46.98	72.59	49.39	29 31	49.56	17 9

NOTE.—The last column indicates the number of years covered by the observa-
tions. The temperatures are by the standard of Fahrenheit's thermometer.
    The figures in the second column indicate the elevation above the sea-level of
each place named in the table.

II.—NORTH AND SOUTH AMERICA.

NOTE.—The sign — indicates a temperature below Zero.

Places.	Lati-tude.	Heig't Feet.	Spring.	Sum-mer.	An-tumn.	Win-ter.	Year.	No. of Years and Mos.
BAHAMA ISLANDS :	° ′	°	°	°	°	°	°	
Nassau.................	25 05	80	78.62	84.50	80.55	74.70	79.50	3 11
BERMUDA ISLANDS :								
Bermuda...............	32 23	......	65.19	77.43	72.80	62.42	69.46	12 9
BRAZIL :								
Rio de Janeiro.........	—22 54	......	77.81	72.37	76.09	82.45	77.18	12 0
BRITISH NORTH AMERICA :								
Boothia Felix..........	69 59	......	— 5.30	38.04	9.69	—27.71	+ 3.68	2 6
Northumberland Sound.	76 52	......	— 3.18	33.12	4.15	—34.35	— 0.07	1 0
BUENOS AYRES :								
Buenos Ayres..........	—34 37	......	64.50	52.60	60.66	73.40	62.79	1 6
CARRIBBEAN ISLANDS :								
Antigua	17 09	......	77.77	80.63	81.73	77.37	79.38	1 0
Guadaloupe............	15 59	......	78.21	81.26	80.43	76.32	79.05	3 0
St. Thomas............	18 21	......	81.91	82.79	82.88	80.51	82.02	1 11
St. Vincent............	13 10	......	80.81	82.16	82.40	79.70	81.27	8 0
CHILI :								
Valparaiso...	—33 02	......	61.42	56.82	61.54	....	....	1 6
COSTA RICA :								
San José..............	9 54	3772	71.08	69.17	67.97	68.32	69.23	4 1
CUBA :								
Havana..............	23 09	......	78.88	83.94	79.73	73.66	79.05	11 3
ECUADOR :								
Quito..................	— 0 14	8970	60.96	60.08	63.50	59.72	60.89	2 3
GREENLAND :								
Godthaab.............	64 10	......	23.26	40.62	29.14	14.14	26.79	14 6
Upernavik.............	72 47	......	+ 6.95	38.07	20.22	—12.47	13.04	5 0
GUATEMALA :								
Guatemala..........	14 35	4961	68.00	67.28	66.03	63.72	66.20	4 0
GUIANA (BRITISH) :								
Demerara............	6 43	.. ...	81.17	81.33	81.33	79.00	80.71	1 6
GUIANA (DUTCH)								
Paramaribo.....	5 44	......	79.33	80.51	82.73	78.64	80.30	2 0
HONDURAS :								
Belize................	17 29	......	80.31	83 18	80.50	76.00	80.00	1 0
ICELAND :								
Reikjavik.............	64 00	......	37.04	53.54	37.94	29.18	39.43	14 6
JAMAICA :								
Kingston..............	18 00	50	78.07	81.00	79.75	76.16	78.77	1 0
MEXICO :								
Matamoras............	25 49	55	75.94	84.97	76.98	64.29	75.54	9 2
Mexico City..........	19 27	7663	64.30	63.51	59.90	56.68	61.10	3 11
Vera Cruz............	19 12	26	77.00	81.92	78 26	70.88	77.02	13 0
NEW BRUNSWICK :								
St. John.............	45 22	135	36.83	57.59	44.97	21.05	40.11	7 0
NEWFOUNDLAND :								
St. Johns.	47 34	170	36.73	57.52	45.45	25.07	41.20	7 1
NEW GRANADA :								
Aspinwall....	9 21	6	79.70	79.22	78.71	78.88	79.13	5 10
Bogota	4 36	8863	59.54	59.54	58.10	59.13	59.09	1 4
NOVA SCOTIA :								
Halifax	44 39	8	38.82	61.72	48.74	25.28	43.64	10 6
ONTARIO :								
Hamilton..............	43 15	300	41.34	69.79	50.45	27.35	48.03	13 6
Toronto...............	43 39	342	40.73	64.99	46.90	24.07	44.17	31 0
PERU :								
Lima..................	—12 03	530	78.44	68.06	69.14	77.60	73.31	2 0
PORTO RICO :								
Porto Rico.............	18 29	......	79.00	86.89	81.56	78.05	81.37	5 0
PRINCE EDWARD ISLAND :								
Charlottetown	46 12	......	39.00	65.73	47.59	23.34	43.93	1 0
QUEBEC :								
Montreal	45 31	57	43.71	70.77	46.94	17.19	44.65	27 0
Quebec...............	46 49	300	38.63	65.34	43.97	13.32	40.31	10 0
SAN DOMINGO :								
San Domingo..........	18 29	......	85.56	79.25	78.40	82.63	81.46	1 0
URUGUAY :								
Montevideo...	—34 54	......	68.00	57.33	64.67	77.33	66.83	1 0
VENEZUELA :								
Caracas...............	10 31	2900	71.65	73.00	72.71	69.71	71.77	1 2

RAINFALL IN THE UNITED STATES.

These figures of the average Annual Rainfall at the places named are from "Tables of the Precipitation of Rain and Snow in the United States," by C. A. Schott, published by the Smithsonian Institution, Washington, D. C.

Inches.	Inches.	Inches.
Baltimore 41.10	Fort Marcy, N. Mex..16.65	New Bedford, Mass ..41.42
Baton Rouge, La.....60.16	Ft.Massachusetts,Col.17.06	New Haven, Conn....44.43
Boston.... ....44.99	Fort Myers, Fla......56.55	New Orleans, La.....51.05
Buffalo, N. Y........33.84	Fort Randall, Dak....16.51	New York...........43.21
Burlington, Vt...... 34.15	Fort Smith, Ark......40.96	Penn Yan, N. Y.....28.42
Brunswick, Me...... 44.68	Fort Snelling, Minn..25.11	Peoria, Ill...........35.83
Charleston, S. C.....43.63	Ft.Towson, Ind. Ter..57.08	Philadelphia... .....44.05
Cleveland, Ohio.....37.61	Ft Vancouver,Wash.T.38.84	Pittsburgh, Pa........37.09
Cincinnati... ......44.87	Fortress Monroe 47.04	Providence, R. I......41.51
Dalles, Or...........21.74	Gaston, N. C.........43.40	Richmond, Ind......43.32
Detroit, Mich... .....30.05	Hanover, N. H...... 40.32	Sacramento, Cal......19.56
Fort Bliss, Tex... ... 9.56	Huntsville, Ala......54.88	Salt Lake, Utah.....23.85
Fort Bridger, Utah... 6.12	Key West, Fla......36.23	San Francisco, Ca...21.69
Fort Brown, Tex.....33.44	Macinac, Mich......23.96	San Diego, Cal....... 9.16
Ft. Colville, Wash. T. 9.83	Marietta, Ohio 42.70	Savannah, Ga... ....48.32
Fort Craig, N. Mex...11.67	Meadow Valley, Cal..57.03	Sitka, Alaska... ....83.39
Fort Defiance, Ariz...14.21	Memphis, Tenn......45.46	Springdale, Ky.......48.59
Fort Garland, Col.... 6.11	Milwaukee, Wis......30.40	St. Louis, Mo........42.18
Ft.Gibson,Indian Ter.36.37	Muscatine, Iowa.... .42.88	Washington, Ark.....54.50
Fort Hoskins, Or.....66.71	Mt. Vernon Ars'l, Ala.66.14	Washington, D. C....37.52
Fort Kearney, Neb...25.25	Natchez, Miss........53.55	WhiteSulp.Spring,Va.37.54
Fort Laramie, Wy....15.16	Neah Bay, Wash.Ter.123.35	
Ft. Leavenworth,Kan.31.74	Newark, N. J.... ....44.85	

Average Annual Rainfall in Some Other Parts of America.

Inches.	Inches.	Inches.
Bermuda............ 55.34	Maranham 277.00	St.John's,Newfound. 58.30
Cayenne............ 116.00	Rio Janeiro......... 59.02	Toronto, Canada.... 35.17
Cordova, Mex. 112.08	San Domingo 107.06	Vera Cruz, Mex.....183.90
Havana............. 91.02	St. John's, N. Bruns. 51.12	

Average Annual Rainfall in Europe.

From Knight's Mechanical Dictionary, 1876.

Inches.	Inches.	Inches.
Aberdeen, Scotland.. 28.87	Cork, Ireland....... 40.02	Marseilles, France .. 23.04
Armagh, Ireland.... 36.12	Copenhagen, Den.. . 18.35	Milan, Italy......... 38.01
Bath, England 30.03	Dublin, Ireland 21.01	Naples.............. 29.61
Bergen, Norway..... 88.61	Geneva, Switzerland. 31.07	Paris............... 22.64
Berlin, Prussia...... 23.56	Glasgow, Scotland... 21.33	Prague, Austria..... 14.01
Bordeaux, France... 31.00	Limerick, Ireland ... 35.00	Rome............... 30.86
Borrowdale, Eng....141.54	Lisbon, Portugal.... 27.01	Stockholm, Sweden.. 20.04
Brussels, Belgium... 28.06	Liverpool........... 34.05	St. Petersburg...... 17.03
Cambridge, England. 24.09	London.............. 24.04	Truro, England..... 44.00
Cracow, Austria 13.08	Manchester, Eng.... 36.02	York, England. 23.00
Coimbra, Portugal ..118.08	Mannheim, Ger..... 22.47	

TONNAGE OF THE UNITED STATES, 1789-1877.

Comparative View of the Distribution of the Tonnage of the United States Merchant Marine, employed in the Foreign Trade, the Coastwise Trade, and the Fisheries, each Year, from 1789 to 1877.

Compiled from the Annual Report of the Register of the Treasury, 1877.

Years.	Foreign Trade.	Coastwise Trade.	Whale Fisheries.	Cod and Mackerel Fisheries.	Sail.	Steam.	Total.	Annual Increase or Decrease per cent.
	Tons.	Tons.	Tons.	Tons.	Tons.	Tons.	Tons.	
1789	123,893	68,607	......	9,062	201,562	......	201,562	......
1790	346,254	103,775	......	28,348	478,377	......	478,377	137.83
1791	363,110	106,494	......	32,542	502,146	......	502,146	4.96
1792	411,438	120,957	......	32,062	564,457	......	564,457	12.35
1793	367,734	122,071	......	30,959	520,764	......	520,764	— 7.74
1794	438,863	162,578	4,120	23,048	628,618	......	628,618	20.71
1795	529,471	184,398	8,163	30,933	747,965	......	747,965	19.00
1796	576,733	217,841	2,864	34,962	831,900	......	831,900	11.22
1797	597,777	237,403	1,104	40,628	876,912	......	876,912	5.41
1798	603,376	251,443	763	42,746	898,328	......	898,328	2.49
1799	657,142	246,640	5,647	29,979	939,408	......	939,408	4.57
1800	667,107	272,492	3,406	29,427	972,492	......	972,492	3.52
1801	630,558	274,551	3,085	39,382	947,576	......	947,576	— 2.56
1802	557,760	249,623	3,201	41,522	892,106	......	892,106	— 5.85
1803	585,910	290,060	12,390	51,812	949,172	......	949,172	6.39
1804	660,514	317,537	12,339	52,011	1,042,401	......	1,042,404	1.00
1805	744,224	332,663	6,015	57,465	1,140,367	......	1,140,367	9.40
1806	798,507	340,540	10,507	59,183	1,208,737	......	1,208,737	5.99
1807	840,163	349,028	9,051	70,306	1,268,548	......	1,268,548	4.95
1808	765,252	420,819	4,526	51,998	1,212,595	......	1,242,595	— 2.04
1809	906,855	405,163	3,777	34,487	1,350,282	......	1,350,282	8.66
1810	981,019	405,347	3,589	34,828	1,424,783	......	1,424,783	5.51
1811	763,607	420,362	5,299	43,231	1,232,502	......	1,232,502	—13.49
1812	758,636	477,972	2,930	30,459	1,269,997	......	1,269,997	2.95
1813	672,700	470,109	2,042	20,877	1,166,628	......	1,166,628	— 8.14
1814	674,633	466,150	562	17,855	1,159,209	......	1,159,209	— 0.63
1815	854,295	475,666	1,230	36,937	1,368,128	......	1,368,128	18.03
1816	800,700	522,665	1,168	47,626	1,372,219	......	1,372,219	0.29
1817	804,851	525,030	5,224	64,807	1,399,912	......	1,399,912	0.20
1818	589,954	549,374	16,750	69,107	1,225,185	......	1,225,185	—10.34
1819	581,230	571,058	82,386	76,078	1,260,752	......	1,260,752	0.04
1820	583,657	588,025	36,445	72,040	1,280,167	......	1,280,167	1.54
1821	593,825	614,845	27,995	62,293	1,298,958	......	1,298,958	1.47
1822	613,068	624,189	18,216	69,226	1,324,699	......	1,324,699	1.98
1823	600,003	617,805	40,503	78,255	1,311,687	21,879	1,330,566	0.89
1824	636,807	641,563	33,346	77,447	1,367,553	21,610	1,389,163	3.94
1825	667,408	640,861	33,379	81,462	1,400,049	23,061	1,423,110	2.44
1826	696,221	722,340	41,974	73,656	1,500,132	34,059	1,534,191	7.80
1827	701,517	780,259	45,892	83,939	1,580,409	40,198	1,620,607	5.63
1828	757,998	842,006	54,801	85,687	1,701,974	39,418	1,741,392	7.45
1829	592,859	508,858	57,284	101,797	1,206,761	54,037	1,260,798	—27.60
1830	537,563	516,979	39,705	97,529	1,127,304	64,472	1,191,776	— 5.47
1831	538,136	539,724	82,797	107,189	1,233,401	34,445	1,267,846	6.38
1832	614,121	649,627	73,246	102,458	1,348,636	90,814	1,439,450	13.53
1833	648,869	744,199	101,636	111,447	1,504,301	101,850	1,606,151	11.59
1834	749,378	783,619	108,424	117,496	1,636,093	122,814	1,758,907	9.51
1835	788,173	797,338	97,649	141,781	1,702,127	122,814	1,824,941	3.13
1836	753,094	873,023	146,254	109,731	1,736,546	145,556	1,882,102	3.13
1837	683,205	956,981	129,137	127,363	1,741,921	154,765	1,896,686	0.24
1838	702,062	1,041,105	124,860	126,713	1,802,217	193,423	1,995,640	5.22
1839	702,400	1,153,552	132,285	108,242	1,801,541	204,938	2,006,479	5.05
1840	762,838	1,176,694	136,927	104,305	1,978,455	202,309	2,180,764	4.02
1841	788,398	1,107,068	157,405	77,873	1,955,656	175,088	2,130,744	— 2.30
1842	823,746	1,045,753	151,990	70,902	1,862,730	229,661	2,092,391	— 1.80
1843	856,930	1,076,156	152,517	73,000	1,921,736	236,867	2,158,603	3.16
1844	900,471	1,109,615	168,614	101,396	2,007,926	272,170	2,280,096	5.63
1845	904,476	1,223,218	190,903	98,404	2,090,983	326,019	2,417,002	6.00

TONNAGE OF THE UNITED STATES, 1789-1877—(*Continued*),

Years.	Foreign Trade.	Coast-wise Trade.	Whale Fish-eries.	Ccd and Mack-erel-Fish-eries.	Sail.	Steam.	Total.	Annual Increase or Decrease per cent.
	Tons.	Tons.	Tons.	Tons.	Tons.	Tons.	Tons.	
1846......	943,307	1,315,577	187,420	115,781	2,214,192	347,893	2,562,085	6.00
1847......	1,047,454	1,488,601	193,859	109,132	2,434,205	404,841	2,839,046	10.81
1848......	1,168,707	1,659,317	192,613	133,406	2,726,151	427,891	3,154,042	11.09
1849......	1,258,756	1,770,376	180,186	124,698	2,871,621	462,395	3,334,016	5.71
1850......	1,439,694	1,797,825	146,017	151,918	3,010,020	525,434	3,535,454	6.04
1851......	1,544,663	1,899,970	181,644	146,156	3,188,832	583,607	3,772,439	6.70
1852......	1,705,650	2,055,873	193,798	183,119	3,504,200	634,240	4,138,440	9.70
1853......	1,910,471	2,134,258	193,203	169,078	3,802,392	604,618	4,407,010	6.49
1854......	2,151,918	2,322,114	181,901	146,969	4,126,295	676,607	4,802,902	8.96
1855......	2,348,358	2,543,255	186,848	133,540	4,441,716	770,285	5,212,001	8.53
1856......	2,302,190	2,247,663	189,461	132,339	4,198,576	673,077	4,871,653	2 60
1857......	2,268,196	2,336,609	195,842	140,196	4,235,059	705,784	4,940,843	1.41
1858......	2,301,148	2,401,220	198,594	148,846	4,321,418	728,390	5,049,808	2.20
1859......	2,321,674	2,480,929	185,728	156,707	4,376,285	768,753	5,145,038	1.90
1860......	2,379,396	2,644,867	166,841	162,764	4,485,931	867,937	5,353,868	4.06
1861......	2,496,894	2,704,724	145,734	192,461	4,662,609	877,204	5,539,813	3.47
1862......	2,173,537	2,616,716	117,714	204,197	4,401,701	710,463	5,112,164	— 4.51
1863......	1,926,886	2,960,633	99,228	168,309	4,579,537	575,519	5,155,056	0.84
1864......	1,486,749	3,245,265	95,145	159,241	4,026,065	960,335	4,986,400	— 3.85
1865......	509,199	1,016,199	1,380	53,216	1,212,805	367,189	1,570,994	} 2.21
1865......	1,009,151	2,365,323	80,136	53,278	2,816,833	699,950	3,516,788	
1866......	1,031,541	2,162,220	76,900	97,728	2,442,212	926,267	3,368,479	} —15.42
1866......	356,215	557,401	28,180	503	785,254	157,045	942,299	
1867......	1,300,852	2,528,214	52,384	76,065	2,834,535	1,122,980	3,957,515	} — 0.12
1867......	214,796	132,176				278,072	68,900	346,972	
1868......	1,400,940	2,702,140	71,343	83,857	3,118,895	1,199,415	4,318,310	} 1.10
1868......	33,449					33,449		33,449	
1869......	1,496,220	2,515,515	70,202	62,704	3,041,083	1,103,568	4,144,641	— 4.76
1870......	1,448,846	2,638,247	67,954	91,460	4,171,412	1,075,095	4,246,507	2.46
1871......	1,363,652	2,764,600	61,490	92,865	3,194,970	1,087,637	4,282,607	0.85
1872......	1,359,040	2,929,552	51,608	97,547	3,326,194	1,111,553	4,437,747	3.62
1873......	1,378,533	3,163,220	44,755	100,519	3,539,584	1,156,443	4,696,027	5.82
1874......	1,389,815	3,293,439	39,108	78,290	3,615,042	1,185,610	4,800,652	2.23
1875......	1,515,598	3,219,698	38,229	80,207	3,085,064	1,168,668	4,853,732	1.13
1876......	1,553,705	2,598,835	39,116	87,802	3,107,086	1,172,372	4,279,458	—11.63
1877......	1,611,193	2,540,322	40,593	91,085	3,071,404	1,171,196	4,242,600	— 0.85

Steam Vessels built in the United States during the Year ended June 30, 1877.

CLASS OF VESSELS.	Number.	Tonnage.
River steamers, side-wheel......................	44	17,932.62
River steamers, stern-wheel....................	107	17,201.27
River steamers, propellers......................	93	4,026.80
Lake steamers, propellers.	14	2,386.41
Ocean steamers, side-wheel.....................	1	29.05
Ocean steamers, propellers.....................	6	5,338.27
Total..............................	265	47,514.51

Number and Tonnage of Steam Iron Vessels built in the United States during the Year ended June 30, 1877.

Ports.	Number.	Tons.
Philadelphia...................................	4	4,894.45
Wilmington....................................	2	899.85
Baltimore.....................................	1	133.11
Total.......:............................	7	5,927.41

SHIP-BUILDING IN THE UNITED STATES, 1815-1877.

Statement Showing the Number and Class of Vessels Built, and the Tonnage thereof, in the United States from 1815 to 1877, inclusive.

From the Annual Report of the Register of the Treasury.

Year.	Ships and Barks.	Brigs.	Schooners.	Sloops, Canal Boats and Barges.	Steamers.	Total Number of Vessels Built.	Total Tonnage.
							Tons.
1815.....	136	234	681	274	....	1,315	154,624
1816.....	76	122	781	434	....	1,403	131,668
1817.....	84	86	559	394	....	1,073	86,393
1818.....	53	85	428	332	....	898	82,421
1819.....	53	82	473	243	....	851	79,817
1820.....	21	60	301	152	....	534	47,784
1821.....	43	89	247	127	....	506	55,856
1822.....	64	131	260	168	....	623	75,346
1823.....	55	127	260	165	15	622	75,007
1824.....	56	156	377	166	26	781	90,939
1825.....	56	197	538	168	35	994	114,997
1826.....	71	187	482	227	45	1,012	126,438
1827.....	55	153	464	241	38	951	104,342
1828.....	73	108	474	196	33	884	93,375
1829.....	44	68	485	145	43	785	77,098
1830.....	25	56	403	116	37	637	58,094
1831.....	72	95	416	94	34	711	85,762
1832.....	152	143	568	122	100	1,065	144,539
1833.....	144	167	625	185	65	1,188	161,626
1834.....	98	94	497	180	68	937	118,330
1835.....	25	50	301	100	30	506	46,238
1836.....	98	65	444	164	125	890	113,627
1837.....	67	72	507	168	135	949	122,987
1838.....	66	79	501	153	90	889	113,135
1839.....	83	80	439	122	125	858	120,999
1840.....	97	109	878	224	64	872	118,309
1841.....	114	101	310	157	78	760	118,893
1842.....	116	91	272	404	137	1,021	129,063
1843.....	58	34	138	173	79	482	43,617
1844.....	73	47	204	279	163	766	103,537
1845.....	124	87	822	342	163	1,038	146,018
1846.....	100	164	576	355	225	1,420	188,203
1847.....	151	168	689	392	198	1,598	243,732
1848.....	254	174	701	547	175	1,851	318,075
1849.....	198	148	623	370	208	1,547	256,577
1850.....	247	117	547	290	259	1,360	272,218
1851.....	211	65	522	326	233	1,367	298,203
1852.....	255	79	584	267	259	1,444	351,493
1853.....	269	95	681	394	271	1,710	425,571
1854.....	334	112	661	386	281	1,774	535,616
1855.....	381	126	605	669	253	2,047	583,450
1856.....	306	103	594	479	221	1,703	469,393
1857.....	251	58	504	258	263	1,334	378,804
1858.....	222	46	431	400	236	1,225	242,286
1859.....	89	28	297	284	172	870	156,001
1860.....	110	86	372	289	264	1,071	212,892
1861.....	110	38	360	371	264	1,143	233,194
1862.....	62	17	207	397	183	864	175,075
1863.....	97	34	212	1,113	307	1,823	310,884
1864.....	112	45	322	1,389	498	2,366	415,740
1865.....	109	46	369	853	411	1,788	383,805
1866*....	96	61	457	926	348	1,889	336,146
1867.....	93	70	517	657	180	1,519	303,528
1868.....	80	48	500	848	236	1,802	285,304
1869.....	91	36	506	816	277	1,720	275,230
1870.....	73	27	519	709	290	1,618	276,953
1871.....	40	14	498	901	302	1,755	273,226
1872.....	15	10	426	900	292	1,643	209,032
1873.....	28	9	611	1,221	402	2,271	359,245
1874.....	71	22	655	995	404	2,147	432,725
1875.....	114	22	502	840	323	1,301	237,538
1876.....	76	5	424	260	338	1,112	203,585
1877.....	71	4	337	352	265	1,029	176,592

* New measurement from 1866.

NUMBER AND DISTRIBUTION OF THE SHIPPING OF THE UNITED STATES, JUNE 30, 1877.

From the Annual Report of the Register of the Treasury, December, 1877.

STATES AND TERRITORIES.	Sailing Vessels.		Steam Vessels.		Canal-boats.		Barges.		Total.	
	No.	Tons.	No.	Tons.	No.	Tons.	No.	Tons.	No.	Tons.
Alabama..............	67	8,954	33	5,799	....	......	7	886	107	15,639
Alaska.......	10	135	1	46	....	......			11	181
California............	803	131,262	169	50,081	....	......	65	8,733	1,037	190,076
Connecticut..........	731	51,450	89	27,953	1	120	24	4,367	845	83,890
Delaware............	163	11,859	20	3,490	....	......	6	705	189	16,065
District of Columbia..	73	2,637	28	5,918	....	......	1	168	102	8,723
Florida..............	258	13,714	66	7,172	....	......			324	20,886
Georgia.............	76	11,405	27	8,597	....	......	3	298	106	20,300
Illinois............	306	70,098	158	22,015	....	......	55	11,514	519	103,627
Indiana.............	.....	....	54	5,671	....	......	22	2,575	76	8,246
Iowa.................	.....	....	47	3,909	....	......			47	3,909
Kentucky............	.....	....	41	10,115	....	......	21	1,475	62	11,591
Louisiana............	434	42,738	174	42,820	....	......	9	1,445	617	87,003
Maine	2,790	504,943	91	17,854	....	......	1	152	2,882	522,949
Maryland............	1,654	91,375	118	35,699	....	......	1	32	1,773	127,105
Massachusetts	2,454	442,068	136	41,244	....	......	7	2,097	2,597	485,409
Michigan............	456	55,103	378	63,241	....	......	141	35,075	975	153,419
Minnesota...........	2	79	44	3,881	....	......	15	1,468	61	5,427
Mississippi...........	109	3,257	37	4,342	....	......	14	675	160	8,274
Missouri.............	.....	....	174	66,229	....	......	238	81,660	412	147,890
Nebraska............	.....	....	24	5,047	....	......			24	5,047
New Hampshire......	77	12,000	4	264	....	......			81	12,263
New Jersey........ ...	906	57,887	92	16,458	150	15,056	65	10.088	1,222	99,488
New York............	3,135	682,870	1,008	408,237	810	62,833	541	126,857	5,494	1,280,637
North Carolina.......	308	10,140	23	2,013	....	......			330	12,153
Ohio	254	63,001	215	60,622	....	......	81	20,192	550	143,815
Oregon......	44	2,720	74	24,409	....	......	19	5,243	137	32,373
Pennsylvania.........	918	169,890	483	130,630	25	3,808	402	76,543	1,828	380,821
Rhode Island.........	238	18,164	50	23,685	....	......			288	41,849
South Carolina.......	178	8,741	36	4,837	....	......			214	13,578
Tennessee............	.....	....	87	13,708	....	......			87	13,708
Texas...............	251	9,842	38	5,239	....	......	5	685	294	15,767
Vermont	11	564	5	2,520	1	77			17	3,161
Virginia.............	1,024	26,735	86	7,231	....	......	9	822	1,119	34,788
Washington Territory.	72	23,536	38	5,305	....	......	3	86	113	28,927
West Virginia........	.....	.. ..	131	15,456	....	......	158	15,712	289	31,168
Wisconsin	284	53,472	116	19,448	....	......	1	27	401	72,947
Total.:.............	**18,081**	**2,580,388**	**4,395**	**1,171,196**	**996**	**81,394**	**1,914**	**409,620**	**25,386**	**4,242,599**
SUMMARY.										
Atlantic & Gulf Coasts	15,548	2,098,341	2,090	656,316	524	43,920	684	146,287	18,886	2,944,865
Pacific Coast	929	157,653	282	79,841	....	......	87	14,002	1,298	251,596
Northern Lakes.......	1,604	324,394	923	201,045	472	37,474	192	47,207	3,191	610,160
Western Rivers.......	.....	....	1,110	233,954	....	......	951	202,064	2,061	436,018
Total	**18,081**	**2,580,388**	**4,395**	**1,171,196**	**996**	**81,394**	**1,914**	**409,620**	**25,386**	**4,242,599**

NOTE.—Fractions of tons are omitted in the table.

Number and Tonnage of Vessels built in the United States during the Year ended June 30, 1877.

From the Annual Report of the Register of the Treasury, December, 1877.

STATES AND TERRITORIES.	Sailing Vessels.		Steam Vessels.		Canal-boats.		Barges.		Total.	
	No.	Tons.	No.	Tons.	No.	Tons.	No.	Tons.	No.	Tons.
SUMMARY.										
Atlantic & Gulf coasts..	496	97,177.55	89	17,164.27	12	1,157.93	23	4,777.79	620	120,277.54
Pacific coast...........	56	6,467.70	21	4,894.75	....	....	8	1,356.02	84	12,718.47
Northern lakes..........	29	2,695.64	39	3,801.95	17	1,863.01	4	551.50	89	8,903.00
Western rivers...........	.....	....	113	21,653.54	....	....	119	13,039.41	232	34,692.95
Total................	**581**	**106,339.89**	**265**	**47,514.51**	**29**	**3,021.84**	**154**	**19,724.72**	**1,029**	**176,591.96**

PAY TABLE OF THE NAVY.

	At Sea.	On Shore Duty.	On Leave or Walting Orders.
Admiral..	$13,000	$13,000	$13,000
Vice-Admiral	9,000	8,000	6,000
Rear-Admirals.	6,000	5,000	4,000
Commodores....................................	5,000	4,000	3,000
Captains.......................................	4,500	3,500	2,800
Commanders....................................	3,500	3,000	2,300
Lieutenant-Commanders—			
First four years after date of commission...	2,800	2,400	2,000
After four years from date of commission...	3,000	2,600	2,300
Lieutenants—			
First five years.............................	2,400	2,000	1,600
After five years.............................	2,600	2,200	1,800
Masters—			
First five years.	1,800	1,500	1,200
After five years.............................	2,000	1,700	1,400
Ensigns—			
First five years.............................	1,200	1,000	800
After five years.............................	1,400	1,200	1,000
Midshipmen....................................	1,000	800	600
Cadet Midshipmen............................	500	500	500
Mates...	900	700	500
Medical and Pay Directors and Medical and Pay Inspectors and Chief Engineers, having the same rank at sea....................................	4,400	....	....
Fleet Surgeons, Fleet Paymasters, and Fleet Engineers—	4,400	....	....
Surgeons, Paymasters, and Chief Engineers—........			
First five years after date of commission....	2,800	2,400	2,000
Second five years...........................	3,200	2,800	2,400
Third five years.............................	3,500	3,200	2,600
Fourth five years.	3,700	3,600	2,800
After twenty years...........................	4,200	4,000	3,000
Passed Assistant Surgeons, Passed Assistant Paymasters, and Passed Assistant Engineers—			
First five years after date of appointment...	2,000	1,800	1,500
After five years...	2,200	2,000	1,700
Assistant Surgeons, Assistant Paymasters, and Assistant Engineers—			
First five years after date of appointment...	1,700	1,400	1,000
After five years.............................	1,900	1,600	1,200
Chaplains—			
First five years.............................	2,500	2,000	1,600
After five years.............................	2,800	2,300	1,900
Boatswains, Gunners, Carpenters and Sail-makers—			
First three years.............................	1,200	900	700
Second three years..........................	1,200	1,000	800
Third three years	1,400	1,300	900
Fourth three years..........................	1,600	1,300	1,000
After twelve years...........................	1,800	1,600	1,200
Cadet Engineers (after examination).	1,000	800	600

	On shore duty.	On leave or waiting orders.
Naval Constructors—		
First 5 years....$3,200	$2,200	
Second 5 years.. 3,400	2,400	
Third 5 years... 3,700	2,700	
Fourth 5 years.. 4,000	3,000	
After 20 years... 4,200	3,200	
Ass't Naval Constructors—		
First 4 years.... 2,000	1,500	
Second 4 years.. 2,200	1,400	
After 8 years.... 2,600	1,900	
Secretary to Admiral and Vice Admiral............................$2,500		
Secretaries to Commanders of Squadrons..........................2,000		
Secretary to Naval Academy 1,800		

Clerks to Commanders of Squadrons and Vessels....	$750
First Clerks to Commandants of Navy Yards.................	1,500
Second Clerks to Commandants of Navy Yards.................	1,200
Clerk, Mare Island Navy Yard.....	1,800
Clerk to Commandants Naval Stations................	1,500
Clerks to Paymasters at Navy Yards—	
Boston, New York, Philadelphia and Washington..............	1,600
Mare Island	1,800
Kittery, Norfolk and Pensacola..	1,400
At other Stations..............	1,300

The pay of Seamen is $258, and of ordinary seamen $210 per annum.

NOTE.—The navy spirit ration was totally abolished July 1, 1870, and in lieu thereof the navy ration is 30 cents per day.

398   AN AMERICAN ALMANAC FOR 1878.

THE NAVY OF THE UNITED STATES.

From the Annual Report of the Secretary of the Navy, December, 1877.

THE navy consists of 67 steam and 23 sailing vessels, 23 iron-clads, 2 torpedo, 1 ferry, and 26 tug boats.

The active list of the navy is composed of 1 admiral, 1 vice-admiral, 11 rear-admirals, 25 commodores, 50 captains, 90 commanders, 80 lieutenant-commanders, 280 lieutenants, 100 masters, 71 ensigns, 77 midshipmen, 43 cadet-midshipmen, and 213 cadet-midshipmen on probation at the Naval Academy, all of whom are officers of the line.

Of the staff, there are 1 surgeon-general, 14 medical directors, 15 medical inspectors, 50 surgeons, 53 passed assistant-surgeons, 44 assistant-surgeons, 1 paymaster-general, 12 pay-directors, 13 pay-inspectors, 50 paymasters, 30 passed assistant-pay-masters, 20 assistant-paymasters ; 1 engineer-in-chief, 69 chief-engineers, 97 passed assistant-engineers, 43 assistant-engineers, 19 cadet-engineers, and 63 cadet-engineers on probation at the Naval Academy ; 24 chaplains, 12 professors of mathematics, 1 secretary for the admiral and 1 for the vice-admiral; 1 chief-constructor, 10 naval constructors, 5 assistant-constructors, and 9 civil engineers.

The warrant-officers consist of 54 boatswains, 50 gunners, 50 carpenters, 41 sail-makers, and 45 mates.

There were in the service on the 24th day of November, 1877, 7012 enlisted men and boys.

The retired list is composed of 41 rear-admirals, 26 commodores, 15 captains, 13 commanders, 14 lieutenant-commanders, 6 lieutenants, 13 masters, 5 ensigns, 2 midshipmen, 3 surgeons-general, 18 medical directors, 1 medical inspector, 2 surgeons, 2 passed assistant-surgeons, 5 assistant-surgeons, 3 paymasters-general, 5 pay-directors, 3 paymasters, 2 passed assistant-paymasters, 2 assistant-paymasters, 5 chief-engineers, 17 passed assistant-engineers, 23 assistant engineers, 1 chief-constructor, 4 naval constructors, 7 chaplains, 4 professors of mathematics, 9 boatswains, 5 gunners, 11 carpenters, and 12 sailmakers.

The active list is therefore composed of 829 officers of the line, 534 officers of the staff, and 249 warrant-officers—total, 1672 officers of all grades.

The retired list is composed of 135 officers of the line, 103 officers of the staff, 27 warrant-officers, and 4 professors of mathematics.

NAVY OFFICERS.

From the Navy Register of the U. S., July, 1877.

ADMIRAL.

Name.	Present Duty, Station, or Residence.	Whence Appointed.	Original Entry into the Service.	Date of Present Commission.	Total Sea Service. Years.
David D. Porter...	Special Duty, Washington	Penn...	1829....	Aug. 15, 1870	23

VICE-ADMIRAL.

| Stephen C. Rowan | Port Admiral, New York. | Ohio. ... | 1826.. . | Aug. 15, 1870 | 25 |

REAR-ADMIRALS—Active List (11).

John Rodgers.........	Sup't Naval Observatory........	D. C..	1828.	Dec. 31, 1869	23
John L. Worden	Commanding European Station.	N. Y.	1834.	Nov. 20, 1872	21
William Reynolds.....	Commanding Asiatic Station....	N. Y.	1831.	Dec. 12, 1873	20
William E. LeRoy ...	Newburgh, N. Y...............	N. J.	1832.	April 5, 1874	27
J. R. Madison Mullany.	Gov. Naval Asylum, Philadelphia	Conn.	1832.	June 5, 1874	25
C. R. P. Rodgers	Superintendent Naval Academy.	Ohio.	1833.	June 14, 1874	26
Stephen D. Trenchard.	Com'dg North Atlantic Station.	N. Y.	1834.	Aug. 10, 1875	26
Alexander Murray.....	Com'dg North Pacific Station...	Penn.	1835.	April 26, 1876	18
George H. Preble.....	Com'dg South Pacific Station..	Me...	1835.	Sept. 30, 1876	23
Thomas H. Patterson..	President Board Examiners.....	La...	1836.	1877	20
John C. Howell........	Chief Bureau Yards and Docks.	Penn.	1836.	1877	21

COMMODORES—Active List (25).

Daniel Ammen........	Chief Bureau Navigation........	Ohio..	1836.	April 1, 1872	21
Edward T. Nichols....	Brooklyn, N. Y................	Ga..	1836.	May 24, 1872	22
Robert H. Wyman.....	In charge Hydrographic Office...	N. H.	1837.	July 19, 1872	20
George B. Balch.......	Member Light-House Board	Ala .	1837.	Aug. 13, 1872	20
Thomas H. Stevens....	Special duty, Norfolk Harbor...	Conn.	1836.	Nov. 20, 1872	18
Foxhall A. Parker.....	Com'dt Navy Yard, Boston.....	Va...	1837.	Nov. 25, 1872	18
John Guest............	Beltsville, Md.................	Ark..	1837.	Dec. 12, 1872	21
John M. B. Clitz	Com'g Nav. Sta., Pt. Royal, S.C.	Mich.	1837.	Dec. 23, 1872	22
Andrew Bryson.......	Philadelphia, Pa..............	N. Y.	1837.	Feb. 14, 1873	23
Donald McN. Fairfax..	Cheshire, Conn...............	N. C.	1837.	Aug. 24, 1873	20
James H. Spotts.......	San Francisco, Cal...........	Ky...	1837.	Sept. 25, 1873	21
J. W. A. Nicholson....	Com'dt Navy Yard, New York..	N. Y.	1838.	Nov. 8, 1873	22
George H. Cooper.....	Light-House Inspector..........	N. Y.	1837.	June 5, 1874	23
John C. Beaumont....	Chief Signal-Officer............	Penn.	1838.	June 14, 1874	22
Chas. H. B. Caldwell..	Com'dg South Atlantic Station..	Conn.	1838.	June 14, 1874	20
John C. Febiger.......	Com'dt Navy Yard, Washington	Ohio.	1838.	Aug. 9, 1874	25
Peirce Crosby	Lexington, Ky.................	Penn.	1838.	Oct. 3, 1874	22
J. Blakeley Creighton.	Com'dt Navy Yard, Norfolk, Va.	R. I..	1838.	Nov. 9, 1874	23
Aaron K. Hughes.....	Greenwich, N. Y..............	N. Y.	1838.	Feb. 4, 1875	18
Edmund R. Colhoun..	Member Board Examiners... ...	Mo..	1839.	April 26, 1876	17
Charles H. Baldwin....	Member Board Examiners....	N. Y.	1839.	Aug. 8, 1876	14
Robert W. Shufeldt...	Chief Bu. Equip't and Recruiting	N. Y.	1839.	Sept. 21, 1876	16
Alexander C. Rhind..	New York...................	Ala..	1838.	Sept. 30, 1876	19
George M. Ransom....	Commanding *Franklin*........	Ohio.	1839.	1877	22
William F. Spicer....	Winchester, Mass.............	N. Y.	1839.	1877	20

THE NAVIES OF THE WORLD.
Compiled from Official Documents.

COUNTRIES.	No. of Vessels.	No. of Men.	Cost of Navy. Dollars.	COUNTRIES.	No. of Vessels.	No. of Men.	Cost of Navy. Dollars.
Argentine Republic....	28	3,135	842,362	Japan..........	21	3,944	2,700,000
Austria-Hungary	68	6,319	4,705,095				Army and
Belgium.................	10	172	....	Mexico.........	4	......	Navy.
Bolivia.............. ...	37						10,554,745
Brazil.......	63	6,184	9,994,147	Netherlands....	105	4,906	5,780,216
Canada (Dominion).....	7	......	....	Norway........	119	4,342	652,840
Chili	15	840	....	Peru............	18		
China	38	......	....	Portugal	37	3,853	1,585,494
Denmark.	33	1,125	1,200,000	Roumania	9	266	
Egypt.................	14	......	....	Russia	223	30,039	20,030,704
France	226	50,517	33,178,699	Spain	138	14,648	6,536,315
Germany...............	60	8,051	1,192,325	Sweden	141	6,141	1,352,792
Gt. Britain & Ireland....	531	81,447	56,445,000	Turkey........	170	6,000	
Greece	21	652	891,978	United States..	146	8,684	16,077,974
Italy	66	11,880	7,543,388				

POST-OFFICE STATISTICS OF THE UNITED STATES— 1790-1877.

Number of Post-Offices, Extent of Post-Routes, and Revenue and Expenditures of the Post-Office Department; with the Amount paid to Postmasters and for Transportation of the Mail, since 1790.

Years.	No. of Post-Offices.	Extent of Post-Routes in Miles.	Revenue of the Department	Expenditure of the Department	Amount paid for Salaries of Postmast'rs	Amount paid for Transport'n of the Mail.
1790 ...	75	1,875	$37,935	$32,140	$8,198	$22,081
1795.....	453	13,207	160,620	117,893	30,272	75,359
1800.....	903	20,817	280,804	213,994	69,243	128,644
1805.....	1,558	31,076	421,373	377,367	111,552	239,635
1810.....	2,300	36,406	551,684	495,969	149,438	327,966
1815.....	3,000	43,748	1,043,065	748,121	241,901	487,779
1816.....	3,260	48,673	961,782	804,422	265,944	521,970
1817.....	3,459	52,089	1,002,973	916,515	303,916	589,189
1818.....	3,618	59,473	1,130,235	1,035,832	346,429	664,611
1819.....	4,000	67,586	1,204,737	1,117,861	375,828	717,881
1820.....	4,500	72,492	1,111,927	1,160,926	352,395	782,425
1821.....	4,650	78,808	1,059,037	1,181,283	337,599	815,681
1822.....	4,709	82,763	1,117,490	1,167,572	355,299	788,618
1823.....	4,043	84,860	1,130,115	1,156,995	360,462	767,464
1824.....	5,182	84,860	1,197,758	1,188,019	383,804	768,939
1825.....	5,677	94,052	1,306,525	1,229,043	411,183	785,646
1826.....	6,150	94,052	1,447,703	1,366,712	447,727	885,100
1827.....	7,003	105,336	1,524,633	1,468,959	486,411	942,345
1828.....	7,530	105,336	1,659,915	1,689,945	548,049	1,086,313
1829.....	8,004	115,000	1,707,418	1,782,132	559,237	1,153,646
1830.....	8,450	115,176	1,850,583	1,932,708	595,231	1,274,009
1831.....	8,686	115,486	1,997,811	1,936,122	635,028	1,252,226
1832.....	9,205	104,466	2,258,570	2,266,171	715,481	1,482,507
1833.....	10,127	119,916	2,617,011	2,930,414	826,283	1,894,688
1834.....	10,693	119,916	2,823,749	2,910,605	897,317	1,925,544
1835.....	10,770	112,774	2,993,356	2,757,350	945,418	1,719,007
1836.....	11,091	118,264	3,408,323	3,841,766	812,803	1,638,052
1837.....	11,767	141,242	4,236,779	3,544,630	891,352	1,996,727
1838.....	12,519	134,818	4,238,733	4,430,662	933,948	3,131,906
1839.....	12,780	133,999	4,484,657	4,636,536	980,000	3,285,622
1840.....	13,468	155,739	4,543,522	4,718,236	1,028,925	3,293,876
1841.....	13,778	155,026	4,407,726	4,499,523	1,018,645	3,150,375
1842.....	13,733	149,732	4,546,849	5,674,752	1,147,256	3,087,790
1843...	13,814	142,295	4,296,225	4,374,754	1,426,394	2,947,319
1844.....	14,103	144,687	4,237,238	4,296,513	1,359,316	2,938,551
1845.....	14,183	143,940	4,289,841	4,320,732	1,409,875	2,905,504
1846.....	14,601	152,865	3,487,199	4,084,297	1,042,079	2,716,673
1847.....	15,146	153,818	3,955,893	3,979,570	1,060,228	2,476,455
1848.....	16,159	163,208	4,371,077	4,326,850	....	2,804,703
1849.....	16,749	163,703	4,905,176	4,479,049	1,320,921	2,577,407
1850.....	18,417	178,672	5,552,971	5,212,953	1,549,376	2,965,786
1851.....	19,793	196,290	6,727,867	6,278,402	1,781,646	3,538,064
1852.....	20,901	214,284	6,925,971	7,108,459	1,296,765	4,225,311
1853.....	22,320	217,743	5,940,725	7,982,957	1,406,477	4,906,808
1854.....	23,548	219,935	6,955,586	8,577,424	1,707,708	5,401,382
1855.....	24,410	227,908	7,342,136	9,968,342	2,135,835	6,076,395
1856.....	25,565	239,642	7,620,822	10,405,286	2,102,891	6,765,639
1857.....	26,586	242,601	8,053,952	11,508,058	2,285,610	7,239,333
1858.....	27,977	260,603	8,186,793	12,722,470	2,355,016	8,346,054
1859.....	28,539	260,052	8,068,484	15,754,093	2,453,901	7,157,699
1860.....	28,498	240,594	8,518,067	19,170,610	2,552,808	8,808,710
1861.....	28,586	140,139	8,349,296	13,606,759	2,514,157	5,309,454
1862.....	28,875	134,013	8,299,821	11,125,364	2,340,767	5,833,834
1863.....	29,047	139,598	11,163,790	11,314,207	2,876,083	5,740,576
1864.....	28,878	139,171	12,438,254	12,644,786	3,174,326	5,818,469
1865.....	29,550	142,340	14,556,159	13,604,728	3,383,350	6,246,994
1866.....	23,828	180,921	14,386,986	15,852,079	3,454,677	7,630,474
1867.....	25,163	203,345	15,237,027	19,235,483	4,033,728	9,336,245
1868.....	26,481	216,928	16,292,601	22,730,593	4,255,311	10,296,056
1869.....	27,106	223,731	18,344,511	23,698,131	4,546,958	10,106,501
1870.....	28,492	231,232	19,772,221	23,998,837	4,673,466	10,984,653
1871.....	30,045	238,359	20,037,045	24,390,104	5,028,382	11,529,395
1872.....	31,863	251,398	21,915,426	26,658,192	5,121,665	15,547,821
1873.....	33,244	256,210	22,996,742	29,084,945	5,725,468	16,161,034
1874.....	34,294	269,097	26,477,072	32,126,413	5,818,472	18,881,319
1875.....	35,517	277,873	26,791,390	33,611,309	7,049,936	18,777,201
1876.....	36,383	281,798	27,815,903	33,263,488	7,397,897	18,361,043
1877. ...	37,315	292,820	27,468,323	33,486,322	7,295,251	18,529,238

UNITED STATES POSTAL REGULATIONS.
First Class Mail Matter.

LETTERS.—This class includes letters and any thing of which the Postmaster can-not ascertain the contents without destroying the wrapper, or any thing unsealed which may be wholly or partly in writing—except book-manuscript, corrected proofs passing between authors and publishers, and postal cards. Postage, 3 cents each half ounce, or for each fraction above half an ounce. On local or drop letters, at free-delivery offices, 2 cents. At offices where no free-delivery by carrier, 1 cent. Postal cards, 1 cent.

Registered letters, 10 cents in addition to the proper postage.

The Post-Office Department or its revenue is not by law liable for the loss of any registered mail matter.

Second Class.

REGULAR PUBLICATIONS.—This class includes all newspapers, periodicals, or matter exclusively in print and regularly issued at stated periods from a known office of publication or news agency. Postage, on daily or weekly issues, 2 cents a pound or fraction thereof. On periodicals issued less frequently than once a week, 3 cents a pound or fraction thereof.

Third Class.

Mail matter of the third class is divided as follows :

One cent for two ounces.—Almanacs, books (printed), calendars, catalogues, cor-rected proofs, hand-bills, magazines, when not sent to regular subscribers, maps (lithographed or engraved), music (printed sheet), newspapers, when not sent to regular subscribers, occasional publications, pamphlets, posters, proof-sheets, pro-spectuses, and regular publications designed primarily for advertising purposes, or for free circulation, or for circulation at nominal rates.

One cent for each ounce.—Blank books, blank cards, book manuscript, card-boards, and other flexible material, chromo-lithographs, circulars, engravings, en-velopes, flexible patterns, letter envelopes, letter paper, lithographs, merchandise, models, ornamented paper, postal cards, when sent in bulk and not addressed, photographic views, photographic paper, printed blanks, printed cards, sample cards, samples of ores, metals, minerals, and merchandise, seeds, cuttings, bulbs, roots, and scions, stereoscopic views.

All packages of matter of the third class must be so wrapped or enveloped, with open sides or ends, that their contents may be readily examined by postmasters without destroying the wrappers.

Matter of the second and third classes containing any writing whatever, will be charged with letter postage, except as follows:

The sender may write his name or address therein, or on the outside, with the word "from" preceding the same, or may write briefly on any package the number and names of the articles inclosed.

Postal Money Orders.

An order may be issued for any amount, from *one cent to fifty dollars* inclusive, but fractional parts of a cent cannot be included.

The Fees for orders are : On orders not exceeding $15...............10 cents.
" " over $15 and not exceeding $30....15 "
" " over 30   " " 40....20 "
" " over 40   " " 50....25 "

When a larger sum than fifty dollars is required, additional orders must be ob-tained ; but no more than *three* orders will be issued in one day from the same post-office to the same remitter in favor of the same payee.

Free Delivery.

The free delivery of mail matter at the residences of the people desiring it is required by law in every city of 50,000 or more population, and may be established at every place containing not less than 20,000 inhabitants. The present number of free-delivery offices is 87.

The franking privilege was abolished July 1, 1873, but the following mail-mat-ter may be sent free by legislative saving-clauses, viz. :

1. All public documents, printed by order of Congress.
2. Seeds transmitted by the Commissioner of Agriculture, or by any member of Congress, procured from that department.
3. All newspapers sent to subscribers within the county where printed.
4. Letters and packages relating exclusively to the business of the Government of the United States, mailed only from an Executive Department, or a bureau or office of the same, in specially printed envelopes.

All communications to Government officers, and to or from members of Con-gress, are required to be prepaid by stamps.

RATES OF FOREIGN POSTAGE.

From the United States Official Postal Guide, October, 1877.

The standard single rate is ½ ounce avoirdupois.

* Prepayment optional in case of country marked with a star, embraced in the Postal Union Treaty of 1874. When not prepaid, double rates are collected.

Destination.	Letters Cts.	Newspapers Cts.
Africa, British Possessions on W. Coast, by British Mail	15	4
Africa, Spanish Possessions on Northern Coast	*5	2
Argentine Confederation...	27	4
Australia, except New South Wales and Queensland, U. S. Mail	5	2
Austria	*5	2
Azores	*5	2
Balearic Isles	*5	2
Belgium	*5	2
Bermuda	5	2
Bolivia, British Mail, viâ Aspinwall	17	4
Brazil, British Mail	*10	4
British Columbia	3	1
Buenos Ayres	27	4
Burmah, German Mail	17	3
" British Mail, viâ Brindisi	*10	4
Canada	3	1
Canary Islands	*5	2
Cape of Good Hope	15	4
Carthagena, New Grenada	13	4
Ceylon, British Mail, viâ Southampton	*10	4
Chili, British Mail	17	4
China, viâ San Francisco	10	2
Costa Rica, direct Mail, viâ Aspinwall	5	2
Cuba, direct Mail	5	2
Curaçoa, British Mail, viâ St. Thomas	13	4
Denmark	*5	2
E. Indies, viâ Southampton	27	4
Ecuador	20	2
Egypt	*5	2
England	*5	2
Faroe Islands	*5	2
Fiji Islands, direct, viâ San Francisco	5	2
Finland	5	2
France	*5	2
French Colonies	*10	4
Gambia, British Mail	*10	4
Germany	*5	2
Gibraltar, British Mail	*5	2
Gold Const, British Mail	15	4
Grand Duchy of Finland	*5	2
Great Britain	*5	2
Greece	*5	2
Greenland	*5	2
Greytown, British Mail	13	4
Guadaloupe, " "	*10	4
Guatemala, direct Mail	10	2
Guiana, British, French and Dutch	13	4
Havana	5	2
Hawaiian Kingdom, dir. Mail	6	1
Haytl, by direct steamer	5	2
Hong Kong, Canton, Swatow, Amoy, and Foo Chow, viâ San Francisco	*10	4
Iceland	13	4
India, British Mail	*10	4
Ireland	5	2
Italy	*5	2
Jamaica	*5	2
Japan, dir., viâ S. Francisco	*10	4
Java, British Mail, viâ Southampton	*10	4
Liberia, British Mail, viâ Southampton	15	4
Luxembourg	*5	2
Madeira	*5	2
Malta	*5	2
Martinique, British Mail, viâ St. Thomas	*10	4
Mexico, by sea	10	2
" overland	3	1
Morocco, British Mail	*10	4
" Western Coast— Spanish Postal Stations	*5	2
Nassau, N. P	3	2
Netherlands	*10	4
New Brunswick	3	1
New Foundland	6	2
New Grenada, direct Mail	5	2
New South Wales, direct M.	12	2
New Zealand, direct Mail	12	2
Nicaragua, direct	5	2
Norway	*5	2
Nova Scotia	3	1
Panama, direct Mail	5	2
Paraguay, U. S. Packet	27	4
Peru, British Mail	17	4
Poland	5	2
Porto Rico, British Mail, viâ St. Thomas	*10	4
Portugal	*5	2
Prince Edward Island	3	1
Queensland	12	2
Roumania	*5	2
Russia	*5	2
Salvador, direct Mail	10	2
Sandwich Islands, direct Mail, viâ San Francisco	6	1
Scotland	5	2
Servia	5	2
Shanghai	5	2
Siam, dir. from S. Francisco	10	2
Sierra Leone, British Mail, viâ Southampton	15	4
Spain	*5	2
St. Domingo, direct Steamer	5	2
St. Helena, British Mail	15	4
Sweden	*5	2
Switzerland	*5	2
Tangiers, viâ Spain	*5	2
Tripoli, Italian Mail	7	3
Tunis, Italian Mail	7	3
Turkey	*5	2
Turk's Island, British Mail	13	4
Uruguay	23	4
Van Diemen's Land	5	2
Venezuela, British Mail, viâ St. Thomas	13	4
Victoria	5	2
West Indies, British Mail, viâ St. Thomas	13	4
West Indies, direct Mail	5	2
" " French Colonies, viâ France	10	4
Zanzibar, British Mail, viâ Southampton	15	4

UNITED STATES PATENT-OFFICE BUSINESS.

Comparative Statement of the Business of the Office from 1837 to 1877, inclusive.
From the Official Gazette of the United States Patent Office, 1877.

Year.	Appli- cations.	Caveats Filed.	Patents Issued.	Cash Received.	Cash Expended.	Surplus.
1837...................	....	....	435	$20,289 08	$33,506 98	....
1838...................	....	....	520	42,123 54	37,402 10	$4,721 44
1839...................	....	....	425	37,260 00	34,543 51	2,716 49
1840...................	735	228	473	38,056 51	39,020 67	....
1841...................	847	312	495	40,413 01	52,666 87	....
1842...................	761	391	517	36,505 68	31,241 48	5,264 20
1843...................	819	315	531	35,315 81	30,776 96	4,538 85
1844...................	1,045	380	502	42,509 26	36,244 73	6,264 53
1845...................	1,246	452	502	51,076 14	39,395 65	11,680 49
1846...................	1,272	448	619	50,264 16	46,158 71	4,105 45
1847...................	1,531	553	572	63,111 19	41,878 85	21,232 84
1848...................	1,628	607	660	67,576 69	58,905 84	8,670 85
1849...................	1,955	595	1,070	80,752 98	77,716 44	3,036 54
1850...................	2,193	602	995	86,927 05	80,100 95	6,816 13
1851...................	2,258	760	869	95,738 61	86,916 93	8,821 60
1852...................	2,639	996	1,020	112,656 34	95,916 91	16,739 43
1853...................	2,673	901	958	121,527 45	132,869 83	....
1854...................	3,324	868	1,902	163,789 84	167,146 32	....
1855...................	4,435	906	2,024	216,459 35	179,540 33	36,919 02
1856...................	4,960	1,024	2,502	192,588 02	199,931 02	....
1857...................	4,771	1,010	2,910	196,132 01	211,582 09	....
1858...................	5,364	934	3,710	203,716 16	193,193 74	10,522 42
1859...................	6,225	1,097	4,538	245,942 15	210,278 41	35,663 74
1860	7,653	1,084	4,819	256,352 59	252,820 80	3,531 79
1861...................	4,643	700	3,340	137,354 44	221,491 91	....
1862...................	5,088	824	3,521	215,754 99	182,810 39	32,944 60
1863...................	6,014	787	4,170	195,593 29	189,414 14	6,179 15
1864...................	6,932	1,063	5,020	240,919 98	229,868 00	11,051 98
1865...................	10,664	1,937	6,616	348,791 84	274,199 34	74,592 50
1866...................	15,269	2,723	9,450	495,665 83	361,724 28	133,941 10
1867...................	21,276	3,597	13,015	646,581 92	639,263 32	7,318 60
1868...................	20,420	3,705	13,378	681,565 86	628,679 77	52,886 09
1869..................	19,271	3,624	13,986	693,145 81	486,430 78	206,715 03
1870...................	19,171	3,273	13,321	669,456 76	557,149 19	112,307 57
1871...................	19,472	3,366	13,033	678,716 46	560,595 08	118,121 38
1872...................	18,246	3,090	13,590	699,726 39	665,591 36	34,135 03
1873..........	20,414	3,248	12,864	703,191 77	691,178 98	12,012 79
1874............	21,602	3,181	13,599	738,278 17	679,288 41	58,989 76
1875...................	21,638	3,094	16,288	743,453 36	721,657 71	21,795 65
1876...................	21,425	2,697	17,026	757,987 65	652,542 60	105,445 05
1877...................	19,914	2,658	14,459	714,964 73	609,043 24	105,921 49

SCHEDULE OF UNITED STATES PATENT FEES.

On filing each application for a Patent (17 years)............................$15
On issuing each Original Patent. 20
On application for Re-issue..30
On each Caveat...10
On appeal to Examiner-in-chief...10
On appeal to Commissioner of Patents.....................................20
On filing a Disclaimer..10
On application for Design (3½ years)......................................10
On application for Design (7 years)..15
On application for Design (14 years)......................................30
On each Trade Mark (30 years)..25
On each Label (28 years).. ... 6

OFFICERS OF THE SMITHSONIAN INSTITUTION.

Secretary—Joseph Henry.
Assistant Secretary—Spencer F. Baird.
Chief Clerk—William J. Rhees.

Executive Committee. { Peter Parker, John Maclean, George Bancroft.

REGENTS OF THE INSTITUTION.

Morrison R. Waite, Chief-Justice of the U. S., member of the House.
T. W. Ferry, President of the Senate, *pro tem.*
H. Hamlin, member of the Senate.
R. E. Withers, member of the Senate.
A. A. Sargent, member of the Senate.
Hiester Clymer, member of the House.
Alex. H. Stephens, member of the House.

James A. Garfield, member of the House.
John Maclean, Princeton, N. J.
Peter Parker, Washington, D. C.
George Bancroft, Washington, D. C.
Asa Gray, Cambridge, Mass.
J. D. Dana, New Haven, Conn.
Henry Coppée, Bethlehem, Pa.

THE COPYRIGHT LAWS OF THE UNITED STATES.

EVERY applicant for a copyright must state distinctly the name and residence of the claimant, and whether the right is claimed as author, designer, or proprietor. No affidavit or formal application is required.

A printed copy of the title of the book, map, chart, dramatic or musical composition, engraving, cut, print, or photograph, or a description of the painting, drawing, chromo, statue, statuary, or model or design for a work of the fine arts, for which copyright is desired, must be sent by mail or otherwise, prepaid, addressed "LIBRARIAN OF CONGRESS, WASHINGTON, D. C." This must be done before publication of the book or other article.

A fee of 50 cents, for recording the title of each book or other article, must be inclosed with the title as above, and 50 cents in addition (or one dollar in all) for each certificate of copyright under seal of the Librarian of Congress, which will be transmitted by return mail.

Within ten days after publication of each book or other article, two complete copies must be sent prepaid, to perfect the copyright, with the address "LIBRARIAN OF CONGRESS, WASHINGTON, D. C."

Without the deposit of copies above required the copyright is void, and a penalty of $25 is incurred.

No copyright is valid unless notice is given by inserting in every copy published, "Entered according to act of Congress, in the year ——, by ——, in the office of the Librarian of Congress, at Washington ;" or, at the option of the person entering the copyright, the words : "Copyright, 18—, by ——."

The law imposes a penalty of $100 upon any person who has not obtained copyright who shall insert the notice "Entered according to act of Congress," or "Copyright," or words of the same import, in or upon any book or other article.

Each copyright secures the exclusive right of publishing the book or article copyrighted for the term of twenty-eight years. Six months before the end of that time, the author or designer, or his widow or children, may secure a renewal for the further term of fourteen years, making forty-two years in all.

Any copyright is assignable in law by any instrument of writing, but such assignment must be recorded in the office of the Librarian of Congress within sixty days from its date. The fee for this record and certificate is one dollar.

A copy of the record (or duplicate certificate) of any copyright entry will be furnished, under seal, at the rate of fifty cents.

Copyrights cannot be granted upon Trade-marks, nor upon Labels intended to be used with any article of manufacture. If protection for such prints or labels is desired, application must be made to the Patent Office, where they are registered at a fee of $6 for labels and $25 for trade-marks.

PATENTS ISSUED IN 1876 TO RESIDENTS OF EACH STATE.

The proportion of patents to population is shown in last column.

STATES, ETC.	No. of Patents.	One to every—	STATES, ETC.	No. of Patents.	One to every—
Alabama	46	21,673	Montana Territory	3	13,296
Arizona Territory	2	20,855	Nebraska	40	3,233
Arkansas	23	21,064	Nevada	21	2,796
California	423	1,376	New Hampshire	106	3,003
Colorado	21	2,246	New Jersey	685	1,328
Connecticut	736	730	New Mexico Territory	1	111,308
Dakota Territory	10	4,050	New York	3,914	1,121
Delaware	35	3,572	North Carolina	51	21,007
Dist. of Columbia	197	668	Ohio	1,195	2,230
Florida	22	8,556	Oregon	24	4,243
Georgia	63	18,795	Pennsylvania	1,895	1,859
Idaho Territory	5	4,116	Rhode Island	231	941
Illinois	1,208	1,957	South Carolina	31	22,751
Indiana	425	3,054	Tennessee	107	11,762
Iowa	425	2,810	Texas	108	7,582
Kansas	83	4,498	Utah Territory	14	7,113
Kentucky	163	8,104	Vermont	111	2,978
Louisiana	107	6,793	Virginia	145	8,449
Maine	178	3,522	Washington Territory	5	7,486
Maryland	273	2,800	West Virginia	54	8,185
Massachusetts	1,587	918	Wisconsin	303	3,515
Michigan	426	2,787	Wyoming Territory	10	1,151
Minnesota	164	2,720	U. S. Army	7	....
Mississippi	42	19,712	U. S. Navy	1	....
Missouri	423	4,069	U. S. in general	16,239	2,398

THE ARMIES OF THE WORLD.

Compiled from Official Documents.

COUNTRIES.	Regular Army.	War Footing.	Cost of Army.
			Dollars.
Argentine Republic..........	8,283	....	{ Army and Navy, 4,514,018
Austria-Hungary................. .	296,218	1,021,692	50,690,000
Belgium..........................	46,277	103,683	8,787,909
Bolivia..........	4,022	....	1,126,916
Brazil............	16,500	32,000	10,862,496
Canada (Dominion)	3,000	635,000	1,013,944
Chili............	3,516	29,274	....
China.........	700,000	1,260,000	....
Colombia	2,600	30,000	288,000
Denmark.......................	35,703	50,000	2,406,109
Egypt...........	62,920	128,000	{ Army and Navy, 4,452,422
France.........................	470,600	1,750,000	100,007,623
Germany.......................	419,650	1,034,524	92,573,403
Great Britain and Ireland.........	133,720	370,561	65,161,015
Greece.........................	12,397	30,000	1,494,860
India, British.................. ...	58,170	144,700	76,875,960
Italy...........................	199,577	867,509	37,983,755
Japan..........................	35,380	50,240	7,506,000
Luxembourg....................	513	....	100,480
Mexico	22,337	....	{ Army and Navy, 10,554,745
Netherlands....................	61,803	160,000	10,266,990
Norway........................	12,750	18,000	1,480,760
Persia.........................	28,400	108,500	3,400,000
Peru...........................	13,200	....	....
Portugal.......................	35,733	75,000	4,342,929
Roumania......................	130,158	144,668	3,310,198
Russia........................	787,900	1,671,674	144,215,615
Servia.........................	14,150	150,000	869,138
Spain..........................	330,000	400,000	49,146,491
Sweden........................	36,495	156,970	3,579,940
Switzerland....	100,102	203,262	2,419,213
Turkey.........................	157,667	618,100	24,783,095
United States.........	20,000	2,893,469	37,082,735
Uruguay.......................	4,060	24,000	{ Army and Navy, 2,364,100
Venezuela....	5,494	....	....

COTTON CROP OF THE UNITED STATES FOR 48 YEARS.

YEARS ENDING SEPTEMBER 1.

From the Commercial and Financial Chronicle.

Year.	Bales.	Year.	Bales.	Year.	Bales.	Year.	Bales.
1829	870,415	1841	1,634,945	1853	3,262,882	1866	2,193,987
1830	976,845	1842	1,683,574	1854	2,930,027	1867	2,019,774
1831	1,038,848	1843	2,378,875	1855	2,847,389	1868	2,593,993
1832	987,487	1844	2,030,409	1856	3,527,845	1869	2,439,039
1833	1,070,438	1845	2,394,503	1857	2,939,519	1870	3,154,946
1834	1,205,324	1846	2,100,537	1858	3,113,962	1871	4,352,317
1835	1,254,328	1847	1,778,651	1859	3,851,481	1872	2,974,351
1836	1,360,752	1848	2,347,634	1860	4,669,770	1873	3,930,508
1837	1,422,930	1849	2,728,596	1861	3,656,006	1874	4,170,388
1838	1,801,497	1850	2,096,706	1862		1875	3,832,991
1839	1,360,532	1851	2,355,257	to	} No record	1876	4,669,288
1840	2,177,835	1852	3,015,029	1865		1877	4,485,000

NOTE.—The average net weight per bale is 440 lbs.

DEBTS, REVENUES, EXPENDITURES, AND COMMERCE OF NATIONS.

Compiled from the Almanach de Gotha, the Statistical Abstract of the United Kingdom, and from Official Documents. The figures are for the latest attainable years as to each country.

COUNTRIES.	Public Debt.	Revenue.	Expenditures.	Imports.	Exports.
	$	$	$	$	$
Argentine Republic.	68,416,043	20,683,537	20,663,337	34,910,290	44,041,131
Austria proper......	1,419,096,072	186,776,170	202,035,039	....	....
Austria-Hungary....	205,999,970	60,000,000	58,845,695	258,450,000	204,800,000
Belgium...	232,684,553	50,048,972	49,045,128	258,504.000	222,920,400
Bolivia	17,500,000	2,929,574	4,505,504	5,750,000	5,000,000
Brazil..............	368,351,139	72,548,451	67,789,297	88,045,520	104,232,800
Canada..............	112,248,378	22,700,000	24,100,000	93,200,000	89,851,328
Chili...............	50,677,600	21,294,383	22,052,187	39,050,197	37,139,061
China..............	3,200,000	230,000,000	....	105,000,000	114,000,000
Colombia	15,399,304	8,114,619	2,779,410	6,949,028	9,994,286
Denmark	52,000,000	13,464,066	13,074,620	60,311,240	83,933,640
Ecuador............	17,500,000	20,800,000	21,500,455	7,596,264	3,913,536
Egypt..............	450,540,000	54,820,818	54,737,670	29,000,000	68,000,000
France	4,695,600,000	514,605,716	519,334,162	4,111,000	9,280,000
Germany	30,000,000	135,584,249	135,000,000	918,850,000	608,200,000
Gt.Britain & Ireland.	3,625,296,585	392,825,180	390,626,140	1,869,695,885	1,283,853,010
Greece..............	40,012,000	7,765,360	7,632,768	790,085,000	713,978,200
Guiana.............	460,000	1,580,000	4,580,000	1,811,770	2,241,040
Hawaiian Islands...	548,022	504,095	460,000	1,682,000	2,090,000
Hungary Proper ..	274,358,915	106,069,258	116,902,036	....	....
India, British......	576,634,330	252,649,885	272,503,145	179,000,000	282,600,000
Italy...............	1,977,117,845	279,550,000	278,121,440	265,899,000	243,371,000
Japan..............	148,924,725	63,120,600	62,993,850	24,087,515	27,669,465
Luxembourg........	2,400,000	1,438,660	1,409,344	....	....
Mexico.....	205,500,000	23,807,671	24,891,522	29,062,407	31,659,151
Netherlands........	391,242,322	43,973,341	48,785,061	275,416,000	261,750,000
Norway............	13,526,128	11,364,220	10,726,500	52,017,280	33,933,640
Paraguay...........	12,098,417	600,000	750,000	565,595	607,653
Peru...............	213.482,680	29,801,195	33,755,375	....	37,500,000
Persia..............	No debt.	8,240,000	8,750,000	5,625,000	2,813,000
Portugal............	428,977,613	29,566,816	29,720,336	58,131,520	26,448,600
Roumania..........	60,000,000	19,578,885	19,578,885	16,200,000	28,440,000
Russia..............	1,420,092,043	409,377,280	410,557,408	365,426,400	422,966,400
Servia	5,000,000	2,968,422	2,934,779	6,197,000	5,500,000
Siam...............	....	4,000,000	4,000,000	7,100,000	8,300,000
Spain..............	2,401,612,001	131,500,000	131,824,000	114,000,000	90,000,000
Sweden	39,241,142	23,563,201	21,872,193	85,906,800	62,532,960
Switzerland........	6,225,000	8,297,480	8,524,400	Not given.	Not given.
Turkey.............	1,012,772,200	88,764,050	140,000,000	72,430,000	....
United States	2,046,027,066	269,000,587	238,660,009	492,090,406	658,637,457
Uruguay............	43,615,000	6,965,683	6,800,000	21,917,800	16,953,000
Venezuela..........	62,659,687	3,549,000	3,642,500	12,000,000	17,000,000
Total debts.......	22,937,086,780				

RANKS AND NUMBER PENSIONED FOR EACH RANK OF THE ARMY, JUNE 30, 1877.

	President of the United States.	General Officers.	Colonels.	Lieutenant-Colonels.	Majors.	Sergeons.	Captains.	Chaplains.	First Lieutenants.	Assistant burgeons.	Second Lieutenants.	Enlisted men—Army.	Total Army.
ARMY—													
Invalid................	....	15	173	251	247	109	2,106	53	2,122	114	1,648	103,347	114,199
Widows, etc...........	1	67	225	211	287	197	1,745	87	1,411	159	963	91,772	97,6 5
Total.................	1	82	398	462	534	279	3,851	140	3,533	273	2,611	195,160	211,724

NOTE.—Those pensioned for service in the War of 1812 (17,114) are not included in the above. The above does not include the pay of officers retired from service.

PRICES OF GOVERNMENT LOANS IN LONDON, DEC. 1, 1877.

Compiled from the Investor's Monthly Manual, issued by The Economist, London.

Countries.	Interest, per cent.	Issue Price.	Selling Price.
Argentine—	6	75	73
Public Works, 1871	6	88½	63
Austria—			
Consols	5	....	57
Australia (South)	6	....	106
Belgian—			
4½ per cents	4½	....	102
3 per cents	3	75½	76½
Bolivian	6	68	24
Brazilian—			
5 per cent 1871	5	89	92
4½ per cent	4½	88	88
British—			
3 per cent. Consols	3	....	96¾
New 3 per cents	3	....	95⅝
British Columbian—			
6 per cents	6	....	105
Buenos Ayres—			
6 per cents	6	89½	89½
Canadian Dominion—			
6 per cents	6	....	106
4 per cents	4	90	92
Cape of Good Hope—			
6 per cent	6	....	115
Ceylon—			
6 per cents	6	....	108
Chilian—			
7 per cents	7	92	102⅜
6 per cents	6	84	99
4½ per cent	4½	....	78
Chinese—			
8 per cents	8	....	102
Colombian—			
4½ per cent	4½	....	87
Costa Rica—			
6 per cents	6	72	11
Danish—			
4 per cents	4	....	....
Dutch—			
4 per cents	4	101	101
Egyptian—			
9 per cents	9	90	75
7 per cents	7	93	73
French—			
5 per cent National, 1871-2	} 5	82½	} 106
5 per cent National, 1872		84½	
4½ per cent Treasury	4½	....	99
Greek—			
5 per cents	5	...	12
Guatemala—			
6 per cents	6	70⅛	22
Honduras—			
10 per cent Railway Loan	10	80	3
Hungarian—			
6 per cent Treasury bonds	6	91½	86
5 p. c. Treas. bonds, 1873	5	....	64
India—			
5 per cents	5	....	106
Italian—			
6 per cents	6	81⅜	102½
5 per cents	5	71	71¾
Jamaica—			
4 per cent guar	4	104	106
Japanese—			
9 per cent Customs Loan	9	98	110
Mexican—			
3 per cents	3	60	3½
Moorish—			
5 per cents	5	85	99
Norwegian—			
4½ per cents	4½	96½	96½
Paraguayan—			
8 per cent Public Works	8	6	80
Peruvian—			
6 per cent Railway Loans	6	81¼	12⅜
5 per cent Consols	5	77½	11
Portuguese—			
6 per cents	6	....	97
3 per cents	3	40	50
Russian—			
5 per cent Consols		89	76
4½ per cents	4½	92	75
3 per cents	3	66¼	55
San Domingo—			
6 per cents	6	70	5
Sardinian—			
5 per cents	5	85	88
Spanish—			
6 per cents	6	80	68
5 per cents	5	80	95
3 per cents	3	....	13
Swedish—			
5 per cents	5	90	105½
4½ per cents	5	92	97½
Turkish—			
6 per cents	6	60½	10
5 per cents	5	50	10
United States—			
5-20 Bonds, 1865	6	par	105½
5-20 Bonds, 1867	6	par	108¾
10-40 Bonds	5	par	108½
4½ per cent Funded, 1876	4½	par	104¼
4 per cent Funded, 1877	4	par	
Uruguay—			
6 per cents	....	72	23
Venezuela—			
6 per cents	....	60	10⅜

HIGHEST AND LOWEST PRICES OF ACTIVE STOCKS AT THE NEW YORK STOCK EXCHANGE FROM 1860 to 1877.

Name of Stock.	1860.		1861.		1862.		1863.		1864.		1865.		1866.		1867.		1868.	
	H.	L.	H.	L.	H.	L.	H.	L.	H.	L.	H.	L.	H.	L.	H.	L.	H.	L.
Adams Express	....	....	....	....	....	....	....	....	....	....	....	....	104	61	84½	55	82½	46
American Express	....	....	....	....	....	....	....	....	....	....	....	....	105	75	82¾	54¾	77½	40
Central of New Jersey	....	....	....	....	....	....	....	....	....	....	....	....	132½	104	125	115	124½	110¾
Chicago, Milwaukee and St. Paul	....	....	....	....	....	....	....	....	....	....	....	....	64½	41	53⅝	25	111	47
" " " pref.	....	....	....	....	....	....	....	....	....	....	....	....	75	55	70½	47½	112	63¼
Chicago and Northwestern	....	....	....	....	....	....	....	....	88	34	40½	20	62½	25½	65¼	29⅝	97¾	58¾
" " pref.	....	....	....	....	....	....	50½	16	97	61	71⅞	48	84½	52⅛	83	56¼	98⅛	68
Chicago and Rock Island	84¼	42½	62	30¾	85⅛	50	123½	82¼	149⅝	85¼	113⅛	81¾	123½	90	105	85	118	85
Delaware, Lackawanna and Western	99	54	82	65	130	83	198	130	265	195	225	185	162½	125½	130	110	132	107½
Erie	43	8⅛	40½	17	65¼	33⅝	122	66	126⅛	82	98½	44¼	97⅜	57½	77½	52¾	82⅛	37¼
Hannibal and St. Joseph	....	....	....	....	....	....	....	....	....	....	....	....	60	80	52	45	91	51
Harlem	24	8	17	8¾	25⅛	12	170	27½	285	86⅛	77	75	97	97	118½	95	131½	112
Lake Shore	....	....	....	....	....	....	....	....	....	....	....	....	....	....	....	....	102⅛	95
Michigan Central	73⅓	25	61⅓	39¾	93	47	128¾	91	157	115	118¼	90⅓	117¾	100¾	114	102	129	106½
New York Central	92⅛	69	82½	68	107¾	79⅝	140	107	145	109	119	80	123½	86⅝	118½	95¾	159⅝	110⅛
Ohio and Mississippi	....	....	....	....	....	....	....	....	69	32	34⅓	19½	36⅛	24¼	30	22	34⅝	28
Pacific Mail	107⅓	70	100	50	137	91	248	136¼	325	214	329	151	234	159¾	173½	108¼	130¼	88
Panama	146½	106	121	97½	170	110	200	171	300	200	270	200	270	239	312	354	369	290
Quicksilver	....	....	....	....	....	....	....	....	....	....	....	....	58	36¾	45½	15	32⅛	19⅝
Toledo, Wabash and Western	....	....	....	....	....	....	86	39⅞	75⅛	52	55	39	55½	31	53⅛	34	67	42½
United States Express	....	....	....	....	....	....	....	....	....	....	....	....	80	70	81⅝	54	80¼	41
Wells-Fargo Express	....	....	....	....	....	....	....	....	....	....	....	....	....	....	70¼	42	49½	22
Western Union Telegraph	....	....	....	....	....	....	....	....	....	....	....	....	70	44	50⅝	30⅛	39⅛	33

PRICES OF ACTIVE STOCKS—(*Continued*).

NAME OF STOCK.	1869. H.	1869. L.	1870. H.	1870. L.	1871. H.	1871. L.	1872. H.	1872. L.	1873. H.	1873. L.	1874. H.	1874. L.	1875. H.	1875. L.	1876. H.	1876. L.	1877. H.*	1877. L.
Adams Express	69½	48	69	60⅜	91⅜	64½	99⅜	88¾	100¼	76	120	92½	104½	98	114	100	105	91
American Express	40⅝	40⅜	†	†	7	7	†	†	70¼	41	65½	58½	65	50	67	55	60⅛	43¼
Atlantic and Pacific Telegraph	....	....	....	....	....	....	....	....	....	....	20	14	29½	17½	22	14½	25	15½
" " " pref.	....	....	....	....	37⅛	35	....	....	38⅞	10	22	10⅛	18	3⅜	7	1	....	....
Central of New Jersey	122⅝	85¾	110⅜	92	115	100	118⅝	98	106½	85	109½	98	120	99⅝	109⅞	20⅞	37¾	6
Chicago and Northwestern	94	62	85⅛	67	91⅛	53	100	66⅜	85	31½	62¼	34¾	48⅞	33⅜	45¼	35⅛	43⅜	15
" " pref.	106¼	73⅛	92⅞	80¼	125	81⅜	94½	83⅞	116	53	74⅞	48	62¾	46	67⅛	55⅝	69½	37¾
Chicago and Rock Island	133⅝	101⅛	125⅜	101⅞	126	93⅛	117¼	105	117⅜	83¼	109⅝	92⅛	109⅝	100⅛	111⅛	98¼	105½	82⅜
Chicago, Milwaukee and St. Paul	84⅞	60	75	52⅞	64⅞	48¾	64⅛	52	62¼	21⅛	49⅜	31¼	40⅛	28⅝	46⅞	18⅛	42⅛	11
" " " " pref.	96⅝	74	89¼	71⅝	93	71¾	82⅞	72⅛	79½	43¾	74⅜	48	67⅛	51	84⅜	49⅜	73	40⅞
Col., Chicago and I. C.	59	19	22⅜	15⅛	21⅝	15¾	42⅜	19¾	43⅞	15⅝	32⅝	8	9¾	8	6¼	2½	79	40½
Delaware, Lackawanna and Western	120½	104¾	112⅜	100⅜	111¼	102⅞	112⅜	91	106	79½	112⅞	99	123	106⅛	120⅞	64⅜	77	30⅞
Erie	48⅜	21	28⅛	20⅛	84¾	19	75	30⅛	69¼	35⅝	51⅛	26	35½	12¼	23⅞	7⅜	15	4⅝
Hannibal and St. Joseph	139	90	121½	97	106	50½	57⅜	20	52⅛	15	34¼	22⅛	30⅛	15⅜	22⅝	10½	15⅜	7
Harlem	168¾	123	150	120	135	117⅛	120¾	107½	139	90	134⅞	118¾	138	127½	145	130⅝	147	135
Lake Shore	110⅜	75⅛	102	84	116	84⅝	98¼	86⅛	97¾	57¼	84⅝	67⅞	80⅛	51⅛	68⅝	43¾	73⅞	45
Michigan Central	217⅞	145	126	116	126	114	120	113	111	65	95½	68⅛	82¼	53	65½	34⅝	74¼	35⅝
N. Y. Central and Hudson River	217⅜	154⅛	*102½	86	103½	90⅜	101½	91¾	106½	77⅞	105⅝	95⅞	107⅜	100	117½	96	109¼	85⅛
Ohio and Mississippi	39	22⅛	41¾	23⅞	55	27¾	51¾	41¼	49⅝	21	36	21⅜	82¾	14¾	24⅜	5	11⅞	2⅛
Pacific Mail	123¾	42	46⅜	30¾	53⅛	39½	102⅜	53	76⅞	24	51½	33⅝	45⅜	30⅞	39⅞	16⅛	26¼	12⅞
Pacific of Missouri	....	....	....	....	....	....	60	54¾	60½	27⅛	48	29¾	55	7½	16	1½	....	....
Panama	348	183	175	70	75	49	150	72	130	76	118	101	172	110¾	140	122	130	80
Quicksilver	26	12	15½	4¼	27⅛	5	49¼	25½	46½	18	86⅛	22¾	35	13	20¼	10⅛	....	....
" pref.	....	....	18	9	33	7½	59	30	57	25	48	29	44	20	....	....	....	....
Toledo, Wabash and Western	86	42½	61⅜	42½	71⅝	48¼	79¾	66½	75¾	32¾	55⅛	18⅜	21⅜	2⅛	8	¾	20½	⅛
Union Pacific	....	....	27⅛	9	37⅞	11⅛	42	28⅞	39½	14¾	38¾	23	82¾	36	74½	57¾	73	59¾
United States Express	78	48½	56	32	66	33⅛	88½	63	82	44¾	73	60	65	41⅛	76¾	49⅜	59¾	36
Wells-Fargo Express	37½	16	42¼	12⅜	58⅛	35	95	56⅛	86	56	64	69⅛	92⅛	71	90	79	90	81
Western Union Telegraph	44⅝	32	46½	30⅛	71⅝	44⅛	82⅛	67½	94⅜	43⅛	83⅛	68	84⅜	70¾	80½	66⅞	84⅝	56

* Hudson River Railroad consolidated with New York Central. † No sales reported.

HIGHEST AND LOWEST PRICES OF UNITED STATES SECURITIES FOR EIGHTEEN YEARS, 1860-1877.

Compiled from the Commercial and Financial Chronicle.

SALES AT THE NEW YORK STOCK EXCHANGE.

YEARS	6s of 1868 Coup. H.	6s of 1868 Coup. L.	5s of 1874 Coup. H.	5s of 1874 Coup. L.	6s of 1881 Coup. H.	6s of 1881 Coup. L.	6s of 1881 Reg. H.	6s of 1881 Reg. L.	6s (5-20 years), Coupon. 1862 H.	1862 L.	1864 H.	1864 L.	1865 H.	1865 L.	1865 new H.	1865 new L.	1867 H.	1867 L.	1868 H.	1868 L.	5s, 10-40. Coup. H.	Coup. L.	Reg. H.	Reg. L.	5s of 1881, Funded. Coup. H.	Coup. L.	Currency Sixes. H.	Currency Sixes. L.	Fund. 4½s of 1891. Reg. H.	Reg. L.	4s of 1907, Funded. Reg. H.	Reg. L.
1860	109¾	99	99	90																												

NOTE.—It is to be understood that the prices quoted were in currency.

UNITED STATES CURRENCY VALUE OF GOLD.

Giving the Currency Price in Dollars of One Hundred Dollars in Gold in the New York Market, averaged by Months and Years, from Jan. 1, 1862, to Jan. 1, 1878.

PERI-ODS.	1862.	1863.	1864.	1865.	1866.	1867.	1868.	1869.	1870.	1871.	1872.	1873.	1874.	1875.	1876.	1877.
Jan...	102.5	145.1	155.5	216.2	140.1	134.6	138.5	135.6	121.3	110.7	109.1	112.7	111.4	112.5	112.8	106.2
Feb..	103.5	160.5	158.6	205.5	138.4	137.4	141.4	134.4	119.5	111.5	110.3	114.1	112.3	114.5	113.4	105.2
Mar..	101.8	154.5	162.9	173.8	130.5	135	139.5	131.3	112.6	111	110.1	115.5	112.1	115.5	114.3	104.8
Apr. .	101.5	151.5	172.7	148.5	127.3	135.6	138.7	132.9	113.1	110.6	111.1	117.8	113.4	114.8	113.2	106.2
May..	103.3	148.9	176.3	135.6	131.8	137	139.6	139.2	114.7	111.5	113.7	117.7	112.4	115.8	112.7	106.5
June.	106.5	144.5	210.7	140.1	148.7	137.5	140.1	138.1	112.9	112.4	113.9	116.5	111.3	117		111.9	105.5
July..	115.5	130.6	258.1	142.1	151.6	139.4	142.7	136.1	116.8	112.4	114.3	115.7	110	114.8	111.8	105.6
Aug..	114.5	125.8	254.1	143.5	148.7	140.8	145.5	134.2	117.9	112.4	114.4	115.4	109.7	113.5	110.8	104.6
Sept..	118.5	134.2	222.5	143.9	145.5	143.4	143.6	136.8	114.8	114.5	113.5	112.7	109.7	115.8	109.7	103.5
Oct...	128.5	147.7	207.2	145.5	148.3	143.5	137.1	130.2	112.8	113.2	113.2	108.9	110	116.5	110.7	102.9
Nov..	131.1	148.0	233.5	147	143.8	139.6	134.4	126.2	111.4	111.2	112.9	108.6	110.9	115.2	109.1	102.9
Dec...	132.3	151.1	227.5	146.2	136.7	134.8	135.2	121.5	110.7	109.3	112.2	110		111.7	113.9	108	102.7
Aver'ge of year	113.3	145.2	203.3	157.3	140.9	138.2	139.7	133		114.9	111.7	112.4	113.8	111.2	115.1	111.5	104.7

NOTE.—According to the officially-published quotations of the gold market in New York, the currency price of $100 gold reached its maximum on the 11th day of July, 1864, the quotations for that day ranging from $276 to $285. The average price of $100 gold for the month of July, 1864, was $258.10.

GOLD VALUE OF UNITED STATES CURRENCY.

Giving the Gold Price in Dollars of One Hundred Dollars in Currency in the New York Market, averaged by Months and Years, from Jan. 1, 1862, to Jan. 1, 1878.

PERI-ODS.	1862.	1863.	1864.	1865.	1866.	1867.	1868.	1869.	1870.	1871.	1872.	1873.	1874.	1875.	1876.	1877.
Jan...	97.6	68.9	64.3	46.3	71.4	74.3	72.2	73.7	82.4	90.3	91.7	88.7	89.7	88.9	88.6	94.1
Feb..	96.6	62.3	63.1	48.7	72.3	72.8	70.7	74.4	83.7	89.7	90.7	87.6	89.1	87.3	88.2	95
Mar..	98.2	64.7	61.4	57.5	76.6	74.1	71.7	76.2	88.8	90.1	90.8	86.6	89.2	86.6	87.4	95.4
Apr..	98.5	66	57.9	67.3	78.6	73.7	72.1	75.2	88.4	90.4	90	84.9	88.2	87.1	88.3	94.1
May..	96.8	67.2	56.7	73.7	75.9	73	71.6	71.8	87.2	89.7	88	85	89.9	86.3	88.7	93.9
June.	93.9	69.2	47.5	71.4	67.2	72.7	71.4	72.4	88.6	89	87.8	85.8	90	85.4	89.4	94.8
July .	86.6	76.6	38.7	70.4	66	71.7	70.1	73.5	85.6	89	87.5	86.4	91	87.2	89.5	94.7
Aug..	87.3	79.5	39.4	69.7	67.2	71	68.6	74.4	84.8	89	87.4	86.7	91.2	88.1	90.2	95.7
Sept..	84.4	74.5	44.9	69.5	68.7	69.7	69.6	73.1	87.1	87.3	88.1	88.7	91.2	86.4	91.1	96.6
Oct...	77.8	67.7	48.3	68.7	67.4	69.7	72.9	76.8	88.7	88.3	88.3	91.8	91	85.8	90.1	97.2
Nov..	76.3	67.6	42.8	68	69.5	71.6	74.4	79.2	89.8	89.9	88.6	92.1	90.2	86.7	91.6	97.2
Dec. .	75.6	66.2	44	68.4	73.2	74.2	74	82.3	90.3	91.5	89.1	90.9	89.6	87.8	92.5	97.3
Aver'ge of year	88.3	68.9	49.2	63.6	71	72.4	71.6	75.2	87	89.5	89	87.9	89.9	86.9	89.6	95.5

STATE CAPITALS AND GOVERNORS IN 1878.

State.	Capital.	Governor.	Years of Term.	Term Began.	Term Ends.	Salary.
Alabama........	Montgomery ...	Geo. S. Houston, D...	2	Nov. 22, '76	Nov. 24, '78	$3,000
Arkansas........	Little Rock.....	W. R. Miller, D......	2	Jan. 8, '77	Jan. 8, '79	3,500
California......	Sacramento.....	William Irwin, D.....	4	Dec. 4, '75	Dec. 1, '79	7,000
Colorado...... ..	Denver	John L. Routt, R.....	2	Nov. 1, '76	Jan. 14, '79	3,000
Connecticut.....	Hartford	Rich. D. Hubbard, D.	2	Jan. 3, '77	Jan. 8, '79	2,000
Delaware.......	Dover.....	John P. Cochran, D..	4	Jan. '75	Jan. '79	2,000
Florida........	Tallahassee.....	George F. Drew, D...	4	Jan. 1, '77	Jan. '81	3,500
Georgia........	Atlanta........	Alfred H. Colquitt, D.	4	Jan. 1, '77	Jan. 1, '81	4,000
Illinois........	Springfield.... .	Shelby M. Cullom, R.	4	Jan. 1, '77	Jan. 1, '81	6,000
Indiana........	Indianapolis....	Jas. D. Williams, D...	4	Jan. 8, '77	Jan. 3, '81	6,000
Iowa...........	Des Moines.....	John H. Gear, R......	2	Jan. 14, '78	Jan. 11, '80	3,000
Kansas........	Topeka..... ...	Geo. T. Anthony, R.	2	Jan. 8, '77	Jan. 13, '79	3,000
Kentucky..... ..	Frankfort.....	Jas. B. McCreary, D.	4	Aug. 31, '75	Sept. 2, '79	5,000
Louisiana.......	New Orleans ...	Francis T. Nicholls, D	4	Jan. 8, '77	Jan. 8, '81	8,000
Maine..........	Augusta........	Selden Connor, R....	1	Jan. 2, '78	Jan. 1, '79	2,500
Maryland.......	Annapolis......	John Lee Carroll, D..	4	Jan. '76	Jan. '80	4,500
Massachusetts..	Boston...........	Alex. H. Rice, R.....	1	Jan. 2, '78	Jan. 1, '79	5,000
Michigan.......	Lansing........	Chas. M. Croswell, R.	2	Jan. 1, '77	Jan. 1, '79	1,000
Minnesota......	St. Paul........	J. S. Pillsbury, R	2	Jan. 7, '78	Jan. '80	3,000
Mississippi	Jackson........	John M. Stone, D....	4	Jan. 7, '78	Jan. '82	4,000
Missouri........	Jefferson City..	John S. Phelps, D....	4	Jan. 3, '77	Jan. 5, '81	5,000
Nebraska.......	Lincoln..	Silas Garber, R.......	2	Jan. 10, '77	Jan. 7, '79	2,500
Nevada.........	Carson City ...	Louis R. Bradley, D..	4	Jan. 5, '75	Jan. 7, '79	6,000
New Hampshire	Concord.... ...	Benj. F. Prescott, R..	1	June 7, '77	June '78	1,000
New Jersey.....	Trenton........	Geo. B. McClellan, D.	3	Jan. 15, '78	Jan. 18, '81	5,000
New York......	Albany.........	Lucius Robinson, D..	3	Jan. '77	Jan. '80	10,000
North Carolina.	Raleigh	Zebulon B. Vance, D.	4	Jan. 1, '77	Jan. 1, '81	4,000
Ohio..........	Columbus......	Richard M. Bishop, D.	2	Jan. 9, '78	Jan. 14, '80	4,000
Oregon........	Salem..........	S. F. Chadwick, D....	4	Sept. '74	Sept. '78	1,500
Pennsylvania...	Harrisburg.. ...	John F. Hartranft, R.	3	Jan. 17, '76	Jan. 15, '79	10,000
Rhode Island...	Newp't & Prov.	Chas. C. Van Zandt, R.	1	May 29, '77	May 28, '78	1,000
South Carolina.	Columbia..... ..	Wade Hampton, D...	2	Dec. 14, '76	Dec. '79	3,500
Tennessee......	Nashville.......	James D. Porter, D...	2	Jan. 15, '77	Jan. '79	4,000
Texas..........	Austin........	R. B. Hubbard, D	2	Dec. 1, '76	Jan. 15, '79	4,000
Vermont........	Montpelier.... .	Horace Fairbanks, R.	2	Oct. 4, '76	Oct. 2, '78	1,000
Virginia........	Richmond......	F. W. M. Holliday, D.	4	Jan. 1, '78	Jan. 1, '82	5,000
West Virginia..	Wheeling.......	Hy. M. Mathews, D...	4	Mar. 4, '77	Mar. 4, '81	2,700
Wisconsin......	Madison........	William E. Smith, R..	2	Jan. 7, '78	Jan. '80	5,000

Democratic Governors, 24.   Republican Governors, 11.

Governors of the Territories in 1878.

Territory.	Capital.	Governor.	Years of Term.	Term Began.	Term Ends.	Salary.
Arizona........	Tucson.........	John P. Hoyt, R......	4	April 5, '77	April 5, '81	$2,600
Dakota........	Yankton........	John L. Pennington, R.	4	Jan. 1, '74	Jan. 1, '78	2,600
Idaho........	Boise City......	Mason Brayman, R..	4	July 24, '76	July 24, '80	2,600
Montana.......	Helena	Benjamin F. Potts, R.	4	July 13, '74	July 13, '78	2,600
New Mexico...	Santa Fé.	Samuel B. Axtell, R..	4	July 1, '75	July 1, '79	2,600
Utah..........	Salt Lake City,.	George W. Emery, R.	4	July 1, '75	July 1, '79	2,600
Washington....	Olympia........	Elisha P. Ferry, R...	4	April 26, '76	April 26, '80	2,600
Wyoming......	Cheyenne......	John M. Thayer, R...	4	Feb. 10, '75	Feb. 10, '79	2,600

LEGISLATURES AND ELECTIONS OF STATES.

States.	Sessions.	Next Legislature Meets.	Limit of Session.	Term of Sen.	Term of Rep.	Salary.	Next Election.
Alabama	Bien.	Nov. 12, '78	50 days.	4	2	$4 per day & 10 c. mileage.	Bien. Aug. 5, '78
Arkansas	Bien.	Jan. 13, '79	60 days.	4	2	$6 per day.	Bien. Sept. 3, '78
California	Bien.	Dec. 3, '77	120 days.	4	2	$10 per day & $3 for 20 m. travel	Bien. Sept. 6, '79
Colorado	Bien.	Jan. 1, '79	40 days.	4	2	$4 per day.	Bien. Oct. 1, '78
Connecticut	Ann.	Jan. 9, '78	None.	2	1	$270 and mileage.	Bien. Nov. 5, '78
Delaware	Bien.	Jan. 7, '79	None.	4	2	$3 per day & mil'ge.	Bien. Nov. 5, '78
Florida	Bien.	Jan. 1, '79	60 days.	4	2	$6 per day.	Bien. Nov. 5, '78
Georgia	Bien.	Jun. 9, '78	40 days.	4	2	$4 per day & mil'ge.	Bien. Oct. 2, '78
Illinois	Bien.	Jan. 8, '79	None.	4	2	$5 per day & 10 c. mileage & $50.	Bien. Nov. 5, '78
Indiana	Bien.	Jan. 2, '79	60 days.	4	2	$5 per day.	Bien. Oct. 8, '78
Iowa	Bien.	Jan. 14, '78	None.	4	2	$550.	Bien. Oct. 8, '78
Kansas	Bien.	Jan. 14, '79	50 days	4	2	$3 per day for 50 d.	Bien. Nov. 5, '78
Kentucky	Bien.	Dec. 31, '77	60 days.	4	2	$5 per day.	Bien. Aug. 4, '79
Louisiana	Ann.	Jan. 7, '78	60 days.	4	2	$8 per day and mileage.	Bien. Nov. 4, '78
Maine	Ann.	Jan. 2, '78	None.	1	1	$150.	Ann. Sept. 9, '78
Maryland	Bien.	Jan. 2, '78	90 days.	4	2	$5 per day and mileage.	Bien. Nov. 4, '79
Massachus'tts	Ann.	Jan. 2, '78	None.	1	1	$650.	Ann. Nov. 5, '78
Michigan	Bien.	Jan. 1, '79	None.	2	2	$3 per day.	Bien. Nov. 5, '78
Minnesota	Bien.	Jan. 8, '78	60 days.	2	1	$5 per day and 15 c.	Ann. Nov. 5, '78
Mississippi	Ann.	Jan. 8, '78	None.	4	2	$500	Bien. Nov. 4, '79
Missouri	Bien.	Jan. 8, '79	70 days.	4	2	$5 per day.	Bien. Nov. 5, '78
Nebraska	Bien.	Jan. 7, '79	40 days.	2	2	$3 per day.	Bien. Nov. 5, '78
Nevada	Bien.	Jan. 6, '79	60 days.	4	2	$8 per day and 40 c. mileage.	Bien. Nov. 5, '78
N. Hampshire	Bien	June 5, '78	None.	1	1	$3 per day and mileage.	Bien. Mar. 12, '78
New Jersey	Ann.	Jan. 8, '78	None.	3	1	$500.	Ann. Nov. 5, '78
New York	Ann.	Jan. 1, '78	None.	2	1	$1,500.	Ann. Nov. 5, '78
N. Carolina	Bien.	Jan. 8, '79	60 days.	2	2	$4 per day and 10 c. mileage.	Bien. Nov. 5, '78
Ohio	Bien.	Jan. 7, '78	None.	2	2	$5 per day and $3 for 25 m.	Ann. Oct. 14, '78
Oregon	Bien.	Sept. 9, '78	40 days	4	2	$3 per day & $3 for 20 m.	Bien. June 3, '78
Pennsylvania	Bien.	Jan. 1, '78	None.	4	2	$1,000.	Ann. Nov. 5, '78
Rhode Isla'd*	Ann.	Jan. 22, '78	None.	1	1	$1 per day and 8 c. mileage.	Ann. April 3, '78
S. Carolina	Ann.	Nov. 27, '77	None.	4	2	$5 per day and 10 c. mileage.	Bien. Nov. 5, '78
Tennessee	Bien.	Jan. 1, '79	75 days.	2	2	$4 per day and 16 c. mileage.	Bien. Nov. 5, '78
Texas	Bien.	Jan. 8, '79	60 days.	4	2	$5 per day.	Bien. Nov. 5, '78
Vermont	Bien.	Oct. 2, '78	None.	2	2	$3 per day.	Bien. Sept. 3, '78
Virginia	Bien.	Dec. 5, '77	90 days.	4	2	$540.	Bien. Nov. 4, '79
West Virginia	Bien.	Jan. 8, '79	45 days.	4	2	$4 per day.	Bien. Oct. 6, '78
Wisconsin	Ann.	Jan. 9, '78	None.	2	1	$350.	Ann. Nov. 5, '78
TERRITORIES.							
Arizona	Bien.	Jan. 6, '79	40 days.	2	2		Bien. Nov. 5, '78
Dakota	Bien.	Jan. 14, '79	40 days.	2	2		Bien. Nov. 5, '78
Idaho	Bien.	Jan. 14, '78	40 days.	2	2		Bien. Nov. 4, '79
Montana	Bien.	Jan. 13, '79	40 days.	2	2	$6 per day and mileage.	Bien. Nov. 5, '78
New Mexico	Bien.	Dec. 2, '78	40 days.	2	2		Bien. Nov. 5, '78
Utah	Bien.	Jan. 14, '78	40 days.	2	2		Ann. Aug. 5, '78
Washington	Bien.	Oct. 6, '79	40 days.	2	2		Bien. Nov. 5, '78
Wyoming	Bien.	Nov. 4, '79	40 days.	2	2		Ann. Sept. 3, '78

* The Rhode Island Legislature is required to meet annually the last Tuesday in May, at Newport, and an adjourned session to be holden annually at Providence.

STATE DEBTS, VALUATION, AND TAXES.

THE following statistics of the finances of the thirty-eight States in the Union have been derived in most cases from the officers of the States themselves.

STATES.	Date of Statement.	Amount of State Debt. Funded.	Unfunded.	Amount Raised by Taxation Last Year.	Amount of Taxable Property as Assessed. Real.	Personal.	State Tax Per Cent on $100.
		$	$	$	$	$	Cts.
Alabama....	.... 1876.	14,061,670			83,851,252	76,200,000	75
Arkansas...	Sept. 30, 1877.	4,153,035	13,967,012	457,450	61,960,452	32,692,425	60
California..	June 30, 1877.	3,411,000		4,105,884	454,641,311	140,431,866	73½
Colorado...	Nov. 1, 1876.	None.	50,000	74,000	25,584,069	18,545,536	15
Connect't ..	Dec. 1, 1876.	5,014,500		705,024	238,027,082	106,379,945	15
Delaware...	....	1,000,000 (?)					50
Florida.....	Jan. 1, 1877.	1,259,600	43,392	225,000	19,713,462	10,197,091	70
Georgia	Jan., 1877.	11,135,500			146,041,809	90,811,941	50
Illinois.....	Jan. 1, 1876.	796,330	None.	2,640,025	931,199,308	197,291,421	36
Indiana.....	Nov. 1, 1877.	1,097,755		1,395,484	638,246,860	222,362,781	13
Iowa.......	Oct. 30, 1877.	545,435	341,000	(?) 750,000	324,698,364	79,971,680	20
Kansas.....	Nov. 1, 1877.	1,235,975		714,549	94,586,003	29,246,313	55
Kentucky..	Oct. 10, 1876.	2,477,000	183,394	1,586,138	211,508,998	396,534,486	40
Louisiana..	May 31, 1876.	9,318,343	2,548,812	2,473,629	139,220,457	35,485,337	14½
Maine	Jan. 1, 1877.	5,920,400		675,173	224,579,509 (Real & Personal.)	547,044,271	30
Maryland ..	.... 1877.	10,296,522*			1,191,499,228 (Real & Personal.)	508,965,487	17¾
Massac'ts ..	Jan. 1, 1877.	33,550,464†	17,072	1,800,000	630,000,000 (Real & Personal.)		10
Michigan...	Sept. 30, 1877.	1,391,150		1,071,021	274,417,873	77,362,451	17
Minnesota..	Sept. 30, 1877.	2,252,057		788,943	95,097,480	35,702,040	21½
Mississippi.	January, 1877.	3,226,847		856,049	606,086,786 (Real & Personal.)		65
Missouri...	Jan. 1, 1877.	17,248,000		2,843,953	37,975,987	33,335,592	40
Nebraska ..	Oct. 31, 1877.	599,267		968,873	16,820,394	12,744,289	63¼
Nevada.....	Nov. 21, 1877.	840,400		287,347	199,000,353 (Real & Personal.)		90
N.Hamps...	June 1, 1877.	3,576,390	94,084	400,000	445,918,221	160,497,340	50
N. Jersey ..	Jan. 1, 1877.	2,396,300		1,715,552	2,376,252,178	379,488,140	35
N. York....	Sept. 30, 1877.	10,957,055	926,695	8,529,174	91,679,918	56,884,630	81½
N.Carolina.	Sept. 30, 1877.	4,120,100	24,937,045	533,635	1,084,796,732	490,524,810	38
Ohio	Nov. 15, 1877.	6,479,505		4,581,235	41,107,140 (Real & Personal.)		29
Oregon.....	.... 1874.	597,865		315,000	No Tax on Real Estate.		62½
Pennsylv'a.	Oct. 1, 1877.	23,374,876		574,817	159,382,242		30
Rhode Isl'd	Sept. 11, 1877.	2,541,500		492,352	194,122,716	75,760,344	15
S.Carolina..	Oct. 31, 1876.	7,109,250	979,484	1,124,587	82,980,307	43,704,948	1.00
Tennessee..	Jan. 1, 1877.	23,212,006	2,000,000	1,452,676	212,224,546	24,354,966	10
Texas......	Sept. 1, 1877.	5,070,261	220,000	1,396,170	83,174,600	174,457,409	50
Vermont..	.... 1877.		171,000	370,394	81,198,291	18,519,312	30
Virginia....	Sept. 30, 1877.	29,350,816	4,188,141	2,679,339	242,756,548	78,560,940	50
West. Va...	Creation of State Debt by Constitution prohibited			322,462	109,713,997	87,477,083	80
Wisconsin..	Sept. 30, 1877.	2,252,057		840,999	274,417,873	77,362,481	15
		251,569,741	50,667,131	49,760,934	$16,256,084,501		

* The State of Maryland held $4,454,570 in interest-paying securities of corporations, besides $22,957,935 in unproductive securities.

† Massachusetts held $11,440,917 in sinking fund, January 1, 1877.

Historical and Statistical Table of the United States and Territories, showing the Area of each in Square Miles and in Acres; the Date of Organization of Territories; Date of Admission of New States into the Union, with the Statutory References for each.

Corrected from Report of Commissioner of the General Land Office.

THE THIRTEEN ORIGINAL STATES.	Ratified the Constitution.	Area of the Original States.	
		In Square Miles.	In Acres.
New Hampshire	June 21, 1788	9,280	5,939,200
Massachusetts	Feb. 6, 1788	7,800	4,992,000
Rhode Island	May 29, 1790	1,306	835,840
Connecticut	Jan. 9, 1788	4,750	3,040,000
New York	July 26, 1788	47,000	30,080,000
New Jersey	Dec. 18, 1787	8,320	5,324,800
Pennsylvania	Dec. 12, 1787	46,000	29,440,000
Delaware	Dec. 7, 1787	2,120	1,356,800
Maryland	April 28, 1788	11,124	7,119,360
Virginia—East and West	June 25, 1788	61,352	39,265,280
North Carolina	Nov. 21, 1789	50,704	32,450,560
South Carolina	May 23, 1788	34,000	21,760,000
Georgia	Jan. 2, 1788	58,000	37,120,000

STATES ADMITTED.	Act Organizing Territory.	U. S. Statutes.		Act Admitting State.	U. S. Statutes.		Admission Took Effect.	Area of Admitted States and Territories.	
		Vol.	P.		Vol.	P.		In Sq. Miles.	In Acres.
Kentucky	(Out of Va.)			Feb. 4, 1791	1	189	June 1, 1792	37,680	24,115,200
Vermont				Feb. 18, 1791	1	191	Mar. 4, 1791	10,212	6,535,680
Tennessee	(Out of N. C.)			June 1, 1796	1	491	June 1, 1796	45,600	29,184,000
Ohio	Ord'n'e of 1787			Apr. 30, 1802	2	173	Nov. 29, 1802	39,964	25,576,960
Louisiana	March 3, 1805	2	331	Apr. 8, 1812	2	701	Apr. 30, 1812	41,346	26,461,440
Indiana	May 7, 1800	2	58	Dec. 11, 1816	3	399	Dec. 11, 1816	33,809	21,637,760
Mississippi	April 7, 1798	1	549	Dec. 10, 1817	3	472	Dec. 10, 1817	47,156	30,179,840
Illinois	Feb. 3, 1809	2	514	Dec. 3, 1818	3	536	Dec. 3, 1818	55,410	35,462,400
Alabama	March 3, 1817	3	371	Dec. 14, 1819	3	608	Dec. 14, 1819	50,722	32,462,080
Maine	(Out of Mass.)			Mar. 3, 1820	3	544	Mar. 15, 1820	35,000	22,400,000
Missouri	June 4, 1812	2	743	Mar. 2, 1821	3	645	Aug. 10, 1821	65,350	41,824,000
Arkansas	March 2, 1819	3	493	June 15, 1836	5	50	June 15, 1836	52,198	33,406,720
Michigan	Jan. 11, 1805	2	309	Jan. 26, 1837	5	144	Jan. 26, 1837	56,451	36,128,640
Florida	Mar. 30, 1822	3	654	Mar. 3, 1845	5	742	Mar. 3, 1845	59,268	37,931,520
Iowa	June 12, 1838	5	235	Mar. 3, 1845	5	742	Dec. 28, 1846	55,045	35,228,800
Texas				Dec. 29, 1845	9	108	Dec. 29, 1845	274,356	175,587,840
Wisconsin	April 20, 1836	5	10	Mar. 3, 1847	9	178	May 29, 1848	53,924	34,511,360
California				Sept. 9, 1850	9	452	Sept. 9, 1850	188,981	120,947,840
Minnesota	March 3, 1849	9	403	May 4, 1858	11	285	May 11, 1858	83,531	53,459,840
Oregon	Aug. 14, 1848	9	323	Feb. 14, 1859	11	383	Feb. 14, 1859	95,274	60,975,360
Kansas	May 30, 1854	10	277	Jan. 29, 1861	12	126	Jan. 29, 1861	80,891	51,769,976
West Virginia	(Out of Va.)			Dec. 31, 1862	12	633	June 19, 1863	23,000	14,720,000
Nevada	March 2, 1861	12	209	Mar. 21, 1864	13	30	Oct. 31, 1864	112,090	71,737,741
Nebraska	May 30, 1854	10	277	Feb. 9, 1867	14	391	Mar. 1, 1867	75,995	48,636,800
Colorado	Feb. 28, 1861	12	172	Mar. 3, 1875	18	474	Aug. 1, 1876	104,500	66,880,000

POPULATION, CAPITALS, AND AREA OF PRINCIPAL NATIONS.

Countries.	Capital.	Last Census.	Population.	Area Square Miles.	Inhabitants to the Square Mile.
Argentine Republic	Buenos Ayres	1875	1,715,681	871,000	1.96
Austria-Hungary	Vienna	1869	35,904,435	226,406	158.58
Belgium	Brussels	1866	4,839,094	11,412	424.03
Bolivia	La Paz	1861	1,742,352	473,300	3.70
Brazil	Rio de Janeiro	1872	10,108,291	3,275,326	3.08
Canada, Dominion of	Ottawa	1871	3,602,321	3,483,952	1.03
Chili	Santiago	1875	2,068,447	130,977	15.79
Chinese Empire	Pekin	Est.	433,500,000	3,924,627	110.45
Colombia	Bogota	1870	2,951,311	432,400	6.07
Egypt	Cairo	Est.	5,252,000	212,600	24.70
Denmark	Copenhagen	1870	1,912,142	14,553	131.32
Ecuador	Quito	1875	866,137	218,984	3.49
France	Paris	1876	36,905,788	201,900	182.79
Germany	Berlin	1875	42,727,360	212,091	201.45
Great Britain and Ireland	London	1871	31,628,338	121,230	268.08
Greece	Athens	1870	1,457,894	19,941	72.96
India, British	Calcutta	1871	190,663,623	950,919	200.50
Italy	Rome	1875	27,482,174	112,677	243.91
Japan	Yeddo	1874	33,625,678	156,604	214.71
Mexico	Mexico	1871	9,276,079	1,030,442	9.00
Morocco	Morocco	Est.	6,000,000	219,000	27.39
Netherlands	Amsterdam	1876	3,865,456	20,527	188.31
Norway	Christiania	1876	1,807,555	122,280	14.78
Paraguay	Asuncion	1873	221,079	57,303	3.85
Persia	Teheran	Est.	6,500,000	648,000	10.03
Peru	Lima	1876	2,673,075	502,760	5.31
Portugal	Lisbon	1872	4,429,332	36,510	121.31
Russian Empire	St. Petersburg	1876	86,952,347	8,404,767	10.34
Roumania	Bucharest	1873	5,073,000	16,817	301.65
Servia	Belgrade	1874	1,352,822	19,721	68.50
Siam	Bangkok	Est.	6,300,000	250,000	25.20
Spain	Madrid	1870	16,835,506	182,758	92.11
Sweden	Stockholm	1876	4,429,713	170,980	25.90
Switzerland	Berne	1876	2,759,854	15,233	181.17
Turkey	Constantinople	Est.	31,939,738	1,812,048	17.62
Uruguay	Montevideo	1876	445,000	70,000	6.35
United States	Washington	1870	38,925,598	3,603,884	10.80
Venezuela	Caracas	1873	1,784,197	368,235	4.92

Amount of United States Coin Bonds Outstanding, January 1, 1878.

Title of Loan.	Int.	When Redeemable.	Interest Payable.	Registr'd.	Coupon.	Total.
Loan of Feb., 1861 ('81's)	6		Jan. & July	$13,820,000	$4,595,000	$18,415,000
Oregon War Debt	6		Jan. & July		945,000	945,000
Loan of July & Aug., 1861 ('81's)	6	After June 30, 1881	Jan. & July	126,295,100	63,036,250	189,321,350
Loan of 18-5('81's)	6	After June 30, 1881	Jan. & July	53,919,400	21,080,600	75,000,000
Ten - forties of 1864	5	After Mar. 1, 1874	Mar. & Sep.	142,552,750	52,013,550	194,566,300
Consols of 1865 (5-20's)	6	After July 1, 1870	Jan. & July	47,046,960	69,856,400	116,903,350
Consols of 1867 (5-20's)	6	After July 1, 1872	Jan. & July	98,557,400	212,029,800	310,617,200
Consols of 1868 (5-20's)	6	After July 1, 1873	Jan. & July	15,750,500	21,714,800	37,465,300
Funded Loan of 1881 (5's)	5	After May 1, 1881	F.M.A.& N.	221,238,300	287,202,050	508,440,350
Funded Loan of 1891 (4½'s)	4½	After Sept. 1, 1891	M.J.S. & D.	118,474,200	81,525,800	200,000,000
Funded Loan of 1907 (4's)	4	After July 1, 1907	J.A.J. & O.	61,044,400	13,855,600	74,900,000
				$998,979,000	$827,834,850	$1,726,833,550

Currency 6's issued to Pacific Railroads, 30 years, from 1865 to 1869 ... $64,623,512

INDEX.